What others are saying ab

"Takes the standard timber book to the next level. Many subjects and examples not found in other books."

Clayton A. Pharaoh, S.E., California Polytechnic State University, San Luis Obispo

"We look forward to your publication as a significant tool in the preparation of better educated professionals."

Richard R. Chapman, Simpson Strong-Tie Company, Inc.

"[I] was favorably impressed with the degree of detail and analysis . . . I believe your book should fit well into the available reference materials for wood frame construction . . . Your audience should include not only the student academic community, but also the practicing engineer!"

Barry H. Welliver, S.E., Consulting Engineer

"Your book fills the long existing gap of step by step presentation of solutions of most of the common and some not so common problems encountered in the design of wood structures. I find your book to be a "must" tool for the student of wood design and a very valuable addition to the library of the practicing structural engineer."

James A. Kaslan, S.E., Kaslan Associates, Inc.

Acknowledgments

I sincerely wish to thank all of the fine individuals and organizations who contributed to the writing of this manual. First my appreciation to my editor, Deborah Tranelli, who put in long hours proof reading this manual in a gallant attempt to correct my self-acknowledged horrific spelling. To Clay (good to his word) Pharaoh who took the time from his busy teaching schedule at Cal Poly San Luis Obispo to read the manuscript and give an in-depth peer review of the material. He is simply the best. To the American Plywood Association and their outstanding engineers, Fulton Dessler and Ken Andreason who were always giving of their time and expertise - a fine organization and a great group of engineers. To the insightful Ron Demczak, who bestows such delicious tidbits of wisdom that they may last all year long. And, finally, to my mom and dad, Ray and Alice Duquette. Their courage in the face of personal adversity, gentle love and support have proven an inspiration to me all of my life. To all these fine individuals, I extend my sincere thanks, as I am deeply indebted and grateful to them .

TIMBER SOLUTIONS MANUAL

David W. Duquette P.E.

Solutions in this manual are written for individuals who require further practice in homework, undergraduate, PE or SE Examination level problems. The problems in this manual are not meant as a substitute for, or to supplant texts or manuals in the field of timber engineering. The Publisher and the Author believe that the solutions are reliable but not intended to cover all possible applications of Timber Engineering. Employment of this manual presupposes that you, the user, assume all responsibility for its use. The publisher, author, distributors, or other related individuals or organizations do not assume or accept any responsibility or liability for negligence, errors, oversight, omissions or damages in the use of this manual arising from the employment of the solutions or in the preparation of engineering plans or designs. This manual is published for the express use of being a study aid and is not intended to render professional engineering services. Requirement of these services necessitates the engagement of a licensed professional.

Timber Solutions Manual

Printed in the United States of America

Library of Congress Catalog Card Number: 96-93136

ISBN: 0-9656181-0-2

PUBLISHED BY:

Da Vinci Publishing
New York, New York

Table of Contents

Preface

This Manual has been written to aid students, engineers, builders and architects in solving problems in Timber Design Engineering. Its primary purpose is to supplement existing texts and manuals in the field and to provide practical solutions to the problems found in course homework, undergraduate test preparation, actual engineering practice, and PE Exam and SE Exam preparation. As the NCEE has copyright privileges on its tests, it is not possible to cite exact problems for the PE and SE level examinations. However, the problems in this manual are designed to be similar to, and at a comparable level of complexity as with those found on the National Exams. Wher ever possible, this manual incorporates the recent changes in the 1991 NDS (National Design Specifications) and the seismic design changes in the 1991 and 1994 UBC (Uniform Building Code).

Each Chapter is arranged in increasing complexity from entry level timber engineering course work problems to SE level exam problems. Many of the problems have been solved by a computer spreadsheet. Both intermediate and final values have been rounded and will vary slightly with actual hand calculations. Problems that are often found in practice are also placed toward the ends of their respective chapters. Every effort has been made to use standard methodology found in actual practice in the solution of the problems. It has been said that engineering is more an art than a science. There are many ways to solve these problems and engineers differ in their approach. As long as you are accurate, safe and economic in your designs, you will not stray too far from the fold. Keep in mind that my approach serves as a basis for study and practice in the Art of Timber Engineering Design.

Nomenclature

A area (in^2, ft^2)
a dimension of member (in.)
a horizontal distance to load for bracket columns (in.)
A_c area of concrete footing in pole design (ft^2)
A_g gross cross-sectional area of a tension or compression member (in^2)
A_h projected area of hole caused by drilling or routing to accommodate bolts or other fasteners at net section (in^2)
A_h gross cross-sectional area of main wood member (in^2)
A_n cross-sectional area of notched member (in^2)
A_n area of steel member (in^2)
A_s sum of gross cross-sectional areas of side member(s) (in^2)
A_{web} cross-sectional area of the web of a steel W-shaped beam or wood I joist (in^2)
b breadth (width) of rectangular member (in)
b width of column flange (in)
b length of shearwall parallel to lateral force; distance between chords of shearwall (ft)
b width of horizontal diaphragm; distance between chords of horizontal diaphragm (ft)
B_t allowable tension on anchor bolt embedded in concrete or masonry
B_v allowable shear on anchor bolt embedded in concrete or masonry
C compressive force (lb)
C pole circumference at point of maximum moment (in)
C code coefficient representing seismic design response spectrum value
c distance from neutral axis to outer surface of beam (in)
c buckling and crushing interaction factor for columns
C_b bearing area factor
C_c curvature factor
C_{co} seasoning conditioning factor for round timber piles
C_{cs} critical section factor for round timber piles
C_D duration-of-load factor
C_d penetration depth factor for connections
C_{di} diaphragm factor for nailed connections
C_{dt} constant for tapered beam deflection
C_e wind force combined height, exposure, and gust factor coefficient
C_{eg} end grain factor for connections
C_F size factor for sawn lumber
C_f form factor for bending stress
C_{fu} flat use factor for bending stress
C_g group action factor for connections
C_s shear stress adjustment factor
C_I interaction stress factor
C_l beam stability factor
C_m wet service factor for high-moisture conditions
C_p column stability factor
C_p ponding magnification factor
C_p seismic response coefficient for determining force on a portion of a structure
C_q wind pressure coefficient
C_r reduction factor for double-tapered curved beams

C_r	repetitive-member factor (bending stress) for dimension lumber
C_{sp}	single pile factor for timber piles
C_{st}	metal side plate factor for 4 in. shear plate connections
C_T	buckling stiffness factor for 2x4 and smaller dimension lumber in trusses
C_t	seismic coefficient depending on type of LFRS used to calculate period of vibration T
C_{tn}	toenail factor for nail connections
C_u	untreated factor for timber piles
C_V	volume factor for glulams
C_x	spaced column fixity factor
C_y	factor for tapered beam deflection
C_Δ	geometry factor for connections
$C_{\Delta e}$	edge distance factor
$C_{\Delta s}$	spacing factor
D	diameter (in)
d	depth of rectangular beam cross-section (in)
d	least dimension of rectangular compression member associated with axis of column buckling(in)
d	pennyweight of nail or spike
d	dimension of wood member for shrinkage calculation (in)
d_b	arch depth at base (in)
d_c	depth of cross section at centerline (in)
d_{cb}	approximate centerline depth for pitched and tapered curved beams (in)
d_{crt}	minimum centerline depth due to radial tension for pitched and tapered curved beams (in)
d_e	effective depth of member at a connection (in)
d_{eb}	factor for calculation depth of pitched and tapered curved beams (in)
d_{eff}	approximate effective centerline deflection for pitched and tapered curved beams (in)
d_n	effective depth of member remaining at a notch (in)
d_t	depth of tangent point (in)
d_x	width of rectangular column parallel to y axis, used to calculate column slenderness ratio about x axis
d_y	width of rectangular column parallel to x axis, used to calculate column slenderness ratio about y axis
d_1	shank diameter of lag bolt (in)
d_2	pilot hole diameter for the threaded portion lag bolt (in)
d_1, d_2	cross-sectional dimensions of rectangular compression member in planes of lateral support (in)
E	lateral force due to earthquake (lb,k)
E	length of tapered tip of lag bolt (in)
E,E´	tabulated and allowable modulus of elasticity (psi,ksi)
E_{axial}	modulus of elasticity of glulam for axial deformation calculation (psi,ksi)
E_m	modulus of elasticity of main member (psi,ksi)
E_s	modulus of elasticity of side member (psi,ksi)
E_x	modulus of elasticity about x axis (psi,ksi)
E_y	modulus of elasticity about y axis (psi,ksi)
e	eccentricity of load (in)
F	force or load (lb,k)
F_b, F_b'	tabular and allowable bending design value (psi,ksi)
F_{be}	critical buckling (Euler) value for bending member (psi,ksi)
F_{bx}, F_{bx}'	tabulated and allowable bending stress about strong (x) axis (psi,ksi)

F_{by}, F_{by}'	tabulated and allowable bending stress about strong (y) axis (psi,ksi)
F_{b1}'	allowable edgewise bending design value F'bx (psi, ksi)
F_{b2}'	allowable flatwise bending design value F'by (psi,ksi)
F_b^*	tabulated bending stress multiplied by all applicable adjustment factors except CL (psi,ksi)
F_b^{**}	tabulated bending stress multiplied by all applicable adjustment factors except CV (psi,ksi)
F_c, F_c'	tabular and allowable compression parallel to grain design value (psi,ksi)
F_{cE}	critical buckling design value for compression members (psi,ksi)
F_{cE1}, F_{cE2}	critical buckling design value for compression member in planes of lateral support (psi,ksi)
F_c^*	tabulated compression stress parallel to grain multiplied by all applicable adjustment factors except Cp (psi,ksi)
$F_{c\perp}, F_{c\parallel}$	tabular and allowable design value in compression perpendicular to grain (psi,ksi)
$F_{c\perp 0.2}, F'_{c\perp 0.2}$	reduced and allowable compression stress perpendicular to rain deformation limit of 0.02 in. (psi,ksi)
F_e	dowel bearing strength (psi,ksi)
F_{em}	dowel bearing strength of main member (psi,ksi)
F_{es}	dowel bearing strength of side member (psi,ksi)
$F_{e\parallel}$	dowel bearing strength parallel to grain for bolt or lag screw connections (psi,ksi)
$F_{e\perp}$	dowel bearing strength perpendicular to grain for bolt or lag screw connections (psi,ksi)
$F_{e\theta}$	dowel bearing strength at an angle to grain for bolt or lag screw connections (psi,ksi)
F_g, F_g'	tabular and allowable end grain in bearing parallel to grain (psi,ksi)
F_p	allowable bearing stress for fastener in steel member (psi,ksi)
F_{px}	seismic story force at level x for designing the horizontal diaphragm (lb,k)
F_{rt}, F_{rt}'	tabular and allowable design value in radial tension (psi,ksi)
F_t	that portion of the seismic base shear V applied to top level in addition to seismic force given by Fx or Fpx distributions (lb,k)
F_t, F_t'	tabular and allowable tension parallel to grain stress (psi,ksi)
F_u	ultimate tensile strength for steel (psi,ksi)
F_v, F_v'	tabular and allowable design value shear parallel to grain stress (horizontal shear) (psi, ksi)
F_x	seismic story force at level x for designing vertical elements (shearwalls) in LFRS (lb,k)
F_y	yield strength (psi,ksi)
F_{yb}	bending yield strength of fastener (psi,ksi)
F_θ'	allowable bearing stress at angle to grain theta (psi,ksi)
f_b	actual (computed) bending stress (psi,ksi)
f_{bx}	actual (computed) bending stress about strong (x) axis (psi,ksi)
f_{by}	actual (computed) bending stress about strong (y) axis (psi,ksi)
f_{b1}	edgewise bending stress Fbx (psi,ksi)
f_{b2}	flatwise bending stress Fby (psi,ksi)
f_c	actual (computed) compression stress parallel to grain (psi,ksi)
$f_{c\perp}$	actual (computed) compression stress perpendicular to grain (psi,ksi)
f_g	actual (computed) bearing stress parallel to grain (psi,ksi)
f_o	reference stress for pitched and tapered curved beams (psi,ksi)
f_r	radial stress in curved bending member (psi, ksi)
f_{rt}	radial tension stress (psi, ksi)
f_s	stress in reinforcing steel (psi,ksi)
f_s	torsional stress (psi, ksi)
f_t	actual (computed) tension stress in a member parallel to grain (psi, ksi)

f_v	actual (computed) shear stress parallel to grain (horizontal shear) in a beam using full design loads (psi, ksi)
f_v'	reduced (computed) shear stress parallel to grain (horizontal shear) in a beam obtained by neglecting the loads within distance d of face of support (psi, ksi)
G	specific gravity
G	shear modulus (modulus of rigidity) (psi, ksi)
g	gauge of screw
g	acceleration of gravity
h	height of crown of arch (ft)
h	building of height of wind pressure zone (ft)
h	height of shearwall
h_a	height of apex for pitched and tapered curved beams (in.)
h_i, h_x	height above base to level i level x (ft)
h_n	height above base to *n*th or uppermost level in building (ft)
h_s	height of soffit at midspan for pitched and tapered curved beams (in)
I	initial moisture content (below 30%) (%)
I	moment of inertia (in4)
I	importance coefficient for seismic force
I	importance coefficient for wind force
I_k, I_g	ration of moment of inertia of knots to moment of inertia of gross cross section
K	bending stress factor for pitched and tapered curved beams
K	code multiplier for DL for use in beam deflection calculations to account for creep effects
K	framing coefficient from old seismic base shear formula
K_S	effective section modulus for plywood (in3)
K_{bE}	Euler buckling coefficient for beams
K_{cE}	Euler buckling coefficient for columns
K_D	diameter coefficient for wood screw, nail and spike connections
K_e	effective length factor for column end conditions (bucking length coefficient for columns)
K_f	column stability coefficient for bolt and nail built-up columns
K_L	loading coefficient for evaluating volume effect factor Cv for glulam beams
K_m	moisture content coefficient for sawn lumber truss compression chord
K_r	radial stress factor
K_T	truss compression chord coefficient for sawn lumber
K_v	shear coefficient
K_x	spaced column fixity coefficient
K_1, K_2	coefficients for truss deflection
K_θ	angle to grain coefficient for bolt and lag screw connections
k	change in member thickness for arch deflection (%)
L	span length of bending member (ft)
L	span or length (ft)
L	distance between points of lateral support of compression members (ft)
L_c	length from tip of pile to critical section (ft)
L_c	length between tangent points for pitched and tapered curved beams (ft)
L_c	cantilever length in cantilever beam system (ft)
L_e	effective length for shear (ft)
ℓ	span length of bending member (in)
ℓ	length between points of lateral support of compression member (in)
ℓ	length (ft)
ℓ	length of bolt in main or side members (in)

ℓ	length of fastener (in)
ℓ	unbraced length of column (in)
ℓ/D	bolt slenderness ratio
ℓ_b	bearing length (in)
ℓ_c	clear span (in)
ℓ_c	effective length of compression member (in)
ℓ_c	effective span length of bending member (in)
ℓ_c	effective unbraced length of compression side of beam (in)
ℓ_{e1}, ℓ_{e2}	effective length of compression member in planes of lateral support (in)
ℓ_e/d	slenderness ratio of compression member
$(\ell_e/d)_x$	slenderness ratio of column for buckling about strong (x) axis
$(\ell_e/d)_y$	slenderness ratio of column for buckling about weak (y) axis
ℓ_m	length of bolt in wood main member (in)
ℓ_n	length of notch (in)
ℓ_s	total length of bolt in wood side member(s) (in)
ℓ_t	length of tapered leg for pitched and tapered curved beams (in)
ℓ_u	laterally unsupported span length of bending member (in)
ℓ_u	laterally braced length of compression side of beam (in)
ℓ_x	unbraced length of column considering buckling about strong (x) axis (in)
ℓ_y	unbraced length of column considering buckling about weak (y) axis (in)
ℓ_1, ℓ_2	distances between points of lateral support of compression member in planes 1 and 2 (in)
ℓ_3	distance from center of spacer block to centroid of group of split ring or shear plate connectors in end block for a spaced column (in)
M	bending moment (in-lb, in-k, ft-lb, ft-k)
M	mass
M	moment capacity (in-lb)
M_p	plastic moment capacity (in-lb, in-k)
M_y	yield moment (in-lb, in-k)
m	final moisture content (below 30%) (%)
N	fastener value for angle with direction of grain (lb)
N	normal reaction (lb, k)
N	number of fasteners in connection
N, N´	nominal and allowable lateral design value at angle to grain θ for a single split ring or shear plate connector (lb)
n	number of fasteners in row
n	number of stories (seismic forces)
P	total concentrated load, axial load or force (lb)
P	design wind pressure (psf)
P	penetration depth of fastener into wood member (in)
P	fastener value for load acting parallel to grain
P, P´	nominal and allowable withdrawal design value for fastener, lbs. per inch of penetration
P, P´´	nominal and allowable lateral design value parallel to grain for a single split ring or shear plate connector (lb)
P_u	collapse load (ultimate load capacity)
Q	fastener value for load acting perpendicular to grain (lb)
Q	statical moment of area about the neutral axis (in3)

Q, Q'	nominal and allowable lateral design value perpendicular to grain for a single split ring or shear plate connector (lb)
q	perpendicular-to-grain component of lateral force z on one fastener
q	soil bearing pressure (psf)
q_a	soil bearing pressure under axial loads (psf)
q_b	soil bearing pressure caused by overturning moment (psf)
R	radius of curvature of inside face of lamination (in)
R	nominal calculated resistance of structure (see LRDF)
R	reaction (lb, k)
R	reduction (percent) of roof or floor live load
R_b	slenderness ratio of laterally unbraced beam
R_h	horizontal reaction (lb)
R_m	radius of curvature of centerline of curved member (in)
R_s	reduction in snow load (psf per degree of roof slope over 20 degrees)
R_w	seismic structural system quality factor
R_v	vertical reaction (lb)
R_1	seismic force generated by mass of wall that is parallel to earthquake force being considered
r	radius of gyration (in)
S	section modulus (in3)
S	seismic coefficient for soil characteristics for a site
S	shrinkage of wood member (in)
SG	specific gravity
SG_m	specific gravity of main member
SG_s	specific gravity of side member
SV	shrinkage value for wood due to 1 percent change in moisture content (in/in)
S_B	allowable soil-bearing capacity for poles (psf)
S_m	shrinkage form initial moisture condition to final moisture content *m* (%)
So	total shrinkage form table 2.3 (%)
S_o, $S_{1\text{-}4}$	allowable lateral soil-bearing pressure for poles (psf)
s	length of arch segment (in)
s	center-to-center spacing between adjacent fasteners in a row (in)
s	length of unthreaded shank of lag bolt (in)
T	applied torque (in-k)
T	tensile force (lb, k)
T	fundamental period of vibration of structure in direction of seismic force under consideration (sec)
t	thickness (in)
t	fire resistance rating (min.)
t	thickness of column flange (in)
t	thickness of beam flange (in)
t	thickness of lamination (in)
t_m	thickness of main member (in)
t_s	thickness of side member (in)
t_{washer}	thickness of washer (in)
u	force in truss member caused by unit load (lb)
V	shear force in a beam, diaphragm, or shearwall (lb, k)
V	seismic base shear (lb, k)
V	basic wind speed (mph)

V'	reduced shear in beam determined by neglecting load within *d* from face of supports (lb, k)
v	unit shear in horizontal diaphragm or shearwall (lb/ft, k/ft)
v_2	unit shear in second-floor diaphragm (lb/ft, k/ft)
v_{2r}	unit shear in shearwall between second floor and roof levels (lb/ft, k/ft)
v_{12}	unit shear in shearwall between first floor and second floor levels (lb/ft, k/ft)
v_r	unit shear in roof diaphragm (lb/ft, k/ft)
W	weight of structure of total seismic dead load (lb, k)
W	total uniform load (lb, K)
W, W'	nominal and allowable withdrawal design value for fastener, lbs per inch of penetration
W_{DL}	dead load of structure (lb, k)
W_{foot}	dead load of footing or foundation (lb, k)
W_p	weight of portion of structure (element or component) (lb,k, lb/ft, k/ft, psf)
W_r	total DL tributary to roof level (lb, k)
W_r'	that portion of Wr which generates seismic forces in roof diaphragm (lb, k)
W_1	DL of 1 ft. wide strip tributary to story level in direction of seismic force (lb/ft, k/ft)
W_2	total DL tributary to second-floor horizontal diaphragm (lb/ft, k/ft)
w	uniformly distributed load or force (lb/.ft, k/ft, psf, ksf)
w	tabulated withdrawal design value for single fastener (lb/in of penetration)
w_i, w_x	tributary weight assigned to story level *i*, level *x* (lb, k)
w_{px}	weight of diaphragm and elements tributary thereto at level x (lb, k, lb/ft, k/ft)
w_r	uniform load to roof horizontal diaphragm (lb/ft, k/ft)
w_2	uniform load to second-floor horizontal diaphragm (lb/ft, k/ft)
X	distance (ft)
x	distance (ft)
x	distance from beam support face to load (in)
x	horizontal location (in, ft)
x	width of triangular soil bearing pressure diagram (ft)
y	vertical location (in, ft)
y	wall height of arch (ft)
Z	plastic section modulus (in3)
Z	seismic zone factor
Z, Z'	nominal and allowable lateral design value for single fastener in a connection (lb)
ZIC/R_w	seismic base shear coefficient
Z'_α	allowable resultant design value for lag bolt subjected to combined lateral and withdrawal loading (lb)
$Z_{m\perp}$	nominal lateral design value for single bolt or lag bolt in wood-to-wood connection with main member loaded perpendicular to grain and side member loaded parallel to grain (lb)
$Z_{s\parallel}$	nominal lateral design value for single bolt or lag bolt in wood-to-wood connection with main member loaded parallel to grain and side member loaded perpendicular grain (lb)
$Z_\parallel$	nominal lateral design value for single bolt or lag bolt connection with all wood members loaded parallel to grain (lb)
$Z_\perp$	nominal lateral design value for single bolt or lag bolt in wood-to-metal connection with wood member(s) loaded perpendicular to grain (lb)
α	angle measure (degrees)
Δ	deflection (in)
ΔH	horizontal movement (in)
ΔC	change in moisture content of wood member (percent)
Δc	centerline deflection (in)
#	lbs.

√	ok
○	PE level problem
●	SE level problem

Note: SE and PE level problems (or sections of those problems) are often interchangable at exam level.

Alphabetical List of Problem Topics

Alphabetical List of Problem Topics

Alphabetical List of Problem Topics

Alphabetical List of Problem Topics

1. Structural Behavior and Design Loads

PROBLEM 1.1

Beam Deflection Using the "K" Factor.

A young architect in your office is designing her first small office building and asks you to quickly double check her basic deflection criteria on some floor joists (before the inclusion of adjustment factors). She wants you to determine both the allowable and actual deflection for the floor joist shown below. Use the 1994 TCM "K" factor criteria for both seasoned and unseasoned wood.

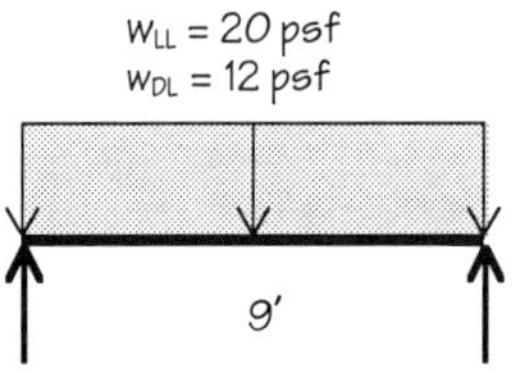

ASSUME

DF - L No. 1.
2x12 @ 16 in o/c.
Beam wt. included in DL.
Increased stiffness required.

NDS T1B, T4A

SOLUTION

$I = 178\ in^4$

$E = 1.6e3$ ksi

TCM T4.4

When considering deflection for sensitive beams or joists of a floor area, the TCM requires us to satisfy these deflection criteria for increased stiffness:

$$\Delta_{LL} \le L/480$$

$$\Delta_{TL} \le L/360$$

The UBC deflection values differ slightly, see T16-E

Calc actual deflection ($\Delta_{LL}, \Delta_{D+L}$)

Calc tributary loads on per foot basis:

$w_{LL} = 1.33(.02) = .027$ klf

$w_{DL} = 1.33(.012) = .016$ klf

Per TCM criteria:

$$\Delta_{LL} = \frac{5w\ell^4}{384EI} = \frac{5(.027)9^4(1728)}{384(1.6e3)178} = .014 \text{ in}$$

When using beam formulas pay strict attention to the units of both the variables and the answers. The Number 1728 is 12 cubed and commonly use in practice to ease the insertion of "w" in pounds per foot and the span in feet. We can ratio the above to simplify our work:

$$\Delta_{TL} = .014\left(\frac{w_{TL}}{w_{LL}}\right) = .014\left(\frac{20+12}{20}\right) = .022 \text{ in}$$

Do not go crazy about "sig-figs". You will be fooling your-self with an inflated view of accuracy if you attach too many digits to your work. Since I like to work in kips, I usually have 3 to the right for loads (or forces) and 2 to the right for answers (unless it is a deflection or an intermediary number). As you can see, it's a matter of style. Choose something that is realistic and that you are comfortable with. Be consistent.

> Actual LL deflection = .015 in
> Actual DL + LL deflection = .025 in

Find K

Wood has the tendency to creep under a long term sustained dead load. To adjust for this tendency of long term creep, the TCM uses the value "K". In many instances the live load is also long term (therefore sustained) and will contribute to creep. The code leaves this adjustment up to the judgment of the designer as it does not specifically address it. The term "K" is directly affected by the moisture content of wood, and thus the code values for "K" are: TCM T4.4

K = 1.0 (seasoned) the above deflection is the same

= .5 (unseasoned)

$$\Delta_{LL+KDL} = .014\left(\frac{.5(12)+20}{20}\right) = .018 \text{ in}$$

Ck deflection

In practice (if economics permit), you should consider designing beams a bit stiffer than is required by local codes in both high traffic and in low traffic areas (See TCM Table 4.4). This is done to increase user comfort and, at the same time, build confidence in the performance of the structure. Your efforts will go a long way in establishing your reputation as a good and conscientious engineer (in the eyes the building owner or project developer). For example: When a beam supports both a well-traveled hallway and an office work area, it needs to be a little stiffer. This helps to insure that the office workers are not disturbed by the vibrations of the hallway traffic. Consideration should also be given to members over windows where long term creep might impede their operation.

$\Delta_{LL} = .014 \text{ in} < l/480 = 9(12)/480 = .23 \text{ in}$ √

Apply K factor (to more stringent NDS defl. criteria)

TCM T4.3

$\Delta_{TL} = \Delta_{LL+KDL}$

$= .022 \text{ in} \le l/360 = 9(12)/360 = .3 \text{ in}$ √ (seasoned)

$= .018 \text{ in} < .3 \text{ in}$ (unseasoned) √

The allowable deflection for DL + LL and KDL + LL is the same

> Allowable LL defl = .23 in
> Allowable DL + LL defl = .3 in

NDS 3.5.2

Where critical, your design should take creep into account. The NDS uses the more conservative approach of:

$\Delta_{TL} = LL + 1.5DL$ (seasoned)

$= LL + 2DL$ (unseasoned)

Fall seven times, stand up eight.

JAPANESE PROVERB

PROBLEM 1.2

Tributary areas and roof live load reduction loading for various members.

You are part of a team project to design a strip mall for a major supermarket chain. The lead engineer asks you to determine the tributary areas and loading for the roof members of the supermarket floor plan (sketch shown below) using 1994UBC methods 1 & 2.

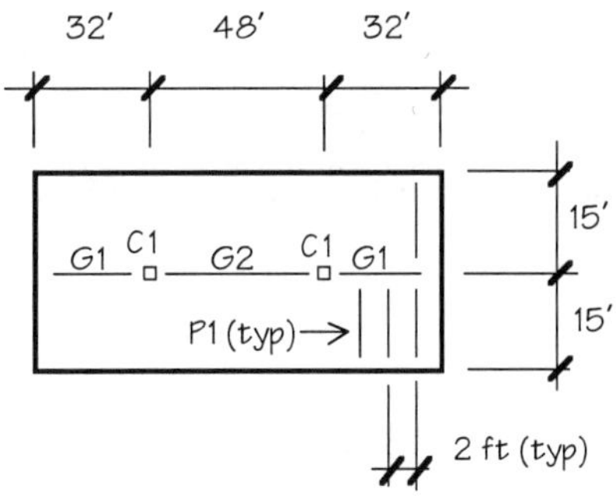

FLOOR FRAMING PLAN

ASSUME

DL = .012 ksf.
Flat roof sloped to prevent ponding.

SOLUTION

As an engineer, you must continuously ask yourself the questions: Is this calculation value reasonable as compared to like structures and circumstances? Does it look right? If it does not, or you question the value, recheck your calculations.

Calculate Tributary areas (TA)

$P1 = 15(2) = 30 \text{ ft}^2$

$G1 = 32(15) = 480 \text{ ft}^2$

$G2 = 48(15) = 720 \text{ ft}^2$

$C1 = 1/2(48+32)15 = 600 \text{ ft}^2$

Method 1

Calculate Reduced Live Load (RLL)

$TA_{P1} = 30 < 200 \Rightarrow 20 \text{ psf}$ UBC T16-C

$TA_{G1} = 480 < 600 \Rightarrow 16 \text{ psf}$

$TA_{G2} = 720 > 600 \Rightarrow 12 \text{ psf}$

$TA_{C1} = 600 = 600 \Rightarrow 16 \text{ psf}$

Calculate w, P Loads

$w_{P1} = (20+12)2 = 64 \text{ lb/ft}$

$w_{G1} = (16+12)15 = 420 \text{ lb/ft}$

w_{G2} = (12+12)15 = 360 lb/ft

P_{C1} = (16+12)600 = 16800 lbs

Trib load w_{P1} = 64 lb/ft
Trib load w_{G1} = 420 lb/ft
Trib load w_{G2} = 360 lb/ft
Trib load w_{PC1} = 16800 lbs

UBC 1606

Method 2 reduced live load (RLL)

TA_{P1} = 30 < 150 no reduction allowed

⇒ LL = 20 psf

w = 64 lb/ft same as above

TA_{G1} = 480 > 150 (reduction permitted)

R = r(A-150) = .08(480-150) = 26.4% controls

R = 23.1(1 + DL/LL) = 23.1(1+12/20) = 36.96% > 26.4%

R = 40% > 26.4%

Using smallest reduction

RLL = 20(1.0-.264) = 14.72 psf

w = (14.7+12)15 = 401 lb/ft

TA_{G2} = 720 >150

R = .08(720-150) = 45.6%

R = 36.96% same as above < 45.6%

R = 40% > 36.96%

37% controls (rounded)

RLL = 20(1.0-.37) = 12.6 psf

w = (12.6+12)15 = 369 lb/ft

TA_{C1} = 600> 150

R = .08(600-150) = 36%

R = 36.96% > 36%

R = 40% > 36%

36% controls

RLL = 20(1.0-.36) = 12.8 psf

P = (12.8+12)600 = 14880 lbs

It is not uncommon for you to receive and work off of plans that do not indicate the location or weight of mechanical or air-conditioning equipment. Make sure you incorporate the actual weight and location in your final design.

Trib load w_{P1} = 64 lb/ft
Trib load w_{G1} = 401 lb/ft
Trib load w_{G2} = 369 lb/ft
Trib load w_{PC1} = 14880 lbs

As you can see from comparing the two methods, Method 1 tends to be the more conservative approach. It is easier to use and is widely employed in practice. The use of either Method 1 or Method 2 is permitted by code. However, the combination of the two methods is strictly prohibited.

Many designers employ Method 1 first. If the selected beam does not work or is not economic, they then try Method 2. In general, the employment of a methodology that progressively uses "ok", but less conservative numbers is commonly known in practice as "making the numbers scream".

Alternate (for method 2)

The 1994 UBC sec. 1607 provides an alternate equation for method 2 if the infulence area is ≥ 400 ft^2. As an example for C1 we have:

A_I = 4(600) = 2400

L = reduced LL in psf

$$= L_o\left(.25+\frac{15}{\sqrt{A_I}}\right) = 20\left(.25+\frac{15}{\sqrt{2400}}\right)$$

= 11.12 psf < 12.8 psf

We can see by the comparison of the results of method 2 and the alternate equation that the original equation is more conservative in nature.

I am looking for a lot of men who have an infinite capacity to not know what can't be done.

HENRY FORD

PROBLEM 1.3

Sloped load on pitched roof.

The architectural designer in your office is working on a second story addition to an existing garage. He needs you to determine the roof load with respect to the horizontal plane and with respect to the roof slope so that he can rough out his design to submit it to you for review.

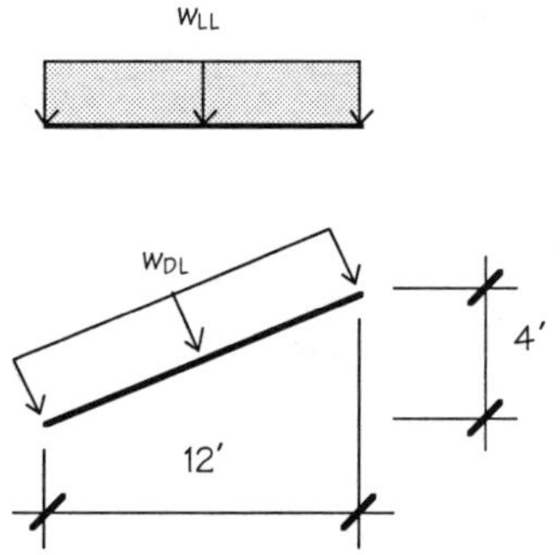

ASSUME

RLL = 20 psf.
Roof wt. = 12 psf.

SOLUTION

It's always a good idea to examine the unit weight of the material you are using for your calcs. In a short time this experience will allow you to get a feel for the unit weight of similar components of like buildings. This procedure thus becomes a sort of "soft" quality control check because you will have developed and recognized a reasonable range of weights for a given type of structure.

Material weights are usually taken from standard tables that give the weight of the material when it is laying flat. Live loads are given with respect to the horizontal (flat). Therefore, for inclined surfaces we must calculate the total weight with either the material translated to the LL (horizontal) or the LL translated to the material weight for the stated slope of the roof.

Resolve the geometry and force triangles

Determine the loads with respect to the horizontal plane and along the slope of the member using similar triangles.

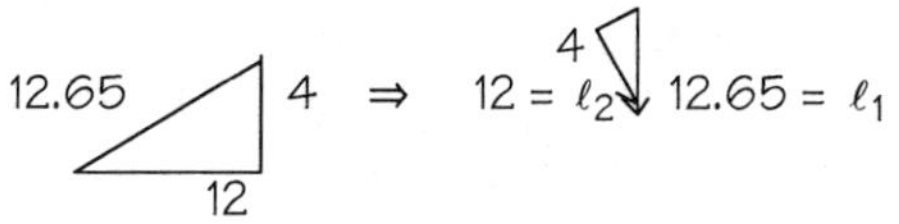

Calc load with respect to horizontal plane

Both the LL and the DL are gravity forces that act in a downward direction.

$$w_{TL} = w_{DL}\left(\frac{\ell_1}{\ell_2}\right) + w_{LL}$$

$$= \frac{12(12.65)}{12} + 20 = 32.6 \text{ psf} \quad (w_{DL} \text{ gets larger})$$

Graphically we have:

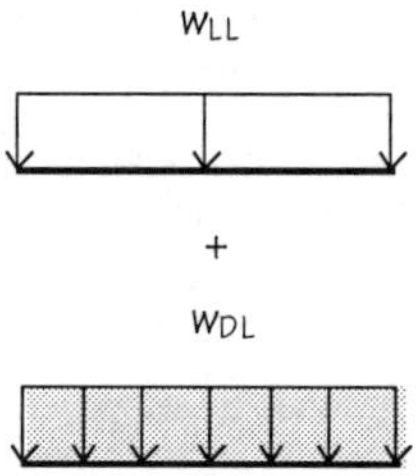

TL with respect to the horiz. = 33 psf

Calc load with respect to the slope

$$w_{TL} = w_{LL}\left(\frac{\ell_2}{\ell_1}\right) + w_{DL}$$

$$w_{LL} = 20\left(\frac{12}{12.65}\right) + 12 = 31.97 \text{ psf}$$

Load with respect to the slope = 32 psf

Note that for calculations relating to the horizontal plane you use the horizontal length. Use the length of the member along its surface when calculating with respect to the slope of the member. Also note that a convenient point at which we can consider the roof "flat" (for the purposes of determining loads) is a 4:12 pitched roof. If this is done it will result in an error of about 5% (12.65/12 = 1.05) for the DL portion of the total load, or about 2 to 3% overall for typical residential roofs. This is considered within the spirit of the code.

The first step in designing the roofs of buildings is to estimate the weight of the material the members have to support. In your estimation of the weight of roofing material, take in to account that UBC (chap 32) allows the roof to be replaced. Many roofers will install the new roof (asphaltic, wood shingle, or built-up) on top of the existing roof material. This effectively doubles the material weight of that part of the roof estimate. Many designers take this in to account initially and conservatively apply a min. of 2 layers of roofing when estimating the roofing material.

Vibration

Vibrating equipment will result in added loads to the structure above the weight of the unit itself. The TCM (sec. 4.1.17) recommends that you should double the weight of the vibratory equipment when considering these loads, consider the loosening of connections, use vibration base isolators and consider human comfort as an effective model for design.

□
□
□

Advice is what we ask for when we already know the answer but wish we didn't.

ERICA JONG

PROBLEM 1.4

Snow load on 1-story structure.

Determine the design load w, the moment M, and the shear V, in the horizontal plane and along the slope of the roof for the structure shown.

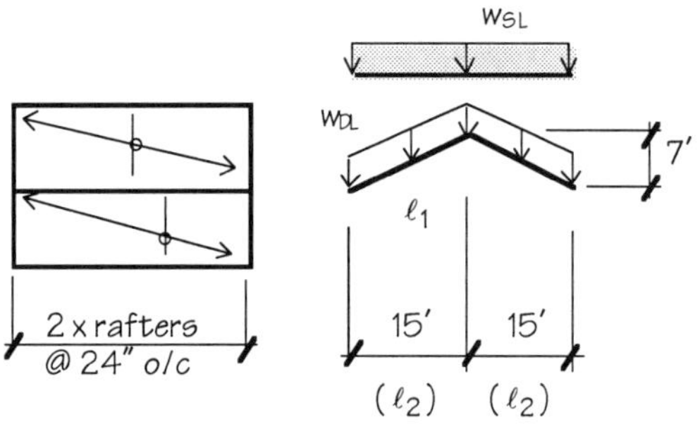

ASSUME

Roof wt = 10 psf.
Snow load = 50 psf.

SOLUTION

Initially, you should check with the local building official to get a feel for local snow and wind loads. For future reference, record and file what they tell you (names, date, info., etc.)

Check reduction for snow weight

slope = $\theta = \tan^{-1}(7/15) = 25.0° > 20°$

∴ A snow load reduction may be used. UBC1605.4

$$R_s = \left(\frac{S}{40}\right)-\left(\frac{1}{2}\right)=\left(\frac{50}{40}\right)-\left(\frac{1}{2}\right)$$

= .75 psf/degree over 20°

$w_{SL} = 50 - .75(25-20) = 46.3$ psf

Reduced snow load = 46.3 psf

Check load along horizontal plane

Using similar triangles:

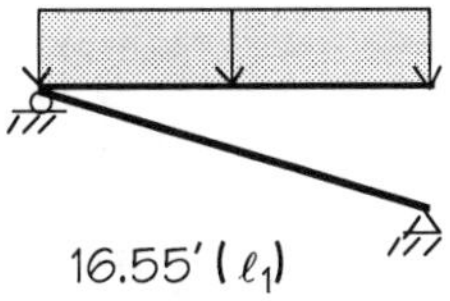

$$w_{TL} = 2(w_{SL} + w_{DL}) = 2\left(w_{DL}\left(\frac{\ell_1}{\ell_2}\right) + w_{SL}\right)$$

$$= 2\left(10\left(\frac{16.55}{15}\right) + 46.3\right) = 114.1 \text{ plf}$$

$$V = \frac{wL}{2} = \frac{.114(15)}{2} = .86^{k}$$

$$M = \frac{wL^2}{8} = \frac{.114(15)^2}{8} = 3.21^{k\,ft}$$

> Along the horiz. plane:
> w_{SL} = 114 plf
> $V = .86^{k}$
> $M = 3.2^{k\,ft}$

<u>**Check load along slope**</u>

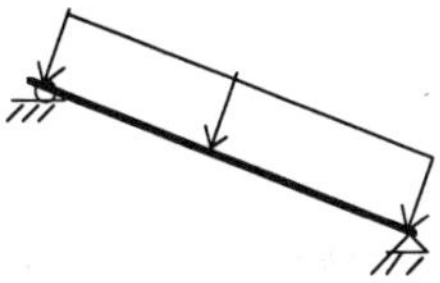

$$w_{SL} = 46.2\left(\frac{15}{16.55}\right) = 41.96 \text{ plf}$$

Use normal component as shown

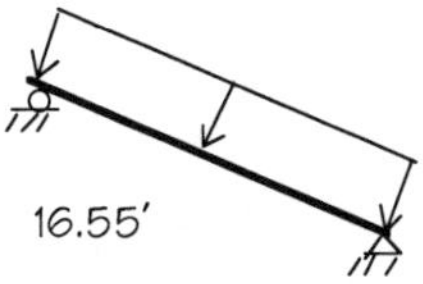

Force triangle

$$= 2\left(w_{SL}\left(\frac{\ell_2}{\ell_1}\right) + w_{DL}\right)$$

$$= 2\left(41.6\left(\frac{15}{16.55}\right) + 10\right) = 96 \text{ plf}$$

$$V = \frac{wL}{2} = \frac{.096(16.55)}{2} = .79^{k}$$

This is the theoretically correct value for shear.

$$M = \frac{wL^2}{8} = \frac{.096(16.55)^2}{8} = 3.29^{k\,ft}$$

> Along the slope:
> w_{SL} = 96 plf
> $V = .79^{k}$
> $M = 3.3^{k\,ft}$

Note that the moments are about the same. The shears, however, are different. The horizontal plane method is a bit easier to apply. It is the method preferred in practice as it gives a conservative value for shear.

Unless you are using a computer and have translated the loads for the slope, the deflection is to difficult to calculate. A simple and conservative approach is to use a flat model to determine the deflection for the beam.

Strong lives are motivated by dynamic purposes.

KENNETH HILDEBRAND

PROBLEM 1.5

Floor live load reduction for various members of one level.

The principal of your firm needs you to determine the reduced floor live load for the selected members of the 2-story residence shown below.

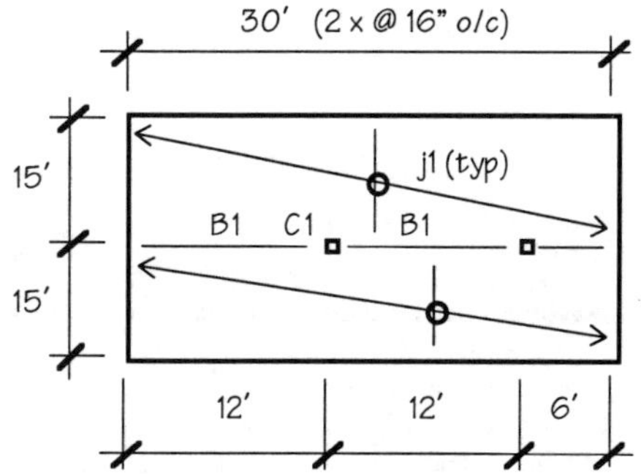

Floor Framing Plan

ASSUME

Loads from one level.
DL = 14 psf.
LL from UBC T-23A.

SOLUTION

Recall that the UBC code does not allow a live load reduction for areas of public assembly or when the live load exceeds 100 psf.

J1

$TA_{J1} = 15(16/12) = 20\ ft^2 < 150\ ft^2$

∴ no reduction allowed

FLL = 40 psf UBC T16-C

$w_{TL} = (40 + 14)16/12 = 72$ plf

No reduction allowed
$w_{TL} = 72$ plf

B1

$TA_{B1} = 15(12) = 180\ ft^2 > 150\ ft^2$

$R = r(A - 150)$

$= .08(180 - 150) = 2.4\ \%$

$R = 23.1\left(1 + \frac{DL}{FLL}\right)$ UBC 1606

$= 23.1\left(1 + \frac{14}{40}\right) = 31.2\ \% > 2.4\%$

$R = 40\ \% > 2.4\%$ governs

reduced FLL = 40(1 - .024) = 39.0 psf

$w_{TL} = 15(39 + 14) = 795$ plf

Reduction allowed
$w_{TL} = 795$ plf

C1

$TA_{C1} = 180\ ft^2$ (same as B1)

reduced FLL = 39 psf

P = 180(39 + 14) = 9540 lbs

Reduction allowed
P = 9540 lb

The 1995 UBC sec. 1607 provides an alternate equation for method 2 if the influence area is $\geq 400\ ft^2$. Since our largest influence area is $< 400\ ft^2$ we can not use the alternate formula (see prob. 1.2).

Although we have covered only vertical (gravity) loads thus far, keep in mind that lateral loads may also affect the member you are designing. It is convenient to first design for vertical loads then do a lateral analysis so that you can design for those forces. This is because you use the ever present gravity loads to calc the lateral forces. Many designers prefer to use the term "load" when talking about gravity forces and the term "force" when talking about wind or seismic forces.

User Comfort

User comfort is an important issue that rarely gets the consideration it deserves. Many designers are so intent upon meeting the critical criteria of timber engineering that the actual use of the building escapes them. Live load deflection is directly related to user comfort and is dealt with when one uses the span ratio limits found in TCM Table 4.3 and 4.4. Table 4.4 is used when stiffer floors are desired.

Creep

The subject of creep will be visited many times in this manual. Elastic deformation occurs when the wood member is initially loaded and rebounds to its original geometry when unloaded. If the load is maintained, there will occur inelastic deflection (which is called creep or time-dependent deformation). This time-dependent deformation occurs whether the load is large or small. It can be estimated at equal to the initial instantaneous deformation. Creep is independent of species. The variations in temperature and humidity will exacerbate the detrimental effects of creep. On the other hand, according to the Wood Handbook, a 50 degrees F rise in temperature may cause creep to increase by 2 to 3 times the normal value. If the wood is "green" it may creep 4 to 6 times its initial deformation. What is interesting to note is that unloading the member results in the immediate recovery of elastic deformation and, in time, about 1/2 the creep deformation. Again, the temperature and the humidity will influence the effects of creep by increasing the magnitude or the deformation recovery. See prob. 1.1.

Age

Wood's mechanical properties fluctuate little with time. In fact, it takes several centuries for wood to exhibit a serious loss in strength.

The great thing in this world is not so much where we are, but in what direction we are moving.

OLIVER WENDELL HOLMES

PROBLEM 1.6

Wind loads on various heights of buildings.

Determine the horizontal wind load for the buildings shown below. Use the 1994 UBC Method 2 and incremental step loadings.

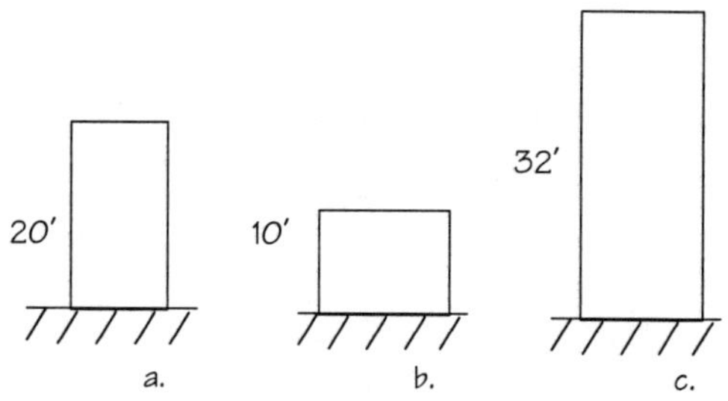

ASSUME

Projected area method for primary frames.

	a.	b.	c.
basic wind speed (mph)	70	90	70
exposure	D	C	B
I	1.0	1.0	1.0

SOLUTION

Find C_q

$10<20<32<40 \Rightarrow C_q = 1.3$ UBC Method 2

Building profile a.

From the chart above we get at each UBC increment:

UBC 1618, T16-F,G,H,K

$P_{15} = 1.39(1.3)12.6(1.0) = 22.8$ psf

$P_{20} = C_e C_q q_s I = 1.45(1.3)12.6(1.0) = 23.8$ psf

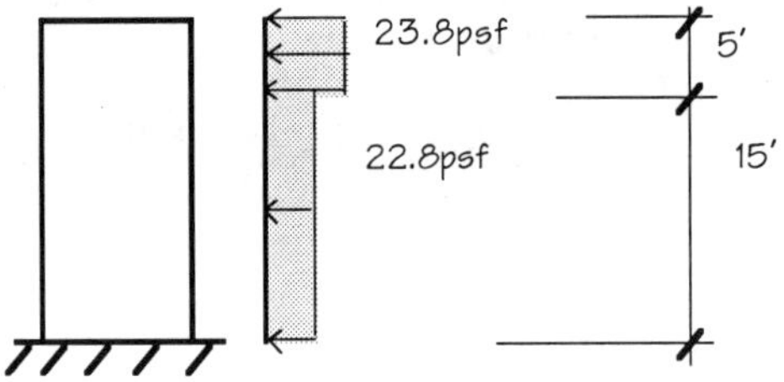

Building profile b.

$P_{10} = 1.06(1.3)20.8(1.0) = 28.7$ psf

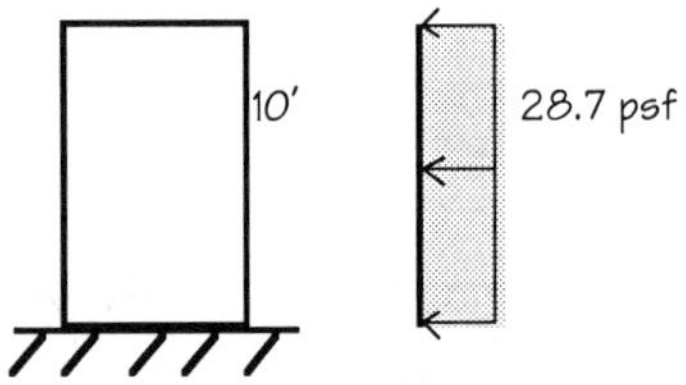

Building profile c.

$P_{15} = .62(1.3)12.6(1.0) = 10.2$ psf

$P_{20} = .67(1.3)12.6(1.0) = 11$ psf

$P_{25} = .72(1.3)12.6(1.0) = 11.8$ psf

$P_{30} = .76(1.3)12.6(1.0) = 12.4$ psf

$P_{32} \Rightarrow$ interpolate

$$\left.\begin{matrix} 30 & .76 \\ 32 & x \\ 40 & .84 \end{matrix}\right] \rightarrow x = .78$$

$P_{32} = .78(1.3)12.6(1.0) = 12.8$ psf

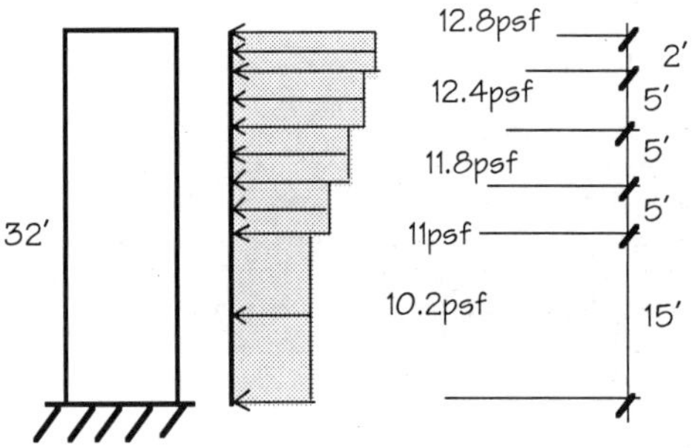

Note however, that the code allows interpolation above 15'. This implies that the above examples are conservative. If each level above 15 ft. is interpolated, we get a loading diagram like this:

UBC T116-G

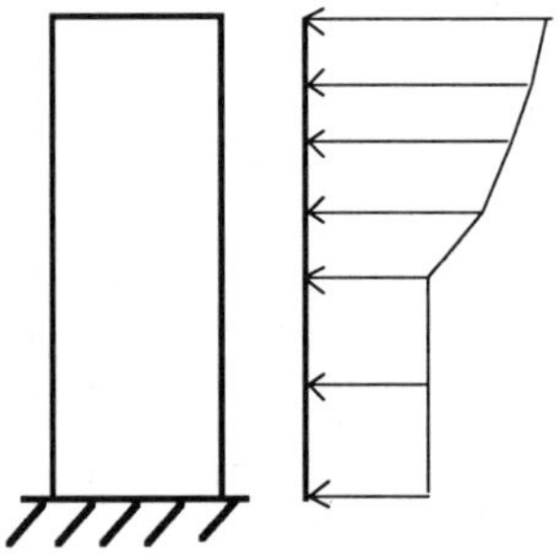

If the structure is tall and encompasses many UBC height increments, it would be inefficient to use either of the above diagrams (in practice). This is because of the amount of time it takes to do such calculations. To simplify the calculations, many engineers opt for the more conservative approach of assigning higher values for longer lengths (heights).

The real secret of success is enthusiasm.

WALTER CHRYSLER

PROBLEM 1.7

Wind loads to buildings with pitched roofs.

For the primary frames of the buildings shown below, determine the lateral wind load to the roof and to the combination of windward walls and the roof.

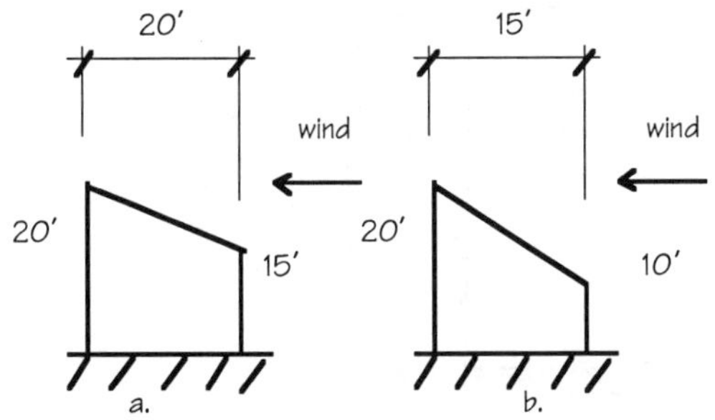

a.	b.
Use UBC method 2 (projected area method)	Use UBC method 2 (projected area method) and UBC method 1 (normal force method)

ASSUME

- Exposure C.
- Basic wind speed = 80 mph.
- I = 1.0.
- Closed structures.
- Non- rigid frame.

SOLUTION

Building a.

Method 2

Apply load to horizontal projection of roof and walls.

$P_{15} = C_e C_q q_s I = 1.06(1.3)16.4(1.0) = 22.6$ psf

The UBC allows the mid-height of the roof to be used. Use of 20 ft for C_e is considered conservative.

$P_{20} = 1.13(1.3)16.4(1.0) = 24.1$ psf

UBC 1618, T16-F, G, H, K

Force applied to lateral load system using:

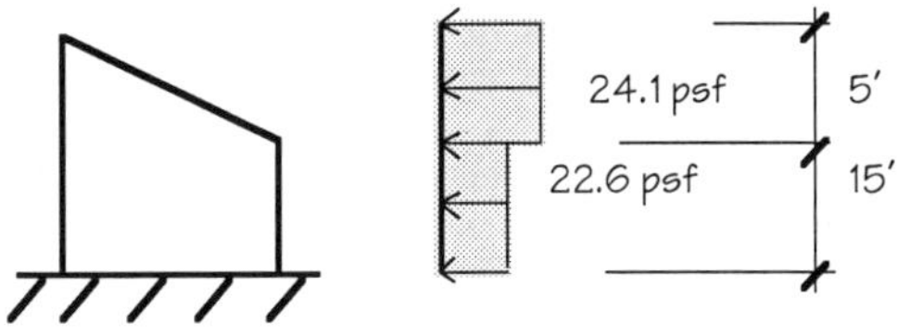

> Method 2 yields $P_{15} = 22.6$ psf, $P_{20} = 24.1$ psf

Building b.

Method 2

Note that this method gives an inaccurate joint moment in rigid gable frames. Hence it is not allowed to be applied in conjunction with them.
From above we get:

$P_{15} = 22.6$ psf

$P_{20} = 24.1$ psf

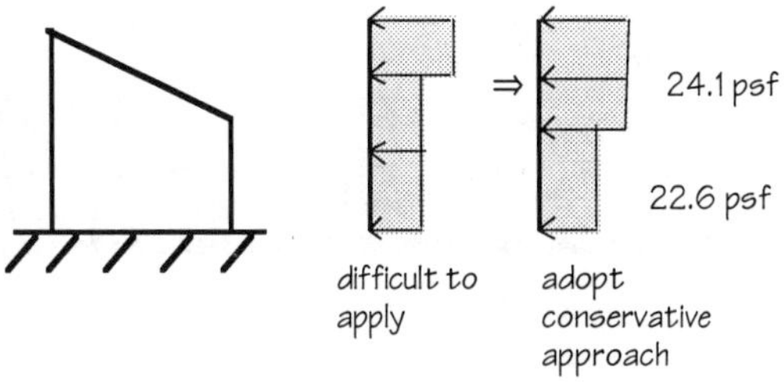

> Method 2 yields $P_{15} = 22.6$ psf
> $P_{20} = 24.1$ psf (same as above but adopting conservative approach)

Method 1

$$\text{slope} = \tan^{-1}\left(\frac{20-10}{20}\right) = 26.6°$$

2:12 < 26.6 < 9:12

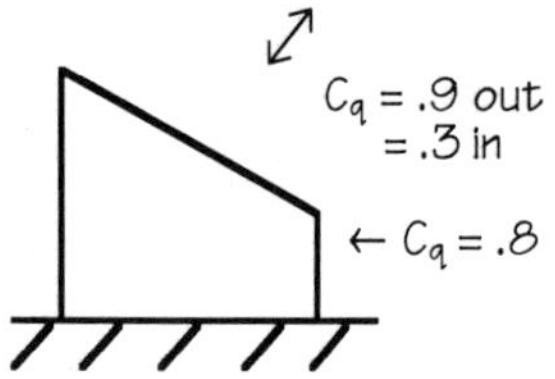

$P_{10} = .8(1.3)16.4(1.0) = 17.1$ psf

$P_{20\,in} = .3(1.3)16.4(1.0) = 6.4$ psf (in)

$P_{20\,out} = .9(1.3)16.4(1.0) = 19.2$ psf (out)

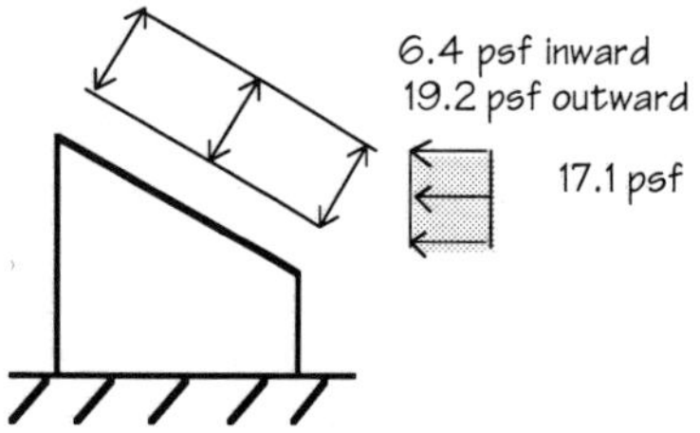

Method 1 yields for the roof:
6.4 psf inward
19.2 psf outward
For the wall:
P_{10} = 17.1 psf inward

□
□
□

A man is rich in proportion to the number of things which he can afford to let alone.

THOREAU

PROBLEM 1.8

Moment stability of basic shearwall due to wind.

Define the basic formulas required to determine the overall moment of stability of the simple wall shown below. Lateral and uplift forces are due to wind.

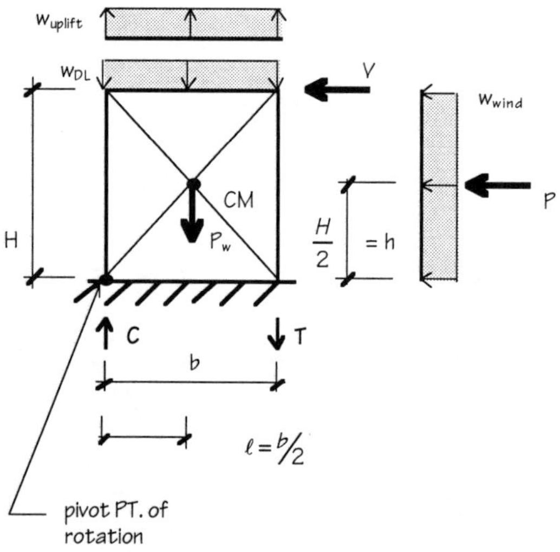

SOLUTION

Analyzing a shearwall requires that you must examine all loads and the potential force transfer points of the shearwall system. Pay particular attention to the connection of the roof system to the shearwall because the code requires the simultaneous examination of both lateral and uplift forces caused by wind. If it turns out that force transfer is possible (but not going to be ok), stabilize the roof by using ties. This stabilization check must be included in the

UBC 1619.1, 1631.1

stability check. A simple example of this procedure follows:

w_{uplift}	Uplift forces caused by suction on the roof elements and transferred to the shearwall system.
w_{DL}	The tributary DL of the roof/ceiling element acting on the shearwall.
CM	Center of mass of shearwall.
P_w	Resultant DL of wall acting at the CM. P_w = Area (wall wt. in psf)
C or T	Resultant force couple of shearwall.
V	Lateral load of other elements. This force is transferred via the diaphragm.
w_{wind}	Tributary lateral pressure acting on the shearwall.
P	Resultant of w_{wind}

GOM	Gross Overturning Moment
RM	Resisting Moment
DOM	Design Overturning Moment
FS	Factor of Safety =1.5 = 3/2 (wind) = 1.18 (seismic)

$$GOM = Ph + VH + \frac{w_{uplift} b^2}{2}$$

$$RM = \frac{w_{DL} b^2}{2} + P_w\left(\frac{b}{2}\right)$$

The mandate of the moment stability comparison is that net system effect be balanced out with the appropriate factor of safety for overturning. If you overestimate the dead load resistance, your calculation becomes unconservative with respect to this stability check. The uplift force on the overall shearwall system must be less than or equivalent to the resistive force times a factor of safety.

$$GOM \le \tfrac{2}{3}\ RM = .67\ RM \text{ (wind forces)}$$

$$GOM \le .85\ RM \text{ (seismic forces)}$$

If this force is exceeded, then the DL weight of the foundation can be added to the RM calculation (with the addition of connective hardware such as holdowns). If this does not fill the requirements of stability, then something else is done, like lengthening the shearwall to increase the RM or making the foundation larger to add resistive weight. The DOM is used to calculate the uplift force "T" required to size the holdown and check the boundary elements of the shearwall. The holdown connects the shearwall to the massive resistive weight of the foundation below. For wind:

$$DOM = GOM - \tfrac{2}{3}\ RM$$

$$T = \tfrac{DOM}{b}$$

The overall system must be stable and contain the appropriate FS. Thus:

$$GOM \le \tfrac{2}{3}\ RM \text{ (wind forces)}$$

Structural system thinking

Conceptually, try to think of your structure as a system of individual members positively linked together to transfer applied loads or forces. Don't just think of the individual components that you are being paid to design.

You are required to provide a direct and continuous path from the source of the load to the ground for both vertical and lateral forces. It is the paths and elements that essentially makeup the vertical and lateral systems. With vertical loads the path becomes obvious. However, with lateral loads it is not so obvious, and you must be on the alert for possible breaks and weak points along the transfer path.

In order to have continuous force transfer, the elements and connective hardware must be in physical contact with each other. This obvious concept reveals the error in thinking when we look at individual elements rather than the flow of force in systematic terms. You don't just design elements of a system, you design a cohesive system of elements.

□
□
□

There is only one success, to be able to spend your life in your own way.

CHRISTOPHER MORLEY

PROBLEM 1.9

Shearwall basic formulas.

For a simple shearwall, define the basic length of the shearwall required. Find the design tension force and simple compression force in terms of unit shear.

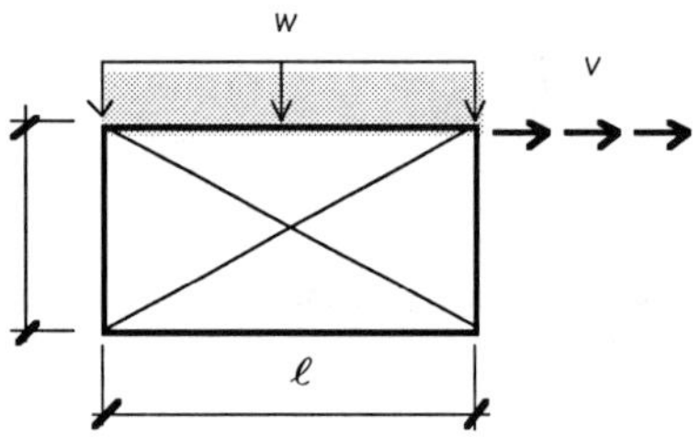

ASSUME

Wind force.
Neglect wall weight (consv.).

SOLUTION

Find ℓ_R

UBC 1619.1

$GOM = Vh = v\,\ell h$

$$\tfrac{2}{3}\,RM = \frac{2}{3}\left(\frac{w\ell^2}{2}\right) = \frac{w\ell^2}{3}$$

For stability $GOM \le \tfrac{2}{3}\,RM$

$$v\,\ell h = \frac{w\ell^2}{3}$$

Solve for ℓ_R for given v,w

$$vh = \frac{w\ell}{3} \quad \text{solving gives}$$

$$\ell_R = \frac{3vh}{w} \text{ (lenght of SW required)}$$

Find T

$$T = \frac{DOM}{\ell} = \frac{GOM - \tfrac{2}{3}\,RM}{\ell}$$

$$= \frac{v\ell h - \frac{w\ell^2}{3}}{\ell} \quad \text{solving gives}$$

$$T = vh - \frac{wL}{2} \text{ (tension force required)}$$

Find C

w_{trib} = The tributary gravity load proximate to the chord of the shearwall (before T exists).

But if T, then $\frac{w\ell}{2}$

$$C = \frac{GOM}{\ell} + w_{trib} = \frac{v\ell h}{\ell} + w_{trib}$$

$$C = vh + w_{trib}$$

Under the ASD approach (as outlined in the code), the structure remains in the elastic range of the material. When a large earthquake occurs the structure can go into the inelastic range of the material. Here the Code assumes that sufficient detailing of the connections will provide the required ductility to keep the structure safe. It is your responsibility to insure that the detailing of the connections provides a direct and continuous path for lateral force transfer.

Load Duration and Combination Factors

The UBC Sec. 1603.5 states that allowable stresses (and soil-bearing values) for working stress design can be increased by 1/3 for wind or earthquake forces whether the forces act alone or are combined with vertical loads. Traditionally, this increase has been applied to all materials and soil-bearing values. Since this 1.33 (load duration factor) increase is the same as the past C_D (load combination factor) increase of 1.33, it is often confused, and one or the other is not used. This is, of course, a conservative error and only makes the structure less economic and more safe. The 1991 NDS maintains that both increases can be used since they are two different adjustments. The 1991 NDS recommends that the material property adjustment factor C_D be changed from 1.33 to 1.6 for wind and seismic forces. This is due to the fact that wood can support higher stresses for short amounts of time. You should verify the acceptance of C_D = 1.6 with your local building officials. Recall that the UBC limits the use of the load duration factor of 1.33 for certain seismic zones and forms of building irregularity.

Shearwall sheathing materials

Shearwalls are essentially vertical diaphragms that are designed to resist lateral forces in the plane of (parallel to) the wall. There are many types of materials that are allowed by code to be used in the construction of a shearwall on wood stud walls. Some of the more typical materials are:

- Fiberboard. See UBC Table 23 - I - P.
- Particleboard. See UBC Table 23 - I - K - 2.
- Plywood. Minimum requirements are 5/16 inch thick and 3/8 inch thick plywood for studs at 16 and 24 inches on center respectively. See UBC sec. 2314.3 and Table 23 - I - K - 1.
- Plaster/stucco.
- Diagonal planks. Usually 1 inch sheathing laid at 45 degrees to vertical studs with a minimum of two 8d nails for 6 inch wide boards; three 8d nails at 8 inch or wider boards with additional requirements by the UBC sec. 23114.2.
- Drywall/gypsum wallboards.

The most commonly used shearwall materials today are plywood, drywall/gypsum wallboards and OSB particleboard.

Perfections of means and confusion of goals seem -in my opinion- to characterize our age.

ALBERT EINSTEIN

<u>PROBLEM</u> 1.10

Seismic coefficient determination for various zones.

You just landed an important engineering position with the home office of a firm that has branches in four different states. Each state lies in a different primary seismic zone. Since your overseeing job requires you to perform a quick seismic quality control check of the work in all four states, you need to get a ballpark idea of the seismic zones' coefficients.

Determine the seismic coefficient (regular structures) for the following:

a. ASSUME

Zone 1.
Essential Facility.
Ply SW 3 stories or less.
C = 2.75.

b. ASSUME

Zone 2A.
Hazardous Facility.
Other light framing SW.
C = 2.75.

c. ASSUME

Zone 3.
Special occupancy.
Concrete SW.
C = 2.75.

d. ASSUME

Zone 4.
STD occupancy.
Masonry SW.
C = 2.75.

SOLUTION

Zone 1

$$V = \frac{ZICW}{R_w} = \frac{.075(1.25)2.75W}{8} = .032W$$ UBC 1628.2.1

.032 seismic coefficient for Zone 1

The value of C does not have to exceed 2.75. It may be used as a maximum with any code circumstances.

Zone 2a

$$V = \frac{.015(1.25)2.75W}{6} = .009W$$ UBC T16-I

.009 seismic coefficient for Zone 2a

Zone 3

$$V = \frac{.3(1.0)2.75W}{6} = .138W$$

.138 seismic coefficient for Zone 3

Zone 4

$$V = \frac{.4(1.0)2.75W}{6} = .183W$$

.183 seismic coefficient for Zone 4

Over the years it has become apparent that certain types of buildings perform better than others during an earthquake. These structures are called "regular" by the code. They tend to be symmetric and without discontinuities. When a building does not possess these qualities (and when they reside in certain seismic zones) the code penalizes these "irregular" structures by enforcing higher coefficients.

The coefficients for Z are representative of the effective peak ground accelerations for their respective zones. These coefficients can be likened to g factors that are applied to the base of the structure before it is amplified by dynamic properties or geology. The peak ground accelerations are based on a 475-year recurrence of that peak. A 10% probability exists that the peak will be exceeded in 50 years.

Vertical seismic ground motion

Although certain recorded earthquakes have had large vertical ground motion (i.e. Northridge, CA), usually vertical ground motion caused by a seismic event is considerably less than that of the horizontal movement caused by the same event. It is for this reason that we normally do not consider the effects of vertical seismic forces (see UBC 1628.10) Furthermore, because we design primarily for gravity forces, a typical structure has more intrinsic vertical strength and stability built into the design that is used to resist the smaller vertical seismic forces.

Computer spreadsheets

The 1991 NDS incorporated sweeping changes in the design of wood structures and elements. There is little doubt that the added complexity will require the use of computer programs and self-authored (in-house) computer spreadsheets to fully realize the technical advances in wood engineering.

You can purchase computer wood engineering programs to solve many of the problems found in practice. However, it is highly recommended that the reader acquire the skills of basic spreadsheet usage.

Once you have solved a problem on the computer spreadsheet it can be saved and used as a template for other comparable problems you might run into in your practice. Furthermore, computer spreadsheets are not only used to directly solve a multitude of complex problems, but can be used to solve other problems indirectly (with logical test- making decision parameters).

Love is but the discovery of ourselves in others, and the delight in the recognition.

ALEXANDER SMITH

PROBLEM 1.11

Seismic and wind comparison normal to tilt-up wall.

One of your staff architects needs to know the design forces for a one-story strip mall for a preliminary job proposal. She wants you to determine the design forces normal to the indicated wall in the transverse direction. She also wants you to determine the reaction at the roof and slab.

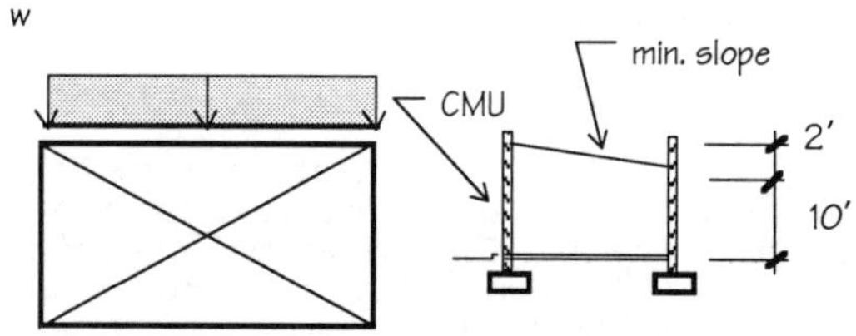

ASSUME

Exposure C (method 2).
Basic wind speed = 70 mph.
I = 1.0.
Closed structure.
RDL = .012 ksf.
$Wall_{DL}$ = .08 ksf.
Zone 4.

SOLUTION

Wind

UBC 1618, T16-F,G,H

Look @ 1 square ft of wall for: wind to main wall, and to the parapet respectively. Using Method 2:

$P = C_e C_q q_S I$ which implies

$w_1 = 1.06(1.3)12.6(1.0) = 17.4$ psf

$w_2 = 1.06(1.2)12.6(1.0) = 16.0$ psf

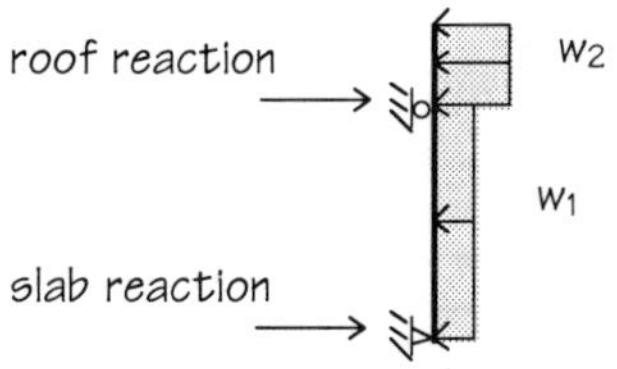

These forces are considered to act inwards or outwards depending on whether the wind is acting leeward or windward.

> Wind force to parapet = 16.0 psf
> Wind force to wall = 17.4 psf

Seismic

UBC 1603.2

The structures that are most likely governed by seismic forces are made of heavy materials like CMU, concrete, or brick. Wood structures are lighter and will be governed by wind forces more often than not. Look @ 1 square ft of wall for seismic to main wall and to the parapet respectively.

UBC T16-I,L,O

$F_p = ZIC_pW_p$ which implies

$w_1 = .4(1.0).75(.08) = .024$ ksf

$w_2 = .4(1.0)2.0(.08) = .064$ ksf

These forces are inwards or outwards.

Summary

> At main wall design (w_1)
> seismic governs over wind,
> .024 > .017
> At parapet wall design (w_2)
> seismic governs over wind,
> .064 > .016

Reaction at roof and slab

Note that the code (UBC) requires that C_p be increased 50 percent in the center half of flexible diaphragms when considering anchorage forces at the horizontal diaphragm level. Therefore, our anchorage values must be adjusted later for a flexible diahpragm.

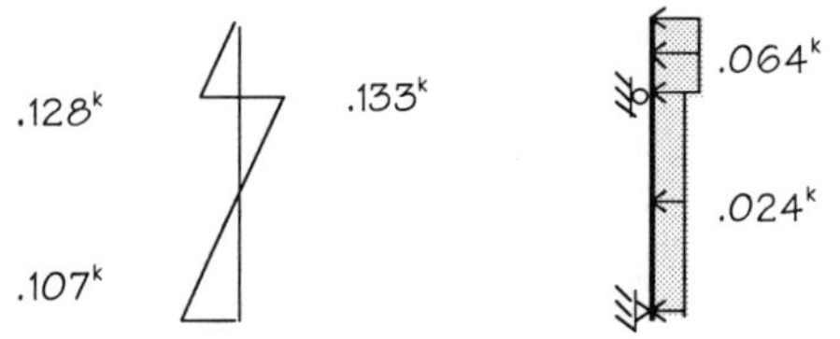

The reaction to the roof is .261 klf, which is greater than the code minimum requirement of .2 klf. The reaction to the slab is .107 klf. This assumes the wall spans vertically. Remember that the wall could have been designed to span horizontally to pilasters. In this case the concentrated forces would accumulate at the pilasters.

Concerns for man and his fate must always form the chief interest of all technical endeavors. Never forget this in the midst of your diagrams and equations.

ALBERT EINSTEIN

PROBLEM 1.12

Panelized roof system loading comparison.

Examine the difference between: a uniform load using AISC Table of Concentrated Load Equivalents, a uniform load calculated as the unit load times the tributary width to the girder, and a point load for a panelized roof system shown below.

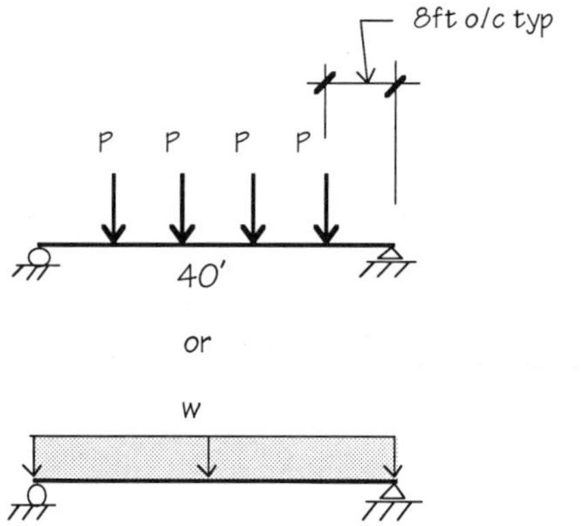

ASSUME

Panelized roof system.
$P = 4.1^k$ (reduced LL included).
Girder tributary width = 16 ft.
$TL = DL + LL_{reduced} = .032$ ksf.

SOLUTION

Point loads

P has been derived from TL: $P = .032(8)16 = 4.1^k$

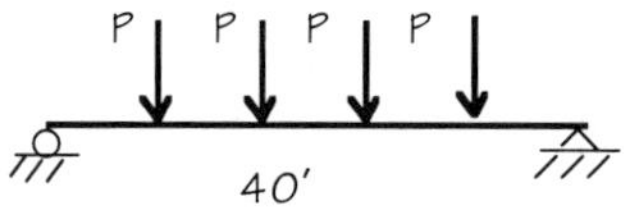

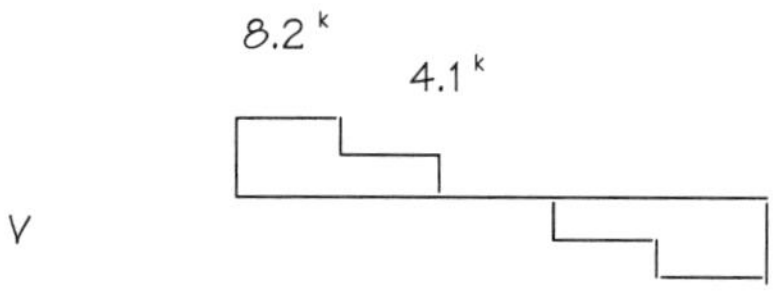

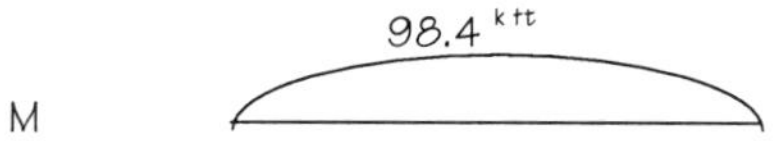

Uniform load

Per AISC's Table of Concentrated Load Equivalents, the equivalent simple span uniform load in kips is equal to P(f) where f = the uniform load equivalent. For this load condition: AISC 2-113 (8th ed.)

$w = Pf = 4.1(4.8)/ 40 = .492$ klf

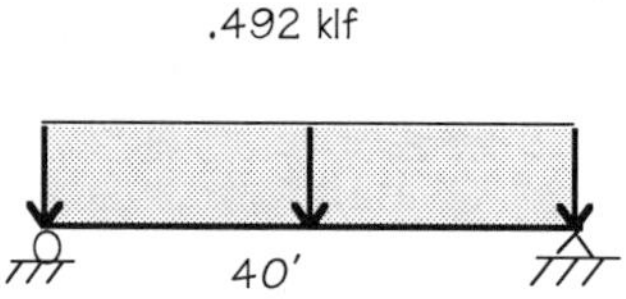

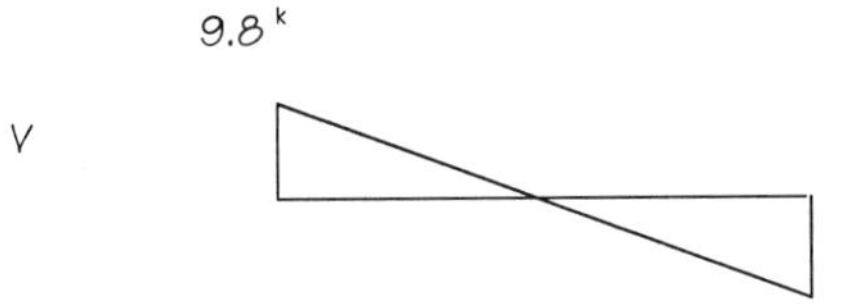

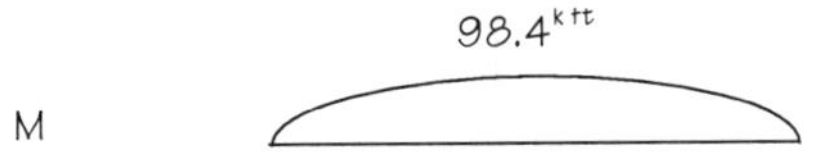

Uniform load using tributary area

w = TL(girder tributary width)

= .032(16) = .512 klf (consv.)

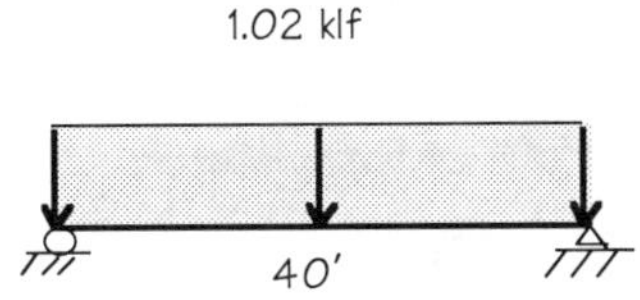

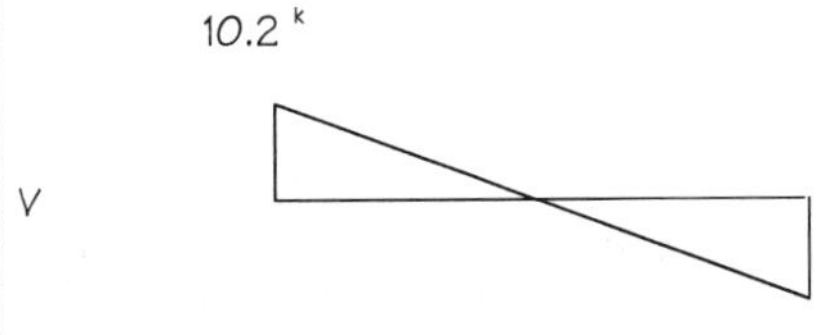

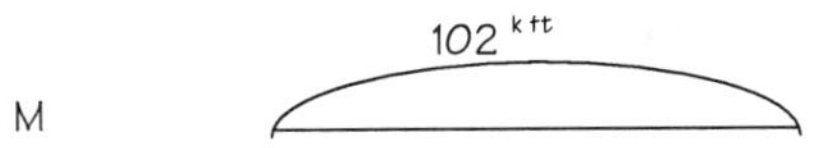

Summary

The most accurate analysis is the point load method. The AISC method is next. The girder tributary width method is the most conservative approach and is widely used in practice. In choosing one or the other approach consider the criteria of time and money. If you do not have the time do the conservative method. If you are trying to save some construction costs use the point load method. Remember that the reduced LL is based upon the tributary area of the member being designed. In most panelized systems purlins are at 8 ft o/c and subpurlins are at 24 in o/c.

Ah, but a man's reach should exceed his grasp, Or what's a heaven for.

ROBERT BROWNING

PROBLEM 1.13

Base shears for wind and seismic loads.

Determine whether wind or seismic base shear governs (in the transverse direction) for the one-story strip mall structure shown below. Use a simple approximate method.

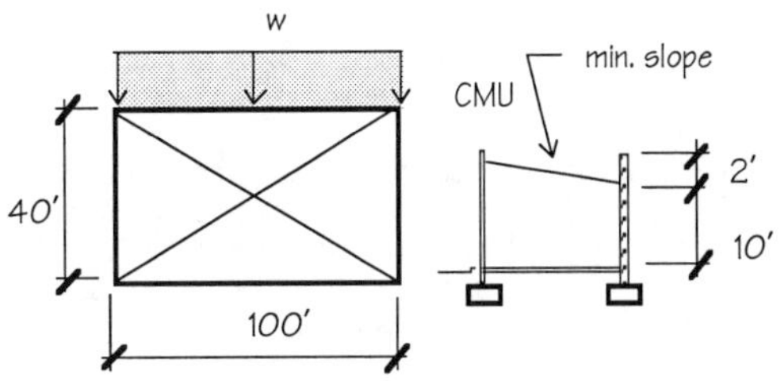

ASSUME

Exposure C (method 2).
Basic wind speed = 70 mph.
I = 1.0.
Closed structure.
RDL = .012 ksf.
$Wall_{DL}$ = .08 ksf.
Zone 4.

SOLUTION

UBC 1619

The code requires that the building be simultaneously considered for both lateral and vertical wind pressures. Consider only affects of lateral here.

Ck wind

Look @ a 1 ft strip of building for wind tributary to diaphragm.

UBC 1618, T16-F,G,H

$P_{wind} = C_eC_qq_sI$

$= 1.06(1.3)12.6(1.0) = 17.4$ psf

Many designers approximate the load w by just taking 1/2 the vertical span of the wall and adding the height of the parapet. Thus:

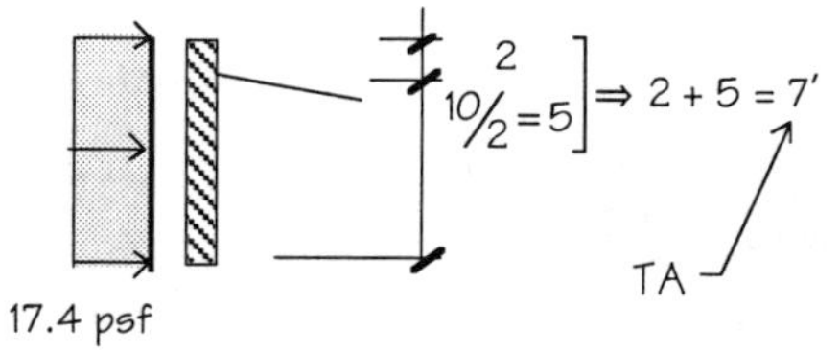

$w = P(TA) = .0174(7)$

$= .122$ klf < .2 code min UBC Sec. 1611).

Which is the load to the roof diaphragm.

Ck Seismic

Look @ a 1 ft. strip for seismic to compare with wind to see which governs the design of the elements. Note that since the base shear coefficient and the story coefficients are equal for a one-story building, our task is greatly simplified as compared to a multi-story building. This allows the base shear coefficient $(ZIC)/R_w$ to be used directly to compute the uniform force to the horizontal diaphragm.

$V = \frac{ZICW}{R_w}$ c max = 2.75   UBC 1628.2.1

$V = \frac{.4(1.0)2.75W}{6} = .183W$

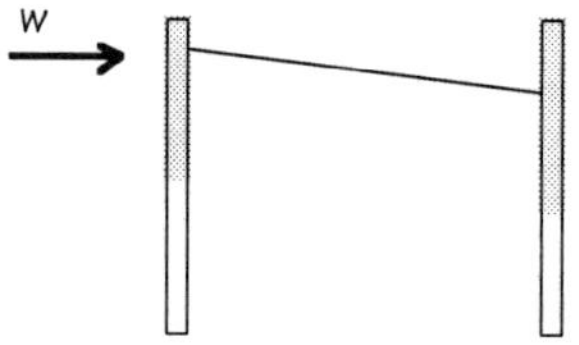

The longitudinal exterior walls are seismically loading the diaphragm. If there were interior longitudinal walls, they too would load the diaphragm as well. Simply put, walls with their plane in the direction of the seismic force can offer resistance to the force. Walls perpendicular to the force cannot offer resistance, so their inertial (seismic) load has to be carried through the horizontal diaphragm to other walls that are shear walls. Note: Interior walls which are seismically attached to a roof or floor should have their inertial force added to the diaphragm's seismic load.

$W = Wall_{DL}$(wall trib. of both walls)

$= .08(7)2 = 1.12$ klf

W_{diaph} = diaph length (diaph DL)

$= 40(.012) = .48$ klf

$w_{seismic} = .183(1.12 + .48)$

$= .183(1.6)$

$= .293$ klf $> w_{wind}$

∴ Seismic governs.

The value of .183 for the base shear coefficient is very common for concrete or masonry structures with a wood roof, and represents approximately 18% of the gravity force applied laterally to the horizontal diaphragm.

Note that w is usually larger in the longitudinal (longer) direction and smaller in the transverse direction. This is due to the estimation of DL being the same over the given area. Hence the seismic force is directly proportional to the length of the floor or roof.

Calc diaph. shear

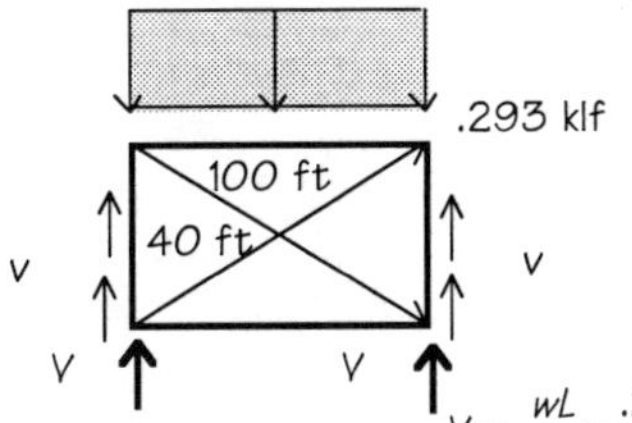

$V = \frac{wL}{2} = \frac{.29(100)}{2} = 14.5^k$

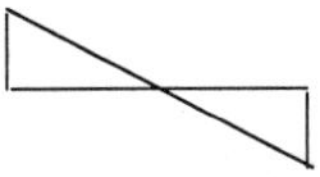

v = 14.5/40 = .363 klf (unit shear)

Calc shear in wall (Due to inertial load of wall itself)

Use full height of wall (consv.)

$TA_{wall} = 12(40) = 480\ ft^2$

$R_{wall} = .183(480).08 = 7.03^k$

Calc base shear

$V_{base} = V + R_{wall} = 14.5 + 7.03 = 21.5^k$

Base shear $V = 21.5^k$

Calc unit base shear

$v = \frac{V}{b} = \frac{21.5}{40} = .54\ klf$

Unit base shear v = .54 klf

Analysis comparison

To get a feel for the accuracy of the approximate methodology of the analysis that we used for this problem, let's do a comparison with a more direct and exact method. Using the AITC Beam Formula Tables (or a computer program), analyze the subject wall as a vertical beam with a 2 foot cantilever. For wind we have:

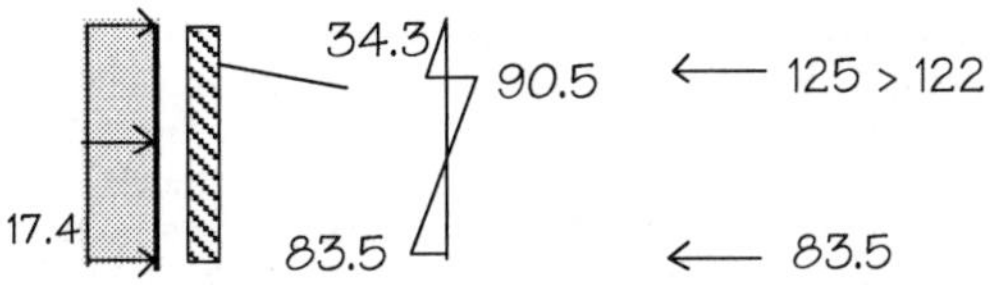

125/122 = 1.02 Which implies 2% over.

Hence the approximate method yields an error of 2% in this case (if other walls are run, it's as much as 10%). Since we have the same geometry (with different forces) for the seismic lateral loading, we again have a 2% error when we calculate the seismic resultants as well.

Summary

We see that the approximate method compares well with the more exact method we used in our comparison. Although the approximate method is commonly used in practice, it should only be used provided you understand the limitations of the procedure. This is true of any procedure or computer program. Failure to understand the intrinsic limitations of a formula, a procedure, or a computer program, can lead to unrecognized systematic error that will taint your calculations and impugn your reputation as a professional engineer. Many college professors advise against using a formula (or a computer program) that you cannot understand and replicate yourself.

R_w - structural system quality factor

The structural system quality factor is located in the denominator of the formula for the base shear coefficient. Mathematically, as Rw gets larger the base shear coefficient, and hence the base shear itself, gets smaller.

This reflects the judgment of the authoring agencies that certain representative structural system types will perform better under lateral load than other structural system types. Take, for example, a building frame system compared to a bearing wall system.

The building frame system has the vertical load "resistive" path elements separated from the lateral load "resistive" path elements (neglecting the horizontal diaphragms). The frame itself takes the vertical or gravity loads to the ground while the non-bearing shearwall elements take the lateral forces to the ground.

In a bearing wall system the bearing walls take both vertical and lateral loads to the ground. It is the judgment of the authoring agencies that if an individual element of the lateral force system fails in a building frame system, the net catastrophic effect will be lessened due to the separate load paths. Plainly put, a failure of a lateral element in a building frame system does not necessarily cause a localized collapse of the proximate vertical elements.

This theory is based upon empirical evidence and observation of numerous structures undergoing earthquakes (both real and simulated). It is for these reasons that a larger R_w is awarded to structural systems with a better performance (actual and anticipated) record.

Basically, this sense of redundancy is expressed in structural engineering in two ways. First, we only calculate quantifiable load paths through selected members. We ignore all other partial resistive elements and paths when fulfilling code requirements. Therefore, there exists a certain amount of redundancy in most structures which allows the structure to be "stronger" than our calcs show. Secondly, sometimes we incorporate secondary systems for critically important elements, members or systems to provide additional factors of safety.

When the eagles are silent the parrots begin to jabber.

SIR WINSTON CHURCHILL

<u>PROBLEM</u> 1.14

Critical lateral load distribution for 2-story plywood sheathed structure.

Determine the critical lateral load w in the transverse direction and distribute it to the floors and walls of the 2 - story structure shown below.

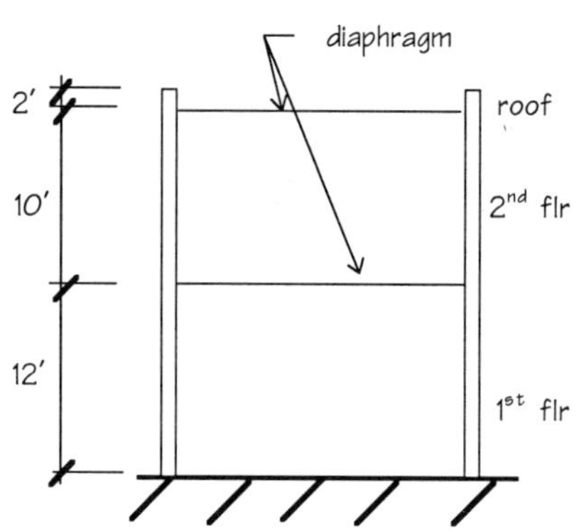

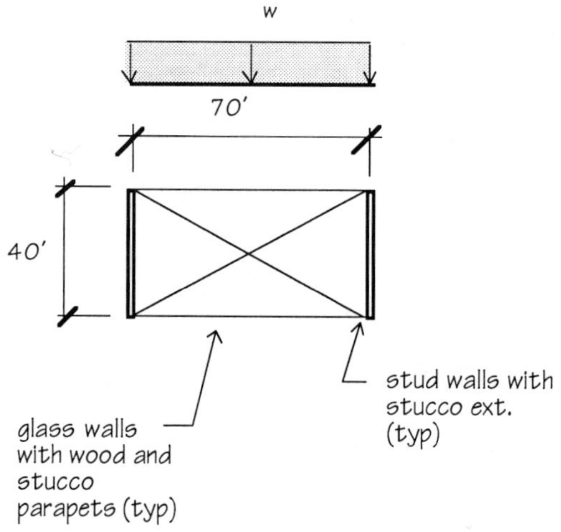

ASSUME

Standard occupancy.
No openings on transverse walls.
RDL = 16 psf.
FDL = 12 psf.
Wall DL = 16 psf.
Glass wall DL = 8 psf.
No snow load.
Zone 3.
Basic wind speed = 90 mph (method 2).
Exposure B.
Shear paneled walls.

Interior partitions (office building).
$C = 2.75$, $F_t = 0$.

SOLUTION

UBC 1618, T16-F,G,H

Ck wind (1′ strip)

$P = C_e C_q q_s I$

$= C_e(1.3)20.8(1.0) = 27\,C_e$

$P_{15} = 27(.62) = 16.8$ psf

$P_{20} = 27(.67) = 18.1$ psf

$$P_{24} \Rightarrow \left.\begin{matrix} 20 & .67 \\ 24 & x \\ 25 & .72 \end{matrix}\right] \rightarrow x = .71$$

or use 25′ consv.

$P_{24} = 27(.71) = 19.2$ psf

Wind loads

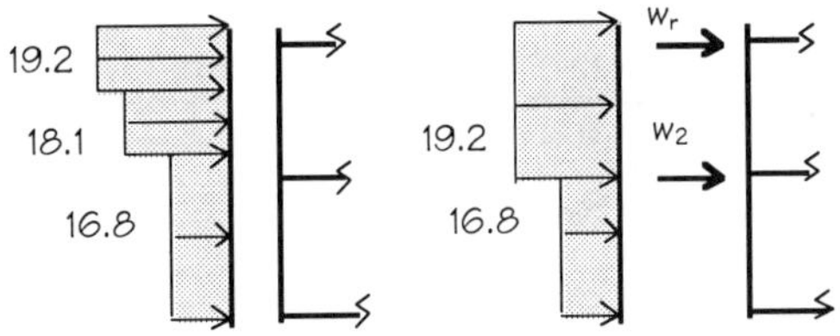

actual code consv. case

For ease of calc, use consv. case.

$$w_r = 19.2\left(\frac{10}{2}+2\right) = 134.4 \text{ plf}$$

$$w_2 = 19.2\left(\frac{10}{2}\right)+16.7\left(\frac{12}{2}\right) = 196.2 \text{ plf}$$

> Wind loads are:
> $w_r = 134.4$ plf
> $w_2 = 196.2$ plf

Ck seismic (1′ strip)

UBC 1628.2.1

$$V = \frac{ZICW}{R_w} = \frac{.3(1.0)2.75W}{8} = .103W$$

The seismic base shear coefficient = .103

Calc trib mass (wts) to roof

In this example, neglect the difference between a glass wall or a stucco wall at parapet level.

2-walls roof

$$W_1 = 2\left(\frac{10}{2}+2\right)8+40(16) = 752 \text{ plf}$$

If interior walls were present, 1/2 of their mass would be applied to the roof diaphragm. It would be conservative to assume that 1/2 the required seismic partition load should be applied to the roof diaphragm. Many partition walls are short and terminate below the level of the ceiling. UBC 1604.4

Total seismic mass to the roof diaphragm

$W_r' = 70(.75) = 52.5^k$

Total mass tributary to roof (includes mass of the transverse shear walls).

$W_r = 52.5 + 2(7).016(40) = 61.5^k$

This method is illustrated in the "Design of Wood Structures" by Breyer. However, some engineers believe it is conservative to include the transverse walls in the total mass tributary to the roof. This is because the shear wall mass is resisted by the shear wall itself. Thus the story forces will be slightly larger due to the conservative approach. It is left to the reader to choose which method to employ in practice.

Calc trib mass (wts) to second floor

The code requires that a 10 psf seismic partition load be applied to the floor diaphragm. UBC 1628.2

2 walls floor partition

$$W_1 = 2\left(\frac{10}{2}+\frac{12}{2}\right)16+40(12) + 10(40) = 1232 \text{ plf}$$

Total mass to the 2nd floor diaphragm

$W_2' = 70(1.23) = 86.1^k$

Total mass tributary to the 2nd floor (includes mass of the transverse shear walls).

$W_2 = 86.1 + 2(11).016(40) = 100.2^k$

Develop Seismic Table

For ease of calculation this table is used to summarize the results as we arrive at the numbers.

Use tabular form:

story	h_x	w_x k	$w_x h_x$	F_x k	story V k
roof	22	61.5	1353	8.8	
					8.8
2nd	12	100.2	1202	7.9	
					16.7
1st	0				
		161.7	2555	16.7	

Calc. base shear from col. 3 and the seismic coef.

$V = .103(161.7) = 16.7^k$

Calc. Fx story forces (story coefficients)

UBC 1628.5

These forces will be used for the design of shear walls.

$$F_x = \frac{(V-F_t)w_x h_x}{\sum w_i h_i} \qquad F_t = 0$$

$$F_x = \left(\frac{(V-F_t)h_x}{\sum w_i h_i}\right)w_x = \left(\frac{(16.7-0)h_x}{2555}\right)w_x$$

$= (.00654h_x)w_x$ (story coefficient)

Apply to each level of the building

$F_r = (.00654(22))61.5 = .14(61.5) = 8.8^k$

$F_2 = (.00654(12))100.2 = .08(100.2) = 7.9^k$

16.7

These story forces should total the value for the base shear. Summing up all the story forces above each level gives the story shear between their respective levels. (see col. 5 above). Col. 6 progressively records the total story shears between levels of the structure

$F_r = .14w_r$
$F_2 = .08w_2$

Calc. F_{px} forces (story coefficients)

UBC 1631.2.9

$$F_{px} = \left(\frac{F_t + \sum_{i=x}^{n} F_i}{\sum_{i=x}^{n} w_i}\right)w_{px}$$

Ck F_{px} code limits

$(.35ZI)w_{px} \le F_{px} \le (.75ZI)w_{px}$

$(.35(.3)1.0)w_{px} \le F_{px} \le (.75(.3)1.0)w_{px}$

$(.105)w_{px} \le F_{px} \le (.225)w_{px}$

$F_{pr} = \left(\frac{F_r}{w_r}\right)w_{pr} = \left(\frac{8.8}{61.5}\right)w_{pr} = .14\ w_{pr}$ Which equals F_r above.

$(.105)w_{px} \le .14\ w_{pr} \le (.225)w_{px}$

$$F_{p2} = \left(\frac{F_r + F_2}{w_r + w_2}\right)w_{p2}$$

$$= \left(\frac{8.8+7.9}{61.5+100.2}\right)w_{p2} = .103\ w_{p2}$$

$(.105)w_{px} \ge .103\ w_{p2} \le (.225)w_{px}$

Since the $.35ZIw_{px}$ code min. is greater than F_{p2}, use the $.35ZIw_{px}$ min.

$F_{pr} = .14w_{pr}$
$F_{p2} = .105\ w_{p2}$

Calc. force to roof diaphragm

Compare seismic force to wind forces applied to roof diaphragm. Using F_{px} coefficient for the uniform seismic force load gives:

$w_{pr} = .14W_1 = .14(.75) = .105$ klf < .134 klf (wind)

Wind governs at roof diaphragm

Calc. force to 2nd floor diaphragm

Compare seismic force to wind forces applied to diaphragm. Using F_{px} coefficient for the uniform seismic force load gives:

$w_{p2} = .105W_1 = .105(1.23) = .129$ klf < .196 klf (wind)

Wind governs at 2nd floor diaphragm

Diaphragm loads

Diaphragms are designed using F_{px} criteria (if it governs). Distribute the critical wind load (governs here) to roof and 2nd floor diaphragms. The diaphragms are designed as if they were horizontal "I" beams. The plywood acts like the web, the double top plates act like flanges and the shear walls resist the forces like reactions.

Note that these forces are slightly larger because we added 1/2 the mass of the transverse walls into the total mass for this level.

Calc. roof and 2nd floor diaphragm shears

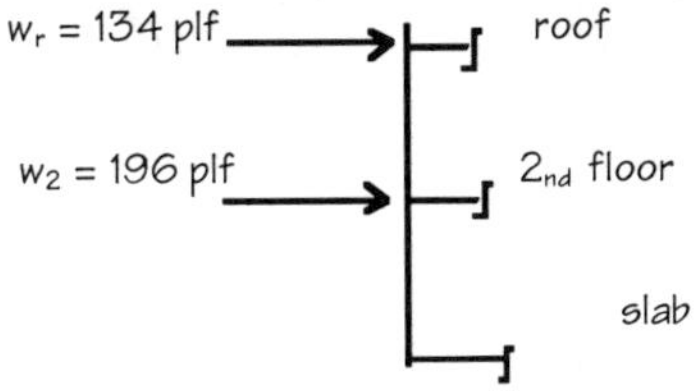

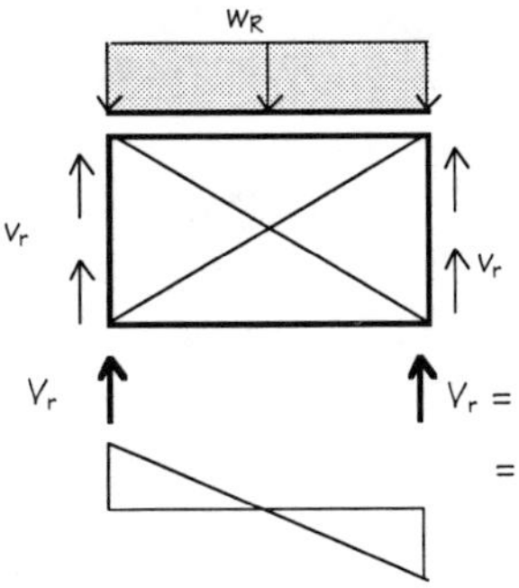

$V_r = \frac{4.7}{40} = .118 \text{ klf}$

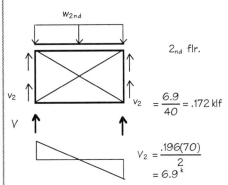

$V_r = \frac{wL}{2} = \frac{.134(70)}{2} = 4.7^k$

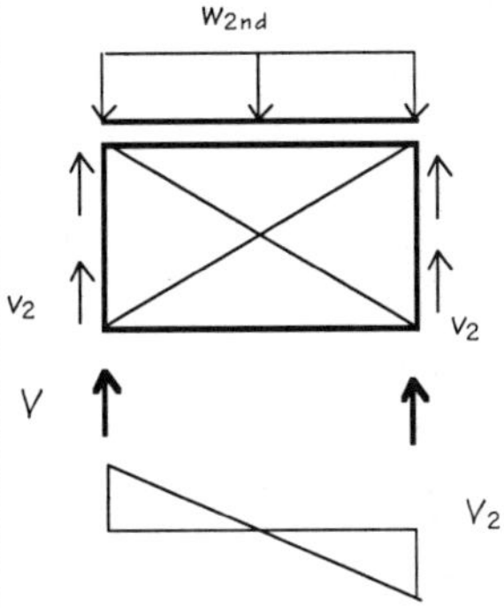

$V_2 = \frac{6.9}{40} = .172 \text{ klf}$

$V_2 = \frac{.196(70)}{2} = 6.9^k$

Calc. F_x forces (story coefficients)

These forces are used to compute the forces for shear wall design.

$w_r = w_{pr} = .105 \text{ klf} < .139 \text{ klf}$ wind governs

The 2nd story coefficients are not equal, so recalc w_2 using F_x story coefficients.

$w_2 = .08W_1 = .08(1.23) = .098 \text{ klf} < .196 \text{ klf}$

Wind governs both roof and 2nd floor diaphragms

Even though wind governs for the diaphragms above, it is possible that when we add the inertial load of the shearwall that seismic will govern. So in our ck, we need to apply the seismic diaphragm shears and the inertial force generated by the mass of top half of the shear walls. Recalc the diaphragm reaction shears thus:

$V_r = \frac{wL}{2} = \frac{.105(70)}{2} = 3.7^k$

$V_2 = \frac{.098(70)}{2} = 3.4^k$

Calc inertial force of shearwall

$R_2 = .15w = .14\left(.016\left(\frac{10}{2}+2\right)40\right) = .63^k$

$$R_1 = .08w = .08\left(.016\left(\frac{10}{2}+\frac{12}{2}\right)40\right) = .56^k$$

<u>Calc shears at mid-height of shearwalls</u>

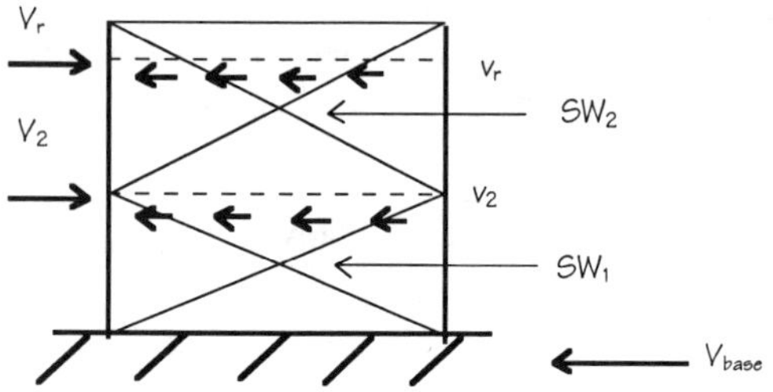

b

Shear in walls

$SW_2 = V_r + R_2$

$= 3.7 + .63 = 4.3^k < 4.7^k$ (wind)

$SW_1 = V_r + R_2 + V_2 + R_1$

$= 4.3 + 3.4 + .56$

$= 8.3^k < 4.7 + 6.9 = 11.6^k$ (wind)

∴ Wind still controls the lateral design of this building. We can see however that it is possible to have wind govern over some elements and seismic to govern over the design of others. Remember that both wind and seismic are not applied simultaneously

> In summary the diaphragm design unit shears are:
> $v_r = .118$ klf
> $v_2 = .172$ klf
> The design shear at the shearwalls are:
> $SW_2 \Rightarrow v_2 = .118$ klf
> $SW_1 \Rightarrow v_1 = 11.6/40 = .29$ klf

□
□
□

People are always blaming their circumstances for what they are. I don't believe in circumstances. The people who get on in this world are the people who get up and look for the circumstances they want, and, if they can't find then, make them.

GEORGE BERNARD SHAW

<u>PROBLEM</u> 1.15

Critical lateral load distribution for 2-story CMU structure.

Determine the critical lateral load w in the transverse direction and distribute it to the floors and walls of the 2 - story structure shown below.

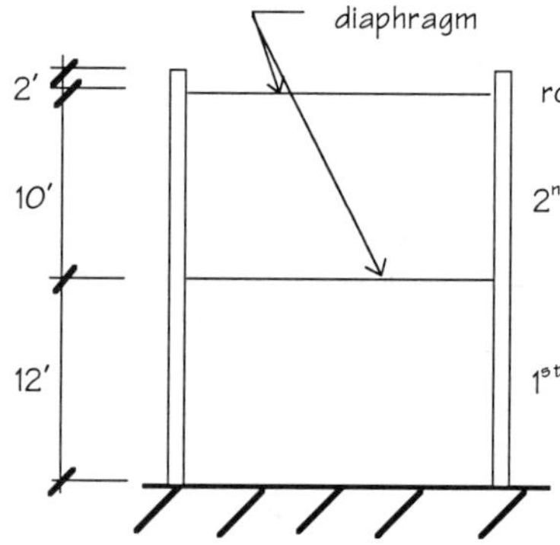

<u>Elevation</u>

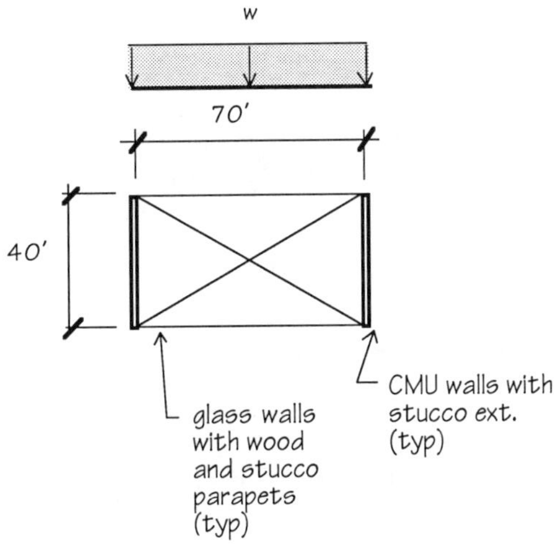

ASSUME

Standard occupancy.
No openings on transverse walls.
RDL = 16 psf.
FDL = 12 psf.
Wall DL = 92 psf.
Glass wall DL = 8 psf.
No snow load.
Zone 4.
Basic wind speed = 70 mph (method 2).
Exposure B.
Interior partitions (office building).
$C = 2.74$, $F_t = 0$.

SOLUTION

Ck wind (1′ strip)

UBC 1618, T16-F, G, H

$P = C_e C_q q_s I$

$= C_e(1.3)12.6(1.0) = 16.4\,C_e$

$P_{15} = 16.4(.62) = 10.2$ psf

$P_{20} = 16.4(.67) = 11.0$ psf

$$P_{24} \Rightarrow \left.\begin{matrix} 20 & .67 \\ 24 & x \\ 25 & .72 \end{matrix}\right] \rightarrow x = .71$$

or use 25′ (consv.)

$P_{24} = 16.4(.71) = 11.6$ psf

Wind loads

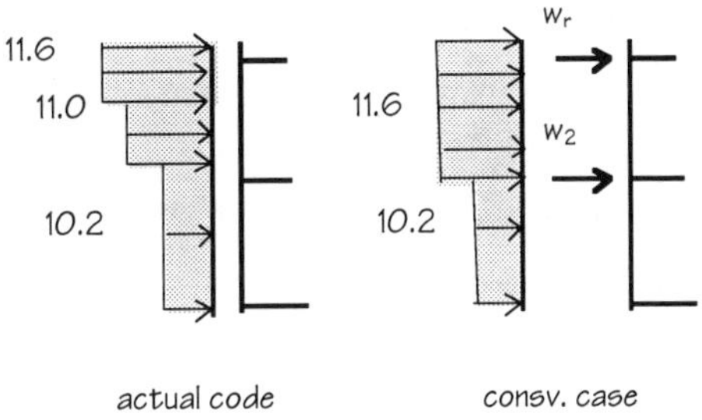

Use consv. case for ease of calc.

$$w_r = 11.6\left(\frac{10}{2}+2\right) = 81 \text{ plf}$$

$$w_2 = 11.6\left(\frac{10}{2}\right)+10.2\left(\frac{12}{2}\right) = 119 \text{ plf}$$

> Wind loads are
> $w_r = 81$ plf
> $w_2 = 119$ plf

Ck seismic (1′ strip)

UBC 1628.2.1

$$V = \frac{ZICW}{R_w} = \frac{.4(1.0)2.75W}{6} = .183W$$

The seismic base shear coefficient = .183

Note that for diaphragm and connective design forces the UBC sec. 1631.2.9.3 requires that $R_w \leq 6$ if the flexible diaphragm supports masonry or concrete walls. Since our example does not support walls of this type our R_w is not bound by this constraint.

Calc trib mass (wts) to roof

UBC 1628.5

In this example, neglect the difference of the glass wall or the stucco wall at parapet level.

2-walls roof

$$W_1 = 2\left(\frac{10}{2}+2\right)8 + 40(16) = 752 \text{ plf}$$

If interior walls were present, 1/2 of their mass would be applied to the roof diaphragm. It would be conservative to assume that 1/2 the required seismic partition load be applied to the roof diaphragm. Many partition walls are short and terminate below the level of the ceiling.

Total seismic mass to the roof diaphragm

$W_r' = 70(.75) = 52.5^k$

Total mass tributary to roof (includes mass of the transverse shear walls).

UBC 1628.2

$W_r = 52.5 + 2(7).092(40) = 104.0^k$

See prob. 1.14.

Calc trib mass (wts) to second floor

The code requires that a 10 psf seismic partition load be applied to the floor diaphragm.

$$W_1 = 2\left(\frac{10}{2}+\frac{12}{2}\right)16 + 40(12) + 10(40) = 1232 \text{ plf}$$

Total mass to the 2nd floor diaphragm

$W_2' = 70(1.23) = 86.1^k$

Total mass tributary to 2nd floor (includes mass of the transverse shear walls).

$W_2 = 86.1 + 2(11).092(40) = 167.1^k$

Develop Seismic Table

For ease of calculation, this table is used to summarize the results as we arrive at the numbers.

Use tabular form.

story	h_x '	w_x ^{k}	$w_x h_x$	F_x ^{k}	story V^k
roof	22	104	2288	23.9	
					23.9
2nd	12	167	2004	21.7	
					45.6
1st	0	–			
		271	4292	45.6	

Calc. base shear From col. 3 and seismic coefficient.

$V = .183(271) = 49.6^k$

Calc. Fx story forces (story coefficients)

UBC 1628.5

These forces will be used for the design of shear walls.

$$F_x = \frac{(V-F_t)w_x h_x}{\sum w_i h_i} \qquad F_t = 0$$

$$F_x = \left(\frac{(V-F_t)h_x}{\sum w_i h_i}\right)w_x = \left(\frac{(49.6-0)h_x}{4292}\right)w_x$$

$$= (.01156h_x)w_x \qquad \text{(story coefficient)}$$

Apply to each level of the building:

$F_r = (.01156(22))104 = .254(104) = 26.4^k$

$F_2 = (.01156(12))167 = .139(167) = 23.2^k$

$\overline{\ 49.6}$

These story forces should total the value for the base shear. Summing up all the story forces above each level gives the story shear between their respective levels.

$F_r = .254w_r$
$F_2 = .139w_2$

Calc. F_{px} forces (story coefficients)

UBC 1631.2.9

$$F_{px} = \left(\frac{F_t + \sum_{i=x}^{n} F_i}{\sum_{i=x}^{n} w_i}\right)w_{px}$$

$(.35ZI)w_{px} \le F_{px} \le (.75ZI)w_{px}$

$(.35(.4)1.0)w_{px} \le F_{px} \le (.75(.4)1.0)w_{px}$

$(.14)w_{px} \le F_{px} \le (.3)w_{px}$

$$F_{pr} = \left(\frac{F_r}{w_r}\right)w_{pr} = \left(\frac{26.4}{104}\right)w_{pr} = .254\,w_{pr}$$

$(.14)w_{px} \le .254\,w_{pr} \le (.3)w_{px}$

$$F_{p2} = \left(\frac{F_r+F_2}{w_r+w_2}\right)w_{p2} = \left(\frac{26.4+23.2}{104+167}\right)w_{p2} = .183\,w_{p2}$$

$(.14)w_{px} \le .183\, w_{p2} \le (.3)w_{px}$ √

Calc. force to roof diaphragm

Compare seismic force to wind forces applied to roof diaphragm. Using F_{px} coefficient for the uniform seismic force load gives:

$w_{pr} = .254W_1 = .254(.75) = .19 \text{ klf} > .081 \text{ klf}$ (wind)

Seismic governs at roof diaphragm

Calc. force to 2nd floor diaphragm

Compare seismic force to wind forces applied to 2nd floor diaphragm. Using F_{px} coefficient for the uniform seismic force load gives:

$w_{p2} = .19W_1 = .19(1.23) = .234 \text{ klf} > .119 \text{ klf}$ (wind)

Seismic governs at 2nd floor diaphragm

Diaphragm loads

UBC 1611

Diaphragms are designed using F_{px} criteria (if it governs). Distribute critical seismic load to roof and 2nd floor diaphragms. The diaphragms are designed as if they were horizontal "I" beams. The plywood acts like the web, the double top plates act like flanges and the shear walls resist the forces like reactions.

Calc. roof and 2nd floor diaphragm shears

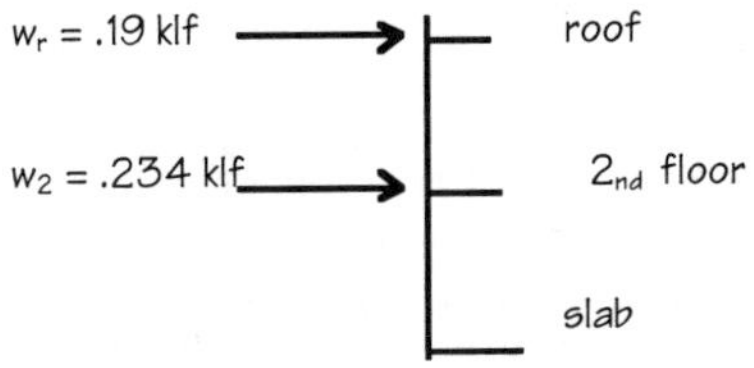

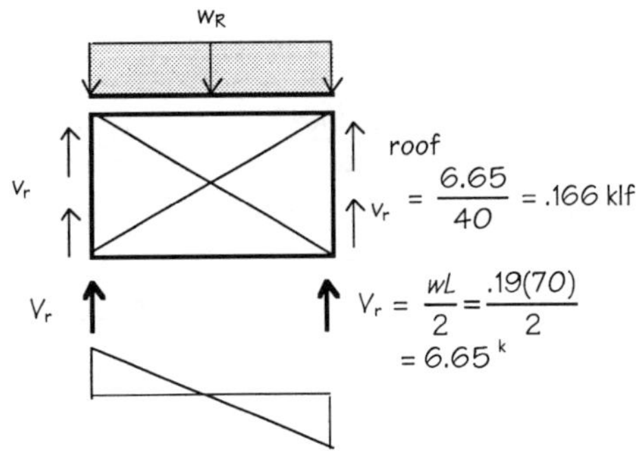

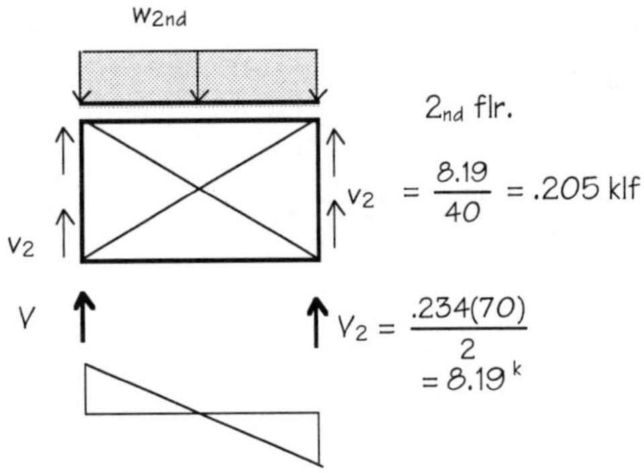

Calc F_x forces (story coefficients)

These forces are used to compute the forces for shear wall design.

$w_r = w_{pr} \Rightarrow F_x = F_{px} \Rightarrow V_r = V_{pr} \Rightarrow v_r = v_{pr}$

The 2nd story coefficients are not equal, so recalc. w_2 using F_x story coefficient

$w_2 = .139(1.23) = .171 \text{ klf} > .112 \text{ klf}$

$$V_2 = \frac{.171(70)}{2} = 5.99^k$$

$$v_2 = \frac{5.99}{40} = .15 \text{ klf}$$

Seismic governs

Calc inertial force of shearwalls

$$R_2 = .254w = .254\left(.092\left(\frac{10}{2}+2\right)40\right) = 6.52^k$$

$$R_1 = .139w = .139\left(.092\left(\frac{10}{2}+\frac{12}{2}\right)40\right) = 5.67^k$$

Calc shears at mid-height of shearwalls

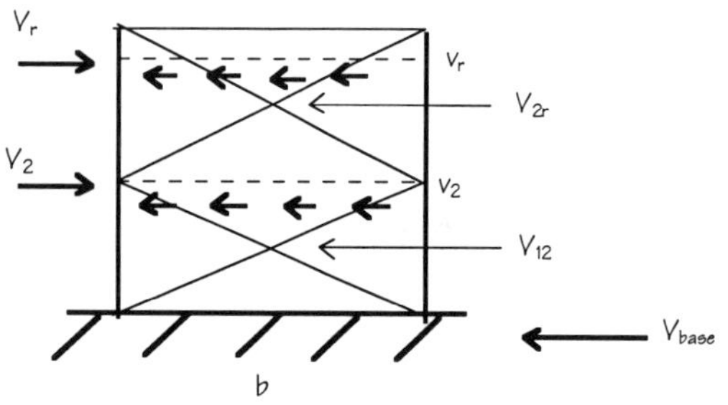

Shear in walls

$$V_{2r} = V_r + R_2 = 6.65 + 6.52 = 13.17^k$$

$$V_{12} = V_r + R_2 + V_2 + R_1 = 13.17 + 8.19 + 5.67 = 27.03^k$$

Unit shear in walls

$$v_{2r} = \frac{13.17}{40} = .329 \text{ klf}$$

$$v_{12} = \frac{27.03}{40} = .676 \text{ klf}$$

∴ Seismic controls the lateral design of this building. We can see, however, that it is possible have wind govern over some elements and seismic to govern over the design of others. If seismic governs and we are designing a warehouse, the code would require that W include 25% of the live load. Recall that the UBC Table 16-C footnote requires that C_p (for anchorage forces) be increased 50% in the center half of a flexible diaphragm. Also note the UBC Sec. 1611 requires a min. of 200 plf for anchorage forces of concrete or masonry walls.

In summary the diaphragm unit design shears are:
v_r = .166 klf
v_2 = .205 klf
The design shear at the shearwalls are:
v_{2r} = .329 klf
v_{12} = .676 klf

Construction sites

It is a good idea for you to visit as many construction sites as possible (preferably your own). This gives you first-hand knowledge of actual methods and practices used in construction. Pay strict attention to the detailing of the structure as it relates to a continuous path for force transfer. A direct and continuous path greatly effects the structure's ability to resist seismic (or wind) forces.

The heights by great men reached and kept were not attained by sudden flight, but they, while their companions slept, were toiling upward in the night.

HENRY WADSWORTH LONGFELLOW

2. Design of Beams

Chapter Problems	Page	Prob.
Beam analysis for simple loads using AITC formulas	2-3	2.1
Beam design for "rough" sawn repetitive members	2-21	2.13
Beam design for double cantilever using semigraphical method of analysis	2-50	2.25
Beam design for non-repetitive members with shear modification	2-6	2.17
Beam design for repetitive members	2-17	2.11
Beam design for repetitive members (Adjustment factor practice)	2-24	2.15
Beam design for repetitive members in wet use condition	2-22	2.14
Beam design for sloped roof rafters	2-19	2.12
Beam design for snow loaded members	2-25	2.16
Bearing parallel to grain adjustment	2-8	2.4
Bearing perpendicular to grain adjustment	2-9	2.5
Bearing perpendicular to grain adjustment for glulam	2-11	2.6
Bi-axial bending	2-61	2.30
Cantilevered glulam beam design	2-53	2.26
Double tapered glulam beam	2-64	2.31
Glulam beam design along with the checking of the purlins and subpurlins	2-35	2.21
Glulam beam design for curved member of pedestrian bridge	2-47	2.24
Glulam beam design for fully supported member	2-28	2.18
Glulam beam design that is laterally supported at 16 ft o/c	2-32	2.20
Glulam beam design that is laterally supported at 8 ft o/c	2-30	2.19
Glulam beam design with cantilever beam/simple beam configuration	2-42	2.23
Load combination comparisons for typ elements	2-5	2.2
Maximum joist spacing for concrete formwork	2-57	2.28
Maximum uniform roof load for a simple beam	2-56	2.27
Notched (top side) beam adequacy using 1991 NDS	2-15	2.9
Notched beam adequacy using 1991 NDS	2-12	2.7

Chapter Problems

Chapter Problems	Page	Prob.
Notched circular beam adequacy using 1991 NDS	2-13	2.8
Panelized roof system design	2-38	2.22
Pitched and tapered curved glulalm beam	2-73	2.34
Pitched and tapered curved glulam beam with attached haunch	2-69	2.33
Shear Modification of loads for simple beam	2-16	2.10
Single tapered glulam beam	2-66	2.32
Sloped and notched rafter with hankinsons using 1991 NDS criteria	2-7	2.3
Tapered end cuts of glulam roof beam	2-59	2.29

PROBLEM 2.1

Beam analysis for simple loads using AITC formulas.

Find the maximum bending stress, shear stress and deflection of the beams shown below. Assume that the beam is a 4 x 10 wood member with an E = 1.6 e3 ksi. Neglect beam weight.

a.

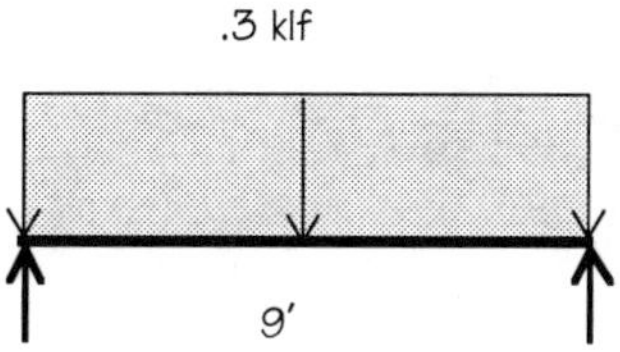

b.

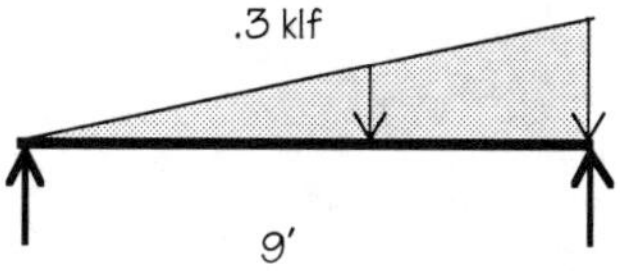

c.

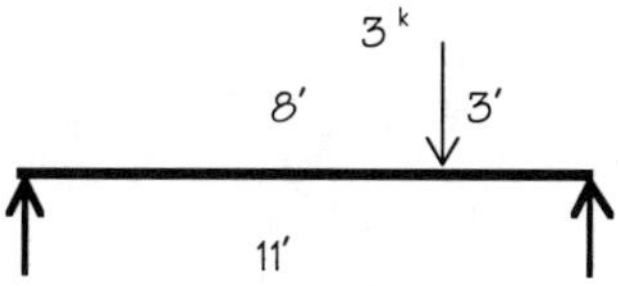

d.

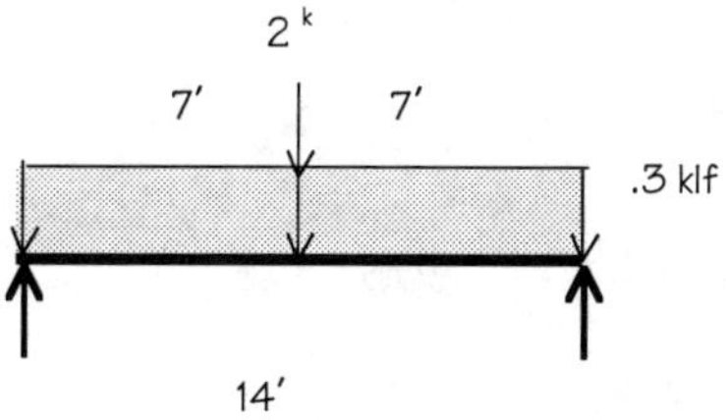

e.

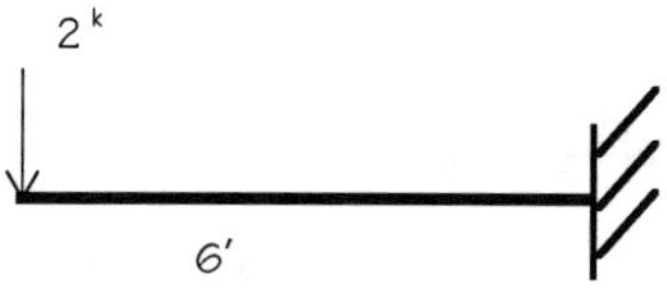

f.

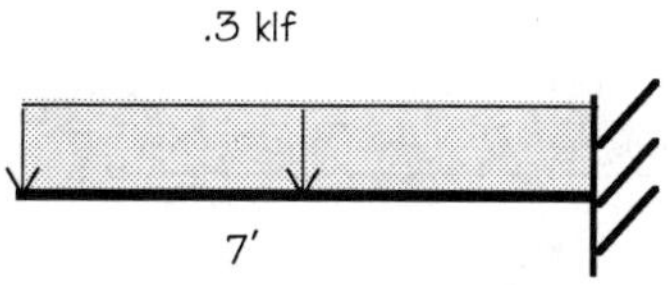

g.

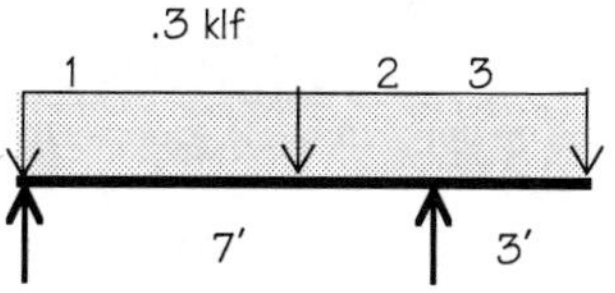

(omit Δ in g.)

a. S4S dressed size = $3\frac{1}{2} \times 9\frac{1}{4}$

$A = 32.38\ in^2$

$I = 230.8\ in^4$

$S = 49.91\ in^3$ NDS T1B

Assume $w_{4x10} = 7.9$ plf

$$V_{max} = \frac{wL}{2} = \frac{.3(9)}{2} = 1.35^{\,k}$$

$$M_{max} = \frac{wL^2}{8} = \frac{.3(9)^2}{8} = 3.04^{\,k\,ft}$$ AITC 8.13

$$f_v = \frac{1.5(V)}{A} = \frac{1.5(1.35)}{32.38} = .06 \text{ ksi}$$

Use a factor of 12 for unit conversion.

$$f_b = \frac{M}{S} = \frac{3.04(12)}{49.91} = .73 \text{ ksi}$$

Use a factor of 1728 for unit conversion.

$$\Delta = \frac{5w\ell^4}{384EI} = \frac{5(.3)9^4(1728)}{384(1.6e3)230.8} = .12 \text{ in}$$

b. $W = \frac{w\ell}{2} = \frac{.3(9)}{2} = 1.35^{k}$

$$V_{max} = \frac{2W}{3} = \frac{2(1.35)}{3} = .9^{k}$$

$$M_{max} = .1283W\ell = .1283(1.35)9 = 1.56^{k\,ft}$$

$$f_v = \frac{1.5(.9)}{32.38} = .042 \text{ ksi}$$

$$f_b = \frac{1.56(12)}{49.91} = .375 \text{ ksi}$$

$$\Delta = \frac{.01304w\ell^3}{EI} = \frac{.01304(1.35)9^3 1728}{1.6e3(230.84)} = .06 \text{ in}$$

c. $V_{max} = \frac{3(8)}{11} = 2.18^{k}$

$$M_{max} = \frac{3(8)3}{11} = 6.55^{k\,ft}$$

$$f_v = \frac{1.5(2.11)}{32.38} = .1 \text{ ksi}$$

$$f_b = \frac{6.55(12)}{49.91} = 1.57 \text{ ksi}$$

$$\Delta = \frac{Pab(a+2b)[3a(a+2b)]^{1/2}}{27EI\ell}$$

$$= \frac{3(4)9(4+2(9))[3(4)(4+2(9))]^{1/2}}{27(1.6e3)230.8(13)} = .0003 \text{ in}$$

d. Combine beam 7 and formulas.

$$V_{max} = \frac{wL}{2} + \frac{P}{2} = \frac{.3(14)}{2} + \frac{2}{2} = 3.1^{k}$$

$$M_{max} = \frac{wL^2}{8} + \frac{P\ell}{4} = \frac{.3(14)^2}{8} + \frac{2(14)}{4} = 14.4^{k\,ft}$$

$$f_v = \frac{1.5(V)}{A} = \frac{1.5(3.1)}{32.38} = .14 \text{ ksi}$$

$$f_b = \frac{M}{S} = \frac{14.4(12)}{49.91} = 3.7 \text{ ksi}$$

$$\Delta = \frac{5w\ell^4}{384EI} + \frac{P\ell^3}{48EI}$$

$$= \frac{5(.3)14^4(1728)}{384(1.6e3)230.8} + \frac{2(14)^3}{48(1.6e3)230.8} = .7 \text{ in}$$

e.

$$V = P = 2^{k}$$

$$M = Pb = 2(6) = 12^{k\,ft}$$

$$f_v = \frac{1.5(2)}{32.38} = .09 \text{ ksi}$$

$$f_b = \frac{2(12)}{49.9} = .48 \text{ ksi}$$

$$\Delta = \frac{P\ell^3}{3EI} = \frac{2(6)^3 1728}{3(1.6e3)230.8} = .67 \text{ in}$$

f.

$$V = w\ell = .3(7) = 2.1^{k}$$

$$M = \frac{w\ell^2}{2} = \frac{.3(7)^2}{2} = 7.35^{k\,ft}$$

$$f_v = \frac{1.5(2.1)}{32.38} = .1 \text{ ksi}$$

$$f_b = \frac{7.35(12)}{49.9} = 1.77 \text{ ksi}$$

$$\Delta = \frac{w\ell^4}{8EI} = \frac{.3(7)^4 1728}{8(1.6e3)230.8} = .42 \text{ in}$$

g.

$$V_1 = \frac{w(\ell^2 - a^2)}{2\ell} = \frac{.3(7^2 - 3^2)}{2(7)} = .86^{k}$$

$$V_2 = wa = .3(3) = .9^{k}$$

$$V_3 = \frac{w(\ell^2 + a^2)}{2\ell} = \frac{.3(7^2 + 3^2)}{2(7)} = 1.24^{k} \text{ controls}$$

$$M_{12} = \frac{w(\ell+a)^2(\ell-a)^2}{8\ell^2} = \frac{.3(7+3)^2(7-3)^2}{8(7)^2} = 1.22^{k\,ft}$$

$$M_3 = \frac{wa^2}{2} = \frac{.3(3)^2}{2} = 1.35^{k\prime}$$

$$f_v = \frac{1.5(V)}{A} = \frac{1.5(1.24)}{32.4} = .06 \text{ ksi}$$

$$f_b = \frac{M}{S} = \frac{1.35(12)}{49.9} = .3 \text{ psi}$$

In this example we examined one of the methods of calculating the stresses required for the design of a beam. The AITC Beam Formulas are useful for the analysis of simple loads and load combinations. Where more complicated loading patterns or support conditions arise (as in actual practice), the employment of the computer is the method of choice for their solution.

Units in formulas

Be sure to pay strict attention to the units of the symbols for the loads, weight and dimensions given in the General Nomenclature section of the AITC when using the Beam Formula Table. You must convert over the formulas to the units that you are using. For instance, we normally talk of a uniform load as being in klf (kips per linear foot of span). The span length for a bending member is given in inches in the "1. Simple Beam- Uniformly Distributed Load Formula". So you would be in error if you combined the two without the use of a conversion coefficient.

General considerations

Four factors are generally considered in the design of wood beams: bending, shear, deflection and bearing. When we size a member we look at the first three of the four factors. Bending and shear have to do with the stresses of the member under load. Deflection is limited by code criteria and is a reflection of not only user comfort, but the critical strain limitations of cosmetic building materials (like plaster ceilings). Bearing limitations are concerned with support conditions.

The design process is often viewed as the iterative process of selecting a trial size member (for the given loads and support conditions) and checking it in each of the above categories. If somewhere in the process the member fails to meet the critical design criteria, the design is revised so that a new trial member is chosen and the process is repeated until all design criteria are met.

There is a difference in approach when you are designing a beam and when you are to perform an analysis of an existing beam. It is simpler to do an analysis of an existing beam because many of the pertinent characteristics of the beam are known. The main idea is found in how you solve with or work with the formulas. A simple example will illustrate the point. Consider the bending (flexure) check of an existing member. We know the loads and the section modulus. We use the loads to calculate the moment and plug it into the formula $\frac{M}{S}$ to obtain the bending stress (f_b) of the member. We then compare this actual bending stress to the allowable bending stress (F_b'). If $f_b < F_b'$, the bending stress is ok and we may move on to one of the other factors. If it is not ok (greater than) we revise the design trial size and recheck it in an iterative manner. Now consider the bending check in the design process. We still have the calculated moment but we have no section modulus. We make an educated guess of the pertinent allowable bending adjustment factors (design coefficients) to calculate the allowable bending stress (F_b'). We then use the formula $\frac{M}{F_b'} = S_R$ to obtain the required section modulus. We then select a size member that has a section modulus greater than required, recheck our assumptions and proceed in an iterative manner as described above.

Life is like a dogsled team. If you ain't the lead dog, the scenery never changes.

LEWIS GRIZZARD

PROBLEM 2.2

Load combination comparisons for typ. elements.

Determine the critical load combination for:

a. The rafter shown below.

b. The beam shown below with w_{RDL} = 18 psf, w_{RLL} = 16 psf.

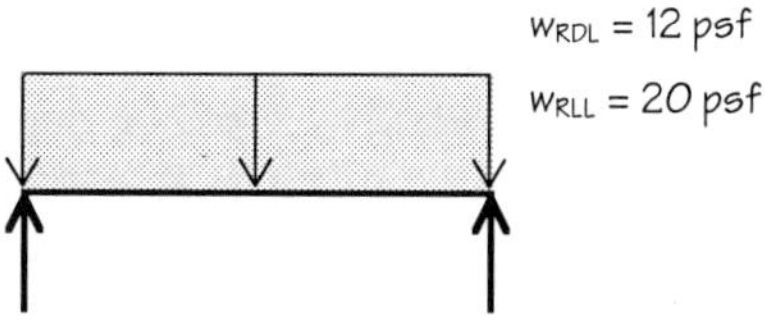

ASSUME

No ponding, no plaster.
Rafter at 24 " o/c.
Beam trib width = 8 ft.
Full lateral support from plywood.
Rafter wt include in DL above.
EMC <19%.
Normal temperature conditions.
Commercial building.

SOLUTION

It is often possible to tell which load combination governs just by looking at the relative magnitudes of both the loads and C_D. If the one load is much larger than the other it will obviously govern. If it's too close to call by inspection, then a convenient way to tell is shown below:

UBC 1603.6, NDS B.2

a. DL

$C_D = .9$

$w_{DL} = 2(12) = 24$ plf

Ratio the load thus:

$$\frac{24}{.9} = 26.7 \text{ plf}$$

DL + LL

$C_D = 1.25$

$w_{LL} = 2(20) = 40$ plf

Ratio the load thus:

$$\frac{40}{1.25} = 32.0 \text{ plf} > 26.7 \text{ plf}$$

Comparison reveals DL+LL controls

b. DL

$C_D = .9$

$w_{DL} = 8(18) = 144$ plf

Ratio the load thus:

$$\frac{144}{.9} = 160 \text{ plf}$$

DL + LL

$C_D = 1.25$

$w_{LL} = 8(16) = 128$ plf

Ratio the load thus:

$$\frac{128}{1.25} = 102 \text{ plf} < 160 \text{ plf}$$

Comparison reveals DL governs

Load Duration vs Load Combination factor?

Both of these allowable stress adjustment factors are to be used for wind or seismic loading. The load duration factor (C_D) is given in the NDS Appendix B.2, the TCM Table 4.1 and the UBC Sec. 2304.3.4.2.

Sec. 1.4.4 and sec. 2.3.2.3 of the NDS states that the load duration factor and the load combination factor are independent of each other and are permitted to be used simultaneously together for design calculations. For years these two factors have been thought of as the same allowable stress increase because they both had coefficients of 1.33. In 1991 the NDS attempted to clarify this with the section noted above, while at the same time bumping up the load duration factor (C_D) to 1.6 times the allowable stress.

Appendix B, Sec. B4 of the NDS justifies this distinction by explaining that the load combination factor is based upon the reduced probability for the simultaneous loading of a member with multiple design loads. The load duration factor (C_D) is based upon the relationship of the strength of wood and the amount of time that member is stressed under a particular load. The load duration factor (C_D) is the reflection of the specific material properties of wood and is to be used only with wood as it relates as a structural member. The load combination factor, however, is meant to be applied to all structural materials. So, it is possible to use the 1.33 coefficient for a seismic tie connector while using 1.33(1.6) coefficient for the wood member itself.

You can always use the load combination factor of 1.33 (with adherence to ASCE 7 provisions), as it has been adopted by most of the building officials in the country. But the wheels of progress sometimes move slowly, so you are cautioned to check with your local building official to verify the 1.6 increase and whether you may use both increases simultaneously. Note that the 94 UBC uses the 1.6 increase for wind members only. Also be sure to check the UBC (sec. 1628.7.2 etc.) for the restrictions in the 1.33 increase in areas of high seismic risk and building with irregularities.

It is your work in life that is the ultimate seduction.

PABLO PICASSO

PROBLEM 2.3

Sloped and notched rafter with hankinsons using 1991 NDS criteria.

Find the actual bearing stress and the allowable bearing stress for both the roof beam and its support. Do not use bearing area adjustment. The reaction of the beam is 3 kips.

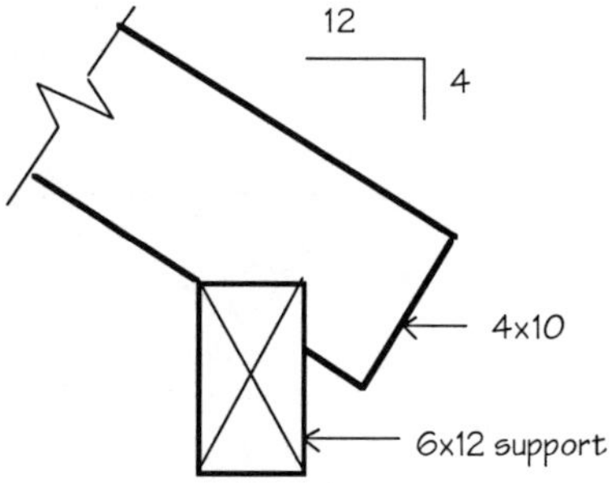

ASSUME

DF-L No. 1.
Load is DL + RLL.
EMC < 19%.
Normal temperature.

SOLUTION

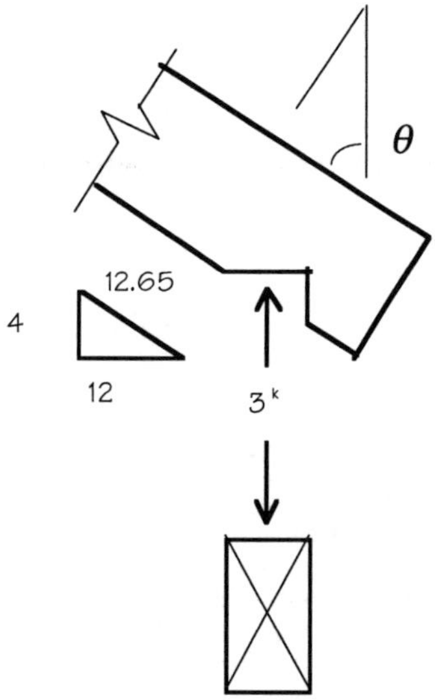

$$\theta = \cos^{-1}\left(\frac{4}{12.65}\right) = 71.566°, \quad \text{or } \sin^{-1}\left(\frac{12}{12.65}\right)$$

Actual Bearing

Same for both but the allowables are different.

$$f_g = P/A = 3/3.5(5.5) = .156 \text{ ksi}$$

Actual bearing f_g = .156 ksi NDS T2.3.1

Allowable bearing at 4 x 10

Assume no steel base plate. Infers $f_g < .75F_g'$ (see NDS 3.10.1.3) NDS 3.10.3

$$F_g' = .75F_g(C_D)C_t = .75(1.45)1.25(1.0) = 1.36 \text{ ksi}$$

$$F_{c\perp}' = F_{c\perp}(C_M)C_t(C_b) = .625(1.0)1.0(1.0) = .625 \text{ ksi}$$

$$F_\theta = \frac{F_g' F_{c\perp}'}{F_g' \sin^2\theta + F_{c\perp}' \cos^2\theta}$$

Since $\sin\left(\sin^{-1}\left(\frac{12}{12.65}\right)\right) = 12/12.65$

$$F_\theta = \frac{1.36(.625)}{1.36\left(12/12.65\right)^2 + .625\left(12/12.65\right)^2}$$

$= .48 \text{ ksi} > .156 \text{ ksi}$ √

Bearing at 4x10 ok

NDS T2.3.1

Allowable bearing at 6 x 12

Assume no steel bearing plate.

$F'_{c\perp} = F_{c\perp}(C_M)C_t(C_b) = .625(1.0)1.0(1.0)$

$= .625 \text{ ksi} > .156 \text{ ksi}$ √

Bearing at 6x12 ok

If a steel base plate were used in this example it would serve to increase the area that is bearing upon the 6x12. This increases the allowable load. Although no increase in bearing area would be realized for the 4x10 rafter, note that the .75 coefficient would be removed and therefore an increase of 25% could be gained.

Notching

Generally speaking, you should avoid the notching of beams or members whenever and whereever possible. It is not uncommon for the trades to cut or notch repetitive members like floor joists or wall studs to accommodate electrical or mechanical systems. The wood industry has become concerned over this practice even when the member is lightly loaded (low percentage of its carrying capacity) because of the serious nature of cutting or notching main or engineered members.

Always insist upon putting a note on your building plans that prohibits the practice of cutting or notching structural members. If required for specific members, detail the procedure and location on the plans.

There is more to life than increasing its speed.

GANDHI

PROBLEM 2.4

Bearing parallel to grain adjustment.

For the column shown below, calculate the allowable bearing "P" both without a steel base plate and then with a steel base plate.

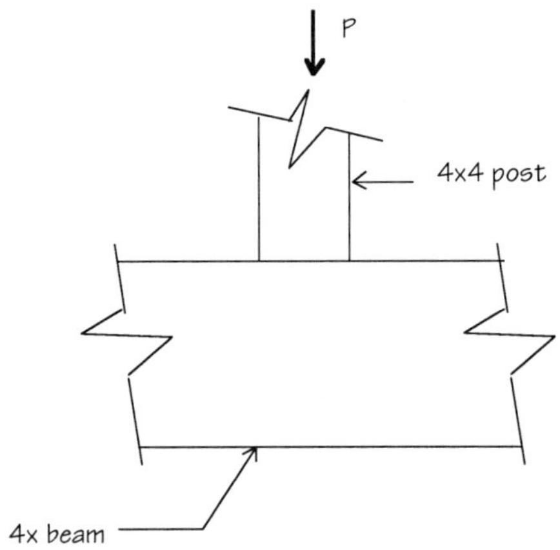

ASSUME

Neglect C_b increase.
Normal temperature conditions.
Supports roof loads.
Same A with or without base plate.

SOLUTION

Without base plate NDS 3.10.1.3

$F_g' = F_g(C_D)C_t = 1.45(1.25)1.0 = 1.81$ ksi

Since no base plate implies fg < .75Fg', it follows that:

$P \le .75F_g'(A) = (.75)1.81(3.5(3.5)) = 16.63^k$

NDS T2.3.1

Allowable bearing without base plate = 16.63^k

With base plate

$F_g' = F_g(C_D)C_t = 1.45(1.25)1.0 = 1.81$ ksi

$P \le F_g'(A) = 1.81(3.5(3.5)) = 22.2^k$

Allowable bearing with base plate = 22.2^k

Parallel to grain bearing

This type of stress ordinarily applies to members under compression. The usual examples of this type of stress are found in posts or columns in the vertical direction and in compression chords in the horizontal direction. It is important to have the member(s) cut square so that full bearing is achieved without any creation of incidental eccentric moments that would cause the shifting of the joints involved.

Parallel to grain stress does not usually control the design of such members because of the influence of other compelling factors and criteria. The allowable stress will possibly control the design when the member approaches a large load capacity for its size. A typical instance is when heavy floor loads are applied to 2x4 construction grade stud walls.

Professional Ethics

On the road to accomplishing your goal of becoming a licensed professional engineer (P.E.) and, eventually, a licensed structural engineer (S.E.), you should take the time to consider the professional ethical responsibilities of theengineering practice.

Once in practice, you enter into the realm of the professional engineering community. You may at times represent the community in both your personal and professional lives. You should conduct yourself with professionalism, integrity and concern for public welfare.

You should always tell the truth. To state the facts as you honestly see them. Moreover, you must make honesty, equal justice and courtesy the foundation of your ethical philosophy. An engineer should foster an interest in his fellow man not passively, but in active observance of a lifestyle that marshals these characteristics to the benefit of the public and of humanity in general.

When you receive the honor of being licensed by your state, you have entered into a social and public trust. The state grants you rights and privileges as an engineer and expects you to discharge your duties and to conduct yourself and your business at a level of public responsibility, integrity, and with impartial fairness to all concerned. Ethically speaking, an engineer applies his special knowledge not only to enhance the lives of his clients and business, but to the greater benefit of humanity.

An engineer strives to uphold the honor and dignity of the engineering profession while disassociating himself from any disreputable enterprise or questionable individuals.

The only man who is really free is the one who can turn down an invitation to dinner without giving an excuse.

JULES RENARD

PROBLEM 2.5

Bearing perpendicular to grain adjustment.

For the loading condition shown below, calculate the allowable bearing "P", both with and without the adjustment.

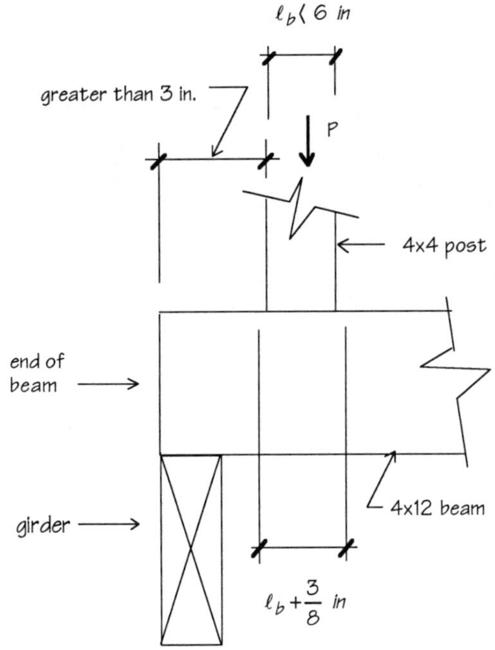

ASSUME

Dry service conditions.
Normal temperature conditions.
DF-L No 1.

SOLUTION

Recall that no adjustment is made for duration of load (C_D) for the design values when considering bearing (compression perpendicular to grain).

Without adjustment

NDS T2.3.1

$F'_{c\perp} = F_{c\perp}(C_M)C_t(C_b) = .625(1.0)1.0(1.0) = .625$ ksi

$P \le F'_{c\perp}(A) = .625(3.5(3.5)) = 7.66^k$

> Bearing without adjustment = .625 ksi
> P without adjustment = 7.66^k

With adjustment

NDS 2.3.10

$$C_b = \frac{\ell_b + .375}{\ell_b}$$

$$C_b = \frac{3.5 + .375}{3.5} = 1.11$$

$F'_{c\perp} = .625(1.0)1.0(1.11) = .69$ ksi

$P = .69(3.5(3.5)) = 8.5^k$

> Bearing with adjustment = .69 ksi
> P with adjustment = 8.5^k

It is obvious that a slight increase is awarded when the adjustment factor is used. Note that since the increase is small and that it is conservative not to use it, many design offices do not use it. It saves time.

Round bearing areas

The bearing area factor may be used for round contact surface areas. In doing so the TCM recommends that the length of bearing (ℓ_b) equal the diameter of the footprint (like the contact surface area of a washer or round pole).

Bearing stress

It should be noted that construction methods and construction tolerances can produce slight mis-alignments in joints. This causes eccentric loading. Even if the member is perfectly aligned, it will bend slightly under its service load. As the member bends it rotates on the inner edge of its bending curve. This edge will receive greater bearing pressure due to this rotation. However, no allowance is given for this fact and the full contact area of the member is used when calculating the bearing area.

Bearing stress is usually concerned with the service of the structure and not safety issues. It is associated with the amount of deformation the member undergoes under load. The bearing stress values that are cited in the NDS limit the amount of deformation to the ASTM D143 0.04 in restriction. Adherence to the bearing stress requirements will produce the reasonableperformance of a building under normal service loads.

If the bearing stress limitations are not taken into account, large service loads can reduce the performance of the structure and cause cosmetic damage in the form of cracks in plaster, etc.

Member availability

Although not pertinent to this problem, the engineer should check the availability of any larger size or special order members prior to finalization of the design process. Failure to do so could result in embarrassing and costly delays in the field.

We're all in this alone.

LILY TOMLIN

PROBLEM 2.6

Bearing perpendicular to grain adjustment for glulam.

The principal of the firm wants you to understand the significance of using the C_b factor for glulam beams. For the loading condition of the glulam beam shown below, she wants you to calculate the allowable bearing "P", both with and without the adjustment.

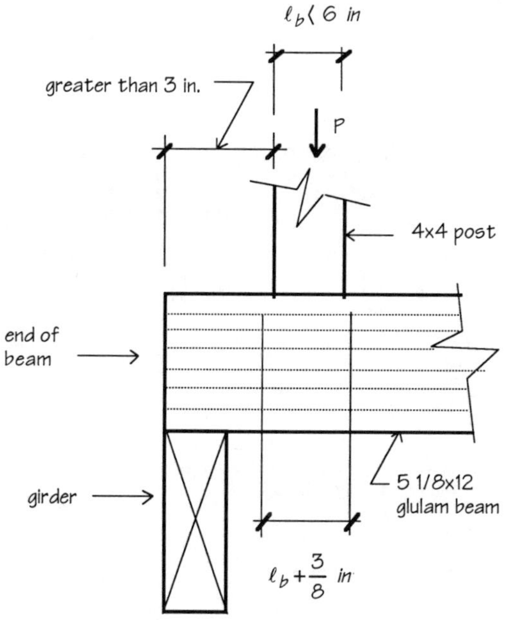

ASSUME

Dry service conditions.
Normal temperature conditions.
24F-V8.

SOLUTION

Without adjustment NDS T2.3.1

Calc adjusted design value:

$$F'_{c\perp} = F_{c\perp}(C_M)C_t(C_b) = .65(1.0)1.0(1.0) = .65 \text{ ksi}$$

Calc maximum load:

$$P \le F'_{c\perp}(A) = .65(3.5(3.5)) = 7.96^k$$

> Allowable bearing without adjustment P = 7.96 k

With adjustment NDS 2.3.10

Calc bearing perpendicular to grain adjustment factor:

$$C_b = \frac{\ell_b + .375}{\ell_b} = \frac{3.5 + .375}{3.5} = 1.11$$

Calc adjusted design value:

$$F'_{c\perp} = .65(1.0)1.0(1.11) = .72 \text{ ksi}$$

Calc maximum load:

$$P = .72(3.5(3.5)) = 8.82^k$$

> Allowable bearing with adjustment P = 8.82 k

A slight increase is awarded when the adjustment factor is used. Since the increase is small (and that it is conservative not to use it) many offices do not use the factor because of the time it saves.

Note also that with a glulam beam you could have a condition where $F_{c\perp}$ is different on one side of the beam than on the other of the beam. For instance, with a 24F-V3, the compression laminations are of lesser quality than the tension laminations. Which means that even if the bottom reaction point (positive moment implies tension side is on bottom) is ok for bearing, the top might not be. Thus:

$$F_{c\perp} = .65 \text{ ksi (tension lams)}$$
$$= .56 \text{ ksi (compression lams)}$$

You must be on the lookout for conditions like thiswhether or not you are going to use the adjustment on glulam beams. Also, be aware that you must let the construction crew know which side of the glulam beam is placed up.

Professional life

An engineer should extend cooperation with other engineers in the service of the profession. The exchange of information (or valuable experience) should be given freely so as to benefit the profession as a whole. Contributions can be at many levels. These may vary from assistance given to our many engineering societies, to providing school educational programs with talks or seminars.

Any conduct that may discredit the dignity or honor of the profession should be avoided at all costs. The continuity of your ethical behavior should be consistent and weave a tight pattern as it flows through the fabric of your life. In essence, you should act with the same standard of excellence of ethical conduct in your professional life as you do in your personal and business lives.

□
□
□

We are here on earth to do good to others. What the others are here for; I don't know.

W. H. AUDEN

○ PROBLEM 2.7

Notched (top side) beam adequacy *using 1991 NDS.*

Due to an error in elevation the field construction crew decided to notch a very short main beam. Because of scheduling and the amount of construction completed (that it supports), they ask you determine if it's ok. You know that it is o.k. in bending and deflection, but need to check the adequacy of the notched beam in shear (as it's shown below).

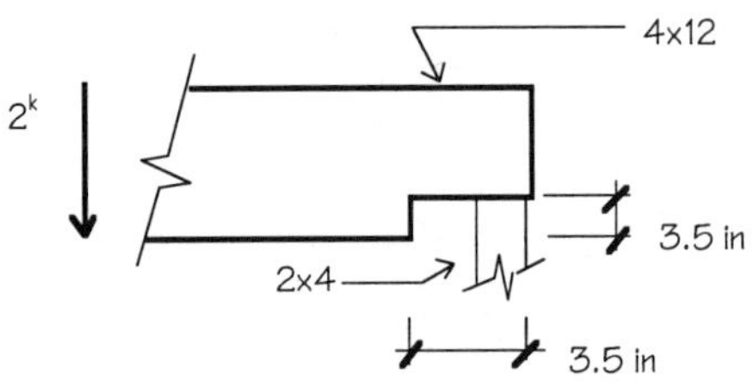

ASSUME

DF-L No.3.
DL + RLL controls.
EMC < 19%.

SOLUTION

The NDS suggests that notching of bending elements is to be avoided whenever possible. It's not that you cannot do it, it's that you shouldn't, especially on the tension side of the element.

Shear

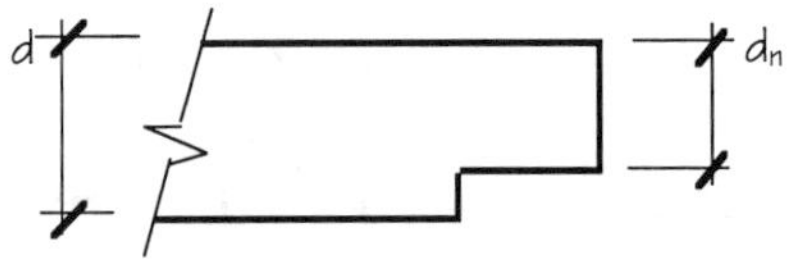

$$f_v = \left(\frac{3V}{2bd_n}\right)\left(\frac{d}{d_n}\right)$$ NDS 3.4.4

$$= \left(\frac{3(2)}{2(3.5)(11.25-3.5)}\right)\left(\frac{11.25}{(11.25-3.5)}\right) = .16 \text{ ksi}$$

$$F_v' = F_v C_D C_M C_t C_H = .095(1.25)1.0(1.0)1.0$$

$= .119$ ksi $< .16$ ksi **NG!**

Shear NG!

NDS T2.3.1

Ck notch

$$\frac{11.25}{4} = 2.81 \text{ in} < 3.5 \text{ in} \quad \textbf{NG!}$$

Not only is the allowable shear capacity of the beam exceeded, but it does not meet the NDS 3.2.3.2 recommended ratio.

Although this does not happen often, it happens often enough. It is important that you keep your cool and maintain your integrity. If there is a way you can think of that will remedy the problem (like an additional post under the full section) and no other problems occur (like a large eccentric load on the footing), consider doing it. But remember, you take the liability for all field changes that you approve. Be sure, and above all, be safe.

Public relations

As an engineer, you have a public trust to uphold. With this trust comes certain responsibilities and obligations. When possible, one of your obligations is to extend the knowledge that the public has of the engineering profession. If you are knowledgeable on a specific subject, speak out about it to increase the public's awareness.

Be alert for any exaggerations that might be made by other individuals or other engineers that would discredit the engineering profession. It is your responsibility to publicly correct these statements with the truth that is founded in your own personal knowledge, and not hearsay.

Regardless of who is the engineer of record, an engineer is ultimately responsible of his work. You should, with honest conviction, be concerned with the safety, health and welfare of the public in general; and, specifically, those who may come in contact with, or be affected by, your work.

An engineer should not publicly assert his opinion about any aspect of engineering unless he personally knows all of the facts that relate to the subject under consideration.

Destiny is not a matter of chance; it is a matter of choice. It is not a thing to be waited for; it is a thing to be achieved.

WILLIAM JENNINGS BRYAN

● PROBLEM 2.8

Notched circular beam adequacy using 1991 NDS.

You are working with an architect who is designing a log cabin home. She wants you to determine the adequacy (in shear) for the notched circular beam shown below.

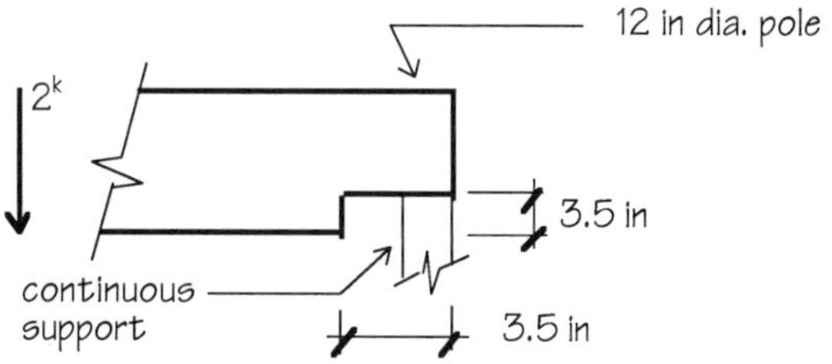

ASSUME

DF-L No. 3.
DL + RLL controls.
EMC < 19%.

SOLUTION

The NDS suggests that notching of bending elements is to be avoided whenever possible. It's not that you cannot do it, it's that you should not, especially on the tension side of the element.

Shear

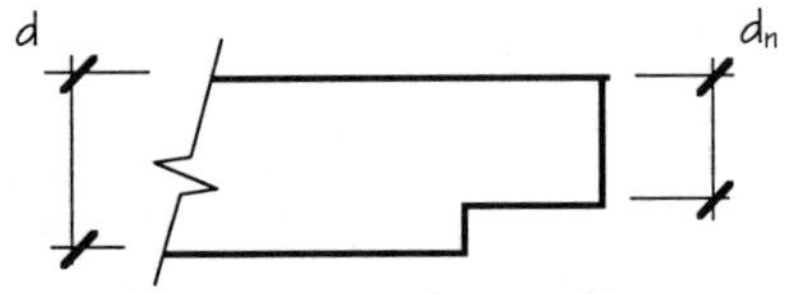

$$A_n = \frac{\pi D^2}{4} = \frac{\pi(12)^2}{4} = 113.1 \text{ in}^2$$

NDS 3.4.4

$$f_v = \left(\frac{3V}{2A_n}\right)\left(\frac{d}{d_n}\right) = \left(\frac{3(2)}{2(113.1)}\right)\left(\frac{12}{(12-3.5)}\right) = .037 \text{ ksi}$$

NDS 2.3.1

$$F_v' = F_v C_D C_M C_t C_H = .095(1.25)1.0(1.0)1.0$$

$$= .119 \text{ ksi} > .037 \text{ ksi}$$

Shear ok

Ck notch

$$\frac{12}{4} = 3 \text{ in} < 3.5 \text{ in} \quad \textbf{NG!}$$

The allowable shear capacity of the beam is ok, but the beam does not meet the NDS recommended ratio of the notch itself.

The beam is NG because it does not met the NDS 3.2.3.2 recommended ratio for the notch.

Stress concentrations (stress riser) around the area of the notch cause a reduction in strength of bending elements. Recall that the notch also reduces the depth of the beam for shear resistance as well. Thus horizontal shear will adversely react with bending induced cross grain tension(tension perpendicular to grain) to cause the localized splitting of the member around the notch. If severe, the splitting can propagate and cause a reduction in bending capacity, and may induce catastrophic collapse of the member. In these circumstances, consideration should be given to reducing the stress riser by tapering the notch or reducing the tendency of the wood to split with the addition of tension perpendicular to grain reinforcing bolts or lag screws.

The AITC does not recommend the notching of large glulam beams. Note that a reduced bearing capacity in the glulam is caused by lesser quality material in the inner portions of the cut (see NDS 3.2.3.3).

Ethics and attitude

Here are some simple ethical rules and attitudes to consider:

- Be courteous and pleasant to all.
- Do not show favoritism; treat everyone honestly and fairly.
- Show respect for the rights and opinions of others.
- Keep your word and perform your obligations to the best of your ability.
- Nurture a good reputation. Set an example for others.
- Show loyalty to your employer and friends.
- Comply with the laws and regulations of the state and engineering profession.
- Practice engineering faithfully and sincerely.
- Pay attention to the details.
- Be proud, proficient and punctual in your work.
- Use common sense.
- Listen to others.
- Learn to talk intelligently about engineering.
- Do not gossip about others.
- Do not use sarcastic or profane language.

Almost every man wastes part of his life in attempts to display qualities which he does not possess.

SAMUEL JOHNSON

● PROBLEM 2.9

Notched (top side) beam adequacy using 1991 NDS.

Determine the adequacy in shear for the notched beam shown below.

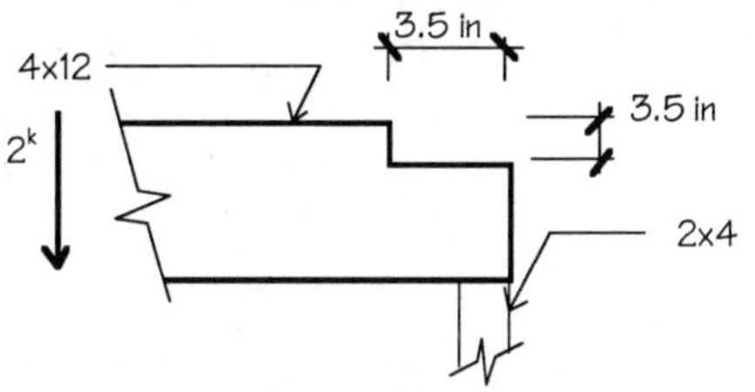

ASSUME

DF-L No. 3.
DL + RLL controls.
EMC < 19 %.

SOLUTION

This condition is less severe because the notch is on the top compression side of the beam.

NDS 2.3.1

$F_v' = F_v C_D C_M C_t C_H = .095(1.25)1.0(1.0)1.0 = .119$ ksi

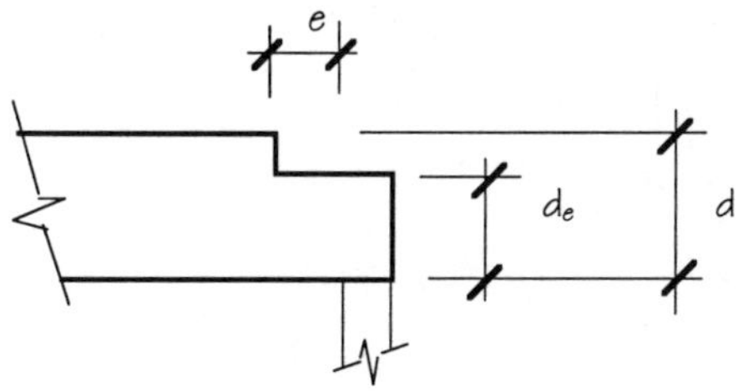

TCM 5.4.5

$$f_v = \frac{3R_v}{2b\left(d-\left(\frac{d-d_e}{d_e}\right)e\right)} = \frac{3(2)}{2(3.5)\left(11.25-\left(\frac{11.25-7.75}{7.75}\right)3.5\right)}$$

$= .089 < .119^k$

But NDS 3.2.3.2 implies:

$\frac{d}{6} = \frac{11.25}{6} = 1.88$ in < .35 **NG!**

> Beam is ok in shear, but NG due to its notch exceeding NDS requirements

Severe notching (TCM method)

Although it is not desirable to do so, if the notch cut to the edge of the support length (e) exceeds the depth of the material remaining after the notch (d_e) the above equation in not used. The following example will illustrate the procedure.

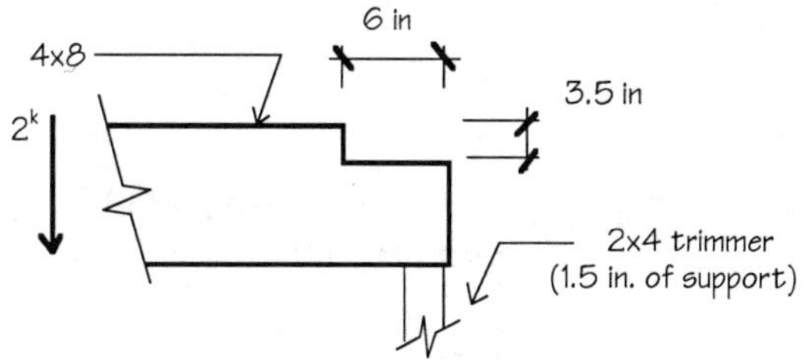

ASSUME

DF-L No. 3.
DL + RLL controls.
EMC < 19 %.

SOLUTION

$F_v' = F_v C_D C_M C_t C_H = .095(1.25)1.0(1.0)1.0 = .119$

Check $e > d_e$?

$e = 6 - 1.5 = 4.5$ in

$d_e = 7.25 - 3.5 = 3.75$ in < 4.5 in

Since $e > d_e$ compute f_v using d_e thus:

$f_v = \frac{1.5V}{A} = \frac{1.5(2)}{3.75(3.5)} = .23 \text{ ksi} > .119 \text{ ksi}$ **NG!**

Check 40% requirement (AITC sec. 5.4.5)

The depth of the notch on the top side of a beam is not allowed to exceed 40% of the depth of the beam.

$.4(7.25) = 2.9 \text{ in} < 3.5 \text{ in}$ **NG!**

> Beam **NG** in shear. The value of the allowable shear is exceeded and the depth of the notch is too deep for this beam.

For certain situations the NDS and TCM requirements and recommendations are not necessarily in agreement. Many designers simple choose one of the methods and stick to it in order to develop a consistent methodology.

Eighty percent of success is showing up.

WOODY ALLEN

PROBLEM 2.10

Shear Modification of loads for simple beam.

Calculate the permitted reduction in shear for the simple beam shown below.

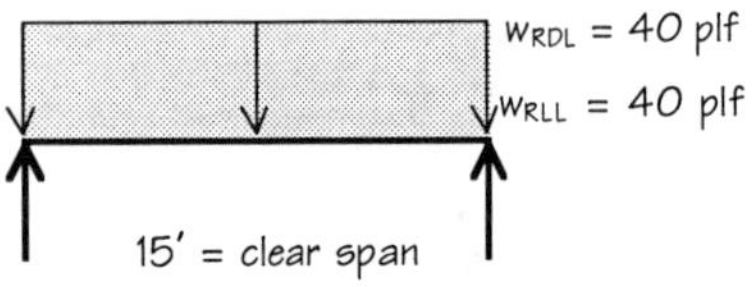

ASSUME

Shear is critical.
4x4 post.
4x12 beam.

SOLUTION

Office practice dictates that the most expeditious evaluation of shear is to use the maximum shear from the shear diagram when plugging into the shear stress formula. The NDS allows the maximum design shear to be modified (or reduced) in stress calculations. The NDS recognizes that arch action (or, more technically, diagonal compression) occurs within the beam. This action allows the vertical load to transfer through the beam so that horizontal shear stress may be ignored (for the loads about the section). To save time, many designers use the reduction only when shear becomes critical (short spans with heavy loads). Thus:

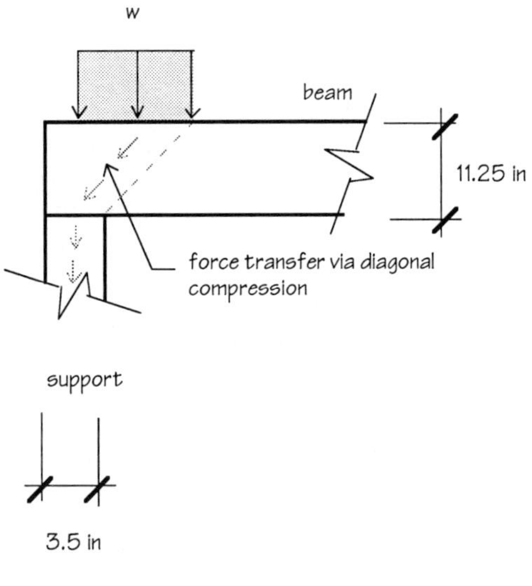

Diagram of modified load

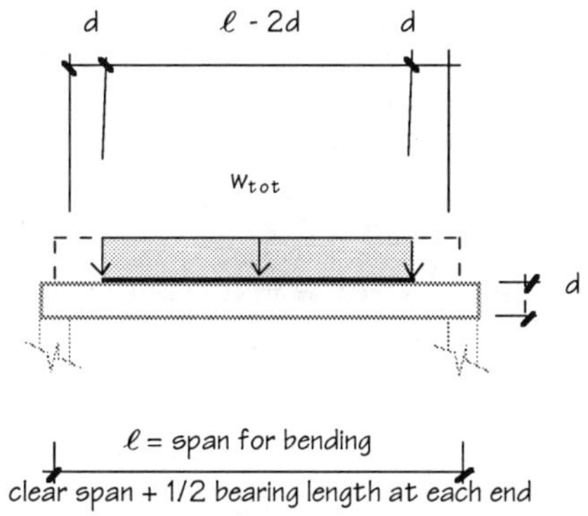

Uniform and concentrated loads may be reduced by this procedure when calculating the maximum design shear. Note that the loads must be applied to the top of the beam for the modification to be allowed.

Diagram of modified shear

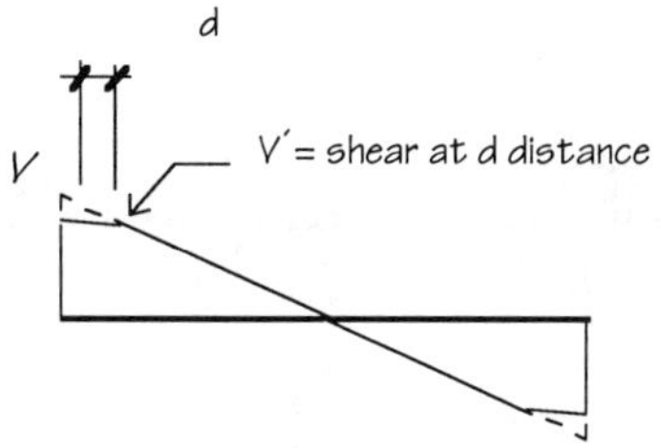

DL + RLL controls by inspection.

Ck shear modification loading

NDS 3.4.3(a)

$w = w_{RDL} + w_{RLL} = 40 + 40 = 80$ plf

$$V = \frac{w\ell}{2} = \frac{(.08)15}{2} = .6^k \quad \text{(conservative)}$$

$$V' = \frac{w\left(15 + \frac{3.5}{12}\right)}{2} - w\left(\frac{d + \frac{3.5}{2}}{12}\right)$$

$$= \frac{.08\left(15 + \frac{3.5}{12}\right)}{2} - .08\left(\frac{11.25 + \frac{3.5}{2}}{12}\right)$$

$$= .525^k$$

$V' = .53^k$ design shear

He deserves Paradise who makes his companions laugh.

THE KORAN

PROBLEM 2.11

Beam design for repetitive members.

You are designing a residence. Currently you are working on the garage roof rafter design (which is sloped for drainage). Design the repetitive roof rafter as shown below.

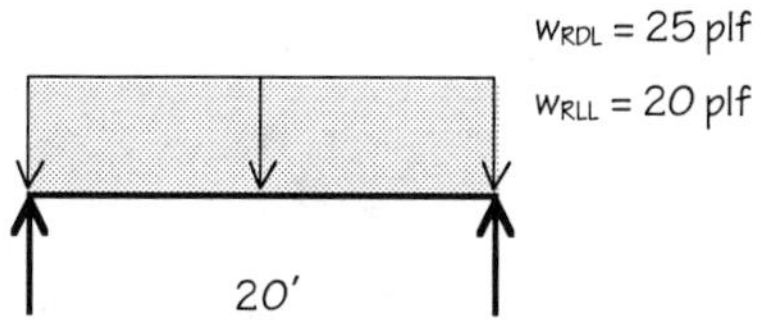

ASSUME

No ponding, no plaster.
Rep. member. at 24 " o/c.
DF - L No. 1.
Full Lat. support from plywood.
Neglect rafter wt.
EMC < 19%.
Normal temp. conditions.
Commercial building.

SOLUTION

$F_b = 1.0$ ksi
$F_v = .095$ ksi
$E = 1.7e3$ ksi

DL + RLL controls by inspection

Assume the rafter is relatively long so that either M or Δ will control.

Bending

NDS T2.3.1 Roof rafters are usually 2x8, 10, or 12's depending on the span and load. Since the span is 20 ft, a 2x8 will probably be unsatisfactory. Assume the selected section will have a C_F of 1.1 (2x10). If the actual C_F is not 1.1 adjust it and re-ck the calc. This assumes that this procedure is an iterative process.

$$F_b' = F_b C_D C_M C_t C_L C_F C_r = 1.0(1.25)1.0(1.0)1.0(1.1)1.15$$

$$= 1.58 \text{ ksi}$$

$$M = \frac{w\ell^2}{8} = \frac{(.025+.02)20^2}{8} = 2.25^{\text{ k-ft}}$$

NDS 3.3.2

$$S_R = \frac{12M}{F_b'} = \frac{12(2.25)}{1.58} = 17.09 \text{ in}^3$$

try $S_{2\times10} = 21.39 \text{ in}^3 > 17.09 \text{ in}^3$ √

$I = 98.9 \text{ in}^4$

$A = 13.88 \text{ in}^2$

If the member had not been a 2x10, then it would have had a different C_F. With a new C_F, the allowable bending stress would have had to have been changed accordingly.

Bending ok

Ck shear

NDS T2.3.1 Unless shear is going to be a problem (e.g., a large load and a relatively short span), do not use a shear modification.

$$F_v' = F_v(C_D)C_M(C_t)C_H = .095(1.25)1.0(1.0)1.0 = .119 \text{ ksi}$$ NDS 3.4.2

$$V = \frac{w\ell}{2} = \frac{(.025+.02)20}{2} = .45^{\text{ k}}$$

$$A_R = \frac{1.5(V)}{F_v'} = \frac{1.5(.45)}{.119} = 5.67 \text{ in}^2 < 13.88 \quad \surd$$

Shear ok

Ck defl. (based on TCM)

Progressive collapse by the accumulation of water is known as ponding failure. Water is trapped and causes excessive deflection which in turn allows more water to be trapped. The cycle continues until failure occurs. Positive slope on all roofs is recommended to properly drain the roof so that ponding does not occur. NDS T4.3

$$E' = E(C_M)C_t = 1.7e3(1.0)1.0 = 1.7e3 \text{ ksi}$$

$$\Delta_{LL} = \frac{5w\ell^4}{384EI} = \frac{5(.02)20^4(1728)}{384(1.7e3)98.93}$$

$$= .43 \text{ in} < \ell/240 = 20(12)/240 = 1 \text{ in} \quad \surd$$

$$\Delta_{TL} = \Delta_{LL}\left(\frac{w_{TL}}{w_{LL}}\right) = .43\left(\frac{.025}{.02}\right) = .54 \text{ in}$$

$$\ell/180 = 20(12)/180 = 1.33 \text{ in} > .5 \text{ in} \quad \surd$$

Deflection ok

Ck bearing

Since the support conditions are not known, determine the minimum bearing length.

$$F_{c\perp}' = F_{c\perp}(C_M)C_t(C_b) = .625(1.0)1.0(1.0) = .625 \text{ ksi}$$ NDS T2.3.1

$$\ell_{b\ min} = \frac{R}{bF_{c\perp}'} = \frac{.45}{1.5(.625)} = .48 \text{ in}$$

Use 2x10 DF-L No. 1 at 24 in o/c with a minimum bearing length of .5 in. MC ≤ 19%

When I played pro football, I never set out to hurt anybody deliberately . . . unless it was, you know, important, like a league game or something.

DICK BUTKUS

PROBLEM 2.12

Beam design for sloped roof rafters.

Design a sloped roof rafter as shown.

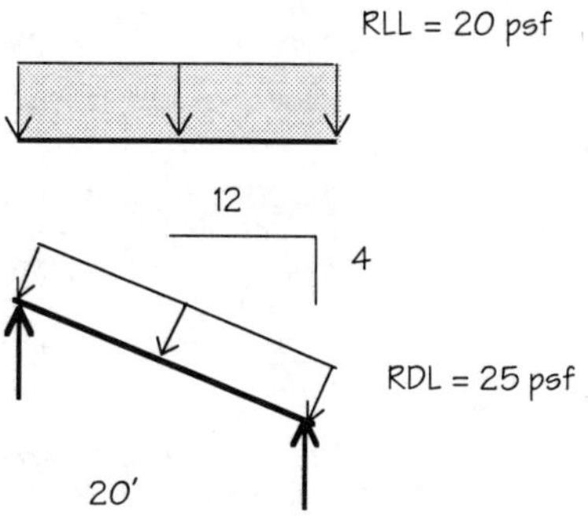

ASSUME

No ponding, no plaster.
Rep. mem. at 16 " o/c.
DF - L No. 1.
Full Lat. support from plywood.
Neglect rafter wt.
EMC <19%.
Normal temp. conditions.
Commercial building.
Neglect deflection.

SOLUTION

$F_b = 1.0$ ksi
$F_v = .095$ ksi
$E = 1.7e3$ ksi

Use Horizontal plane method

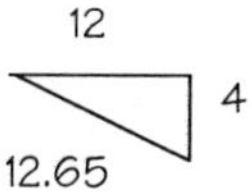

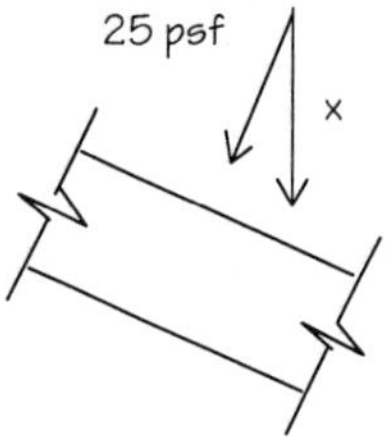

$$\Rightarrow \frac{x}{12.65} = \frac{25}{12}$$

for 16 in spc'g

$$x = 1.33\left(\frac{25(12.65)}{12}\right) = 35.1 \text{ plf}$$

$$w_{LL} = 1.33(.02) = .027 \text{ klf}$$

$$w_{DL} = .035 \text{ klf}$$

DL + RLL controls by inspection. Assume the rafter is relatively long so that either M or Δ will control. It is common for a building to be reroofed without the removal of the old roofing material. Engineers often include additional dead loads in the original design loads in anticipation of this common practice. Do not include these additional loads when performing uplift calculations.

The loads are $w_{LL} = .027$ klf
$w_{DL} = .035$ klf

Ck Bending

NDS 2.3.1

As previously stated, roof rafters are usually 2x8, 10, or 12's depending on the span and load. Since the span is 20 ft, a 2x8 will probably be unsatisfactory.

NDS 3.3.2

Assume the selected section will have a C_F of 1.1 (2x10). If the actual C_F is not 1.1, adjust it and re-ck the calc. This assumes that this procedure is an iterative process.

$$F_b' = F_b C_D C_M C_t C_L C_F C_r = 1.0(1.25)1.0(1.0)1.0(1.1)1.15$$

$= 1.58$ ksi

$$M = \frac{w\ell^2}{8} = \frac{(.035+.027)20^2}{8} = 3.1^{\text{k-ft}}$$

$$S_R = \frac{12M}{F_b'} = \frac{12(3.1)}{1.58} = 23.5 \text{ in}^3$$

try $S_{2\times10} = 21.39 \text{ in}^3 < 23.5 \text{ in}^3$ **NG!**

try $S_{2\times12} = 31.64 \text{ in}^3 > 23.5 \text{ in}^3$ √

$I = 178 \text{ in}^4$

$A = 16.88 \text{ in}^2$

The member was not a 2x10, so we will have to recalc with a new C_F:

$$F_b = 1.0(1.25)1.0(1.0)1.0(1.0)1.15 = 1.44 \text{ ksi}$$

$M = 3.1^{\text{k-ft}}$

$$S_R = \frac{12(3.1)}{1.44} = 25.8 \text{ in}^3 < 31.64 \text{ in}^3 \quad √$$

> Bending ok

Ck Shear

NDS 2.3.1

Unless shear is going to be a problem (e.g. there is a large load and a relatively short span), do not use a shear modification.

NDS 3.4.2

$$F_v' = F_v(C_D)C_M(C_t)C_H = .095(1.25)1.0(1.0)1.0 = .119 \text{ ksi}$$

$$V = \frac{w\ell}{2} = \frac{(.035+.027)20}{2} = .62^{k}$$

$$A_R = \frac{1.5(V)}{F_v'} = \frac{1.5(.62)}{.119} = 7.8 \text{ in}^2 < 16.88 \quad √$$

> Shear ok

Ck Bearing

Since the support conditions are not known, determine the minimum bearing length.

NDS T2.3.1

$$F_{c\perp}' = F_{c\perp}(C_M)C_t(C_b) = .625(1.0)1.0(1.0) = .625 \text{ ksi}$$

$$\ell_{b\,min} = \frac{R}{bF_{c\perp}'} = \frac{.62}{1.5(.625)} = .66 \text{ in}$$

> Use 2x12 DF- L No. 1 at 16 in o/c with a minimum bearing length of .66 in. MC ≤ 19%

Structural Design Engineering

It is important to understand the difference between the design process we are taught in school, and the requirements of a holistic, systematic approach in the "real world".

In the reality of office practice, the design engineer begins her thinking by examining the building structure in terms of a set of interactive primary and secondary system (and subsystem) requirements. She will think in terms of solutions that will satisfy the criteria of the architect, the builder, applicable codes and, in general, good engineering practice. This preferred thinking will tend to proceed from the general to the more specific. In other words, from the overall system requirements to the detailed requirements that comprise the components of those systems and subsystems.

This approach is in contrast to how we learn and assimilate the knowledge of structural engineering in school. There we are taught (by necessity) to manipulate and design component by component. A kind of reverse thinking from that of the actual office practice design process of engineering a building. In school we learn how to design the individual elements of a structure like beams and columns. We learn about the generalities of vertical load resistive systems, and about the specifics of lateral load resistive systems. We learn about codes and materials. We learn about construction processes and techniques. All of this learning in terms of individual components tends to create the habit of having our thinking "flow" from the specific to the general. This is in direct opposition to the natural form of thinking found in practice. The problem is exacerbated by the sheer amount of technical information a student is required to assimilate during the academic process.

You can achieve higher levels of accomplishment in your engineering career if you understand the importance of these issues. You must first be capable of understanding complicated structural systems in an effort to recognize the fundamental rather than the detailed issues of the problem criteria. Then you must devise a strategy for resolving them. Your purpose is to develop an overall approach to manage or design specific technical ideas and components.

Young engineers just starting out are frequently referred to as "human calculators" - no decision making, just grunt work. The responsible decisions for the job are made by a project engineer who has more "experience". By cultivating this holistic thinking process (that flows from the general to the specific), you can get a head start on bridging the "experience" gap while you're still in the academic arena. If you are just out of school or in practice, there is no time like the present to re-examine your approach to the design process. May the flow be with you!

It matters not whether you win or lose: what matters is whether I win or lose.

DARIN WEINBERG

PROBLEM 2.13

Beam design for "rough" sawn repetitive members.

Design the rough sawn roof beam as shown below.

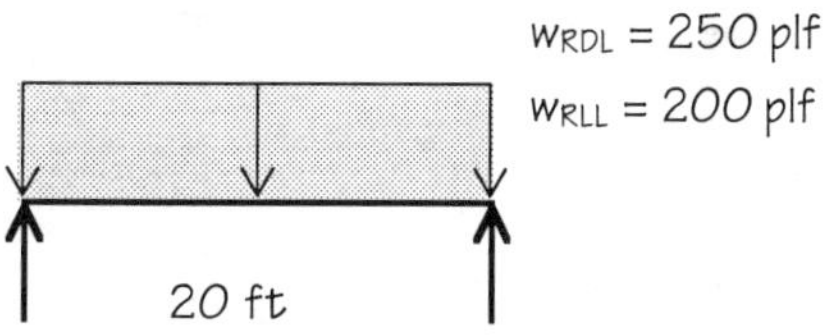

ASSUME

No ponding, no plaster.
Rep. mem. at 24 " o/c.
DF - L No. 1.
Full Lat. support from plywood.
Member weight included in DL.
EMC <19%.
Normal temp. conditions.
Commercial building (with roof-top storage).

SOLUTION

F_b = 1.35 ksi
F_v = .085 ksi
E = 1.7e3 ksi

DL + RLL controls by inspection.

Assume the beam is relatively long so that either M or Δ will control. Remember that rough size lumber is about an 1/8 in larger than the dressed size of lumber, so calculate the approximate requirements and ck to see if a smaller size will work.

Bending

Since the span is 20 ft assume a selected section will have a C_F of 1.0. If the actual C_F is not 1.0, adjust it and re-ck the calc. This assumes that this procedure is an iterative process. NDS T2.3.1

$$F_b' = F_b C_D C_M C_t C_L C_F C_r$$

= 1.35(1.25)1.0(1.0)1.0(1.0)1.15 = 1.94 ksi

$$M = \frac{w\ell^2}{8} = \frac{(.25+.2)20^2}{8} = 22.5^{\text{ k-ft}}$$ NDS 3.3.2

$$S_R = \frac{12M}{F_b'} = \frac{12(22.5)}{1.94} = 139.2 \text{ in}^3$$

A rough sawn beam has properties greater than tabulated values for dressed sizes so if the dressed sizes work the rough is ok.

try: $S_{6\times14}$ = 167.1 in^3 > 139.2 in^3 √
I = 1127.7 in^4
A = 74.3 in^2

A 6x12 has an S of 121.2 that obviously would not be helped much by an increase of an 1/8 in. As an exercise we will calc it anyway.

$$S_{6x12\ rough} = \frac{bd^2}{6} = \frac{5.63(11.63)^2}{6} = 126.9\ in^3 < S_R$$

NG!

Ck actual C

$$C_F = \left(\frac{12}{d}\right)^{1/9} = \left(\frac{12}{11.63}\right)^{1/9} = 1.0\ \checkmark$$

Bending ok

Ck shear

NDS T2.3.1

Unless shear is going to be a problem (e.g., a large load and a relatively short span) do not use a shear modification. If you hold the shear mod. in reserve, so to speak, you can save yourself some time in the office. If you need it, it's there like a good friend.

NDS 3.3.2

$$F_v' = F_v(C_D)C_M(C_t)C_H = .085(1.25)1.0(1.0)1.0 = .106\ ksi$$

$$V = \frac{w\ell}{2} = \frac{(.25+.2)20}{2} = 4.5^k$$

$$A_R = \frac{1.5(V)}{F_v'} = \frac{1.5(4.5)}{.106} = 63.7\ in^2 < 74.3\ in^2\ \checkmark$$

Shear ok

Ck Defl. (based on TCM)

NDS T4.3

$$E' = E(C_M)C_t = 1.7e3(1.0)1.0 = 1.7e3\ ksi$$

$$\Delta_{LL} = \frac{5w\ell^4}{384EI} = \frac{5(.2)20^4(1728)}{384(1.7e3)1127.7}$$

$$= .38\ in < \ell/240 = 20(12)/240 = 1\ in\ \checkmark$$

$$\Delta_{TL} = \Delta_{LL}\left(\frac{w_{TL}}{w_{LL}}\right) = .38\left(\frac{.45}{.2}\right) = .86\ in$$

$$\ell/180 = 20(12)/180 = 1.33\ in > .86\ in\ \checkmark$$

Deflection ok

Ck bearing

Since the support conditions are not known, determine the minimum bearing length.

NDS T2.3.1

$$F_{c\perp}' = F_{c\perp}(C_M)C_t(C_b) = .625(1.0)1.0(1.0) = .625\ ksi$$

$$\ell_{b\ min} = \frac{R}{bF_{c\perp}'} = \frac{4.5}{5.63(.625)} = 1.3\ in$$

Use 6x14 rough sawn DF-L No. 1 with a minimum bearing length of 1.5 in. MC ≤ 19%

The thing always happens that you really believe in; and the belief in a thing makes it happen.

FRANK LLOYD WRIGHT

PROBLEM 2.14

Beam design for repetitive members in wet use condition.

A fellow staff engineer is swamped with small project deadlines. He asks you to design the rough sawn roof rafter of a fast food restaurant as shown below.

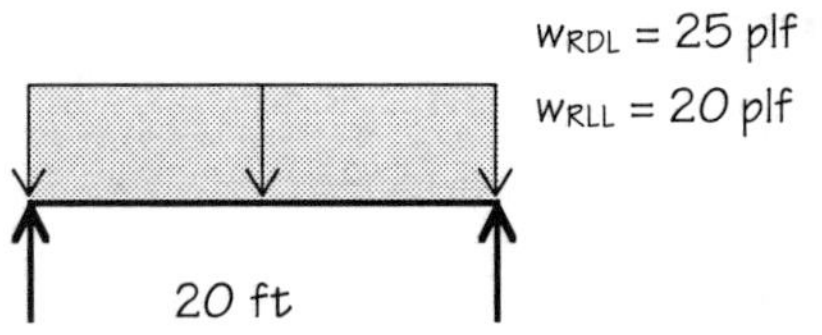

ASSUME

No ponding, no plaster.
Repetitive members at 12" o/c.
DF - L No. 2.
Full Lat. support from plywood.

Neglect rafter wt.
EMC >19%.
Normal temp. conditions.
Commercial building.

SOLUTION

$F_b = .875$ ksi
$F_v = .095$ ksi
$E = 1.6e3$ ksi

DL + RLL controls by inspection.

Assume rafter is relatively long so that either M or Δ will control.

Bending

NDS T2.3.1

Roof rafters are usually 2x8, 10, or 12's depending on the span and the load. Since the span is 20 ft, a 2x8 will probably be unsatisfactory. Assume the selected section will have a C_F of 1.1 (2x10). If the actual C_F is not 1.1, adjust it and re-ck the calc. This assumes that this procedure is an iterative process. Note that EMC >19% affecting C_M.

$F_b{}' = F_b C_D C_M C_t C_L C_F C_r$

The NDS (Table 4A) stipulates that C_M =.85 when used with F_b, unless $F_b C_F \le 1150$ psi, then CM = 1.0 (as in our case)

$F_b = .875(1.25)1.0(1.0)1.0(1.1)1.15 = 1.4$ ksi

NDS 3.3.2

$$M = \frac{w\ell^2}{8} = \frac{(.025+.02)20^2}{8} = 2.25^{\text{ k-ft}}$$

$$S_R = \frac{12M}{F_b'} = \frac{12(2.25)}{1.4} = 19.3 \text{ in}^3$$

try $S_{2\times10} = 21.39 \text{ in}^3 > 19.3 \text{ in}^3$ √
$I = 98.9 \text{ in}^4$
$A = 13.88 \text{ in}^2$

If the member had not have been a 2x10, then it would have had a different C_F. With a new C_F, the allowable bending stress would had to have been changed (and checked) accordingly.

Bending ok

Ck shear

NDS T2.3.1

Most practicing engineers do not use the shear modification unless they can foresee that shear is going to be a problem. From NDS Table 4A, $C_M = .97$

$$F_v' = F_v(C_D)C_M(C_t)C_H = .095(1.25).97(1.0)1.0 = .12 \text{ ksi}$$

$$V = \frac{w\ell}{2} = \frac{(.025+.02)20}{2} = .45^{\text{ k}}$$

NDS 3.4.2

$$A_R = \frac{1.5(V)}{F_v'} = \frac{1.5(.45)}{.12} = 5.63 \text{ in}^2 < 13.88 \ \surd$$

Shear ok

Ck defl. (based on TCM)

EMC >19% affects C_M here as well.

NDS T4.3

$$E' = E(C_M)C_t = 1.6e3(.9)1.0 = 1.44\,e3 \text{ ksi}$$

$$\Delta_{LL} = \frac{5w\ell^4}{384EI} = \frac{5(.02)20^4(1728)}{384(1.44e3)98.93}$$

$$= .51 \text{ in} < \ell/240 = 20(12)/240 = 1 \text{ in} \ \surd$$

$$\Delta_{TL} = \Delta_{LL}\left(\frac{w_{TL}}{w_{LL}}\right) = .51\left(\frac{.045}{.02}\right) = 1.15 \text{ in}$$

$$\ell/180 = 20(12)/180 = 1.33 \text{ in} > 1.15 \text{ in} \ \surd$$

Deflection ok

Ck bearing

Since the support conditions are not known, determine the minimum bearing length. $C_M = .67$

NDS T2.3.1

$$F_{c\perp}' = F_{c\perp}(C_M)C_t(C_b) = .625(.67)1.0(1.0) = .42 \text{ ksi}$$

$$\ell_{b\,min} = \frac{R}{bF_{c\perp}'} = \frac{.45}{1.5(.42)} = .71 \text{ in}$$

Use 2x10 DF-L No. 1 at 24 in o/c with a minimum bearing length of .75 in. MC ≥ 19%

Regret for the things we did can be tempered by time; it is regret for the things we did not do that is inconsolable.

SYDNEY J. HARRIS

PROBLEM 2.15

Beam design for repetitive members (Adjustment factor practice).

Design the roof rafter as shown.

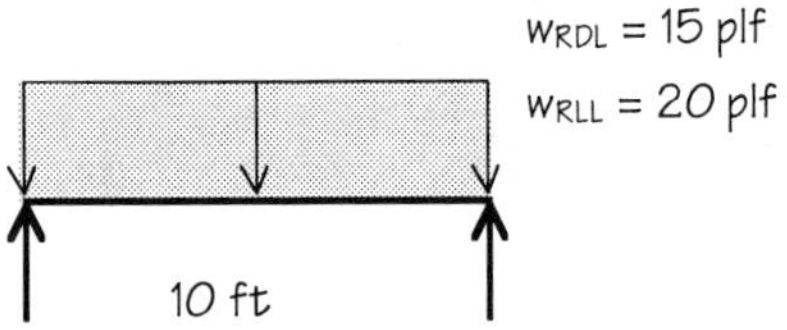

ASSUME

- No ponding, plaster ceiling.
- 2x8 rep. member at 16" o/c.
- DF - L No. 3.
- Full Lat. support from plywood.
- Neglect rafter wt.
- EMC > 19%.
- 100°F < temp. conditions < 125° F.
- Commercial building.
- Both ends sit on 2x4 bearing walls.

SOLUTION

F_b = .5 ksi
F_v = .095 ksi
E = 1.4e3 ksi

DL + RLL controls by inspection.

Assume that either M or Δ will control.

Bending

$F_b' = F_b C_D C_M C_t C_L C_F C_r$

The NDS stipulates that C_M =.85 when used with F_b, unless $F_b C_F \le 1150$ *psi*, $C_M = 1.0$. NDS Table 2.3.4 gives C_t = .7 for our temperature range. Assume C_F = 1.2 — NDS T2.3.1

F_b =.5(1.25).85(.7)1.0(1.2)1.15 = .51 ksi — NDS 3.3.2

$$M = \frac{w\ell^2}{8} = \frac{(.015+.02)10^2}{8} = .44^{\text{ k-ft}}$$

$$S_R = \frac{12M}{F_b'} = \frac{12(.44)}{.51} = 10.4 \text{ in}^3$$

try $S_{2\times8}$ = 13.1 in³ > 10.4 in³ √
I = 47.6 in⁴
A = 10.9 in²

Actual C_F = 1.2 √

Bending ok

Ck shear

As stated in the previous problems, unless there is a large load on a relatively short span, do not use a shear modification. — NDS 2.3.1

$F_v' = F_v(C_D)C_M(C_t)C_H$ =.095(1.25).97(.7)1.0 = .08 ksi — NDS 3.4.2

$$V = \frac{w\ell}{2} = \frac{(.015+.02)10}{2} = .18^{\text{ k}}$$

$$A_R = \frac{1.5(V)}{F_v'} = \frac{1.5(.18)}{.08} = 3.38 \text{ in}^2 < 13.88 \text{ in} \ \surd$$

Shear ok

Ck defl. (based on TCM)

$E' = E(C_M)C_t$ = 1.4e3(.9).9 = 1.13e3 ksi — NDS 2.3.1

$$\Delta_{LL} = \frac{5w\ell^4}{384EI} = \frac{5(.02)10^4(1728)}{384(1.13e3)47.6}$$

$$= .08 \text{ in} < \ell/240 = 10(12)/240 = .5 \text{ in} \ \surd$$ — NDS T4.3

$$\Delta_{TL} = \Delta_{LL}\left(\frac{w_{TL}}{w_{LL}}\right) = .08\left(\frac{.035}{.02}\right) = .14 \text{ in}$$

$$l/180 = 10(12)/180 = .67 \text{ in} > .14 \text{ in} \quad \checkmark$$

Deflection ok

Ck bearing

NDS 2.3.1

$$F'_{c\perp} = F_{c\perp}(C_M)C_t(C_b)$$

NDS 2.3.10

$$C_b = \frac{\ell_b + .375}{\ell_b} = \frac{3.5+.375}{3.5} = 1.11$$

$$F'_{c\perp} = .625(.67).7(1.11) = .33 \text{ ksi}$$

$$f_{c\perp} = \frac{.18}{1.5(3.5)} = .03 \text{ ksi} < .33 \text{ ksi}$$

2x8 ok

If the rafter had failed in shear, we would have to change the size because the allowable shear remains constant and is not affected by grade. If we had a problem in bending or deflection, we would have the option of changing the size or grade of the lumber.

Crowns in sawn beams

Prior to their installation in the structure, it is common for sawn members to have some amount of curvature along their length. A note should be placed on the plans that states that the crown of the beam be turned up so that you get the benefit of this natural camber.

**Do not be too timid and squeamish about your actions.
All life is an experiment.**

RALPH WALDO EMERSON

PROBLEM 2.16

Beam design for snow loaded members.

Design the roof rafter as shown.

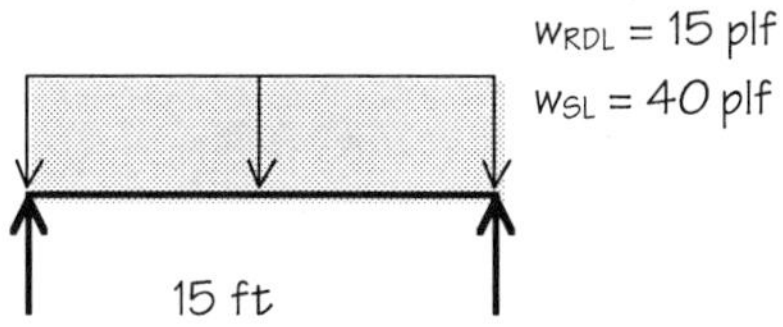

ASSUME

- No ponding, no plaster.
- Rep. mem. at 16 " o/c.
- Hem-fir No. 1.
- Full Lat. support from plywood.
- Neglect rafter wt.
- EMC >19%.
- Normal temp. conditions.
- Commercial building.

SOLUTION

F_b = .95 ksi
F_v = .075 ksi
E = 1.5e3 ksi

DL + SL controls by inspection.

Assume the rafter is relatively long so that either M or Δ will control.

Bending

Roof rafters are usually 2x8, 10, or 12's depending on the span and load. Since the span is 20 ft, a 2x8 will probably be unsatisfactory. Assume the selected section will have a C_F of 1.1 (2x10). If the actual C_F is not 1.1, adjust it and re-ck the calc. This assumes that this procedure is an iterative process. NDS 2.3.1

$$F_b' = F_b C_D C_M C_t C_L C_F C_r$$

C_M = .85, but when $F_bC_F \le 1.15$ ksi, C_M = 1.0

$F_bC_F = .95(1.1) = 1.05 \text{ ksi} < 1.15 \text{ ksi} \Rightarrow C_M = 1.0$

$$F_b = .95(1.15)1.0(1.0)1.0(1.1)1.15 = 1.38 \text{ ksi}$$

We can not reduce the snow load because our assumed roof pitch is below 20 degrees.

$M = \dfrac{w\ell^2}{8} = \dfrac{(.015+.04)15^2}{8} = 1.55^{\,k\text{-}ft}$

NDS 3.3.2

$S_R = \dfrac{12M}{F_b'} = \dfrac{12(1.55)}{1.38} = 13.5 \text{ in}^3$

try $S_{2\times8} = 13.1 \text{ in}^3 < 13.5 \text{ in}^3$ **NG!**

In practice, it is not unusual to accept a 6% overage from the requirement. It is considered to be in the spirit of the code to do so.

13.5/13.1 = 1.03 ⇒ 3% over requirement

However, for a 2x8 $C_F = 1.2$

$\Rightarrow S_R = 13.5\left(\dfrac{1.1}{1.2}\right) = 12.4 \text{ in}^3 < 13.1 \text{ in}^3$ √

$I = 47.6 \text{ in}^4$

$A = 10.9 \text{ in}^2$

Since the member was not a 2x10, we had to change to a different C_F. With a new C_F, the allowable bending stress changed accordingly. Note that many engineers use an alternate method of selecting a trial section. It is common to calculate the S_RC_F that is required and look up that value in a precalculated chart (like the one found in the appendix). In many cases, this will reduce the iterative requirements of the method presented in this problem.

Bending ok

Ck shear

NDS 2.3.1

Do not use the shear modification.

$F_v' = F_v(C_D)C_M(C_t)C_H = .075(1.15).97(1.0)1.0 = .084 \text{ ksi}$

NDS 3.4.2

$V = \dfrac{w\ell}{2} = \dfrac{(.015+.04)15}{2} = .41^k$

$A_R = \dfrac{1.5(V)}{F_v'} = \dfrac{1.5(.41)}{.084} = 7.3 \text{ in}^2 < 10.9$ √

Shear ok

Ck defl. (based on TCM)

NDS 2.3.1

$E' = E(C_M)C_t = 1.5e3(.9)1.0 = 1.35e3 \text{ ksi}$

$\Delta_{SL} = \dfrac{5w\ell^4}{384EI} = \dfrac{5(.04)15^4(1728)}{384(1.35e3)47.6} = .71 \text{ in} < \ell/240$

$= 15(12)/240 = .75 \text{ in}$ √

NDS T4.3

$\Delta_{TL} = \Delta w_{SL}\left(\dfrac{w_{TL}}{w_{SL}}\right) = .71\left(\dfrac{.055}{.04}\right) = .98 \text{ in}$

$\ell/180 = 15(12)/180 = 1.0 \text{ in} > .98 \text{ in}$ √

Deflection ok (but close)

Ck bearing

NDS 2.3.1

Since the support conditions are not known, determine the minimum bearing length.

$F_{c\perp}' = F_{c\perp}(C_M)C_t(C_b) = .405(.67)1.0(1.0) = .27 \text{ ksi}$

$\ell_{b\,min} = \dfrac{R}{bF_{c\perp}'} = \dfrac{.41}{1.5(.27)} = 1.01 \text{ in}$

Our selection reflects the interst of most individuals who deal with the design and construction of structures. Namely that the economics of the design are a big concern.

Use 2x8 Hem fir No. 1 at 16 in o/c
with a minimum bearing length of 1 in.
MC ≥ 19%

Life teaches us to be less harch with ourselves and with others.

GOETHE

PROBLEM 2.17

Beam design for non-repetitive member with shear modification.

Design a beam utilizing shear modification for the following as shown.

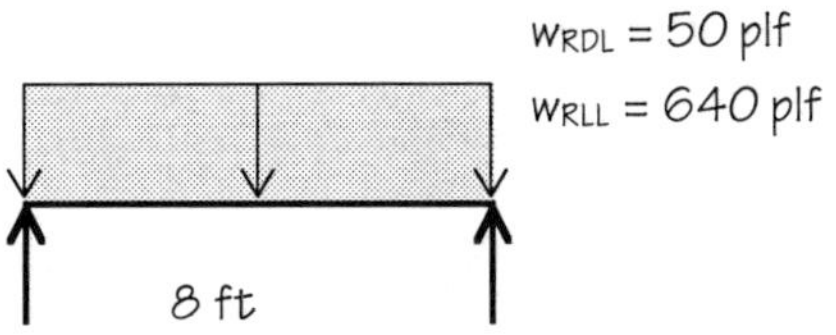

ASSUME

No ponding, no plaster.
DF - L No. 1.
Full Lat. support from plywood.
Neglect beam wt.
EMC <19%.
Normal temp. conditions.
Commercial building.

SOLUTION (assume 4x member)

F_b = 1.0 ksi
F_v = .095 ksi
E = 1.7e3 ksi

DL + RLL controls by inspection. Assume the beam is relatively short and has a large loading so that V will control.

Ck shear without shear modification

NDS 2.3.1

$$F_v' = F_v(C_D)C_M(C_t)C_H = .095(1.25)1.0(1.0)1.0 = .119 \text{ ksi}$$

$$V = \frac{w\ell}{2} = \frac{(.050+.64)8}{2} = 2.8^{k}$$

NDS 3.4.2

$$A_R = \frac{1.5(V)}{F_v'} = \frac{1.5(2.8)}{.119} = 35.3 \text{ in}^2$$

try $A_{4\times 12} = 39.4 \text{ in}^3 > 35.3 \text{ in}^3$ √
$I = 415.3 \text{ in}^4$
$S = 73.8 \text{ in}^2$

Shear ok

Ck with Shear Modification

NDS 3.4.3(a)

$$V' = V - w_T\left(\frac{d}{12}\right) = 2.8 - .69\left(\frac{11.25}{12}\right) = 2.2^{k}$$

$$A_R = \frac{1.5(V)}{F_v} = \frac{1.5(2.2)}{.119} = 27.7 \text{ in}^2$$

So, our original selection is ok, but might not be the least possible here because it is in the 4x range; A_{4x10} = 32.38 in.

$$A_R = \frac{1.5\left(2.8 - .69\left(\frac{9.25}{12}\right)\right)}{.119} = 28.6 \text{ in}^2 < 35.3 \text{ in}^3 \text{ NG!}$$

Our original selection is ok in shear

Bending

Assume the selected section will have a C_F of 1.1 (4x12). If the actual C_F is not 1.1, adjust it and re-ck the calc. This assumes that this procedure is an iterative process. NDS 2.3.1

$$F_b' = F_b C_D C_M C_t C_L C_F C_r = 1.0(1.25)1.0(1.0)1.0(1.1)$$

NDS 3.3.2

$$= 1.38 \text{ ksi}$$

$$M = \frac{w\ell^2}{8} = \frac{(.05+.64)8^2}{8} = 5.5^{\text{k-ft}}$$

$$S_R = \frac{12M}{F_b'} = \frac{12(5.5)}{1.38} = 47.8 \text{ in}^3 < 73.8 \text{ in}^3 \ \surd$$

If the member had not been a 4x12, then it would have had a different C_F. With a new C_F, the allowable bending stress would had to have been changed accordingly, as well.

Bending ok

Ck defl. (based on TCM)

NDS 2.3.1

$$E' = E(C_M)C_t = 1.7e3(1.0)1.0 = 1.7e3 \text{ ksi}$$

$$\Delta_{LL} = \frac{5w\ell^4}{384EI} = \frac{5(.64)8^4(1728)}{384(1.7e3)415.3}$$

$$= .08 \text{ in} < \ell/240 = 8(12)/240 = .4 \text{ in} \ \surd$$

$$\Delta_{TL} = \Delta_{LL}\left(\frac{w_{TL}}{w_{LL}}\right) = .08\left(\frac{.69}{.64}\right) = .09 \text{ in}$$

$$\ell/180 = 8(12)/180 = .53 \text{ in} > .09 \text{ in} \ \surd$$

Deflection ok

Ck bearing

Since the support conditions are not known, determine the minimum bearing length. Remember to use the full R whether the shear modification controlled the size of the member or not.

NDS T2.3.1

$$F'_{c\perp} = F_{c\perp}(C_M)C_t(C_b) = .625(1.0)1.0(1.0) = .625 \text{ ksi}$$

$$\ell_{b\ min} = \frac{R}{bF'_{c\perp}} = \frac{2.8}{3.5(.625)} = 1.3 \text{ in}$$

Use 4x12 DF-L No. 1 with a minimum bearing length of 1.3 in. MC ≤ 19%

If at first you don't succeed, find out if the loser gets anything.

BILL LYON

PROBLEM 2.18

Glulam beam design for fully supported member.

You are working on a 2-story structure. Part of your responsibility is to design the floor beam as shown.

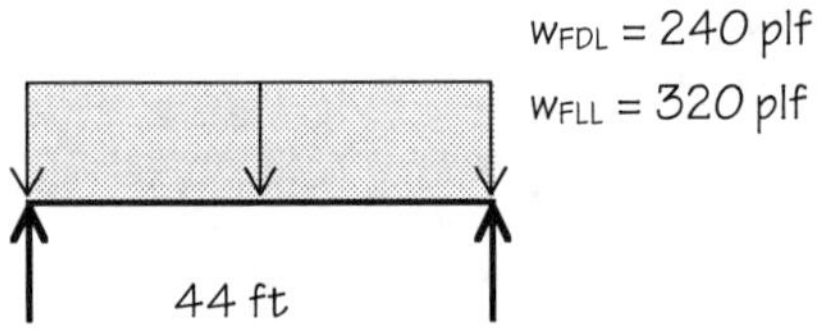

ASSUME

No ponding, plaster ceiling.
Full Lat. support from plywood.
Design for self wt.
EMC < 19%.
Normal temp. conditions.
Commercial building.
24F-V4 glulam.

SOLUTION

F_b = 2.4 ksi (T), 1.2 ksi (compression zone in tension)
F_v = .165 ksi
E = 1.8e3 ksi

DL + LL controls by inspection.

The beam is long so either M or Δ will control.

Bending

Lateral stability implies:

$$F_b' = F_b C_D C_M C_t C_L$$ NDS T2.3.1

Since the plywood roof diaphragm fully supports the top compression side of the beam (the top side is in compression with a positive moment), the unbraced length is zero. Hence lateral buckling is prevented and C_L = 1.0. Therefore, we need only consider the volume factor (C_v) when a beam is fully supported.

Volume effect:

$$F_b' = F_b C_D C_M C_t C_V$$

Assume the selected glulam will have a C_V of .82. If the actual C_V is not .82, adjust it and re-ck the calc. This trial procedure is an iterative process. NDS 3.3.4

$$F_b = 2.4(1.0)1.0(1.0).82 = 1.97 \text{ ksi}$$

$$M = \frac{w\ell^2}{8} = \frac{(.24+.32)44^2}{8} = 135.5^{\text{ k-ft}}$$

$$S_R = \frac{12M}{F_b'} = \frac{12(135.5)}{1.97} = 825.4 \text{ in}^3$$

try $S_{5\times31\text{-}5/8} = 833.5 \text{ in}^3 > 825.4 \text{ in}^3$ √

$I = 13180 \text{ in}^4$

$A = 158.1 \text{ in}^2$

Assume that the self weight of the glulam is about 40 pcf = .023 pci.

self weight = .023(158.1)12 = 43.6 plf

$$S_R = 825.4\left(\frac{.604}{.56}\right) = 890.3 \text{ in}^3 > 833.5 \text{ in}^3 \quad \textbf{NG!}$$

We could further check to see if our first trial size C_v would help.

Determine the actual C_V (K_L = 1.0)

NDS 5.3.2

$$C_V = K_L\left(\frac{21}{L}\right)^{1/10}\left(\frac{12}{d}\right)^{1/10}\left(\frac{5.125}{b}\right)^{1/10}$$

$$C_V = 1.0\left(\frac{21}{44}\right)^{1/10}\left(\frac{12}{31.63}\right)^{1/10}\left(\frac{5.125}{5}\right)^{1/10} = .85 > .82 \;\checkmark$$

By inspection we can see that it is only a small increase in percentage S_R and probably will not help us.

Try $S_{5\times 34\text{-}3/8} = 984.7 \text{ in}^3 > 825.4 \text{ in}^3$ ✓

$I = 16920 \text{ in}^4$

$A = 171.9 \text{ in}^2$

self weight = .023(171.9)12 = 47.8 plf

$$S_R = 825.4\left(\frac{.608}{.56}\right) = 896.1 \text{ in}^3 < 984.7 \text{ in}^3 \;\checkmark$$

Determine the actual C_V (K_L = 1.0)

$$C_V = K_L\left(\frac{21}{L}\right)^{1/10}\left(\frac{12}{d}\right)^{1/10}\left(\frac{5.125}{b}\right)^{1/10}$$

$$C_V = 1.0\left(\frac{21}{44}\right)^{1/10}\left(\frac{12}{34.38}\right)^{1/10}\left(\frac{5.125}{5}\right)^{1/10} = .9 > .82 \;\checkmark$$

Which implies that our assumption was conservative and that our trial size is ok.

Bending ok

When the lateral support is relatively closely spaced (say 2 to 4 feet in general), the beam stability factor (C_L) approaches unity. As the unsupported length gets longer, the beam stability factor (C_L) gets smaller. If the beam is judiciously laterally supported, we can generally say that the volume factor (C_v) controls over the beam stability factor (C_L). The beam stability factor (C_L), will control when the beam is laterally supported at longer lengths.

<u>Ck shear</u>

It is considered conservative not to use the shear modification.

NDS T2.3.1

$$F_V' = F_V(C_D)C_M(C_t) = .165(1.0)1.0(1.0) = .165 \text{ ksi}$$

NDS 3.3.2

$$V = \frac{w\ell}{2} = \frac{(.608)44}{2} = 13.4^{k}$$

$$A_R = \frac{1.5(V)}{F_V'} = \frac{1.5(13.4)}{.165} = 121.8 \text{ in}^2 < 171.9 \text{ in}^2 \;\checkmark$$

Shear ok

<u>Ck defl.</u> (based on TCM)

$$E' = E(C_M)C_t = 1.8e3(1.0)1.0 = 1.8e3 \text{ ksi}$$

NDS T2.3.1

$$\Delta_{LL} = \frac{5w\ell^4}{384EI} = \frac{5(.32)44^4(1728)}{384(1.8e3)16920}$$

$$= .89 \text{ in} < \ell/360 = 44(12)/360 = 1.47 \text{ in} \;\checkmark$$

NDS T4.3

$$\Delta_{DL} = \Delta_{w:LL}\left(\frac{w_{DL}}{w_{LL}}\right) = .89\left(\frac{.29}{.32}\right) = .81 \text{ in}$$

camber = 1.5 Δ_{DL} = 1.5(.81) = 1.2 in

Deflection ok

Deflection is more critical and restrictive in the case of a floor beam. It is the choice of some designers to check deflection before they check the shear stress in a floor beam. This procedure may save you some time in actual engineering practice.

Glued plywood flooring

Some designers prefer to achieve better performance of the building by gluing the plywood flooring to the structural framing system. This is a conservative measure that adds stiffness to the floor through composite action. When this technique is employed the designer should ignore the composite behavior of the system when they are checking for deflection limitations.

<u>Ck bearing</u>

Since the support conditions are not known, determine the minimum bearing length.

NDS T2.3.1

$$F'_{c\perp} = F_{c\perp}(C_M)C_t(C_b) = .65(1.0)1.0(1.0) = .65 \text{ ksi}$$

$$\ell_{b\ min} = \frac{R}{bF'_{c\perp}} = \frac{13.4}{5(.65)} = 4.1 \text{ in}$$

> Use 5x34-3/8 24F-V4 glulam with a minimum bearing length of 4.1 in. Camber = 1.25 in

Design tips

Cost-efficient glulam designs are obtained with the use of simple guidelines. The engineer should strive to provide enough lateral support to the compression side of the glulam so that little or no reduction is required when considering the lateral stability of the beam. The bearing ends of the beam should be held rigid enough so that rotation or rolling of the ends do not occur.

A common means of (compression side) lateral support for the top side of a simple beam is the use of plywood roof or floor sheathing. This assumes that the top sides of the intermediate rafters or joists are flush with the top of the beam. Thus, the plywood nailing is into the beam and provides full lateral support. If the rafters or joists are placed on top of the beam, their spacing will constitute the unbraced length (provided the connections furnish adequate lateral restraint of the beam).

A plywood diaphragm is a good approach to realizing full lateral stability for the beam. If planks are utilized for the diaphragm, special attention must be given to the nailing patterns. Moment couples must be created by the use of nailed joints so that the system provides adequate lateral stability from diaphragm rigidity.

You will note that the stress was specified in the assumptions of the problem. It is common practice to select a tabular bending stress before a trial size is determined and used for the other stress checks.

□
□
□

Results! Why man, I have gotten a lot of results. I know several thousands things that won't work.

THOMAS A. EDISON

PROBLEM 2.19

Glulam beam design that is laterally supported at 8 ft o/c.

Design the floor beam as shown below.

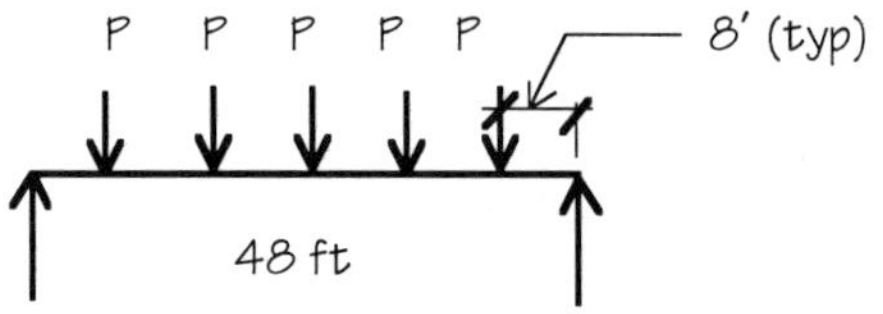

ASSUME

No ponding, plaster ceiling.
Lateral support from supported beams.
Design for self wt.
EMC < 16%.
Normal temp. conditions.
Commercial building.
24F-V4 glulam.
$P = 3.1^k$.
DL/LL = .75.

SOLUTION

F_b = 2.4 ksi (T), 1.2 ksi (compression zone in tension)
F_v = .165 ksi
E_x = 1.8e3 ksi, E_y = 1.4e3 ksi

DL + LL controls by inspection.

The beam is long so either M or Δ will control.

Bending

We must check both lateral stability and volume effect. For lateral stability, we assume a trial beam size (from the volume effect trial beam) to get a slenderness ratio (R_B), then re-check it in an iterative manner.

Volume effect:

NDS T2.3.1

$F_b' = F_b C_D C_M C_t C_V$

Assume the selected glulam will have a C_V of .82. If the actual C_V is not .82 adjust it and re-ck the calc. This trial procedure is an iterative process.

$F_b = 2.4(1.0)1.0(1.0).82 = 1.97$ ksi

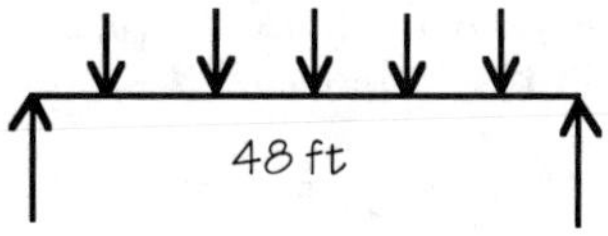

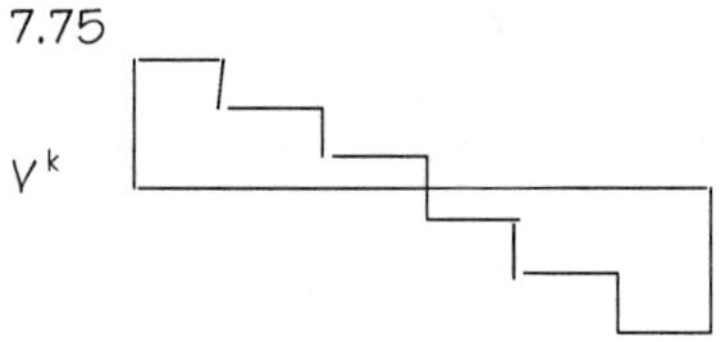

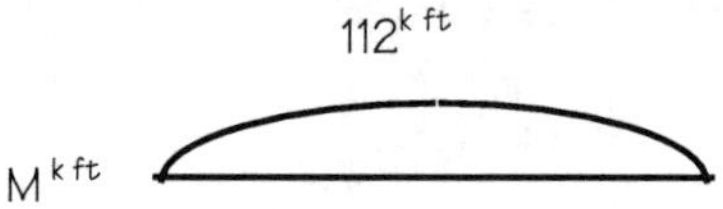

$$S_R = \frac{12M}{F_b'} = \frac{12(112)}{1.97} = 682.2 \text{ in}^3$$

try $S_{5 \times 30\text{-}1/4} = 762.6 \text{ in}^3 > 682.2 \text{ in}^3$ √

From experience, we have chosen one lamination larger than required for S_R. This is to account for the additional self wt. which is yet to be calculated.

I = 11530 in^4

A = 151.3 in^2

Assume that the self weight of the glulam is about 40 pcf = .023 pci.

NDS 3.3.2

self weight = .023(151.3)12 = 42 plf

$$M = 112 + \frac{.042(48)^2}{8} = 124.1^{k\,ft}$$

$$S_R = 682.2\left(\frac{124.1}{112}\right) = 755.9 \text{ in}^3 < 762.6 \text{ in}^3 \ \surd$$

Determine the actual C_V (K_L = 1.0)

NDS 5.3.2

$$C_V = K_L\left(\frac{21}{L}\right)^{1/10}\left(\frac{12}{d}\right)^{1/10}\left(\frac{5.125}{b}\right)^{1/10}$$

$$C_V = 1.0\left(\frac{21}{48}\right)^{1/10}\left(\frac{12}{30.25}\right)^{1/10}\left(\frac{5.125}{5}\right)^{1/10} = .84 > .82$$

Which implies that our assumption was conservative and that our trial size is ok. √

Ck Lateral Stability

NDS T2.3.1

$F_b' = F_b C_D C_M C_t C_L$

Unbraced length ℓ_u = 8 ft = 96 in

For 5 equal concentrated loads at the 1/6 pts with lateral support at those 1/6 pts.

NDS T3.3.3

$\ell_e = 1.73\,\ell_u = 1.73(96) = 166.1$ in

$$R_B = \sqrt{\frac{\ell_e d}{b^2}} = \sqrt{\frac{166.1(30.25)}{5^2}} = 14.2 < 50 \ \surd$$

This beam is subject to lateral torsional buckling. Because of this movement (in the y axis plane) we need to consider the stability with E_y.

NDS T2.3.1

$E' = E_y(C_M)C_t = 1.4e3(1.0)1.0 = 1.4e3$ ksi

$$F_{bE} = \frac{K_{bE}E'y}{R_B^2} = \frac{.609(1.4e3)}{14.2^2} = 4.23 \text{ ksi}$$

$F_b^* = F_{bx}C_D C_M C_t = 2.4(1.0)1.0(1.0) = 2.4$ ksi

NDS 3.3.3.8

$$C_L = \frac{1+\left(F_{bE}/F_{bx}^*\right)}{1.9} - \sqrt{\left(\frac{1+\left(F_{bE}/F_{bx}^*\right)}{1.9}\right)^2 - \frac{\left(F_{bE}/F_{bx}^*\right)}{.95}}$$

$$C_L = \frac{1+\left(4.23/2.4\right)}{1.9} - \sqrt{\left(\frac{1+\left(4.23/2.4\right)}{1.9}\right)^2 - \frac{\left(4.23/2.4\right)}{.95}}$$

$= .95 > .84$

∴ Volume effect (C_v) governs over stability. Our trial section was determined using volume effect so we are ok.

> Bending ok

NDS T2.3.1

Ck shear

$F_v' = F_v(C_D)C_M(C_t) = .165(1.0)1.0(1.0) = .165$ ksi

NDS 3.4.2

$$V = 7.75 + \frac{w\ell}{2} = 7.75 + \frac{(.042)48}{2} = 8.76^k$$

$$A_R = \frac{1.5(V)}{F_v'} = \frac{1.5(8.76)}{.165} = 79.6 \text{ in}^2 < 151.3 \text{ in}^2 \ \checkmark$$

> Shear ok

NDS T2.3.1

Ck defl. (based on TCM)

$E' = E(C_M)C_t = 1.8e3(1.0)1.0 = 1.8e3$ ksi

$\Delta_{TL} = 2.18$ in (from comptr output)

Since the ratio DL/LL = .75 ,

This implies TL/LL = 1.75

NDS T4.3

$$\Delta_{LL} = \Delta_{TL}\left(\frac{w_{LL}}{w_{TL}}\right) = 2.18\left(\frac{1}{1.75}\right)$$

$$= 1.25 \text{ in} < \ell/360 = 48(12)/360 = 1.6 \text{ in} \ \checkmark$$

$$\Delta_{DL} = \Delta_{LL}\left(\frac{w_{DL}}{w_{LL}}\right) = 1.25(.75) = .94 \text{ in}$$

camber = 1.5 Δ_{DL} = 1.5(.94) = 1.41 in

> Deflection ok

Ck bearing

Since the support conditions are not known, determine the minimum bearing length.

$F_{c\perp}' = F_{c\perp}(C_M)C_t(C_b) = .65(1.0)1.0(1.0) = .65$ ksi

$$\ell_{b\ min} = \frac{R}{bF_{c\perp}'} = \frac{8.76}{5(.65)} = 2.7 \text{ in}$$ NDS T2.3.1

> Use 5x30-1/4 24F-V4 glulam with a minimum bearing length of 10 in. Camber = 1.5 in

□
□
□

You have no idea what a poor opinion I have of myself, and how little I deserve it.

W. S GILBERT

● PROBLEM 2.20

Glulam beam design that is laterally supported at 16 ft o/c.

Design the floor beam as shown below.

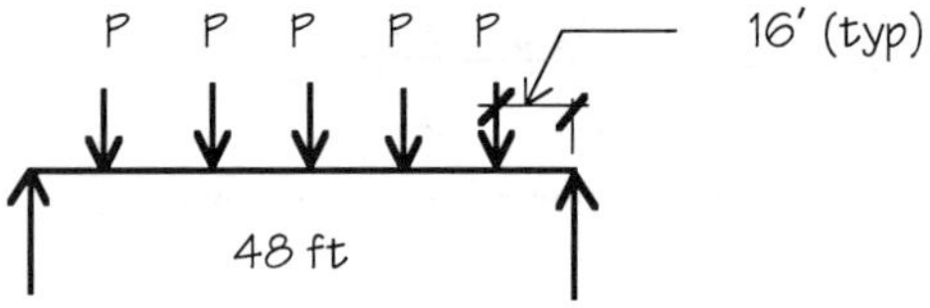

ASSUME

- No ponding, no plaster ceiling.
- Lateral support at 16 ft o/c.
- Design for self wt.
- EMC < 16%.
- Normal temp. conditions.
- Commercial building.
- 24F-V4 glulam.

$P = 3.1^k$.
DL/LL = .75.

SOLUTION

F_b = 2.4 ksi (T), 1.2 ksi (compression zone in tension)
F_v = .165 ksi
E_x = 1.8e3 ksi, E_y = 1.4e3 ksi

DL + LL controls by inspection

The beam is long so either M or Δ will control.

Bending

NDS T2.3.1 We must check both lateral stability and volume effect. For lateral stability, we assume a trial beam size (from the volume effect trial beam) to get a slenderness ratio R_B, then recheck it in an iterative manner.

Volume effect:

$$F_b' = F_b C_D C_M C_t C_V$$

Assume the selected glulam will have a C_V of .82. If the actual C_V is not .82 adjust it and re-ck the calc. This trial procedure is an iterative process.

$$F_b = 2.4(1.0)1.0(1.0).82 = 1.97 \text{ ksi}$$

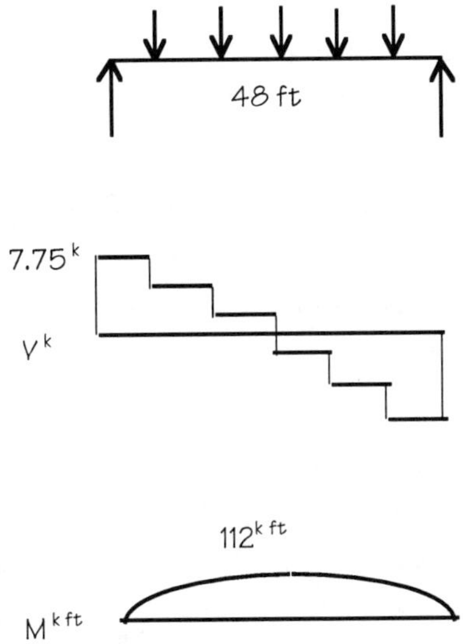

$$S_R = \frac{12M}{F_b'} = \frac{12(112)}{1.97} = 682.2 \text{ in}^3$$

try $S_{5 \times 30\text{-}1/4} = 762.6 \text{ in}^3 > 682.2 \text{ in}^3$ √

This is one lamination larger than required from S_R to account for the additional self wt. to be calc.

$$I = 11530 \text{ in}^4$$
$$A = 151.3 \text{ in}^2$$

Assume that the self weight of the glulam is about 40 pcf = .023 pci.

self weight = .023(151.3)12 = 42 plf

$$M = 112 + \frac{.042(48)^2}{8} = 124.1^{k\,ft}$$ NDS 3.3.2

$$S_R = 682.2\left(\frac{124.1}{112}\right) = 755.9 \text{ in}^3 < 762.6 \text{ in}^3 \text{ √}$$

Determine the actual C_V (K_L = 1.0)

$$C_V = K_L\left(\frac{21}{L}\right)^{1/10}\left(\frac{12}{d}\right)^{1/10}\left(\frac{5.125}{b}\right)^{1/10}$$ NDS 5.3.2

$$C_V = 1.0\left(\frac{21}{48}\right)^{1/10}\left(\frac{12}{30.25}\right)^{1/10}\left(\frac{5.125}{5}\right)^{1/10} = .84 > .82$$

Which implies that our assumption was conservative, and that our trial size is ok √

Ck Lateral Stability

$$F_b = F_b' = F_b C_D C_M C_t C_L$$ NDS T2.3.1

Unbraced length ℓ_U = 16 ft = 192 in

For 5 equal concentrated loads at the 1/6 pts with lateral support at those 1/6 the pts.

$$\ell_e = 1.73\,\ell_U = 1.73(192) = 332.2 \text{ in}$$

$$R_B = \sqrt{\frac{\ell_e d}{b^2}} = \sqrt{\frac{332.2(30.25)}{5^2}} = 20 < 50 \text{ √}$$ NDS 3.3.3.6

This beam is subject to lateral torsional buckling. Because of this movement (in the y axis plane), we need to consider the stability with E_y NDS T2.3.1

$$E' = E_y(C_M)C_t = 1.4e3(1.0)1.0 = 1.4e3 \text{ ksi}$$

$$F_{bE} = \frac{K_{bE}E_y'}{R_B^2} = \frac{.609(1.4e3)}{20^2} = 2.13 \text{ ksi}$$

NDS 3.3.3.8

$F_b^* = F_{bx}C_DC_MC_t = 2.4(1.0)1.0(1.0) = 2.4$ ksi

$$C_L = \frac{1+\left(F_{bE}/F_{bx}^*\right)}{1.9} - \sqrt{\left(\frac{1+\left(F_{bE}/F_{bx}^*\right)}{1.9}\right)^2 - \frac{\left(F_{bE}/F_{bx}^*\right)}{.95}}$$

$$C_L = \frac{1+\left(2.13/2.4\right)}{1.9} - \sqrt{\left(\frac{1+\left(2.13/2.4\right)}{1.9}\right)^2 - \frac{\left(2.13/2.4\right)}{.95}} = .76 < .84$$

∴ Stability governs over volume effect. Our trial section was determined using volume effect so we must re-evaluate. This is an illustration that in practice it is more economic to reduce your unbraced length to a reasonable distance (like 8 ft). It is also a demonstration of the amount of extra work performed by you if you do not.

R_B is a fundamental criteria of lateral stability (for buckling). Since it is sensitive to beam width, select a wider glulam.

NDS T2.3.1

Volume effect:

$$F_b' = F_bC_DC_MC_tC_V$$

Assume the selected glulam will have a C_V of .82. If the actual C_V is not .82 adjust it and re-ck the calc. This trial procedure is an iterative process.

$S_R = 682.2$ in^3

try $S_{6\text{-}3/4 \times 27\text{-}1/2} = 850.8$ in^3 > 682.2 in^3 √

NDS 3.3.4

This is about 2 laminations larger than required from S_R to account for the additional self wt. to be calc.

I = 11700 in^4

A = 185.6 in^2

Assume that the self weight of the glulam is about 40 pcf = .023 pci.

self weight = .023(185.6)12 = 51.2 plf

$$M = 112 + \frac{.051(48)^2}{8} = 126.7^{\,k\,ft}$$

$$S_R = 682.2\left(\frac{126.7}{112}\right) = 771.7 \text{ in}^3 < 850.8 \text{ in}^3 \;√$$

NDS 5.3.2

Determine the actual C_V (K_L = 1.0)

$$C_V = K_L\left(\frac{21}{L}\right)^{1/10}\left(\frac{12}{d}\right)^{1/10}\left(\frac{5.125}{b}\right)^{1/10}$$

$$C_V = 1.0\left(\frac{21}{48}\right)^{1/10}\left(\frac{12}{27.5}\right)^{1/10}\left(\frac{5.125}{6.75}\right)^{1/10} = .82 = .82$$

Which implies that our assumption was ok √

<u>Ck Lateral Stability</u>

$\ell_e = 332.2$ in

$$R_B = \sqrt{\frac{\ell_e d}{b^2}} = \sqrt{\frac{332.2(27.5)}{6.75^2}} = 14.2 < 50 \;√$$ NDS 3.3.3.6

$E' = 1.4e3$ ksi

$$F_{bE} = \frac{K_{bE}E_y'}{R_B^2} = \frac{.609(1.4e3)}{14.2^2} = 4.23 \text{ ksi}$$ NDS 3.3.3.8

$F_b^* = F_{bx}C_DC_MC_t = 2.4(1.0)1.0(1.0) = 2.4$ ksi

$$C_L = \frac{1+\left(4.2/2.4\right)}{1.9} - \sqrt{\left(\frac{1+\left(4.2/2.4\right)}{1.9}\right)^2 - \frac{\left(4.2/2.4\right)}{.95}} = .94 > .84$$

∴ Curently, volume effect governs over stability. Our trial section was determined using volume effect, so we are ok.

Bending ok

<u>Ck shear</u> NDS T2.3.1

$$F_V' = F_V(C_D)C_M(C_t) = .165(1.0)1.0(1.0) = .165 \text{ ksi}$$

$$V = 7.75 + \frac{w\ell}{2} = 7.75 + \frac{(.051)48}{2} = 8.97^{\,k}$$ NDS 3.4.2

$$A_R = \frac{1.5(V)}{F_V'} = \frac{1.5(8.97)}{.165} = 81.5 \text{ in}^2 < 185.6 \text{ in}^2 \;√$$

Shear ok

<u>Ck defl.</u> (based on TCM)

$E' = E(C_M)C_t = 1.8e3(1.0)1.0 = 1.8e3$ ksi NDS T2.3.1

$\Delta_{TL} = 2.15$ in (from comptr output)

Since the ratio DL/LL = .75

this implies TL/LL = 1.75

$$\Delta_{LL} = \Delta_{TL}\left(\frac{w_{LL}}{w_{TL}}\right) = 2.15\left(\frac{1}{1.75}\right)$$

$= 1.23 \text{ in} < \frac{l}{240} = \frac{48(12)}{240} = 2.4 \text{ in}$ √

$$\Delta_{DL} = \Delta_{LL}\left(\frac{w_{DL}}{w_{LL}}\right) = 1.23(.75) = .92 \text{ in}$$

camber = 1.5 Δ_{DL} = 1.5(.92) = 1.38 in

Deflection ok

Ck bearing

Since the support conditions are not known, determine the minimum bearing length.

NDS T2.3.1

$$F'_{c\perp} = F_{c\perp}(C_M)C_t(C_b) = .65(1.0)1.0(1.0) = .65 \text{ ksi}$$

$$\ell_{b\,min} = \frac{R}{bF'_{c\perp}} = \frac{8.97}{6.75(.65)} = 2.0 \text{ in}$$

Use 6-3/4x27-1/2, 24F-V4 glulam with a minimum bearing length of 2 in. Camber = 1.38 in

Death is not the greatest loss in life. The greatest loss is what dies inside us while we live.

NORMAN COUSINS

● PROBLEM 2.21

Glulam beam design along with the checking of the purlins and subpurlins.

You are part of a design team of a large commercial project. The tasking is broken down into various components and phases. You are to design the glulam beam as shown. Check size of purlins and subpurlins.

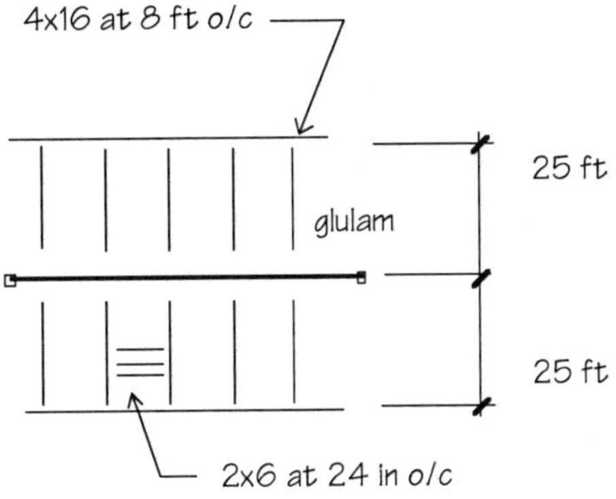

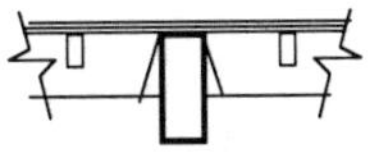

ASSUME

- DL to subpurlin = 9 psf.
- DL to purlin = 11 psf.
- DL to glulam = 13 psf.
- LL uses UBC Method 1.
- EMC < 19%.
- Self wts included in psf above.
- Commercial building.
- Design for glulam self wt, EMC < 16%.
- DF - L No. 1 at purlin and subpurlin.
- 24F - V4 glulam, DL/LL = .75.
- Defl. ok at 2x & 4x.
- No ponding, plaster ceiling.
- Lateral support from beams at glulam.
- Normal temp. conditions.

SOLUTION

LL uses UBC Method 1.

$w_{2x6} = 2(20 + 9) = 58$ plf

$w_{4x16} = 8(20 + 11) = 248$ plf

$TA_{glulam} = 48(25) = 1200 \text{ ft}^2$

$w_{glulam} = 25(12 + 13) = 625$ plf

Ck 2x6

$F_b = 1.0$ ksi
$F_v = .095$ ksi
$E = 1.7e3$ ksi
$S = 7.56 \text{ in}^3$
$A = 8.25 \text{ in}^2$

Ck Bending $C_F = 1.3$ — NDS T2.3.1

Assume full lateral support from the plywood diaphragm.

$F_b' = F_b C_D C_M C_t C_L C_F C_r = 1.0(1.25)1.0(1.0)1.0(1.3)1.15$

$= 1.87$ ksi

NDS 3.3.2

$$M = \frac{w\ell^2}{8} = \frac{(.058)8^2}{8} = .46^{\text{ k-ft}}$$

$$S_R = \frac{12M}{F_b'} = \frac{12(.46)}{1.87} = 2.95 \text{ in}^3 < 7.56 \text{ in}^3 \ \checkmark$$

Bending ok

Ck Shear — NDS T2.3.1

$F_v' = F_v(C_D)C_M(C_t)C_H = .095(1.25)1.0(1.0)1.0 = .119$ ksi

$$V = \frac{w\ell}{2} = \frac{(.058)8}{2} = .23^{\text{ k}}$$

NDS 3.4.2

$$A_R = \frac{1.5(V)}{F_v'} = \frac{1.5(.23)}{.119} = 2.9 \text{ in}^2 < 8.25 \text{ in}^3 \ \checkmark$$

Shear ok, which implies that the 2x6 is ok

Ck 4x16 (assume full lateral support)

$F_b = 1.0$, ksi, (non-rep mem, over 24" o/c)
$F_v = .095$ ksi
$E = 1.7e3$ ksi
$S = 135.7 \text{ in}^3$
$A = 53.4 \text{ in}^2$

Ck Bending ($C_F = 1.0$) — NDS T2.3.1

$F_b' = F_b C_D C_M C_t C_L C_F C_r = 1.0(1.25)1.0(1.0)1.0(1.0)1.0$

$= 1.25$ ksi

$$M = \frac{w\ell^2}{8} = \frac{(.248)25^2}{8} = 19.4^{\text{ k-ft}}$$

$$S_R = \frac{12M}{F_b'} = \frac{12(19.4)}{1.25} = 186.2 \text{ in}^3 > 135.4 \text{ in}^3 \ \textbf{NG!}$$

NDS 3.3.2

Try 6x18

$C_F = (12/d)^{1/9} = (12/17.5)^{1/9} = .96$

$F_b = 1.35$, ksi, (non-rep mem, over 24" o/c)
$F_v = .085$ ksi
$E = 1.6e3$ ksi
$S = 280.7 \text{ in}^3$
$A = 96.3 \text{ in}^2$

$F_b = 1.35(1.25)1.0(1.0)1.0(.96)1.0 = 1.62$ ksi

$$S_R = \frac{12(19.4)}{1.62} = 143.7 \text{ in}^3 < 280.7 \text{ in}^3 \ \checkmark$$

Bending ok

Ck Shear — NDS T2.3.1

$F_v' = F_v(C_D)C_M(C_t)C_H = .085(1.25)1.0(1.0)1.0 = .106$ ksi

$$V = \frac{w\ell}{2} = \frac{(.248)25}{2} = 3.1^{\text{ k}}$$

NDS 3.4.2

$$A_R = \frac{1.5(V)}{F_v'} = \frac{1.5(3.1)}{.106} = 43.9 \text{ in}^2 < 96.3 \text{ in}^3 \ \checkmark$$

Shear ok for 6x18, which infers 6x18 ok

Glulam (uses glulam from previous problem)

$F_b = 2.4$ ksi (T), 1.2 ksi (compression zone in tension)
$F_v = .165$ ksi
$E_x = 1.8e3$ ksi, $E_y = 1.4e3$ ksi

DL + LL controls by inspection.

The beam is long so either M or Δ will control.

Bending

We must check both lateral stability and volume effect. For lateral stability, we assume a trial beam size (from the volume effect trial beam) to get a slenderness ratio R_B, then re-check it in an iterative manner.

Volume effect: — NDS T2.3.1

$F_b' = F_b C_D C_M C_t C_V$

Assume the selected glulam will have a C_V of .82. If the actual C_V is not .82 adjust it and re-ck the calc. This trial procedure is an iterative process.

NDS 5.3.2

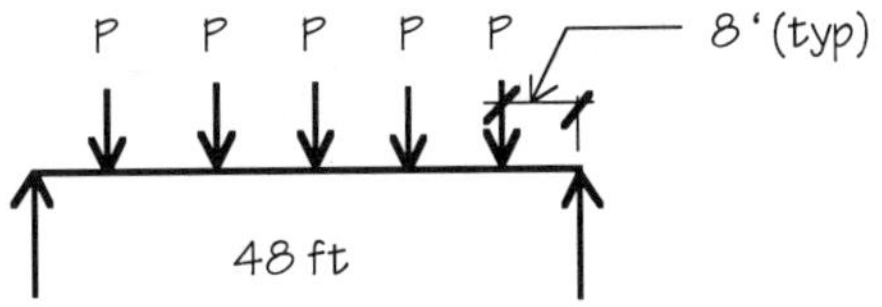

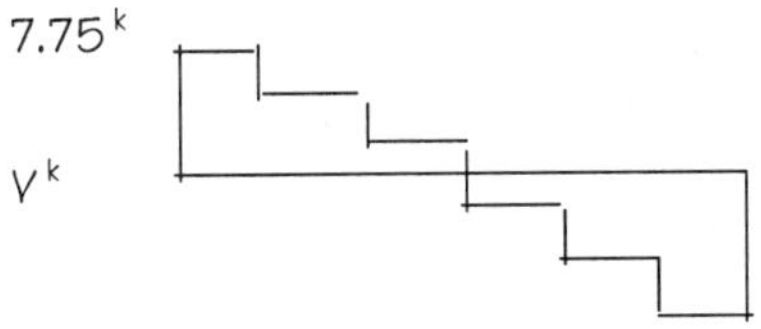

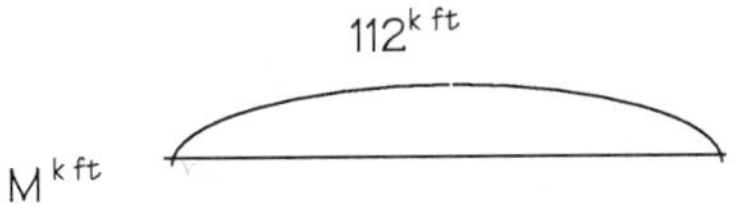

NDS 3.3.2

$P = 3.1^k$ (from 6x18)

$F_b = 2.4(1.0)1.0(1.0).82 = 1.97$ ksi

$$S_R = \frac{12M}{F_b'} = \frac{12(112)}{1.97} = 682.2 \text{ in}^3$$

try $S_{5 \times 30\text{-}1/4} = 762.6 \text{ in}^3 > 682.2 \text{ in}^3$ √

This is one lamination larger than required from S_R. This is to account for the additional self weight which is yet to be calculated.

$I = 11530 \text{ in}^4$

$A = 151.3 \text{ in}^2$

Assume that the self weight of the glulam is about 40 pcf = .023 pci.

self weight = .023(151.3)12 = 42 plf

$$M = 112 + \frac{.042(48)^2}{8} = 124.1^{k\,ft}$$

$$S_R = 682.2\left(\frac{124.1}{112}\right) = 755.9 \text{ in}^3 < 762.6 \text{ in}^3 \quad √$$

Determine the actual C_V ($K_L = 1.0$)

$$C_V = K_L\left(\frac{21}{L}\right)^{1/10}\left(\frac{12}{d}\right)^{1/10}\left(\frac{5.125}{b}\right)^{1/10}$$

$$C_V = 1.0\left(\frac{21}{48}\right)^{1/10}\left(\frac{12}{30.25}\right)^{1/10}\left(\frac{5.125}{5}\right)^{1/10} = .84 > .82$$

Which implies that our assumption was conservative, and that our trial size is ok. √

<u>Ck Lateral Stability</u>

NDS T2.3.1

$$F_b' = F_b C_D C_M C_t C_L$$

Unbraced length $\ell_U = 8 \text{ ft} = 96 \text{ in}$

For 5 equal concentrated loads at the 1/6 pts with lateral support at those 1/6 pts.

$$\ell_e = 1.73\,\ell_U = 1.73(96) = 166.1 \text{ in}$$

NDS 3.3.3.6

$$R_B = \sqrt{\frac{\ell_e d}{b^2}} = \sqrt{\frac{166.1(30.25)}{5^2}} = 14.2 < 50 \quad √$$

This beam is subject to lateral torsional buckling. Because of this movement in the y axis plane, we need to consider the stability with E_y

$$E' = E_y(C_M)C_t = 1.4e3(1.0)1.0 = 1.4e3 \text{ ksi}$$

$$F_{bE} = \frac{K_{bE}E'_y}{R_B^2} = \frac{.609(1.4e3)}{14.2^2} = 4.23 \text{ ksi}$$

$$F_b^* = F_{bx}C_D C_M C_t = 2.4(1.0)1.0(1.0) = 2.4 \text{ ksi}$$

NDS 3.3.3.8

$$C_L = \frac{1+\left(F_{bE}/F_{bx}^*\right)}{1.9} - \sqrt{\left(\frac{1+\left(F_{bE}/F_{bx}^*\right)}{1.9}\right)^2 - \frac{\left(F_{bE}/F_{bx}^*\right)}{.95}}$$

$$C_L = \frac{1+(4.23/2.4)}{1.9} - \sqrt{\left(\frac{1+(4.23/2.4)}{1.9}\right)^2 - \frac{(4.23/2.4)}{.95}}$$

$= .95 > .84$

∴ Volume effect governs over stability. Our trial section was determined using volume effect, so we are ok.

Bending ok

Ck shear

NDS T2.3.1

Unless shear is going to be a problem, like if there is a large load and a relatively short span, do not use a shear modification (conservative).

$$F_v' = F_v(C_D)C_M(C_t) = .165(1.0)1.0(1.0) = .165 \text{ ksi}$$

NDS 3.4.2

$$V = 7.75 + \frac{w\ell}{2} = \frac{(.042)48}{2} = 8.76^k$$

$$A_R = \frac{1.5(V)}{F_v'} = \frac{1.5(8.76)}{.165} = 79.6 \text{ in}^2 < 151.3 \text{ in}^2 \quad \surd$$

Shear ok

Ck defl. (based on TCM)

NDS T2.3.1

$E' = E(C_M)C_t = 1.8e3(1.0)1.0 = 1.8e3$ ksi

$\Delta_{TL} = 2.18$ in (from comptr output)

Since the ratio DL/LL = .75

this implies TL/LL = 1.75

$$\Delta_{LL} = \Delta_{TL}\left(\frac{w_{LL}}{w_{TL}}\right) = 2.18\left(\frac{1}{1.75}\right)$$

$$= 1.25 \text{ in} < \ell/360 = 48(12)/360 = 1.6 \text{ in} \quad \surd$$

$$\Delta_{DL} = \Delta_{LL}\left(\frac{w_{DL}}{w_{LL}}\right) = 1.25(.75) = .94 \text{ in}$$

camber = 1.5 Δ_{DL} = 1.5(.94) = 1.41 in

Deflection ok

Ck bearing

Since the support conditions are not known, determine the minimum bearing length.

NDS T2.3.1

$$F_{c\perp}' = F_{c\perp}(C_M)C_t(C_b) = .65(1.0)1.0(1.0) = .65 \text{ ksi}$$

$$\ell_{b\ min} = \frac{R}{bF_{c\perp}'} = \frac{8.76}{5(.65)} = 2.7 \text{ in}$$

Use 5x30-1/4 24F-V4 glulam with a minimum bearing length of 2.7 in. Camber = 1.5 in

□
□
□

Do not fear death so much, but rather the inadequate life.

BERTOLT BRECHT

○ PROBLEM 2.22

Panelized roof system design.

Size the selected members for the panelized roof system shown below.

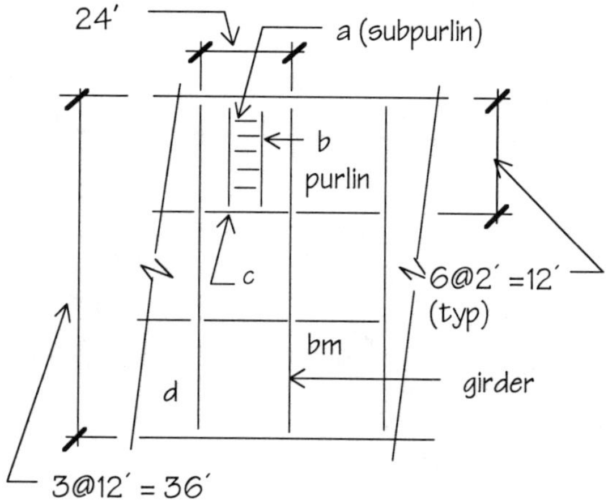

ply 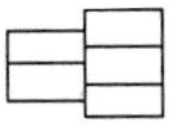

ASSUME

- 1/2 in STR. 1 ply with 10d @ 6 in o/c.
- DF - L No. 2, purlins and subpurlins.
- DF - L Dense No 1 beams.
- 24F - V8 glulam girders.
- LL uses UBC Method 1.
- EMC < 19% (dimension lumber).
- Commercial building.
- Design for glulam self wt, EMC < 16%.
- No ponding, no plaster ceiling.
- Lateral support from beams at glulam.
- Normal temp. conditions.
- Composite roof, DL = 2.2 psf.
- Neglect insulation and sprinklers.

SOLUTION

a. Subpurlin (assume 2x6)

Calc loads

DL	roofing	2.2 psf
	1/2 " ply	1.5
	2x4 @ 24 in o/c	.7
	misc.	2.6
		7.0
LL		20 psf
		27 psf

$TA = 2(8) = 16\ ft^2$ (no reduction allowed)

$w = 2(.027) = .054$ klf

$F_b = .875$ ksi	$S = 7.56\ in^3$
$F_v = .095$ ksi	$A = 8.25\ in^2$
$E = 1.6e3$ ksi	$I = 20.8\ in^4$

Ck Bending $C_F = 1.3$

Assume full lateral support from the plywood diaphragm.

NDS T2.3.1

$$F_b' = F_b C_D C_M C_t C_L C_F C_r$$

$$= .875(1.25)1.0(1.0)1.0(1.3)1.15 = 1.64 \text{ ksi}$$

$$M = \frac{w\ell^2}{8} = \frac{(.054)8^2}{8} = .43^{\text{ k-ft}}$$

$$S_R = \frac{12M}{F_b'} = \frac{12(.43)}{1.64} = 3.1\ in^3 < 7.56\ in^3\ \checkmark$$ NDS 3.3.2

Bending ok

Ck Shear

$$F_v' = F_v(C_D)C_M(C_t)C_H = .095(1.25)1.0(1.0)1.0 = .119 \text{ ksi}$$ NDS T2.3.1

$$V = \frac{w\ell}{2} = \frac{(.054)8}{2} = .22^{\text{ k}}$$

$$A_R = \frac{1.5(V)}{F_v'} = \frac{1.5(.22)}{.119} = 2.8\ in^2 < 8.25\ in^3\ \checkmark$$ NDS 3.4.2

Shear ok

Ck Defl.

$$E' = E(C_M)C_t = 1.6e3(1.0)1.0 = 1.6e3 \text{ ksi}$$ NDS T2.3.1

$$\Delta_{TL} = \frac{5w\ell^4}{384EI} = \frac{5(.054)8^4(1728)}{384(1.6e3)20.8}$$

$$= .15 \text{ in} < \frac{L}{180} = \frac{8(12)}{180} = .53 \text{ in}\ \checkmark$$

$$\Delta_{LL} = \left(\frac{LL}{DL+LL}\right)\Delta_{DL+LL} = \left(\frac{20}{27}\right).15$$

$$= .11 \text{ in} < \frac{L}{240} = \frac{8(12)}{240} = .4 \text{ in}\ \checkmark$$

Deflection ok

Chose Hgr

$R_{\text{simp LUP 26 with 10d}} = .88^k > .22$

Use 2x6 DF - L No. 2 @24" o/c with simpson LUP26 with 10d

b. Purlin (assume 4x10)

$TA = 8(12) = 96\ ft^2 < 200$

No reduction allowed per method 1.

Calc loads

previous	7 psf
4x8 @ 8' o/c	1
LL	20 psf
	28 psf

w = 8(.028) = .224 klf

F_b = .875 ksi S = 49.9 in^3
F_v = .095 ksi A = 32.4 in^2
E = 1.6e3 ksi I = 230.8 in^4

Ck Bending $C_F = 1.2$

Assume full lateral support from the plywood diaphragm and subpurlins.

NDS T2.3.1

$$F_b' = F_b C_D C_M C_t C_L C_F C_r = .875(1.25)1.0(1.0)1.0(1.2)1.0$$

= 1.3 ksi

$$M = \frac{w\ell^2}{8} = \frac{(.224)12^2}{8} = 4.03^{\text{k-ft}}$$

NDS 3.3.2

$$S_R = \frac{12M}{F_b'} = \frac{12(4.03)}{1.3} = 37.2 \text{ in}^3 < 49.9 \text{ in}^3 \ \surd$$

Bending ok

Ck Shear

NDS T2.3.1

$$F_v' = F_v(C_D)C_M(C_t)C_H = .095(1.25)1.0(1.0)1.0 = .119 \text{ ksi}$$

$$V = \frac{w\ell}{2} = \frac{(.224)12}{2} = 1.3^{k}$$

NDS 3.4.2

$$A_R = \frac{1.5(V)}{F_v'} = \frac{1.5(1.3)}{.119} = 16.4 \text{ in}^2 < 32.4 \text{ in}^3 \ \surd$$

Shear ok

Ck Defl.

NDS T2.3.1

$$E' = E(C_M)C_t = 1.6e3(1.0)1.0 = 1.6e3 \text{ ksi}$$

$$\Delta_{TL} = \frac{5w\ell^4}{384EI} = \frac{5(.224)12^4(1728)}{384(1.6e3)230.8}$$

$$= .28 \text{ in} < \frac{L}{180} = \frac{12(12)}{180} = .8 \text{ in} \ \surd$$

$$\Delta_{LL} = \left(\frac{LL}{DL+LL}\right)\Delta_{DL+LL} = \left(\frac{20}{28}\right).28$$

$$= .2 \text{ in} < \frac{L}{240} = \frac{12(12)}{240} = .6 \text{ in} \ \surd$$

Deflection ok

Chose Hgr

$R_{\text{simp LUS48 with 16d}} = 1.69^k > 1.3$

Use 4x10 DF - L No. 2
@8 ft o/c with
simpson LUS48 with 16d

c. Beam (assume 2 psf)

TA = 12(24) = 288 ft^2 > 200

⇒ LLR = 16 psf (method 1)

Calc loads

previous	8 psf
beam	2
RLL	16 psf
	26 psf

P = 8(12).026 = 2.5^k

F_b = 1.55 ksi
F_v = .085 ksi
E = 1.7e3 ksi

DL + RLL controls by inspection. Assume M or Δ will control.

Bending

Assume the selected section will have a C_F of .9. If the actual C_F is not .9 adjust it and re-ck the calc. This assumes that this procedure is an iterative process. NDS T2.3.1

$$F_b' = F_b C_D C_M C_t C_L C_F C_r$$

= 1.55(1.25)1.0(1.0)1.0(.9)1.0 = 1.74 ksi

M = Pa = 2.5(8) = 20$^{\text{k-ft}}$

NDS 3.3.2

$$S_R = \frac{12M}{F_b'} = \frac{12(20)}{1.74} = 137.9\ in^3$$

try $S_{6x14} = 167.1\ in^3 > 137.9\ in^3$ √

$A = 74.3\ in^2$

$I = 1127.7\ in^4$

self wt. = 18 plf

NDS 4.3.2.2

Our assumption was a psf at 2 pts along the beam, 2(96)2 = 384 lbs for the beam wt. Since 18(24) = 432 lbs for the beam wt. we are a little low. Say ok.

$C_F = (12/d)^{1/9} = (12/13.5)^{1/9} = .99 > .9$ √

Bending ok

Ck shear (without shear modification)

NDS T2.3.1

$$F_V' = F_V(C_D)C_M(C_t)C_H = .085(1.25)1.0(1.0)1.0 = .106\ ksi$$

$$V = \frac{w\ell}{2} + 2.5 = \frac{(.018)24}{2} = 2.7^k$$

NDS 3.4.2

$$A_R = \frac{1.5(V)}{F_V'} = \frac{1.5(2.7)}{.106} = 38.2\ in^2 < 74.3\ in^2 \ √$$

Shear ok

Ck defl. (based on TCM)

NDS T2.3.1

$$E' = E(C_M)C_t = 1.7e3(1.0)1.0 = 1.7e3\ ksi$$

$$\Delta_{TL} = \frac{Pa(3\ell^2 - 4a^2)}{24EI} = \frac{2.5(8)(3(24)^2 - 4(8)^2)1728}{24(1.7e3)1127.7}$$

$$= 1.1\ in < \ell/180 = 24(12)/180 = 1.6\ in \ √$$

$$\Delta_{LL} = \Delta_{TL}\left(\frac{w_{LL}}{w_{TL}}\right) = 1.1\left(\frac{16}{26}\right)$$

$$= .68\ in < \ell/240 = 24(12)/240 = 1.2\ in \ √$$

Deflection ok

Chose Hgr

$R_{simp\ HU614Tf} = 4.8^k > 2.5^k$ √

Use 6x14 Df-L dense No 1 with simpson HU614TF Hgr

d. Girder (assume 3 psf)

$TA = 24(36) = 864\ ft^2 > 600$

$\Rightarrow LLR = 12$ psf (method 1)

Calc loads

previous	10 psf (could reduce)
beam	3
RLL	12 psf
	25 psf

$F_b = 2.4$ ksi (T)
$F_v = .165$ ksi
$E_x = 1.8e3$ ksi, $E_y = 1.6e3$ ksi

DL + LL controls by inspection

The beam is long so either M or Δ will control

Bending

Usually we must check both lateral stability and volume effect. For lateral stability, we must assume a trial beam size (from the volume effect trial beam) to get a slenderness ratio R_B, then recheck it in an iterative manner. However, since the plywood roof diaphragm fully supports the top compression side of the beam, the unbraced length is zero. Hence lateral buckling is prevented and $C_L = 1.0$. Therefore in general, we need only consider the volume factor when a beam is fully supported.

Volume effect:

$$F_b' = F_b C_D C_M C_t C_V$$

Assume the selected glulam will have a C_V of .82. If the actual C_V is not .82 adjust it and re-ck the calc. This trial procedure is an iterative process. NDS T2.3.1

$w = 8(.025) = .2$ klf

$P = .025(8)2(2)6 = 4.8^{k\,ft}$

$$M = \frac{w\ell^2}{8} + Pa = = \frac{.2(36)^2}{8} + 4.8(12) = 90.0^{k\,ft}$$

A conservative alternative is to assume a uniform load this essentially moves more load to the center of the beam which in turn increases the M. Thus:

NDS 3.3.2

$$M = \frac{w\ell^2}{8} = \frac{.025(24)36^2}{8} = 97.2^{kft} \quad \text{consv.}$$

$$F_b = 2.4(1.25)1.0(1.0).82 = 2.46 \text{ ksi}$$

$$S_R = \frac{12M}{F_b'} = \frac{12(97.2)}{2.46} = 474.1 \text{ in}^3$$

try $S_{5\text{-}1/8 \times 27} = 622.7 \text{ in}^3 > 474.1 \text{ in}^3$ √

$I = 8406 \text{ in}^4$

$A = 138.4 \text{ in}^2$

Assume that the self weight of the glulam is about 40 pcf = .023 pci.

self weight = .023(138.4)12 = 38 plf < 24(3) = 72 plf √

Determine the actual C_V (K_L = .96 consv.)

NDS 5.3.2

$$C_V = K_L\left(\frac{21}{L}\right)^{1/10}\left(\frac{12}{d}\right)^{1/10}\left(\frac{5.125}{b}\right)^{1/10}$$

$$C_V = 1.0\left(\frac{21}{36}\right)^{1/10}\left(\frac{12}{27}\right)^{1/10}\left(\frac{5.125}{5.125}\right)^{1/10} = .87 > .82$$

Which implies that our assumption was conservative, and that our trial size is ok √

> Bending ok

Ck shear

NDS T2.3.1

Unless shear is going to be a problem (e.g. there is a large load and a relatively short span), do not use a shear modification (conservative).

$$F_v' = F_v(C_D)C_M(C_t) = .165(1.25)1.0(1.0) = .206 \text{ ksi}$$

NDS 3.4.2

$$V = 4.8 + \frac{w\ell}{2} = 4.8 + \frac{(.2)36}{2} = 8.4^{k}$$

or a consv. approach

$$V = \frac{w\ell}{2} = \frac{.025(24)36}{2} = 10.8^{\,k} \quad \text{consv.}$$

$$A_R = \frac{1.5(V)}{F_v'} = \frac{1.5(10.8)}{.206} = 78.6 \text{ in}^2 < 151.3 \text{ in}^2 \ \surd$$

> Shear ok

Ck defl. (based on TCM)

$E' = E(C_M)C_t = 1.8e3(1.0)1.0 = 1.8e3$ ksi NDS T2.3.1

$$\Delta = \frac{5w\ell^4}{384EI} + \frac{Pa(3\ell^2 - 4a^2)}{24EI}$$

$$\Delta_{LL} = \frac{5(.2)36^4(1728)}{384(1.8e3)8406} + \frac{4.8(12)\left(3(36)^2 - 4(12)^2\right)1728}{24(1.8e3)8406}$$

$$= 1.4 \text{ in} < \ell/240 = 36(12)/240 = 1.8 \text{ in} \ \surd$$

$$\Delta_{DL} = \Delta_{LL}\left(\frac{w_{DL}}{w_{LL}}\right) = 1.4\left(\frac{13}{12}\right) = 1.52 \text{ in}$$

camber = 1.5 Δ_{DL} = 1.5(1.52) = 2.28 in

> Deflection ok.
> Use 5-1/8x27 24F-V8 glulam
> Camber = 2.28 in

Only two things are infinite, the universe and human stupidity, and I'm not sure about the former.

ALBERT EINSTEIN

PROBLEM 2.23

Glulam beam design with cantilever beam/simple beam configuration.

Design a cantilever beam system as shown. Investigate camber only.

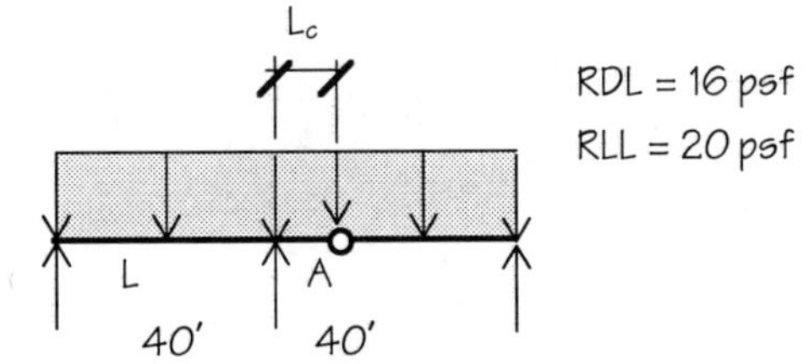

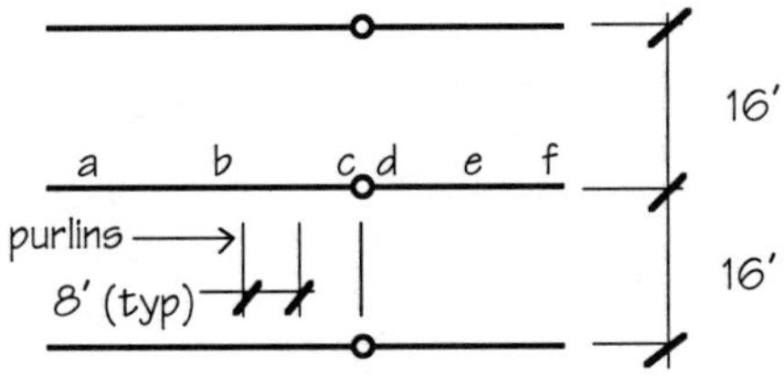

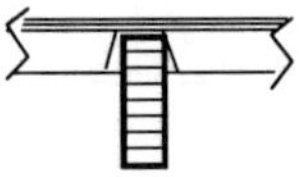

ASSUME

No ponding, no plaster.
24F - V8 glulam.
Glulam wt included in DL.
Full lateral support from plywood.
Normal temp. conditions.
Commercial building.
EMC < 16%.

SOLUTION

Cantilever systems are used on roofs. They are not used on floors because they tend to transmit vibrations (which will be disturbing to the occupants of the building) easily. The TCM therefore recommends simply supported spans for floors.

$w_{DL} = 16(.016) = .256$ klf
$w_{LL} = 16(.02) = .32$ klf

However, the code (UBC T16-C) allows a reduced LL to 12 psf so:

$w_{LL} = 16(.012) = .192$ klf

$L_c = .172L = .172(40) = 6.88$ ft balanced

(most efficient if only balanced load case)

$L_c = .2L = .2(40) = 8$ ft unbalanced governs

(most efficient if both balanced and unbalanced load cases)

By code, DL + LL and DL + unbalanced LL must be considered for roofs if the LL < 20 psf. The TCM *(Cantilever Beam Coefficients)* gives the recommended lengths for cantilever systems.

DL + LL case 1

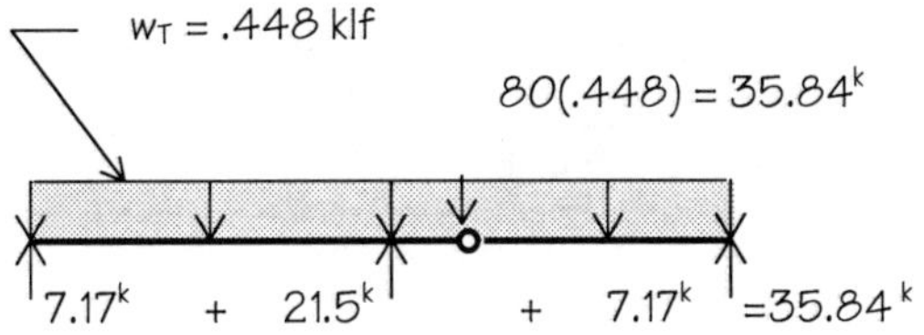

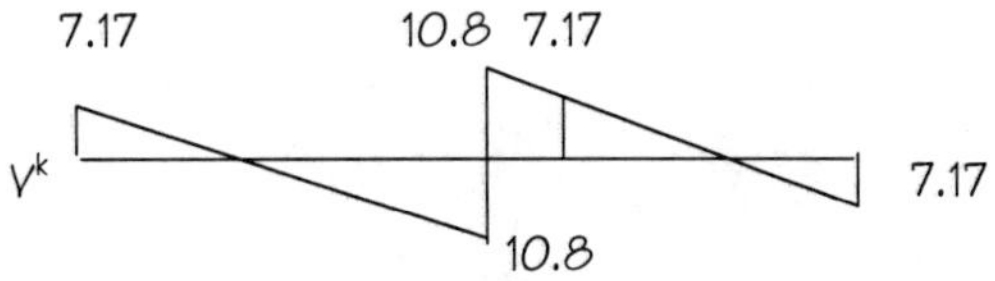

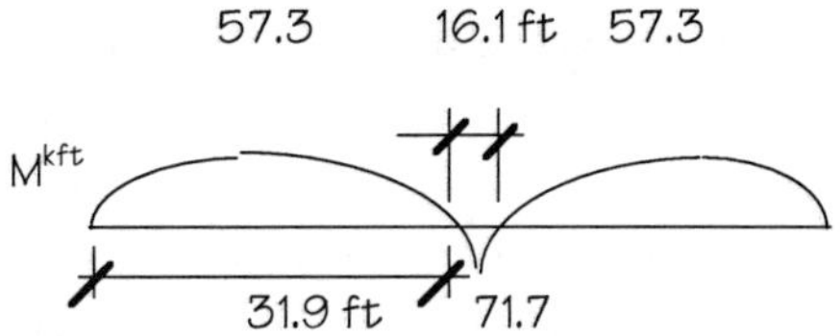

The balanced case can produce maximum shear/reactions, moment and deflection.

DL + unbal LL case 2

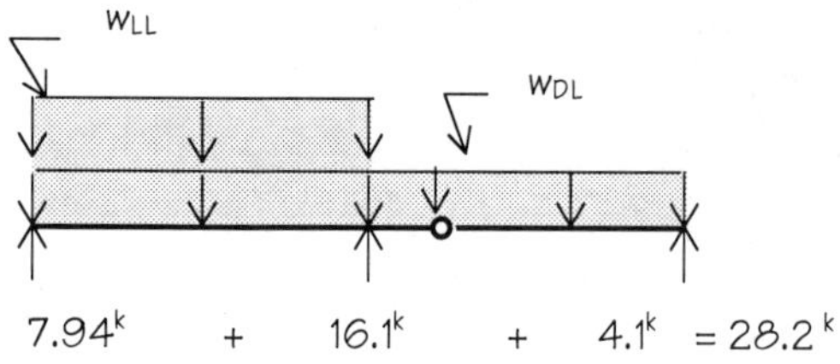

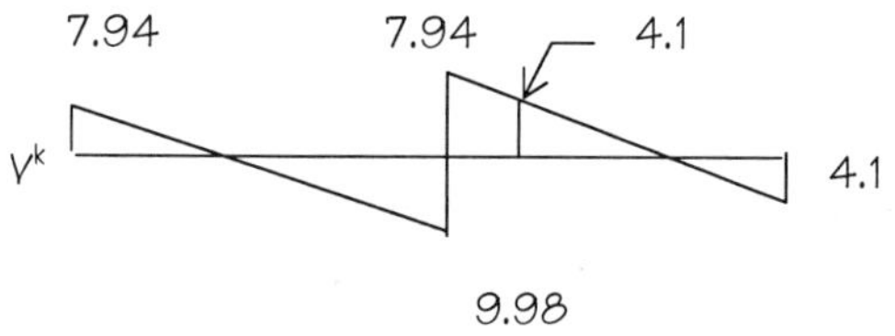

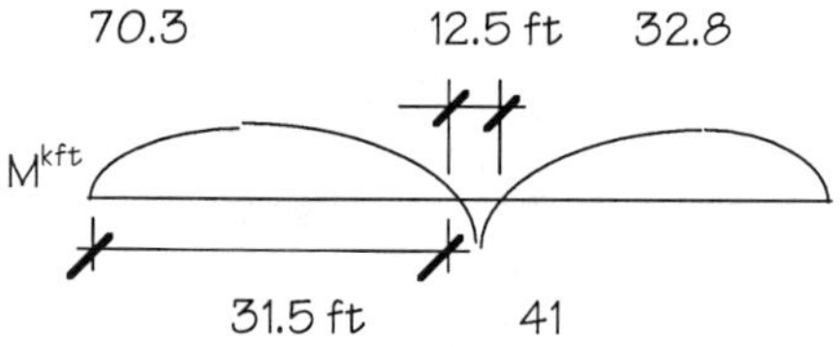

Produces maximum M on left span.

DL + unbal LL case 3

Produces maximum M on right span and maximum unbraced length for the negative moment (could be critical for stability). Since uplift at "a" might be a concern, this produces the minimum reaction at "a".

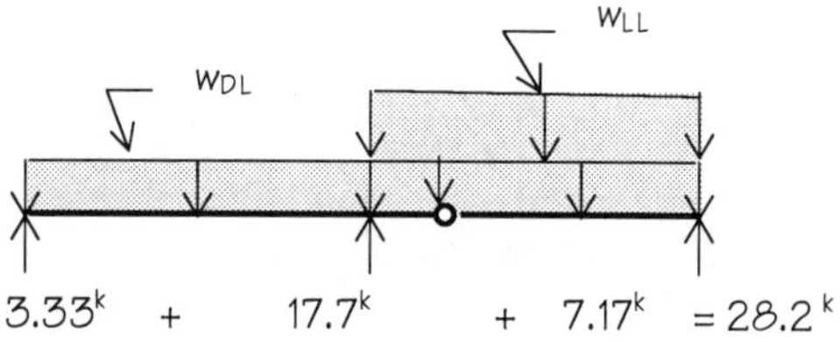

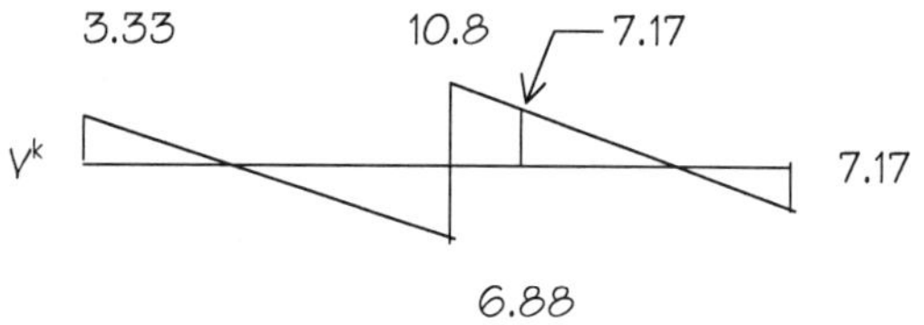

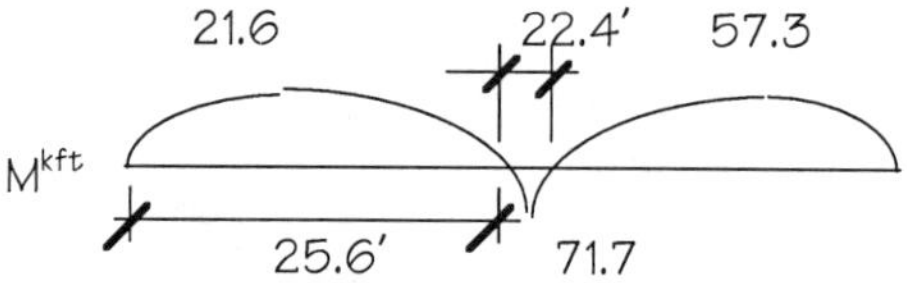

Note that case 3 does not give Max M, V or critical case for the unbraced length of the compression side. Therefore, we could have omitted case 3.

Mem DF (assume full lateral support)

Bending

F_b = 2.4 ksi
F_v = .165 ksi
E = 1.8e3 ksi

Lateral stability implies:

$F_b' = F_b C_D C_M C_t C_L$ NDS T2.3.1

Since the plywood roof diaphragm fully supports the top compression side of the beam (the top side is in compression with a positive moment), the unbraced length is zero. Hence lateral buckling is prevented and C_L = 1.0. Therefore in general, we need only consider the volume factor when a simple span beam is fully supported.

Volume effect:

$F_b' = F_b C_D C_M C_t C_V$

Assume the selected glulam will have a C_V of .82. If the actual C_V is not .82 adjust it and re-ck the calc. This trial procedure is an iterative process.

$F_b = 2.4(1.25)1.0(1.0).82 = 2.46$ ksi

NDS 3.3.2

$M = 57.3^{k\text{-}ft}$

$S_R = \frac{12M}{F_b'} = \frac{12(57.3)}{2.46} = 279.5\ in^3$

try $S_{5\text{-}1/8 \times 19\text{-}1/2} = 324.8\ in^3 > 279.5\ in^3$

$I = 3167\ in^4$

$A = 99.94\ in^2$

Determine the actual C_V ($K_L = 1.0$)

NDS 5.3.2

$$C_V = K_L\left(\frac{21}{L}\right)^{1/10}\left(\frac{12}{d}\right)^{1/10}\left(\frac{5.125}{b}\right)^{1/10}$$

$$C_V = 1.0\left(\frac{21}{40-8}\right)^{1/10}\left(\frac{12}{19.5}\right)^{1/10}\left(\frac{5.125}{5.125}\right)^{1/10} = .91 > .82$$

Which implies that our assumption was conservative, which means that our trial size is ok.

Bending ok

Ck shear

NDS T2.3.1

Unless shear is going to be a problem, like if there is a large load and a relatively short span, do not use a shear modification (conservative).

$F_V' = F_V(C_D)C_M(C_t) = .165(1.25)1.0(1.0) = .206$ ksi

NDS 3.4.2

$V = 7.17^k$

$A_R = \frac{1.5(V)}{F_V'} = \frac{1.5(7.17)}{.206} = 52.2\ in^2 < 99.9\ in^2$

Shear ok

Ck Defl./ camber

Deflection calculations on cantilever systems can be complicated. Normally they are done with the aid of the computer. Here we will just investigate camber as an exercise.

$$\Delta_{DL} = \frac{5w\ell^4}{384EI} = \frac{5(.256)32^4(1728)}{384(1.8e3)2491} = 1.35\ in$$

camber = $1.5\,\Delta_{DL} = 1.5(1.35) = 2.03$ in

Use 5-1/8x19-1/2, 24F - V8 glulam with camber = 2.03 in

Mem AC

Bending

F_b = 2.4 ksi (T), 2.4 ksi (compression zone in tension)
F_v = .165 ksi
E_x = 1.8e3 ksi, E_y = 1.6e3 ksi

Assume either M or Δ will control.

In this type of problem we have 2 different values for F_b. One for the tensionon the top side and one for the tension on the side of the glulam beam. This essentially requires us to look at doing 2 separate bending calcs for the 2 different M's (in the positive and negative areas of bending). We must check both lateral stability and volume effect. For lateral stability, we must assume a trial beam size (from the volume effect trial beam) to get a slenderness ratio R_B, then recheck it in an iterative manner.

Bending (positive moment)

Remember that the bottom of the beam is laterally unsupported (except, possibly, at the reaction points). The top of the beam is laterally supported by the roof plywood diaphragm. This implies that the unbraced length for the positive moment (compression) area is zero because it has continuous lateral support provided by the roof diaphragm. So C_L goes to "1" and lateral stability does not control. This lessens our work hereto just considering volume effect.

Volume effect:

$F_b' = F_b C_D C_M C_t C_V$ NDS T2.3.1

Assume the selected glulam will have a C_V of .82. If the actual C_V is not .82 adjust it and re-ck the calc. This trial procedure is an iterative process.

$F_b = 2.4(1.25)1.0(1.0).82 = 2.46$ ksi

$+M = 70.3^{kft}$, $-M = 71.7^{kft}$

Use of -M implies a consv. approach (for this area but this reduces our calc for next area).

NDS 3.3.2

$$S_R = \frac{12M}{F_b'} = \frac{12(71.7)}{2.46} = 349.8 \text{ in}^3$$

try $S_{5\text{-}1/8 \times 21} = 376.7 \text{ in}^3 > 349.8 \text{ in}^3$ √

$I = 3955 \text{ in}^4$

$A = 107.6 \text{ in}^2$

Determine the actual C_V ($K_L = 1.0$)

NDS 5.3.2

$$C_V = K_L\left(\frac{21}{L}\right)^{1/10}\left(\frac{12}{d}\right)^{1/10}\left(\frac{5.125}{b}\right)^{1/10}$$

L = 31.5 ft (distance between points of zero moment)

$$C_V = 1.0\left(\frac{21}{31.5}\right)^{1/10}\left(\frac{12}{21}\right)^{1/10}\left(\frac{5.125}{5.125}\right)^{1/10} = .91 > .82$$

Which implies that our assumption was conservative, and that our trial size is ok.

Bending ok

Bending (negative moment)

The compression side of the beam (bottom) is unsupported from the column to the inflection pt., and from the column to the hinge.

Volume effect:

The maximum distance between points of zero moment is 22.4 ft < 31.5 ft. This implies that since we used -M, our trial +M beam is ok here.

Ck Lateral Stability

NDS T2.3.1

$$F_b' = F_b C_D C_M C_t C_L$$

For a smaller beam size (and economy) place lateral brace at the first purlin 8 ft from column between A & C.

NDS 3.3.3.6

$\Rightarrow \ell_{u\,max} = 8 \text{ ft} = 96 \text{ in}$

$$\frac{\ell_u}{d} = \frac{96}{21} = 4.6 < 7 \quad √$$

$$\ell_e = 2.06\ell_u = 2.06(96) = 198 \text{ in}$$

$$R_B = \sqrt{\frac{\ell_e d}{b^2}} = \sqrt{\frac{198(21)}{5.125^2}} = 12.6 < 50 \quad √$$

This beam is subject to lateral torsional buckling. Because of this movement in the y axis plane, we need to consider the stability with E_y

NDS T2.3.1

$$E' = E_y(C_M)C_t = 1.6e3(1.0)1.0 = 1.6e3 \text{ ksi}$$

$$F_{bE} = \frac{K_{bE}E'_y}{R_B^2} = \frac{.609(1.6e3)}{12.6^2} = 6.14 \text{ ksi}$$

$$F_b^* = F_{bx}C_D C_M C_t = 2.4(1.25)1.0(1.0) = 3.0 \text{ ksi}$$

NDS 3.3.3.8

$$C_L = \frac{1+\left(F_{bE}/F_{bx}^*\right)}{1.9} - \sqrt{\left(\frac{1+\left(F_{bE}/F_{bx}^*\right)}{1.9}\right)^2 - \frac{\left(F_{bE}/F_{bx}^*\right)}{.95}}$$

$$C_L = \frac{1+\left(6.14/3\right)}{1.9} - \sqrt{\left(\frac{1+\left(6.14/3\right)}{1.9}\right)^2 - \frac{\left(6.14/3\right)}{.95}} = .96 > .82 \quad √$$

∴ Volume effect governs over stability. Our trial section was determined using volume effect of .82 so we are a little conservative.

Bending ok

Ck shear

Unless shear is going to be a problem (e.g., if there is a large load and a relatively short span), do not use a shear modification (conservative).

NDS T2.3.1

$$F_v' = F_v(C_D)C_M(C_t) = .165(1.25)1.0(1.0) = .206 \text{ ksi}$$

$V = 10.8^k$

NDS 3.4.2

$$A_R = \frac{1.5(V)}{F_v'} = \frac{1.5(10.8)}{.206} = 78.6 \text{ in}^2 < 107.6 \text{ in}^2 \quad √$$

Shear ok

Ck Defl./camber @ b

$$\Delta_{DL_{ad}} = \left(\frac{wx}{24EIL}\right)\left(L^4 - 2L^2x^2 + Lx^3 - 2A^2L^2 + 2A^2x^2\right) +$$

$$\frac{PAx}{6EIL}\left(L^2 - x^2\right)$$

$$= \frac{.256(20)12\left(40^4 - 2(40)^2 20^2 + 40(20)^3 - 2(8)^2 40^2 + 2(8)^2 20^2\right)}{24(1.8e3)2490(240)} +$$

$$\frac{4.1(8)20}{6(1.8e3)2490(40)}\left(40^2 - 20^2\right) = 1.29 \text{ in}$$

camber = $1.5\ \Delta_{DL} = 1.51.29 = 1.93$

Ck Defl/camber @ d

$$\Delta DL_D = \frac{wx\left(4A^2L - L^3 + 6A^2x - 4Ax^2 + x^3\right)}{24EI} +$$

$$\frac{Px\left(2AL + 3Ax - x^2\right)}{6EI}$$

$$= \frac{.256(8)\left(4(8)^2 40 - 40^3 + 6(8)^2 8 - 4(8)8^2 + 8^3\right)}{24(1.8e3)3167} +$$

$$\frac{4.1(8)\left(2(8)40 + 3(8)8 - 8^2\right)}{6(1.8e3)3167} = -4.5e\text{-}5 \text{ in}$$

No camber required.

> Use 5-1/8x21, 24F - V8
> glulam with Knee braces @
> the column and 1st purlin @ 8 ft
> from col. @ a-c.
> Camber$_{ac}$ = 1.93 in between A and C

He who has a why to live can bear almost any how.

NIETZSCHE

PROBLEM 2.24

Glulam beam design for curved member of pedestrian bridge.

Determine the size of the curved glulam beam for the pedestrian walk bridge shown. Bracing and connections ok.

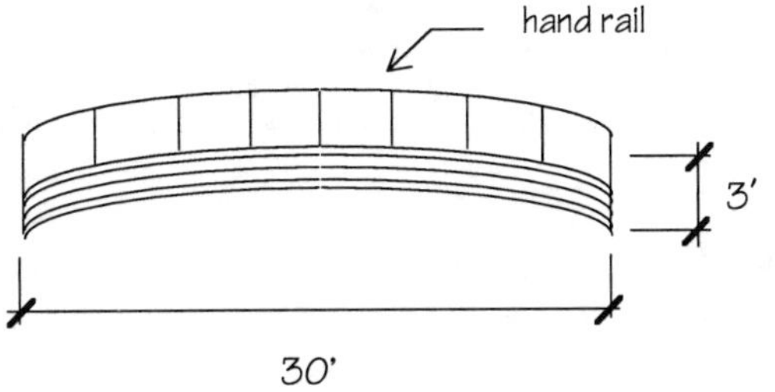

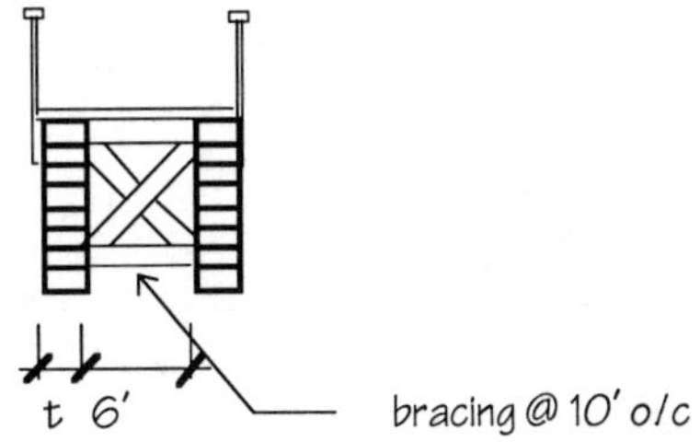

ASSUME

- Wet condition properties.
- L/240 defl. criteria.
- UBC T23A sidewalk LL.
- DL = 80 psf (including glulam).
- Neglect impact loads.
- 24F -V8 glulam.
- Lat. support @ supports.

SOLUTION

Loads

DL	80 psf
LL	250 psf
	330 psf

No reduction for public assembly or LL>100psf
w = 3(.33) = .99 klf

Bending

F_b = 2.4 ksi (T), 2.4 ksi (compresive zone in tension)
F_v = .165 ksi
E_x = 1.8e3 ksi, E_y = 1.6e3 ksi

DL + LL controls by inspection
The beam is long so either M or Δ will control

We must check both lateral stability and volume effect. For lateral stability we must assume a trial beam size (from the volume effect trial beam) to get a slenderness ratio R_B, then re-check it in an iterative manner.

NDS T2.3.1

Volume effect:

$$F_b' = F_b C_D C_M C_t C_V C_c$$

Calc C_c factor

$$C_c = 1 - 2000\left(t/R\right)^2 \quad \Rightarrow \text{need } R = \text{radius}$$

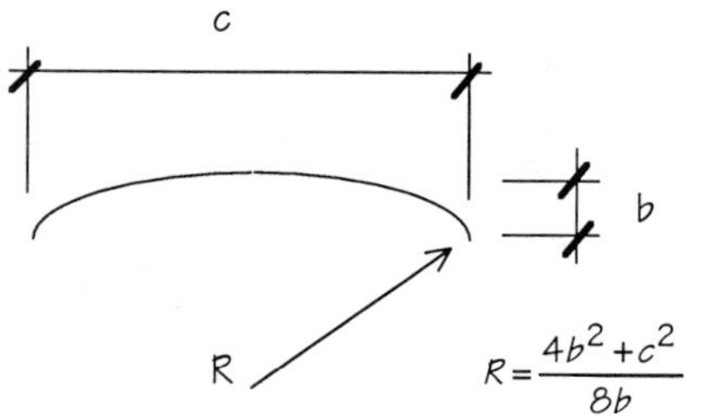

$$R = \frac{4b^2 + c^2}{8b}$$

$$R = \frac{4(3)^2 + (30)^2}{8(3)} = 39 \text{ ft}$$

$$C_c = 1 - 2000\left(5.125/12(39)\right)^2 = .76$$

NDS 3.3.2

Assume the selected glulam will have a C_V of .85. If the actual C_V is not .85 adjust it and re-ck the calc. This trial procedure is an iterative process.

$$F_b = 2.4(1.0).8(1.0).85(.76) = 1.24 \text{ ksi}$$

$$M = \frac{w\ell^2}{8} = \frac{.99(30)^2}{8} = 111.4^{\text{ k ft}}$$

$$S_R = \frac{12M}{F_b'} = \frac{12(111.4)}{1.24} = 1078 \text{ in}^3$$

try $S_{6\text{-}3/4 \times 31\text{-}1/2} = 1116 \text{ in}^3 > 1078 \text{ in}^3$ √

$I = 17580 \text{ in}^4$

$A = 212.6 \text{ in}^2$ NDS 5.3.2

Determine the actual C_V (K_L = 1.0)

$$C_V = K_L\left(\frac{21}{L}\right)^{1/10}\left(\frac{12}{d}\right)^{1/10}\left(\frac{5.125}{b}\right)^{1/10}$$

$$C_V = 1.0\left(\frac{21}{30}\right)^{1/10}\left(\frac{12}{31.5}\right)^{1/10}\left(\frac{5.125}{6.75}\right)^{1/10} = .85 = .85$$ NDS T2.3.1

Which implies that our trial size is ok. √

Ck Lateral Stability

$$F_b' = F_b C_D C_M C_t C_L C_c$$

Unbraced length ℓ_U = 10 ft = 120 in NDS 3.3.3.6

For a uniformly distributed load:

$$\frac{\ell_u}{d} = \frac{120}{31.5} = 3.8 < 7 \quad \surd$$

$$\ell_e = 1.33\,\ell_U = 1.33(120) = 159.6 \text{ in}$$

$$R_B = \sqrt{\frac{\ell_e d}{b^2}} = \sqrt{\frac{159.6(31.5)}{6.75^2}} = 10.5 < 50 \quad \surd$$ NDS T2.3.1

This beam is subject to lateral torsional buckling. Because of this movement in the y axis plane, we need to consider the stability with E_y.

$$E' = E_y(C_M)C_t = 1.6e3(.83)1.0 = 1.33e3 \text{ ksi}$$

$$F_{bE} = \frac{K_{bE}E'y}{R_B^2} = \frac{.609(1.33e3)}{10.5^2} = 7.3 \text{ ksi}$$ NDS 3.3.3.8

$$F_b^* = F_{bx}C_D C_M C_t C_c = 2.4(1.0).8(1.0).76 = 1.5 \text{ ksi}$$

$$C_L = \frac{1 + \left(F_{bE}/F_{bx}^*\right)}{1.9} - \sqrt{\left(\frac{1 + \left(F_{bE}/F_{bx}^*\right)}{1.9}\right)^2 - \frac{\left(F_{bE}/F_{bx}^*\right)}{.95}}$$

$$C_L = \frac{1 + (7.3/1.5)}{1.9} - \sqrt{\left(\frac{1 + (7.3/1.5)}{1.9}\right)^2 - \frac{(7.3/1.5)}{.95}} = .99 > .85$$

∴ Volume effect governs over stability. Our trial section was determined using volume effect, so we are ok.

NDS 5.4.1.1

Bending ok

Ck radial stress

$$f_R = \frac{3M}{2Rbd} = \frac{3(111.4)12}{2(39)12(6.75)31.5} = .02 \text{ ksi}$$

$$F'_{rt} = .015C_DC_MC_t = .015(1.0).8(1.0)$$

$= .012$ ksi< f_R ⇒ NG!

We can either provide radial reinforcement or increase the size/depth of the beam.

Increase size

Try $8\frac{3}{4}\times42$

$S = 2573 \text{ in}^3 > S_R$
$A = 367.5 \text{ in}^2$
$I = 54020 \text{ in}^4$

$$f_R = \frac{3(111.4)12}{2(39)12(8.75)42} = .0117 \text{ ksi} < .012 \text{ ksi} \quad \surd$$

NDS T2.3.1

Radial stress ok

Ck Shear

Don't use a shear modification (conservative).

NDS 3.4.2

$$F'_V = F_V(C_D)C_M(C_t) = .165(1.0).875(1.0) = .14 \text{ ksi}$$

$$V = \frac{w\ell}{2} = \frac{.99(30)}{2} = 14.9^k$$

$$A_R = \frac{1.5(V)}{F'_V} = \frac{1.5(14.9)}{.14} = 159.6 \text{ in}^2 < 367.5 \text{ in}^2 \quad \surd$$

Shear ok

Ck Defl.

$$\Delta_{LL} = \frac{5w\ell^4}{384EI} = \frac{5(.75)30^4(1728)}{384(1.8e3)54020} = .14 \text{ in}$$

$$\frac{L}{240} = \frac{12(30)}{240} = 1.5 \text{ in} > .14 \text{ in} \quad \surd$$

Use 8-3/4x40-1/2, 24F-V8 glulam beam

Alt. design (provide radial reinf.)

The NDS recommends that the EMC < 12%. Since our problem assumes wet conditions, radial reinforcement may cause excessive cracking and should therefore be avoided. For an exercise, we will assume dry conditions and do the alternative design as if C_M = 1.0. NDS T5.11

$$f_R/_{in} = .02(6.75) = .135 \text{ kli}$$

Assume 1 in dia. Lag bolts with:

$P_{all\,t}$ for bolt = 9.56^k

P_{all} withdrawal = .636

For wood / in embedment above NA with C_D = 1.0

$$Penn._{eff} = \frac{31.5}{2} - 2 = 13.75 \text{ in}$$ (keep 2 in clear from edge)

$P_{all} = .636(13.75) = 8.75^k < P_{all\,bolt}$

⇒ Wood governs over bolt.

$$spc'g = \frac{P_{all\ withdrawal}}{f_R/_{in}} = \frac{8.75}{.135} = 64.8 \text{ in}$$ say 60 in o/c

Align bolts radially with respect to curve.

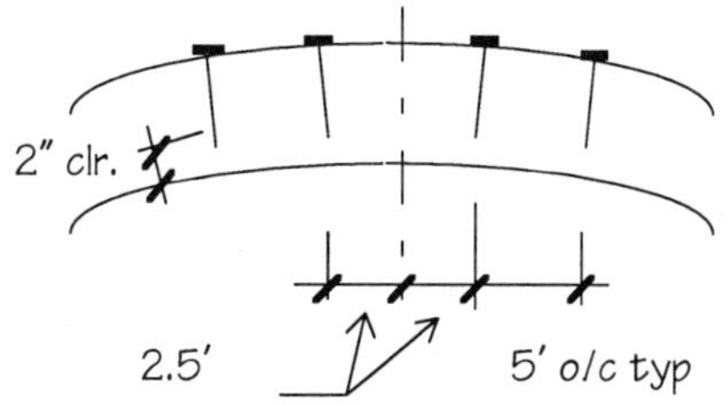

Bolts are spaced and centered so that they resist the total f_r ,< Fr max with reinf. ok

Ck Net effective section in bending

Since we have altered the section our bending resistance has been reduced. The top of the beam is in compression with the predrilled hole "filled" with the lag. Its portion above the NA is thought to be "intact". The bottom of the beam is in tension so the hole is not "filled".

Calc new section modulus

If we assume that the hole goes all the way through we might save ourselves some work.

$$S_{net} = \frac{bd^2}{6} = \frac{(6.75-1)31.5^2}{6}$$

$= 950.9 \text{ in}^3 < 1078 \text{ in}^3$ **NG!**

Since the S was not as great as required by code we need to calc S the long way.

Find centroid (from bottom)

$$\bar{Y} = \frac{\sum A\bar{y}}{\sum A} = \frac{6.75(31.5)15.75 - 1(15.75)7.875}{6.75(31.5) - 1(15.75)} = 16.38 \text{ in}$$

16.38 - 15.75 = .63 in

Using parallel axis theorem

$$I = \sum\left(\left(\frac{bd^3}{12}\right) + Ad^2\right) =$$

$$\left(\left(\frac{6.75(31.5)^3}{12}\right) + 6.75(31.5).63^2\right) -$$

$$\left(\left(\frac{1(15.75)^3}{12}\right) + 1(15.75)\left(15.75/2 + .63\right)^2\right) = 16503 \text{ in}^4$$

$$S = \frac{I}{c}$$

$$S_{top} = \frac{16503}{31.5 - 16.38} = 1091 \text{ in}^3$$

$$S_{bott} = \frac{16503}{16.38} = 1008 \text{ in}^3 < 1078 \text{ in}^3$$

Which is less than required.

Try smaller bolt

$$1078 = \frac{bd^2}{6} = \frac{(31.5)^2(6.75 - x)}{6}$$

x = 6.75 - 6.51 = .24 in (to small) **NG!**

Try increasing width (assume DL constant).

$$1078 = \frac{(31.5)^2(x-1)}{6}$$

x = 7.5 in say 8.75x31.5

New spacing

$$spc'g = \frac{P_{all\ bolt}}{f_R/in} = \frac{8.75}{.02(8.75)} = 50 \text{ in o/c}$$

> For alt., use 1 in dia lag bolts at 50 in o/c in 8.75x31.5 24F-V8 glulam beam

▯
▯
▯

Common sense is not so common.

VOLTAIRE

● PROBLEM 2.25

Beam design for double cantilever using semigraphical method of analysis.

Design the double cantilever beam shown below. Use semigraphical method of analysis. Do not skip load beam. Use first design iteration only.

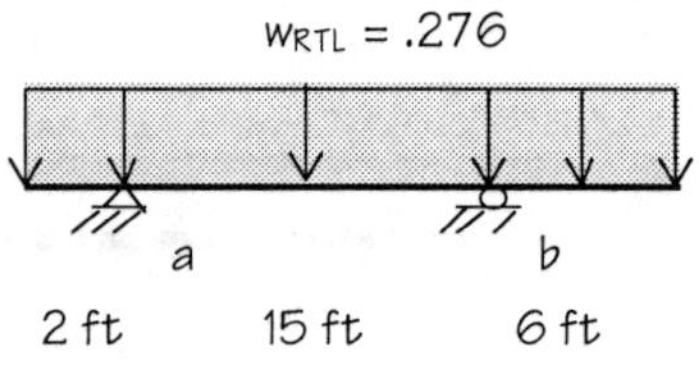

ASSUME

DF - L No. 1.
Normal temp. conditions.
Full lateral support.
Non rep. mem.
No ponding, no plaster.
Defl. ok.
EMC < 19%.
Neglect beam wt.

SOLUTION

$$\sum \overset{+}{M_a} \curvearrowright = 0$$

$$\Rightarrow \frac{.276(15+6)^2}{2} - \frac{.276(2)^2}{2} - 15R_b = 0$$

$$R_b = \frac{60.8 - .6}{15} = 4.02^k$$

$$R_a = (2 + 15 + 6).276 - 4.02 = 2.33^k$$

The semigraphical method of analysis is a useful tool to have in your arsenal of test taking methods. The method is well outlined in **The Basics of Structural Analysis** by Botwin and Murnen.

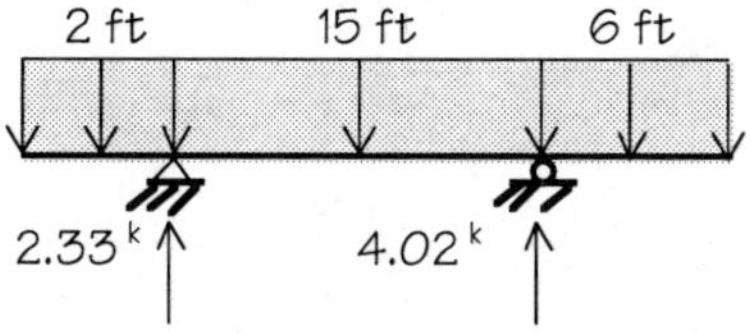

-W	-.276	-.276	-.276	dv/dx
$-\int wdx$	-.55	-4.14	-1.66	ΔV

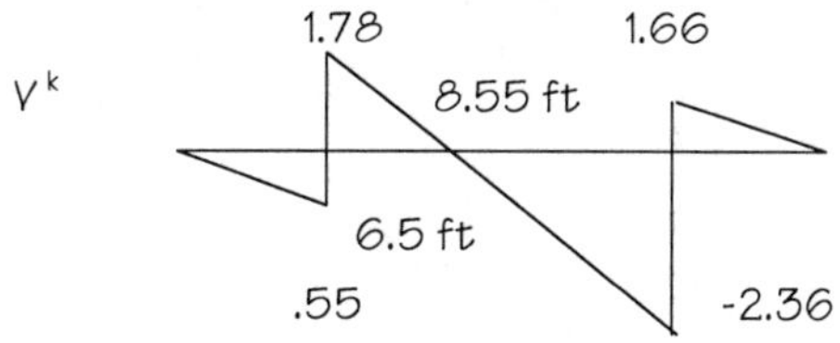

V	-.55	1.78 0	-2.36	1.66	dm/dx
$\int Vdx$	-.55	5.47	-10.09	4.98	ΔM

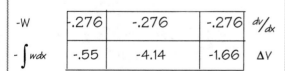

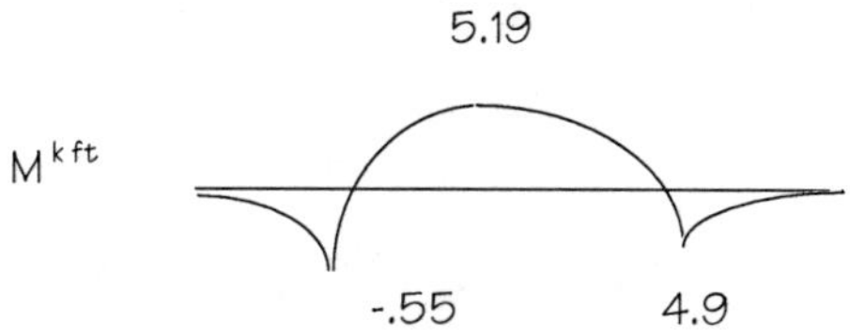

Use Semigraphical Method

Bending (assume 4 x) NDS T2.3.1

F_b = 1.0 ksi
F_v = .095 ksi
E = 1.7e3 ksi

DL + LL controls by inspection. Assume either M or Δ will control.

In this type of problem we have 2 different values for F_b. One for the +M which has full lateral support for the compression side, and one for the -M that does not have support for the compression side of the beam. This essentially requires us to look at doing 2 separate bending calc's for the 2 different M's (in the positive and negative areas of bending).

Bending (positive moment)

Remember that the bottom of the beam is laterally unsupported except at the reaction points. The top of the beam is laterally supported by the roof plywood diaphragm. This implies that the unbraced length for the positive moment area is zero because it has continuous lateral support provided by the roof diaphragm. So C_L goes to one in the +M calculation. Assume the selected section will have a C_F of 1.1 (4x12). If the actual C_F is not 1.1, adjust it and re-ck the calc. This assumes that this procedure is an iterative process (although in this problem we are to perform a first iteration only).

$S = 106.3\ in^3$
$A = 47.2\ in^2$
$I = 717.6\ in^4$

$F_b' = F_b C_D C_M C_t C_L C_F C_r = 1.0(1.25)1.0(1.0)1.0(1.1)1.0$

$= 1.38$ ksi

$M = 5.2^{\text{k-ft}}$

NDS 3.3.2

$$S_R = \frac{12M}{F_b'} = \frac{12(5.2)}{1.38} = 45.2\ in^3 < 106.3\ in^3\ \checkmark$$

If the member had not been a 4x12, then it would have had a different C_F. With a new C_F, the allowable bending stress would have had to been changed accordingly.

We could continue here and finish the positive moment bending calc but notice that the positive moment is about the same as the negative moment. If we did finish the calc, we would enter into the negative moment calcs with a trial size based upon that +M and just have to change it because F_b for the negative moment is smaller and that the unbraced length is larger. Let's save ourselves some work and go to the negative calc. now, and return here later as a ck, if required.

NDS T2.3.1

Bending (negative moment)

$F_b' = F_b C_D C_M C_t C_L C_F C_r$

Unbraced length $\ell_U = 6$ ft $= 72$ in

$$\frac{\ell_U}{d} = \frac{72}{11.25} = 6.4 < 7$$

NDS 3.3.3.6

$\ell_e = 1.33\ell_U = 1.33(72) = 95.8$ in

NDS T2.3.1

$$R_B = \sqrt{\frac{\ell_e d}{b^2}} = \sqrt{\frac{95.8(11.25)}{3.5^2}} = 9.4 < 50\ \checkmark$$

This beam is subject to lateral torsional buckling. Because of this movement in the y axis plane, we need to consider the stability with E_y. Since $E_y = E_x$:

$E' = E_y(C_M)C_t = 1.7e3(1.0)1.0 = 1.7e3$ ksi

$$F_{bE} = \frac{K_{bE}E'y}{R_B^2} = \frac{.438(1.7e3)}{9.4^2} = 8.4\ \text{ksi}$$

$F_b^* = F_{bx}C_D C_F = 1.0(1.25)1.1 = 1.4$ ksi

NDS 3.3.3.8

$$C_L = \frac{1+\left(F_{bE}/F_{bx}^*\right)}{1.9} - \sqrt{\left(\frac{1+\left(F_{bE}/F_{bx}^*\right)}{1.9}\right)^2 - \frac{\left(F_{bE}/F_{bx}^*\right)}{.95}}$$

$$C_L = \frac{1+\left(8.4/1.4\right)}{1.9} - \sqrt{\left(\frac{1+\left(8.4/1.4\right)}{1.9}\right)^2 - \frac{\left(8.4/1.4\right)}{.95}} = .99$$

$\therefore F_b = 1.0(1.25)1.0(1.0).99(1.1)1.0 = 1.36$ ksi

$M = 4.9^{k}$ft

$$S_R = \frac{12M}{F_b'} = \frac{12(4.9)}{1.36} = 43.2\ in^3 < 106.3\ in^3\ \checkmark$$

Bending ok. consv.

If our trial beam size was inadequate because of the beam stability factor (C_L), we would then resize it. Increasing the depth would not be appropriate because R_B is based on the ratio d/b^2. As d gets larger, R_B gets larger. As R_B gets larger, F_{bE} gets smaller. This smaller value then causes the beam stability factor (C_L) to be reduced. The net result would be that we are going the wrong way. We need to make the member "squattier". So, if this buckling case occurs, try making the beam section wider.

Ck shear

Do not use a shear modification (conservative).

$F_v' = F_v(C_D)C_M(C_t) = .095(1.25)1.0(1.0) = .119$ ksi NDS T2.3.1

$V = 2.4^{k}$

$$A_R = \frac{1.5(V)}{F_v'} = \frac{1.5(2.4)}{.119} = 30.25\ in^2 < 47.2\ in^2\ \checkmark$$ NDS 3.4.2

Shear ok

NDS T2.3.1

Ck bearing

Since the support conditions are not known, determine the minimum bearing length.

$$F'_{c\perp} = F_{c\perp}(C_M)C_t(C_b)$$

$$F'_{c\perp} = .625(1.0)1.0(1.0) = .625 \text{ ksi}$$

$$\ell_{b\ \min} = \frac{R}{bF'_{c\perp}} = \frac{2.4}{3.5(.625)} = 1.1 \text{ in}$$

> Use 4x12, DF-L No 1 beam with a minimum bearing length of 1.1 in

I don't want any yes-men around me. I want everybody to tell me the truth even if it costs them their jobs.

SAMUEL GOLDWYN

○ PROBLEM 2.26

Cantilevered glulam beam design.

Design the roof beam as shown below.

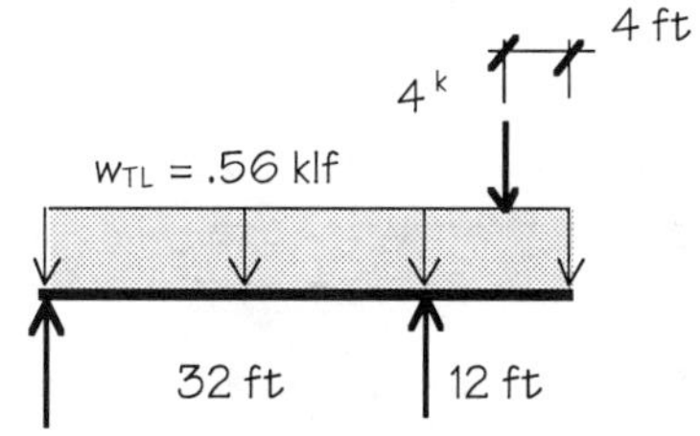

ASSUME

No ponding, no plaster ceiling.
Lateral support at supports.
Design for self wt.
EMC < 16%.
Normal temp. conditions.
Commercial building.
24F-V1 glulam.
Tension lams on bottom.
DL/LL = .75.
Neglect skip loading and unbalanced LL.

SOLUTION

F_b = 2.4 ksi (T), 1.2 ksi (compression zone in tension)
F_v = .165 ksi
E_x = 1.7e3 ksi, E_y = 1.4e3 ksi

DL + LL controls by inspection. Assume either M or Δ will control.

In this type of problem we have 2 different values for F_b. One for the tension on the top side and one for the tension on the bottom side of the glulam beam. This essentially requires us to look at doing 2 separate bending calcs for the 2 different M's (in the positive and negative areas of bending). We must check both lateral stability and volume effect. For lateral stability, we must assume a trial beam size (from the volume effect trial beam) to get a slenderness ratio R_B, then re-check it in an iterative manner.

Bending (positive moment)

Remember that the bottom of the beam is laterally unsupported except at the reaction points. The top of the beam is laterally supported by the roof plywood diaphragm. This implies that the unbraced length for the positive moment area is zero because it has continuous lateral support provided by the roof diaphragm. So C_L goes to one and lateral stability does not control. This lessens our work here to just considering volume effect.

Volume effect:

NDS T2.3.1

$$F_b' = F_b C_D C_M C_t C_V$$

Assume the selected glulam will have a C_V of .82. If the actual C_V is not .82 adjust it and re-ck the calc. This trial procedure is an iterative process.

$$F_b = 2.4(1.25)1.0(1.0).82 = 2.46 \text{ ksi}$$

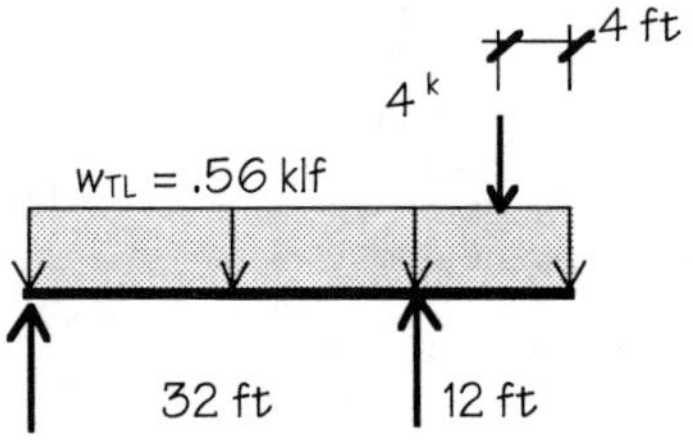

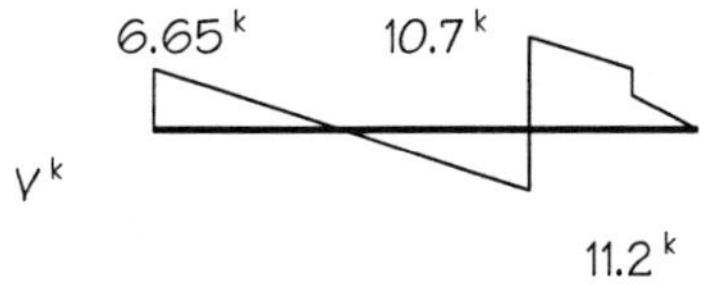

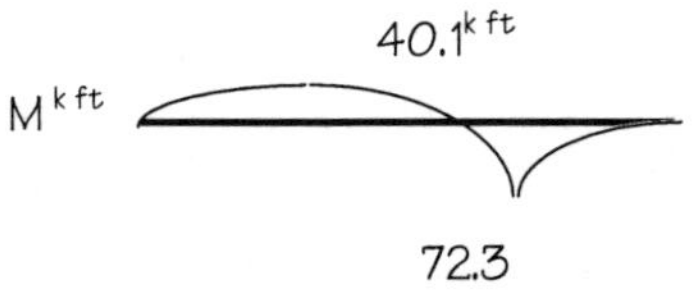

We could continue here and finish the positive moment bending calc. But notice that the positive moment is considerably less than the negative moment. If we did finish the calc we would enter into the negative moment calcs with a trial size based upon a much smaller M and have to change it. Also note that because F_b for the negative moment is smaller and that the unbraced length is larger, it would further contribute to the need to re-size the trial beam. Let's save ourselves some work and go to the negative calc. now, and return here later as a ck if required.

Bending (negative moment)

Volume effect:

$$F_b' = F_b C_D C_M C_t C_V$$

Assume the selected glulam will have a C_V of .82. If the actual C_V is not .82 adjust it and re-ck the calc. This trial procedure is an iterative process. NDS T 2.3.1

$$F_b = 1.2(1.25)1.0(1.0).82 = 1.23 \text{ ksi}$$

$$M = 72.3^k \text{ ft}$$

$$S_R = \frac{12M}{F_b'} = \frac{12(72.3)}{1.23} = 705.4 \text{ in}^3$$ NDS 3.3.2

try $S_{5\text{-}1/8 \times 31\text{-}1/2} = 847.5 \text{ in}^3 > 705.4 \text{ in}^3$ √

This is one lamination larger than required from S_R to account for the additional self weight to be calc'd.

$$I = 13350 \text{ in}^4$$

$$A = 161.4 \text{ in}^2$$

Assume that the self weight of the glulam is about 40 pcf = .023 pci.

self weight = .023(161.4)12 = 45 plf

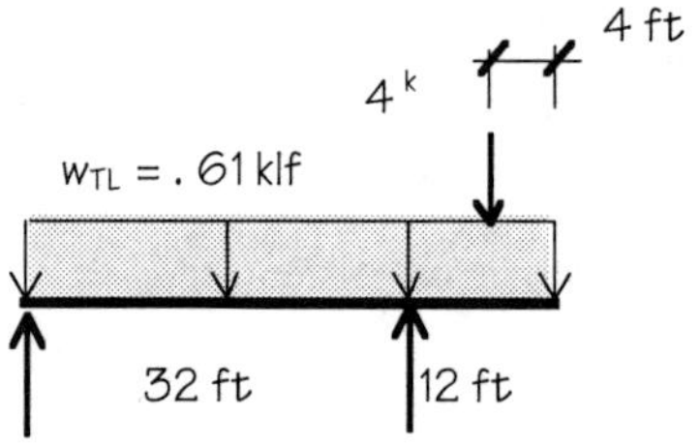

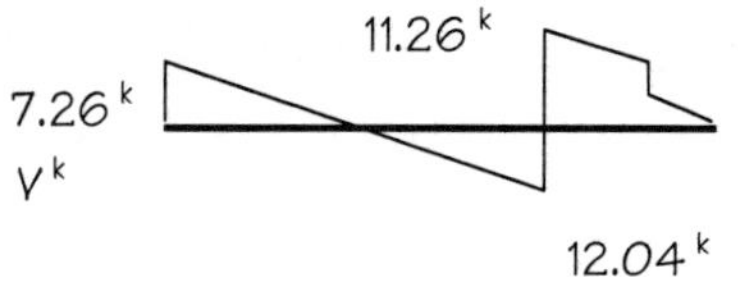

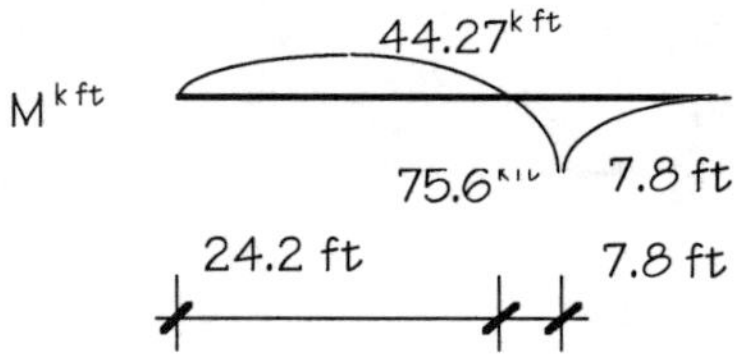

NDS 3.3.2 $S_R = 705.4\left(\frac{75.6}{72.3}\right) = 737.6 \text{ in}^3 < 847.5 \text{ in}^3$ √

Determine the actual C_V ($K_L = 1.0$)

NDS 5.3.2 $$C_V = K_L\left(\frac{21}{L}\right)^{1/10}\left(\frac{12}{d}\right)^{1/10}\left(\frac{5.125}{b}\right)^{1/10}$$

L = 7.8 + 12 = 19.8 ft (distance between points of zero moment)

$$C_V = 1.0\left(\frac{21}{19.8}\right)^{1/10}\left(\frac{12}{31.5}\right)^{1/10}\left(\frac{5.125}{5.125}\right)^{1/10} = .91 > .82$$

Which implies that our assumption was conservative, and that our trial size is ok. √

Ck Lateral Stability

NDS T2.3.1 $F_b' = F_b C_D C_M C_t C_L$

Unbraced length ℓ_U = 12 ft = 144 in

$$\frac{\ell_U}{d} = \frac{144}{31.5} = 4.57 < 7$$

NDS 3.3.3.6 $\ell_e = 2.06\ell_U = 2.06(144) = 296.6$ in

$$R_B = \sqrt{\frac{\ell_e d}{b^2}} = \sqrt{\frac{296.6(31.5)}{5.125^2}} = 18.9 < 50 \;\checkmark$$

This beam is subject to lateral torsional buckling. Because of this movement in the y axis plane, we need to consider the stability with E_y.

NDS T2.3.1 $E' = E_y(C_M)C_t = 1.4e3(1.0)1.0 = 1.4e3$ ksi

$$F_{bE} = \frac{K_{bE}E'y}{R_B^2} = \frac{.609(1.4e3)}{18.9^2} = 2.39 \text{ ksi}$$

$F_b^* = F_{bx}C_DC_MC_t = 1.2(1.25)1.0(1.0) = 1.5$ ksi

NDS 3.3.3.8 $$C_L = \frac{1+\left(F_{bE}/F_{bx}^*\right)}{1.9} - \sqrt{\left(\frac{1+\left(F_{bE}/F_{bx}^*\right)}{1.9}\right)^2 - \frac{\left(F_{bE}/F_{bx}^*\right)}{.95}}$$

$$C_L = \frac{1+(2.39/1.5)}{1.9} - \sqrt{\left(\frac{1+(2.39/1.5)}{1.9}\right)^2 - \frac{(2.39/1.5)}{.95}}$$

= .93 > .91 < .82 √

∴ Volume effect governs over stability. Our trial section was determined using volume effect of .82 so we are a little conservative.

Bending (returning to positive moment)

Volume effect:

NDS T2.3.1 $F_b' = F_b C_D C_M C_t C_V$

Assume a C_V of .82

$F_b = 2.4(1.25)1.0(1.0).82 = 2.46$ ksi

M = 44.3 ^{k}ft

NDS 3.3.2 $$S_R = \frac{12M}{F_b'} = \frac{12(44.3)}{2.46} = 216.1 \text{ in}^3$$

try $S_{5\text{-}1/8 \times 31\text{-}1/2} = 847.5 \text{ in}^3 > 216.1 \text{ in}^3$ √

Determine the actual C_V ($K_L = 1.0$)

$$C_V = K_L\left(\frac{21}{L}\right)^{1/10}\left(\frac{12}{d}\right)^{1/10}\left(\frac{5.125}{b}\right)^{1/10}$$

NDS 5.3.2 L = 24.2 ft (distance between points of zero moment)

Note that to use the simpler L = 32 ft is considered conservative.

$$C_V = 1.0\left(\frac{21}{24.2}\right)^{1/10}\left(\frac{12}{31.5}\right)^{1/10}\left(\frac{5.125}{5.125}\right)^{1/10} = .90 > .82$$

Which implies that our assumption was conservative, and that our trial size is ok. √

Bending ok

Ck shear

Do not use a shear modification (conservative).

NDS T2.3.1 $F_v' = F_v(C_D)C_M(C_t) = .165(1.25)1.0(1.0) = .206$ ksi

$V = 12.04^k$

$$A_R = \frac{1.5(V)}{F_v'} = \frac{1.5(12.04)}{.206} = 87.7 \text{ in}^2 < 161.4 \text{ in}^2 \;\checkmark$$

Shear ok

Ck defl. (based on TCM)

NDS T2.3.1 $E' = E(C_M)C_t = 1.7e3(1.0)1.0 = 1.7e3$ ksi

$\Delta_{TL} = .27$ in (pos M, from comptr output)

$\Delta_{TL} = .19$ in (neg M, from comptr output)

Since the ratio DL/LL = .75, this implies TL/LL = 1.75

$$\Delta_{LL} = \Delta_{TL}\left(\frac{w_{LL}}{w_{TL}}\right) = .27\left(\frac{1}{1.75}\right)$$

$$= .15 \text{ in} < \ell/240 = \frac{32(12)}{240} = 1.6 \text{ in} \ \checkmark$$

$$\Delta_{DL} = \Delta_{LL}\left(\frac{w_{DL}}{w_{LL}}\right) = .15(.75) = .11 \text{ in}$$

camber = 1.5 Δ_{DL} = 1.5(.11) = .17 in

Negative moment deflection ok by insp. Both deflections are not great enough to effect the camber.

Deflection ok

Ck bearing

Since the support conditions are not known, determine the minimum bearing length.

NDS T2.3.1

$$F'_{c\perp} = F_{c\perp}(C_M)C_t(C_b) = .65(1.0)1.0(1.0) = .65 \text{ ksi}$$

$$\ell_{b\ min} = \frac{R}{bF'_{c\perp}} = \frac{23.3}{5.125(.65)} = 6.99 \text{ in}$$

Use 5.125x31-1/2 24F-V1 glulam with a minimum bearing length of 7 in. No Camber

□
□
□

It's all right to have butterflies in your stomach. Just get them to fly in formation.

DR. ROB GILBERT

○ PROBLEM 2.27

Maximum uniform roof load for a simple beam.

Determine the maximum uniform roof load that can be superimposed on the header shown below.

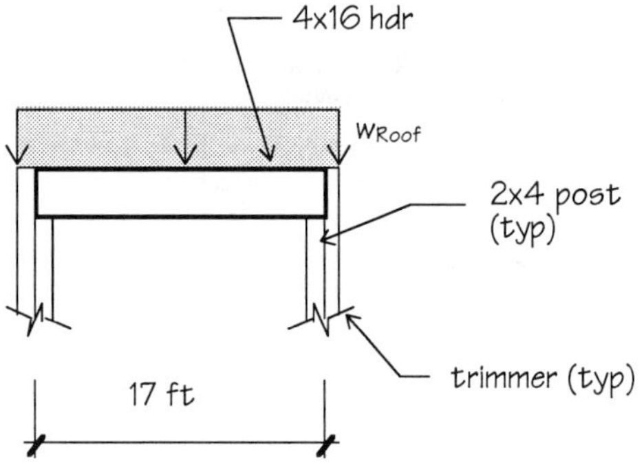

ASSUME

- Use clear span for calcs.
- No ponding.
- DF - L No. 2.
- Full Lat. support from plywood.
- Beam wt = 15 plf.
- EMC > 19%.
- Normal temp. conditions.
- Post does not govern.
- L/360 Defl. criteria.

SOLUTION

F_b = .875 ksi
F_v = .095 ksi
E = 1.6e3 ksi

Since we want to find w_{max} we must work the problem backwards. Perform bending, shear and deflection cks to see which case governs the selected size.

Bending

L = 17 - 2(3.5/12) = 16.42 ft

$$F_b' = F_b C_D C_M C_t C_L C_F C_r$$ NDS T2.3.1

The NDS stipulates that C_M =.85 when used with F_b, unless $F_b C_F \le 1150$ psi, $C_M = 1.0$

$$F_b = .875(1.25)1.0(1.0)1.0(1.0)1.0 = 1.09 \text{ ksi}$$

NDS 3.3.2

$$M = \frac{w\ell^2}{8} = F_bS$$

$$w = \frac{8F_bS}{\ell^2} = \frac{8(1.3)135.7}{12(16.42)^2} = .436 \text{ klf}$$

Maximum bending w = .436 klf

Ck shear

Do not use a shear modification (conservative).

NDS T2.3.1

$$F_v' = F_v(C_D)C_M(C_t)C_H = .095(1.25).97(1.0)1.0 = .115 \text{ ksi}$$

$$V = \frac{w\ell}{2} = \frac{F_vA}{1.5}$$

$$w = \frac{2F_vA}{1.5\ell} = \frac{2(.115)53.4}{1.5(16.4)} = .5 \text{ klf} > .436 \text{ klf}$$

NDS 3.3.2

Bending governs over shear

Ck defl. (based on TCM)

$$\Delta_{allow} = \ell/360 = 12(16.42)/360 = .547 \text{ in}$$

$$E' = E(C_M)C_t = 1.6e3(.9)1.0 = 1.44 \text{ ksi}$$

$$\Delta = \frac{5w\ell^4 1728}{348EI}$$

$$w = \frac{\Delta 348EI}{5\ell^4 1728} = \frac{.547(384)1.44e3(1034)}{5(16.4)^4 1728}$$

$= .5$ klf $> .436$ klf

Bending governs over deflection

Ck bearing

NDS T2.3.1

$A_{contact} = 5.25 \text{ in}^2$

$$F_{c\perp}' = F_{c\perp}(C_M)C_t(C_b)$$

$$C_b = \frac{\ell_b + .375}{\ell_b} = \frac{1.5 + .375}{1.5} = 1.25$$

NDS 2.3.10

$$F_{c\perp}' = .625(.67)1.0(1.25) = .52 \text{ ksi}$$

$$P = AF_{c\perp} = \frac{w\ell}{2}$$

$$w = \frac{2AF_{c\perp}}{\ell} = \frac{2(5.25).52}{16.4} = .334 \text{ klf} < .436 \text{ klf}$$

∴ bearing governs

Max uniform load

$w_{max} = w - w_{4x16} = .334 - .015 = .319$ klf

The maximum superimposed load w = 319 plf is due to bearing

□
□
□

Courage is doing what you're afraid to do. There can be no courage unless you're scared.

EDDIE RICKENBACKER

PROBLEM 2.28

Maximum joist spacing for concrete formwork.

Determine:

a. The maximum joist spacing.
b. Jst size with spacing of 36 in o/c.

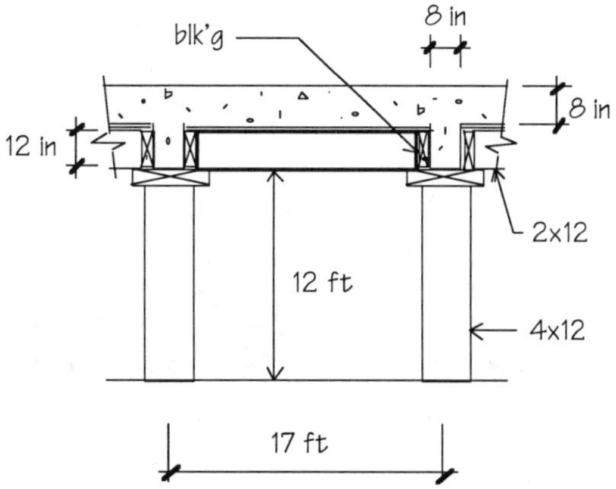

ASSUME

$C_D = 1.0$.
DF - L No. 1.
Full Lat. support from plywood.
EMC < 19%.
Normal temp. conditions.
Other mems. do not govern.
$\Delta_{allow} = L/480$.
$w_{conc} = 150$ pcf.
$w_{ply} = 2$ psf.
$w_{jst} = 5$ psf.
Pin/pin column.
Loads stay the same if mem. changes.
Bearing does not control.
Spacing greater 24 in o/c.

SOLUTION

a. Joist spacing

$F_b = 1.0$ ksi
$F_v = .095$ ksi
$E = 1.8e3$ ksi

Since we want to find jst spc'g$_{max}$ we must work the problem backwards. Perform bending, shear and deflection cks to see which case governs the selected size.

Bending

$S = 31.64$ in^3
$A = 16.88$ in^2
$I = 178$ in^4

$L = 10 - 8/12 = 9.33$ ft

NDS T2.3.1

$w = (8/12).15 + .002 + .005 = .107$ ksf

spc'g = s ⇒ sw = .107 s ksf

NDS 3.3.2

$F_b{}' = F_b C_D C_M C_t C_L C_F C_r = 1.0(1.0)1.0(1.0)1.0(1.0)1.0$

$= 1.0$ ksi

$$M = \frac{w\ell^2}{8} = \frac{sw\ell^2}{8} = SF_b$$

$$s = \frac{8F_bS}{w\ell^2} = \frac{8(31.6)1.0}{.107(9.33)^2} = 27.1 \text{ in o/c}$$

Maximum bending s_R = 27.1 in o/c

NDS T2.3.1

Ck shear

Do not use a shear modification (conservation).

$$F_v' = F_v(C_D)C_M(C_t)C_H = .095(1.0)1.0(1.0)1.0 = .095 \text{ ksi}$$

NDS 3.4.2

$$V = \frac{w\ell}{2} = \frac{F_vA}{1.5} \Rightarrow A = \frac{1.5V}{F_v} = \frac{1.5\left(w\ell s/2\right)}{F_v}$$

$$s = \frac{2AF_v(12)}{1.5w\ell} = \frac{2(16.9).095(12)}{1.5(.107)9.33} = 25.7 \text{ in} < 27.1 \text{ in}$$

Shear governs over bending

Ck defl. (based on TCM)

$$\Delta_{allow} = 12L/480 = \frac{(12)5\left(\frac{sw}{144}\right)\ell^4}{384EI}$$

$$E' = E(C_M)C_t = 1.8e3(1.0)1.0 = 1.8e3 \text{ ksi}$$

$$s = \frac{12(384)1.8e3(177.98)144}{480(5).107(9.33(12))^3} = 589.8 \text{ in} > 25.7 \text{ in}$$

Shear governs maximum spacing of 25.7 in o/c

b. Joist size with 3 ft spacing

Bending

NDS 3.3.2

assume $C_F = 1.0$

$w = 3(.107) = .321$ klf

$$M = \frac{w\ell^2}{8} = \frac{.321(9.33)^2}{8} = 3.49^{\text{ k ft}}$$

$$S_R = \frac{12M}{F_b} = \frac{12(3.49)}{1.0} = 41.9 \text{ in}^3$$

try 2x14 $S = 43.9$ in^3 > 41.8 in^3
$A = 19.9$ in^2
$I = 290.8$ in^4

$C_F = .9$

$F_b = .9$ ksi

$$S_R = \frac{12M}{F_b} = \frac{12(3.49)}{.9} = 46.5 \text{ in}^3 > 43.9 \text{ in}^3 \textbf{ NG!}$$

try 4x10 $S = 49.9$ in^3
$A = 32.4$ in^2

$I = 230.8 \text{ in}^4$

$C_F = 1.0$

$F_b = 1.0$ ksi

$S_R = 41.9 \text{ in}^3 < 49.9 \text{ in}^3$ √

NDS T2.3.1

Bending ok with 4x10

Ck shear

NDS 3.4.2

$F_v' = F_v(C_D)C_M(C_t)C_H = .095(1.0)1.0(1.0)1.0 = .095$ ksi

$$V = \frac{w\ell}{2} = \frac{.321(9.33)}{2} = 1.5^k$$

$$A_R = \frac{1.5V}{F_v} = \frac{1.5(1.5)}{.095} = 23.7 \text{ in}^2 < 32.4 \text{ in}^2 \ \surd$$

NDS T2.3.1

Shear ok with 4x10

Ck defl. (based on TCM)

$E' = E(C_M)C_t = 1.8e3(1.0)1.0 = 1.8e3$ ksi

$$\Delta_{allow} = \ell/480 = \frac{12(9.33)}{480} = .23 \text{ in}$$

$$I_R = \frac{5w\ell^4 1728}{348E\Delta} = \frac{(5).321(9.33)^4 1728}{384(1.8e3).23}$$

$= 132.2 \text{ in}^4 < 230.8 \text{ in}^4$ √

Defl. ok, use 4x10 Df-l No 1 for 3 ft o/c spc'g

□
□
□

Do or do not. There is no try.

YODA

● PROBLEM 2.29

Tapered end cuts of glulam roof beams.

You are working with an architect on the redesign of an existing roof that has drainage problems. She wants to taper end cut the existing 5x34-3/8 glulam roof beams to increase drainage. Analyze the design shown below.

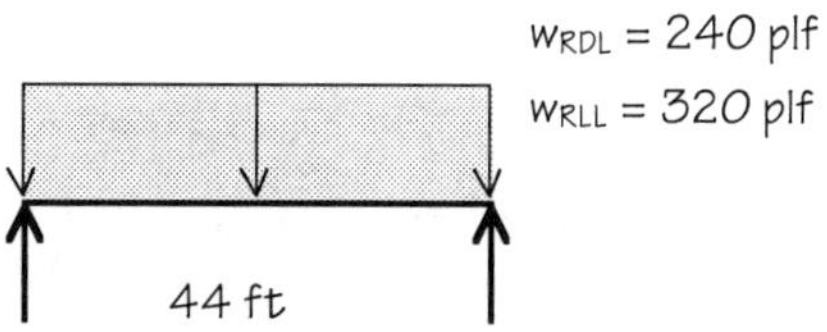

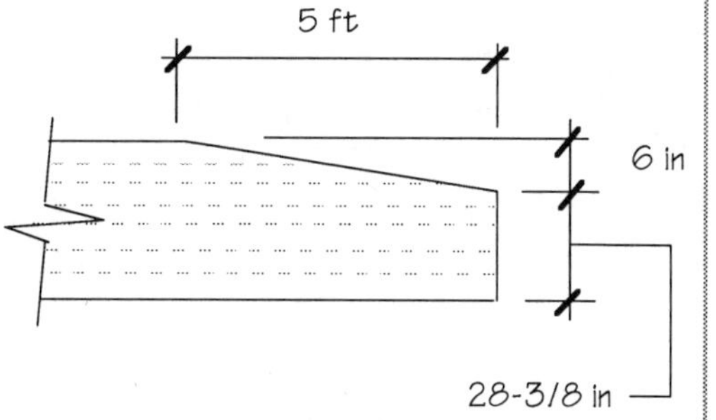

ASSUME

No ponding, plaster ceiling.
Full lateral support from plywood diaphragm.
Previous design ok.
EMC < 19%.
Normal temperature conditions.
Commercial building.
24F-V4 glulam (western species).
Bearing length ok at 12 in

SOLUTION

$F_b = 2.4$ ksi (T), 1.2 ksi (compression zone in tension)
$F_v = .165$ ksi
$E = 1.8e3$ ksi

DL + LL controls by inspection.

The beam is long so either M or Δ will control.

The architect wants to provide extra water head for the new downspouts and scuppers. In cutting the end of the glulam in a sloping manner, the cut will usually be made through the higher strength laminations. The lower strength core laminations will then be exposed resulting in a lower allowable design values than the listed tabular stress values for: the allowable bending stress, the section modulus and the compression perpendicular to grain.

Allowable shear stress (F_v) is unaffected because it is already based on the lower value core laminations. The length of the slope is commonly about 4 to 8 feet long and the depth of the cut rarely exceeds 1/2 the depth of the beam.

From the TCM Table 5.4 for 24F- V4 the adjusted tabular design stresses are:

F_b = 2.2 ksi
E = 1.7e3 ksi
$F_{c\perp}$ = 560 psi

Bending

We will need to check bending at both location "a" and "b".

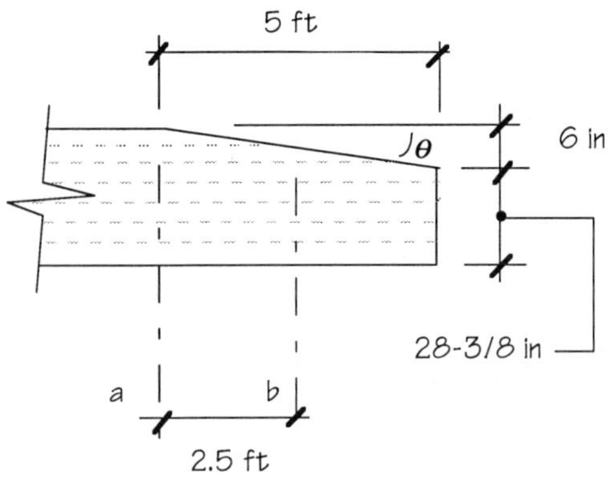

Lateral stability:

The roof diaphragm fully laterally supports the top (compression) side of the beam. Thus the unbraced length is zero. Lateral buckling is prevented and beam stability factor (C_L) = 1.0. Therefore, the volume factor will control when a beam is fully supported.

Volume effect: (K_L = 1.0) NDS 5.3.2

$$C_V = K_L\left(\frac{21}{L}\right)^{1/10}\left(\frac{12}{d}\right)^{1/10}\left(\frac{5.125}{b}\right)^{1/10}$$

$$C_V = 1.0\left(\frac{21}{44}\right)^{1/10}\left(\frac{12}{31.63}\right)^{1/10}\left(\frac{5.125}{5}\right)^{1/10} = .85$$

The interaction stress factor (C_I) and C_v are not simultaneously applied. The combined stresses can be checked by either the interaction equation or the interaction stress factor (C_I). The interaction stress factor is an expression of the interaction equation as a function of slope when solved for the bending stress of tapered beams. NDS Eq5-31

Ck the interaction stress factor C_I

$$\theta = \tan^{-1}\left(\frac{6}{5(12)}\right) = 5.71$$

$$C_I = \frac{1}{\sqrt{1+\left(F_b \tan\left(\theta/F_v\right)\right)^2+\left(F_b \tan^2\left(\theta/F_{c\perp}\right)\right)^2}}$$ NDS T2.3.1

$$= \frac{1}{\sqrt{1+\left(2.2\tan\left(5.71/.165\right)\right)^2+\left(2.2\tan^2\left(5.71/.56\right)\right)^2}}$$

$= .55 < .85$

C_I controls over C_v

$$F_b' = F_b C_D C_M C_t C_I$$

F_b' = 2.2(1.25)1.0(1.0).55 = 1.51 ksi

Ck location "a"

$$M = \frac{(w)x(l-x)}{2} = \frac{(.56)5(44-5)}{2} = 54.6^{\text{ k-ft}}$$

$$S_R = \frac{12M}{F_b'} = \frac{12(54.6)}{1.51} = 433.9 \text{ in}^3 < 984.7 \text{ in}^3 \ \surd$$

Bending ok at location "a"

Ck bending at location "b"

NDS 5.3.2

Calculate C_V at this location.

$$C_V = 1.0\left(\frac{21}{44}\right)^{1/10}\left(\frac{12}{28.38}\right)^{1/10}\left(\frac{5.125}{5}\right)^{1/10} = .85 > .55$$

C_l controls over C_v

$F_b' = 1.51$ ksi

$$M = \frac{(.56)2.5(44-2.5)}{2} = 29.1^{\text{k-ft}}$$

$$S_R = \frac{12M}{F_b'} = \frac{12(29.1)}{1.51} = 231.3 \text{ in}^3$$

$$S = \frac{bd^2}{6} = \frac{5(31.38)^2}{6} = 821 \text{ in}^3 > 231.3 \text{ in}^3 \ \checkmark$$

Bending ok at location b

Ck shear

NDS T2.3.1

Do not use a shear modification (conservative).

$$F_V' = F_V(C_D)C_M(C_t) = .165(1.25)1.0(1.0) = .206 \text{ ksi}$$

$$V = \frac{w\ell}{2} = \frac{(.56)44}{2} = 12.3^{\text{k}}$$

$$A_R = \frac{1.5(V)}{F_V'} = \frac{1.5(12.3)}{.206} = 89.6 \text{ in}^2$$

For shear stress, it is accurate to calculate the new area at the edge of the support. It is conservative to use the dimensions at the end of the beam.

$$A = 28.38(5) = 141.9 \text{ in}^2 > 89.6 \text{ in}^2 \ \checkmark$$

Shear ok. The existing 5x34-3/8 24F-V4 glulam ok with the proposed tapered end cut.

Fear is the main source of superstition, and one of the main sources of cruelty. To conquer fear is the beginning of wisdom.

BERTRAND RUSSELL

○ PROBLEM 2.30

Bi-axial bending.

You are doing pick-up work in your office. A fellow engineer tells you that that he did not size a large "emullion" type support beam found in a 2-story window at a local shopping mall renovation. Determine the size of the beam "a" shown below. For aesthetic reasons, the architect requires that the beam have its longest dimension in the vertical plane.

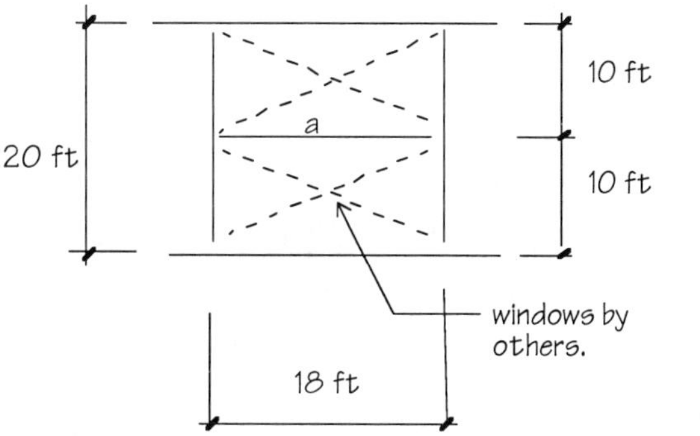

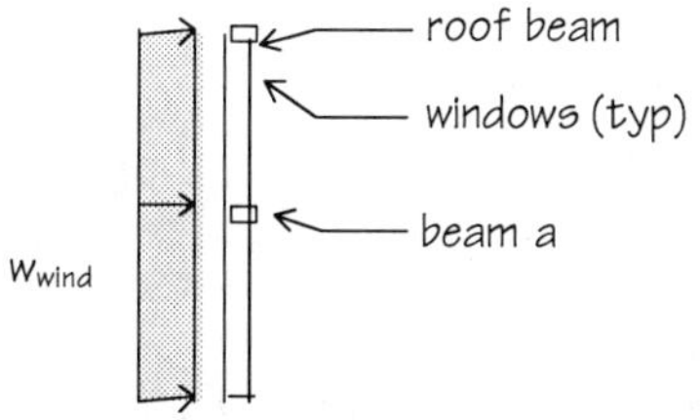

ASSUME

24F - V8 glulam (western species).
w_{wind} = 22.7 psf.
w_{DL} = .10 klf (includes beam DL).
Full height glass DL to beam below.
Wind governs.
EMC < 16%.
Normal temperatures.
Bearing ok.
Window does not transmit roof DL to beam.

SOLUTION

NDS T5A, 1C

F_{vx} = .165 ksi
F_{vy} = .145 ksi
F_{bx} = 2.4 ksi
F_{by} = 1.45 ksi
E_x = 1.8e3 ksi
E_y = 1.6e3 ksi

Ck bending

DL + wind controls by inspection, but we still need to check the DL alone case with C_D = .9

Case 1 (DL)

M about the x-axis:

$$M = \frac{w\ell^2}{8} = \frac{.1(18)^2}{8} = 4.1 \text{ k ft}$$

NDS T2.3.1

Assume the selected glulam will have a C_V of .85. If the actual C_V is not .85, adjust it and re-ck the calc. This trial procedure is an iterative process.

$F_b' = F_b C_D C_M C_t C_v$ = 2.4(.9)1.0(1.0).85 = 1.84 ksi

$$S_R = \frac{12M}{F_b'} = \frac{12(4.1)}{1.84} = 26.7 \text{ in}^3$$

try $S_{5\text{-}1/8 \times 12}$ = 123.0 in^3 > 26.7 in^3 √

I = 738.0 in^4

A = 61.5 in^2

NDS 5.3.2

Determine the actual C_V (K_L = 1.0)

$$C_V = K_L\left(\frac{21}{L}\right)^{1/10}\left(\frac{12}{d}\right)^{1/10}\left(\frac{5.125}{b}\right)^{1/10}$$

$$C_V = 1.0\left(\frac{21}{18}\right)^{1/10}\left(\frac{12}{12}\right)^{1/10}\left(\frac{5.125}{5.125}\right)^{1/10} = 1.02$$

Which implies that our trial size is ok. √

Ck Lateral Stability

$F_b' = F_b C_D C_M C_t C_L$ NDS T2.3.1

Unbraced length ℓ_U = 18 ft = 216 in

For a uniformly distributed load:

$$\frac{\ell_u}{d} = \frac{216}{12} = 18 > 7$$

$\ell_e = 1.63\,\ell_U + 3d$ = 1.63(216) + 3(12) = 388 in NDS T3.3.3

$$R_B = \sqrt{\frac{\ell_e d}{b^2}} = \sqrt{\frac{388(12)}{5.125^2}} = 13.3 < 50 \ \surd$$

This beam is subject to lateral torsional buckling. Because of this movement in the y axis plane, we need to consider the stability with E_y. NDS T2.3.1

$E' = E_y(C_M)C_t$ = 1.6e3(1.0)1.0 = 1.6e3 ksi

$$F_{bE} = \frac{K_{bE}E_y'}{R_B^2} = \frac{.609(1.6e3)}{13.3^2} = 5.51 \text{ ksi}$$

$F_b^* = F_{bx}C_D C_M C_t$ = 2.4(.9)1.0(1.0) = 2.16 ksi

NDS 3.3.3.8

$$C_L = \frac{1+\left(F_{bE}/F_{bx}^*\right)}{1.9} - \sqrt{\left(\frac{1+\left(F_{bE}/F_{bx}^*\right)}{1.9}\right)^2 - \frac{\left(F_{bE}/F_{bx}^*\right)}{.95}}$$

$$C_L = \frac{1+(5.5/2.16)}{1.9} - \sqrt{\left(\frac{1+(5.5/2.16)}{1.9}\right)^2 - \frac{(5.5/2.16)}{.95}} = .97 > .85$$

∴ Stability governs over volume effect . Our trial section was determined using C_v = .85, so we are ok.

Bending ok for DL alone

Case 2 (DL + wind)

M about the y-axis:

w = .023(10) = .23 klf

$$M = \frac{w\ell^2}{8} = \frac{.23(18)^2}{8} = 9.3 \text{ k ft}$$

d_y = 5.125 in < b_y = 12 in

Which implies that C_L = 1.0. C_v does not apply to elements loaded to their flat side. NDS appendix B.2

We must recalc our values with C_D = 1.6

NDS T2.3.1

Assume the selected glulam will have a C_V of .85. If the actual C_V is not .85, adjust it and re-ck the calc. This trial procedure is an iterative process.

$F_{bx}' = F_b C_D C_M C_t C_L = 2.4(1.6)1.0(1.0).97 = 3.72$ ksi

$$f_{bx} = \frac{12M}{S_x} = \frac{12(4.1)}{123} = .4 \text{ ksi}$$

$F_{by}' = F_b C_D C_M C_t C_L C_{fu} = 1.45(1.6)1.0(1.0)1.0(1.1)$

$= 2.6$ ksi

$S_y = 52.5$ in^3

$I_y = 134.6$ in^4

$$f_{by} = \frac{12M}{S_y} = \frac{12(9.3)}{52.5} = 2.13 \text{ ksi}$$

NDS 3.9.2

Combined stress

$$\left(\frac{f_c}{F_c'}\right)^2 + \frac{f_{b1}}{F_{b1}'\left(1-\left(f_c/F_{cE1}\right)\right)} + \frac{f_{b2}}{F_{b2}'\left(1-\left(f_c/F_{cE2}\right)-\left(f_{b1}/F_{bE}\right)^2\right)} \le 1.0$$

Where the subscript 1 = x and subscript 2 = y. Because we have a bi-axial bending, the above reduces to:

$$\frac{f_{bx}}{F_{bx}'} + \frac{f_{by}}{F_{by}'\left(1-\left(f_{bx}/F_{bE}\right)^2\right)} \le 1.0$$

$$\left(\frac{.4}{3.72}\right)^2 + \frac{2.13}{2.6\left(1-\left(.4/5.5\right)^2\right)} = .84 < 1.0 \ \checkmark$$

This member is currently working at 84% capacity.

Bending ok for 5-1/8 x 12 glulam

Ck defl.

Based on TCM Table 4.4 we consider the use of $\frac{\ell}{360}$ as our deflection limit. In this problem it is conservative to use a value of K = 1.0.

Strong axis deflection

$E' = E(C_M)C_t = 1.8e3(1.0)1.0 = 1.8e3$ ksi

$$\Delta_{DL} = \frac{5w\ell^4}{384EI} = \frac{5(.1)18^4(1728)}{384(1.8e3)738}$$

$= .18 \text{ in} < \ell/360 = 18(12)/360 = .6$ in $\checkmark$

Cambering a glulam beam 1.5 times the DL deflection should bring about a roughly level beam for the effects of long term deflection and creep. NDS T2.3.1

camber = $1.5\,\Delta_{DL} = 1.5(.18) = .27$ in

Weak axis deflection

$E' = E(C_M)C_t = 1.6e3(1.0)1.0 = 1.6e3$ ksi

$$\Delta_{wind} = \frac{5w\ell^4}{384EI} = \frac{5(.23)18^4(1728)}{384(1.6e3)134.6}$$

$= 2.52 \text{ in} > \ell/480 = 18(12)/480 = .45$ in **NG!**

Find I_R

$$I_R = \frac{5w\ell^4}{384E(\ell/480)} = \frac{5(.23)18^4(1728)}{384(1.6e3).45} = 754.5 \text{ in}^4$$

It is obvious that the critical bending stress lies in the horizontal plane (wind). Normally we would flip the beam around to make it carry the critical load more efficiently. However, the architect requires the present orientation of the beam. Re-select wider beam with larger I.

Try 8-3/4x15, I = 837.4 in4 > 753.8 in^4 $\checkmark$

Deflection ok with 8-3/4x15 glulam

The preceding checks before re-sizing are ok by inspection.

Ck shear

Unless shear is going to be a problem (e.g. if there is a large load and a relatively short span), do not use a shear modification (conservative). NDS T2.3.1

$F_V' = F_V(C_D)C_M(C_t) = .165(1.6)1.0(1.0) = .26$ ksi

It is considered conservative to add shears parallel to grain in bi-axial bending.

$$V = \frac{(w_{wind}+w_{DL})\ell}{2} = \frac{(.23+.1)18}{2} = 2.97^k$$

$$A_R = \frac{1.5(V)}{F_V'} = \frac{1.5(2.97)}{.26} = 17.1 \text{ in}^2 < 131.3 \text{ in}^2 \ \checkmark$$

Shear ok

You gain strength, courage and confidence by every experience in which you really stop to look fear in the face. You are able to say to yourself, "I lived through this horror. I can take the next thing that comes along." You must do the thing you think you cannot do.

ELEANOR ROOSEVELT

PROBLEM 2.31

Double tapered glulam beam.

A contractor wants you to design the roof of her material and equipment storage facility with double tapered glulam beams. Design the beams for the criteria shown on the following page.

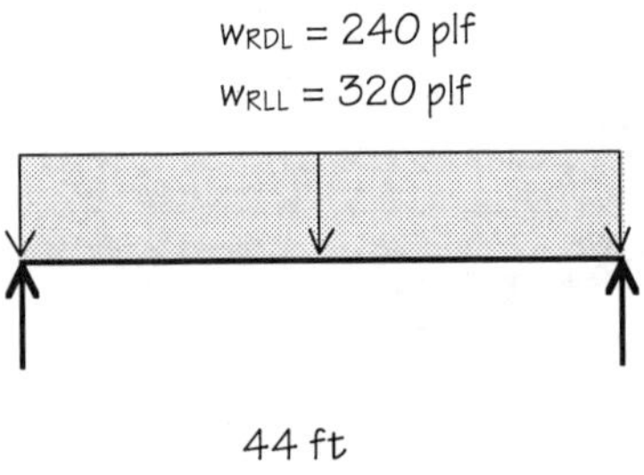

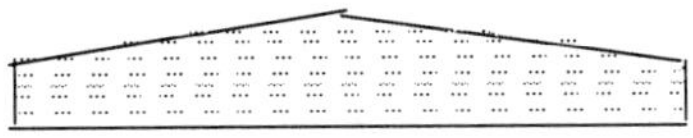

ASSUME

No ponding, non-plaster ceiling.
Full lateral support from plywood diaphragm.
EMC < 19%.
Normal temperature conditions.
Commercial building.
Allowable equal to 24F-V8 glulam (western species).
Roof slope = 1:12.

SOLUTION

NDS T5A

F_b = 2.4 ksi
F_v = .165 ksi
E = 1.8e3 ksi
$f_{c\perp}$ = .65 ksi

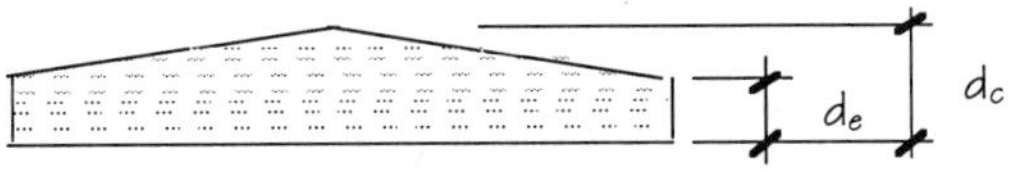

DL + LL controls by inspection.

Some contractors like using tapered glulam roof beams. This type of glulam automatically provides the proper roof pitch that will help facilitate drainage. Contractors like this because it tends to simplify TOB (top of beam) heights.

When you design a tapered glulam the manufacturer will construct the glulam with the "compression side" grade value for the entire taper. If requested, you may have the glulam taper cut similar to an end cut of a standard glulam combination. Remember, in cutting the end of the glulam in a sloping manner, the cut will usually be made through the higher strength laminations. The lower strength core laminations will then be exposed. This results in lower allowable design values than the listed tabular stress values for: the allowable bending stress, the section modulus and the compression perpendicular to grain. Check TCM Table 5.4 for the adjusted design values.

Allowable shear stress (F_v) is unaffected because it is already based on the lower value core laminations.

Use glulam with "compression" side grade throughout taper.

End depth (using shear)

It is conservative to assume L_e = 44 ft because it neglects bearing support. Assume 5-1/8 in width.

NDS T2.3.1

$$V = \frac{w\ell_e}{2} = \frac{(.56)44}{2} = 12.3^k$$

$$F_V' = F_V(C_D)C_M(C_t) = .165(1.25)1.0(1.0) = .206 \text{ ksi}$$

From TCM 5.10.2 for a uniform load:

$$d = \frac{1.5(V)}{bF_V'} = \frac{1.5(12.3)}{5.125(.206)} = 17.5 \text{ in}^2 \quad \text{use 18 in.}$$

The actual effective length is less than 44 ft not only because of bearing support, but also because of the arch action of the beam. Recall that arch action allows us to use shear modification to further reduce L_e.

> End depth = 18 in.

Deflection

Centerline depth

d_c = de + (span/2) (roof slope)

= 18 + (44(12)/2)(1/12) = 40 in

Determine equivalent prismatic beam

See TCM sec. 5.10.6

TCM 5.10.6

$d = d_e C_{dt}$

$$Cy = \frac{d_c - d_e}{d_e} = \frac{40-18}{18} = 1.22 < 3$$

Which implies:

$C_{dt} = 1 + .62C_y = 1 + .62(1.22) = 1.76$

$d = d_e C_{dt} = 18(1.76) = 31.7$ in

Equivalent I of beam

$$Ie = \frac{bd^3}{12} = \frac{5.125(31.7)^3}{12} = 13605 \text{ in}^4$$

$$\Delta_{TL} = \frac{5w\ell^4}{384EI} = \frac{5(.56)(44)^4 1728}{384(1.8e3)13605}$$

$$= 1.93 \text{ in} < \ell/180 = 44(12)/180 = 2.93 \text{ in} \ \checkmark$$

> Defection ok

Bending

The beam is tapered, so it follows that the maximum stress does not occur in the center of the beam.

Maximum stress depth d TCM 5.10.2

$$d = \frac{d_e}{d_c}(2d_c - d_e) = \frac{18}{40}(2(40)-18) = 27.9 \text{ in}$$

Lateral stability:

The roof diaphragm fully laterally supports the top (compression) side of the beam. Thus the unbraced length is zero. Lateral buckling is prevented and beam stability factor (C_L) = 1.0. Therefore, the volume factor will control when a beam is fully supported.

Volume effect: (K_L = 1.0)

$$C_V = K_L\left(\frac{21}{L}\right)^{1/10}\left(\frac{12}{d}\right)^{1/10}\left(\frac{5.125}{b}\right)^{1/10}$$

NDS 5.3.2

$$C_V = 1.0\left(\frac{21}{44}\right)^{1/10}\left(\frac{12}{27.9}\right)^{1/10}\left(\frac{5.125}{5.125}\right)^{1/10} = .85$$

C_I and C_V are not simultaneously applied. The combined stresses can be checked by either the interaction equation or the interaction stress factor (C_I). The interaction stress factor is an expression of the interaction equation as a function of slope when solved for the bending stress of tapered beams. NDS T2.3.1

TCM 5.10.3

$$F_b' = F_b C_D C_M C_t C_v$$

F_b' = 2.4(1.25)1.0(1.0).85 = 2.55 ksi

TCM 5.10.5

$$f_b = \frac{3W\ell}{4bd_e(2d_c - d_e)}$$

$$= \frac{3(.56(44))44(12)}{4(5.125)18(2(40)-18)} = 1.71 \text{ ksi} < 2.55 \text{ ksi}$$

Maximum bending stress ok

Check actual shear (maximum stress at location d)

$f_v = f_b \tan\theta = 1.71(1/12) = .143 \text{ ksi} < .206 \text{ ksi}$ √

Maximum shear stress ok

Check compression perpendicular to grain

$f_{c\perp} = f_b \tan^2\theta = 1.71(1/12)^2 = .012 \text{ ksi} < .65 \text{ ksi}$

$f_{c\perp}$ ok

Check combined stress

Here we can use either the interaction equation or the interaction stress factor C_I. Do not use C_V, C_L, or C_I with the interaction equation. The interaction equation gives:

$$\frac{f_b^2}{(F_b')^2} + \frac{f_v^2}{(F_v')^2} + \frac{f_{c\perp}^2}{(F_{c\perp}')^2} \le 1.0$$

$$\frac{1.71^2}{(3.0)^2} + \frac{.143^2}{(.206)^2} + \frac{.012^2}{(.65)^2} = .81 < 1.0 \quad \surd$$

Combined stress ok

Camber

$$\Delta_{DL} = \Delta_{TL}\left(\frac{w_{DL}}{w_{TL}}\right) = 1.93\left(\frac{.24}{.56}\right) = .83 \text{ in}$$

Camber at centerline $= 1.5\,\Delta_{DL} = 1.5(.83) = 1.25$ in

Use 1.25 in camber for 5-1/8 wide tapered glulam beam. End depth = 18 in Centerline depth = 40 in. Tapered slope = 1:12

We should be careful to get out of an experience only the wisdom that is in it - and stop there; lest we be like the cat that sits down on a hot stove lid. She will never sit down on a hot stove lid again - and that is well; but also she will never sit down on a cold one any more.

MARK TWAIN

● PROBLEM 2.32

Single tapered glulam beam.

The same contractor who wanted you to design the roof double tapered glulam beams wants you to check out the possibility of using single tapered glulam beams for a 30 ft span. Design the beams for the criteria shown below.

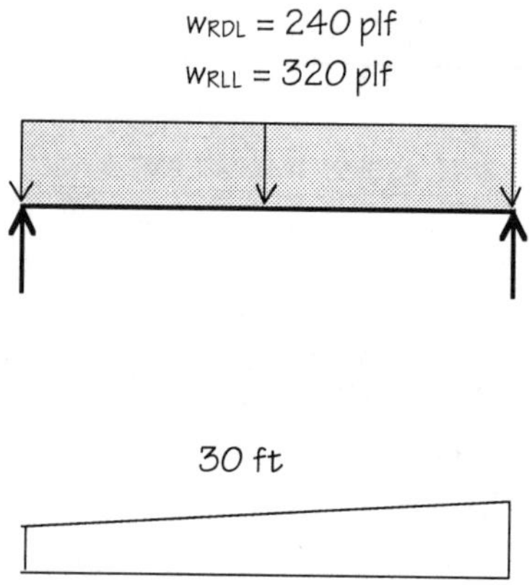

ASSUME

No ponding, non-plaster ceiling.
Full lateral support from plywood diaphragm.
EMC < 19%.
Normal temperature conditions.
Commercial building.
Allowable equal to 24F-V8 glulam (western species).
Roof slope (approx.) = 1:24.

SOLUTION

NDS T5A

$F_b = 2.4$ ksi
$F_v = .165$ ksi
$E = 1.8e3$ ksi
$f_{c\perp} = .65$ ksi

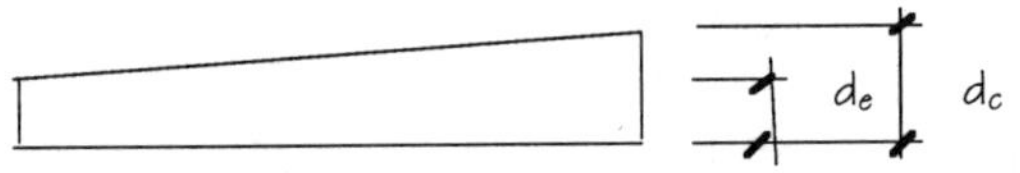

DL + LL controls by inspection.

Some contractors like using tapered glulam roof beams. This type of glulam automatically provides the proper roof pitch that will help facilitate drainage. Contractors like this because it tends to simplify TOB (top of beam) heights.

When you design a tapered glulam the manufacturer will construct the glulam with the compression side grade value for the entire taper. If requested, you may have the glulam taper cut similar to an end cut of a standard glulam combination. Remember, in cutting the end of the glulam in a sloping manner, the cut will usually be made through the higher strength laminations. The lower strength core laminations will then be exposed, resulting in lower allowable design values than the listed tabular stress values for: the allowable bending stress, the section modulus and the compression perpendicular to grain. Check TCM Table 5.4 for the adjusted design values.

Allowable shear stress (F_v) is unaffected because it is already based on the lower value core laminations.

Use glulam with compression side grade throughout taper.

End depth (short side = d_e)

It is conservative to assume L_e = 30 ft because it neglects bearing support. Assume 5-1/8 in width.

$$V = \frac{w\ell_e}{2} = \frac{(.56)30}{2} = 8.4^k$$ NDS T2.3.1

$$F_v' = F_v(C_D)C_M(C_t) = .165(1.25)1.0(1.0) = .206 \text{ ksi}$$

From TCM 5.10.2 for a uniform load.

$$d_e = \frac{1.5(V)}{bF_v'} = \frac{1.5(8.4)}{5.125(.206)} = 11.9 \text{ in}^2 \quad \text{use 12 in.}$$

The actual effective length is less than 30 ft not only because of bearing support but also because of the arch action of the beam. Recall that arch action allows us to use shear modification to further reduce L_e.

End depth (short side) = 12 in

Deflection

End depth (tall side = d_c)

$d_c = d_e$ + (span) (roof slope)

= 12 + (30(12))(1/24) = 27 in

The inefficient use of material indicates that a double taper beam is preferred. However, continue the problem as an example.

Determine equivalent prismatic beam TCM 5.10.6

See TCM sec. 5.10.6

$d = d_e C_{dt}$

$$C_y = \frac{d_c - d_e}{d_e} = \frac{27-12}{12} = 1.25 < 2$$

Which implies:

$C_{dt} = 1 + .43C_y = 1 + .43(1.25) = 1.54$

$d = d_e C_{dt} = 12(1.54) = 18.5$ in

Equivalent I of beam

$$I_e = \frac{bd^3}{12} = \frac{5.125(18.5)^3}{12} = 2704 \text{ in}^4$$

$$\Delta_{TL} = \frac{5w\ell^4}{384EI} = \frac{5(.56)(30)^4 1728}{384(1.8e3)2704}$$

$$= 2.1 \text{ in} > \ell/180 = 30(12)/180 = 2.0 \text{ in} \quad \textbf{NG!}$$

Defection NG, check stresses

Bending

The beam is tapered so it follows that the maximum stress does not occur in the center of the beam.

TCM 5.10.2

Maximum stress depth d

$$d = 2d_e \frac{d_c}{d_e+d_c} = 2(12)\frac{27}{12+27} = 16.6 \text{ in}$$

Lateral stability:

The roof diaphragm fully laterally supports the top (compression) side of the beam. Thus the unbraced length is zero. Lateral buckling is prevented and beam stability factor (C_L) = 1.0. Therefore the volume factor will control when a beam is fully supported.

NDS 5.3.2

Volume effect: (K_L = 1.0)

$$C_V = K_L\left(\frac{21}{L}\right)^{1/10}\left(\frac{12}{d}\right)^{1/10}\left(\frac{5.125}{b}\right)^{1/10}$$

NDS T2.3.1

$$C_V = 1.0\left(\frac{21}{30}\right)^{1/10}\left(\frac{12}{16.6}\right)^{1/10}\left(\frac{5.125}{5.125}\right)^{1/10} = .93$$

C_I and C_V are not simultaneously applied. The combined stresses can checked by either the interaction equation or the interaction stress factor (C_I). The interaction stress factor is an expression of the interaction equation as a function of slope when solved for the bending stress of tapered beams.

TCM 5.10.3

$$F_b' = F_b C_D C_M C_t C_v$$

F_b' = 2.4(1.25)1.0(1.0).93= 2.79 ksi

$$f_b = \frac{3W\ell}{4bd_cd_e}$$

TCM 5.10.5

$$= \frac{3(.56(30))30(12)}{4(5.125)27(12)} = 2.73 \text{ ksi} < 2.79 \text{ ksi}$$

> Maximum bending stress ok

Check actual shear (maximum stress at location d)

$f_v = f_b \tan\theta$ = 2.73(1/24) = .114 ksi < .206 ksi √

> Maximum shear stress ok

Check compression perpendicular to grain

$f_{c\perp} = f_b \tan^2\theta$ = 2.73(1/24)^2 = .005 ksi < .65 ksi

> $f_{c\perp}$ ok

Check combined stress

Here we can use either the interaction equation or the interaction stress factor C_I. Do not use C_V, C_L, or C_I with the interaction equation. The interaction equation gives: TCM 5.10.1

$$\frac{f_b^2}{(F_b')^2} + \frac{f_v^2}{(F_v')^2} + \frac{f_{c\perp}^2}{(F_{c\perp}')^2} \le 1.0$$

$$\frac{2.73^2}{(3.0)^2} + \frac{.113^2}{(.206)^2} + \frac{.005^2}{(.65)^2} = 1.13 > 1.0 \quad \textbf{NG!}$$

Try d_c = 30 in

$$d = 2d_e \frac{d_c}{d_e+d_c} = 2(12)\frac{30}{12+30} = 17.1 \text{ in}$$

The individual stresses are ok by inspection.

$$f_b = \frac{3(.56(30))30(12)}{4(5.125)30(12)} = 2.46 \text{ ksi}$$

$f_v = f_b \tan\theta$ = 2.46(1/24) = .102 ksi

$f_{c\perp} = f_b \tan^2\theta$ = 2.46(1/24)^2 = .004 ksi

$$\frac{2.45^2}{(3.0)^2} + \frac{.102^2}{(.206)^2} + \frac{.004^2}{(.65)^2} = .91 > 1.0 \ \surd$$

> Combined stress ok with increased depth

Camber

Determine equivalent prismatic beam

$d = d_e C_{dt}$

$$C_y = \frac{d_c - d_e}{d_e} = \frac{30-12}{12} = 1.5 < 2$$

Which implies:

$C_{dt} = 1 + .43C_y = 1 + .43(1.5) = 1.65$

$d = d_e C_{dt}$ = 12(1.65) = 19.7 in

Equivalent I of beam

$$I_e = \frac{bd^3}{12} = \frac{5.125(19.7)^3}{12} = 3265 \text{ in}^4$$

$$\Delta_{TL} = \frac{5w\ell^4}{384EI} = \frac{5(.56)(30)^4 1728}{384(1.8e3)3265}$$

$= 1.74 \text{ in} < 2.0 \text{ in}$ √

$$\Delta_{DL} = \Delta_{TL}\left(\frac{w_{DL}}{w_{TL}}\right) = 1.74\left(\frac{.24}{.56}\right) = .75 \text{ in}$$

Camber at centerline = $1.5\,\Delta_{DL} = 1.5(.75) = 1.13$ in

> Use 1.25 in camber for 5-1/8 wide tapered glulam beam.
> Short end depth = 12 in
> Tall end depth = 30 in
> Tapered slope = 1:24 (approx.)

Never put off till tomorrow what you can do the day after tommorrow.

MARK TWAIN

● PROBLEM 2.33

Pitched and tapered curved glulam beam with attached haunch.

An architect wants you to design pitched and tapered curved glulam roof beams for a dining facility. Use the criteria shown to design the glulam with an attached haunch.

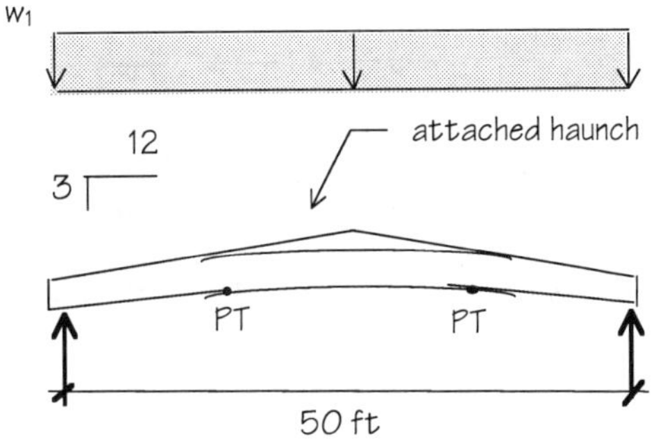

ASSUME

- No ponding, no plaster ceiling.
- Full lateral support.
- w_1 = 32 psf (roof) includes beam weight.
- EMC < 12%.
- Normal temp. conditions.
- Commercial building.
- 24F-V8 glulam.
- Spacing = 16 ft o/c.
- DL/LL = 0.6.

SOLUTION

F_b = 2.4 ksi NDS T2.3.1
F_v = .165 ksi
E_x = 1.8e3 ksi

DL + LL controls by inspection.

Loading

$w = \text{trib } \ell (w_1) = 16(.032) = .51$ klf

End depth (d_e)

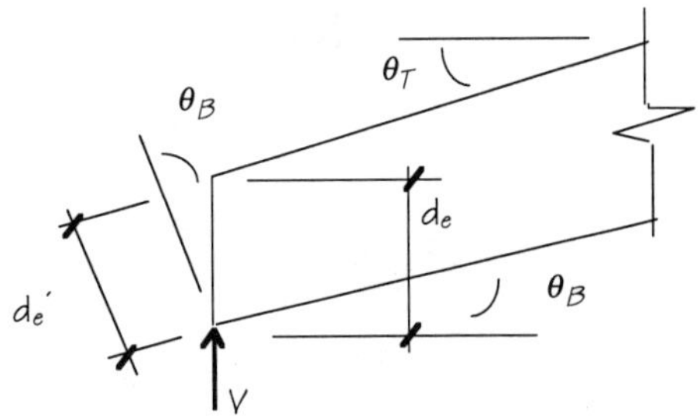

Assume b = 5.125 in.

$$V = \frac{w\ell}{2} = \frac{(.51)50}{2} = 12.8^{k}$$

NDS T2.3.1 $F_v' = F_v(C_D)C_M(C_t) = .165(1.25)1.0(1.0) = .206$ ksi

$$\text{Trial } d_e = \frac{1.5(V)}{bF_v'} = \frac{1.5(12.8)}{5.125(.206)} = 18.2 \text{ in}$$

Use shear modification:

$L_e = L - 2d_e = 50 - 2(18.2/12) = 46.97$ ft say 47 ft

$$V = \frac{(.51)47}{2} = 12^{k}$$

$$d_e = \frac{1.5(V)}{bF_v'} = \frac{1.5(12)}{5.125(.206)} = 17.05 \text{ in}$$

We want to use a glulam that is not cut through a lamination at the end so our d_e has to be in multiples of 1.5 in.

17.05/1.5 = 11.37 laminations, try 12(1.5) = 18 in.

Use d_e = 18 in

Trial d_{cb} (centerline depth from bending)

C_L = 1.0 because the beam is fully supported. Volume effect (C_v) must be checked.

Volume effect:

Assume the selected glulam will have a C_V of .85 and a radius (R) = span = 50 ft. If the actual C_V is not .82 adjust it and re-ck the calc. This trial procedure is an iterative process

NDS 5.3.4

$$C_c = 1 - 2000\left(\frac{t}{R}\right)^2 = 1 - 2000\left(\frac{1.5}{50(12)}\right)^2 = .99$$

NDS T2.3.1 $F_b' = F_bC_DC_vC_c = 2.4(1.25).85(.99) = 2.52$ ksi

$$M = \frac{w\ell^2}{8} = \frac{.51(50)^2 12}{8} = 1913^{\text{k in}}$$

TCM 5.12.6 $\text{Trial } d_{cb} = \sqrt{\frac{6M}{bF_b'}} = \sqrt{\frac{6(1913)}{5.125(2.52)}} = 29.8$ in

Trial $d_{c\Delta}$ (centerline depth from deflection limit)

Assume a 10% increase from the deflection of a straight beam.

$\Delta_{max} = L/180 = 50(12)/180 = 3.33$ in

$$\Delta_{max} = \frac{1.1(5)w\ell^4}{384E'\left(\frac{bd_{c\Delta}^3}{12}\right)}$$ TCM T4.3

Setting the two equations equal and solving gives:

$$d_{c\Delta} = \sqrt[3]{\frac{5.5w\ell^4}{384E'b\Delta_{max}}} = \sqrt[3]{\frac{5.5(.51)(50(12))^4}{384(1.8e3)5.125(3.33)}}$$

= 31.4 in > 29.8 in (deflection controls so far)

Trial d_{crt} (centerline depth from radial stress)

Assume R = R_m = 50 ft.

$F_{rt}' = F_rC_D = .015(1.25) = .019$ ksi

$$\text{Trial } d_{crt} = \frac{3M}{2R_mbF_{rt}'} = \frac{3(1913)}{2(50(12))5.125(.019)} = 49.1 \text{ in}$$ NDS 5.4

This is a little large for this type of member. Since d_{crt} is inversely proportional b and R_m, we can alter either to adjust the depth closer to our other values. Keep b and change R_m by iterative method. Assume $d_c = d_t'$.

31.4/1.5 = 20.9 lams try d_c = 21(1.5) = 31.5 in.

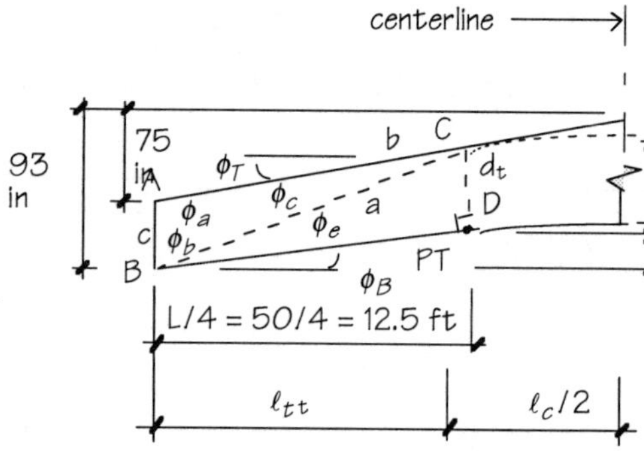

ϕ_T = tan -1 (3/12) = 14.04° TCM 5.12.1.6

ϕ_a = 90 + 14.04 = 104.04°

$a = \sqrt{(12.5(12))^2 + (31.5)^2} = 153.3$ in

$\phi_c = \sin^{-1}\left(\frac{d_e(\sin\phi_a)}{a}\right) = \sin^{-1}\left(\frac{18(\sin 104.04)}{153.3}\right) = 6.54°$

$\phi_b = 180 - \phi_a - \phi_c = 180 - 104.04 - 6.54 = 69.42°$

$\phi_e = \tan^{-1}\left(\frac{d_t'}{\ell/4}\right) = \tan^{-1}\left(\frac{31.5}{12.5(12)}\right) = 11.86°$

$\phi_B = 90 - \phi_b - \phi_c = 90 - 69.42 - 11.86 = 8.72°$

$\ell_t = 12.5(12)\cos\phi_B = 12.5(12)\cos 8.72$

$= 148.27$ in $= 12.4$ ft

$H_t = 12.5(12)\sin\phi_B = 12.5(12)\sin 8.72 = 22.74$ in

$\ell_c = L - 2\ell_t = 50 - 2(12.4) = 25.2$ ft $= 302.4$ in

$b_1 = \frac{\ell_c}{2}\tan\left(\frac{\phi_B}{2}\right) = \frac{302.4}{2}\tan\left(\frac{8.72}{2}\right) = 11.53$ in

$R = \frac{4b_1^2 + \ell_c^2}{8b_1} = \frac{4(11.53)^2 + (302.4)^2}{8(11.53)} = 997.2$ in

$= 83.1$ ft

$R_m = R + d_c/2 = 997.2 + 31.5/2 = 1012.95$ in

$= 84.4$ ft

$d_{crt} = \frac{3(1913)}{2(1012.95)5.125(.019)} = 29.1$ in

This then changes ϕ_B and the PT. The TCM method describes that after several trials a tangent depth and corresponding radius will converge on a number. Since the set of equations seems to yield a divergent series cycle, a simple method is to proceed as follows (see TCM 5.12.7). Take the average of the last 2 successive d_c and d_{crt} to plug in the "a" side equation as shown in the table below.

$d_c = \frac{31.5 + 29.2}{2} = 30.35$ in

Use this in the equation for "a" and follow series convergence to arrive at a value for d_{crt}. Continue until the difference in the average is small - which implies convergence.

d_c	d_{crt}	avg.
31.5	29.2	30.35
30.35	30.488	30.419
30.419	30.405	30.412
30.412	30.413	

Convergence at 30.41 in < 31.39, therefore deflection controls.

$\phi_a = 104.04°$

a = 12.773 ft

$\phi_c = 6.542°$

$\phi_b = 69.418°$

$\phi_e = 11.86°$

$\phi_B = 8.722°$

$\ell_t = 148.265$ in

$H_t = 22.746$ in

$\ell_c = 303.469$ in

$b_1 = 11.572$ in

R = 1000.606 in

$R_m = 84.696$ ft

$f_{rt} = \frac{3M}{2R_m bd} = \frac{3(1913)}{2(84.696)5.125(31.5)12}$

$= .018$ ksi < .019 ksi

> Use $d_t' = d_c = 31.5$ with the geometry shown above

Check deflection (10% higher as before)

$\Delta_{TL} = \frac{1.1(5)w\ell^4}{384E'\left(\frac{bd^3}{12}\right)12} = \frac{1.1(5).51(50(12))^4}{384(1.8e3)\left(\frac{5.125(31.5)^3}{12}\right)12}$

$= 3.28$ in < 3.33 in √

> Deflection ok

Check bending stresses at curved section

$f_b = \frac{6M}{bd^2} = \frac{6(1913)}{5.125(31.5)^2} = 2.26$ ksi

$C_c = .99$

$C_V = K_L\left(\frac{21}{L}\right)^{1/10}\left(\frac{12}{d}\right)^{1/10}\left(\frac{5.125}{b}\right)^{1/10}$ NDS 5.3.2

$$C_V = 1.0\left(\frac{21}{50}\right)^{1/10}\left(\frac{12}{31.5}\right)^{1/10}\left(\frac{5.125}{5.125}\right)^{1/10} = .83$$

The spacing of the connectors of the attached haunch must be checked with regard to lateral stability. Use straight beam equations for this check in the curved area of the beam. Assume that the haunch connectors start at 5 ft on either side of the centerline of the beam.

Unbraced length ℓ_U = 10 ft = 120 in

NDS T3.3.3

$$\frac{\ell_u}{d} = \frac{120}{31.5} = 3.81 < 7$$

$$\ell_e = 2.06\,\ell_U = 2.06(120) = 247.2 \text{ in}$$

$$R_B = \sqrt{\frac{\ell_e d}{b^2}} = \sqrt{\frac{247.2(31.5)}{5.125^2}} = 17.22 < 50 \quad \checkmark$$

This beam is subject to lateral torsional buckling. Because of this movement (in the y axis plane), we need to consider the stability with E_y.

NDS T2.3.1

$$E' = E_y(C_M)C_t = 1.8e3(1.0)1.0 = 1.8e3 \text{ ksi}$$

$$F_{bE} = \frac{K_{bE}E_y'}{R_B^2} = \frac{.609(1.8e3)}{17.22^2} = 3.7 \text{ ksi}$$

$$F_b^* = F_{bx}C_DC_MC_t = 2.4(1.25)1.0(1.0) = 3.0 \text{ ksi}$$

NDS 3.3.3.8

$$C_L = \frac{1+\left(F_{bE}/F_{bx}^*\right)}{1.9} - \sqrt{\left(\frac{1+\left(F_{bE}/F_{bx}^*\right)}{1.9}\right)^2 - \frac{\left(F_{bE}/F_{bx}^*\right)}{.95}}$$

$$C_L = \frac{1+(3.7/3.0)}{1.9} - \sqrt{\left(\frac{1+(3.7/3.0)}{1.9}\right)^2 - \frac{(3.7/3.0)}{.95}} = .89 < .83$$

Therefore C_v controls.

NDS T2.3.1

$$F_b' = F_bC_DC_vC_c = 2.4(1.25).83(.99)$$

$$= 2.47 \text{ ksi} > 2.26 \text{ ksi} \quad \checkmark$$

Bending ok in curved section of beam

Check bending stresses at PT (f_{bt})

Let $\tan\theta = \tan(\phi_T - \phi_B) = \tan(14.04 - 8.72) = .093$

Using TCM Table 5.5 and interpolating:

$$\left.\begin{matrix} .09 & .607 \\ .093 & C_I \\ .095 & .586 \end{matrix}\right] \Rightarrow C_I = .607 + \frac{(.586-.607)(.093-.09)}{.095-.09}$$

$= .594 < .83$ C_I controls

$$F_b' = F_bC_DC_MC_tC_I = 2.4(1.25)1.0(1.0).59 = 1.77 \text{ ksi}$$ NDS T2.3.1

$$M = \frac{w\ell\ell_t}{2} - \frac{w\ell_t^2}{2} = \frac{.51(50)12.4}{2} - \frac{.51(12.4)^2}{2} = 118.9^{\text{ k ft}}$$

$$S_R = \frac{bd^2}{6} = \frac{5.125(31.5)^2}{6} = 848 \text{ in}^3$$

$$f_{bt} = \frac{M}{S} = \frac{118.9(12)}{848} = 1.68 \text{ ksi} < 1.77 \text{ ksi} \quad \checkmark$$

Bending ok at PT

Check bending at 3 pts along leg

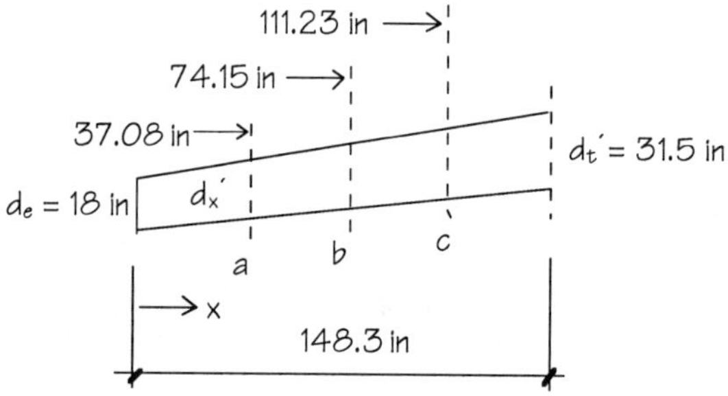

Using TCM equations 5.69 and 5.70 to build a table of values gives:

$$d_x' = \left(d_e + x(\tan\phi_T - \tan\phi_B)\right)\left(\frac{\cos\phi_T}{\cos(\phi_T - \phi_B)}\right)$$ TCM 5.12.7

$$M_x = \frac{.5w}{12}\left(x - .5d_x'(\tan\phi_B)\right)\left(\ell - \left(x - .5d_x'(\tan\phi_B)\right)\right)$$

$$f_b = \frac{6M}{b(d_x')^2}, \quad F_b' = F_b^*(C_v \text{ or } C_I)$$

PT	x	d_x'	M	f_b	C_v	F_b'	f_b/F_b'
a	37.1	21.03	427.4	1.13	.87	1.77	.64
b	74.2	24.53	814.1	1.58	.85	1.77	.89
c	111.2	28.01	1142.2	1.7	.84	1.77	.96
PT	148.3	31.51	1413.3	1.67	.83	1.77	.94

In all cases $F_b' > f_b$ √

> Bending ok at tapered leg

Check radial tension in leg

R_m = 84.7 ft (from above)

NDS 5.4.1

$$f_{rt} = \frac{3M}{2R_m bd} = \frac{3(1913)}{2(84.7)5.125(31.5)12}$$

= .017 ksi < .019 ksi √

> Radial tension ok

Check horizontal movement at supports

$h = H_t + b_1 + d_c/2 = 22.7 + 11.6 + 31.5/2 = 50.05$ in

$$\Delta_H = \frac{2h\Delta_c}{L} = \frac{2(50.05)3.3}{50(12)} = .55 \text{ in}$$

> Provide slotted connection and anti-friction pads for min. 0.55 in

Haunch connection

Try 1/2 in dia. lags at 4 ft o/c (spacing is arbitrary,but must be equal to or less than the assumed spacing above). From TCM Table 5.11:

$T_{allow\ stl} = 2.16^k$

$T_{allow\ wood}$ = .378 kli (withdrawal from table 7.24)

Penetration required = 2.16/.378 = 5.7 in say 6 in

> Use 1/2 in dia. lags with 6 in minimum penetration at 4 ft o/c (counter sink)

I will work in my own way, according to the light that is in me.

LYDIA MARIA CHILD

PROBLEM 2.34

Pitched and tapered curved glulam beam.

Design a pitched and tapered curved glulam for the requirements shown below.

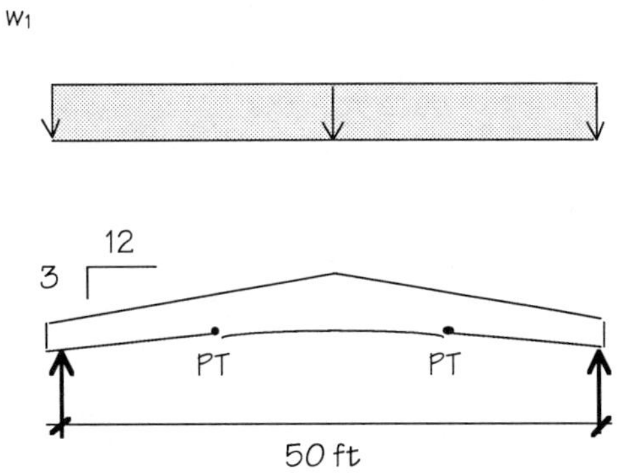

ASSUME

- No ponding, no plaster ceiling.
- Full lateral support.
- w_1 = 32 psf (roof) includes beam weight.
- EMC < 12%.
- Normal temp. conditions.
- Commercial building.
- 24F-V8 glulam.
- Spacing = 16 ft o/c.
- 1-1/2 in lams.
- L/180 maximum deflection.

SOLUTION

NDS T2.3.1

$F_b = 2.4$ ksi
$F_v = .165$ ksi
$E_x = 1.8e3$ ksi
$F_{rt} = 015$ ksi

DL + LL controls by inspection

Loading

$w = \text{trib } \ell (w_1) = 16(.032) = .51$ klf

End depth (d_e)

TCM 5.12.1, 5.12.2

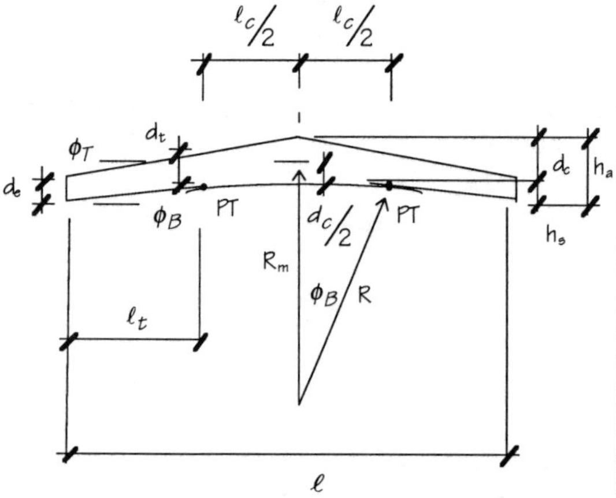

Determine end depth d_e

Assume b = 5.125 in.

$$V = \frac{w\ell}{2} = \frac{(.512)50}{2} = 12.8^{k}$$

$$F_V' = F_v(C_D)C_M(C_t) = .165(1.25)1.0(1.0) = .206 \text{ ksi}$$

$$\text{Trial } d_e = \frac{1.5(V)}{bF_V'} = \frac{1.5(12.8)}{5.125(.206)} = 18.2 \text{ in}$$

Use shear modification

$L_e = L - 2d_e = 50 - 2(18.2/12) = 46.97$ ft say 47 ft

$$V = \frac{(.512)47}{2} = 12.03^{k}$$

$$d_e = \frac{1.5(V)}{bF_V'} = \frac{1.5(12.03)}{5.125(.206)} = 17.09 \text{ in}$$

We want to use a glulam that is not cut through a lamination at the end so our de has to be in multiples of 1.5 in.

17.09/1.5 = 11.39 laminations, try 12(1.5) = 18 in

> Use d_e = 18 in

Trial d_{cb} (centerline depth from bending)

$C_L = 1.0$ because the beam is fully supported. Volume effect (C_v) must be checked.

Volume effect:

Assume the selected glulam will have a C_V of .75. If the actual C_V is not .75 adjust it and re-ck the calc. This trial procedure is an iterative process

$$F_b' = F_b C_D C_V = 2.4(1.25).75 = 2.25 \text{ ksi}$$

$$\phi_T = \tan^{-2}(3/12) = 14.04°$$

Determine D

$$\left.\begin{matrix} 10 & 1.33 \\ 14.04 & x \\ 15 & 1.738 \end{matrix}\right] \quad x = 1.33 + \frac{(1.738-1.33)(14.04-10)}{15-10}$$

x = 1.66

$$M = \frac{w\ell^2}{8} = \frac{.512(50)^2 12}{8} = 1920^{k \text{ in}}$$

$$\text{Trial } d_{cb} = \sqrt{\frac{6MD}{bF_b'}} = \sqrt{\frac{6(1920)1.66}{5.125(2.25)}} = 40.7 \text{ in}$$

> Trial d_{cb} = 40.7 in

Trial $d_{c\Delta}$ (centerline depth from deflection limit)
Assume a 10% increase from the deflection of a straight beam.

$$\Delta_{max} = L/180 = 50(12)/180 = 3.33 \text{ in}$$

$$\Delta_{eff} = \sqrt[3]{\frac{w\ell^3}{6.4E'b\Delta_{max}(\cos\phi_T)^3}}$$

$$= \sqrt[3]{\frac{.512(50)(50(12))^3}{6.4(1.8e3)5.125(3.33)(\cos 14.04)^3}} = 31.3 \text{ in}$$

$d_{c\Delta} = 2d_{eff} - d_e = 2(31.3) - 18$

$= 44.6$ in > 40.7 in deflection controls so far.

Trial $d_{c\Delta} = 44.6$ in

Trial d_{crt} (centerline depth from radial stress)

Assume $R = R_m = 50$ ft.

From TCM Fig. 5.28

A = .058

B = .064

C = .180

$$\frac{d_c}{R_m} = \frac{45}{50(12)} = .075 \Rightarrow K_r = .064$$

$F_{rt}' = F_r C_D = .015(1.25) = .019$ ksi

$$\text{Trial } d_{crt} = \sqrt{\frac{6MK_r}{bF_{rt}'}} = \sqrt{\frac{6(1920).064}{5.125(.015)125}} = 87.6 \text{ in}$$

This is very large for this type of member.

Try radial reinforcement

31.4/1.5 = 20.9 lams try $d_c = 21(1.5) = 31.5$ in.

$F_v/3 = .165/3 = .055$ ksi

$F_{rt}' = 1.25(.055) = .069$ ksi

$$\text{Trial } d_{crt} = \sqrt{\frac{6(1920).064}{5.125(.069)}} = 45.7 \text{ in}$$

45.7/1.5 = 30.5 $\Rightarrow$ 31(1.5) = 46.5 in > 45 in (controls)

Use $d_c = 46.5$ in

Determine h_a, h_s, trial ϕ_B, R

$$h_a = d_e + (\ell/2)\tan\phi_T = 18 + \left(50(12)/2\right)\tan(14.04)$$

$= 93.02$ in

$h_s = h_a - d_c = 93.02 - 46.5 = 46.5$ in

From TCM Fig. 5.29, 5.28

$$\phi_{max} = \sin^{-1}\left(\frac{4Lh_s}{L^2 + 4h_s^2}\right)$$

$\phi_{max} = 14.5° < \phi_T$

$\phi_{min} = 8° < \phi_T$

trial $\phi_B = .45(\phi_{B\,max} + \phi_{B\,min})$

$= .45(14.5 + 8) = 10.13°$

$$R = \frac{h_s - (\ell/2)\tan\phi_B}{1 - \cos\phi_B - \sin\phi_B \tan\phi_B}$$

$$= \frac{46.5 - \left(50(12)/2\right)\tan 10.13}{1 - \cos 10.13 - \sin 10.13 \tan 10.13} = 448.4 \text{ in} = 37.4 \text{ ft}$$

hs = 46.5°, trial $\phi_B = 10.13°$,
R = 37.4 ft

Determine ℓ_t, ℓ_c, ℓ/ℓ_c, d_t, R_M, F_O

$\ell_t = (\ell/2) - R\sin\phi_B = (50(12)/2)$ - SIN 10.13

= 221.1 in = 18.4 ft

$\ell_c = L - 2\ell_t = 50(12) - 2(221.1) = 157.8$ in

$$\frac{\ell}{\ell_c} = \frac{50(12)}{157.8} = 3.8$$

$d_t = d_e + \ell_t(\tan\phi_T - \tan\phi_B)$

$= 18 + 221.1(\tan 14.04 - \tan 10.13) = 33.9$ in

$R_m = R + d_c/2 = 37.4 + 46.5/(2(12))$

= 39.3 ft = 472.1 in

$$f_o = \frac{6M}{bd_c^2} = \frac{6(1920)}{5.125(46.5)^2} = 1.04 \text{ ksi}$$

Check max deflection

$d_{eb} = (d_e + d_c)(.5 + .735\tan\phi_T) - 1.41(d_c)\tan\phi_B$

$= (18 + 46.5)(.5 + .735\tan 14.04) - 1.41(46.5)\tan 10.13$

= 32.4 in

$$\Delta_c = \frac{5w\ell^3}{32E'\left(b\left(d_{eb}\right)^3\right)} = \frac{5(.512)50(50(12))^3}{32(1.8e3)\left(5.125(32.4)^3\right)12}$$

$= 2.75 \text{ in} < 3.33 \text{ in}$ √

Deflection ok

Check bending stresses at centerline

AITC T5.10, determine F, E

10	.927
14.04	F
15	0.0

$$F = .927 + \frac{(0.0 - .927)(14.04 - 10)}{15 - 10} = .178$$

E = 0.0 (by inspection of Table 5.10)

$$K_\theta = D + E\left(\frac{d_c}{R_m}\right) + F\left(\frac{d_c}{R_m}\right)^2 = 1.66 + 0.0 + .178\left(\frac{46.5}{472.1}\right)^2$$

$= 1.66$

$f_b = K_\theta f_o = 1.66(1.04) = 1.73$ ksi

From AITC eq. 4-3

$$C_v = K_L\left(\frac{1291.5}{V}\right)^{1/x} = 1.0\left(\frac{1291.5}{5.125(46.5)50}\right)^{1/10} = .8$$

$F_b' = 2.4(1.25).8 = 2.4 \text{ ksi} > f_b$ √

f_b at centerline ok

Ck f_{bT} at tangent pt

$$d_t' = \left(d_e + \ell_t\left(\tan\phi_T - \tan\phi_B\right)\right)\left(\frac{\cos\phi_T}{\cos(\phi_T - \phi_B)}\right)$$

$$= \left(18 + 221.1(\tan 14.04 - \tan 10.13)\right)\left(\frac{\cos 14.04}{\cos(14.04 - 10.13)}\right)$$

$= 32.9$ in

$$M_t = \frac{w\ell\ell_t}{2} - \frac{w\ell_t^2}{2} = \frac{.512(50)18.4}{2} - \frac{.512(14.4)^2}{2}$$

$= 148.8^{\text{kft}}$

$$f_{bt} = \frac{6M_t 12}{bd_t^2} = \frac{6(148.8)12}{6(32.9)^2} = 1.65 \text{ ksi}$$

C_v must be evaluated for this location.

$$C_V = K_L\left(\frac{1291.5}{V}\right)^{1/x}$$

$$1.0\left(\frac{1291.5}{5.125(32.9)50}\right)^{1/10} = .83$$

$F_b' = 2.4(1.25).83 = 2.49 \text{ ksi} > f_{bt}$ √

f_{bt} at tangent ok

Check bending at 3 pts along leg

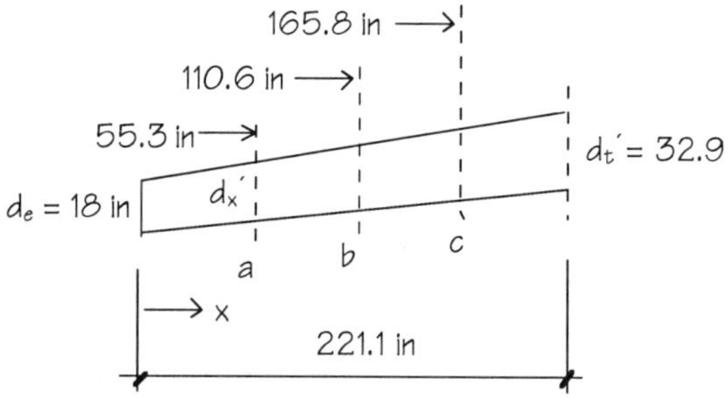

Using TCM equations 5.69 and 5.70 to build a table of values gives:

$$d_x' = \left(d_e + x\left(\tan\phi_T - \tan\phi_B\right)\right)\left(\frac{\cos\phi_T}{\cos(\phi_T - \phi_B)}\right)$$

$$M_x = \frac{.5w}{12}\left(x - .5d_x'\left(\tan\phi_B\right)\right)\left(\ell - \left(x - .5d_x'\left(\tan\phi_B\right)\right)\right)$$

$$f_b = \frac{6M}{b\left(d_x'\right)^2}, \quad F_b' = F_b^*(C_v \text{ or } C_l)$$

PT	x	d_x'	M	f_b	C_v	F_b'	f_b/F_b'
a	55.3	21.3	622.3	1.6	.87	2.61	.61
b	119.6	25.2	1134.5	2.1	.85	2.55	.82
c	165.8	29.0	1520.8	2.12	.84	2.52	.84
PT	221.1	32.9	1777.1	1.9	.83	2.49	.77

In all cases $F_b' > f_b$ √

> Bending ok at tapered leg

Check radial tension at centerline

$$\frac{d_c}{R_m} = \frac{46.5}{37.4(12)} = .1 \Rightarrow K_r = .067$$

$$\frac{\ell}{\ell_c} = \frac{50(12)}{157.8} = 3.8$$

Which is between 3 and 4, implies intrepolation.

$$\left.\begin{matrix} 3.0 & .85 \\ 3.8 & C_r \\ 4.0 & .92 \end{matrix}\right] \quad C_r = .85 + \frac{(.92-.85)(3.8-3.0)}{4-3} = .91$$

$f_{rt} = K_r C_r f_o = .067(.91)1.04$

$= .057$ ksi $< F_{rt}' = .069$ ksi √

> Radial stress ok with reinforcement

Check horizontal movement at supports

$h = H_a - d_c/2 = 93.02 - 46.5/2 = 69.77$ in

$$\Delta_H = \frac{2h\Delta_c}{L} = \frac{2(69.77)2.75}{50(12)} = .64 \text{ in}$$

> Provide slotted connection and anti-friction pads for min. 0.64 in

Radial reinforcement

Radial force/in $= f_{rt}b = .057(5.125) = .292$ kpi

Try 3/4 in dia. lags

From TCM Table 5.11:

$T_{allow\ stl} = 5.265^k$

$T_{allow\ wood} = .641$ kli (withdrawal from table 7.24)

Effective thd. pennetration $= d_c/2 - 2$

$= 46.5/2 - 2 = 21.3$ in

Allowable withdrawable load = 21.3(.641)

$= 1'3.7^k > 5.3^k$

Wood controls.

Max spc'g = 5.265/.292 = 18 in o/c

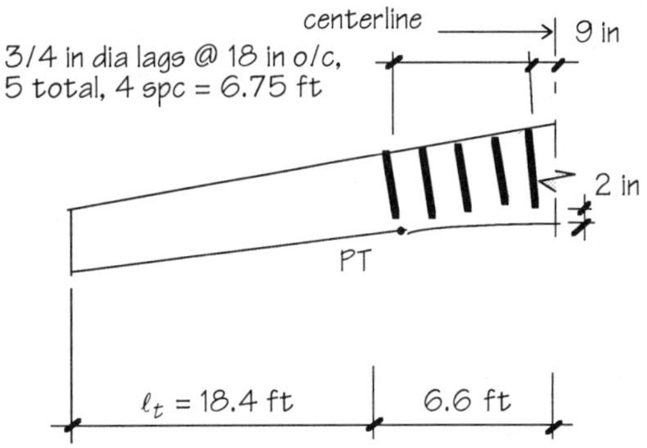

> Use 3/4 in dia lags @ 18 in o/c sym. about centerline, starting @ 9 in on each side of the centerline, screws to extend to 2 in of soffit as shown

Recheck f_b (with reduced section properties @ centerline and PT)

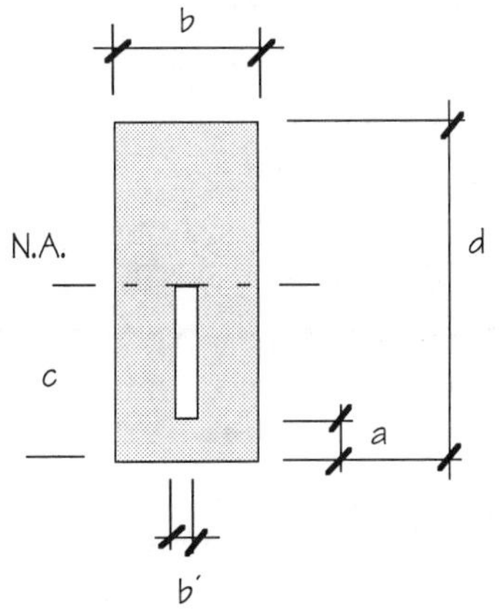

$$c = \frac{bd^2 - b'c^2 + b'a^2}{2(bd - b'c + b'a)}$$

At centerline

$$c = \frac{5.125(46.5)^2 - .75c^2 + .75(2)^2}{2(5.125(46.5) - .75c + .752)} = \frac{-.75c^2 + 11084.5}{(-.75c2 + 479.6)}$$

$0.0 = .75c^2 - 479.6c + 11084.5$

Using the quadratic equation implies

$c = 24.01$ in

$I_{centerline} =$

$$\frac{5.125(46.5)^3}{12} + 5.125(46.5)(.75)^2 - \frac{.75(24-2)^3}{12}$$

$= 42409 \text{ in}^4$

$$f_o = \frac{Mc}{I} = \frac{1920(24)}{42409} = 1.09 \text{ ksi}$$

$f_b = 1.66(1.09) = 1.81 \text{ ksi} < F_b' \; 2.4 \text{ ksi}$ √

Ck @ PT

$$c = \frac{5.125(32.9)^2 - .75c^2 + .75(2)^2}{2(5.125(32.9) - .75c + .752)} = \frac{-.75c^2 + 5550}{(-1.5c + 340)}$$

$0.0 = .75c^2 - 340c + 5550$

Using the quadratic equation implies

$c = 16.96$ in

$$I_{PT} = \frac{5.125(32.9)^3}{12} + 5.125(32.9)(.51)^2 - \frac{.75(16.96-2)^3}{12}$$

$= 15044 \text{ in}^4$

$$f_b = \frac{Mc}{I} = \frac{1777.1(16.96)}{15044} = 2.0 \text{ ksi} < F_b' \; 2.4 \text{ ksi}$$ √

Stresses for reduced section ok

This is the true joy in life, the being for a purpose recognized by yourself as a mighty one; the being thoroughly worn out before you are thrown on the scrap heap; the being a force of nature instead of a feverish selfish little clod of ailments and grievances complaining that the world will not devote itself to making you happy.

GEORGE BERNARD SHAW

3. Combined Bending and Axial Loading

Chapter Problems	Page	Prob.
Bearing plies with combined stress	3-28	3.16
Built-up column maximum vertical load capacity	3-8	3.6
Column design	3-3	3.2
Column stability investigation	3-4	3.3
Combined axial and bending about both axis of a header	3-24	3.14
Combined axial and bending adequacy of a column with new loads and min. eccentricity	3-26	3.15
Combined axial and bending adequacy of a column with side bracket	3-19	3.11
Combined axial and bending adequacy of a column with wind loads from double doors	3-16	3.10
Combined axial and bending adequacy of stud wall	3-14	3.9
Glulam column capacity investigation	3-5	3.4
Round columns	3-21	3.12
Spaced columns	3-23	3.13
Stud wall maximum vertical load carrying capacity	3-6	3.5
Truss lower chord design	3-2	3.1
Truss lower chord design with combined stress of bending and tension	3-9	3.7
Truss top chord design with combined stress of bending and compression	3-11	3.8

PROBLEM 3.1

Truss lower chord design.

Determine the size of the lower chord in the following truss.

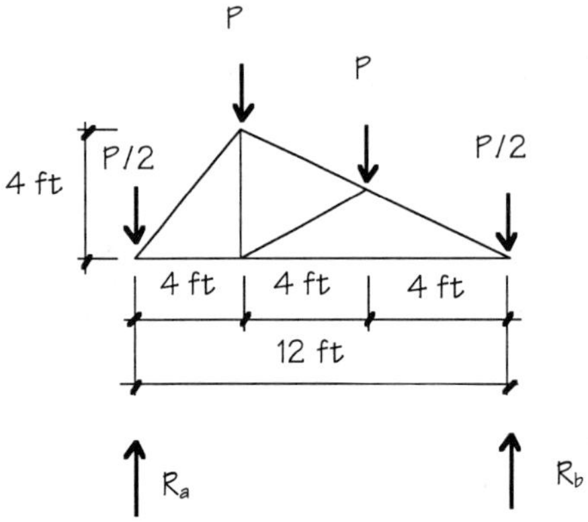

ASSUME

- DF-L No 1.
- $P = 1.5^k$ (RDL + RLL).
- 3/4 in dia. bolts, (1-row) at all connections.
- Pinned joints.
- EMC < 19%.
- Truss wt. included in P above.
- Normal temperatures.

SOLUTION

We can define an axial force element as a member that has a force applied along it's longitudinal centroidal axis. Here we are looking at a tension member of a truss lower chord.

Find reactions

$TL = 3P = 3(1.5) = 4.5^k$

$$R_a = \frac{(4+8)1.5+\left(\frac{1.5}{2}\right)12}{12} = 2.25^k = R_b$$

Resolve pertinent forces

Joint a

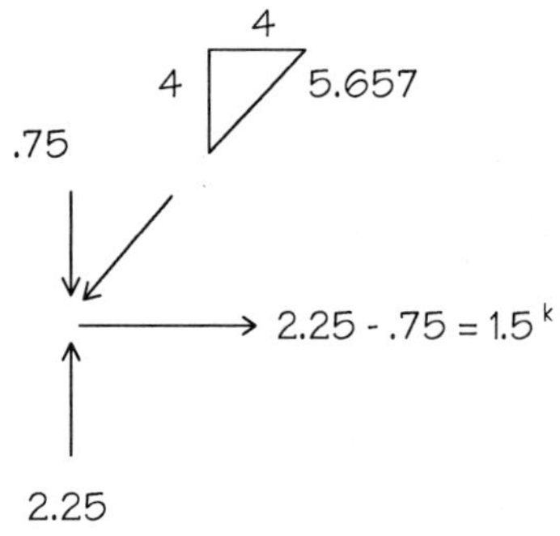

Joint b

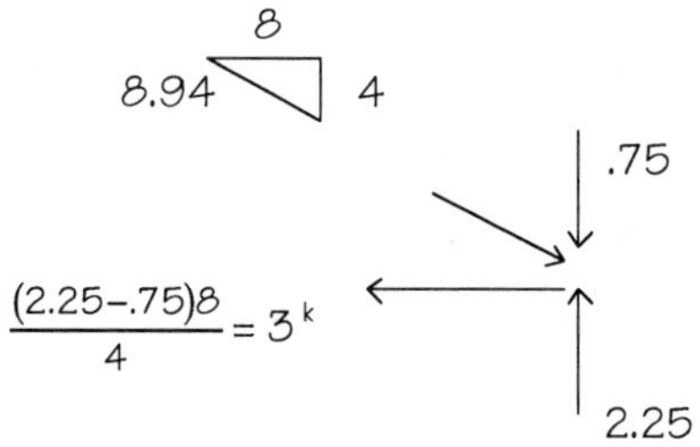

Tension (RDL + RLL governs by insp.) NDS T2.3.1

Assume that $C_F = 1.2$

$F_T' = F_T C_D C_M C_t C_F = .675(1.25)1.0(1.0)1.2 = 1.01$ ksi

$$\text{Req'd } A_n = \frac{P}{F_T'} = \frac{3}{1.01} = 2.97 \text{ in}^2$$

$A_h = (\frac{3}{4} + \frac{1}{8})1.5 = 1.3 \text{ in}^2$

$A_g = A_n + A_h = 2.97 + 1.3 = 4.3 \text{ in}^2$

Try $A_{2x4} = 5.25 \text{ in}^2 > 4.3 \text{ in}^2$ √

Ck actual C_F

$C_F = 1.5 > 1.2$ which implies consv. √

If the actual C_F was smaller than our assumed one we would have had to redo the calc and verify in an iterative manner.

Use 2x4 DF-L No 1 lower chord

Recall that eccentricities at joints are common in the field. These will cause moment stresses at the joints in addition to the analyzed axial stresses of our calcs. A conservative approach should be taken to assure the stability and safety of the system.

I know God will not give me anything I can't handle. I just wish that He didn't trust me so much.

MOTHER TERESA

○ PROBLEM 3.2

Column design.

You are working on the facade of a multi-story department store. Determine the size of the column shown below.

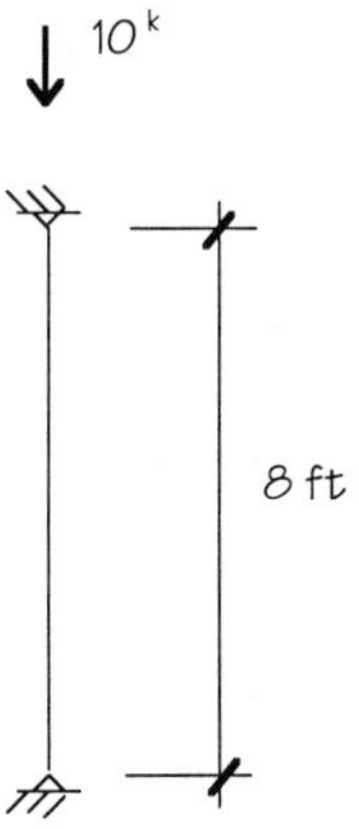

ASSUME

RDL + RLL.
DF-L No 1 column.
Pinned joints.
EMC < 19%.
Normal temperatures.
Neglect bolts holes.

SOLUTION

Column equations evaluate the tendency of the column to buckle along its two axes. The area to be used in this evaluation depends upon the location of any bolt holes. If the hole lies at a point where the column is restrained laterally (braced) we can use the gross area for the stability check. If the hole lies where the column is not braced we must calc using the net area. This type of problem requires an iterative methodology since we must first pre-select a trial size. Essentially, we select a trial size, ck, recalc and re-select as required. Recall that we should always check f_c with the net area without the stability reduction. See Appendix for column trial sizes based upon unbraced height.

Try 4x6

$F_c = 1.45$ ksi
$E = 1.7e3$ ksi
$A = 19.25\ in^2$

Calc the slenderness ratio

This ratio is a primary indicator of a column's tendency to buckle. If $E_x = E_y$, the largest value of the slenderness ratio of both axes is used in the calculation. We can see by inspection that our column will tend to buckle first in the y axis (along the x plane).

$$\left(\frac{\ell_e}{d}\right)_{max} = \left(\frac{K_e \ell}{d}\right)_y = \frac{1(8)12}{3.5} = 27.4$$ NDS T2.3.1

$K_{cE} = 0.3$ (visually graded lumber)

$c = 0.8$ (sawn lumber)

$$E' = EC_M C_t C_T = (1.7e3)1.0(1.0)1.0 = 1.7e3 \text{ ksi}$$

$$F_{cE} = \frac{K_{cE}E'}{\left(\ell_e/d\right)^2} = \frac{.3(1.7e3)}{(27.4)^2} = .68 \text{ ksi}$$

$$F_c^* = F_c C_D C_M C_t C_F = 1.45(1.25)1.0(1.0)1.1 = 1.99 \text{ ksi}$$ NDS 3.7.1.5

$$C_P = \frac{1+\left(F_{cE}/F_c^*\right)}{2c} - \sqrt{\left(\frac{1+\left(F_{cE}/F_c^*\right)}{2c}\right)^2 - \frac{\left(F_{cE}/F_c^*\right)}{c}}$$

NDS T2.3.1

$$C_P = \frac{1+\left(.68/1.99\right)}{2(.8)} - \sqrt{\left(\frac{1+\left(.68/1.99\right)}{2(.8)}\right)^2 - \frac{\left(.68/1.99\right)}{.8}} = .31$$

$F_c' = F_c C_D C_M C_t C_F C_P = 1.45(1.25)1.0(1.0)1.1(.31)$

$= .62$ ksi

Crushing ok by inspection.

$P = F_c' A = .62(19.3) = 11.97^k > 10^k$ √

Use 4x6 DF-L No 1 post

The formula for C_p is known as the column equation. It replaces the 3 previous equations that were used for columns prior to the 1991 NDS. The new equation makes the column curve continuous over the range of slenderness ratios. In the equation above, F_c^* is the allowable for crushing. The behavior of the column is defined in the equation from crushing modes to buckling modes as the slenderness ratio increases.

To laugh often and much; to win the respect of intelligent people and the affection of children; to earn the appreciation of honest critics and endure the betrayal of false friends; to appreciate beauty; to find the best in others; to leave the world a bit better, whether by a healthy child, a garden patch or a redeemed social condition; to know even one life has breathed easier because you have lived. This is to have succeeded.

EMERSON

PROBLEM 3.3

Column stability investigation.

The principal of your firm has accepted work as a expert witness for an insurance company investigation. She has asked you to investigate the subject column (shown) for stability.

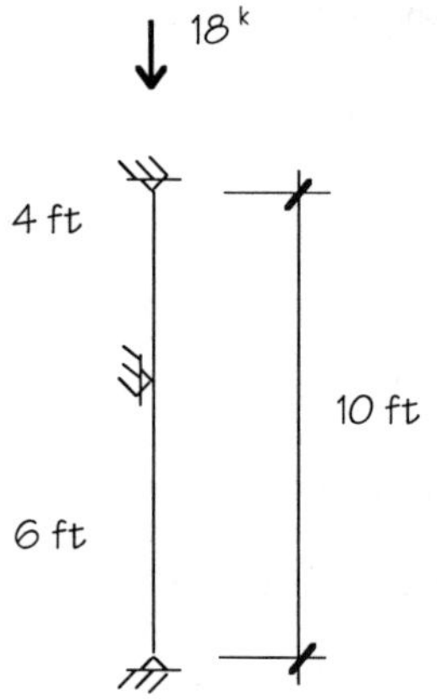

ASSUME

- RDL + RLL.
- DF-L No 1.
- Pinned jts.
- EMC < 19%.
- Normal temperatures.
- All bolts within braced zones.

SOLUTION

Ck 4x6

$F_c = 1.45$ ksi
$E = 1.7e3$ ksi
$A = 19.25$ in^2

Ck y axis (weak axis)

Since $E_x = E_y$ we could just compare $\frac{\ell_e}{d}$ and use the larger value. As an exercise do both.

$$\left(\frac{\ell_e}{d}\right)_y = \left(\frac{K_e\ell}{d}\right)_y = \frac{1(6)12}{3.5} = 20.6$$

NDS T2.3.1

$K_{cE} = 0.3$

$c = 0.8$

$E' = EC_MC_t = (1.7e3)1.0(1.0) = 1.7e3$ ksi

$$F_{cE} = \frac{K_{cE}E'}{\left(\ell_e/d\right)_y^2} = \frac{.3(1.7e3)}{(20.6)^2} = 1.2 \text{ ksi}$$

$F_c^* = F_cC_DC_MC_tC_F = 1.45(1.25)1.0(1.0)1.1 = 1.99$ ksi

NDS 3.7.1.5

$$C_P = \frac{1+\left(F_{cE}/F_c^*\right)}{2c} - \sqrt{\left(\frac{1+\left(F_{cE}/F_c^*\right)}{2c}\right)^2 - \frac{\left(F_{cE}/F_c^*\right)}{c}}$$

$$C_P = \frac{1+\left(1.2/1.99\right)}{2(.8)} - \sqrt{\left(\frac{1+\left(1.2/1.99\right)}{2(.8)}\right)^2 - \frac{\left(1.2/1.99\right)}{,8}} = .5$$

$F_c' = F_cC_DC_MC_tC_FC_P = 1.45(1.25)1.0(1.0)1.1(.5)$

$= .997$ ksi

$P = F_c'A = 1.0(19.3) = 19.3^k > 18^k$ √

Ck x axis (strong axis)

$$\left(\frac{\ell_e}{d}\right)_x = \left(\frac{K_e\ell}{d}\right)_x = \frac{1(10)12}{5.5} = 21.8$$

NDS T2.3.1

$K_{cE} = 0.3$

$c = 0.8$

$E' = EC_MC_t = (1.7e3)1.0(1.0) = 1.7e3$ ksi

$$F_{cE} = \frac{K_{cE}E'}{\left(\ell_e/d\right)_y^2} = \frac{.3(1.7e3)}{(21.8)^2} = 1.07 \text{ ksi}$$

$F_c^* = F_cC_DC_MC_tC_F = 1.45(1.25)1.0(1.0)1.1 = 1.99$ ksi

NDS 3.7.1.5

$$C_P = \frac{1+\left(F_{cE}/F_c^*\right)}{2c} - \sqrt{\left(\frac{1+\left(F_{cE}/F_c^*\right)}{2c}\right)^2 - \frac{\left(F_{cE}/F_c^*\right)}{c}}$$

$$C_P = \frac{1+\left(1.1/1.99\right)}{2(.8)} - \sqrt{\left(\frac{1+\left(1.1/1.99\right)}{2(.8)}\right)^2 - \frac{\left(1.1/1.99\right)}{.8}} = .47$$

$F_c' = F_cC_DC_MC_tC_FC_P = 1.45(1.25)1.0(1.0)1.1(.47)$

$= .94$ ksi

$P = F_c'A = .94(19.3) = 18.1^k > 18^k$ √

Note that strong axis stability governs. Do not forget that bearing may be a problem as well.

4x6 DF-L No 1 post ok.

One can never consent to creep when one feels an impulse to soar.

HELEN KELLER

PROBLEM 3.4

Glulam column capacity investigation.

Investigate the column shown for stability.

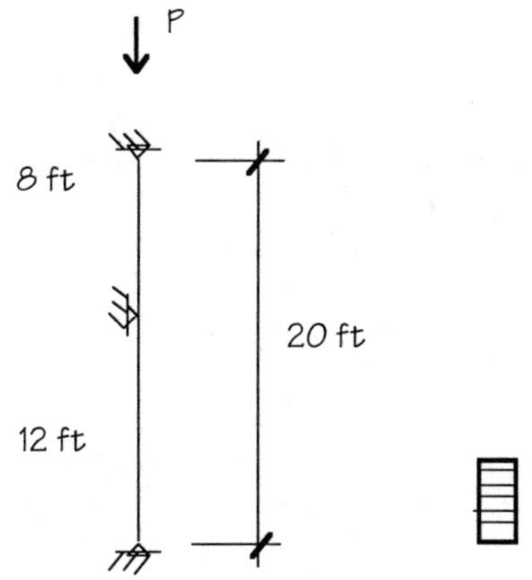

ASSUME

RDL + RLL.
5-1/8x10-1/2.
24F-V5 glulam.
Pinned joints.
EMC < 16%.
Normal temperatures.
All bolts within braced zones.

SOLUTION

Ck 5-1/8x10-1/2

$F_c = 1.45$ ksi
$E_x = 1.7e3$ ksi
$E_y = 1.5e3$ ksi
$A = 53.8\ in^2$

Ck y axis

$$\left(\frac{\ell_e}{d}\right)_y = \left(\frac{K_e \ell}{d}\right)_y = \frac{1(12)12}{5.125} = 28.1$$

NDS T2.3.1 $K_{cE} = 0.418$

$c = 0.9$

$E' = EC_M C_t = (1.5e3)1.0(1.0)1.0 = 1.5e3$ ksi

$$F_{cE} = \frac{K_{cE}E'}{\left(\ell_e/d\right)_y^{\,2}} = \frac{.418(1.5e3)}{(28.1)^2} = .79 \text{ ksi}$$

NDS 3.7.1.5 $F_c^* = F_c C_D C_M C_t = 1.45(1.25)1.0(1.0) = 1.8$ ksi

$$C_P = \frac{1+\left(F_{cE}/F_c^*\right)}{2c} - \sqrt{\left(\frac{1+\left(F_{cE}/F_c^*\right)}{2c}\right)^2 - \frac{\left(F_{cE}/F_c^*\right)}{c}}$$

$$C_P = \frac{1+\left(.79/1.8\right)}{2(.9)} - \sqrt{\left(\frac{1+\left(.79/1.8\right)}{2(.9)}\right)^2 - \frac{\left(.79/1.8\right)}{.9}} = .41$$

Ck x axis

NDS T2.3.1
$$\left(\frac{\ell_e}{d}\right)_x = \left(\frac{K_e \ell}{d}\right)_x = \frac{1(20)12}{10.5} = 22.9$$

$K_{cE} = 0.418$

$c = 0.9$ (for glulam)

$E' = EC_M C_t = (1.7e3)1.0(1.0)1.0 = 1.7e3$ ksi

$$F_{cE} = \frac{K_{cE}E'}{\left(\ell_e/d\right)_y^{\,2}} = \frac{.418(1.7e3)}{(22.9)^2} = 1.4 \text{ ksi}$$

$F_c^* = F_c C_D C_M C_t = 1.45(1.25)1.0(1.0) = 1.8$ ksi

NDS 3.7.1.5
$$C_P = \frac{1+\left(F_{cE}/F_c^*\right)}{2c} - \sqrt{\left(\frac{1+\left(F_{cE}/F_c^*\right)}{2c}\right)^2 - \frac{\left(F_{cE}/F_c^*\right)}{c}}$$

$$C_P = \frac{1+\left(1.4/1.8\right)}{2(.9)} - \sqrt{\left(\frac{1+\left(1.4/1.8\right)}{2(.9)}\right)^2 - \frac{\left(1.4/1.8\right)}{.9}} = .65 > .41$$

The y axis controls stability

$F_c' = F_c C_D C_M C_t C_P = 1.45(1.25)1.0(1.0)\ .41 = .74$ ksi

$P = F_c' A = .74(53.8) = 39.8^k$

Do not forget that bearing may be a problem as well.

$P_{allow} = 39.8^k$

The world is moving so fast these days that the man who says it can't be done is generally interrupted by someone doing it.

HARRY EMERSON FOSDICK

PROBLEM 3.5

Stud wall maximum vertical load carrying capacity.

Determine the maximum gravity load capacity of a typical 2x6 stud wall of DF-L stud grade lumber as shown below.

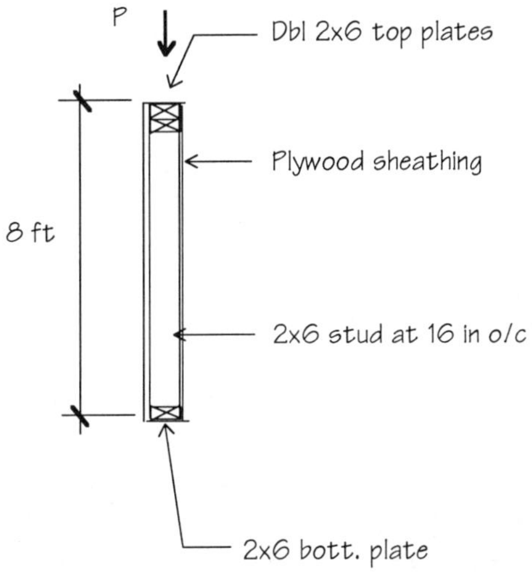

ASSUME

FDL + FLL.
DF-L stud grade.
Pinned joints.
EMC < 19%.
Normal temperatures.
Neglect loading condition of top plate.

SOLUTION

Ck 2x6

$F_c = .825$ ksi
$F_{c\perp} = .625$ ksi
$E = 1.4e3$ ksi
$A = 8.25\ in^2$

Compare slenderness ratios

Lateral support from sheathing gives:

$$\left(\frac{\ell_e}{d}\right)_y = \left(\frac{K_e\ell}{d}\right)_y = \frac{1.0(0)12}{1.5} = 0$$

$$\left(\frac{\ell_e}{d}\right)_x = \left(\frac{K_e\ell}{d}\right)_x = \frac{1.0\left(8-\left(\frac{3(1.5)}{12}\right)\right)12}{5.5} = 16.6$$

$16.6 > 0$

Strong axis governs

Ck capacity NDS T2.3.1

$K_{cE} = 0.3$

$c = 0.8$

$E' = EC_MC_t = (1.4e3)1.0(1.0)1.0 = 1.4e3$ ksi

$$F_{cE} = \frac{K_{cE}E'}{\left(\frac{\ell_e}{d}\right)_y^2} = \frac{.3(1.4e3)}{(16.6)^2} = 1.5 \text{ ksi}$$

$F_c^* = F_cC_DC_MC_tC_F = .825(1.0)1.0(1.0) = .83$ ksi

$$C_P = \frac{1+\left(F_{cE}/F_c^*\right)}{2c} - \sqrt{\left(\frac{1+\left(F_{cE}/F_c^*\right)}{2c}\right)^2 - \frac{\left(F_{cE}/F_c^*\right)}{c}}$$ NDS T2.3.1

$$C_P = \frac{1+\left(1.5/.83\right)}{2(.8)} - \sqrt{\left(\frac{1+\left(1.5/.83\right)}{2(.8)}\right)^2 - \frac{\left(1.5/.83\right)}{.8}} = .85$$

$F_c' = F_cC_DC_MC_tC_FC_P = .825(1.0)1.0(1.0)1.0(.85)$

$= .7$ ksi

$P = F_c'A = .7(8.25) = 5.8^k$

Ck bearing of bott. plate NDS T2.3.1

$$F_{c\perp}' = F_{c\perp}C_MC_tC_b = .625(1.0)1.0\left(\frac{1.5+.375}{1.5}\right)$$

$= .78$ ksi $> .69$ ksi

Stability governs
$P_{allow} = 5.8^k$

To love oneself is the beginning of a lifelong romance.

OSCAR WILDE

PROBLEM 3.6

Built-up column maximum vertical load capacity.

Determine the capacity of the built-up column shown below.

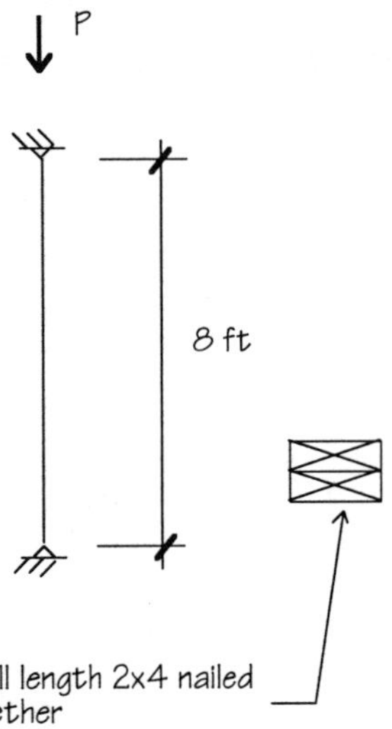

ASSUME

- FDL + FLL.
- DF-L No 1.
- Pinned joints.
- EMC < 19%.
- Normal temperatures.

SOLUTION

The capacity of built-up columns is less than that of a solid column of the same size. This is due to the shear distortion at the connector joints (commonly nails or bolts). Cover plates can improve the capacity somewhat.

$F_c = 1.45$ ksi
$E = 1.7e3$ ksi
$A = 5.25\ in^2$

Compare slenderness ratios

$$\left(\frac{\ell_e}{d}\right)_y = \left(\frac{K_e\ell}{d}\right)_y = \frac{1(8)12}{3} = 32.0$$ NDS 3.7.1.2

$$\left(\frac{\ell_e}{d}\right)_x = \left(\frac{K_e\ell}{d}\right)_x = \frac{1(8)12}{3.5} = 27.4 < 32.0$$

y axis governs

$K_{cE} = 0.3$ NDS T2.3.1

$c = 0.8$

$$E' = EC_MC_t = (1.7e3)1.0(1.0) = 1.7e3$$

$$F_{cE} = \frac{K_{cE}E'}{\left(\ell_e/d\right)^2} = \frac{.3(1.7e3)}{(32)^2} = .5\text{ ksi}$$

$$F_c^* = F_cC_DC_MC_tC_F = 1.45(1.0)1.0(1.0)1.15 = 1.7\text{ ksi}$$

$K_F = 0.6$

$$C_P = K_f\left(\frac{1+\left(F_{cE}/F_c^*\right)}{2c} - \sqrt{\left(\frac{1+\left(F_{cE}/F_c^*\right)}{2c}\right)^2 - \frac{\left(F_{cE}/F_c^*\right)}{c}}\right)$$ NDS 15.3.2.4

$$C_P = .6\left(\frac{1+(.5/1.7)}{2(.8)} - \sqrt{\left(\frac{1+(.5/1.7)}{2(.8)}\right)^2 - \frac{(.5/1.7)}{.8}}\right) = .16$$

$$F_c' = F_cC_DC_MC_tC_FC_P = 1.45(1.0)1.0(1.0)1.15(.16)$$
$$= .27\text{ ksi}$$

$$P = F_c'A = .27(5.25)2 = 2.8^k$$

$P_{allow} = 2.8^k$

The truth is that all of us attain the greatest success and happiness possible in this life whenever we use our native capacities to their greatest extent.

DR. SMILEY BLANTON

PROBLEM 3.7

Truss lower chord design with combined stress of bending and tension.

Determine the size of the lower chord in the following truss. Investigate chord for bending and tension only.

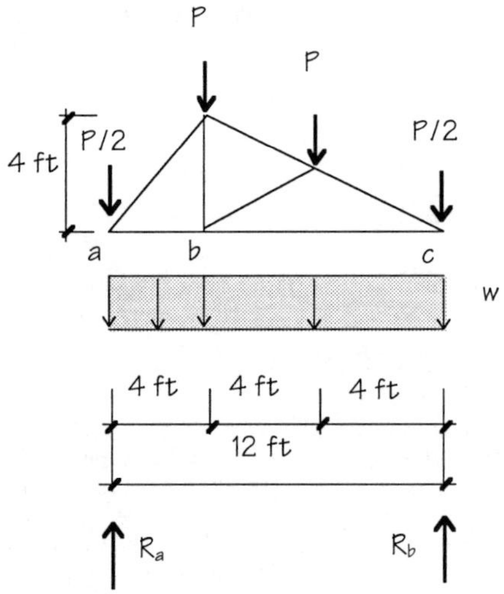

ASSUME

- $P = .51^k$ (RDL + RLL).
- $w = .048$ klf (DL).
- 3/4 in dia. bolts (1-row) at all connections.
- Pinned joints.
- EMC < 19%.
- Truss wt. included in above.
- Normal temperatures.
- Lateral buckling prevented.

SOLUTION

$TL = 3P + 12w = 3(.51) + 12(.048) = 2.1^k$

The distributed load to the bottom chord are converted to concentrated joint forces for analysis using the method of joints.

Find reactions

$$R_c = \frac{(4+8).51 + \left(.51/2\right)12 + 6(.048)4 + 4(.048)12}{12}$$

$= 1.05^k = R_a$

Resolve pertinent forces

Joint a

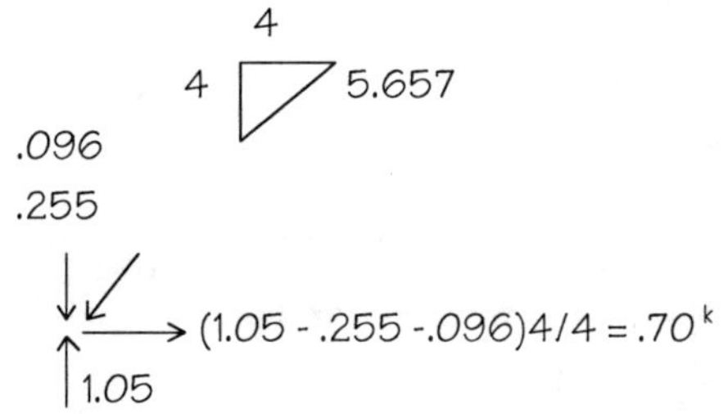

Joint c

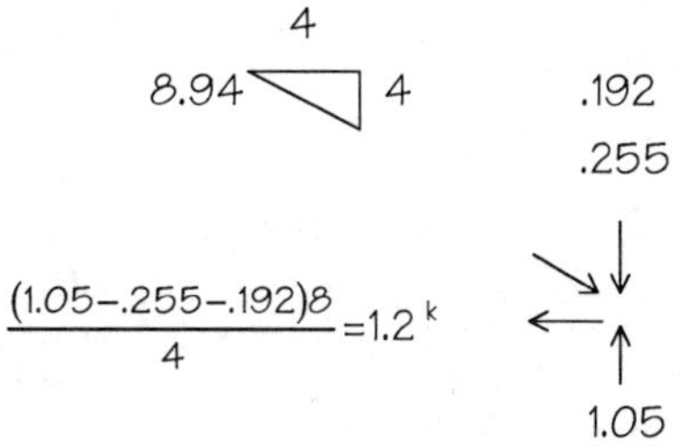

Mem b-c

Assume 2x DF-L No 3, $C_F = 1.3$

$F_t = .325$ ksi
$F_b = .5$ ksi

Tension (RDL + RLL governs by insp.)

Theoretically a pinned connection zone has a moment of zero. Axially at the net section we have:

$F_t' = F_T C_D C_M C_t C_F = .325(1.25)1.0(1.0)1.3 = .53$ ksi

NDS T2.3.1

$$\text{Req'd } A_n = \frac{P}{F_t'} = \frac{1.2}{.53} = 2.27 \text{ in}^2$$

Assume a 1/8 in larger dia. hole for the bolts.

$A_h = (3/4 + 1/8)1.5 = 1.3 \text{ in}^2$

$A_g = A_n + A_h = 2.3 + 1.3 = 3.6 \text{ in}^2$

Try $A_{2x4} = 5.25 \text{ in}^2 > 3.6 \text{ in}^2$ √

$S = 3.06 \text{ in}^3$

Ck actual C_F

$C_F = 1.5 > 1.3$ which implies consv. √

Tension ok at net section for 2x4

Bending (DL)

Lateral buckling is prevented which implies $C_L = 1.0$.

NDS 3.3.2

$$M = \frac{w\ell^2}{8} = \frac{.048(8)^2}{8} = .38^{\text{ k ft}}$$

$$f_b = \frac{M}{S} = \frac{.38(12)}{3.06} = 1.49 \text{ ksi}$$

Since our problem statement and assumptions stated that the load to the bottom chord was due to DL alone, $C_D = .9$ when we check independent bending stress alone.

NDS T2.3.1

$F_b' = F_b C_D C_M C_t C_L C_F C_r = .5(.9)1.0(1.0)1.0(1.5)1.0$

$= .68$ ksi < 1.49 ksi **NG !**

Since we know that we are going to have to satisfy combined stress requirements as well, increase the size and better the grade value. Try 2x6 DF-L No 1. Axial alone ok by inspection.

$F_t = .675$ ksi
$F_b = 1.0$ ksi
$A = 8.25 \text{ in}^2$
$S = 7.56 \text{ in}^3$

$$f_b = \frac{M}{S} = \frac{.38(12)}{7.56} = .6 \text{ ksi}$$

$F_b' = 1.0(.9)1.0(1.0)1.0(1.3)1.0 = 1.17$ ksi $> .6$ ksi √

Bending ok for 2x6 DF-L No 1

Combined stress

Now $C_D = 1.25$, as we are checking combined stresses. Per NDS notation:

$F_b' = F_b^{**} = F_b C_D C_M C_t C_L C_F C_r$

$= 1.0(1.25)1.0(1.0)1.0(1.3)1.0 = 1.63$ ksi

$F_t' = .675(1.25)1.0(1.0)1.3 = 1.1$ ksi

When we examine combined stress we are looking at the point of maximum bending stress as well as maximum tension stress. We, therefore, can use A_g to evaluate f_t. The tensile stress at the midpoint of "bc" is:

$$f_t = \frac{T}{A_g} = \frac{1.2}{8.25} = .15 \text{ ksi}$$

Use interaction equation

$$\frac{f_t}{F_t'} + \frac{f_b}{F_b^{**}} \le 1.0$$

NDS 3.9.1

$$\frac{.15}{1.1} + \frac{.6}{1.63} = .5 < 1.0 \quad √$$

This member is currently working at 50% allowable capacity. We could play with the size and grade to economize the member. This would not normally be done unless many trusses were to be constructed. The rationale goes like this; unless the cost that is going to be saved by changing the size or grade of the member is greater than the engineering design costs to make those changes, leave it as it is.

Do not forget the second interaction equation for tension and bending:

$$\frac{f_b - f_t}{F_b^{**}} \le 1$$

NDS 3.9.1

$$\frac{.6 - .15}{1.63} = .28 < 1.0 \quad √$$

When the member is under bending and tension, the beam stability factor (C_L) is reduced by the tension force. This is because the beam stability factor is a measure of the beam to buckle laterally on the "tension reduced" compression side of the member. Hence the use of the above equation. The volume factor (C_V) thus becomes the more critical factor of the two factors.

2x6 DF-L No 1 ok

Member a-b

Since both T and M are less than that in member b-c, say a-b ok.

> Use 2x6 DF-L No 1 for bottom chord

Far better it is to dare mighty things, to win glorious triumphs even though checkered by failure, than to rank with those poor spirits who neither enjoy nor suffer much because they live in the gray twilight that knows neither victory nor defeat.

THEODORE ROOSEVELT

PROBLEM 3.8

Truss top chord design with combined stress of bending and compression.

Determine the adequacy of the top chords in the following truss. Investigate the chord for bending and compression only.

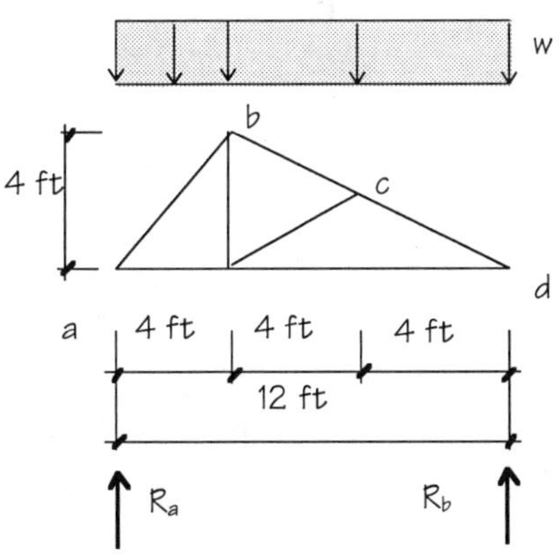

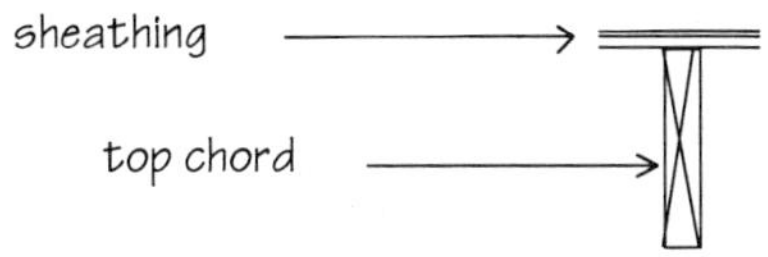

ASSUME

- Shear ok.
- w = .38 klf (RDL + RLL).
- 3/4 in dia. bolts (1-row) at all connections.
- DF-L No 1, 2x10 top chords.
- Pinned joints.
- EMC < 19%.
- Truss wt. included in above.
- Normal temperatures.
- Lateral buckling prevented by plywood.

SOLUTION

The distributed loads to the top chord are converted to concentrated joint forces for analysis using the method of joints.

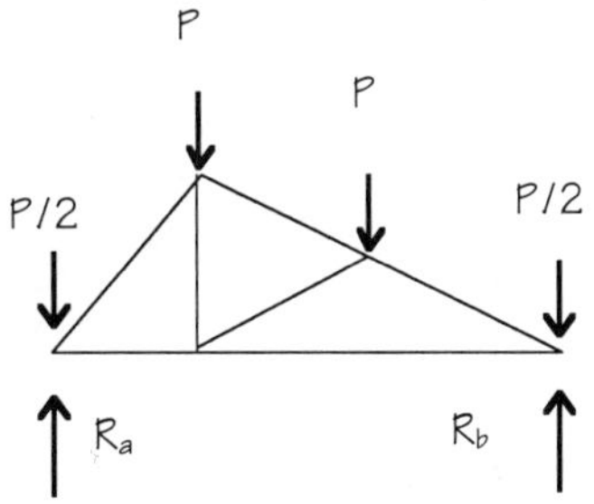

$P = 4(.38) = 1.52^k$

$TL = 3P = 3(1.52) = 4.56^k$

Find reactions

$$R_b = \frac{(4+8)1.52 + \left(\frac{1.52}{2}\right)12}{12} = 2.28^k = R_a$$

Joint a

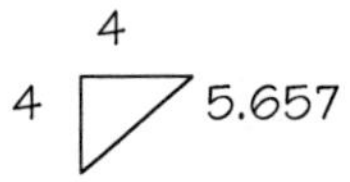

.76

$$\frac{(2.28-.76)5.66}{4} = 2.15^{k}$$

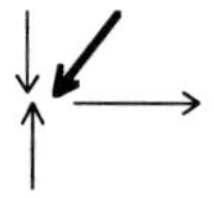

Joint d

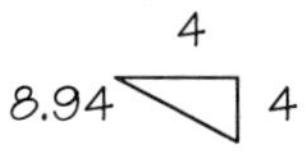

$$\frac{(2.28-.76)8.94}{4} = 3.4^{k}$$

Isolating the right top chord (where P max occurs) gives:

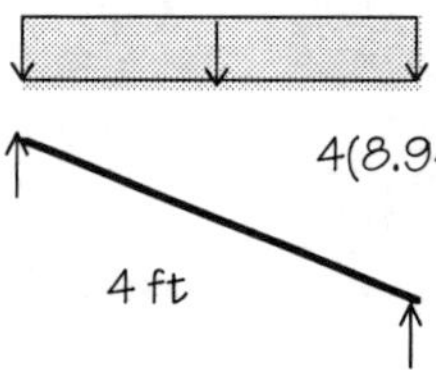

$$M = \frac{w\ell^2}{8} = \frac{.38(4)^2}{8} = .76^{\,k\,ft}$$

Mem b-c

$F_c = 1.45$ ksi
$F_b = 1.0$ ksi
$E = 1.7e3$ ksi
$A = 13.875$ in^2
$S = 21.39$ in^3

Ck axial compression

RDL + RLL governs by insp.

Stability (gross area)

Since lateral buckling is prevented by the sheathing, we can increase the truss chord stiffness by C_T:

$$\left(\ell_e/d\right)_y = 0$$ NDS 3.7.1.2

$$\left(\ell_e/d\right)_x = \left(12(4.47)/9.25\right) = 5.8$$

$$\ell_e = 12(4.47) = 53.6 \text{ in} < 96 \text{ in}$$

$$C_T = 1 + \frac{K_M \ell_e}{K_T E} = 1 + \frac{2.3(53.6)}{.59(1.7e3)} = 1.12$$

$$E' = EC_MC_tC_T = 1.7e3(1.0)1.0(1.12) = 1.9e3 \text{ ksi}$$

$K_{cE} = 0.3$ NDS T2.3.1

$c = 0.8$

$$F_{cE} = \frac{K_{cE}E'}{\left(\ell_e/d\right)_x^2} = \frac{.3(1.9e3)}{(5.8)^2} = 16.9 \text{ ksi}$$

$$F_c^* = F_cC_DC_MC_tC_F = 1.45(1.25)1.0(1.0)1.0 = 1.8 \text{ ksi}$$

$$C_P = \frac{1+\left(F_{cE}/F_c^*\right)}{2c} - \sqrt{\left(\frac{1+\left(F_{cE}/F_c^*\right)}{2c}\right)^2 - \frac{\left(F_{cE}/F_c^*\right)}{c}}$$ NDS 3.7.1.5

$$C_P = \frac{1+(16.9/1.8)}{2(.8)} - \sqrt{\left(\frac{1+(16.9/1.8)}{2(.8)}\right)^2 - \frac{(16.9/1.8)}{.8}} = .98$$

$$F_c' = F_cC_DC_MC_tC_FC_P = 1.45(1.25)1.0(1.0)1.0(.98)$$ NDS T2.3.1

$= 1.77$ ksi

$$P = F_c'A = 1.77(13.88) = 24.6^{k} > 3.4^{k} \;\checkmark$$

Compression ok at gross section

Ck axial at net section (moment = 0)

Theoretically, a pinned connection zone has a moment of zero. There is no reduction for stability because of the bracing at the joint. Axially at the net section we have:

NDS T2.3.1

$F_c' = F_c C_D C_M C_t C_F = 1.45(1.25)1.0(1.0)1.0 = 1.8$ ksi

$\text{Req'd } A_n = \frac{P}{F_c'} = \frac{3.4}{1.8} = 1.9 \text{ in}^2$

$A_h = (3/4 + 1/8)1.5 = 1.3 \text{ in}^2$

$A_g = A_n + A_h = 1.9 + 1.3 = 3.2 \text{ in}^2 < 13.875 \text{ in}^2$ √

Compression ok at net section

Bending (full lateral support)

$f_b = \frac{M}{S} = \frac{.76(12)}{21.4} = .43$ ksi

$F_b' = F_b C_D C_M C_t C_L C_F C_r = 1.0(1.25)1.0(1.0)1.0(1.1)1.0$

$= 1.38$ ksi $> .43$ ksi √

Bending ok

Combined stress

The combined stress interaction equation for bending and compressive stress is more complicated than for bending and tensile stress. This more critical stress occurs due to additional bending from the P-Δ effect.

$f_c = \frac{P}{A_g} = \frac{3.4}{13.875} = .25$ ksi

$C_D = 1.25$ based on the shortest duration for the combination

$F_{cE} = 15.2$ ksi based on the bending axis

Use interaction equation (NDS notation)

$$\left(\frac{f_c}{F_c'}\right)^2 + \frac{f_{b1}}{F_{b1}'\left(1-\left(f_c/F_{cE1}\right)\right)} + \frac{f_{b2}}{F_{b2}'\left(f_c/F_{cE2}\right)-\left(f_{b1}/F_{bE}\right)^2} \le 1.0$$

NDS 3.9.2

Because we have a concentric column force the above reduces to:

$$\left(\frac{f_c}{F_c'}\right)^2 + \frac{f_{b1}}{F_{b1}'\left(1-\left(f_c/F_{cE1}\right)\right)} \le 1.0$$

($F_{cE} = F_{cE1}$ etc. from above)

$$\left(\frac{.25}{1.8}\right)^2 + \frac{.43}{1.38\left(1-\left(.25/15.2\right)\right)} = .34 < 1.0 \quad √$$

This member is currently working at 34% allowable capacity. The design size is conservative and may not be economical based on the situation. In practice the rational goes like this; unless the cost that is going to be saved by changing the size or grade of the member is greater than the engineering design costs to make those changes, leave it as it is.

When the member is loaded in bending and compression the compression reduces the bending tension thus lessening the effect of the volume factor (C_v). The beam stability factor (C_L) thus becomes the more critical of the two factors.

2x10 top chord ok

▯
▯
▯

Procrastination is the fear of success. People procrastinate because they are afraid of the success that they know will result if they move ahead now. Because success is heavy, carries a responsibility with it, it is much easier to procrastinate and live on the "someday I'll" philosophy.

DENIS WAITLEY

PROBLEM 3.9

Combined axial and bending adequacy of stud wall.

Determine the adequacy of the 2x4 stud wall shown below. Investigate studs for bending and compression only. Revise as required.

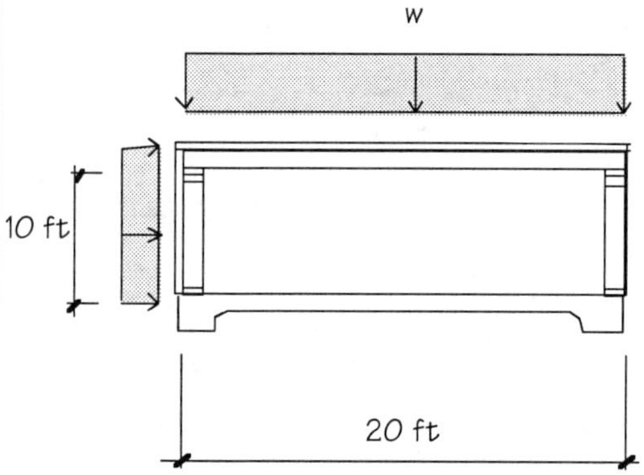

ASSUME

RLL = 12 psf.
RDL = 20 psf.
Wall DL = 16 psf.
P = 22.7 psf (wind).
F_P = 4.8 psf (seismic).
EMC < 19%.
DF-L No stud grade.
Normal temperatures.
Roof rafters at 24 in o/c.
2x4 studs at 16 in o/c.

SOLUTION

F_c = .825 ksi
F_b = .675 ksi
E = 1.4e3 ksi
A = 5.25 in^2
S = 3.06 in^3

Ck axial compression

$w_{RDL} = 10(.012) + 10(.016) = .28$ klf

$w_{RLL} = 10(.02) = .2$ klf

Evaluate load cases

DL ⇒ $1.33(.28) = .37^k$ with $C_D = .9$

DL + RLL ⇒ $1.33(.2 + .28) = .64^k$ with $C_D = 1.25$

Look at ratios (load case/C_D) for comparison to see which case will govern.

$$\frac{.37}{.9} = .41^k$$

$$\frac{.64}{1.25} = .51^k$$

The DL case will govern since .41 < .51. As an exercise perform the calculations for both cases.

DL case

$$f_c = \frac{P}{A_g} = \frac{.28}{5.25} = .053 \text{ ksi}$$

Since lateral buckling is prevented by the sheathing we have: NDS 3.7.1.2

$$\left(\ell_e/d\right)_x = 0$$

$$\left(\ell_e/d\right)_y = \left(10(12)/3.5\right) = 34.3$$

$E' = EC_MC_t = 1.4e3(1.0)1.0 = 1.4e3$ ksi NDS T2.3.1

$K_{cE} = 0.3$

$c = 0.8$

$$F_{cE} = \frac{K_{cE}E'}{\left(\ell_e/d\right)_x^2} = \frac{.3(1.4e3)}{(34.3)^2} = .36 \text{ ksi}$$

$$F_c^* = F_cC_DC_MC_tC_F = .825(.9)1.0(1.0)1.05 = .78 \text{ ksi}$$

$$C_P = \frac{1+\left(F_{cE}/F_c^*\right)}{2c} - \sqrt{\left(\frac{1+\left(F_{cE}/F_c^*\right)}{2c}\right)^2 - \frac{\left(F_{cE}/F_c^*\right)}{c}}$$ NDS 3.7.1.5

$$C_P = \frac{1+(.36/.78)}{2(.8)} - \sqrt{\left(\frac{1+(.36/.78)}{2(.8)}\right)^2 - \frac{(.36/.78)}{.8}} = .41$$

$F_c' = F_cC_DC_MC_tC_FC_P = .825(.9)1.0(1.0)1.05(.41)$

$= .32$ ksi > .053 ksi √

$$\frac{f_c}{F_c'} = \frac{.053}{.32} = .166$$

Axial ok for DL case

DL + RLL case

NDS 3.7.1.2

$$f_c = \frac{P}{A_g} = \frac{.27}{5.25} = .051\ \text{ksi}$$

Since lateral buckling is prevented by the sheathing we have from above:

$$\left(\frac{\ell_e}{d}\right)_x = 0$$

NDS 3.7.1.2

$$\left(\frac{\ell_e}{d}\right)_y = \left(\frac{10(12)}{3.5}\right) = 34.3$$

$E' = EC_MC_t = 1.4e3(1.0)1.0 = 1.4e3$ ksi

$K_{cE} = 0.3$

$c = 0.8$

$$F_{cE} = \frac{K_{cE}E'}{\left(\frac{\ell_e}{d}\right)_x^2} = \frac{.3(1.4e3)}{(34.3)^2} = .36\ \text{ksi}$$

NDS 3.7.1.5

$F_c^* = F_cC_DC_MC_tC_F = .825(1.25)1.0(1.0)1.05 = 1.08$ ksi

$$C_P = \frac{1+\left(F_{cE}/F_c^*\right)}{2c} - \sqrt{\left(\frac{1+\left(F_{cE}/F_c^*\right)}{2c}\right)^2 - \frac{\left(F_{cE}/F_c^*\right)}{c}}$$

$$C_P = \frac{1+\left(.36/1.08\right)}{2(.8)} - \sqrt{\left(\frac{1+\left(.36/1.08\right)}{2(.8)}\right)^2 - \frac{\left(.36/1.08\right)}{.8}} = .31$$

$F_c' = F_cC_DC_MC_tC_FC_P = .825(1.25)1.0(1.0)1.05(.31)$

$= .34$ ksi $> .051$ ksi √

$$\frac{f_c}{F_c'} = \frac{.051}{.34} = .15^k < .166^k$$

DL governs since under its load case the stud is working harder (at a higher percentage of it's capacity) $F_c' > f_c$ √

Axial ok, DL case governs

NDS 3.7.1.2

<u>Ck bearing on wall plates</u>

$$F_{c\perp}' = F_{c\perp}C_MC_tC_b = .625(1.0)1.0\left(\frac{1.5+.375}{1.5}\right)$$

$= .78$ ksi $> .053$ ksi √

Bearing ok

<u>Bending</u>

Full lateral support (of the y axis) is gained from sheathing so $C_L = 1.0$. Wind governs by inspection.

$$M = \frac{w\ell^2}{8} = \frac{22.7(10)^2 1.33}{8(1000)} = .38^{\,k\,ft}$$

$$f_b = \frac{M}{S} = \frac{.38(12)}{3.06} = 1.5\ \text{ksi}$$

$F_b' = F_bC_DC_MC_tC_LC_FC_r = .675(1.6)1.0(1.0)1.0(1.1)1.15$

$= 1.37$ ksi < 1.5 ksi **NG !**

We can either revise the size of the studs or change the grade of the studs (or both).

Revise grade of studs to DF-L No 2

$F_c = 1.3$ ksi
$F_b = .875$ ksi
$E = 1.6e3$ ksi

$F_b' = .875(1.6)1.0(1.0)1.0(1.1)1.15 = 1.8$ ksi > 1.5 ksi √

Previous axial stress ok by inspection.

Bending ok if upgrade studs to DF-L No 2

<u>Combined stress</u>

Since we upgraded the studs we must recalc the DL case. Recall that when calculating the combined stress case we need to consider one C_D throughout the interaction equation. Further note that we need not consider the RLL with lateral forces. This implies that the DL alone case (DL + FLL if we had one) would be used for combined stress calculations regardless of, or whether or not, it governed over the DL + RLL case. NDS 3.9.2

Re-evaluate DL case

$f_c = .053$ ksi

$\left(\frac{\ell_e}{d}\right)_y = 34.3$

$E' = EC_MC_t = 1.6e3(1.0)1.0 = 1.6e3$ ksi

$K_{cE} = 0.3$

$c = 0.8$

$$F_{cE} = \frac{K_{cE}E'}{\left(\frac{\ell_e}{d}\right)_x^2} = \frac{.3(1.6e3)}{(34.3)^2} = .41 \text{ ksi}$$

NDS 3.7.1.5

$F_c^* = 1.3(1.6)1.0(1.0)1.15 = 2.4$ ksi

$$C_P = \frac{1+\left(.41/2.4\right)}{2(.8)} - \sqrt{\left(\frac{1+\left(.41/2.4\right)}{2(.8)}\right)^2 - \frac{\left(.41/2.4\right)}{.8}} = .16$$

$F_c' = F_cC_DC_MC_tC_FC_P = 1.3(1.6)1.0(1.0)1.15(.16)$

$= .38$ ksi

NDS 3.9.2

$$\left(\frac{f_c}{F_c'}\right)^2 + \frac{f_{b1}}{F_{b1}'\left(1-\left(f_c/F_{cE1}\right)\right)} + \frac{f_{b2}}{F_{b2}'\left(f_c/F_{cE2}\right) - \left(f_{b1}/F_{bE}\right)^2} \le 1.0$$

Because we have a concentric column force, the above reduces to:

$$\left(\frac{f_c}{F_c'}\right)^2 + \frac{f_{b1}}{F_{b1}'\left(1-\left(f_c/F_{cE1}\right)\right)} \le 1.0$$

($F_{cE} = F_{cE1}$ etc. from above)

$$\left(\frac{.053}{.38}\right)^2 + \frac{1.5}{1.8\left(1-\left(.053/.41\right)\right)} = .98 < 1.0 \quad \checkmark$$

This member is currently working at 98% allowable capacity.

2x4 stud ok if upgraded to DF-L No 2

What's money? A man is a success if he gets up in the morning and goes to bed at night and in between does what he wants to do.

BOB DYLAN

○ PROBLEM 3.10

Combined axial and bending adequacy of column with wind loads from double doors.

Determine the adequacy of the beam column "a" (center post) shown below. Investigate for bending and compression only.

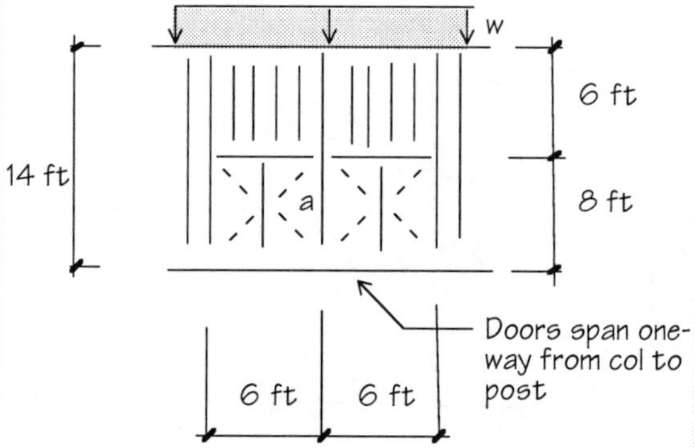

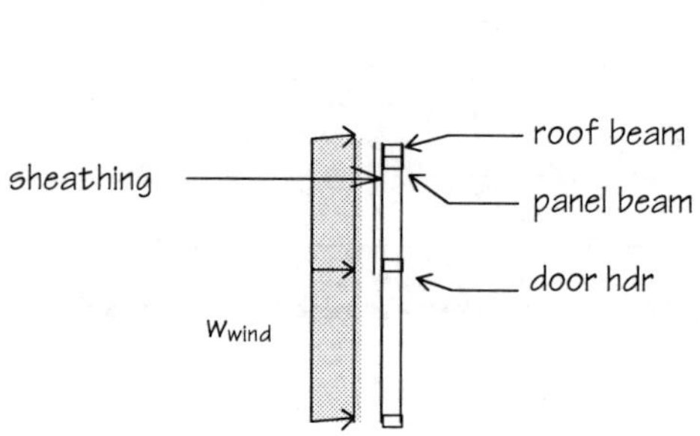

ASSUME

6x10 column.
Df-L No 1.
w_{wind} = 22.7 psf.
w_{RLL} = 32 klf.
w_{RDL} = 19 klf.
Wall DL = 16 psf.
Wind governs.
EMC < 19%.
Normal temperatures.
Neglect door weight.

SOLUTION

F_c = .925 ksi
F_b = 1.35 ksi
E = 1.6e3 ksi
A = 52.25 in^2
S = 82.73 in^3

Load case 1: (gravity loads)

Ck axial compression

RDL + RLL controls by inspection.

$P = P_{wall} + P_{RDL} + P_{RLL}$

$P_{wall} = 6(.016)6 = .58$ klf

$P_{RDL} = 6(.19) = 1.14^k$

$P_{RLL} = 6(.32) = 1.92^k$

$P = .58 + 1.14 + 1.92 = 3.64^k$

$$f_c = \frac{P}{A_g} = \frac{3.64}{52.25} = .07 \text{ ksi}$$

Lateral buckling along the y axis is prevented above the header by the sheathing. This implies that we would have partial fixity at the headerjoint. The recommended K_e = 0.7 (with a unbraced length of 8 ft). A lower value of K_e will give a shorter effective length. And, in effect, says that the particular axis is less sensitive to lateral buckling. In practice it is prudent to be conservative. The question is whether partial fixity is achieved in the field connection and just how much movement (slop) the connection undergoes before it tightens to achieve this partial fixity. The predominate rule of thumb is that unless the joint is engineered for end restraint, do not assume that it is achieved. Therefore, in this case we are justified to neglect the partial fixity and use a K_e of 1.0 and an unbraced length of 8 ft for the y axis. Since $E_x = E_y$ we can look at the slenderness ratios to determine which governs buckling.

NDS 3.7.1.2

$$\left(\frac{K_e \ell}{d}\right)_y = \left(\frac{1.0(8)12}{5.5}\right) = 17.5$$

$$\left(\frac{K_e \ell}{d}\right)_x = \left(\frac{1.0(14)12}{9.5}\right) = 17.7 > 17.5$$

The x axis governs

$E' = EC_MC_t = 1.6e3(1.0)1.0 = 1.6e3$ ksi NDS T2.3.1

$K_{cE} = 0.3$

$c = 0.8$

$$F_{cE} = \frac{K_{cE}E'}{\left(\frac{\ell_e}{d}\right)^2_{max}} = \frac{.3(1.6e3)}{(17.7)^2} = 1.53 \text{ ksi}$$

$C_F = 1.0$ (d < 12 in)

$F_c^* = F_cC_DC_MC_tC_F = .925(1.25)1.0(1.0)1.0 = 1.16$ ksi

$$C_P = \frac{1+\left(\frac{F_{cE}}{F_c^*}\right)}{2c} - \sqrt{\left(\frac{1+\left(\frac{F_{cE}}{F_c^*}\right)}{2c}\right)^2 - \frac{\left(\frac{F_{cE}}{F_c^*}\right)}{c}}$$ NDS 3.7.1.5

$$C_P = \frac{1+\left(\frac{1.5}{1.16}\right)}{2(.8)} - \sqrt{\left(\frac{1+\left(\frac{1.5}{1.16}\right)}{2(.8)}\right)^2 - \frac{\left(\frac{1.5}{1.16}\right)}{.8}} = .77$$ NDS T2.3.1

$F_c' = F_cC_DC_MC_tC_FC_P = .925(1.25)1.0(1.0)1.0(.77)$

$= .89$ ksi $> .07$ ksi √

Axial ok

Load Case 2: (DL + wind)

$C_D = 1.6$

You should verify this number with the local building department before using it in practice.

Ck axial compression

We need not consider the RLL with lateral forces. This implies that the DL alone case (DL + FLL if we had one) would be used for combined stress calculations regardless or whether or not it governed over the DL + RLL case. We must recalc the allowable stress in preparation for the combined stress analysis.

$P = P_{wall} + P_{RDL}$

$P = .58 + 1.14 = 1.72^k$

$$f_c = \frac{P}{A_g} = \frac{1.72}{52.25} = .033 \text{ ksi}$$

NDS T2.3.1 $\left(\frac{K_e \ell}{d}\right)_{max} = 17.7$

$E' = E C_M C_t = 1.6e3$ ksi

$K_{cE} = 0.3$

$c = 0.8$

$$F_{cE} = \frac{K_{cE} E'}{\left(\frac{\ell_e}{d}\right)^2_{max}} = 1.53 \text{ ksi}$$

$C_F = 1.0 \quad (d < 12 \text{ in})$

NDS 3.7.1.5 $F_c^* = F_c C_D C_M C_t C_F = .925(1.6)1.0(1.0)1.0 = 1.48$ ksi

$$C_P = \frac{1+\left(1.53/1.48\right)}{2(.8)} - \sqrt{\left(\frac{1+\left(1.53/1.48\right)}{2(.8)}\right)^2 - \frac{\left(1.53/1.48\right)}{.8}} = .7$$

$F_c' = F_c C_D C_M C_t C_F C_P = .925(1.6)1.0(1.0)1.0(.7)$
$= 1.04 \text{ ksi} > .033 \text{ ksi}$ √

Axial ok

<u>Bending</u> (assume studs at 16 in o/c)

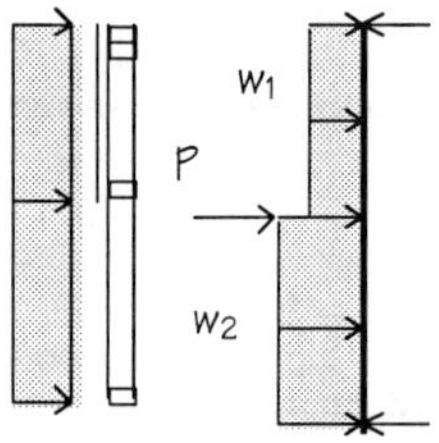

$w_1 = 1.33(.023) = .031$ klf (wall)

$w_2 = 3(.023) = .069$ klf (door)

door wall

$P = 4(3+3).023+3(3+3-1.33).023 = .874^k$

$M = 4.26^{kft}$ (comptr analysis)

$$f_b = \frac{M}{S} = \frac{4.26(12)}{82.73} = .62 \text{ ksi}$$

Considering lateral torsional buckling, we examine the potential movement in the plane of the wall (between door height).

Unbraced length $\ell_U = 8 \text{ ft} = 96$ in

$$\frac{\ell_U}{d} = \frac{96}{9.5} = 10.1 > 7$$

and < 14.3 which implies

$\ell_e = 1.63\ell_U + 3d = 1.63(96) + 3(9.5) = 185$ in NDS 3.3.3.6

$$R_B = \sqrt{\frac{\ell_e d}{b^2}} = \sqrt{\frac{185(9.5)}{5.5^2}} = 7.6 < 50 \ \surd$$

This beam is subject to lateral torsional buckling. Because of this movement in the y axis plane we need to consider the stability with E_y.

$E' = E_y(C_M)C_t = 1.7e3(1.0)1.0 = 1.7e3$ ksi

$$F_{bE} = \frac{K_{bE} E'y}{R_B^2} = \frac{.438(1.6e3)}{7.6^2} = 12.1 \text{ ksi}$$

$C_F = 1.0 \quad (d < 12 \text{ in})$

$F_b^* = F_b C_D C_M C_t C_F = 1.35(1.6)1.0(1.0)1.0 = 2.16$ ksi

$$C_L = \frac{1+\left(F_{bE}/F_{bx}^*\right)}{1.9} - \sqrt{\left(\frac{1+\left(F_{bE}/F_{bx}^*\right)}{1.9}\right)^2 - \frac{\left(F_{bE}/F_{bx}^*\right)}{.95}}$$ NDS 3.3.3.8

$$C_L = \frac{1+\left(12.1/2.16\right)}{1.9} - \sqrt{\left(\frac{1+\left(12.1/2.16\right)}{1.9}\right)^2 - \frac{\left(12.1/2.16\right)}{.95}} = .99$$

$F_b' = F_b C_D C_M C_t C_L C_F C_r = 1.35(1.6)1.0(1.0).99(1.0)1.0$

$= 2.1 \text{ ksi} > .62 \text{ ksi}$ √

Bending ok

<u>Combined stress</u>

Since we upgraded we must recalc DL case.

DL case

$f_c = .033$ ksi

$\left(\frac{\ell_e}{d}\right)_y = 17.7$

$E' = E C_M C_t = 1.6e3(1.0)1.0 = 1.6e3$ ksi

$K_{cE} = 0.3$

$c = 0.8$

The P- Δ effect is about the x axis so we can use our prior calc.

$$F_{cE} = \frac{K_{cE}E'}{\left(\ell_e/d\right)_x^2} = 1.53 \text{ ksi}$$

NDS 3.9.2

$$\left(\frac{f_c}{F_c'}\right)^2 + \frac{f_{b1}}{F_{b1}'\left(1-\left(f_c/F_{cE1}\right)\right)} + \frac{f_{b2}}{F_{b2}'\left(f_c/F_{cE2}\right)-\left(f_{b1}/F_{bE}\right)^2} \le 1.0$$

Because we have a concentric column force the above reduces to:

$$\left(\frac{.033}{1.04}\right)^2 + \frac{.62}{2.1\left(1-\left(.033/1.53\right)\right)} = .30 < 1.0 \quad \surd$$

This member is currently working at 30% allowable capacity. The design size is conservative and may not be economical based upon the situation.

6x10 column ok

Men for the sake of getting a living forget to live.

MARGARET FULLER

PROBLEM 3.11

Combined axial and bending adequacy of a column with a side bracket.

Determine the adequacy of the beam column with a side bracket shown below.

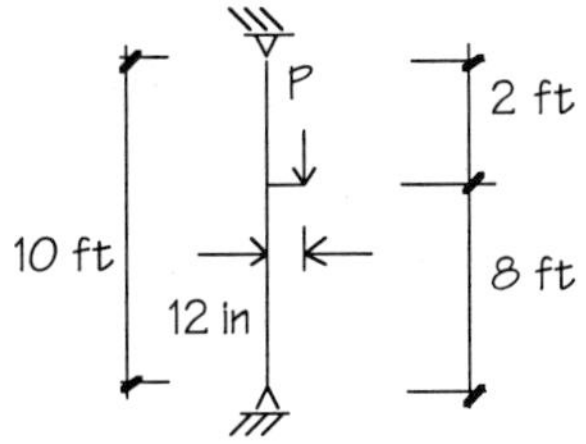

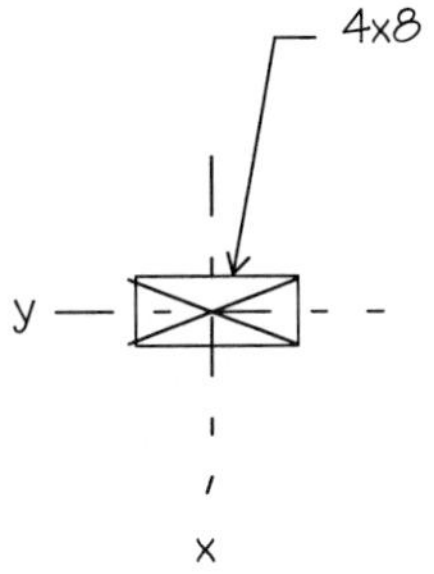

ASSUME

DF-L No 1.
$P = 5^k$ (DL + LL).
EMC < 19%.
Normal temperatures.

SOLUTION

$F_c = 1.45$ ksi
$F_b = 1.0$ ksi
$E = 1.7e3$ ksi
$A = 25.38 \text{ in}^2$
$S_x = 30.7 \text{ in}^3$
$S_y = 14.8 \text{ in}^3$

Ck axial compression

DL + LL controls by inspection.

$$f_c = \frac{P}{A_g} = \frac{5}{25.38} = .197 \text{ ksi}$$

Assume a K_e of 1.0 and an unbraced length of 10 ft for both axes.

NDS 3.7.1.2

$$\left(\frac{K_e\ell}{d}\right)_y = \left(\frac{1.0(10)12}{3.5}\right) = 34.3$$

$$\left(\frac{K_e\ell}{d}\right)_x = \left(\frac{1.0(10)12}{7.125}\right) = 16.8 < 34.3$$

Since $E_x = E_y$, the y axis governs.

NDS T2.3.1

$E' = EC_MC_t = 1.7e3(1.0)1.0 = 1.7e3$ ksi

$K_{cE} = 0.3$

$c = 0.8$

$$F_{cE} = \frac{K_{cE}E'}{\left(\frac{\ell_e}{d}\right)_{max}^2} = \frac{.3(1.7e3)}{(34.3)^2} = .43 \text{ ksi}$$

$C_F = 1.05$

$F_c^* = F_cC_DC_MC_tC_F = 1.45(1.25)1.0(1.0)1.05 = 1.9$ ksi

NDS 3.7.1.5

$$C_P = \frac{1+\left(\frac{F_{cE}}{F_c^*}\right)}{2c} - \sqrt{\left(\frac{1+\left(\frac{F_{cE}}{F_c^*}\right)}{2c}\right)^2 - \frac{\left(\frac{F_{cE}}{F_c^*}\right)}{c}}$$

$$C_P = \frac{1+\left(\frac{.43}{1.9}\right)}{2(.8)} - \sqrt{\left(\frac{1+\left(\frac{.43}{1.9}\right)}{2(.8)}\right)^2 - \frac{\left(\frac{.43}{1.9}\right)}{.8}} = .22$$

NDS T2.3.1

$F_c' = F_cC_DC_MC_tC_FC_P = 1.45(1.25)1.0(1.0)1.05(.22)$

$= .419$ ksi $> .197$ ksi ✓

Axial ok

Bending

NDS 15.4.2

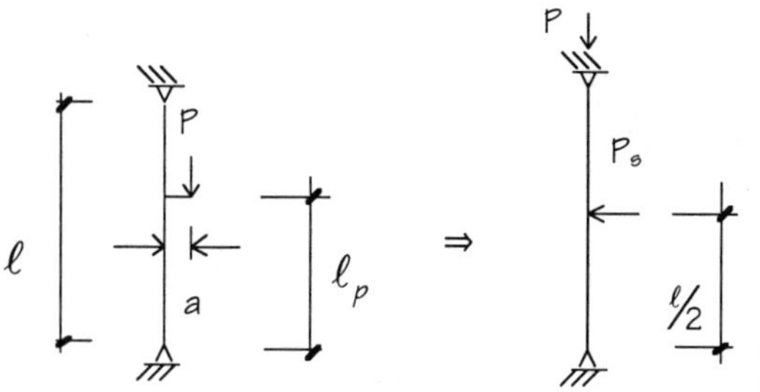

$$P_s = \frac{3Pa\ell_p}{\ell^2} = \frac{3(5)1.0(8)}{(10)^2} = 1.2^{\,k}$$

$$M = \frac{P_s\ell}{4} = \frac{1.2(10)}{4} = 3.0^{\,k\,ft}$$

$$f_{bx} = \frac{M}{S} = \frac{3.0(12)}{30.7} = 1.17 \text{ ksi}$$

Lateral Stability

For potential lateral torsional buckling, the buckling movement will occur about the plane of the y axis.

Unbraced length $\ell_U = 10$ ft $= 120$ in

$$\frac{\ell_U}{d} = \frac{120}{7.125} = 16.8 > 14.3$$

Which implies: NDS T3.3.3

$\ell_e = 1.84\ell_U = 1.84(120) = 220.8$ in

$$R_B = \sqrt{\frac{\ell_e d}{b^2}} = \sqrt{\frac{220.8(7.125)}{3.5^2}} = 11.3 < 50 \ ✓$$ NDS 3.3.3.6

This beam is subject to lateral torsional buckling. Because of this buckling movement about the y axis, we need to consider the stability with E_y.

$E' = E_y(C_M)C_t = 1.7e3(1.0)1.0 = 1.7e3$ ksi NDS T2.3.1

$$F_{bE} = \frac{K_{bE}E'y}{R_B^2} = \frac{.438(1.7e3)}{11.3^2} = 5.8 \text{ ksi}$$

$F_b^* = F_bC_DC_MC_tC_F = 1.0(1.25)1.0(1.0)1.3 = 1.63$ ksi

$$C_L = \frac{1+\left(\frac{F_{bE}}{F_{bx}^*}\right)}{1.9} - \sqrt{\left(\frac{1+\left(\frac{F_{bE}}{F_{bx}^*}\right)}{1.9}\right)^2 - \frac{\left(\frac{F_{bE}}{F_{bx}^*}\right)}{.95}}$$ NDS 3.3.3.8

$$C_L = \frac{1+\left(\frac{5.8}{1.63}\right)}{1.9} - \sqrt{\left(\frac{1+\left(\frac{5.8}{1.63}\right)}{1.9}\right)^2 - \frac{\left(\frac{5.8}{1.63}\right)}{.95}} = .98$$

$F_b' = F_bC_DC_MC_tC_LC_FC_r = 1.0(1.25)1.0(1.0).98(1.3)1.0$ NDS T2.3.1

$= 1.59$ ksi > 1.17 ksi ✓

Bending ok

NDS 3.9.2, 15.4.1

Combined stress

$\left({}^{\ell_e}\!/_{d}\right)_x = 16.8$

$E' = 1.7e3$ ksi

The P- Δ effect is about the x axis so we can use our prior calc. Amplification factor for eccentric bending is thus:

$$F_{cE} = \frac{K_{cE}E'}{\left({}^{\ell_e}\!/_{d}\right)_x^2} = .43 \text{ ksi}$$

The reduced equation for this circumstance is:

$$\left(\frac{f_c}{F_c'}\right)^2 + \frac{f_{b1} + f_c\left({}^{6e_1}\!/_{d_1}\right)\left(1 + 0.234\left({}^{f_c}\!/_{F_{cE1}}\right)\right)}{F_{b1}'\left(1 - \left({}^{f_c}\!/_{F_{cE1}}\right)\right)} \leq 1.0$$

$$\left(\frac{.197}{.42}\right)^2 + \frac{1.17 + .197\left({}^{6(12)}\!/_{7.125}\right)\left(1 + 0.234\left({}^{.197}\!/_{.43}\right)\right)}{1.59\left(1 - \left({}^{.197}\!/_{.43}\right)\right)}$$

$= 4.1 < 1.0$ **NG!**

4x8 column NG!

Every good thought you think is contributing its share to the ultimate result of your life.

GRENVILLE KLEISER

PROBLEM 3.12

Round columns.

The principal of your firm is having her winter cabin in the mountains renovated by a local architect. She has asked you to help her with one of the round columns of the new interior design. Investigate the column (shown) for stability only.

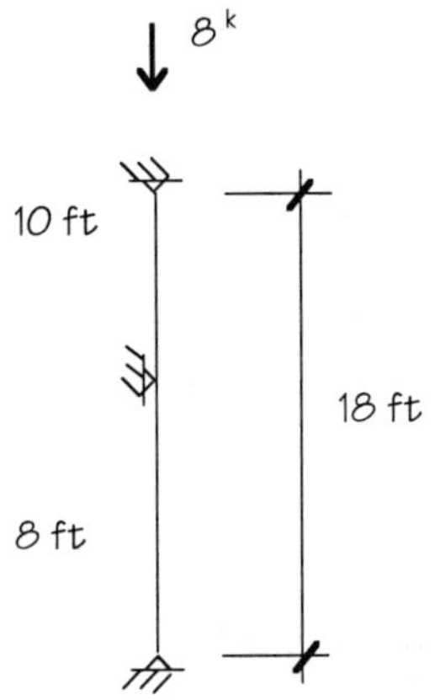

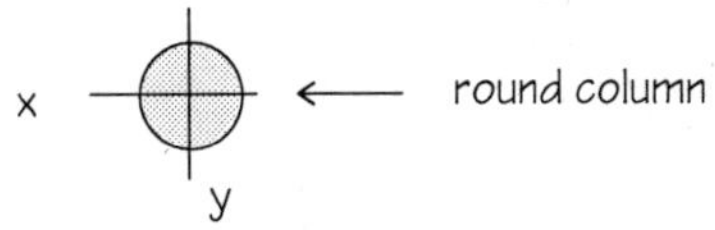

ASSUME

RDL + RLL + FDL + FLL.
DF-L.
Pinned jts.
EMC < 16%.
Normal temperatures.
All bolts within braced zones.
$C_D = 1.0$.

SOLUTION

The load carrying capacity of a round column is generally thought of as equal to a square column that has the same cross-sectional area. To demonstrate this we will do this problem two ways. First we will size the column as if it were square and then select a round column of the same cross sectional area. Then we will redo the problem as a round column and compare the two methods.

Try 6x6 column NDS T6A

Assume DF - L No 1

$F_c = .925$ ksi
$E = 1.6e3$ ksi
$A = 30.25$ in^2 (5.5 x 5.5 square)

Column stability factor

Since Ey = Ex, and the column is square (or round) the 18 foot unbraced length will govern design.

$$\left(\frac{\ell_e}{d}\right) = \left(\frac{K_e\ell}{d}\right) = \frac{1(18)12}{5.5} = 39.3$$

$K_{cE} = 0.3$

NDS T2.3.1

$c = 0.8$

$E' = EC_MC_tC_T = (1.6e3)1.0(1.0)1.0 = 1.6e3$ ksi

$$F_{cE} = \frac{K_{cE}E'}{\left(\ell_e/d\right)_y^2} = \frac{.3(1.6e3)}{(39.3)^2} = .31 \text{ ksi}$$

$F_c^* = F_cC_DC_MC_tC_F = .925(1.0)1.0(1.0)1.0 = .925$ ksi

NDS 3.7.1.5

$$C_P = \frac{1+\left(F_{cE}/F_c^*\right)}{2c} - \sqrt{\left(\frac{1+\left(F_{cE}/F_c^*\right)}{2c}\right)^2 - \frac{\left(F_{cE}/F_c^*\right)}{c}}$$

$$C_P = \frac{1+\left(.31/.925\right)}{2(.8)} - \sqrt{\left(\frac{1+\left(.31/.925\right)}{2(.8)}\right)^2 - \frac{\left(.31/.925\right)}{.8}} = .31$$

NDS T2.3.1

$F_c' = F_cC_DC_MC_tC_FC_P = .925(1.0)1.0(1.0)1.0(.31)$

$= .27$ ksi

$P = F_c'A = .27(30.25) = 8.2^k > 8^k$ √

Convert to equivalent round column area and select diameter.

TCM 5.8.4

$D = 1.128d = 1.128(5.5) = 6.2$ in dia.

Do not forget that bearing may be a problem as well. And that the pole must have the same tabular values as used above.

> 6.2 in dia. pole is equivalent to a 6x6 DF- L No 1 column which is ok

TCM T6A

Try 6.2 in dia. column

See NDS sec 6.1 for round timbers.

$F_c = 1.25$ ksi

$E = 1.5e3$ ksi

$$A = \frac{\pi D^2}{4} = \frac{\pi(6.2)^2}{4} = 30.2 \text{ in}^2$$

$r = D/4 = 6.2/4 = 1.55$ in

TCM 5.8.4

$$\left(\frac{\ell_e}{r}\right) = \left(\frac{K_e\ell}{r}\right) = \frac{1(18)12}{1.55} = 139.4 < 175 \;\surd$$

$K_{cE} = 0.3$

TCM T6.3.1

$c = 0.85$

$E' = EC_t = (1.5e3)1.0 = 1.5e3$ ksi

$$F_{cE} = \frac{12K_{cE}E'}{\left(\ell_e/r\right)^2} = \frac{(12).3(1.5e3)}{(139.4)^2} = .29 \text{ ksi}$$

The design values may be permitted to be increased 0.2% for every foot the critical section is from the tip of the column. Thus C_{cs} is:

TCM T6.3.1

$C_{cs} = 1.0 + L_c(0.002) = 1.0 + 9(0.002) = 1.02$

$F_c^* = F_cC_DC_tC_uC_{sp}C_{cs} = 1.25(1.0)1.0(.8)1.02 = 1.02$ ksi

$$C_P = \frac{1+\left(F_{cE}/F_c^*\right)}{2c} - \sqrt{\left(\frac{1+\left(F_{cE}/F_c^*\right)}{2c}\right)^2 - \frac{\left(F_{cE}/F_c^*\right)}{c}}$$

NDS 3.7.1.5

$$C_P = \frac{1+\left(.29/1.02\right)}{2(.85)} - \sqrt{\left(\frac{1+\left(.29/1.02\right)}{2(.85)}\right)^2 - \frac{\left(.29/1.02\right)}{.85}} = .27$$

$F_c' = F_cC_DC_MC_tC_FC_P = 1.02(.27) = .28$ ksi

$P = F_c'A = .28(30.2) = 8.5^k > 8^k$ √

> 6.2 in dia. pole is ok

As we can see, both methods gave us adjusted values that were greater than the required load. However, the round column design method gives a higher value in this example. In fact, in this case the difference is: 8.5/8.2 = 1.04, implying a 4% increase.

Since it is just as easy to calculate the column as round rather than as square (then converting to round), use the second method for more accuracy.

□
□
□

I am different from Washington; I have a higher, grander standard of principle. Washington could not lie. I can, But I won't.

MARK TWAIN

PROBLEM 3.13

Spaced columns.

The contractor of a project you engineered in the Midwest can not acquire the 10x10 post you specified to meet her construction deadlines. She has asked you to help her by doing the field engineering change order of substituting the 10x10 post with a spaced column consisting of the materials (4x10) she has on hand. Investigate the spaced column (shown) for stability only.

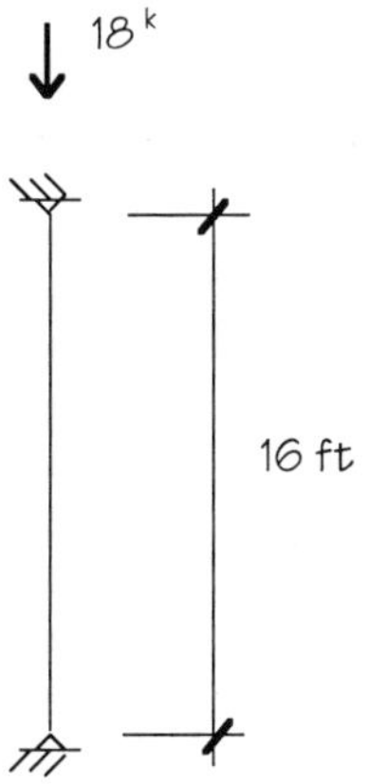

ASSUME

RDL + RLL.
DF-L No 1.
Pinned jts.
EMC < 16%.
Normal temperatures.
All bolts within braced zones.
$C_D = 1.25$.
4x10's on hand.

SOLUTION

Due to the fixity (and shear resistance) at the ends of a spaced column, the capacity of column is increased beyond the individual members that comprise it.

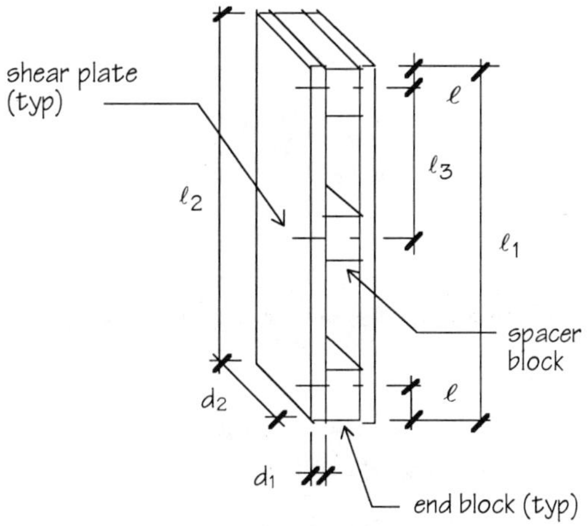

Try 2 - 4x10 spaced column

$F_c = 1.45$ ksi
$E = 1.7e3$ ksi
$A = 32.38 \text{ in}^2$ (one member)

Column stability factor

Buckling about y axis

$$\left(\frac{\ell_e}{d}\right) = \frac{(16)12}{3.5} = 54.9$$

$K_{cE} = 0.3$

$c = 0.8$

Assume the end distance for the shear plate constitutes condition "a" for fixity (K_x = 2.5).

NDS T2.3.1

$$E' = EC_M C_t C_T = (1.7e3)1.0(1.0)1.0 = 1.7e3 \text{ ksi}$$

$$F_{cE} = \frac{K_{cE} K_x E'}{\left(\ell_e/d\right)^2} = \frac{.3(2.5)(1.7e3)}{(54.9)^2} = .42 \text{ ksi}$$

$$F_c^* = F_c C_D C_M C_t C_F = 1.45(1.25)1.0(1.0)1.0 = 1.8 \text{ ksi}$$

NDS 15.2.3.3

$$C_P = \frac{1+\left(F_{cE}/F_c^*\right)}{2c} - \sqrt{\left(\frac{1+\left(F_{cE}/F_c^*\right)}{2c}\right)^2 - \frac{\left(F_{cE}/F_c^*\right)}{c}}$$

$$C_P = \frac{1+(.42/1.9)}{2(.8)} - \sqrt{\left(\frac{1+(.42/1.9)}{2(.8)}\right)^2 - \frac{(.42/1.9)}{.8}} = .21$$

NDS T2.3.1

$$F_c' = F_c C_D C_M C_t C_F C_P = 1.8(.21) = .38 \text{ ksi}$$

$$P = F_c' A2 = .38(25.4)2 = 19.3^k > 18^k \ \checkmark$$

Do not forget to check bearing as it may be a problem as well.

4x8 spaced column ok

Connector design

NDS 15.2.2.5

Our member is in the group B species so:

$$K_s = 8.14\left(\ell_1/d_1 - 11\right) \le 399$$

$$= 8.14(54.9 - 11) = 357 < 399 \ \checkmark$$

Total load to connector

$$K_s A = 357(32.4) = 11567 \text{ lb}$$

NDS T7.3.1

Allowable load for connector

(assume 2- 4 in dia.)

$$2P' = PC_D C_M C_t C_g C_\Delta C_d C_{st}$$

$$= (2)5.26(1.25)1.0(1.0)1.0(1.0)1.0(1.0)$$

$$= 13.2^k < 11.6^k \ \checkmark$$

Use 2 - 4 in dia. split rings

Use spacing specified in NDS Table 10.3.

Love truth, but pardon error.

VOLTAIRE

PROBLEM 3.14

Combined axial and bending about both axis of a header.

You are a lead supervisor in your engineering firm. You need to determine the adequacy of the beam column shown below. Investigate for bending and compression only.

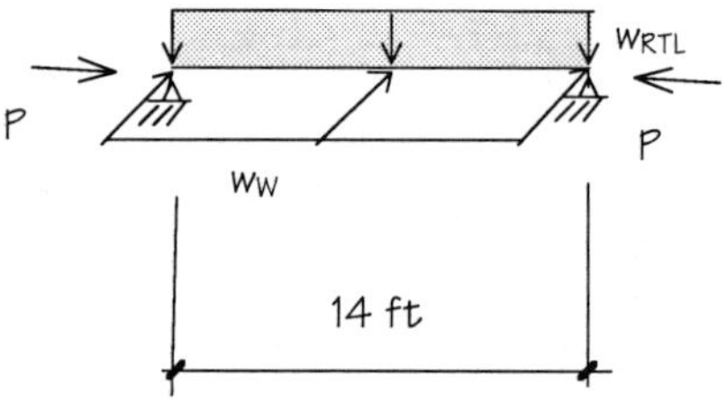

ASSUME

- 6x12 header fully supported by diaphragm.
- DF- L No 1.
- $P = 1.8^k$.
- w_W = .16 klf.
- w_{RTL} = .32 klf.
- LL/DL = 1.7 .
- Wind governs.
- EMC < 19%.
- Normal temperatures.

SOLUTION

$F_c = .925$ ksi
$F_b = 1.35$ ksi
$E = 1.6e3$ ksi
$A = 63.25\ in^2$
$S_x = 121.2\ in^3$
$S_y = 57.98\ in^3$

Load case 1: (gravity loads)

Ck bending

RDL + RLL controls by inspection.

$$M = \frac{w\ell^2}{8} = \frac{.32(14)^2}{8} = 7.84^{\,k\,ft}$$

$$f_b = \frac{M}{S} = \frac{7.84(12)}{121.2} = .78 \text{ ksi}$$

Lateral torsional buckling is prevented by the roof diaphragm which implies $C_L = 1.0$.

$C_F = 1.0$ ($d \leq 12$ in)

NDS T2.3.1 $F_b' = F_bC_DC_MC_tC_LC_FC_r = 1.35(1.25)1.0(1.0)1.0(1.0)1.0$

$= 1.69$ ksi $> .78$ ksi √

Bending ok for case 1

Load Case 2: (RTL + wind)

$C_D = 1.6$

You should verify C_D with the local building department before using it in practice.

Ck axial compression

NDS 3.7.1.2 $$f_c = \frac{P}{A_g} = \frac{1.8}{63.25} = .03 \text{ ksi}$$

$$\left(\frac{K_e\ell}{d}\right)_{max} = \left(\frac{1.0(14)12}{11.5}\right) = 14.6 \text{ in}$$

NDS T2.3.1 $E' = EC_MC_t = 1.6e3(1.0)1.0 = 1.6e3$ ksi

$K_{cE} = 0.3$

$c = 0.8$

NDS 3.7.1.5 $$F_{cE} = \frac{K_{cE}E'}{\left(\frac{\ell_e}{d}\right)^2_{max}} = \frac{.3(1.6e3)}{(14.6)^2} = 2.25 \text{ ksi}$$

$C_F = 1.0$ ($d < 12$ in)

$F_c^* = F_cC_DC_MC_tC_F = .925(1.6)1.0(1.0)1.0 = 1.48$ ksi

$$C_P = \frac{1+\left(2.25/1.48\right)}{2(.8)} - \sqrt{\left(\frac{1+\left(2.25/1.48\right)}{2(.8)}\right)^2 - \frac{\left(2.25/1.48\right)}{.8}}$$

$= .81$

NDS T2.3.1 $F_c' = F_cC_DC_MC_tC_FC_P = 1.48(.81) = 1.2$ ksi $> .03$ ksi √

Axial ok for case 2

Bending

$$M = \frac{w\ell^2}{8} = \frac{.16(14)^2}{8} = 3.9^{\,k\,ft}$$

$$f_b = \frac{M}{S} = \frac{3.9(12)}{57.98} = .81 \text{ ksi}$$

NDS 4.3.3 Considering lateral torsional buckling, we examine the potential movement in the plane of the wall. Here we look at the member with the lateral load applied as if the member were lying flat. The NDS sec. 3.3.1 indicates that $C_L = 1.0$ and no lateral support is required if $d < b$. This is true in our case so $C_L = 1.0$. Also note that $C_{fu} = 1.0$ for a 5x5 or larger member.

NDS T2.3.1 $F_b' = F_bC_DC_MC_tC_LC_FC_rC_{fu}$

$= 1.35(1.6)1.0(1.0)1.0(1.0)1.0(1.0$

$= 2.2$ ksi $> .81$ ksi √

Bending ok for wind case 2

However, we will need F_{bE} for combined stress. Say the unbraced length $\ell_U = 6$ in :

NDS T3.3.3 $$\frac{\ell_U}{d} = \frac{6}{11.5} = .52 > 7$$

$\ell_e = 2.06\,\ell_u = 2.06(6) = 12.4$ in

NDS 3.3.3.6 $$R_B = \sqrt{\frac{\ell_e d}{b^2}} = \sqrt{\frac{12.4(11.5)}{5.5^2}} = 2.2 < 50 \ \surd$$

$E' = E_y(C_M)C_t = 1.6e3(1.0)1.0 = 1.6e3$ ksi

$$F_{bE} = \frac{K_{bE}E'y}{R_B^2} = \frac{.438(1.6e3)}{2.2^2} = 144.8 \text{ ksi}$$

Combined stress

We must recalc the allowable bending stress for DL because we need not consider the RLL with lateral forces. This implies that the DL alone case (DL + FLL if we had one) should be used for combined stress calculations regardless of, or whether or not, it governed over the DL + RLL case. We must recalc the allowable bending stress in preparation for the combined stress analysis.

NDS T2.3.1

$F_b' = F_bC_DC_MC_tC_LC_FC_r = 1.35(1.6)1.0(1.0)1.0(1.0)1.0$

$= 2.16$ ksi

$TL = DL + LL = DL + 1.7DL = .32$

$DL = .12$ klf

$f_b = \frac{.78(.12)}{.32} = .29$ ksi

$f_c = .053$ ksi

$\left(\ell_e/d\right)_y = 17.7$

$E' = EC_MC_t = 1.6e3(1.0)1.0 = 1.6e3$ ksi

$K_{cE} = 0.3$

$c = 0.8$

$F_{cE2} = \frac{K_{cE}E'}{\left(\ell_e/d\right)^2} = \frac{.3(1.6e3)}{\left(168/5.5\right)^2} = .51$ ksi

NDS 3.9.2

$$\left(\frac{f_c}{F_c'}\right)^2 + \frac{f_{b1}}{F_{b1}'\left(1-\left(f_c/F_{cE1}\right)\right)} + \frac{f_{b2}}{F_{b2}'\left(1-\left(f_c/F_{cE2}\right)-\left(f_{b1}/F_{bE}\right)^2\right)} \le 1.0$$

$$\left(\frac{.03}{1.2}\right)^2 + \frac{.81}{2.2\left(1-\left(.03/2.25\right)\right)} + \frac{.29}{2.16\left(1-\left(.03/.51\right)-\left(.81/144.8\right)^2\right)}$$

$= .52 < 1.0$ √

This member is currently working at 51% allowable capacity. The design size is conservative and may not be economical based upon the situation.

6x12 header ok

▯
▯
▯

I am not a pessimist; to perceive evil where it exists is, in my opinion, a form of optimism.

ROBERTO ROSSELLINI

PROBLEM 3.15

Combined axial and bending adequacy of a column with new loads and minimum eccentricity.

An old storage facility column supports 2 floors as shown below. The owners of the building want to check if the column can support additional loads.

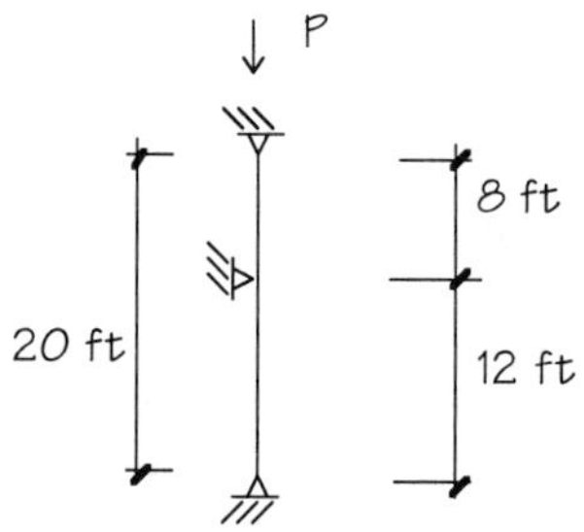

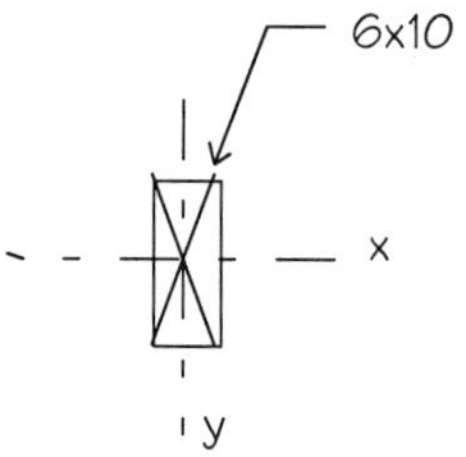

ASSUME

$P_{old} = 10^k$ (DL + LL).
$P_{new} = 5^k$.

DF-L No 1.
EMC < 19%.
Normal temperatures.

SOLUTION

$F_c = 1.0$ ksi
$F_b = 1.2$ ksi
$E = 1.6e3$ ksi
$A = 52.25$ in^2
$S_x = 82.73$ in^3
$S_y = 47.9$ in^3

Ck axial compression

DL + LL controls by inspection.

$$f_c = \frac{P}{A_g} = \frac{15}{52.25} = .29 \text{ ksi}$$

Assume a K_e of 1.0 and a unbraced length of 20 ft for the x axis and 12 ft for the y axis.

NDS 3.7.1.2

$$\left(\frac{K_e\ell}{d}\right)_y = \left(\frac{1.0(12)12}{5.5}\right) = 26.2$$

$$\left(\frac{K_e\ell}{d}\right)_x = \left(\frac{1.0(20)12}{9.5}\right) = 25.3 < 26.2$$

NDS T2.3.1

Since $E_x = E_y$, the y axis (weak axis) governs.

$E' = EC_MC_t = 1.6e3(1.0)1.0 = 1.6e3$ ksi

$K_{cE} = 0.3$

$c = 0.8$

$$F_{cE} = \frac{K_{cE}E'}{\left(\frac{\ell_e}{d}\right)^2} = \frac{.3(1.6e3)}{(26.2)^2} = .7 \text{ ksi}$$

$C_F = 1.0$

$F_c^* = F_cC_DC_MC_tC_F = 1.0(1.25)1.0(1.0)1.0 = 1.25$ ksi

NDS 3.7.1.5

$$C_P = \frac{1+\left(F_{cE}/F_c^*\right)}{2c} - \sqrt{\left(\frac{1+\left(F_{cE}/F_c^*\right)}{2c}\right)^2 - \frac{\left(F_{cE}/F_c^*\right)}{c}}$$

$$C_P = \frac{1+(.7/1.25)}{2(.8)} - \sqrt{\left(\frac{1+(.7/1.25)}{2(.8)}\right)^2 - \frac{(.7/1.25)}{.8}} = .47$$

NDS T2.3.1

$F_c' = F_cC_DC_MC_tC_FC_P = 1.0(1.25)1.0(1.0)1.0\ (.47)$

$= .59$ ksi $> .29$ ksi √

Axial ok

In these types of circumstances the magnitude of the additional loading prompts us to assume that this column is of critical importance to the structure. As the designer you should provide a conservative design with a minimum eccentricity.

Bending (weak axis)

The minimum eccentricity is equal to the larger of 1 in or one-tenth of either side of the principle axis of the column.

$e = .1d = .1(5.5) = .55$ in < 1 in   Use 1 in

$$f_{by} = \frac{Pe_y}{S_y} = \frac{15(1.0)}{47.9} = .31^k$$

Lateral Stability

For potential lateral torsional buckling the movement will occur about the plane of the x axis. Here we look at the member with the lateral load applied as if the member were lying flat. The NDS sec. 3.3.1 indicates that $C_L = 1.0$ and no lateral support is required if $d < b$. This is true in our case so $C_L = 1.0$. Also note that $C_{fu} = 1.0$ for a 5x5 or larger member.

NDS T2.3.1

$F_b' = F_bC_DC_MC_tC_LC_FC_rC_{fu}$

$= 1.2(1.25)1.0(1.0)1.0(1.0)1.0(1.0)$

$= 1.5$ ksi $> .31$ ksi √

Bending ok for eccentricity on y axis

Combined stress for y axis

We will need F_{bEx}.

Unbraced length $\ell_u = 12$ ft $= 144$ in

NDS T3.3.3

$$\frac{\ell_u}{d} = \frac{144}{9.5} = 15.2 > 14.3$$

Which implies:

NDS 3.3.3.6

$\ell_e = 1.84\ell_u = 1.84(144) = 265$ in

$$R_B = \sqrt{\frac{\ell_e d}{b^2}} = \sqrt{\frac{265(9.5)}{5.5^2}} = 9.1 < 50 \quad √$$

$$F_{bE} = \frac{K_{bE}E'y}{R_B^2} = \frac{.3(1.6e3)}{8.8^2} = 6.2 \text{ ksi}$$

Reduced equation is:

TCM 5.9.5

$$\left(\frac{f_c}{F_c'}\right)^2+\frac{f_{b1}+f_c\left(6e_1/d_1\right)\left(1+0.234\left(f_c/F_{cE1}\right)\right)}{F_{b1}'\left(1-\left(f_c/F_{cE1}\right)-\left(\frac{f_{b2}}{F_{bE2}}\right)^2\right)}\le 1.0$$

TCM 15.4.1

$$\left(\frac{.29}{.59}\right)^2+\frac{.31+.29\left(6(1.0)/5.5\right)\left(1+0.234(.29/.7)\right)}{1.5\left(1-(.29/.7)-\left(\frac{0}{6.2}\right)^2\right)}$$

$= .99 < 1.0$ √

Combined stress ok for y axis

Bending (strong axis)

$e = .1d = .1(9.5) = .95 \text{ in} < 1 \text{ in}$ use 1 in

$$f_{by}=\frac{Pe_y}{S_y}=\frac{15(1.0)}{82.7}=.18^{\,k}$$

Lateral Stability

For potential lateral torsional buckling the movement will occur about the plane of the y axis.

NDS T2.3.1

$$F_{bE}=\frac{K_{bE}E'y}{R_B^2}=6.2 \text{ ksi}$$

$F_b^* = F_bC_DC_MC_tC_F = 1.2(1.25)1.0(1.0)1.0 = 1.5$ ksi

NDS 3.3.3.8

$$C_L=\frac{1+\left(F_{bE}/F_{bx}^*\right)}{1.9}-\sqrt{\left(\frac{1+\left(F_{bE}/F_{bx}^*\right)}{1.9}\right)^2-\frac{\left(F_{bE}/F_{bx}^*\right)}{.95}}$$

$$C_L=\frac{1+\left(6.2/1.5\right)}{1.9}-\sqrt{\left(\frac{1+\left(6.2/1.5\right)}{1.9}\right)^2-\frac{\left(6.2/1.5\right)}{.95}}=.98$$

$F_b' = F_bC_DC_MC_tC_LC_FC_r = 1.5(.98)$

$= 1.47 \text{ ksi} > .001^{\,k}$ √

Bending ok for x axis

Combined stress

Amplification factor for eccentric bending

$$\left(\ell_e/d\right)_x=25.3$$

$F_{cE} = .7$ ksi

TCM 15.4.1

$$\left(\frac{f_c}{F_c'}\right)^2+\frac{f_{b1}+f_c\left(6e_1/d_1\right)\left(1+0.234\left(f_c/F_{cE1}\right)\right)}{F_{b1}'\left(1-\left(f_c/F_{cE1}\right)\right)}\le 1.0$$

TCM 5.9.5

$$\left(\frac{.29}{.59}\right)^2+\frac{.18+.29\left(6(1.0)/9.5\right)\left(1+0.234(.29/.7)\right)}{1.47\left(1-(.29/.7)\right)}$$

$= .68 < 1.0$ √

Combined stress ok for x axis. Column ok for new loads

The greatest use of life is to spend it for something that will outlast it.

WILLIAM JAMES

● PROBLEM 3.16

Bearing piles with combined stress.

A scientist approaches your firm and asks you to investigate the possibility of putting some test equipment on top of an old single pile. Investigate the pile for the forces shown below.

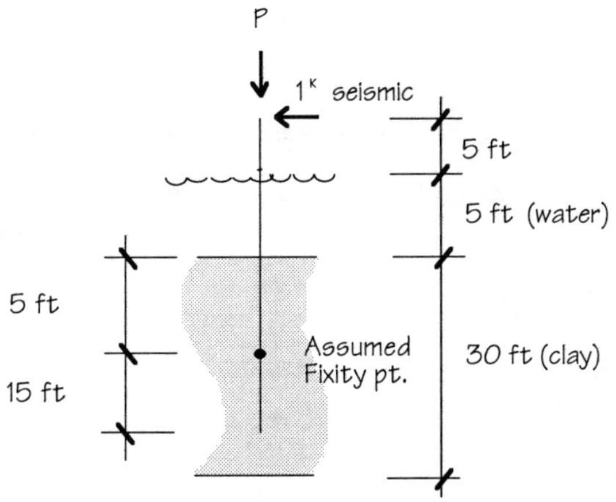

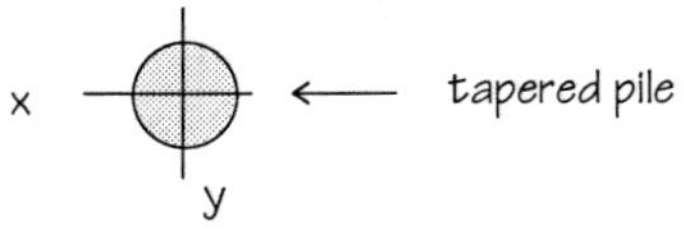

ASSUME

- Neglect lateral except as shown.
- Treated Pacific Coast DF, Class 1 pile.
- $P_{DL} = 6^k$.
- $P_{LL} = 2^k$.
- Neglect pile weight.
- $C_D = 1.33$ (seismic).

SOLUTION

The load caring capacity of a round column is generally thought of as equal to a square column that has the same cross-sectional area.

Tabular values:

NDS T6A

$F_{c\parallel} = 1.25$ ksi
$F_{c\perp} = .23$ ksi
$F_b = 2.45$ ksi (includes form factor C_f)
$E = 1.5e3$ ksi
$F_v = .115$ ksi

Ck axial compression

Evaluate load cases

$DL \Rightarrow 6^k$ with $C_D = .9$

$DL + LL \Rightarrow 8^k$ with $C_D = 1.0$

Look at ratios (load case/C_D) for comparison to see which case will govern.

$$\frac{6}{.9} = 6.7^k < 8^k$$

The DL + LL case will govern.

DL + LL case

Equation 5-16 of the TCM was developed for rectangular sections to determine the point of critical compressive and the combination of compression plus bending stress. Modify and proceed. The problem statement assumes a point of fixity 5 feet below the surface of the clay. Although the clay will provide some lateral support along that length, assume an unbraced length of 15 ft.

A Class 1 pile (TCM Table 6.7) at 30 ft long gives:

$C_{top} = 27$ in. (circumference)
$C_{6\text{-}butt} = 36.5$ in. (circumference 6 ft. from butt)

Rate of change of circumference:

$$\frac{36.5-27}{30-6} = .4 \text{ in./ft.}$$

Circumference at point of fixity:

$$C_{max} = 36.5 - 9(.4) = 32.9 \text{ in}$$

$$D_{max} = C_{max}/\pi = 32.9/3.14 = 10.48 \text{ in. dia.}$$

$$D_{min} = C_{min}/\pi = 27/3.14 = 8.6 \text{ in. dia.}$$

$$D = D_{min} + (D_{max} - D_{min})\left(a - .15\left(\frac{1-D_{min}}{D_{max}}\right)\right)$$

$$= 8.59 + (10.47 - 8.59)\left(.7 - .15\left(\frac{1-8.59}{10.47}\right)\right) = 10.1 \text{ in.}$$

The critical section occurs at:

$$h_c = \frac{D-D_{min}}{D_{max}-D_{min}}(h) = \frac{10.1-8.59}{10.47-8.59}(15)$$

$= 12.0$ ft from top

$$A = \frac{\pi D^2}{4} = \frac{3.14(10.1)^2}{4} = 80.1 \text{ in}^2$$

NDS 3.7.1.2

$$f_c = \frac{P}{A} = \frac{8}{80.1} = .1 \text{ ksi}$$

Since lateral buckling is not prevented, NDS appendix G gives $K_e = 2.1$.

NDS 3.7.1.2

$$\left(\ell_e/_D\right) = \left(^{15(12)2.1}/_{10.1}\right) = 37.4 < 44 \quad \checkmark$$

$E' = EC_MC_t = 1.5e3(1.0)1.0 = 1.5e3$ ksi

$K_{cE} = 0.3$

$c = 0.8$

$$F_{cE} = \frac{12K_{cE}E'}{\left(\frac{\ell_e}{D/4}\right)^2} = \frac{12(.3)1.5e3}{\left(\frac{12(15)2.1}{10.1/4}\right)^2} = .24 \text{ ksi}$$

$C_{cs} = 1.0 + 0.002_{Lc} = 1.0 + 0.002(12.1) = 1.02$

NDS 3.7.1.5

$F_c^* = F_cC_DC_{cs} = 1.25(1.0)1.02 = 1.28$ ksi

$$C_P = \frac{1+\left(F_{cE}/F_c^*\right)}{2c} - \sqrt{\left(\frac{1+\left(F_{cE}/F_c^*\right)}{2c}\right)^2 - \frac{\left(F_{cE}/F_c^*\right)}{c}}$$

$$C_P = \frac{1+\left(.24/1.28\right)}{2(.8)} - \sqrt{\left(\frac{1+\left(.24/1.28\right)}{2(.8)}\right)^2 - \frac{\left(.24/1.28\right)}{.8}} = .18$$

Single pile factor $C_{sp} = .8$

$F_c' = F_cC_DC_{cs}C_{sp}C_P = 1.25(1.0)1.02(.8).18$

$= .18$ ksi $> .1$ ksi $\checkmark$

$$\frac{f_c}{F_c'} = \frac{.1}{.18} = .56 \text{ \% capacity for this load case.}$$

Axial stress ok

Note that compression should also be checked at the top of the pile.

Bending

The bending stress is checked at the critical section.

$M = PL_c = 1.0(12.1) = 12.1^{\text{ k ft}}$

$$f_b = \frac{12M32\pi}{c^3} = \frac{12(12.1)32\pi}{(32.9)^3} = .41 \text{ ksi}$$

$F_b' = F_bC_DC_{sp} = 2.45(1.33).77 = 2.51$ ksi $> .41$ ksi $\checkmark$

Bending stress ok

Combined stress at critical section

Recall that when calculating the combined stress case we need to consider one C_D throughout the interaction equation. Further note that we need not consider the LL with lateral forces. This implies that the DL alone case would be used for combined stress calculations regardless or whether or not it governed over the DL + LL case. NDS 3.9.2

Evaluate DL case

$$f_c = \frac{P}{A} = \frac{6}{80.1} = .075 \text{ ksi}$$

$$\left(\ell_e/_D\right) = 37.4$$

$E' = 1.5$ e3 ksi

$K_{cE} = 0.3$

$c = 0.8$

$F_{cE} = .24$ ksi

$F_c^* = F_cC_DC_{cs} = 1.25(1.33)1.02 = 1.7$ ksi NDS 3.7.1.5

$$C_P = \frac{1+\left(.24/1.7\right)}{2(.8)} - \sqrt{\left(\frac{1+\left(.24/1.7\right)}{2(.8)}\right)^2 - \frac{\left(.24/1.7\right)}{.8}} = .14$$

$F_c' = F_cC_DC_{cs}C_{sp}C_P = 1.25(1.33)1.02(.8).14 = .19$ ksi

$$\left(\frac{f_c}{F_c'}\right)^2 + \frac{f_{b1}}{F_{b1}'\left(1-\left(f_c/F_{cE1}\right)\right)} + \frac{f_{b2}}{F_{b2}'\left(f_c/F_{cE2}\right)-\left(f_{b1}/F_{bE}\right)^2} \leq 1.0$$

Because we have a concentric column force, the above reduces to: NDS 3.9.2

$$\left(\frac{f_c}{F_c'}\right)^2 + \frac{f_{b1}}{F_{b1}'\left(1-\left(f_c/F_{cE1}\right)\right)} \leq 1.0$$

($F_{cE} = F_{cE1}$ etc. from above)

$$\left(\frac{.075}{.19}\right)^2 + \frac{.41}{2.51\left(1-\left(.075/.24\right)\right)} = .39 < 1.0 \quad \checkmark$$

This member is currently working at 39% capacity.

Combined stress ok

Check Embedment (assume movement of 1/2 in.)

S_o = 200 psf (from AITC Table 6.6)

$S_1 = S_O d2/3 = 200(10)2/3 = 1333$ psf

Butt diameter

$$B = \frac{36.5+6(.4)}{\pi} = 12.38 \text{ in.} = 1.03 \text{ ft.}$$

$A = 2.34P/S_1B = 2.34(8)/1.33(1.03) = 13.7$

$$d = \frac{A}{2}\left(1+\sqrt{\frac{1+4.36h}{A}}\right) = \frac{13.7}{2}\left(1+\sqrt{\frac{1+4.36(15)}{13.7}}\right)$$

= 21.9 ft > 10 ft **NG!**

Embedment NG!

Do what you can, with what you have, with where you are.

THEODORE ROOSEVELT

This Page intentionally left blank

There is no good in arguing with the inevitable. The only argument available with an east wind is to put on your overcoat.

JAMES RUSSELL LOWELL

4. Horizontal Diaphragm Design

Chapter Problems	Page	Prob.
Combined stress analysis for a drag strut for a strip mall	4-13	4.10
Diaphragm analysis of building with interior shearwalls	4-3	4.2
Diaphragm analysis with zone nailing	4-12	4.8
Diaphragm deflection	4-31	4.13
Diaphragm design with zone nailing for UBC case 2 & 4	4-16	4.9
Diaphragm design and analysis of roof	4-2	4.1
Diaphragm design of strip mall roof utilizing zone nailing	4-6	4.4
Drag strut design for concrete shearwalls	4-10	4.6
Drag strut force analysis for building with interior shearwalls	4-11	4.7
Horizontal diaphragm with hole proximate to the "loaded" edge of an exterior wall	4-37	4.16
Horizontal diaphragm with hole proximate to the side edge of the exterior wall	4-43	4.17
Horizontal diaphragms with holes	4-24	4.12
Lateral analysis of a nonrectangular L shaped building	4-22	4.11
Methods to calculate drag strut forces	4-9	4.5
Rotation and deflection of open end buildings	4-33	4.14
Rotation of flexible diaphragm	4-5	4.3
Stepped diaphragms	4-35	4.15

PROBLEM 4.1

Diaphragm design and analysis of roof.

Determine the unit shears in the transverse direction for the walls and diaphragm of the one-story structure shown below. Size the diaphragm and calc the chord forces.

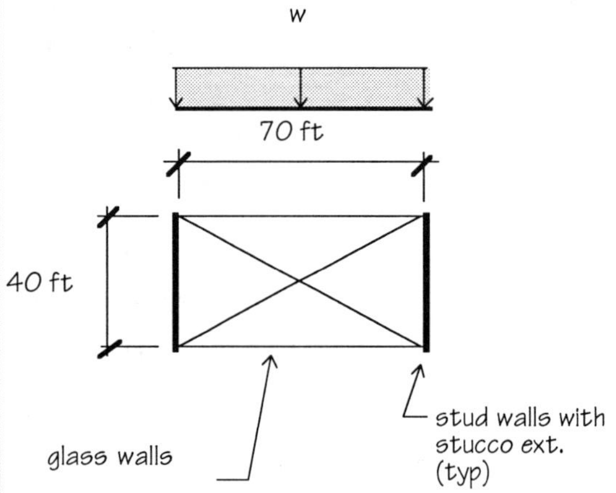

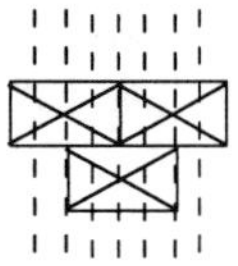

Plywood layout over roof trusses.

ASSUME

- w = .16 klf.
- RLL = 20 psf.
- RDL = 12 psf.
- Standard occupancy.
- No opn'gs on transverse walls.
- Shear paneled walls.
- Roof trusses at 24 in o/c.

SOLUTION

Aspect ratio ck (UBC T23-I-I)

$\frac{70}{40} = 1.75 < 4$ √ UBC T23-I-S-1

Sheathing loads (vertical)

w = .012 + .02 = .032 psf < .04 psf √

Use min. 24/0 1/2 in C-D EXP 1

Diaphragm loads (horizontal)

The diaphragms are designed as if they were horizontal "I" beams. The plywood acts like the web, the chords are likened to flanges, and the shear walls resist the forces like reactions.

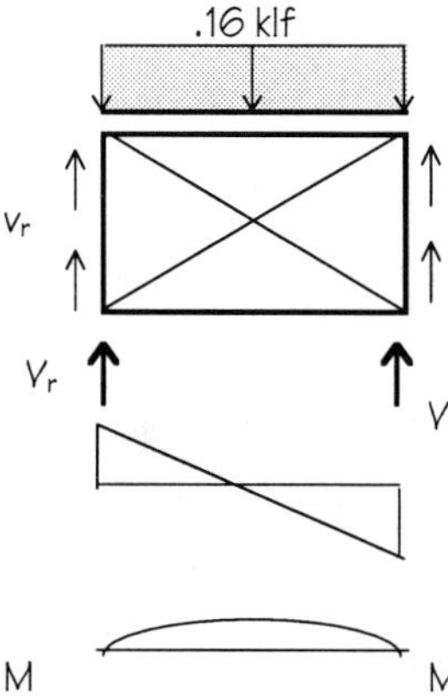

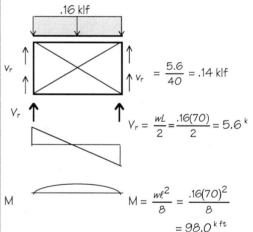

$v_r = \frac{5.6}{40} = .14$ klf

$V_r = \frac{wL}{2} = \frac{.16(70)}{2} = 5.6^{k}$

$M = \frac{w\ell^2}{8} = \frac{.16(70)^2}{8} = 98.0^{k\,ft}$

chord force = $T = C = \frac{M}{b} = \frac{98}{40} = 2.45^{k}$

The lateral force is perpendicular to the continuous panel joint and perpendicular to the potentially unblocked edge. This implies load case 1. UBC T23-I-J-1

v = .14 klf < .24 klf √

For a min. 3/8 in thk. unblocked diaphragm and 2x framing on edge.

Use 15/32-in C-D EXP 1 with 8d at 6,6,12. Blocking not not required with 2x framing on edge

Note that 6,6,12 notation configuration is typical for plywood diaphragm "call outs" in practice. It refers to boundary, all continuous panel edges and other plywood edges, and field nail spacing respectively.

The transverse walls act as reactions to the diaphragm's beam-like action, with a uniformly distributed load w applied. The span of the "beam" is the distance between the shearwalls.

Most people live, whether physically, intellectually or morally, in a very restricted circle of their potential being. They make use of a very small portion of their possible consciousness, and of their soul's resources in general, much like a man who, out of his whole bodily organism, should get into a habit of using and moving only his little finger. Great emergencies and crises show us how much greater our vital resources are than we had supposed.

WILLIAM JAMES

PROBLEM 4.2

Diaphragm analysis of building with interior shearwalls.

Determine the unit shears and chord forces in the transverse direction for the one-story strip mall shown below.

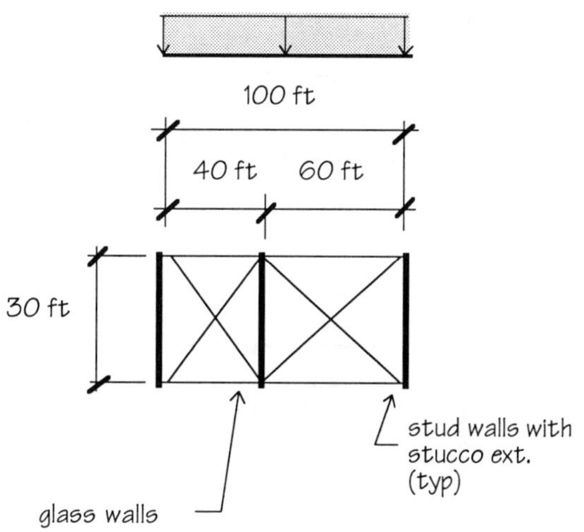

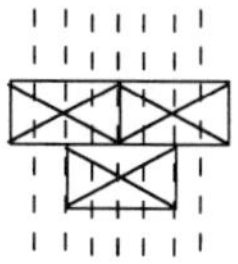

Plywood layout over roof trusses.

ASSUME

Standard occupancy.
No opn'gs on transverse walls.
Shear paneled walls.
Roof trusses at 24 in o/c.

SOLUTION

Aspect ratio ck

$\frac{40}{30} = 1.33 < 4$ √

$\frac{60}{30} = 2 < 4$ √

UBC T23-I-S-1

Diaphragm loads

Analyze the diaphragms as if they were 2 separate simply supported beams. The diaphragms are designed as if they were horizontal "I" beams. The plywood acts like the web, the chords are likened to flanges and the shear walls resist the forces like reactions. Notice that the unit shear for the diaphragm at the center wall will have a right and left side with respect to the wall. This implies that the roof diaphragm is designed as two separate "simple beam" diaphragms, while the interior shear wall has the roof diaphragm unit shears combined to form a wall unit shear.

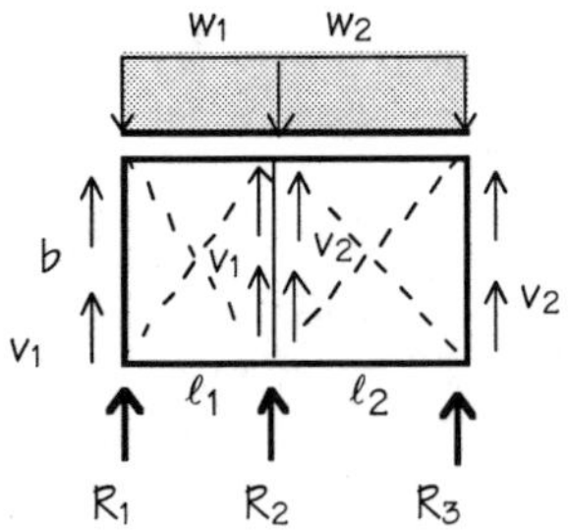

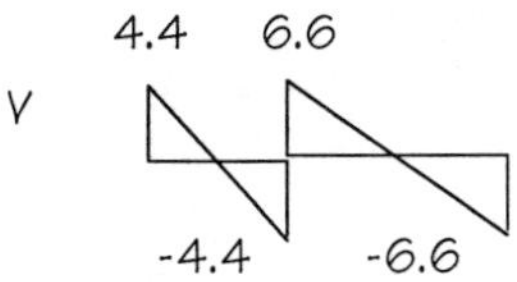

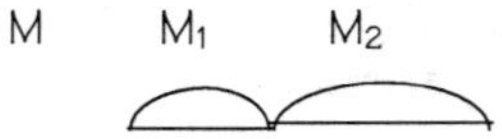

Diaphragm unit shear

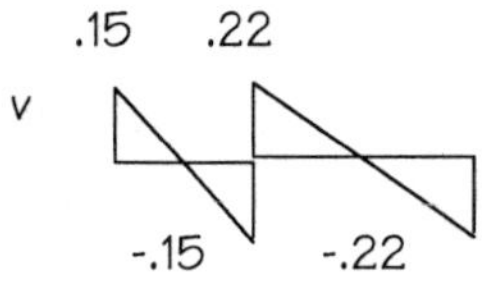

$$v_1 = \frac{w_1\ell_1}{b} = \frac{.22(40)}{30} = .293 \text{ klf}$$

$$v_2 = \frac{w_2\ell_2}{b} = \frac{.22(60)}{30} = .44 \text{ klf}$$

> Diaphragm unit shear $v_1 = .293$ klf
> Diaphragm unit shear $v_2 = .44$ klf

Wall Reactions and wall unit shears

$$R_1 = \frac{w_1\ell_1}{2} = \frac{.22(40)}{2} = 4.4^k$$

$$R_3 = \frac{w_2\ell_2}{2} = \frac{.22(60)}{2} = 6.6^k$$

$$R_2 = R_1 + R_3 = 4.4 + 6.6 = 11.0^k$$

$$v_{R1} = v_1 = .293 \text{ klf}$$

$$v_{R3} = v_2 = .44 \text{ klf}$$

$$v_{R2} = v_{R1} + v_{R3} = .293 + .44 = .733 \text{ klf}$$

> Wall unit shear $v_{R1} = .293$ klf
> Wall unit shear $v_{R3} = .44$ klf
> Wall unit shear $v_{R2} = .733$ klf

Diaphragm chord forces

$$M_1 = \frac{w_1\ell_1^2}{8} = \frac{.22(40)^2}{8} = 44^k$$

$$M_2 = \frac{w_2\ell_2^2}{8} = \frac{.22(60)^2}{8} = 99^k$$

$$T_1 = C_1 = \frac{M_1}{b} = \frac{44}{30} = 1.47^k$$

$$T_2 = C_2 = \frac{M_2}{b} = \frac{99}{30} = 3.3^k$$

> Chord force $T_1 = 1.47^k$
> Chord force $T_2 = 3.3^k$

The only way to avoid being miserable is not to have enough leisure to wonder whether you are happy or not.

GEORGE BERNARD SHAW

PROBLEM 4.3

Rotation of flexible diaphragm.

You are assigned to do the lateral analysis for a small addition to a strip mall. Determine the shearwall forces for the flexible diaphragm shown below.

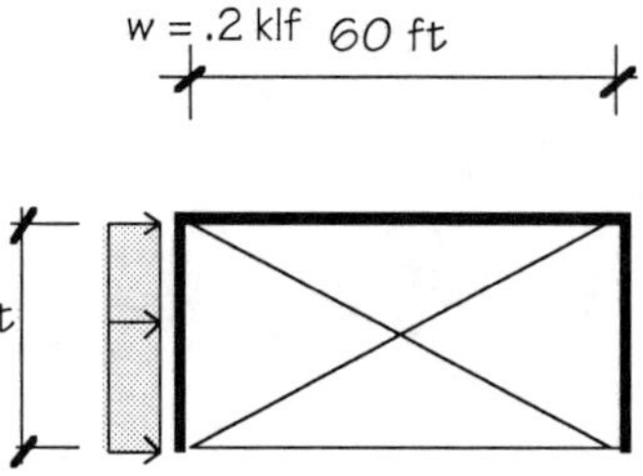

ASSUME

- Roof sloped for drainage.
- Standard occupancy.
- Shear paneled walls.
- Roof trusses at 24 in o/c.
- Neglect deflection.

SOLUTION

Diaphragm unit shear

The store has no effective shearwall in the front. Rotation of the diaphragm can be used to carry the resolved torsional moment to the shear walls. This procedure is not the norm for most buildings because most buildings have shearwalls on all four sides of the structure. Strip malls often have glass fronts which require consideration of resolving the rotational moment through the diaphragm to the 3 existing shearwalls. This procedure is not allowed when the building has concrete or masonry walls and a flexible wood diaphragm.

UBC 2314.1, T23-I-I

Ck code limits and aspect ratio ck

20 ft < 25 ft √

$\frac{60}{20} = 3 < 4$ √

Find rotation and torsional moment

$R = w\,\ell = .2(20) = 4.0^{k}$

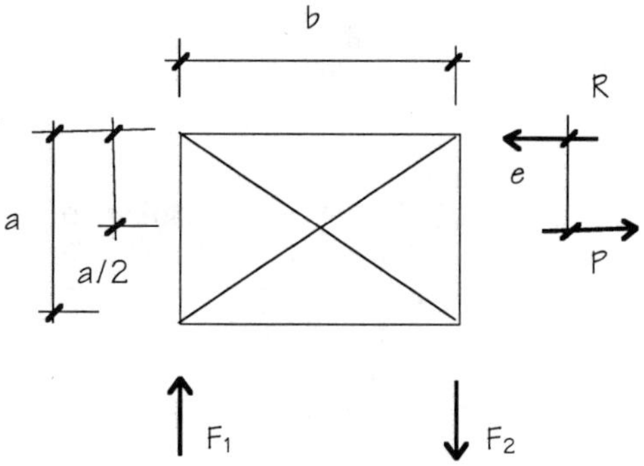

$e = a/2 = 20/2 = 10$ ft

$P = wa = .2(20) = 4.0^{k}$

This force is carried totally by the 60 foot shearwall.

$Me = Pe = T = 4(10) = 40.0^{k\,ft}$

Resolve torsion into couple

$$F_1 = F_2 = \frac{Me}{b} = \frac{T}{b} = \frac{40}{60} = .67^{k}$$

> Forces are as follows:
> $R = 4.0^{k}$
> $F_1 = F_2 = .67$

In general, a diaphragm is referred to as a flexible diaphragm because of the degree of deflection and rotation it has due to in plane lateral forces. The stiffness of a diaphragm ranges from a rigid diaphragm (like a concrete floor) down to a flexible diaphragm (like a wood floor or roof). Wood diaphragms are always considered flexible.

Although you should have this procedure in your engineering arsenal, you should always strive to add a fourth shear resistant element on to the open side of the building. This makes sense when you consider a seismic event where the seismic forces are resolved though the rotational deflection of the building. Our goal should be to provide a safe structure. It is when we have this sort of deflection that wall joints become misaligned or we have unaccounted for prying forces which can cause, or add to causing, a catastrophic collapse.

The method of the enterprising is to plan with audacity, and execute with vigor; and then to treat them as probabilities.

BOVEE

PROBLEM 4.4

Diaphragm design of stripmall roof utilizing zone nailing.

Design the diaphragm for the strip mall shown below.

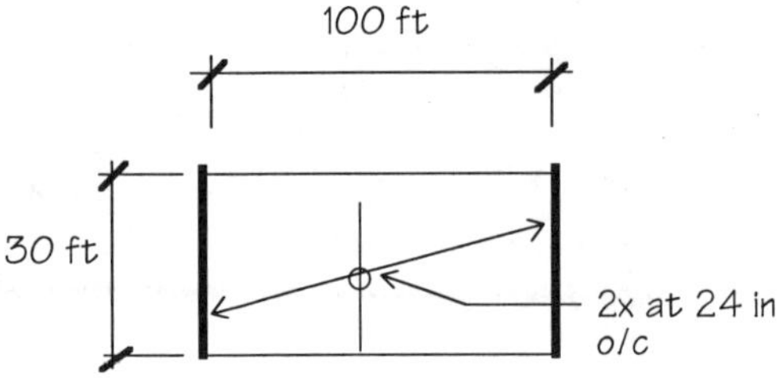

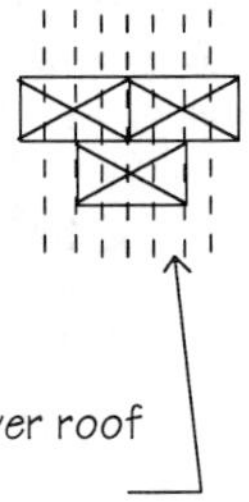

Plywood layout over roof trusses.

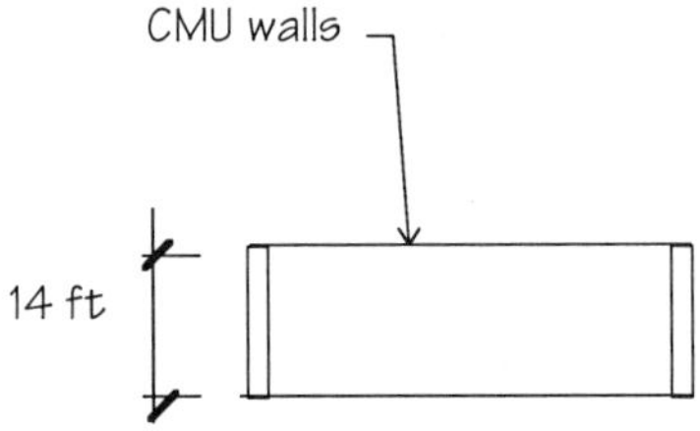

ASSUME

- CMU wt. = 60 psf.
- RLL = 20 psf.
- RDL = 12 psf.
- Roof sloped for drainage.
- 15/32 in C-D EXP 1 plywood.
- 2-#5 chord stl. in CMU (F_s = 20 ksi).
- Zone 4.
- Exposure C (method 2).
- Basic wind speed = 70 mph.
- I = 1.0.
- Closed structure.
- Standard occupancy.
- No opn'gs on trans. walls.
- Shear paneled walls.
- Roof trusses at 24 in o/c.

SOLUTION

Ck wind

Look @ 1 ft strip of building for wind tributary to diaphragm.

UBC1618, T16-F,G,H

$P_{wind} = C_e C_q q_s I = 1.06(1.3)12.6(1.0) = 17.4$ psf

$w = P(TA) = .0174(7) = .122$ klf

Which is the lateral force to the roof diaphragm.

Ck Seismic

Look @ 1' strip for seismic to compare with wind to see which governs the design of the elements. Note that since the base shear coefficient and the story coefficients are equal for a one -story building, our task is greatly simplified as compared to a multi-story building. This allows the base shear coefficient $(ZIC)/R_w$ to be used directly to compute the uniform force to the horizontal diaphragm.

$$V = \frac{ZICW}{R_w}$$

UBC 1628.1 c max = 2.75

$$V = \frac{.4(1.0)2.75W}{6} = .183W$$

The longitudinal exterior walls are seismically loading the diaphragm when considering the transverse direction and visa versa. If there were interior longitudinal walls, they too would load the diaphragm. Simply put, walls with their plane in the direction of the seismic force can offer resistance to the force, but walls perpendicular to the force can't. So, their inertial (seismic) load has to be carried to other walls that are shear walls (through the horizontal diaphragm). Since the diaphragm is shortest in the transverse direction, ck it against wind to see if seismic governs in both directions. If it governs there, it will govern when more diaphragm weight is added in the long direction.

$W = Wall_{DL}$(wall trib. of both walls)

$= .06(7)2 = .84$ klf

W_{diaph} = diaph length (diaph DL)

$= 30(.012) = .36$ klf

$w_{seismic} = .183(.84 + .36) = .183(1.2)$

$= .22$ klf $> .122$ klf

∴ Seismic governs in both directions.

Calc diaph. unit shear

UBC T23-I-1 w_1 aspect ratio = 100/30 = 3.33 < 4 √

$w_1 = .22$ klf $> .2$ klf √

code min. for CMU walls (UBC 1611)

w_2 aspect ratio = 30/100 = .3 < 4 √

$w_2 = .183(.84 + 100(.012)) = .37$ klf

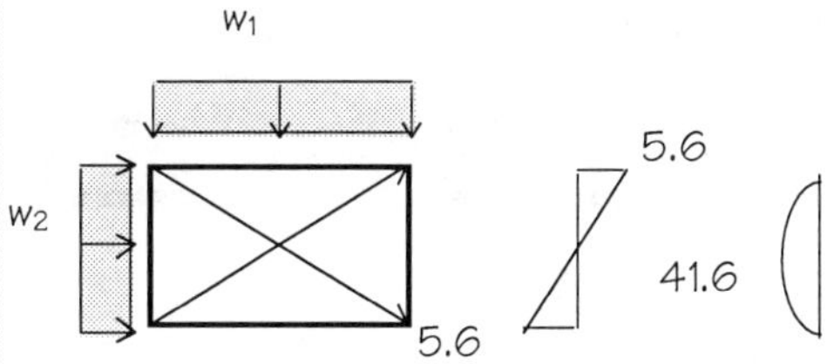

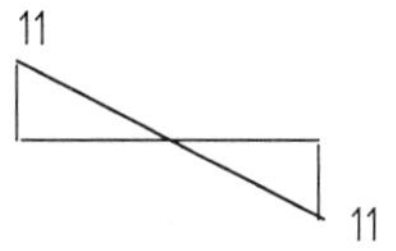

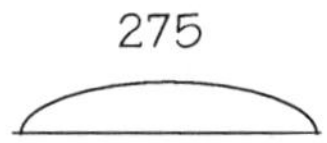

$$V_1 = \frac{w\ell}{2} = \frac{.22(100)}{2} = 11.0^k$$

$$V_2 = \frac{w\ell}{2} = \frac{.37(30)}{2} = 5.6^k$$

$$v_1 = \frac{V}{b} = \frac{11.0}{30} = .367 \text{ klf}$$

$$v_2 = \frac{V}{b} = \frac{5.6}{100} = .056 \text{ klf}$$

$$M_1 = \frac{w\ell^2}{8} = \frac{.22(100)^2}{8} = 275.0^{k\,ft}$$

$$M_2 = \frac{w\ell^2}{8} = \frac{.37(30)^2}{8} = 41.6^{k\,ft}$$

$$T_1 = C_1 = \frac{M_1}{b} = \frac{275}{30} = 9.2^k$$

$T_2 = C_2 = \frac{M_2}{b} = \frac{41.6}{100} = .42^k$

Ck CMU wall stl.

$f_s = \frac{T}{A_s} = \frac{9.2}{2(.31)} = 14.8 \text{ ksi}$

Allowable with 1.33 increase:

$F_s = 20(1.33) = 26.6 \text{ ksi} > 14.8 \text{ ksi}$ √

Chord stl ok

Zone nailing w_1

Use similar triangles to round off location dimensions at different design requirements. Lateral load is perpendicular to the continuous panel joint and potential unblk'd edge (load case 1).

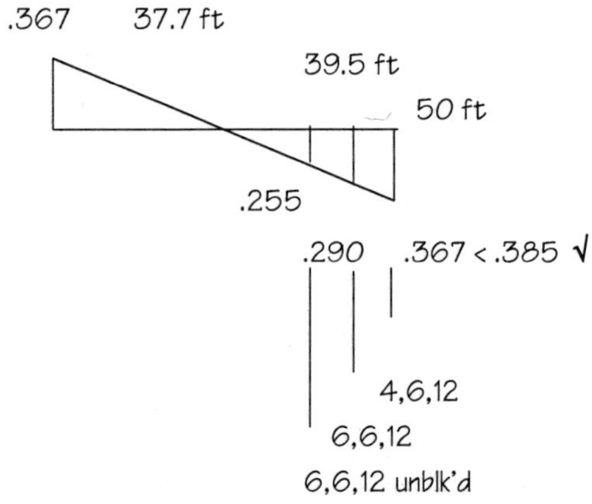

Zone nailing w_2

Use similar triangles to round off location dimensions for different design requirements. Lateral force is parallel to the continuous panel joint and potential unblk'd edge (load case 3).

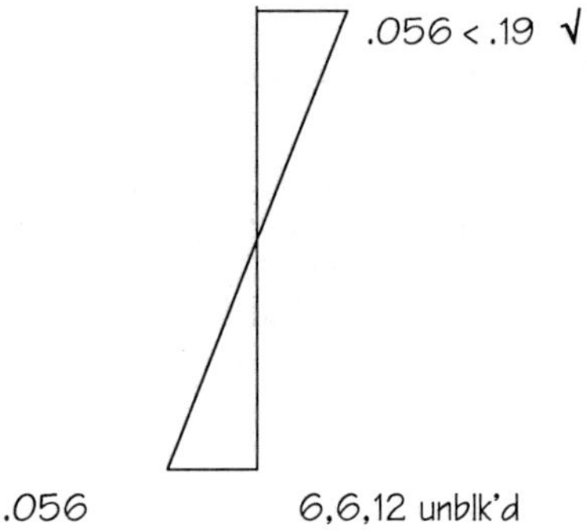

Zone Layout

When you do zone nailing be sure to fully describe its requirements on the structural plans. Since this requires added complications to the construction of the roof, inspection is important to insure proper construction.
Since 39.5 - 37.7 = 1.8 ft is too small, extend 6,4,12 to unblk'd area.

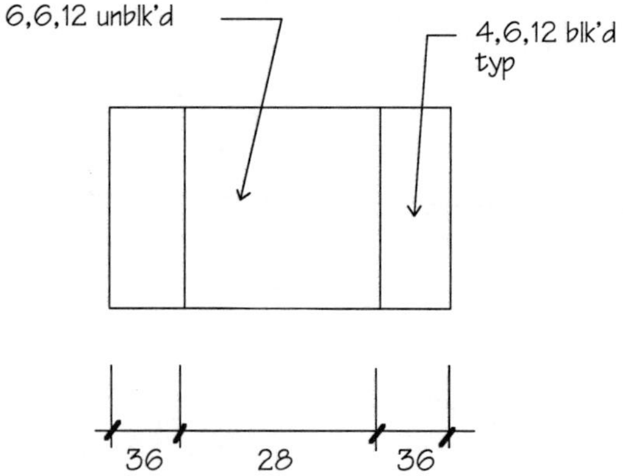

Use 15/32 in C-D EXP 1 with 10d at zone nailing shown above

UBC T23-I-J-1

There is no security on this earth, there is only opportunity.

GENERAL DOUGLAS MACARTHUR

PROBLEM 4.5

Methods to calculate drag strut forces.

Determine the drag strut force in the wood structure shown below.

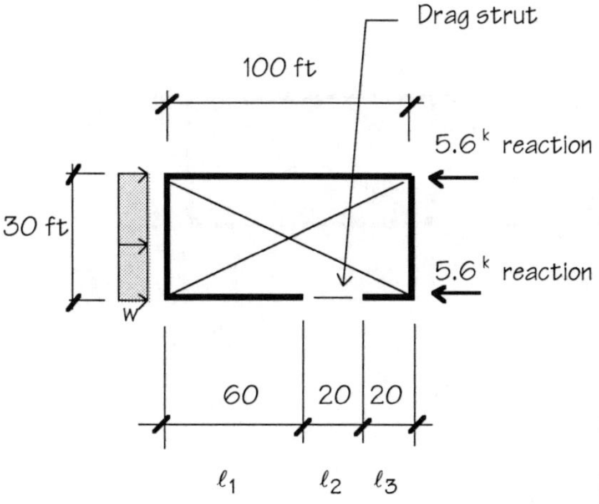

ASSUME

Roof sloped for drainage.
Standard occupancy.
Shear paneled walls.
Roof trusses at 24 in o/c.

SOLUTION

Diaphragm unit shear

$$v = \frac{R}{b} = \frac{5.6}{100} = .056 \text{ klf}$$

Wall unit shear

$$v = \frac{R}{\ell_1 + \ell_3} = \frac{5.6}{60+20} = .07 \text{ klf}$$

Method 1 (FBD approach)

Isolate proximate wall system.

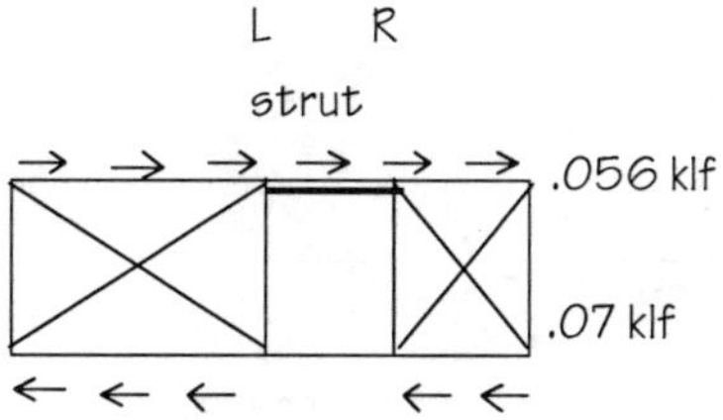

$F_L = 60(.07 - .056) = .84^k$ (tension)
$F_R = 20(.07 - .056) = .28^k$ (compression)

Method 2 (Force diagram)

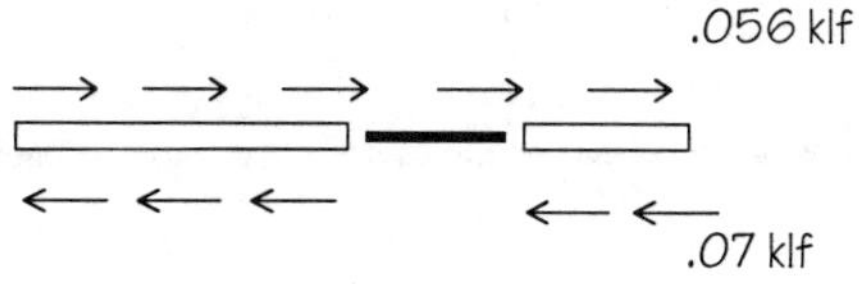

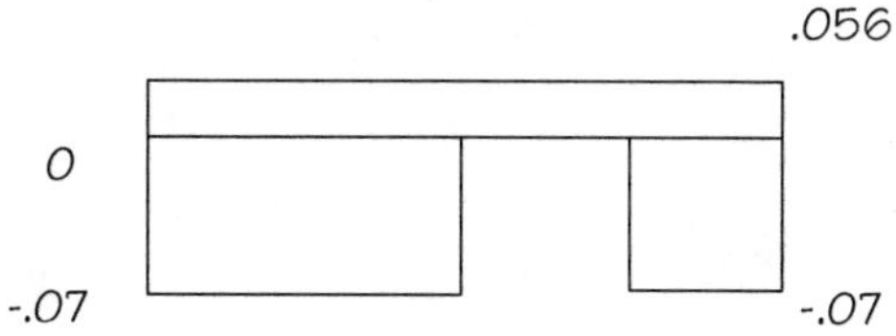

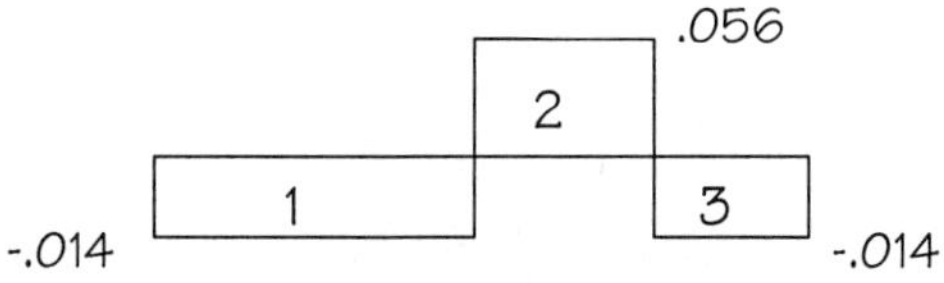

$A_1 = -.014(60) = -.84^k$

$A_2 = .056(20) = 1.12^k$

$A_1 = -.014(20) = -.28^k$

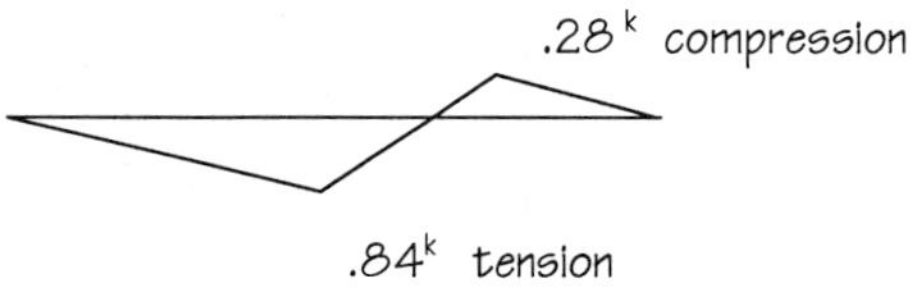

Of the two methods shown thus far, method one is easiest to understand and is quite efficient to use.

Method 3 (conservative approach)

$F_{max} = \ell_2 v = 20(.056) = 1.12^k$ (C or T)

Drag strut forces for the lateral load shown are:
$.84^k$ (tension)
$.28^k$ (compression)
or 1.2^k (consv. for C or T)

Enlighten the people generally, and tyranny and oppressions of body and mind will vanish like evil spirits at the dawn of day.

THOMAS JEFFERSON

PROBLEM 4.6

Drag strut design for concrete shearwalls.

Determine the drag strut force for the previous problem assuming that the walls are concrete and have the unit wall shears shown below. Use Force diagram approach.

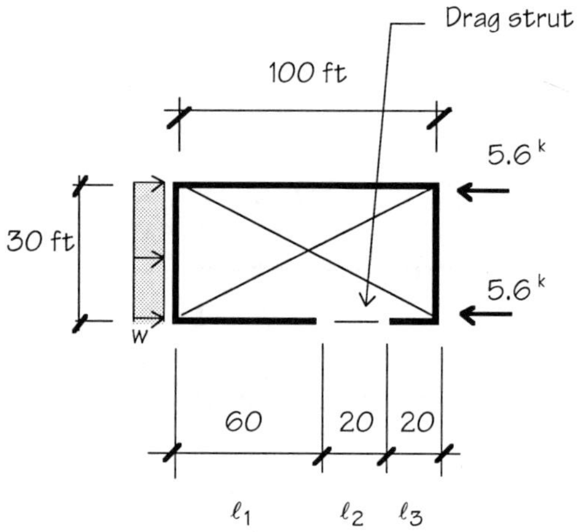

ASSUME

Based upon rigidities of piers:
$v_1 = .073$ klf.
$v_3 = .06$ klf.
Roof sloped for drainage.
Standard occupancy.
Shear paneled walls.
Roof trusses at 24 in o/c.

SOLUTION

Diaphragm unit shear

$$v = \frac{R}{b} = \frac{5.6}{100} = .056 \text{ klf}$$

Method 2 (Force diagram)

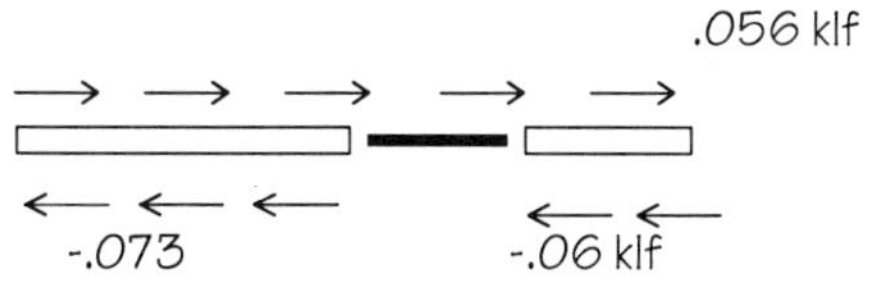

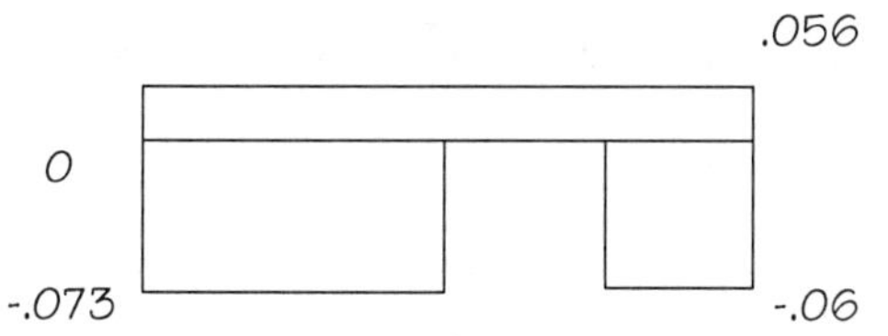

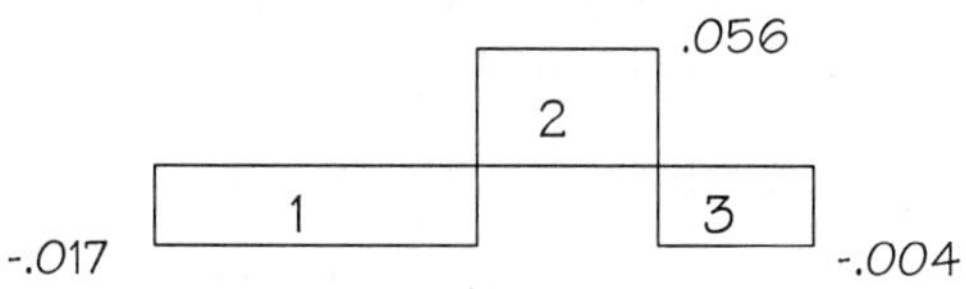

$A_1 = -.017(60) = 1.02^k$

$A_2 = .056(20) = 1.12^k$

$A_1 = -.004(20) = .08^k$

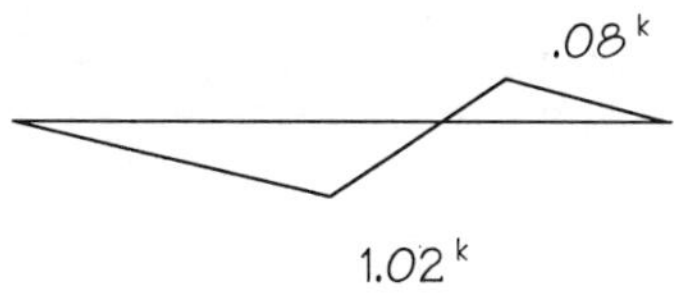

Note how the use of the concrete shearwall (instead of wood) "drew" more force to the longer, more rigid wall. The strut force increased on that end of the drag and decreased at the shorter, less rigid wall end. But the overall collector force remained the same ($A_2 = 1.12^k$).

> Drag strut forces for the lateral load shown are:
> 1.02^k (tension)
> $.08^k$ (compression)

I always wanted to be somebody, but I should have been more specific.

LILY TOMLIN

PROBLEM 4.7

Drag strut force analysis for building with interior shearwalls.

Determine the drag strut force for the interior shearwalls shown below. Use Force diagram approach.

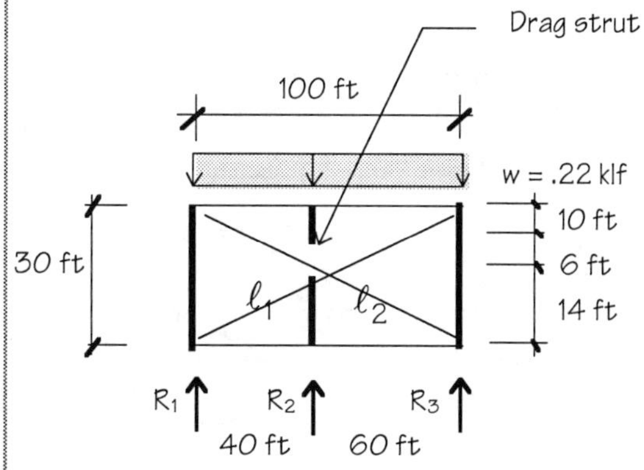

ASSUME

Roof sloped for drainage.
Standard occupancy.
Shear paneled walls.
Roof trusses at 24 in o/c.

SOLUTION

Diaphragm unit shear

Assume that the diaphragm acts like 2 simple beams.

$$R_2 = \frac{w(\ell_1+\ell_2)}{2} = \frac{.22(40+60)}{2} = 11.0^k$$

$$v_2 = \frac{R_2}{b} = \frac{11}{30} = .367 \text{ klf}$$

Strut forces (Force diagram method)

$$v_{2\,walls} = \frac{R_2}{\ell_a+\ell_b} = \frac{11}{10+14} = .458 \text{ klf}$$

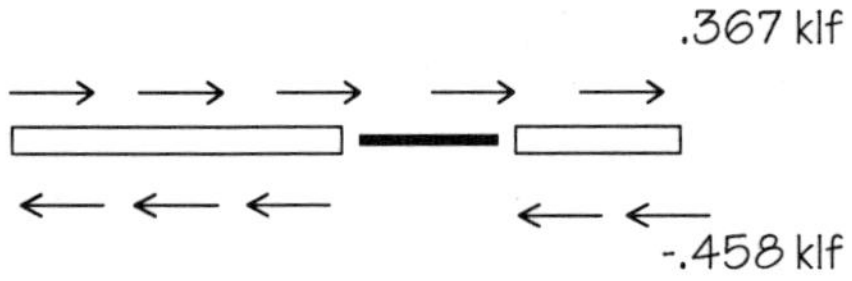

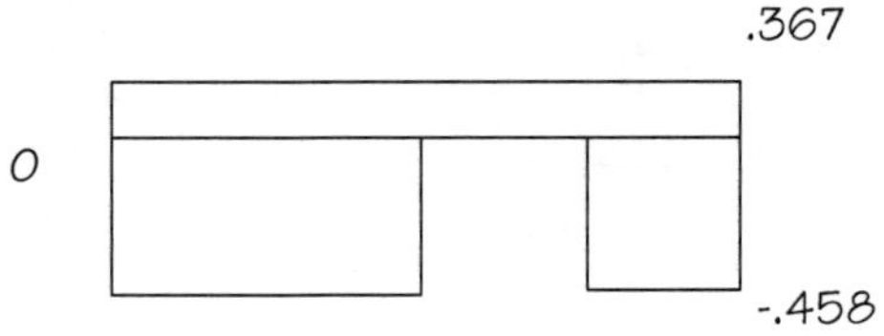

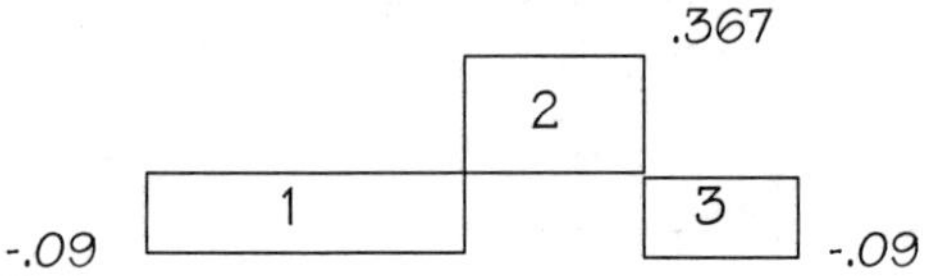

$A_1 = .09(14) = -1.26^k$

$A_2 = .367(6) = 2.2^k$

$A_1 = .09(10) = -.9^k$

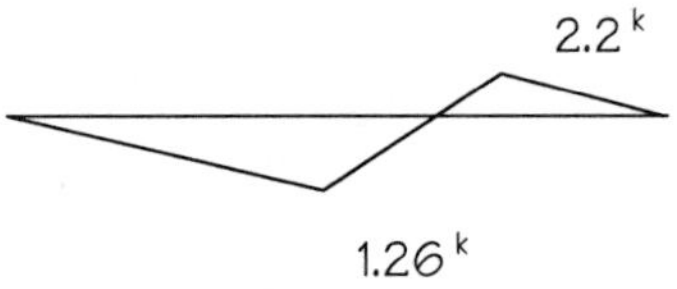

Drag strut forces for the lateral load shown are:
1.26^k (tension)
$.9^k$ (compression)

I can not give you the formula for success, but I can give you the formula for failure - which is: try to please everyone.

HERBERT BAYARD SWOPE

PROBLEM 4.8

Diaphragm analysis with zone nailing.

Determine the roof diaphragm shear, select the plywood and nailing, & calculate the shearwall forces for the strip mall shown below. If at all possible, the contractor would like to use her excess 6d and 3/8 plywood from another job.

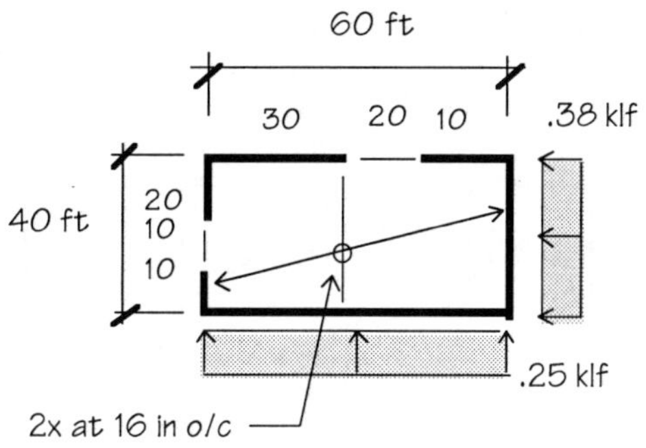

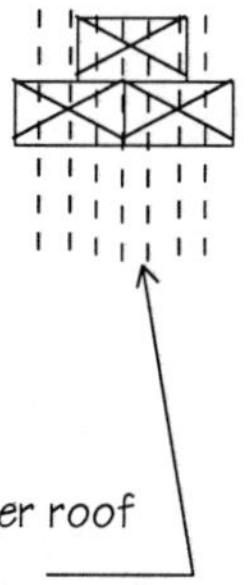

Plywood layout over roof trusses.

ASSUME

Roof sloped for drainage.
3/8 in C-D EXP 1 plywood with 6d.
Shear paneled walls.

SOLUTION

Calc diaph. unit shear

UBC T23-1-I

w_1 aspect ratio = 60/40 = 1.5 < 4 √

w_2 aspect ratio = 40/60 = .67 < 4 √

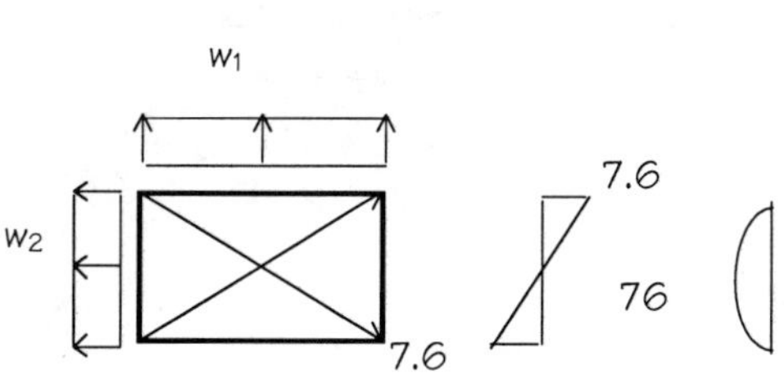

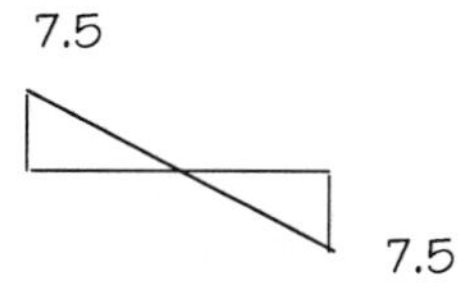

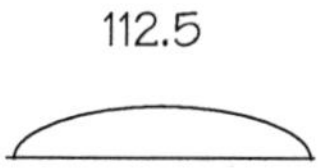

$$V_1 = \frac{w\ell}{2} = \frac{.25(60)}{2} = 7.5^k$$

$$V_2 = \frac{w\ell}{2} = \frac{.38(40)}{2} = 7.6^k$$

$$v_1 = \frac{V}{b} = \frac{7.5}{40} = .188 \text{ klf}$$

$$v_2 = \frac{V}{b} = \frac{7.6}{60} = .127 \text{ klf}$$

$$M_1 = \frac{w\ell^2}{8} = \frac{.25(60)^2}{8} = 112.5^{\ k\,ft}$$

$$M_2 = \frac{w\ell^2}{8} = \frac{.38(40)^2}{8} = 76.0^{\ k\,ft}$$

$$T_1 = C_1 = \frac{M_1}{b} = \frac{112.5}{40} = 2.8^k$$

$$T_2 = C_2 = \frac{M_2}{b} = \frac{76}{60} = 1.3^k$$

Zone nailing w_1

Use similar triangles to round off location dimensions at different design requirements. Lateral load is perpendicular to the continuous panel joint and potential unblk'd edge (load case 1).

UBC T23-I-J-1

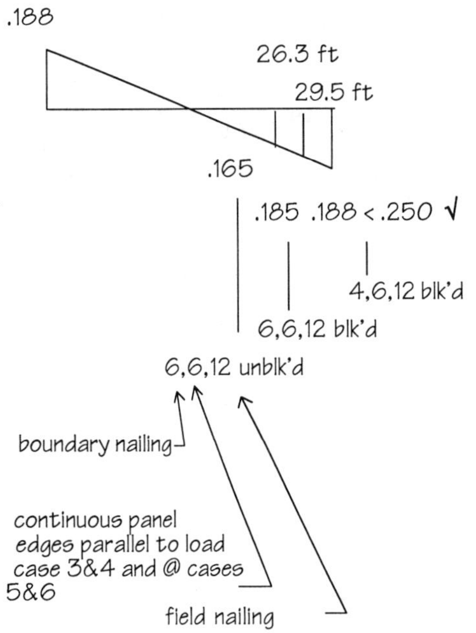

Zone nailing w_2

Use similar triangles to round off location dimensions for different design requirements. Lateral force is parallel to the continuous panel joint and potential unblk'd edge (load case 3).

UBC T23-I-I

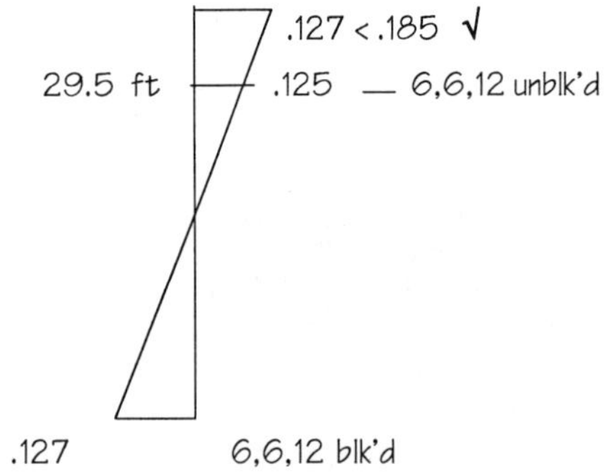

Zone Layout

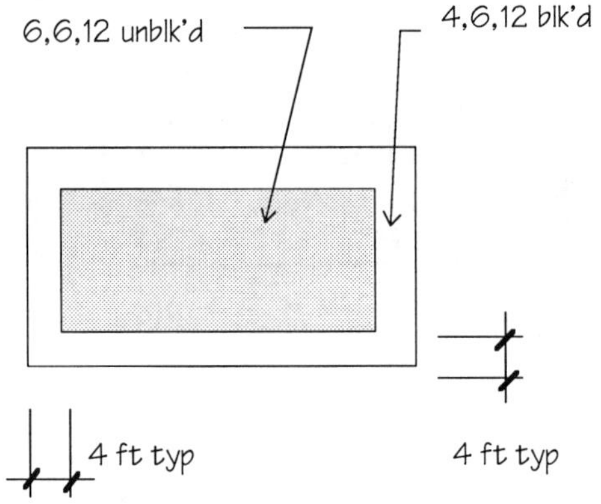

When you do zone nailing, be sure to fully describe its requirements on the structural plans. Since this requires added complications to the construction of the roof, try to keep it simple. We could have made it more complicated by having another zone, but that runs the risk of error in the field. Field inspections are important to insure proper construction.

UBC T23-I-J-1

> Use 3/8 in C-D EXP 1 with 6d at zone nailing shown above

Drag strut force w_1 (Force diagram)

$$v_{1\,walls} = \frac{7.5}{30} = .25 \text{ klf}$$

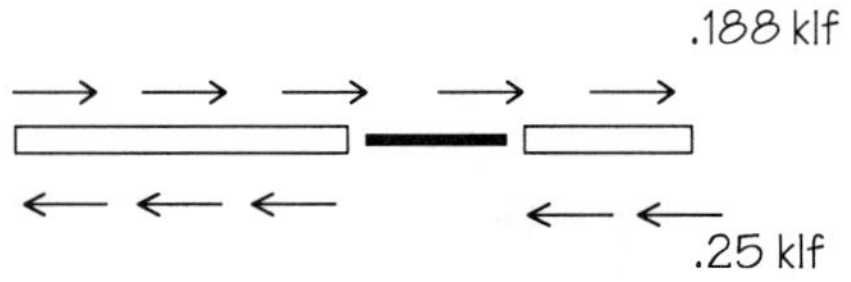

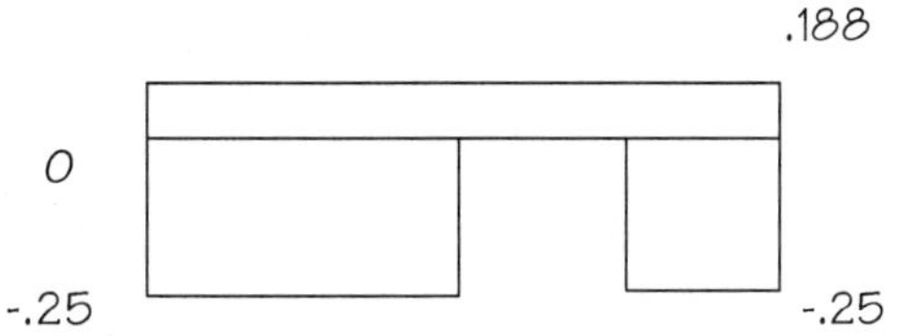

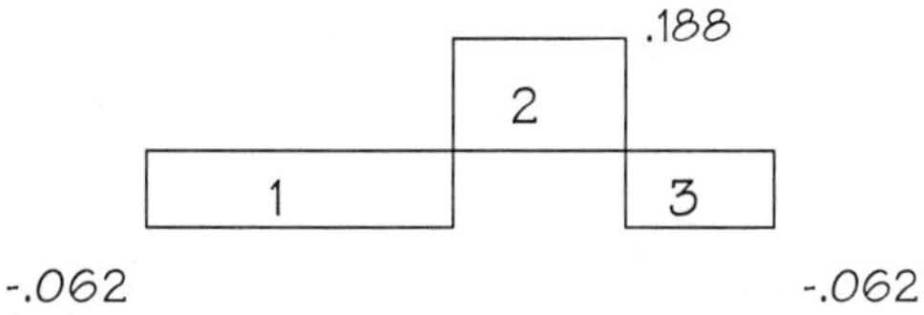

$A_1 = .062(20) = 1.24^k < 1.3^k$

$A_2 = .188(10) = 1.88^k$

$A_3 = .062(10) = .62^k$

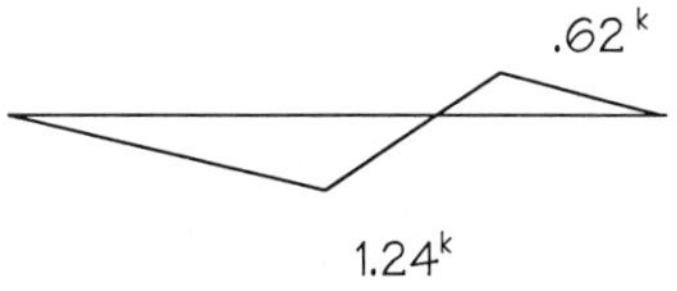

$$M_{20} = \frac{wx(\ell - x)}{2} = \frac{(.38)20(40-20)}{2} = 76.0^{k\,ft}$$

$$T_2 = C_2 = \frac{M_2}{b} = \frac{76}{60} = 1.3^k < 1.24^k$$

∴ chord force governs over drag force for strut

Drag strut force w_2 (Force diagram)

$$v_{1\,walls} = \frac{7.6}{40} = .19 \text{ klf}$$

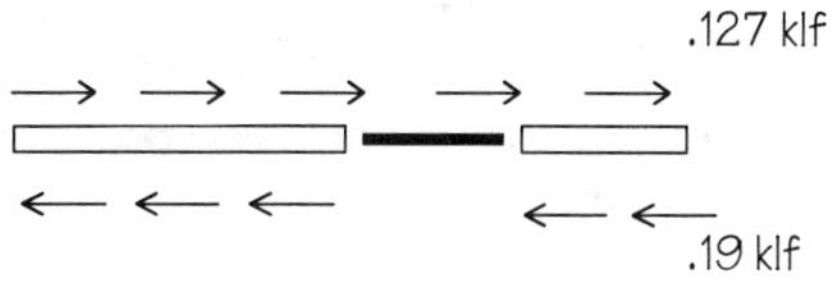

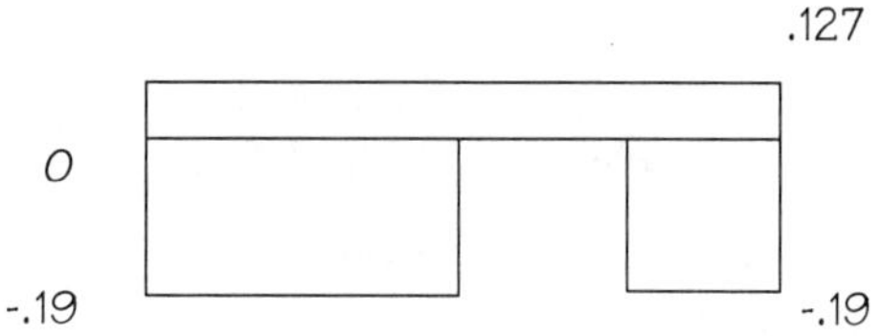

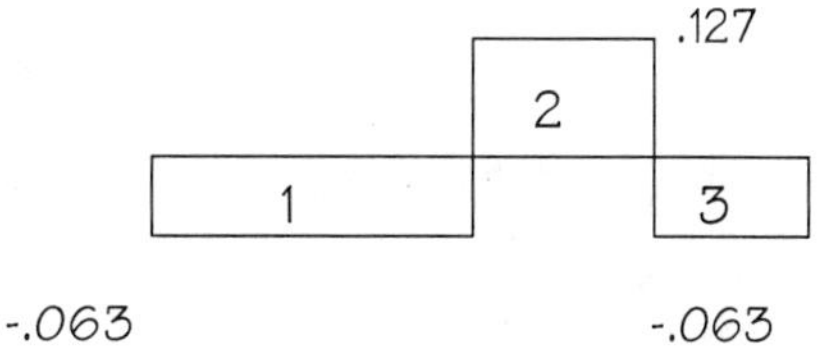

$A_1 = .063(30) = 1.89^k$

$A_2 = .127(20) = 2.54^k$

$A_1 = .063(10) = .63^k$

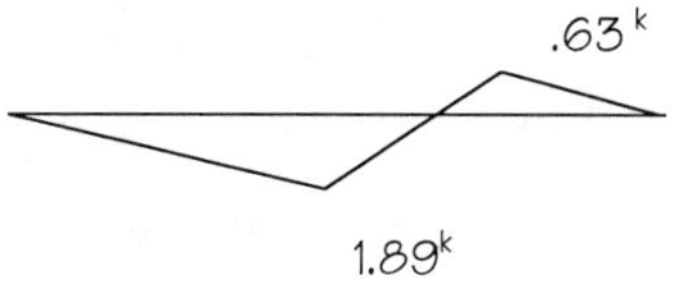

$$M_{20} = \frac{wx(\ell - x)}{2} = \frac{(.25)30(60-30)}{2} = 112.5^{\,k\,ft}$$

$$T_1 = C_1 = \frac{M_1}{b} = \frac{112.5}{40} = 2.8^{\,k} > 1.89^{\,k}$$

> ∴ chord force governs over drag force for strut

The secret of success is constancy of purpose.

BENJAMIN DISRAELI

PROBLEM 4.9

Diaphragm design with zone nailing for UBC case 2 & 4.

Determine the following for the building shown.
- Diaphragm unit shear, plywood and no zone nailing.
- The shearwall forces.
- Chord forces.
- Strut forces.

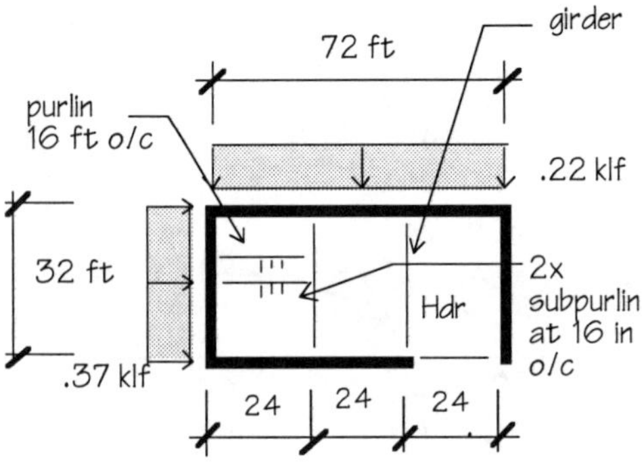

Plywood layout

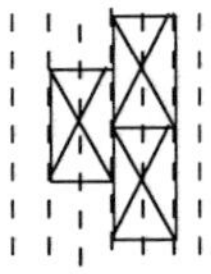

ASSUME

Roof sloped for drainage.
3/8 in C-D EXP 1 plywood with 6d.
Shear paneled walls.

SOLUTION

$$\text{Aspect ratio} = \frac{\ell}{b} = \frac{72}{32} = 2.25 < 4 \quad \checkmark$$

UBC T23-I-I

Calc diaph. unit shear

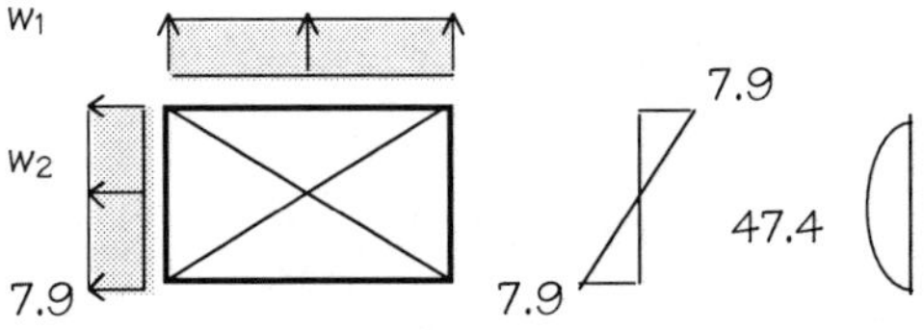

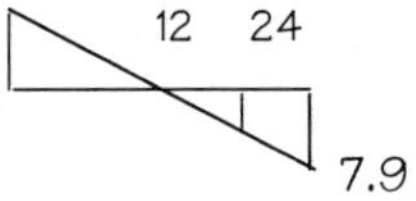

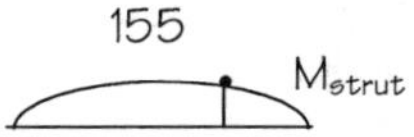

$$V_1 = \frac{w\ell}{2} = \frac{.22(72)}{2} = 7.9^{\,k}$$

$$V_2 = \frac{w\ell}{2} = \frac{.37(32)}{2} = 5.9^{k}$$

$$v_1 = \frac{V}{b} = \frac{7.9}{32} = .247 \text{ klf}$$

$$v_2 = \frac{V}{b} = \frac{5.9}{72} = .082 \text{ klf}$$

$$M_1 = \frac{w\ell^2}{8} = \frac{.22(72)^2}{8} = 142.6^{\text{ k ft}}$$

$$M_2 = \frac{w\ell^2}{8} = \frac{.37(32)^2}{8} = 47.4^{\text{ k ft}}$$

$$T_1 = C_1 = \frac{M_1}{b} = \frac{142.6}{32} = 4.46^{k}$$

$$T_2 = C_2 = \frac{M_2}{b} = \frac{47.4}{72} = .66^{k}$$

Zone nailing w_1

Use similar triangles to round off location dimensions at different design requirements. Lateral load is parallel to the continuous panel joint and perpendicular to the potential unblk'd edge (load case 4).

UBC T23-I-I

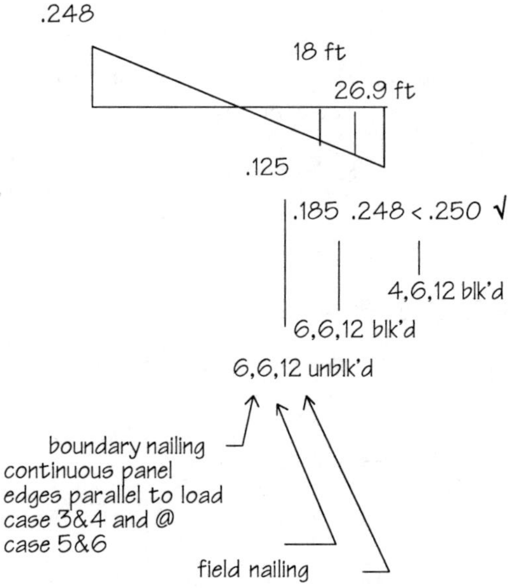

Zone nailing w_2

Use similar triangles to round off location dimensions for different design requirements. Lateral force is perpendicular to the continuous panel joint and parallel to the potential unblk'd edge (load case 2).

UBC T23-I-I

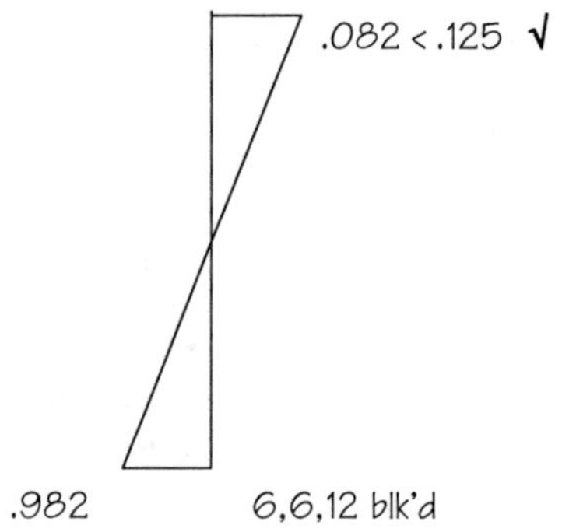

Zone Layout

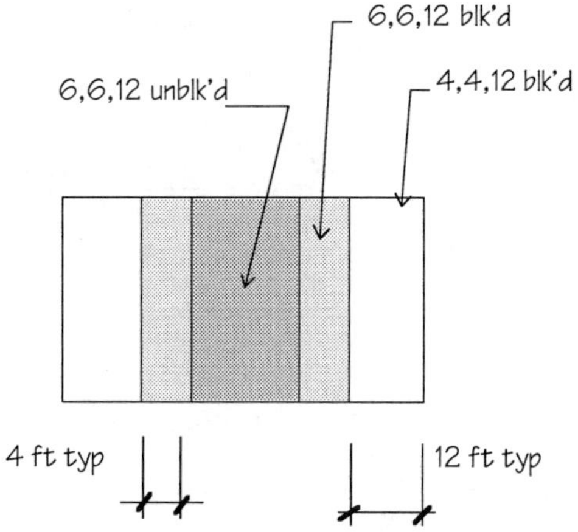

When you do zone nailing be sure to fully describe it's requirements on the structural plans. Since this requires added complications to the construction of the roof, try to keep it simple. We could have made it more complicated by having another zone, but that runs the risk of error. Inspections are important to insure proper construction.

UBC T23-I-J-1

> Use 3/8 in C-D EXP 1 with 6d at zone nailing shown above

Drag strut force w_2 (Force diagram)

$$v_{1\,walls} = \frac{5.92}{48} = .123 \text{ klf}$$

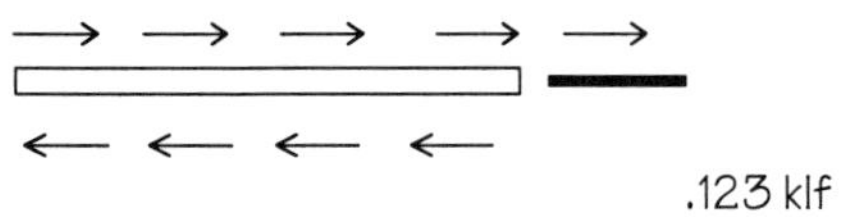

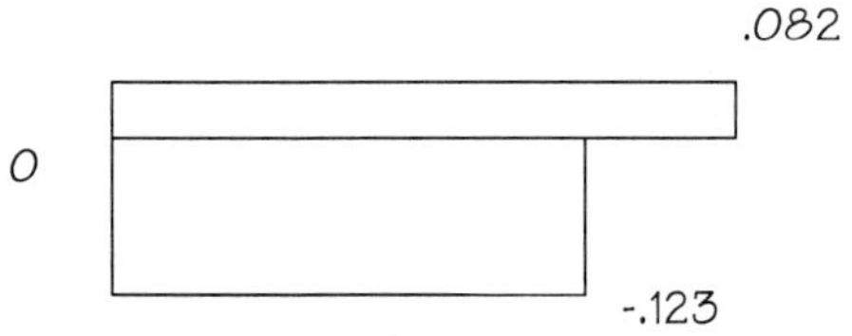

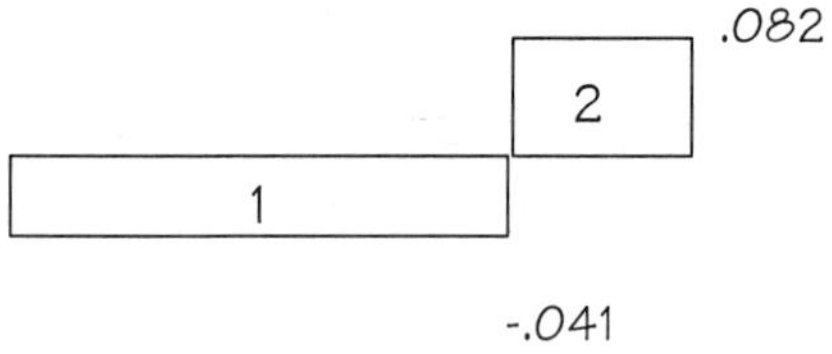

$A_1 = .041(48) = 1.97^k$

$A_2 = .082(24) = 1.97^k$

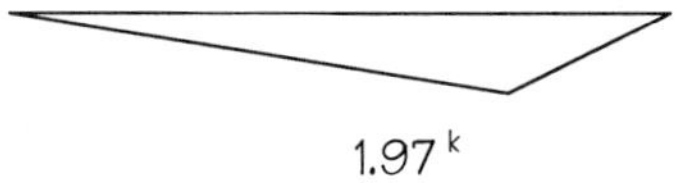

Comparing the chord force at the strut location gives:

$$M_{24} = \frac{wx(\ell - x)}{2} = \frac{(.22)48(72-48)}{2} = 126.7^{k\,ft}$$

$$T_1 = C_1 = \frac{M_1}{b} = \frac{126.7}{32} = 3.96^k > 1.97^k$$

> ∴ chord force governs over drag force for strut

Take what you can use and let the rest go by.

KEN KESEY

PROBLEM 4.10

Combined stress analysis for a drag strut for a strip mall.

Determine the adequacy of the 6x12 drag strut shown below for combine stress of lateral and gravity.

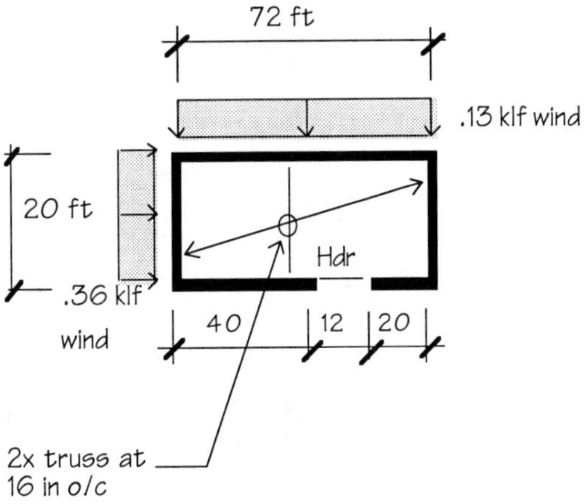

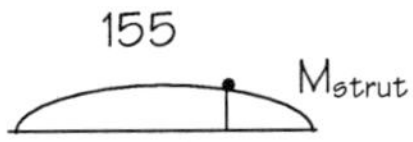

$$V_1 = \frac{w\ell}{2} = \frac{.13(72)}{2} = 4.7^{\,k}$$

$$V_2 = \frac{w\ell}{2} = \frac{.36(20)}{2} = 3.6^{\,k}$$

$$v_1 = \frac{V}{b} = \frac{4.7}{20} = .235 \text{ klf}$$

$$v_2 = \frac{V}{b} = \frac{3.6}{72} = .05 \text{ klf}$$

$$M_1 = \frac{w\ell^2}{8} = \frac{.13(72)^2}{8} = 84.2^{\,k\,ft}$$

$$M_2 = \frac{w\ell^2}{8} = \frac{.36(20)^2}{8} = 18.0^{\,k\,ft}$$

$$T_1 = C_1 = \frac{M_1}{b} = \frac{84.2}{20} = 4.2^{\,k}$$

$$T_2 = C_2 = \frac{M_2}{b} = \frac{18}{72} = .25^{\,k}$$

ASSUME

w_{RDL} = 12 psf.
w_{RLL} = 20 psf.
DF-l No 1 (post and timber grade).
Roof sloped for drainage.
Full lateral support.
EMC < 19 %.

SOLUTION

Calc diaph. unit shear

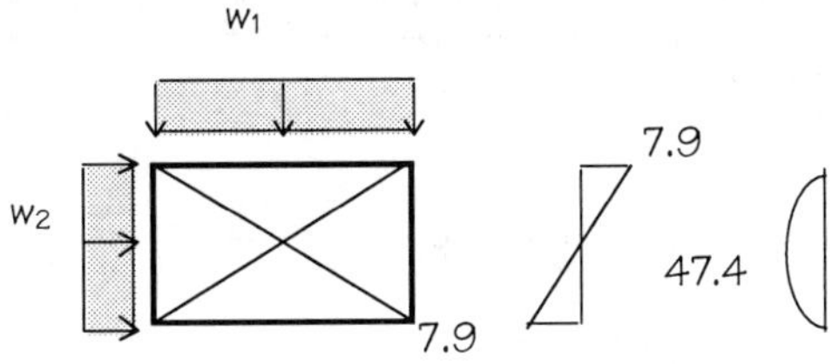

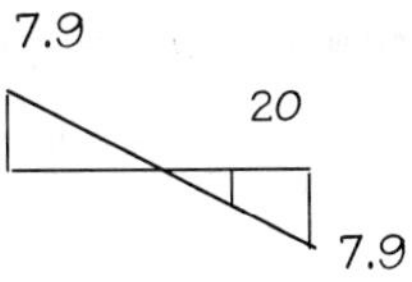

Drag strut force w_2 (Force diagram)

$$v_{1\,walls} = \frac{3.6}{60} = .06 \text{ klf}$$

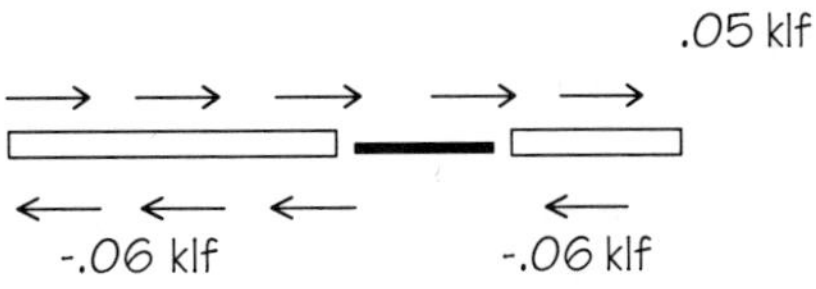

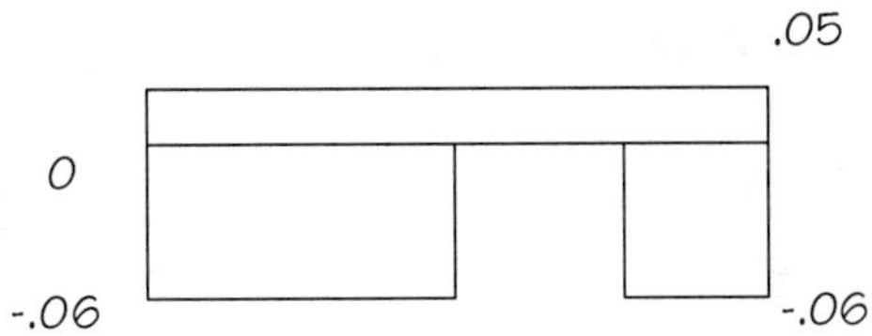

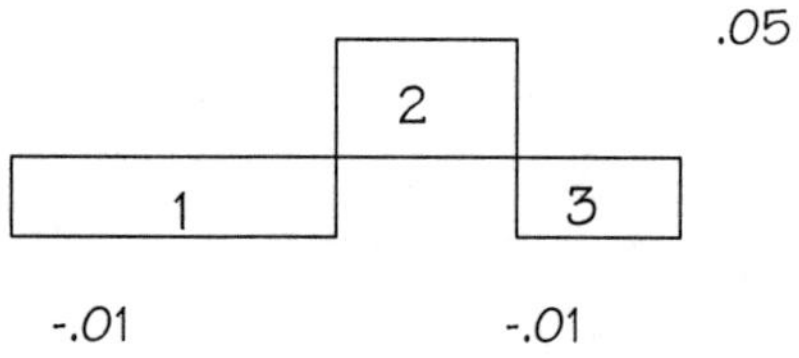

$A_1 = .01(40) = .4^k$

$A_2 = .06(12) = .72^k$

$A_3 = .01(20) = .2^k$

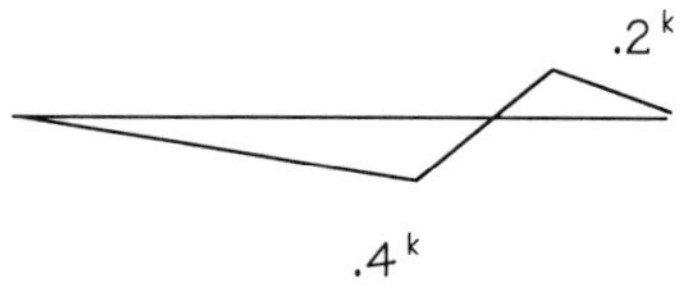

Comparing the chord force at the strut location gives:

$$M_{40} = \frac{wx(\ell - x)}{2} = \frac{(.13)40(72-40)}{2} = 83.2^{k\,ft}$$

$$T_1 = C_1 = \frac{M_1}{b} = \frac{83.2}{20} = 4.16^k > .4^k$$

Chord force governs over drag force for strut

Ck shear

DL + RLL controls by inspection.

$F_c = 1.0$ ksi
$F_{c\perp} = .625$ ksi
$F_v = .085$ ksi
$F_t = .825$ ksi
$F_b = 1.2$ ksi
$E = 1.6e3$ ksi
$A = 63.25$ in^2
$S_x = 121.2$ in^3
$S_y = 57.9$ in^3

$w_{D+L} = 12(.012 + .02) = .38$ klf NDS T2.3.1

$F_v' = F_v(C_D)C_M(C_t)C_H = .085(1.25)1.0(1.0)1.0$

$= .106$ ksi

$$V = \frac{w\ell}{2} = \frac{(.38)12}{2} = 2.28^k$$

$$A_R = \frac{1.5(V)}{F_v'} = \frac{1.5(2.28)}{.106} = 32.3 \text{ in}^2 < 63.3 \text{ in}^3 \ \surd$$

Shear ok

Bending (full lateral support for D + L)

$F_b' = F_bC_DC_MC_tC_LC_FC_r = 1.2(1.25)1.0(1.0)1.0(1.0)$ NDS T2.3.1

$= 1.5$ ksi

$$M = \frac{w\ell^2}{8} = \frac{(.38)12^2}{8} = 6.84^{k\text{-}ft}$$

$$S_R = \frac{12M}{F_b'} = \frac{12(6.84)}{1.5} = 54.7 \text{ in}^3 < 121.2 \text{ in}^3 \ \surd$$

Bending ok

Ck bearing

Since the support conditions are not known, determine the minimum bearing length. Remember to use the full R whether the shear modification controlled the size of the member or not.

$F_{c\perp}' = F_{c\perp}(C_M)C_t(C_b) = .625(1.0)1.0(1.0) = .625$ ksi NDS T2.3.1

$$\ell_{b\,min} = \frac{R}{bF_{c\perp}'} = \frac{2.28}{5.5(.625)} = .66 \text{ in}$$

Use min. bearing of 1.0 in

Ck axial compression

RDL + Lateral governs by insp. NDS 3.7.2.1

Stability (gross area)

Since lateral buckling is prevented by the diaphragm sheathing $\left(\ell_e/d\right)_y = 0$

$$\left(\ell_e/d\right)_x = \left(12(12)/11.5\right) = 12.5$$

$E' = E C_M C_t = 1.6e3(1.0)1.0 = 1.6e3$ ksi

$K_{cE} = 0.3$

$c = 0.8$

$$F_{cE} = \frac{K_{cE}E'}{\left(\ell_e/d\right)_x^2} = \frac{.3(1.6e3)}{(12.5)^2} = 3.1 \text{ ksi}$$

$$F_c^* = F_c C_D C_M C_t C_F = 1.0(1.6)1.0(1.0)1.0 = 1.6 \text{ ksi}$$

NDS 3.7.2.1

$$C_P = \frac{1+\left(F_{cE}/F_c^*\right)}{2c} - \sqrt{\left(\frac{1+\left(F_{cE}/F_c^*\right)}{2c}\right)^2 - \frac{\left(F_{cE}/F_c^*\right)}{c}}$$

$$C_P = \frac{1+\left(3.1/1.6\right)}{2(.8)} - \sqrt{\left(\frac{1+\left(3.1/1.6\right)}{2(.8)}\right)^2 - \frac{\left(3.1/1.6\right)}{.8}} = .86$$

$$F_c' = F_c C_D C_M C_t C_F C_P = 1.0(1.6)1.0(1.0)1.0(.86) = 1.4 \text{ ksi}$$

$$P = F_c' A = 1.4(63.3) = 88.6^k > 4.1^k \quad \checkmark$$

> Compression ok at gross section

Ck axial at net section

Ok by inspection

> Compression ok at net section

Bending (full lateral support DL + lateral)

$$f_b = \frac{M}{S} = \frac{6.84(12)}{121.2} = .68 \text{ ksi}$$

NDS T2.3.1

$$F_b' = F_b C_D C_M C_t C_L C_F C_r = 1.2(1.6)1.0(1.0)1.0(1.0)1.0$$

$$= 1.9 \text{ ksi} > .68 \text{ ksi} \quad \checkmark$$

> Bending (DL + Seismic) ok

Combined stress (DL + lateral compression)

A simple, quick and conservative approach would be to take the max. values for the 2nd second degree equations that are required to solve the combined stress equation thus:

$$f_c = \frac{P}{A_g} = \frac{4.1}{63.3} = .065 \text{ ksi}$$

$C_D = 1.6$ based on the shortest duration for the combination.

$F_{cE} = 3.2$ ksi based on the bending axis

$$\left(\frac{f_c}{F_c'}\right)^2 + \frac{f_{b1}}{F_{b1}'\left(1-\left(f_c/F_{cE1}\right)\right)} + \frac{f_{b2}}{F_{b2}'\left(f_c/F_{cE2}\right) - \left(f_{b1}/F_{bE}\right)^2} \le 1.0$$ NDS 3.9.2

Which reduces to:

$$\left(\frac{f_c}{F_c'}\right)^2 + \frac{f_{b1}}{F_{b1}'\left(1-\left(f_c/F_{cE1}\right)\right)} \le 1.0$$

$$\left(\frac{.065}{1.4}\right)^2 + \frac{.68}{1.9\left(1-\left(.065/3.2\right)\right)} = .45 < 1.0 \quad \checkmark$$

This member is currently working at 37% allowable capacity in this case. The design size is conservative and may not be economic based on the situation. The rationale goes like this: unless the cost that is going to be saved by changing the size or grade of the member is greater than the engineering design costs to make those changes, leave it as it is.

> 6x12 hdr ok for DL + lateral compression

Combined stress (DL + lateral tension)

A simple and quick conservative approach would be to take the max. v values for the 2nd second degree equations that are required to solve the combined stress equation thus:

$$f_t = \frac{P}{A_g} = \frac{4.1}{63.3} = .065 \text{ ksi}$$

$C_D = 1.6$ based on the shortest duration for the combination

$$F_t' = F_t C_D C_M C_t C_F = .825(1.6)1.0(1.0)1.0$$

= 1.32 ksi > .065 ksi √

$$\frac{f_t}{F_t'}+\frac{f_b}{F_b'} = \frac{.065}{1.32}+\frac{.68}{1.9} = .41 < 1.0 \quad √$$

This member is currently working at 41% allowable capacity in this case. The design size is conservative and may not be economically based on the situation. The same rationale above applies. Unless the cost that is going to be saved by changing the size or grade of the member is greater than the engineering design costs to make those changes, leave it as it is.

> 6x12 hdr ok for
> DL + lateral tension

It is the chiefest point of happiness that a man is willing to be what he is.

DESIDERIUS ERASMUS
1465-1536

PROBLEM 4.11

Lateral analysis of a non-rectangular L shaped building.

Analyze the building shown for unit roof shear, chord forces and drag strut connective forces.

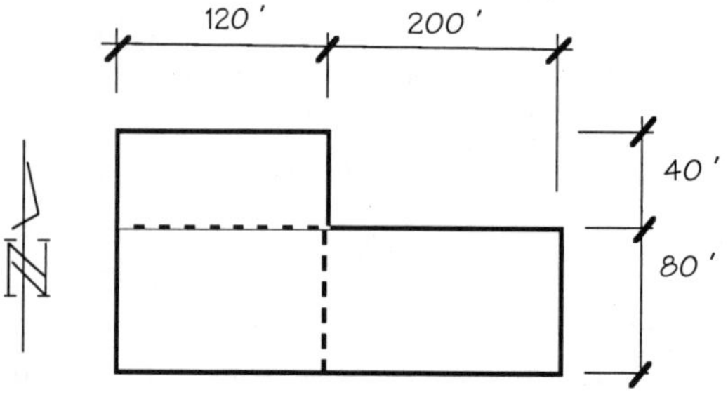

ASSUME

RDL = .012 ksf.
Wall DL = .09 ksf, ht = 16 '.
Neglect wind.
Seismic = .183.

SOLUTION

N/S direction

$$\text{Aspect ratio}_1 = \frac{\ell}{b} = \frac{120}{120} = 1.0 < 4 \quad √$$

NDS T23-I-I

$$\text{Aspect ratio}_2 = \frac{\ell}{b} = \frac{200}{80} = 2.5 < 4 \quad √$$

Calc diaph. unit shear

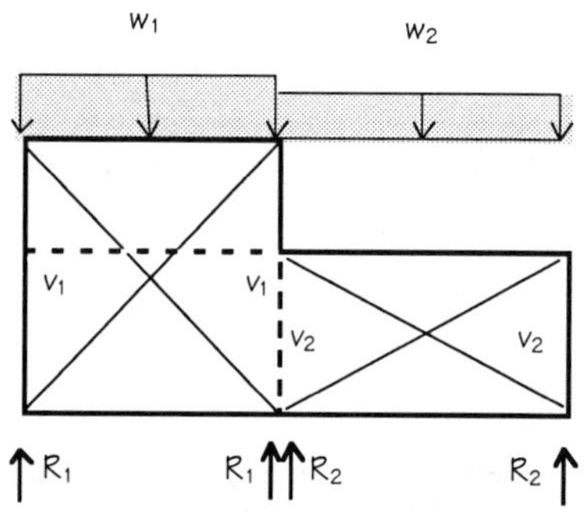

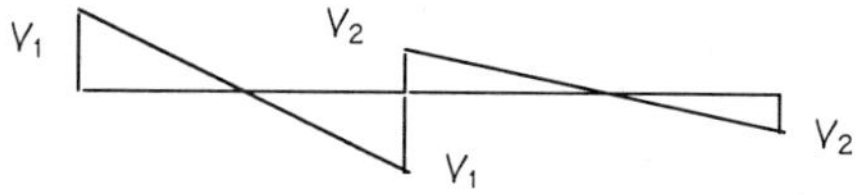

$w_1 = .183(.012(120) + .09(16)) = .527$ klf

$w_2 = .183(.012(80) + .09(16)) = .439$ klf

$R_1 = V_1 = \frac{w\ell}{2} = \frac{.527(120)}{2} = 31.62^k$

$v_1 = \frac{V}{b} = \frac{31.62}{120} = .264$ klf

$M_1 = \frac{w\ell^2}{8} = \frac{.527(120)^2}{8} = 948.6^{\,k\,ft}$

$T_1 = C_1 = \frac{M_1}{b} = \frac{948.6}{120} = 7.91^k$ (chord force)

$R_2 = V_2 = \frac{w\ell}{2} = \frac{.439(200)}{2} = 43.9^k$

$v_2 = \frac{V}{b} = \frac{43.9}{80} = .549$ klf

$M_2 = \frac{w\ell^2}{8} = \frac{.439(200)^2}{8} = 2195^{\,k\,ft}$

$T_2 = C_2 = \frac{M_2}{b} = \frac{2195}{80} = 27.4^k$ (chord force)

$R_1 + R_2 = R_{n/s} = 31.6 + 43.9 = 75.5^k$

Drag strut force

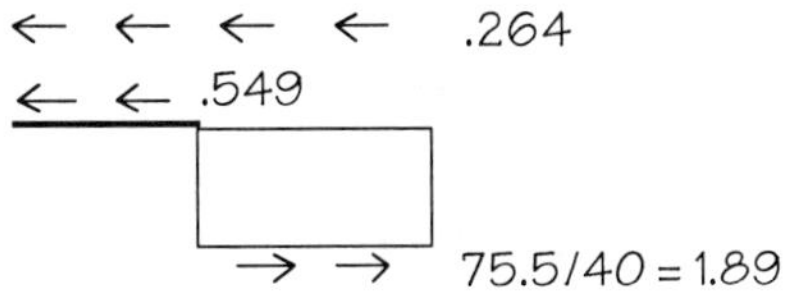

$40(1.89 - .264) = 65.04^k$

or $80(.549 + .264) = 65.04^k$ √

E/W direction

Aspect ratio$_3$ = $\frac{\ell}{b} = \frac{320}{80} = 4.0 = 4$ √

Aspect ratio$_4$ = $\frac{\ell}{b} = \frac{120}{40} = 3.0 < 4$ √

NDS T23-1-1

Calc diaph. unit shear

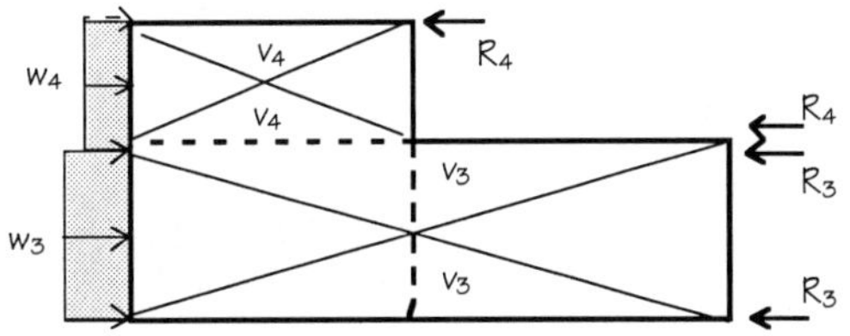

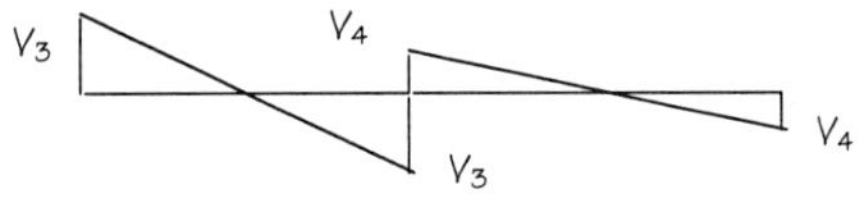

$w_3 = .183(.012(320) + .09(16)) = .966$ klf

$w_4 = .183(.012(120) + .09(16)) = .527$ klf

$R_3 = V_3 = \frac{w\ell}{2} = \frac{.966(80)}{2} = 38.64^k$

$v_3 = \frac{V}{b} = \frac{38.64}{320} = .121$ klf

$M_3 = \frac{w\ell^2}{8} = \frac{.966(80)^2}{8} = 772.8^{\,k\,ft}$

$T_3 = C_3 = \frac{M_1}{b} = \frac{772.8}{320} = 2.42^k$ (chord force)

$R_4 = V_4 = \frac{w\ell}{2} = \frac{.527(40)}{2} = 10.54^k$

$v_4 = \frac{V}{b} = \frac{10.54}{120} = .088$ klf

$M_4 = \frac{w\ell^2}{8} = \frac{.527(40)^2}{8} = 105.4^{\,k\,ft}$

$T_4 = C_4 = \frac{M_2}{b} = \frac{105.4}{120} = .88^k$ (chord force)

$R_3 + R_4 = R_{E/W} = 38.64 + 10.54 = 49.2^k$

Drag strut force

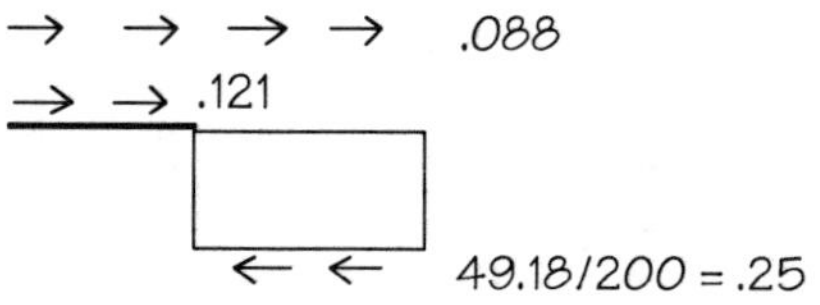

$200(.25 - .121) = 25.8^k$

or $120(.088 + .121) = 25.08^k$ √ **round off error**

▯
▯
▯

First we form habits, then they form us. Conquer your bad habits, or they'll eventually conquer you.

DR. ROB GILBERT

● PROBLEM 4.12

Horizontal diaphragms with holes.

Analyze the effects of the seismic loading on the hole in the roof diaphragm of the strip mall building shown below.

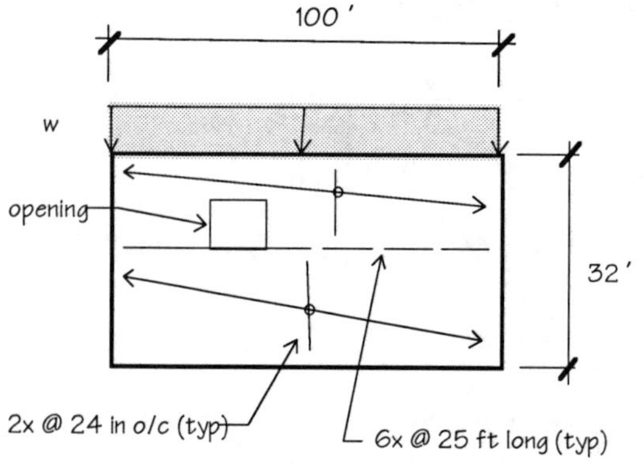

ASSUME

w = .2 klf (.092 diaphragm, .108 walls).
Framing at 2 ft o/c.

SOLUTION

Aspect ratio $= \dfrac{\ell}{b} = \dfrac{32}{16} = 2.0 < 4$ √ NDS T23-I-I

Analyze diaphragm without hole

Obtain chord and unit shear forces at critical locations proximate to the opening. Assume that the seismic loads are applied at the top of the diaphragm. Also note that since we will need local chords at the hole, assume A and D are subdiaphragms with the appropriate code span/depth ratio.

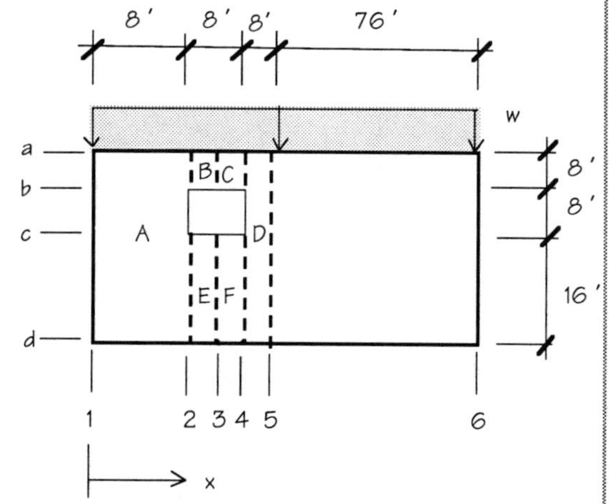

Line 1

$V_1 = V_5 = \dfrac{w\ell}{2} = \dfrac{.2(100)}{2} = 10.0^k$ (shearwall reaction)

$v_1 = \dfrac{V}{b} = \dfrac{10}{32} = .313$ klf (diaphragm unit shear)

Line 2

$V_2 = w\left(\dfrac{\ell}{2} - x\right) = .2\left(\dfrac{100}{2} - 8\right) = 8.4^k$

$$v_2 = \frac{V}{b} = \frac{8.4}{32} = .263 \text{ klf}$$

$$M_2 = \frac{wx}{2}(\ell - x) = \frac{.2(8)}{2}(100-8) = 73.6^{\text{ k ft}}$$

$$F_{2a} = \frac{M_2}{b} = \frac{73.6}{32} = 2.3^{k} \text{ (C)}$$

$$F_{2d} = F_{2a} = 2.3^{k} \text{ (T)}$$

Line 3

$$V_3 = w\left(\frac{\ell}{2} - x\right) = .2\left(\frac{100}{2} - 12\right) = 7.6^{k}$$

$$v_3 = \frac{V}{b} = \frac{7.6}{32} = .238 \text{ klf}$$

$$M_2 = \frac{wx}{2}(\ell - x) = \frac{.2(12)}{2}(100-12) = 105.6^{\text{ k ft}}$$

$$F_{3a} = \frac{M_3}{b} = \frac{105.6}{32} = 3.3^{k} \text{ (C)}$$

$$F_{3d} = F_{3a} = 3.3^{k} \text{ (T)}$$

Line 4

$$V_4 = w\left(\frac{\ell}{2} - x\right) = .2\left(\frac{100}{2} - 16\right) = 6.8^{k}$$

$$v_4 = \frac{V}{b} = \frac{6.8}{32} = .213 \text{ klf}$$

$$M_4 = \frac{wx}{2}(\ell - x) = \frac{.2(16)}{2}(100-16) = 134.4^{\text{ k ft}}$$

$$F_{4a} = \frac{M_4}{b} = \frac{134.4}{32} = 4.2^{k} \text{ (C)}$$

$$F_{4d} = F_{4a} = 4.2^{k} \text{ (T)}$$

Line 5

$$V_5 = w\left(\frac{\ell}{2} - x\right) = .2\left(\frac{100}{2} - 24\right) = 5.2^{k}$$

$$v_5 = \frac{V}{b} = \frac{5.2}{32} = .163 \text{ klf}$$

$$M_5 = \frac{wx}{2}(\ell - x) = \frac{.2(24)}{8}(100-24) = 182.4^{\text{ k ft}}$$

$$F_{5a} = \frac{M_5}{b} = \frac{182.4}{32} = 5.7^{k} \text{ (C)}$$

$$F_{5d} = F_{5a} = 5.7^{k} \text{ (T)}$$

Analyze diaphragm with hole

Obtain the chord and the unit shear forces at the critical locations proximate to opening. The remaining analysis is based upon the guidelines described in ATC-7, *Guidelines for the Design of Wood Sheathed Diaphragms*, and APA research report # 138 *Plywood Diaphragms*, which assume that the diaphragm performs analogous to that of a Vierendeel Truss. Actual tests performed by the APA (see above report) support this assumption. The points of contraflexure of the chords are assumed to be located at 1/2 the hole element length (above and below the hole). Use free body diagrams to calculate the shear and the chord forces at the edge of the opening and the boundaries, using the previous non-opening analysis results at line 3a. Assume the direction of forces and calc as shown below. Forces to the right, down, and clockwise moments are positive. Line 3 above gives our starting values. The actual diaphragm loading is required to calculate localized effects proximate to the hole. Evaluate the approximate seismic loading on the diaphragm as follows:

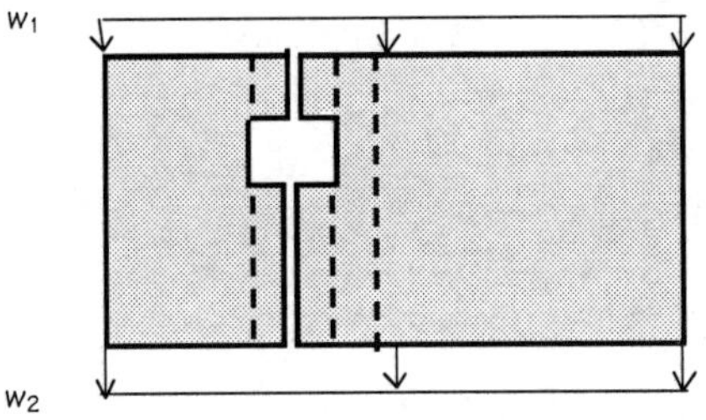

$w_1 = .108/2 + .092(12/32) = .09$ klf

$w_1 = .108/2 + .092(20/32) = .11$ klf

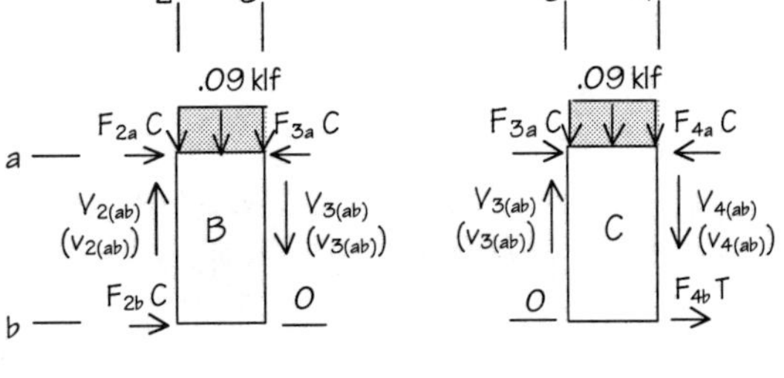

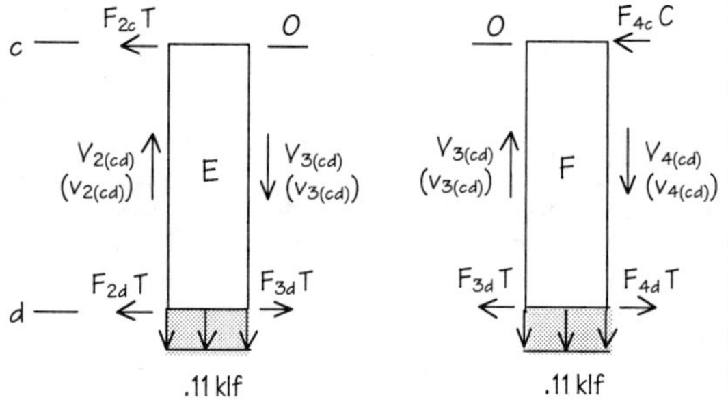

Zone C Due to the point of contraflexure:

$F_{3a} = 3.3^k$ (C), $V_4 = 6.8^k$ from above

$$V_{4(ab)} = \frac{8V_4}{24} = \frac{8(6.8)}{24} = 2.27^k$$

$$v_{4(ab)} = \frac{V}{b} = \frac{2.27}{8} = .284 \text{ klf}$$

$$V_{3(ab)} = 2.27 + 4(.09) = 2.63^k$$

$$v_{3(ab)} = \frac{V}{b} = \frac{2.63}{8} = .329 \text{ klf}$$

$\sum M_{3b} = 0$ gives:

$F_{4a} = (4(2.27) + 8(3.3) + 2(4).09)/8 = 4.53^k$ (C)

$F_{4b} = 4.53 - 3.3 = 1.23^k$ (T)

Zone B

$F_{3a} = 3.3^k$ (C)

$V_{3(ab)} = 2.63^k$

$v_{3(ab)} = .329$ klf

$V_{2(ab)} = 2.63 + 4(.09) = 2.99^k$

$$v_{2(ab)} = \frac{V}{b} = \frac{2.99}{8} = .374 \text{ klf}$$

$F_{2a} = (8(3.3) - 4(2.63) - 2(4).09)/8 = 1.9^k$ (C)

$F_{2b} = 3.3 - 1.9 = 1.4^k$ (C)

Zone F

$F_{3d} = 3.3^k$ (C)

$$V_{4(cd)} = \frac{16V_4}{24} = \frac{16(6.8)}{24} = 4.53^k$$

$$v_{4(cd)} = \frac{V}{b} = \frac{4.53}{16} = .283 \text{ klf}$$

$V_{3(cd)} = 4.53 + 4(.11) = 4.97^k$

$$v_{3(cd)} = \frac{V}{b} = \frac{4.97}{16} = .311 \text{ klf}$$

$F_{4c} = (4(4.53) + 4(2).11)/16 = 1.19^k$ (C)

$F_{4d} = 3.3 + 1.19 = 4.49^k$ (T)

Zone E

$F_{3d} = 3.3^k$ (C)

$V_{3(cd)} = 4.97^k$

$v_{3(cd)} = .311$ klf

$V_{2(cd)} = 4.97 + 4(.11) = 5.41^k$

$$v_{2(cd)} = \frac{V}{b} = \frac{5.41}{16} = .338 \text{ klf}$$

$F_{2c} = (4(4.97) + 4(2).11)/16 = 1.3^k$ (T)

$F_{2d} = 3.3 - 1.3 = 2.0^k$ (T)

Summary of forces at opening gives:

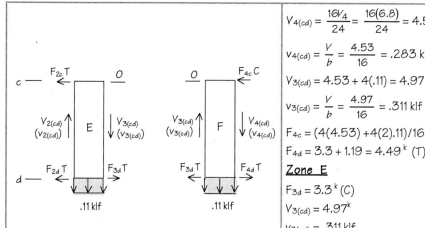

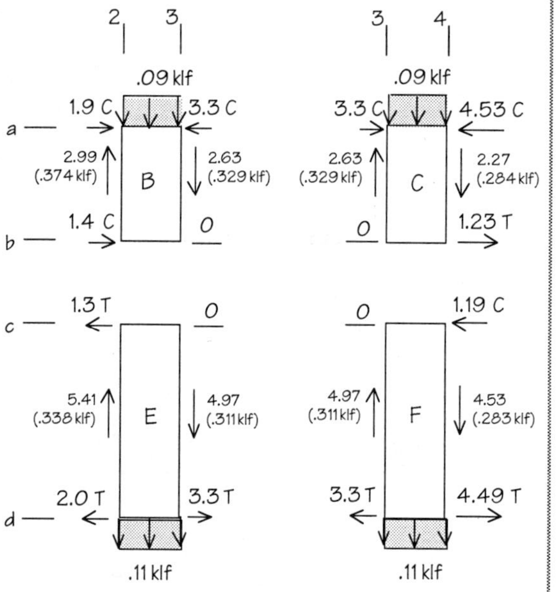

Note that during seismic reversal, the signs of the forces reverse but the absolute value of the forces remains the same.

Calculate net changes in the chord forces.

The net changes in the chord forces will be used to determine the connective hardware at the opening corners.

Diaph. Force Location	Chord Force (kip)		
	Without openings	With openings	Net change
F_2@ a	2.3 C	1.9 C	.4 T
b	0	1.4 C	1.4 C
c	0	1.3 T	1.3 T
d	2.3 T	2.0 T	.3 C
F_4@ a	4.2 C	4.53 C	.33 C
b	0	1.23 T	1.23 T
c	0	1.19 C	1.19 C
d	4.2 T	4.49 T	.29 T

Calculate the net shear forces along chords

The resulting shear forces from chords are dissipated into the subdiaphragms. The length of the connective hardware that dissipates these forces is dependent upon the framing, the allowable shear in the diaphragm, and the allowables of the connective hardware itself. Two typical framing arrangements are as follows:

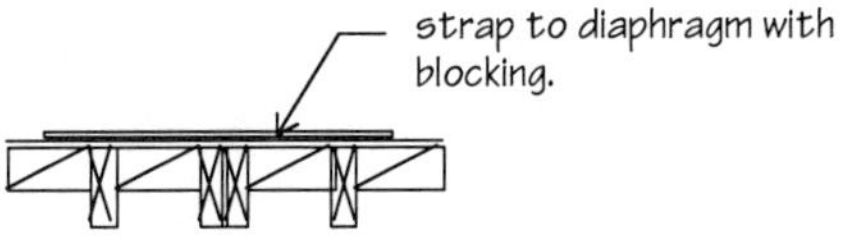

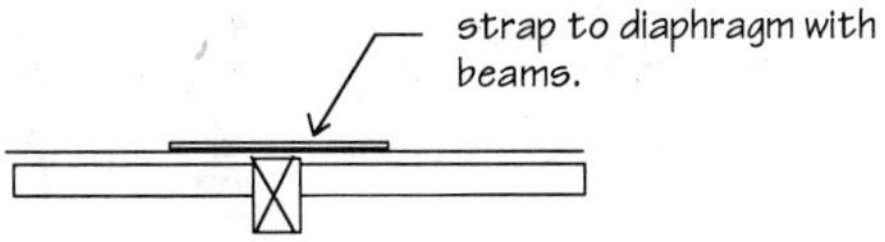

Net shear distribution diagram (tracks internal shear) | Net chord force diagram

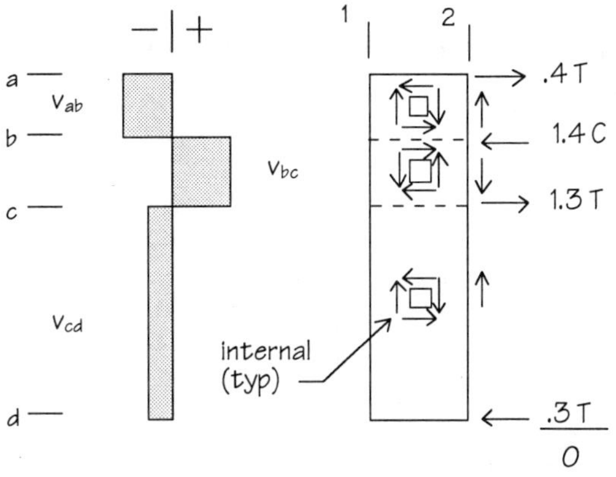

$v_{ab} = -.4/8 = -.05$ klf

$v_{bc} = 1.4/8 - .05 = .125$ klf

$v_{cd} = -1.3/8 + .125 = -.038$ klf

Net shear distribution diagram | Net chord force diagram

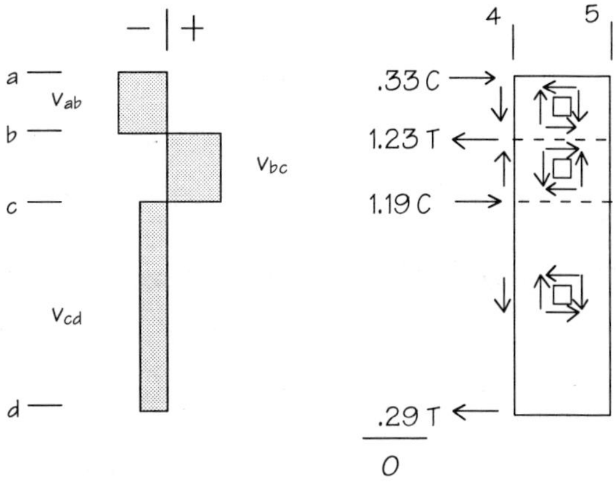

v_{ab} = -.33/8 = -.041 klf

v_{bc} = 1.23/8 - .041 = .113 klf

v_{cd} = -1.19/8 + .113 = -.036 klf

Calc. the resultant shears in the diaphragm.

Using superposition, visually for subdiaphragm 1-2 we have:

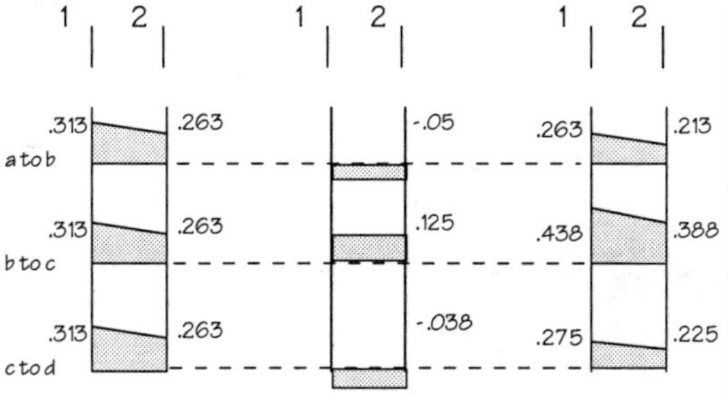

shear diagrams

The other zones are summarized as follows:

		Shear (klf)	
Diaph. shear location	Without openings	With openings	resultant dissipated chord shear
V_1 @ a to b	.313	-.05	.263
@ b to c	.313	.125	.438
@ c to d	.313	-.038	.275
V_2 @ a to b	.263	-.05	.213
@ b to c	.263	.125	.388
@ c to d	.263	-.038	.225
V_4 @ a to b	.213	- .041	.172
@ b to c	.213	.113	.326
@ c to d	.213	- .036	.150
V_5 @ a to b	.163	- .041	.122
@ b to c	.163	.113	.276
@ c to d	.163	- .036	.127

Summary and visualization is difficult at best. As an aid, the following is offered.

← Without hole.

← Segment force zones around hole.

<- - Net chord force change

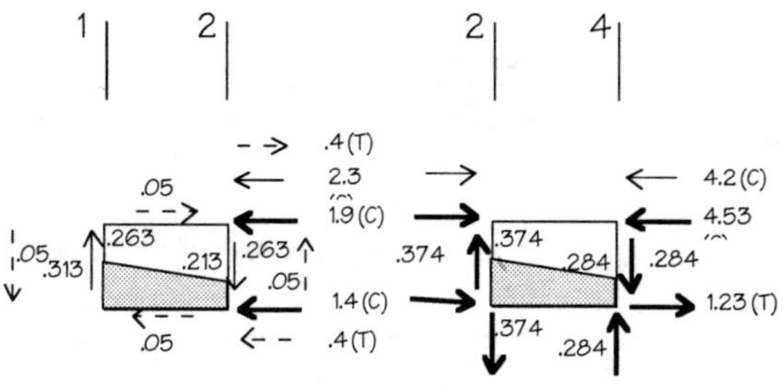

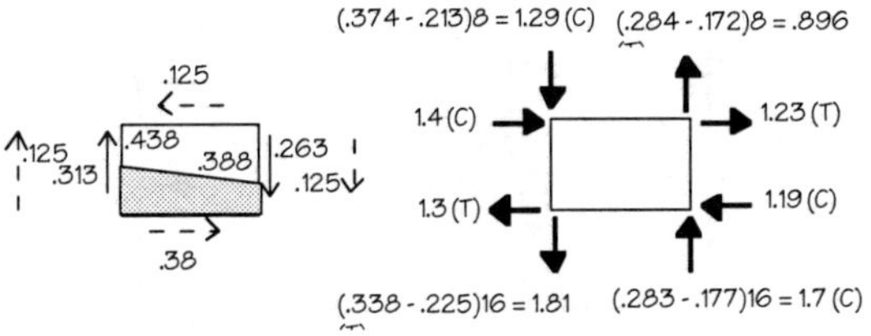

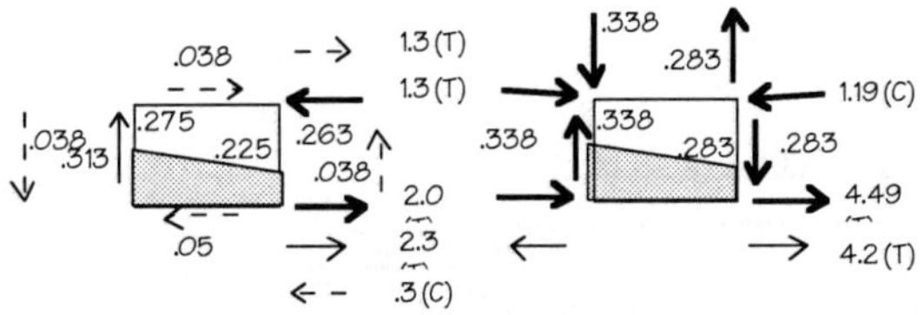

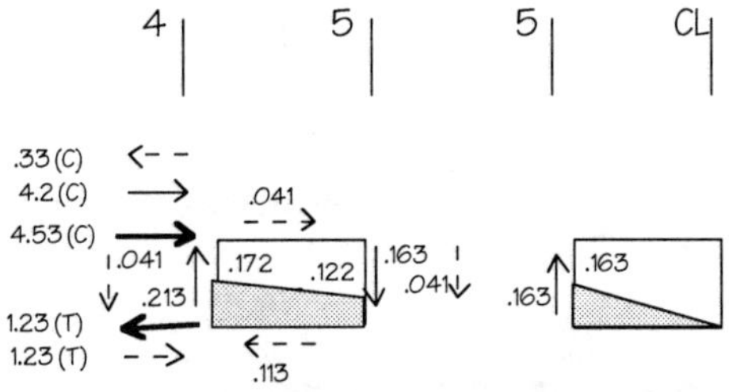

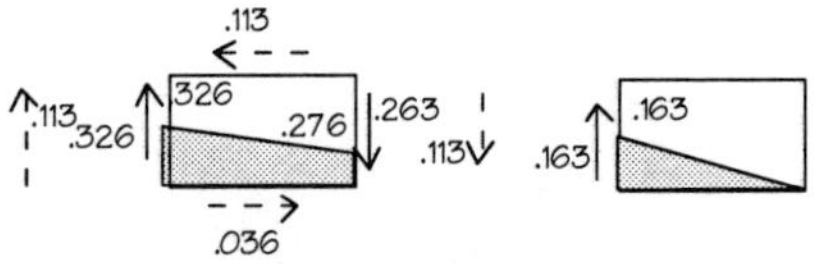

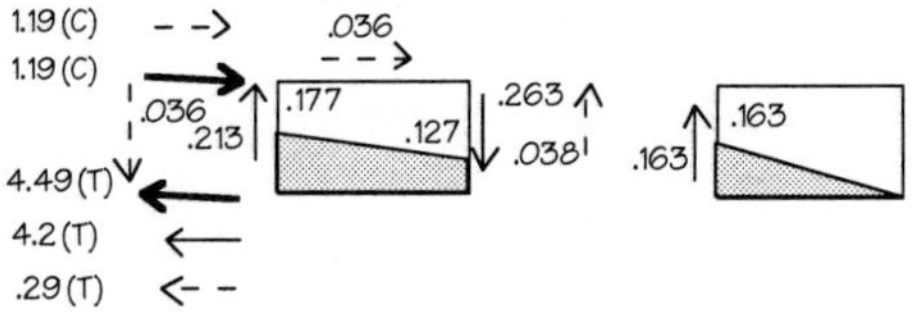

The design shears along chords:

<u>Area a to b</u>

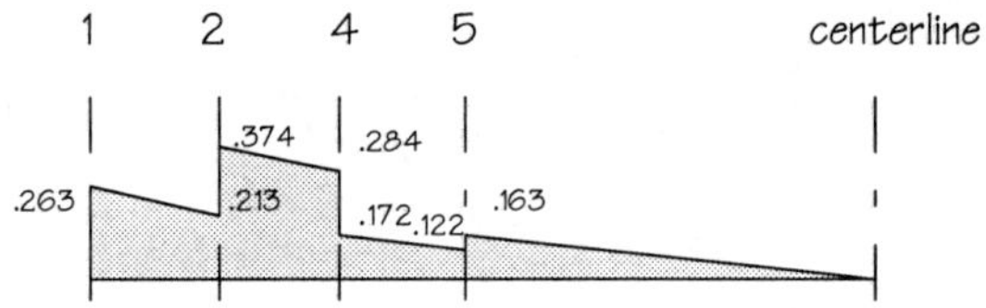

<u>Area b to c</u>

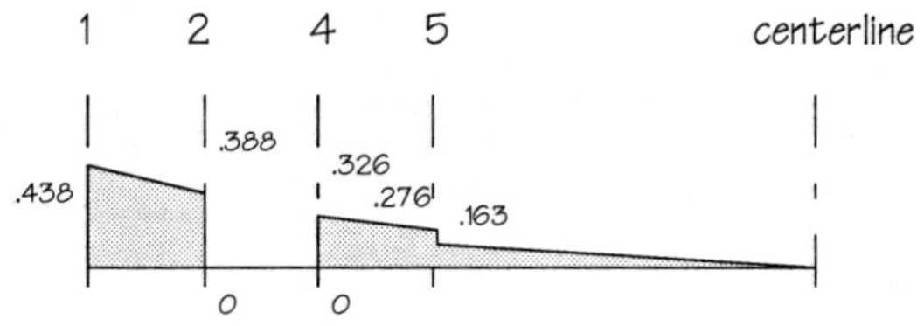

<u>Area c to d</u>

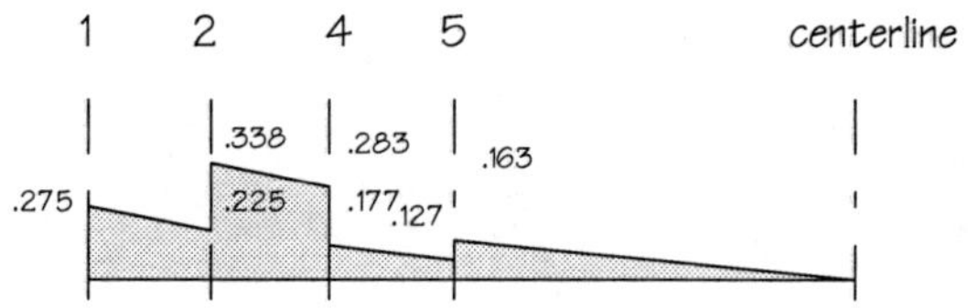

Design shear and force summary.

For design purposes, do not use a design shear value less than the unit shear for the diaphragm without hole analysis. Note that if you attempt to do extensive zone nailing within the drag zone of the hole you will further complicate the analysis to a degree not worth pursuing in practical terms.

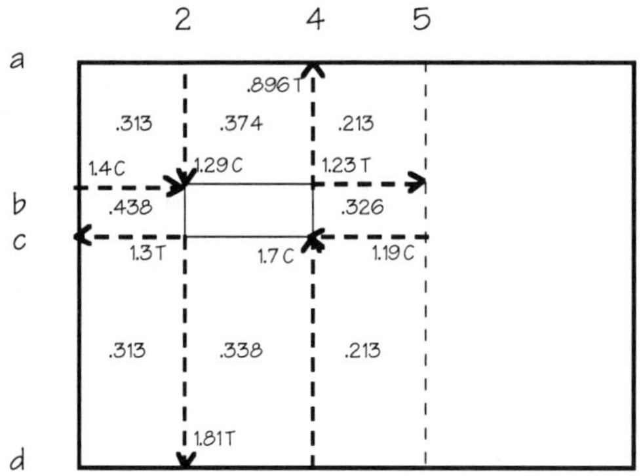

Recall that due to seismic reversal, the shear and chord forces reverse and members and connective hardware must be able to transmit the forces in the opposite direction.

Zone nailing

A simple design enveloping of shears gives:

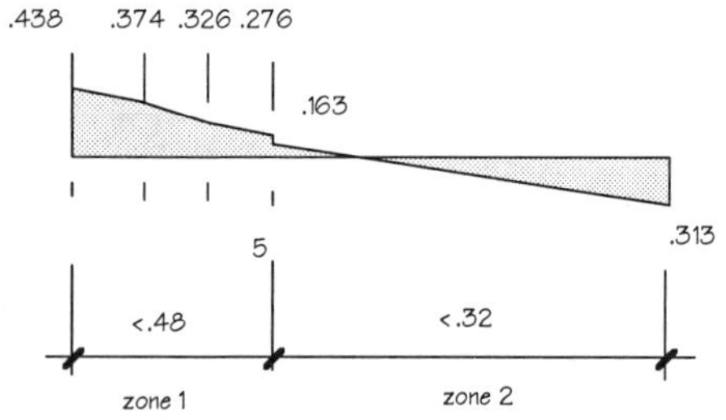

> Zone 1:
> Use 19/32 Str II with 10d @4,6,12 with 3x members.
> Zone 1:
> Use 19/32 Str II with 10d @6,6,12 with 3x members.

Drag ties

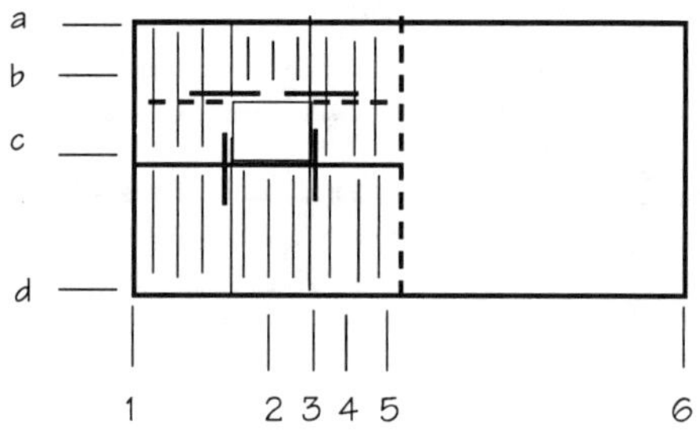

Ties along line 2 and 4

Recall that members from 1 to 5 must be upgraded to 3x. Since the members are continuous from a to c and from c to d, only ties at 4c and 2c are required.

> Use manf. ties with cap > 1.7^k

Ties along b and c

The member is continuous along c. Therefore no tie or strap is required. Tight blocking must be placed along line b to transfer compressive forces and to act as backup blocking for tension straps.

> Use manf. straps with cap. > 1.4^k

Hating people is like burning your own house down to get rid of a rat.

HARRY EMERSON FOSDICK

○ PROBLEM 4.13

Diaphragm deflection.

Determine the deflection of the diaphragm for the building shown below.

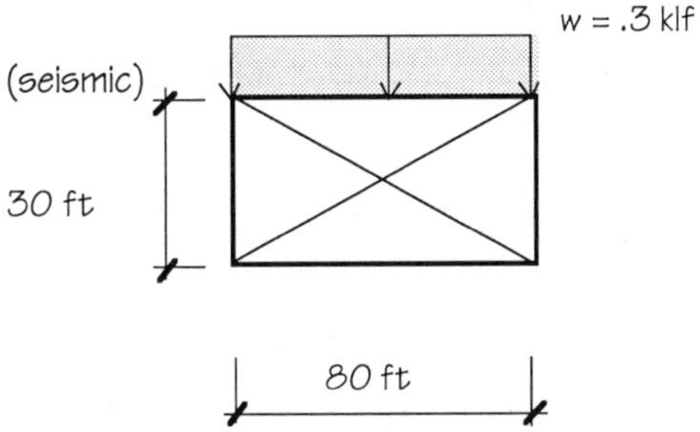

ASSUME

- Neglect wind.
- MC < 19%.
- 3/4 in. dia. MB at chord splices.
- 2-2x6 DF-L No 1 chords.
- 1 in "net" holes for holdowns.
- 1/2 in Str 1 ply with 8d @ 4,6,12 in o/c (blk'd).

NDS T23-1-1

SOLUTION

Ck aspect ratio (used for comparison in this problem)

The aspect ratio is the basic rule of thumb for determining acceptability of diaphragm deflection. It is also the most widely used method because of its ease of employment. This approach relies on the notion that deflection will be reasonable as long as the relative proportions of the diaphragm are limited by traditional ratios. These ratios have historically performed well when used in wood-type structures.

$$\frac{\ell}{b} = \frac{80}{30} = 2.7 < 4 \quad \checkmark$$

Diaphragm loads

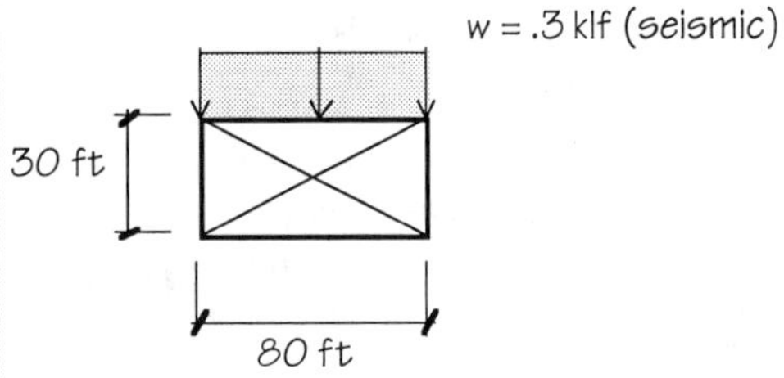

$$V = \frac{w\ell}{2} = \frac{.3(80)}{2} = 12^{k}$$

$$v = \frac{V}{b} = \frac{12}{30} = .4 \text{ klf}$$

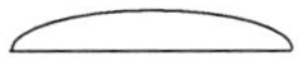

$$M = \frac{w\ell^2}{8} = \frac{.3(80)^2}{8} = 240 \text{ klf}$$

$$T = C = \frac{M}{b} = \frac{240}{30} = 8^{k}$$

$$F_t' = F_t C_D C_F = .675(1.33)1.5 = 1.35 \text{ ksi}$$

$$f_t = \frac{T}{A} = \frac{8}{8.25} = .97 \text{ ksi} < 1.35 \text{ ksi} \quad \checkmark$$

Diaphragm

The formula for the estimated deflection of horizontal diaphragms can be found in Section 25.922 of the 1991 UBC Standard 25-9. Note that in order to use this formula, the shearwall must be uniformly nailed and blocked. Also note that "Simpson Connections" now gives deflection criteria for certain pieces of its hardware (like HD's). The formula is as follows:

$$\Delta_{tot} = \Delta_{bending} + \Delta_{shear} + \Delta_{nail\ slip} + \Delta_{chord\ splice\ slip}$$

$$\Delta = \frac{5v\ell^3}{8EAb} + \frac{vh}{4Gt} + 0.188\ell e_n + \frac{\sum(\Delta_c x)}{2b}$$

v = .4 klf = 400 plf (max. unit shear)

ℓ = 80 ft (wall length)

b = 30 ft (wall width)

A = 8.25 in^2 (chord cross sectional area)

Increase NDS tabular values by 3%. This restores the normal tabular reduction that accounts for shear deflection.

E = 1.7e3(1.03) = 1.75e3 ksi (chord boundary element)

Plywood modulus of rigidity.

G = 90.0 ksi (PDS Table 3)

Plywood effective thickness.

t = .535 in., (PDS Table 2)

Use of Str 1 ply precludes the 20% increase for non Str 1 use. The nail deformation e_n (Table B-4, APA research report # 138) is calculated thus:

$$\frac{load}{nail} = \frac{v}{\#\ 8d/ft} = \frac{.4}{3} = .133^k$$

$$e_n = \left(\frac{v_n}{616}\right)^{3.018} = \left(\frac{133}{616}\right)^{3.018} = .01 \text{ in.}$$

If we were to use the UBC Standards Table 25-9-K and extrapolate for e_n:

$$\begin{array}{ll|l} 120 & .023 & \\ 133 & x & x = .028 \text{ in.} \\ 140 & .031 & \end{array}$$

This is over twice the value of the one given from APA research report # 138. Use APA value for this problem.

The fourth term of the equation estimates the rotation and slip for the tie-down anchorage. If bolts are used at the chord splices, assume that Δ_c = 1/2 of the normal oversize hole value (1/16 in. = .0625 in.) for bolts in holes. If chords are nailed, use a value similar to the previous e_n value.

$\sum(\Delta_c x)$ = Sum of the chord splice slip values multiplied by its distance to the nearest support.

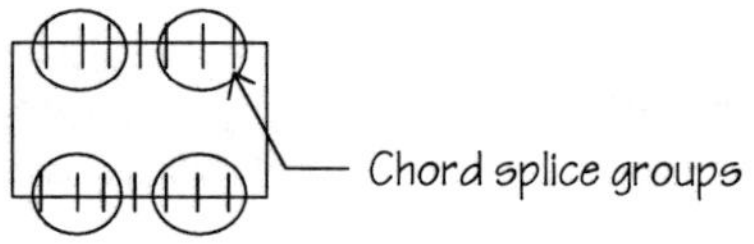

Assume chord splices @ 10 ft o/c with 1/32 in. slip each.

$$\frac{\sum(\Delta_c x)}{2b} = \frac{4\left(\frac{1}{32}\right)(10+20+30)+2\left(\frac{1}{32}\right)40}{2(30)}$$

= .167 in.

$$\Delta_{tot} = \frac{5(400)80^3}{(8)1.75e6(8.25)30} + \frac{400(80)}{(4)90e3(.535)} + 0.188(80).01 + .167$$

= .78 in.

Diaphragm deflection = .78 in.

Note that the aspect ratio is a code requirement and must be satisfied. The calculated deflection of .779 in is difficult to evaluate due to a lack of limiting criteria. The Designer must use her own judgment and experience as to whether the deflection will have deleterious effects on the shearwall or the structure as a whole. Some restrictive deflection criteria on masonry buildings may be found in *Reinforced Masonry Engineering Handbook*, (p. 49) by James E. Amrhein.

When you get right down to the root of the meaning of the word "succeed", you find it simply means to follow through.

F.W. NICHOL

● PROBLEM 4.14

Rotation and deflection of open end buildings.

Determine the deflection of the diaphragm for the open end building shown below.

w = .2 klf (seismic)

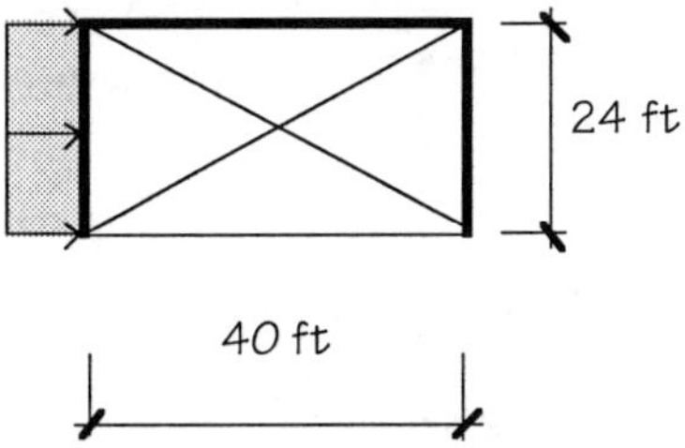

ASSUME

- Neglect wind.
- MC < 19%.
- 3/4 in. dia. MB at chord splices.
- 2-2x6 DF-L No 1 chords.
- 1/16 in oversize holes for holdowns.
- 1/2 in C-D ply with 8d @ 4,6,12 in o/c (blk'd).

SOLUTION

Ck aspect ratio

NDS T23-1-1

The aspect ratio is the basic rule of thumb for determining acceptability of diaphragm deflection. It is also the most widely used method because of its ease of employment. This approach relies on the notion that deflection will be reasonable as long as the relative proportions of the diaphragm are limited by traditional ratios. These ratios have historically performed well when used in wood-type structures. However, in the case where the stability of the structure relies upon rotation, we must adhere to UBC Section 2314.1.

$$24\text{ ft} < 25\text{ ft} < 40\left(\frac{2}{3}\right) = 26.7\text{ ft} \quad \checkmark$$

Diaphragm loads

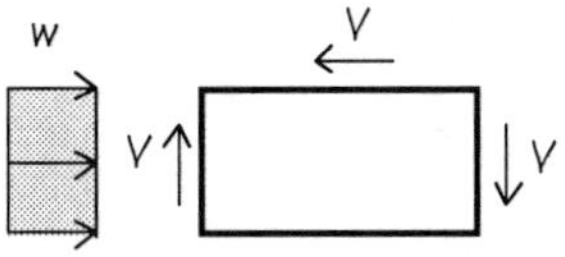

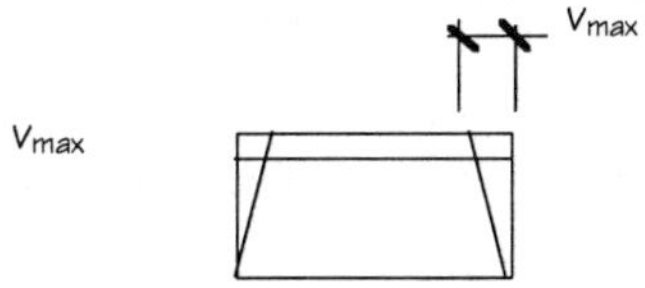

$$v_{max} = \frac{w\ell}{b} = \frac{.2(40)}{24} = .333\text{ klf}$$

$$v = \frac{V}{b} = \frac{12}{30} = .4\text{ klf}$$

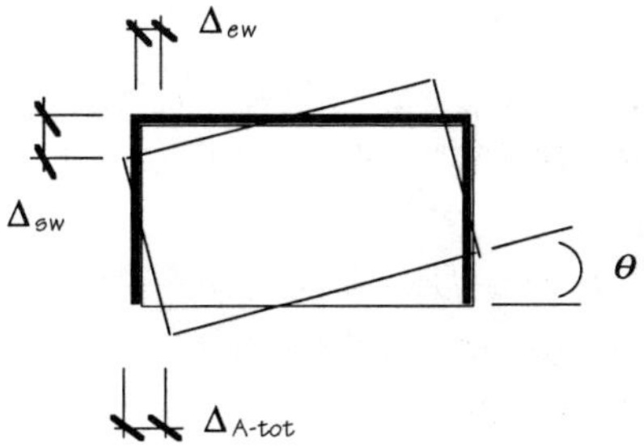

Diaphragm deflection

The formula for the estimated deflection (with rotation considerations) of horizontal diaphragms can be found in the APA Design/Construction Guide publication entitled *Diaphragms.* Note that in order to use this formula the shearwalls and diaphragms must be uniformly nailed and blocked. Since the open (non-restrained) end of the building does not allow for beam action, the diaphragm chord forces are 0. The general formula before reduction, due to the open end, is as follows:

$$\Delta_{tot} = \cancel{\Delta_{bending}}^{0} + \cancel{\Delta_{chord\ splice\ slip}}^{0} + \Delta_{shear} + \Delta_{nail\ slip} + \Delta_{rotation} + \Delta_{end\ wall\ lateral\ translation}$$

$$\Delta_{A-tot} = \overbrace{\frac{v_{max}\ell}{2Gt} + 0.375\ell e_n}^{\text{diaphragm}} + \overbrace{\frac{2\Delta_{sw}\ell}{b} + \Delta_{ew}}^{\text{walls}}$$

Shear deflection Δ_{sw} (side shear wall deflection)

Use $v = \frac{v_{max}}{2} = \frac{.333}{2} = .167$ klf

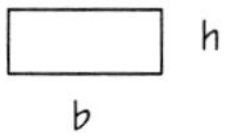

$\Delta_{sw} = \Delta_{bending} + \Delta_{shear} + \Delta_{nail\ slip} + \Delta_{chord\ bolt\ slip}$

$$\Delta_{sw} = \frac{8vh^3}{EAb} + \frac{vh}{Gt} + 0.75he_n + d_a$$

$v = .167$ klf (max. unit shear)
$A = 8.25$ in^2 (chord boundary element)
$h = 10$ ft (wall height)
$b = 24$ ft (wall width)

Estimate the rotation and slip for the tie-down anchorage. Assume 1/16 in. = .0625 in net holes:

$d_a = .0625$ in.
(rotation and slip of tie-down anchorage)
$E = 1.7e3$ ksi (chord boundary element)
Plywood modulus of rigidity.
$G = 90.0$ ksi (Table No. 25-9-J)
Plywood effective thickness.
$t = .535$ in. (Table No. 25-9-H, I)
Nail deformation
(Table B-4, APA research report # 138).

$$\frac{load}{nail} = \frac{v}{\#\ 8d/ft} = \frac{167}{3} = 56\ \#$$

$e_n = 1.2\left(\frac{v_n}{616}\right)^{3.018} = 1.2\left(\frac{56}{616}\right)^{3.018}$ (non Str 1 increase)

$= .001$ in

$$\Delta_{sw} = \frac{8(.167)10^3}{1.7e3(8.25)24} + \frac{.167(10)}{90(.535)} + 0.75(10).001 + .0625$$

$= .109$ in

$\boxed{\Delta_{sw} = .109\ in}$

End wall lateral translation Δ_{ew}

Use $v = v_{max} = .333$ klf

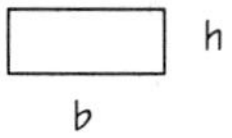

$\Delta_{ew} = \Delta_{bending} + \Delta_{shear} + \Delta_{nail\ slip} + \Delta_{chord\ bolt\ slip}$

$$\Delta_{ew} = \frac{8vh^3}{EAb} + \frac{vh}{Gt} + 0.75he_n + d_a$$

$v = .333$ klf (max. unit shear)
$A = 8.25$ in^2 (chord boundary element)
$h = 10$ ft (wall height)
$b = 40$ ft (wall width)

Estimate the rotation and slip for the tie-down anchorage. Assume 1/16 in. = .0625 in net holes:

$d_a = .0625$ in
(rotation and slip of tie-down anchorage)
$E = 1.7e3$ ksi (chord boundary element)
Plywood modulus of rigidity.
$G = 90.0$ ksi (Table No. 25-9-J)
Plywood effective thickness.
$t = .535$ in. (Table No. 25-9-H, I)
Nail deformation
(Table B-4, APA research report # 138)

$$\frac{load}{nail} = \frac{v}{\#\ 8d/ft} = \frac{333}{3} = 111\ plf$$

$e_n = 1.2\left(\frac{v_n}{616}\right)^{3.018} = 1.2\left(\frac{111}{616}\right)^{3.018}$

(non Str 1 increase)
$= .007$ in.

$$\Delta_{ew} = \frac{8(.333)10^3}{1.7e3(8.25)40} + \frac{.333(10)}{90(.535)} + 0.75(10).007 + .0625$$

$= .19$ in.

$\Delta_{ew} = .19$ in

Total diaphragm deflection

$$\Delta_{A\text{-}tot} = \frac{.333(24)}{2(90).535} + 0.375(24).007 + \frac{2(.109)24}{40} + .19$$

$= .47$ in

Diaphragm deflection = .47 in

Note that the aspect ratio is a code requirement and must be satisfied. The calculated deflection of .418 in. is difficult to evaluate due to a lack of limiting criteria. The Designer must use his own judgment and experience as to whether the deflection will have deleterious effects on the shearwalls, the structure as a whole, or nearby buildings. Some restrictive deflection criteria on masonry buildings may be found in *Reinforced Masonry Engineering Handbook*, (p. 49), by James E. Amrhein.

Even if you're on the right track, you'll get run over if you just sit there.

WILL ROGERS

○ PROBLEM 4.15

Stepped diaphragm.

Analyze the stepped diaphragm below. Make design recommendations to maintain diaphragm integrity.

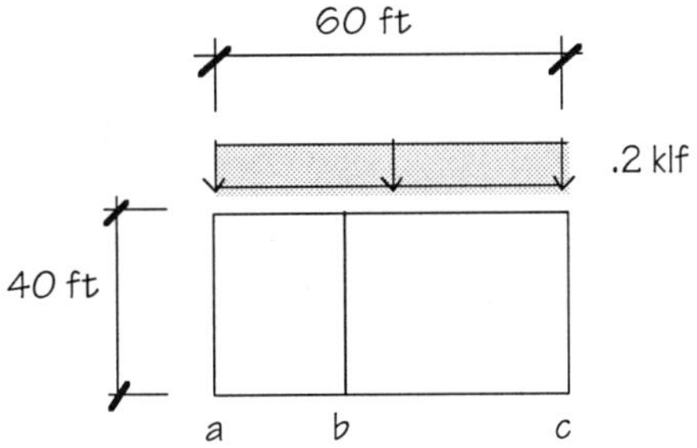

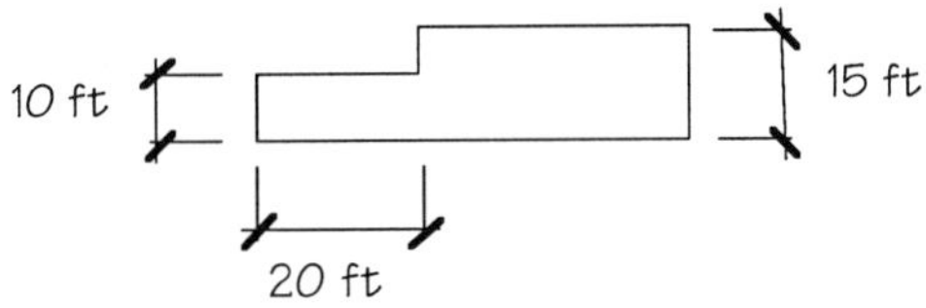

ASSUME

Roof sloped for drainage.
Shearwall: 1/2 in. C-D with 8d @ 6,12 in. o/c.
Diaphragm: 1/2 in. C-D with 8d @ 6,6,12 in. o/c.

SOLUTION

There is an obvious discontinuity at the step of the diaphragm. Diaphragm integrity is interrupted at this point. We must rectify the discontinuity by introducing two structural continuity considerations.

- Diaphragm shear must be transferred from the upper level diaphragm to the lower level diaphragm.
- The chord force of the diaphragm must be transferred from the upper level diaphragm to the lower level diaphragm.

These structural considerations are outlined in the following calculations.

Calc diaph. unit shear

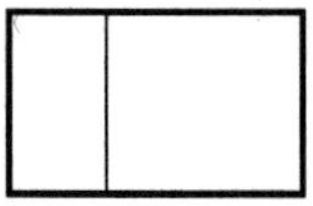

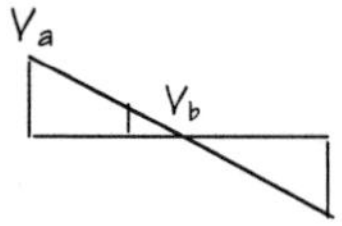

$$V_a = \frac{w\ell}{2} = \frac{.2(60)}{2} = 6.0^{k}$$

$$v_a = \frac{V}{b} = \frac{6.0}{40} = .15 \text{ klf}$$

$$V_b = w\left(\frac{\ell}{2}-x\right) = .2\left(\frac{60}{2}-20\right) = 2.0^{k}$$

$$v_b = \frac{V}{b} = \frac{2.0}{40} = .05 \text{ klf}$$

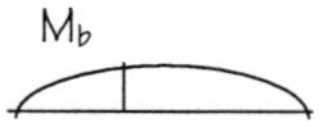

$$M_b = \frac{wx(\ell-x)}{2} = \frac{.2(20)(60-20)}{2} = 80.0^{\text{ k ft}}$$

$$T_b = C_b = \frac{M_b}{b} = \frac{80}{40} = 2.0^{k}$$

$$M_{max} = \frac{w\ell^2}{8} = \frac{.2(60)^2}{8} = 90.0^{\text{k ft}}$$

$$T_{max} = C_{max} = \frac{M_1}{b} = \frac{90}{40} = 2.25^{k}$$

Diaphragm shear transfer

The shear to transfer from the top level to the roof shearwall at "b" and to the lower level roof diaphragms:

$v = .05 \text{ klf} < .26 \text{ klf}$ √

> Use existing specification of 1/2 in C-D plywood with 8d @ 6,12 in o/c for roof level shearwall

Diaphragm chord force transfer

Cut elevation at "b" for free body diagram.

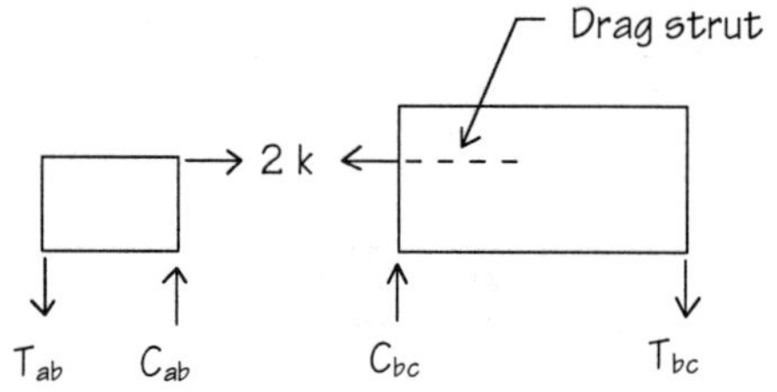

Calculate the moment couple forces:

$T_{ab} = C_{ab} = 2(10)/20 = 1.0^{k}$

$T_{bc} = C_{bc} = 2(10)/40 = .5^{k}$

Max tension or compression $= 1.0 + .5 = 1.5^{k}$

> Provide holdowns at a, b, c and check compression and tension chord struts for seismic reversal forces

Drag strut length.

$$\ell = \frac{2}{.26} = 7.7 \text{ ft}$$

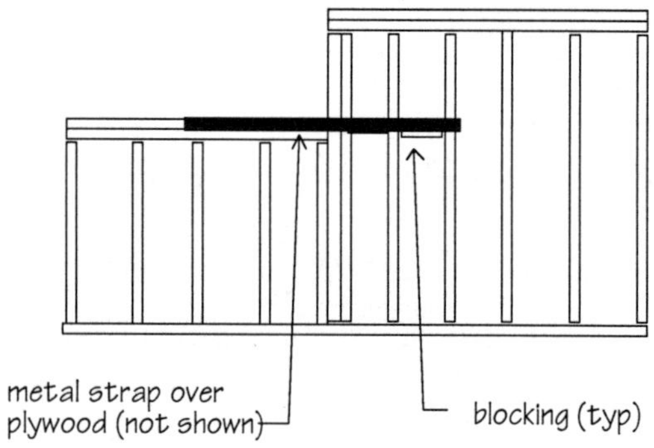

> Use manf. strap.
> Simpson CMST14 = 6.795 ^{k} cap. min.
> and blocking as required for 8 ft min.
> each side of "b"

A stepped diaphragm will tend to increase the cost of construction because of the additional complexity it introduces into the project. Although we can incorporate connective hardware to accommodate the discontinuities, performance (hence risk to the structure and its inhabitants) is decreased by the inclusion of the step. A viable option would be to recommend to simplify the design by the introduction of shear walls at "b". This will enhance the building's performance and potentially decrease the construction costs.

We can endure neither our evils nor their cures.

LIVY
59 B.C. - 17 A.D.

● PROBLEM 4.16

Horizontal diaphragm with hole proximate to the "loaded" edge of aN exterior wall.

Analyze the effects of the seismic loading on the hole in the roof diaphragm of the strip mall building shown below.

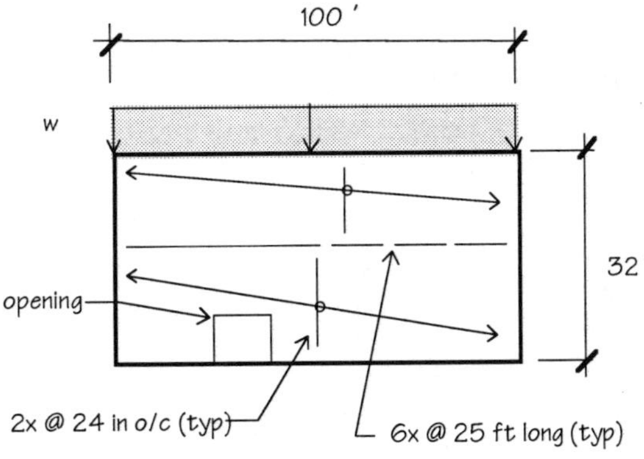

ASSUME

w = .2 klf (.092 diaphragm, .108 walls).
Framing at 2 ft o/c.

SOLUTION

Aspect ratio $= \frac{\ell}{b} = \frac{32}{16} = 2.0 < 4$ √ NDS T23-1-I

Analyze diaphragm without hole

Obtain chord and unit shear forces at critical locations proximate to the opening. Assume that the seismic loads are applied at the top of diaphragm. Also note that since we will need local chords at the hole, assume A and D are subdiaphragms with the appropriate code span/depth ratio.

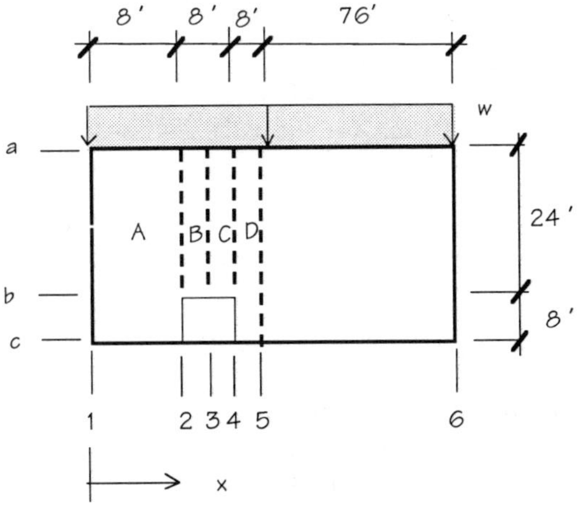

Note that the 8 ft. section at c23 must be capable of taking bending for the wall inertial load.

Line 1

$V_1 = V_5 = \frac{w\ell}{2} = \frac{.2(100)}{2} = 10.0^k$ (shearwall reaction)

$v_1 = \frac{V}{b} = \frac{10}{32} = .313$ klf (diaphragm unit shear)

Line 2

$$V_2 = w\left(\frac{\ell}{2}-x\right) = .2\left(\frac{100}{2}-8\right) = 8.4^k$$

$$v_2 = \frac{V}{b} = \frac{8.4}{32} = .263 \text{ klf}$$

$$M_2 = \frac{wx}{2}(\ell-x) = \frac{.2(8)}{2}(100-8) = 73.6^{k\,ft}$$

$$F_{2a} = \frac{M_2}{b} = \frac{73.6}{32} = 2.3^k \text{ (C)}$$

$$F_{2d} = F_{2a} = 2.3^k \text{ (T)}$$

Line 3

$$V_3 = w\left(\frac{\ell}{2}-x\right) = .2\left(\frac{100}{2}-12\right) = 7.6^k$$

$$v_3 = \frac{V}{b} = \frac{7.6}{32} = .238 \text{ klf}$$

$$M_2 = \frac{wx}{2}(\ell-x) = \frac{.2(12)}{2}(100-12) = 105.6^{k\,ft}$$

$$F_{3a} = \frac{M_3}{b} = \frac{105.6}{32} = 3.3^k \text{ (C)}$$

$$F_{3d} = F_{3a} = 3.3^k \text{ (T)}$$

Line 4

$$V_4 = w\left(\frac{\ell}{2}-x\right) = .2\left(\frac{100}{2}-16\right) = 6.8^k$$

$$v_4 = \frac{V}{b} = \frac{6.8}{32} = .213 \text{ klf}$$

$$M_4 = \frac{wx}{2}(\ell-x) = \frac{.2(16)}{2}(100-16) = 134.4^{k\,ft}$$

$$F_{4a} = \frac{M_4}{b} = \frac{134.4}{32} = 4.2^k \text{ (C)}$$

$$F_{4d} = F_{4a} = 4.2^k \text{ (T)}$$

Line 5

$$V_5 = w\left(\frac{\ell}{2}-x\right) = .2\left(\frac{100}{2}-24\right) = 5.2^k$$

$$v_5 = \frac{V}{b} = \frac{5.2}{32} = .163 \text{ klf}$$

$$M_5 = \frac{wx}{2}(\ell-x) = \frac{.2(24)}{8}(100-24) = 182.4^{k\,ft}$$

$$F_{5a} = \frac{M_5}{b} = \frac{182.4}{32} = 5.7^k \text{ (C)}$$

$$F_{5d} = F_{5a} = 5.7^k \text{ (T)}$$

Analyze diaphragm with hole

Obtain the chord and the unit shear forces at the critical locations proximate to opening. The remaining analysis is based upon the guidelines described in ATC-7, *Guidelines for the Design of Wood Sheathed Diaphragms*, and APA research report # 138 *Plywood Diaphragms*, which assume that the diaphragm performs analogous to that of a Vierendeel Truss. Actual tests performed by the APA (see above report) support this assumption. The points of contraflexure of the chords are assumed to be located at 1/2 the hole element length (above and below the hole). Use free body diagrams to calculate the shear and the chord forces at the edge of the opening and the boundaries, using the previous non-opening analysis results at line 3a. Assume the direction of forces and calc as shown below. Forces to the right, down and clockwise moments are positive. Line 3 above gives our starting values. The actual diaphragm loading is required to calculate localized effects proximate to the hole. Evaluate the approximate seismic loading on the diaphragm as follows:

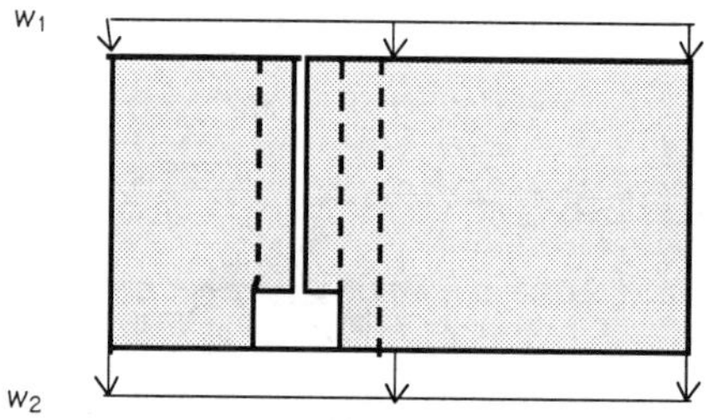

$w_1 = .108/2 + .092(24/32) = .123$ klf

$w_1 = .108/2 + .092(8/32) = .077$ klf

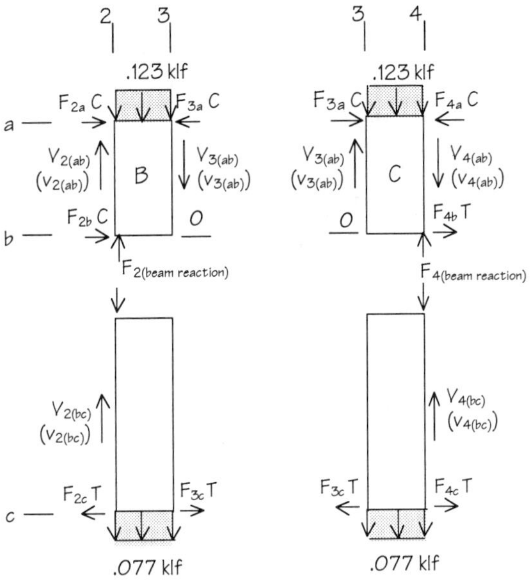

Wall zone at c

$F_{2(beam\ reaction)} = .077(8)/2 = .31^k$

$F_{4(beam\ reaction)} = .31^k$

$F_{3d} = 3.3^k$ (T)

$F_{4d} = 3.3^k$ (T)

$F_{2d} = 3.3^k$ (T)

$V_{4(bc)} = .31^k$

$v_{4(bc)} = \dfrac{V}{b} = \dfrac{.31}{8} = .039$ klf

$V_{2(bc)} = .31^k$

$v_{2(bc)} = .039$ klf

We can either consider the reactions now and enter them in our zone calcs, or consider them at the end. I prefer to add their effects now rather than at a later time.

Zone C Calculate magnitudes.

Due to the point of contraflexure:

$F_{3a} = 3.3^k$ (C), $V_4 = 6.8^k$ from above

$V_{4(ab)} = 6.8^k$

$v_{4(ab)} = \dfrac{V}{b} = \dfrac{6.8}{24} = .283$ klf

$V_{3(ab)} = 6.8 + 4(.123) + .31 = 7.6^k$

$v_{3(ab)} = \dfrac{V}{b} = \dfrac{7.6}{24} = .317$ klf

$\sum M_{3b} = 0$ gives:

$F_{4a} = (4(6.8) + 24(3.3) + 2(4).123 + 4(.31))/24$

$= 4.53^k$ (C)

$F_{4b} = 4.53 - 3.3 = 1.23^k$ (T)

Zone B

$F_{3a} = 3.3^k$ (C)

$V_{3(ab)} = 7.6^k$

$v_{3(ab)} = .317$ klf

Assume that the drag allows the beam reaction full distribution over the diaphragm.

$V_{2(ab)} = 7.6 + 4(.123) + .31 = 8.02^k$

$v_{2(ab)} = \dfrac{V}{b} = \dfrac{8.02}{24} = .334$ klf

$F_{2a} = (24(3.3) - 4(7.29) - 2(4).123)/24 = 2.04^k$ (C)

$F_{2b} = 3.3 - 2.04 = 1.26^k$ (C)

Summary of forces at opening gives:

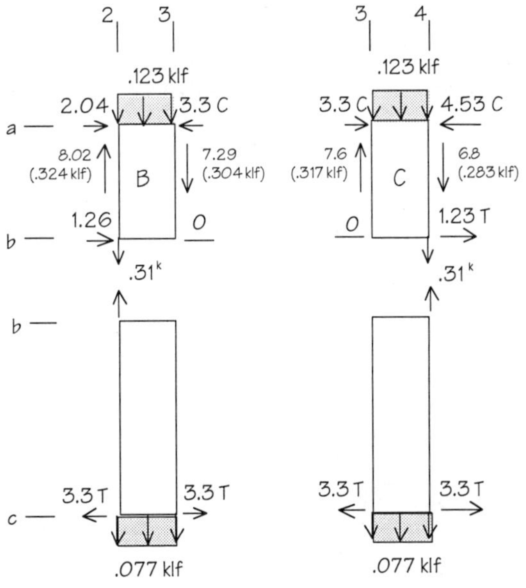

Note that during seismic reversal, the signs of the forces reverse but the absolute value of the forces remains the same.

Calculate net changes in the chord forces.

The net changes in the chord forces will be used to determine the connective hardware at the opening corners.

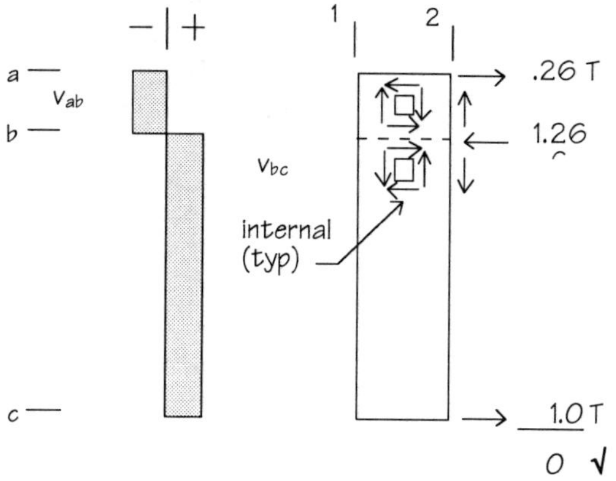

Diaph. Force Location	Chord Force (kip)		
	Without openings	With openings	Net change
F_2@ a	2.3 C	2.04 C	.26 T
b	0	1.26 C	1.26 C
c	2.3 T	3.3 T	1.0 T
F_4@ a	4.2 C	4.53 C	.33 C
b	0	1.23 T	1.23 T
c	4.2 T	3.3T	.9 C

Calculate the net shear forces along chords

$v_{ab} = -.26/8 = -.033$ klf

$v_{bc} = 1.26/8 - .033 = .125$ klf

The resulting shear forces from chords are dissipated into the subdiaphragms. The length of the connective hardware that dissipates these forces is dependent upon the framing, the allowable shear in the diaphragm, and the allowables of the connective hardware itself. Two typical framing arrangements are as follows:

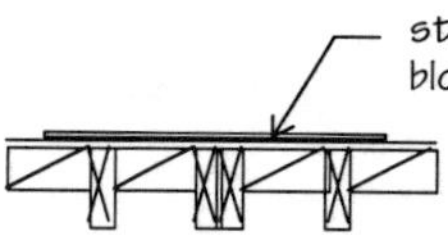

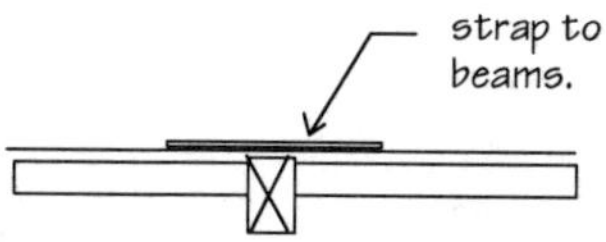

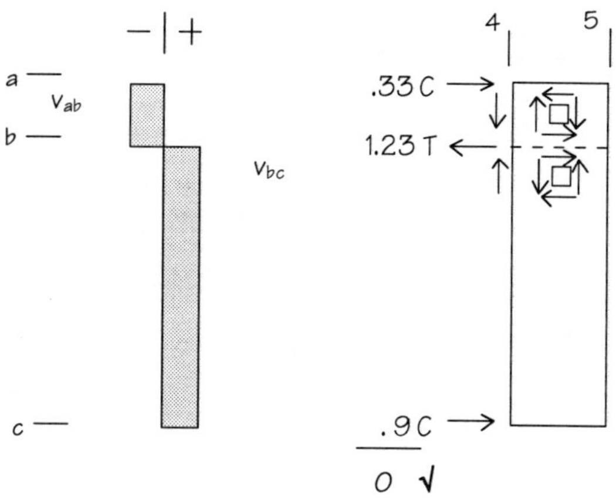

$v_{ab} = -.33/8 = -.041$ klf

$v_{bc} = 1.23/8 - .041 = .113$ klf

Calc. the resultant shears in the diaphragm

Using superposition, visually for subdiaphragm 1-2 we have:

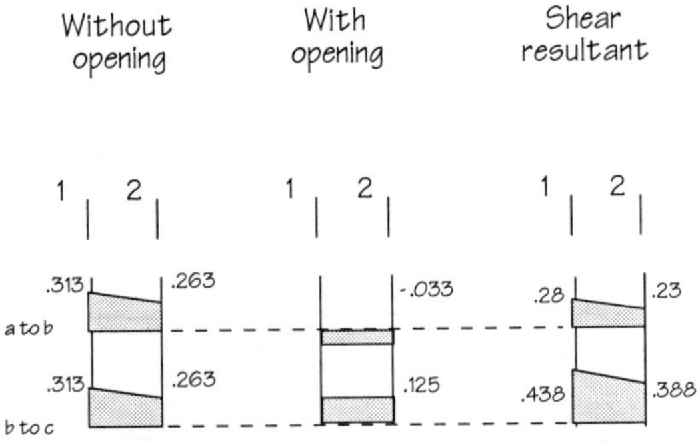

shear diagrams

The other zones are summarized as follows:

Diaph. shear location	Shear (klf)		
	Without openings	With openings	resultant dissipated chord shear
V_1 @ a to b	.313	-.033	.28
@ b to c	.313	.125	.438
V_2 @ a to b	.263	-.033	.23
@ b to c	.263	.125	.388
V_4 @ a to b	.213	- .041	.172
@ b to c	.213	.113	.326
V_5 @ a to b	.163	- .041	.122
@ b to c	.163	.113	.276

Summary and visualization is difficult at best. As an aid, the following is:

← Without hole.

← Segment force zones around hole.

<- - Net chord force change

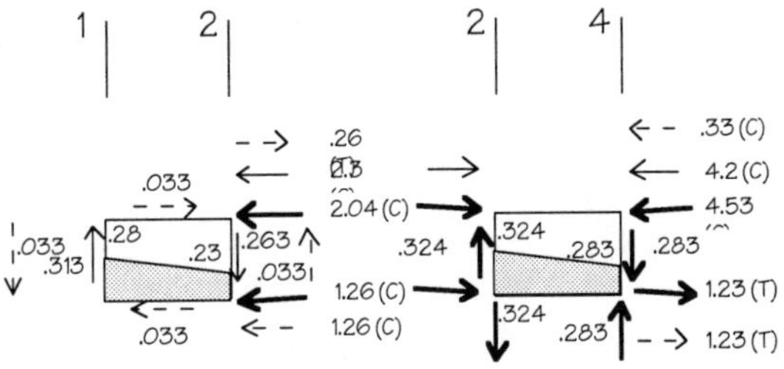

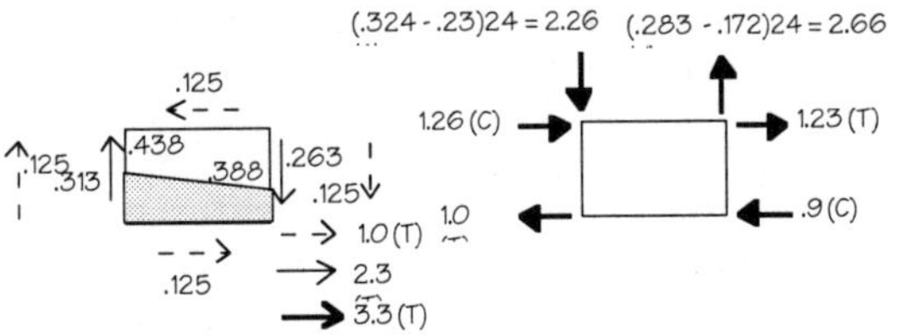

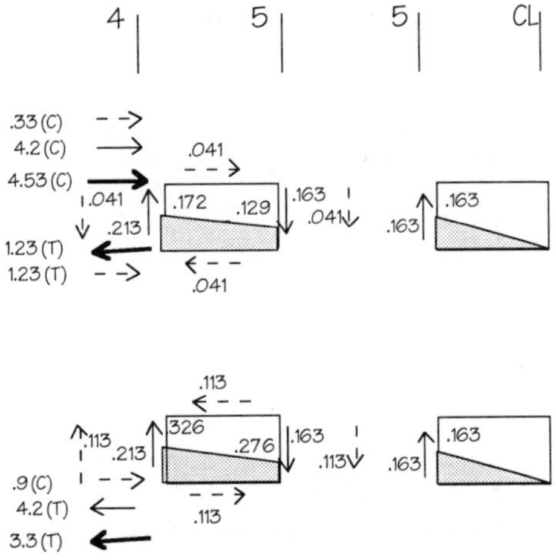

The design resultant shears along chords:

<u>Area a to b</u>

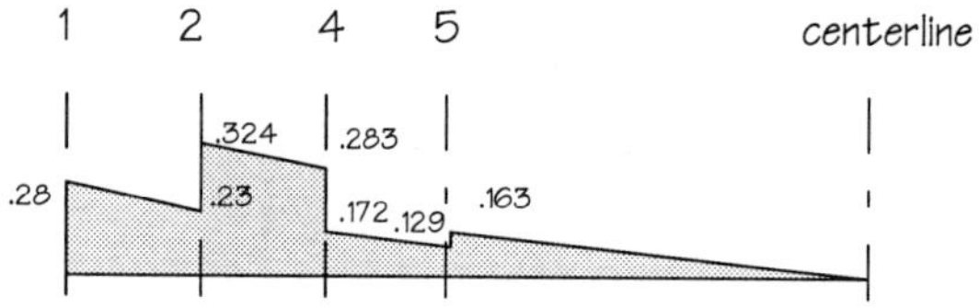

<u>Area b to c</u>

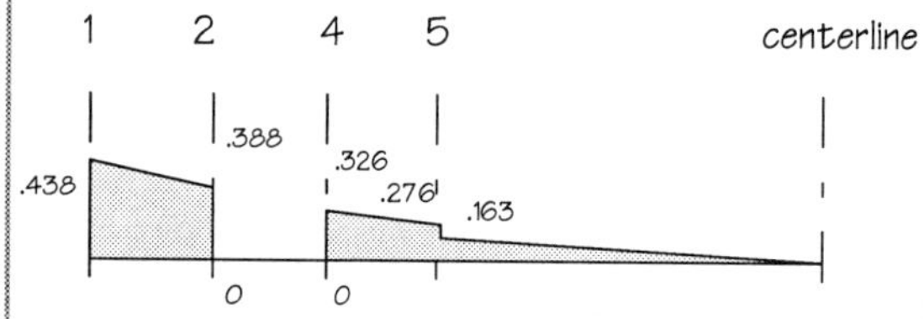

Design shear and force summary

For design purposes, do not use a design shear value less than the unit shear for the diaphragm without hole analysis. Note that if you attempt to do extensive zone nailing within the drag zone of the hole, you will further complicate the analysis to a degree not worth pursuing in practical terms.

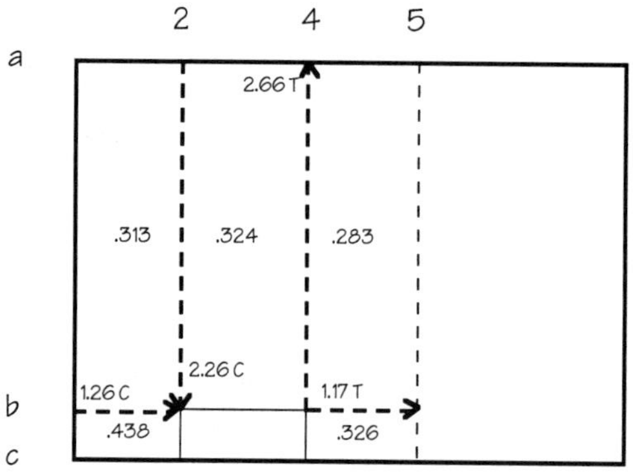

Recall that due to seismic reversal, the shear and chord forces reverse and members and connective hardware must be able to transmit the forces in the opposite direction.

<u>Zone nailing</u>

We can either have special nailing at the drags or use a higher zone. A simple zone design enveloping the shears gives:

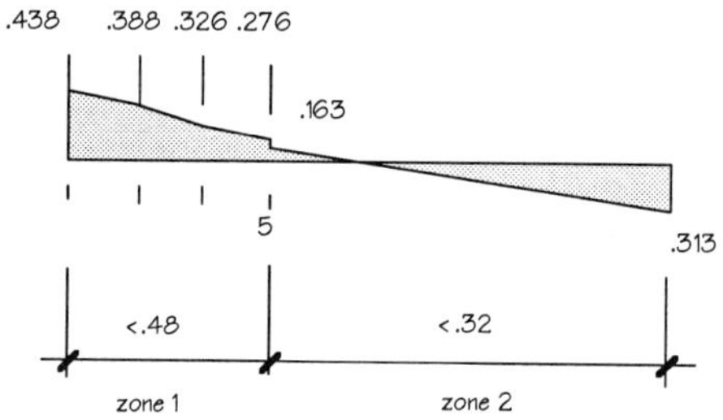

Zone 1:
Use 19/32 Str II with 10d @4,6,12 with 3x members.
Zone 1:
Use 19/32 Str II with 10d @6,6,12 with 3x members.

<u>Drag ties</u>

Ck plan irregularity for opening (UBC Table 23N)

8(8)/32(100) = .02 < .5

If the value were greater than .5 the UBC Sec. 2337(b)9E would not allow a 1.33 (or 1.6) increase factor at zones 3 or 4 for connections.

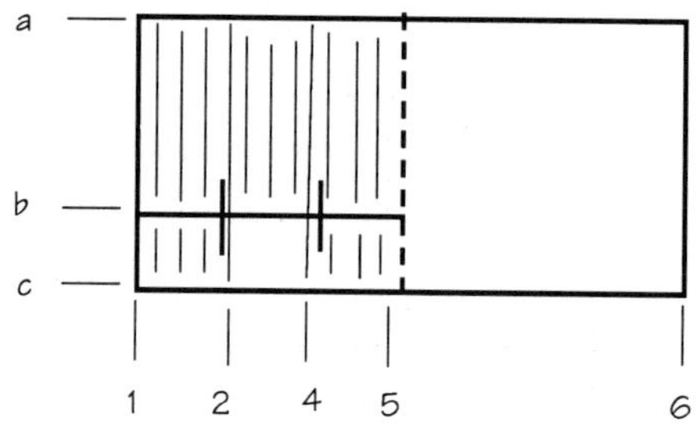

Ties along line 2 and 4

Recall that members from 1 to 5 must be upgraded to 3x. Since the members are continuous from a to b and from b to c, only ties at 4b and 2b are required.
$2.66_k < 6.7^k$ √

> Use manf. ties with cap > 2.7^k
> Simpson CMST14 cap. = 6.7^k

Ties along b and c

The member is continuous along b. Therefore no tie strap is required.

> No strap required due to continuous member

There is no failure except in no longer trying.

ELBERT HUBBARD

● PROBLEM 4.17

Horizontal diaphragm with hole proximate to the side edge of the exterior wall.

Analyze the effects of the seismic loading on the hole in the roof diaphragm of the strip mall building shown below.

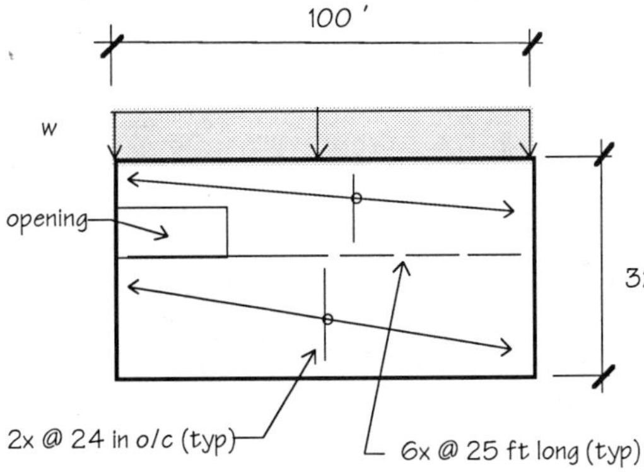

ASSUME

w = .2 klf (.092 diaphragm, .108 walls).
Framing at 2 ft o/c.

SOLUTION

Aspect ratio $= \frac{\ell}{b} = \frac{32}{16} = 2.0 < 4$ √ NDS T23-I-I

Analyze diaphragm without hole

Obtain chord and unit shear forces at critical locations proximate to the opening. Assume that the seismic loads are applied at the top of diaphragm. Also note that since we will need local chords at the hole, assume A and D are subdiaphragms with the appropriate code span/depth ratio.

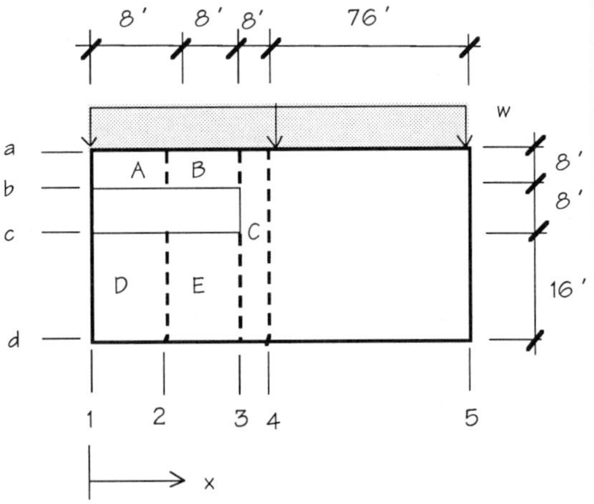

Line 1

$$V_1 = V_5 = \frac{w\ell}{2} = \frac{.2(100)}{2} = 10.0^k \text{ (shearwall reaction)}$$

$$v_1 = \frac{V}{b} = \frac{10}{32} = .313 \text{ klf (diaphragm unit shear)}$$

Line 2 (point of contraflexure)

$$V_2 = w\left(\frac{\ell}{2} - x\right) = .2\left(\frac{100}{2} - 8\right) = 8.4^k$$

$$v_2 = \frac{V}{b} = \frac{8.4}{32} = .263 \text{ klf}$$

$M_2 = \frac{wx}{2}(\ell - x) = \frac{.2(8)}{2}(100-8) = 73.6^{\,k\,ft}$

$F_{2a} = \frac{M_2}{b} = \frac{73.6}{32} = 2.3^{k}$ (C)

$F_{2d} = F_{2a} = 2.3^{k}$ (T)

Line 3

$V_4 = w\left(\frac{\ell}{2} - x\right) = .2\left(\frac{100}{2} - 16\right) = 6.8^{k}$

$v_4 = \frac{V}{b} = \frac{6.8}{32} = .213$ klf

$M_4 = \frac{wx}{2}(\ell - x) = \frac{.2(16)}{2}(100-16) = 134.4^{\,k\,ft}$

$F_{4a} = \frac{M_4}{b} = \frac{134.4}{32} = 4.2^{k}$ (C)

$F_{4d} = F_{4a} = 4.2^{k}$ (T)

Line 4

$V_5 = w\left(\frac{\ell}{2} - x\right) = .2\left(\frac{100}{2} - 24\right) = 5.2^{k}$

$v_5 = \frac{V}{b} = \frac{5.2}{32} = .163$ klf

$M_5 = \frac{wx}{2}(\ell - x) = \frac{.2(24)}{8}(100-24) = 182.4^{\,k\,ft}$

$F_{5a} = \frac{M_5}{b} = \frac{182.4}{32} = 5.7^{k}$ (C)

$F_{5d} = F_{5a} = 5.7^{k}$ (T)

Analyze diaphragm with hole

Obtain the chord and the unit shear forces at the critical locations proximate to the opening. The remaining analysis is based upon the guidelines described in ATC-7, *Guidelines for the Design of Wood Sheathed Diaphragms*, and APA research report # 138 *Plywood Diaphragms*, which assume that the diaphragm performs analogous to that of a Vierendeel Truss. Actual tests performed by the APA (see above report) support this assumption. The points of contraflexure of the chords are assumed to be located at 1/2 the hole element length (above and below the hole). Use free body diagrams to calculate the shear and the chord forces at the edge of the opening and the boundaries, using the previous non-opening analysis results at line 2a. Assume the direction of forces and calc as shown below. Forces to the right, down, and clockwise moments are positive. Line 2 above gives our starting values. The actual diaphragm loading is required to calculate localized effects proximate to the hole. Evaluate the approximate seismic loading on the diaphragm as follows:

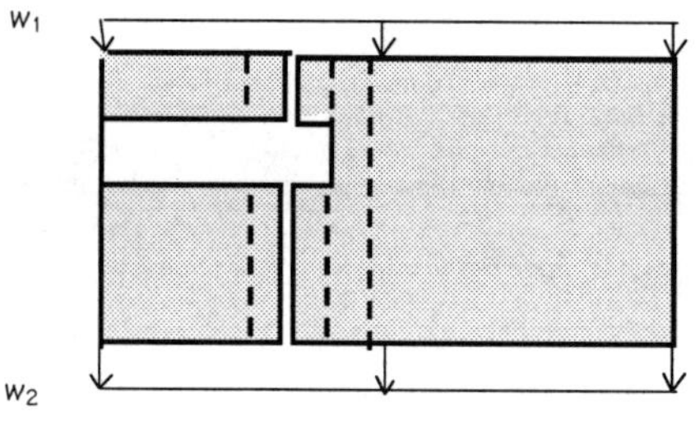

$w_1 = .108/2 + .092(12/32) = .09$ klf

$w_1 = .108/2 + .092(20/32) = .11$ klf

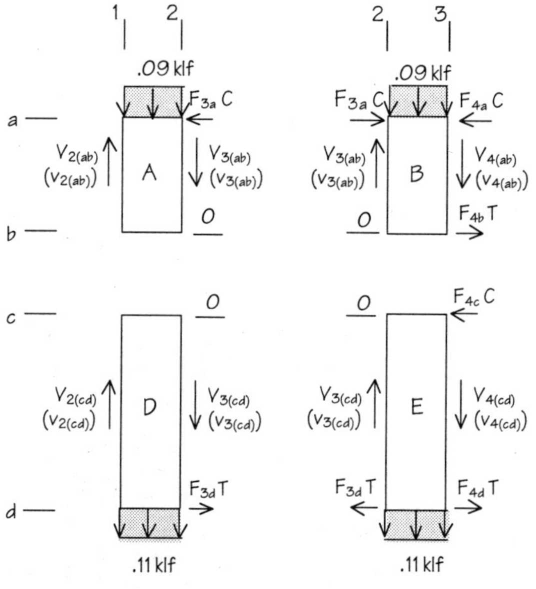

Zone B Calculate magnitudes.

Due to the point of contraflexure:

$F_{2a} = 2.3^{k}$ (C), $V_3 = 6.8^{k}$ from above

$$V_{3(ab)} = \frac{8V_3}{24} = \frac{8(6.8)}{24} = 2.27^k$$

$$v_{3(ab)} = \frac{V}{b} = \frac{2.27}{8} = .284 \text{ klf}$$

$$V_{2(ab)} = 2.27 + 8(.09) = 2.99^k$$

$$v_{2(ab)} = \frac{V}{b} = \frac{2.99}{8} = .374 \text{ klf}$$

$\sum M_{3b} = 0$ gives:

$F_{3a} = (8(2.27) + 8(2.3) + 4(8).09)/8 = 4.93^k$ (C)

$F_{4b} = 4.93 - 2.3 = 2.63^k$ (T)

Zone A

$F_{2a} = 2.3^k$ (C)

$V_{2(ab)} = 2.99^k$

$v_{2(ab)} = .374$ klf

$V_{2(ab)} = 2.99 + 8(.09) = 3.71^k$

$$v_{2(ab)} = \frac{V}{b} = \frac{3.71}{8} = .464 \text{ klf}$$

Zone E

$F_{2d} = 2.3^k$ (C)

$$V_{3(cd)} = \frac{16V_4}{24} = \frac{16(6.8)}{24} = 4.53^k$$

$$v_{3(cd)} = \frac{V}{b} = \frac{4.53}{16} = .283 \text{ klf}$$

$$V_{2(cd)} = 4.53 + 8(.11) = 5.41^k$$

$$v_{2(cd)} = \frac{V}{b} = \frac{5.41}{16} = .338 \text{ klf}$$

$F_{3c} = (8(4.53) + 8(4).11)/16 = 2.49^k$ (C)

$F_{3d} = 2.3 + 2.49 = 4.79^k$ (T)

Zone D

$F_{2d} = 2.3^k$ (C)

$V_{2(cd)} = 5.41^k$

$v_{2(cd)} = .338$ klf

$V_{1(cd)} = 5.41 + 8(.11) = 6.29^k$

$$v_{1(cd)} = \frac{V}{b} = \frac{6.29}{16} = .393 \text{ klf}$$

Summary of forces at opening gives:

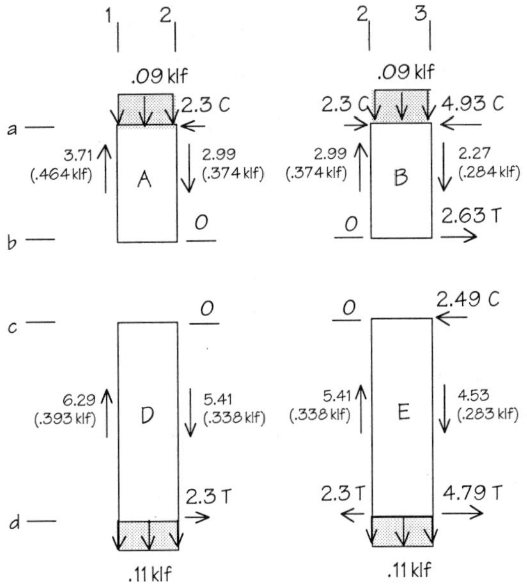

Note that during seismic reversal, the signs of the forces reverse but the absolute value of the forces remain the same.

Calculate net changes in the chord forces.

The net changes in the chord forces will be used to determine the connective hardware at the opening corners.

Diaph. Force Location	Chord Force (kip)		
	Without openings	With openings	Net change
F_3@ a	4.2 C	4.93 C	.73 C
b	0	2.63 T	2.63 T
c	0	2.49 C	2.49 C
d	4.2 T	4.79 T	.59 T

Calculate the net shear forces along chords

The resulting shear forces from chords are dissipated into the subdiaphragms. The length of the connective hardware that dissipates these forces is dependent upon the framing, the allowable shear in the diaphragm, and the allowables of the connective hardware itself. Two typical framing arrangements are as follows:

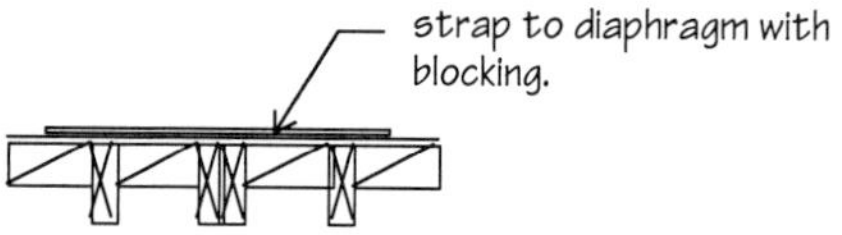

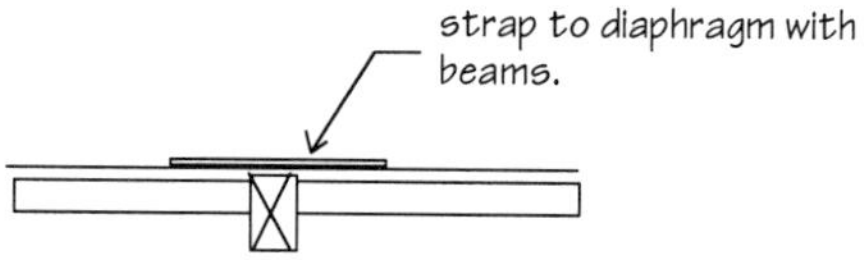

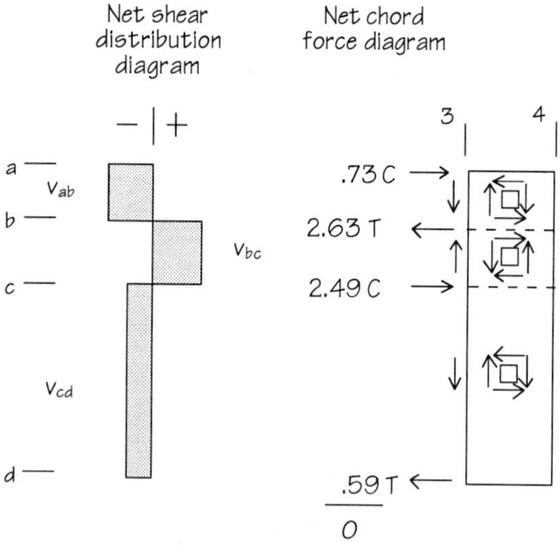

v_{ab} = -.73/16 = -.046 klf

v_{bc} = 2.63/16 - .041 = .118 klf

v_{cd} = -2.49/16 + .118 = -.038 klf

Calc. the resultant shears in the diaphragm

Using superposition, visually for subdiaphragm 1-2 we have:

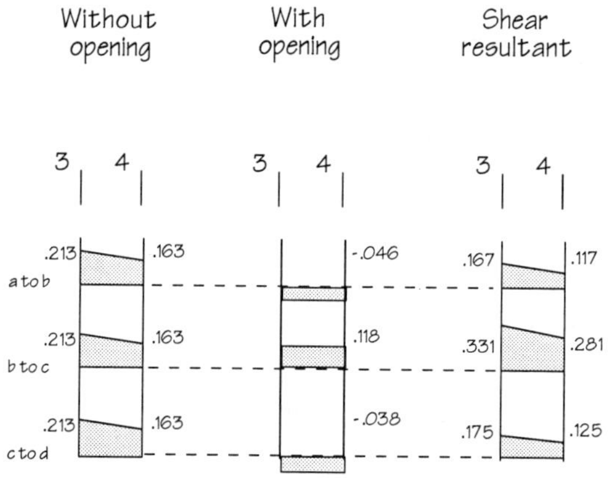

shear diagrams

Summary and visualization are difficult at best. As an aid, the following is offered:

← Without hole.

← Segment force zones around hole.

<- - Net chord force change

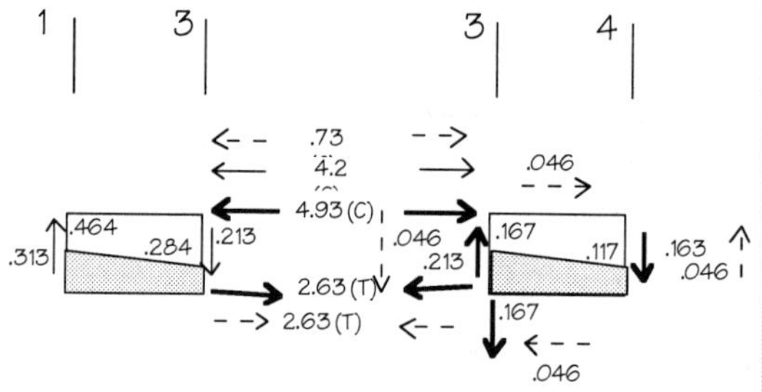

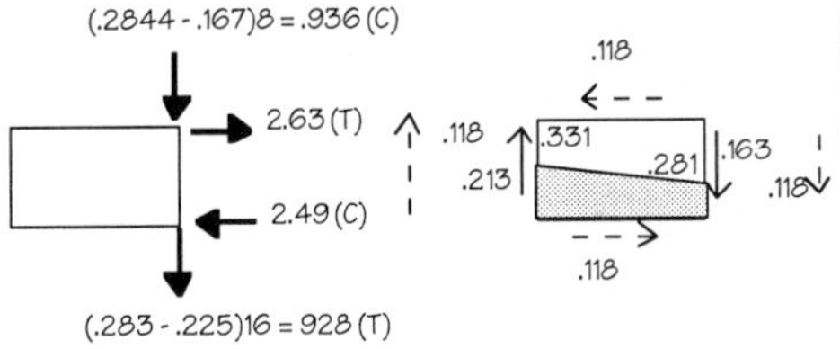

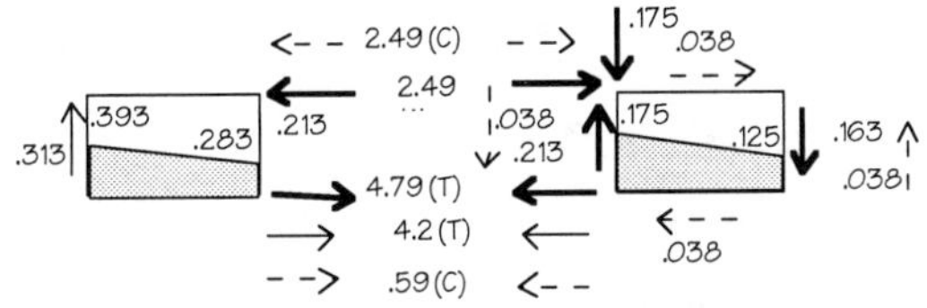

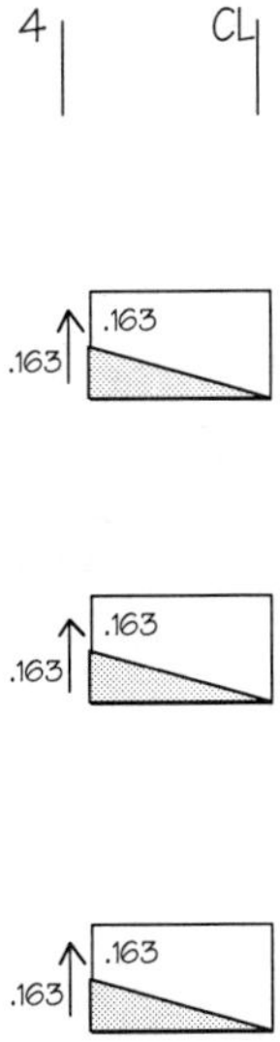

The design resulant shears along chords:

<u>Area a to b</u>

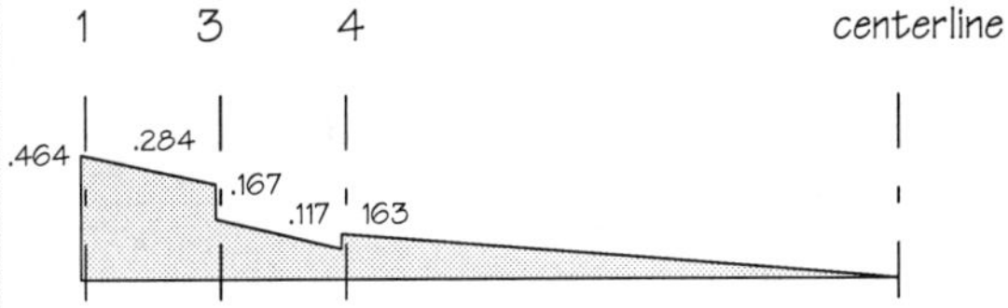

<u>Area b to c</u>

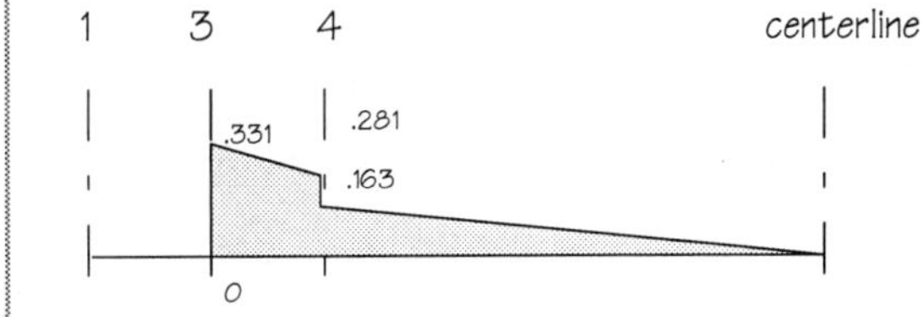

<u>Area c to d</u>

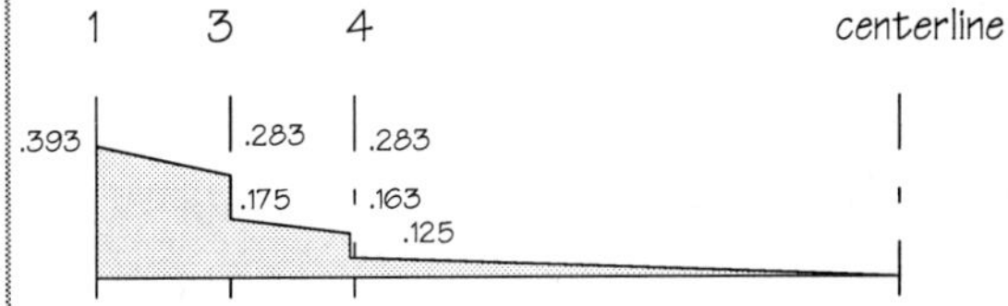

Design shear and force summary

For design purposes do not use a design shear value less than the unit shear for the diaphragm without hole analysis. Note that if you attempt to do extensive zone nailing within the drag zone of the hole, you will further complicate the analysis to a degree not worth pursuing in practical terms.

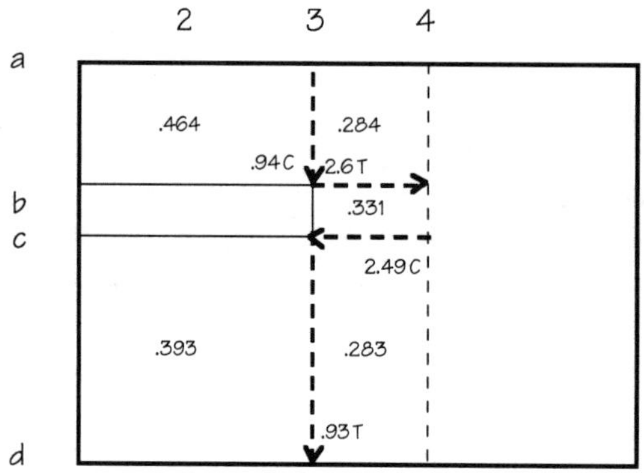

Recall that due to seismic reversal, the shear and chord forces reverse and members and connective hardware must be able to transmit the forces in the opposite direction.

Zone nailing

A simple design for the enveloping of the shears gives:

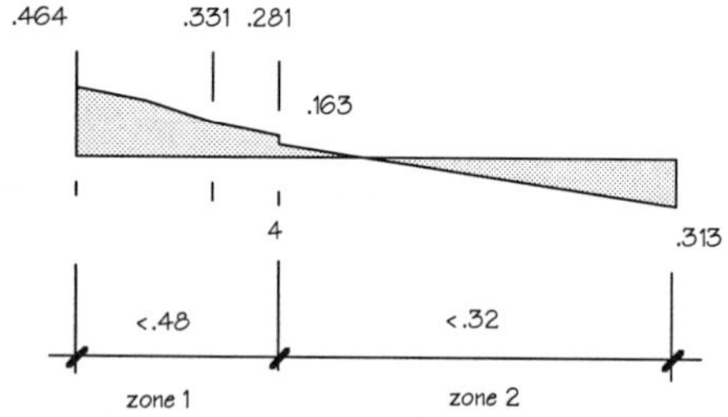

Zone 1:
Use 19/32 Str II with 10d @4,6,12 with 3x members.
Zone 1:
Use 19/32 Str II with 10d @6,6,12 with 3x members.

Drag ties

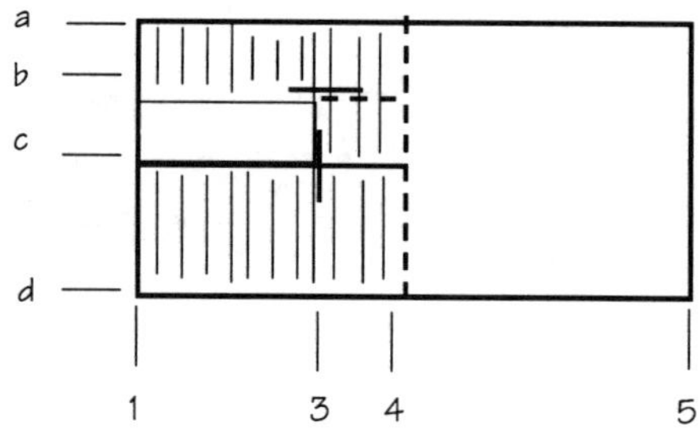

Ties along line 3

Recall that members from 1 to 4 must be upgraded to 3x. Since the members are continuous from a to c and from c to d, only ties at 3c are required.

Use manf. ties with cap. > .94 ^{k}
Simpson CS20 = 1.0 ^{k} cap.

Ties along b and c

The member is continuous along c. Therefore no tie strap is required. Tight blocking must be placed along line b to transfer compressive forces and to act as backup blocking for tension straps.

Use manf. straps with cap. > 2.63 ^{k}
Simpson CMST14 cap. = 6.79 ^{k}

He that lives upon hope will die fasting.

BENJAMIN FRANKLIN

5. Shearwall Design

Chapter Problems	Page	Prob.
Shearwall deflection	5-23	5.10
Shearwall design	5-4	5.2
Shearwall design with plywood on both sides with floor and header loads	5-10	5.5
Shearwall design basics	5-5	5.3
Shearwall design for 2-story configuration	5-13	5.6
Shearwall design of 3 walls in building	5-7	5.4
Shearwall formula basics	5-2	5.1
Shearwall supported by a beam design	5-24	5.11
Shearwall with a hole designed as 2- cantilevers	5-18	5.8
Shearwall with a hole designed as one panel	5-20	5.9
Shearwall with opening on one side	5-27	5.12
Wood moment frame investigation	5-16	5.7

PROBLEM 5.1

Shearwall formula basics.

Determine the forces to design the shearwall shown. Use conservative and dynamic model for comparison.

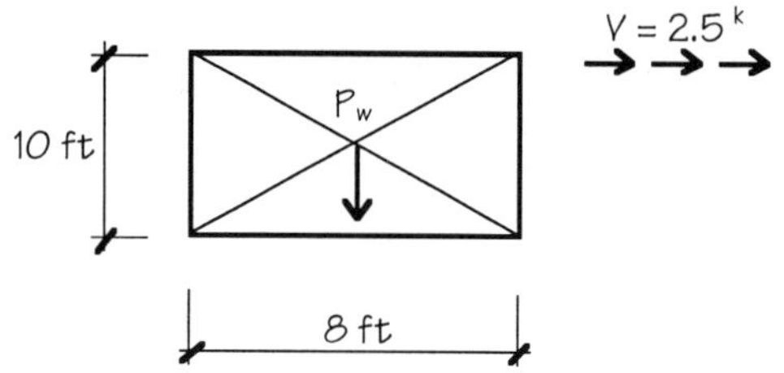

ASSUME

Wall wt = .016 ksf.
V_w= .183W.
Neglect wind.

UBC T23-I-I

SOLUTION

Ck aspect ratio

$$\frac{h}{\ell} = \frac{10}{8} = 1.25 < 3.5 \quad \checkmark$$

Conservative approach (most widely used)

Calc unit base shear

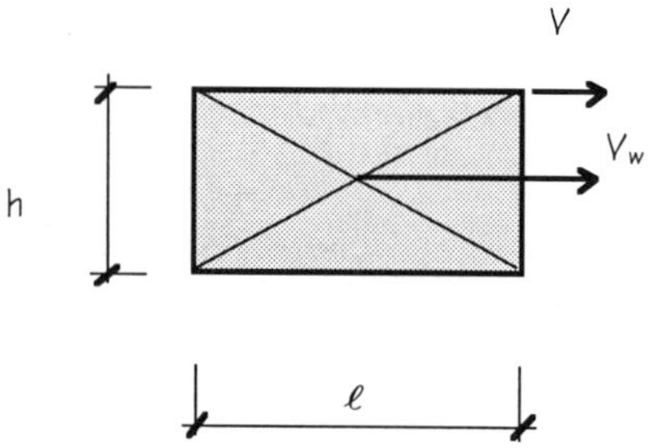

$w_{wall} = .016(10) = .16$ klf

$V_w = .183(10)8(.016) = .23^k$

$V_{base} = V + V_w = 2.5 + .23 = 2.73^k$

To determine shearwall material thickness and nailing requirements, calc the unit base shear.

$$v_{base} = \frac{V_{base}}{\ell} = \frac{2.73}{8} = .341 \text{ klf}$$

The unit base shear is also used to determine anchor bolts and spacing for shear parallel to the wall.

Unit base shear = .341 klf

Calc T/C chord forces

Calc GOM

$GOM = Vh + V_w h/2 = 2.5(10) + .23(10/2) = 26.15^{k\,ft}$

Calc RM

$$.85\,RM = .85\left(\frac{w_{wall}\ell^2}{2}\right) = .85\left(\frac{.16(8)^2}{2}\right) = 4.4^{kft}$$

For stability GOM $\leq$ .85 RM

$26.15^{k\,ft} > 4.4^{kft}$ **NG!**

Since the GOM is larger than the resisting moment we need a holdown. For stability the DL weight of the foundation can be added to the RM calculation. If this does not fill the requirements of stability, then something else is done like; lengthening the shearwall to increase the RM, or making the foundation larger to add resistive weight.

Calc T chord force

$$T = \frac{DOM}{\ell} = \frac{GOM - .85(RM)}{\ell} = \frac{26.15 - 4.4}{8} = 2.7^k$$

Required for Holdown force and HD selection if required.

Holdown tension force required = 2.7 k

Calc C chord force

$$C = \frac{GOM}{\ell} + w_{wall}\ell_{trib} = \frac{26.15}{8} + .16\left(\frac{16}{12}\right) = 3.5^k$$

Used to ck chord stress and ck bearing on mudsill.

Compression force = 3.5 ^{k}

Calc $v_\perp$

Used for unit shear perpendicular to wall. This determines the anchor bolt size and spacing perpendicular to the wall plane.

$V_\perp = V_w$

$$v_\perp = \frac{V_w}{\ell} = \frac{.23}{8} = .029 \text{ klf}$$

Perpendicular unit shear = .029 klf

Dynamic approach

Calc unit base shear

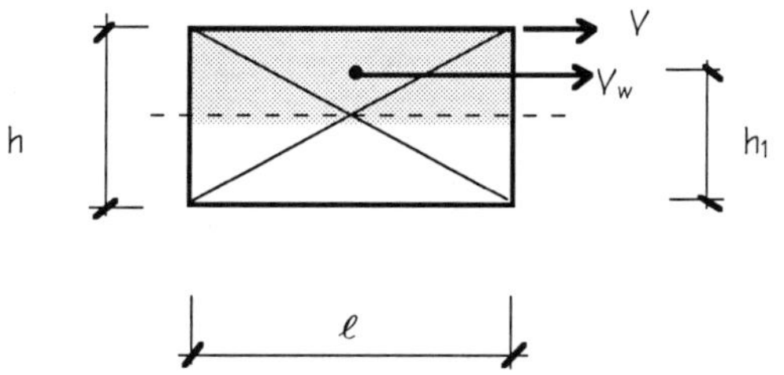

$V_w = .183(5)8(.016) = .12^k$

$V_{base} = V + V_w = 2.5 + .12 = 2.62^k$

An intermediate answer used to determine shearwall material thickness and nailing requirements.

Base shear = 2.62 ^{k}

Calc unit base shear

$$v_{base} = \frac{V_{base}}{\ell} = \frac{2.62}{8} = .33 \text{ klf}$$

The unit base shear is also used to determine anchor bolts and spacing for shear parallel to the wall.

Unit base shear = .33 klf

Calc T/C chord forces

Calc GOM

$GOM = Vh + V_w h_1 = 2.5(10) + .12(7.5) = 25.9^{k\,ft}$

Calc RM

$$.85\,RM = .85\left(\frac{w_{wall}\ell^2}{2}\right) = .85\left(\frac{.16(8)^2}{2}\right) = 4.4^{kft}$$

For stability GOM $\leq$ .85 RM

$25.9^{k\,ft} > 4.4^{kft}$ **NG!**

Again, since the GOM is larger than the resisting moment we need a holdown. For stability the DL weight of the foundation can be added to the RM calculation. If this does not fill the requirements of stability, then something else is done like; lengthening the shearwall to increase the RM, or making the foundation larger to add resistive weight.

Calc T chord force

$$T = \frac{DOM}{\ell} = \frac{GOM - .85(RM)}{\ell} = \frac{25.9 - 4.4}{8} = 2.7^k$$

Required for Holdown force and HD selection if required.

Holdown tension force required = 2.7 ^{k}

Calc C chord force

$$C = \frac{GOM}{\ell} + w_{wall}\ell_{trib} = \frac{25.9}{8} + .16\left(\frac{16}{12}\right) = 3.5^k$$

Used to ck chord stress and ck bearing on mudsill.

Compression force = 3.5 ^{k}

Calc $v_\perp$

Used for unit shear perpendicular to wall. This determines the anchor bolt size and spacing perpendicular to the wall plane. This is the same as above.

$V_\perp = V_w$

$$v_\perp = \frac{V_w}{\ell} = \frac{.23}{8} = .029 \text{ klf}$$

Perpendicular unit shear = .029 klf

The structure remains in the elastic range of the material under the ASD approach outlined in the code. When a large earthquake occurs the structure can go into the inelastic range of the material. Here it is assumed that sufficient detailing of the connections will provide the required ductility to keep the structure safe. In general, you must provide in your detailing (of the connections) a direct and continuous path for lateral force transfer.

Great men are they who see that spiritual is stronger than any material force, that thoughts rule the world.

EMERSON

PROBLEM 5.2

Shearwall design.

Determine the minimum shearwall thickness and nailing if the shearwall material used is:
- C-D plywood with common nails.
- C-D plywood with casing nails.
- Stucco for the shearwall shown below.

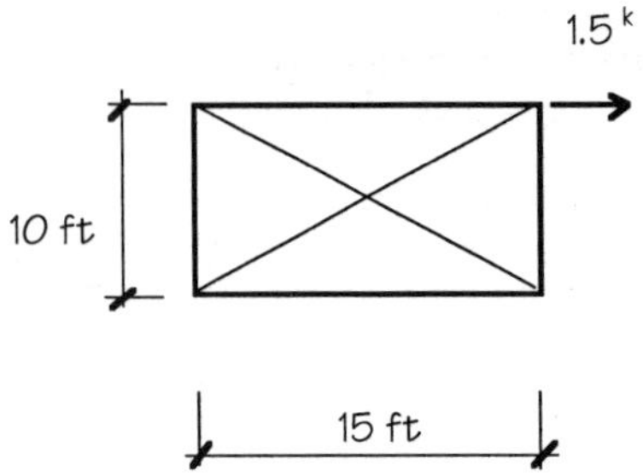

ASSUME

Wall wt = .016 ksf (plywood).
= .02 ksf (stucco).
$V_w = .183W$.
Neglect wind.
MC < 19%.

SOLUTION

Ck aspect ratio

$$\frac{h}{\ell} = \frac{10}{15} = .67 < 3.5 \quad \checkmark$$ UBC T23-I-I

Shearwall with common nails

Use the dynamic approach which utilizes the top half of the shearwall DL for the walls inertial seismic force.

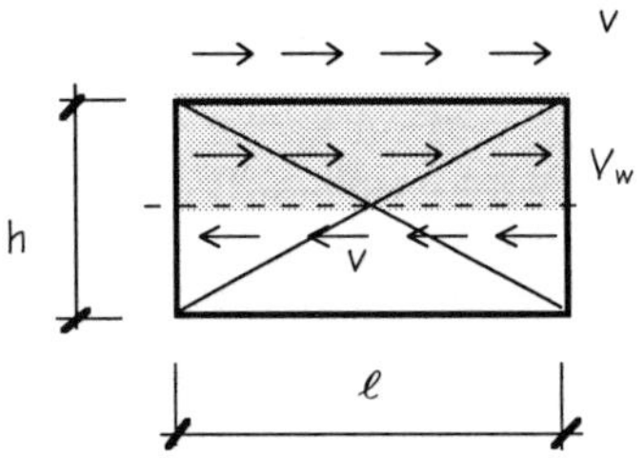

$$v = \frac{1.5}{15} = .10 \text{ klf}$$

$$V_w = .183(10/2)15(.016) = .22^{k}$$

$$v_w = \frac{.22}{15} = .015 \text{ klf}$$

$$v_{base} = v + v_w = .1 + .015 = .115 \text{ klf} < .18 \text{ klf} \quad \checkmark$$ UBC T23-I-K-1

Use 5/16 in C-D EXP 1 plywood with 6d at 6 in o/c, 12 in o/c in field with blocking required

Shearwall with casing nails

Assume the same weight as above regardless of plywood thickness if changed.

v_{base} = .115 klf < .14 klf √

UBC T23-I-K-1

> Use 5/16 in C-D EXP 1 plywood with galvanized 6d at 6 in o/c, 12 in o/c in field with blocking required

Stucco shearwall

v= .10 klf

V_w= .183(10/2)15(.02) = .27 ^{k}

$v_w = \frac{.27}{15} = .018$ klf

$v_{base} = v + v_w = .1 + .018 = .118$ klf < .18 klf √

91 UBC T47-I

> Use expanded metal with 7/8 in thick Portland cement stucco with No 11 gauge, 1-1/2 in long, 7/16 in head nails or No 16 gauge staple with 7/8 in legs at 6 in o/c

□
□
□

Hope is a good breakfast, but it is a bad supper.

FRANCIS BACON
1624

PROBLEM 5.3

Shearwall design basics.

Design the shearwall indicated for the seismic building forces shown below.

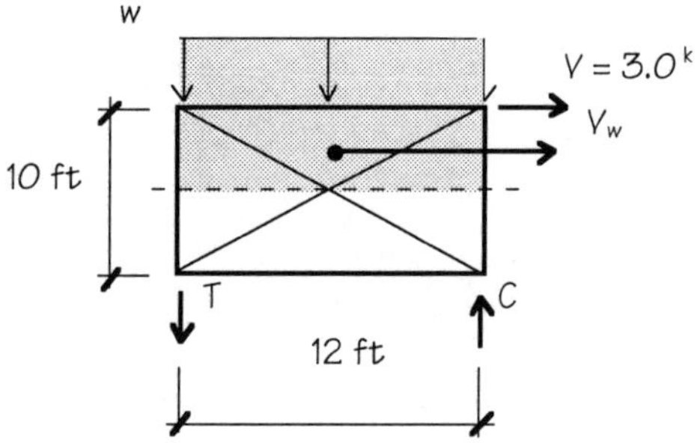

ASSUME

w_{DL} = .12 klf.
w_{LL} = . 2 klf.
Wall wt. = .016 ksf.
V_w = .183W.
Neglect wind.
MC < 19%.
2x4 DF-L stud grade at 16 in o/c.
1 in holes for holdowns.
1/2 in C-D EXP 1 plywood shearwall.
15/16 in AB shear capacity = 2.94 ^{k}.

SOLUTION

Ck aspect ratio

$\frac{\ell}{b} = \frac{12}{10} = 1.2 < 3.5$ √ UBC T23-I-I

Shearwall

Recall that roof LL is omitted when checking the over turning forces for the shearwalls.

Use the dynamic approach which utilizes the top half of the shearwall DL for the wall's inertial seismic force.

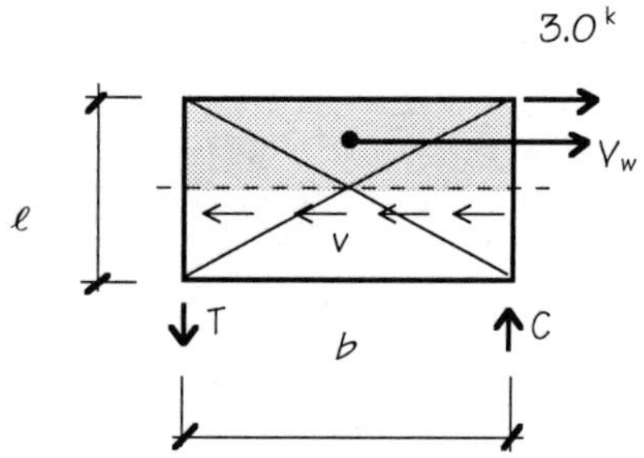

$V_w = .183(10/2)12(.016) = .18^k$

$v_w = \frac{.18}{12} = .015$ klf

$V_{base} = V + V_w = 3.0 + .18 = 3.2^k$

$v_{base} = \frac{V_{base}}{b} = \frac{3.2}{12} = .27$ klf < .46 klf √

UBC T23-I-K-1

> Use 15/32 in C-D EXP 1 plywood with 8d at 4 in o/c, 12 in o/c in field with blocking required

Ck AB

In plane

$Ab_{reqd} = \frac{V_{base}}{V_{AB}} = \frac{3.2}{2.9} = 1.1$ bolts, say 2 bolts

Max spacing = 48 in o/c

Perpendicular to wall

The force is 1/2 of the shearwall inertial weight(lower half) per linear foot.

$v_\perp = v_w = .015$ klf

$v_\perp$ at 48 in o/c = $4(.015) = .06^k < 2.94^k$ √

> Use 5/8 in AB at 48 in o/c

Calc T and C chord forces

We could use the GOM to calc T and C forces. This would be a conservative approach because it does not reduce the T force by the DL. Use the DOM for the calculation of design forces.

$GOM = Vh = 3(10) + .18(7.5) = 31.4^{k\,ft}$

$$RM = \frac{w_{DL}b^2}{2} + \frac{w_{wall}(\ell/2)b^2}{2} = \frac{.12(12)^2}{2} + \frac{.016(10/2)(12)^2}{2}$$

$= 14.4^{k\,ft}$

$DOM = GOM - .85RM = 31.4 - .85(14.4) = 19.2^{k\,ft}$

Since the GOM is larger than the resisting moment we will need a holdown force calc.

$T_{design} = DOM/b = 19.2/12 = 1.6^k$

$$C_{design} = \frac{GOM}{b} + P_{trib} = \frac{31.4}{12} + \frac{1.33(.12 + .016(10))}{2} = 2.8^k$$

> Holdown force required = 1.6^k

Ck T chord

$F_t = .45$ ksi
$F_c = .825$ ksi
$F_{c\perp} = .625$ ksi
$E = 1.4e3$ ksi
$A = 5.25\ in^2$

NDS T2.3.1

Assume 1 in diameter hole for HD

$$f_t = \frac{T}{A_n} = \frac{1.7}{5.25 - (1(1.5))} = .45 \text{ ksi}$$

$F_t' = F_tC_DC_MC_tC_F = .45(1.6)1.0(1.0)1.5$

$= 1.08$ ksi > .45 ksi √

> 2x4 stud ok for tension chord

Ck C chord

Note that some designers use the tributary length of the shearwall to calc the compression DL. This is a conservative approach that assumes that the wall studs do not carry any wall DL. Do not use the .85 multiplier for the compression force. To do so is not conservative. Use a conservative approach where C is calculated for the total height of the stud, but A is calculated at the base.

Compare slenderness ratios

Full lateral support implies:

$$\left(\frac{\ell_e}{d}\right)_y = \left(\frac{K_e\ell}{d}\right)_y = \frac{1.0(0.0)12}{1.5} = 0.0$$

NDS 3.7.1.2

$$\left(\frac{\ell_e}{d}\right)_x = \left(\frac{K_e\ell}{d}\right)_x = \frac{1.0(10)12}{3.5} = 34.3$$

34.3 > 0 strong axis governs

Ck capacity

$K_{cE} = 0.3$

$c = 0.8$

$E' = EC_MC_tC_T = (1.4e3)1.0(1.0)1.0 = 1.4e3$ ksi

NDS T2.3.1

$$F_{cE} = \frac{K_{cE}E'}{\left(\ell_e/d\right)^2} = \frac{.3(1.4e3)}{(34.3)^2} = .36 \text{ ksi}$$

$$F_c^* = F_c C_D C_M C_t C_F = .825(1.6)1.0(1.15) = 1.5 \text{ ksi}$$

It would be conservative to use $C_F = 1.0$

NDS 3.7.1.5

$$C_P = \frac{1+\left(F_{cE}/F_c^*\right)}{2c} - \sqrt{\left(\frac{1+\left(F_{cE}/F_c^*\right)}{2c}\right)^2 - \frac{\left(F_{cE}/F_c^*\right)}{c}}$$

$$C_P = \frac{1+\left(.36/1.5\right)}{2(.8)} - \sqrt{\left(\frac{1+\left(.36/1.5\right)}{2(.8)}\right)^2 - \frac{\left(.36/1.5\right)}{.8}} = .23$$

NDS T2.3.1

$F_c' = F_c C_D C_M C_t C_P = .825(1.6)1.0(1.0)1.15(.23)$

$= .35$ ksi

$P = F_c' A_n = .35(5.25\text{-}1.5) = 1.3^k < 2.8^k$ NG!

Try minimum of 2-2x4 = 2(1.3) = $2.6^k < 2.8^k$ NG!

Try 4x6 chord

$$F_c^* = F_c C_D C_M C_t C_F = .825(1.6)1.0(1.1) = 1.5 \text{ ksi}$$

$$C_P = \frac{1+\left(.36/1.5\right)}{2(.8)} - \sqrt{\left(\frac{1+\left(.36/1.5\right)}{2(.8)}\right)^2 - \frac{\left(.36/1.5\right)}{.8}} = .23$$

$F_c' = F_c C_D C_M C_t C_P = .825(1.6)1.0(1.0)1.1\,(.23) = .33$ ksi

$P = F_c' A_n = .33(19.25 - 1.5(5.5))$

$= 3.6^k > 2.8^k$ √

Chord ok if 4x4 used

NDS T2.3.1

Ck bearing of bottom plate

$F_{c\perp}' = F_{c\perp} C_M C_t C_b = .625(1.0)1.0(1.0)$

$= .625$ ksi $> .33$

Which suggests that chord stability governs over bearing.

NDS T2.3.1

Bearing ok by inspection (also because the bearing area is larger than the area used in the compression chord ck.)

Use 4x6 DF-L stud grade column for shearwall chords

Put all your eggs in one basket and WATCH THAT BASKET!

MARK TWAIN

PROBLEM 5.4

Shearwall design of 3 walls in building.

Design the 3 shearwalls indicated for the building shown below.

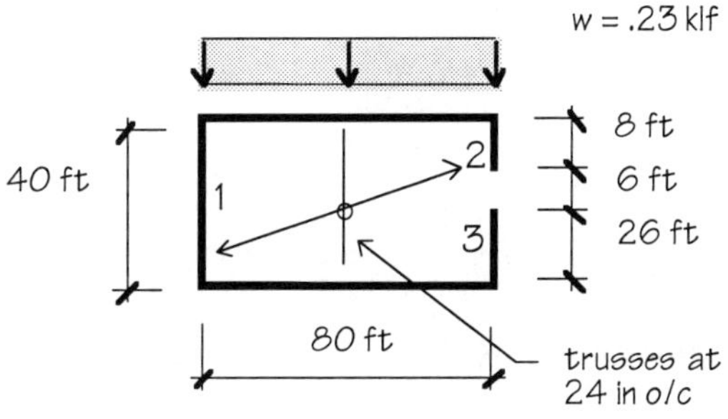

ASSUME

- Wall ht. = 10 ft.
- Wall wt = .016 ksf.
- $V_{wl} = .183W$.
- Neglect wind.
- MC < 19%.
- 2x4 DF-L stud grade studs .
- 1 in holes for holdowns.

SOLUTION

Ck aspect ratios

UBC T23-I-I

$\frac{h}{\ell} = \frac{80}{40} = 2.0 < 4.0$ √ horizontal diaph.

$\frac{h}{\ell} = \frac{10}{8} = 1.25 < 3.5$ √ shortest shearwall length

Diaphragm forces

.23 klf

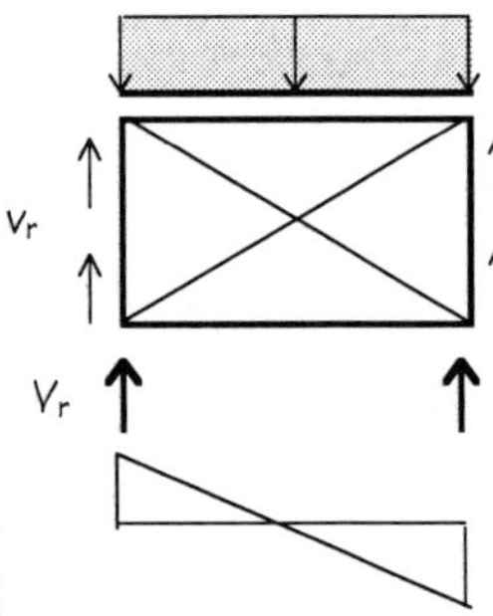

$v_r = \frac{9.2}{40} = .23 \text{ klf}$

$V_r = \frac{wL}{2} = \frac{.23(80)}{2}$

$= 9.2^k$

Shearwall 1

The roof LL is omitted when checking overturning forces for the shearwalls.

Use the dynamic approach which utilizes the top half of the shearwall DL for the walls inertial seismic force.

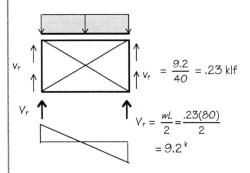

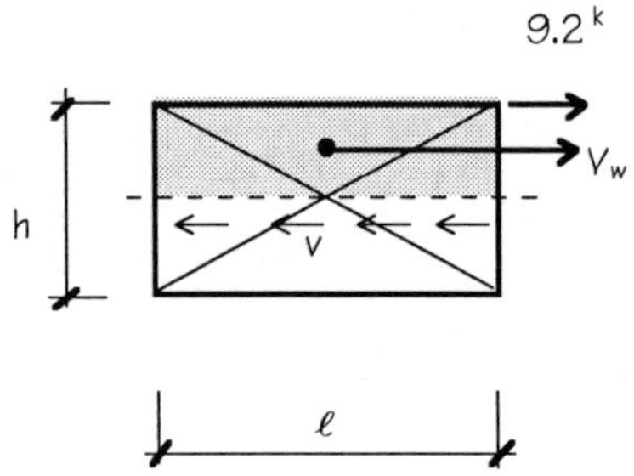

$V_w = .183(10/2)8(.016) = .12^k$

$v_w = \frac{.12}{40} = .003 \text{ klf}$

$V_{base} = V + V_w = 9.2 + .12 = 9.3^k$

$v_{base} = \frac{V_{base}}{\ell} = \frac{9.3}{40} = .23 \text{ klf} < .26 \text{ klf}$ √

Our choices for shearwall materials are voluminous. Although we could use 3/8 in plywood, it is to easy to blow though it with nail guns. It is a personal preference not to use this thickness for shearwalls. For economical reasons we usually try to use the least thick shear material and the largest nail spacing possible.

> Use 15/32 in C-D EXP 1 plywood with 8d at 6 in o/c, 12 in o/c in field with blocking required

UBC T23-I-K-1

Calc T chord forces

Use the GOM to calc T and C forces. This is a conservative approach because it does not reduce the T force by the DL.

$T = C = vh = .23(10) + .003(7.5) = 2.3^k$

$f_t = \frac{T}{A_n} = \frac{2.3}{5.25 - (1(1.5))} = .61 \text{ ksi}$

$F_t' = F_t C_D C_M C_t C_F = .45(1.6)1.0(1.0)1.5$ NDS T2.3.1

$= 1.08 \text{ ksi} > .61 \text{ ksi}$ √

> 2x4 stud ok for tension chord

Calc C chord force

Assume that the studs at 16 in o/c.

$P_{DL} = 2.3 + 10(1.33/2).016 = 2.4^k$

Do not use the .85 multiplier for the compression force. To do so is not conservative.

Ck 2x4 stud

Use conservative approach where P is calculated for the total height of the stud but A is calculated at the base.

$F_c = .825$ ksi
$F_{c\perp} = .625$ ksi
E = 1.4e3 ksi
A = 5.25 in^2

Compare slenderness ratios

NDS 3.7.1.2

$$\left(\frac{\ell_e}{d}\right)_y = \left(\frac{K_e\ell}{d}\right)_y = \frac{1.0(0.0)12}{1.5} = 0.0$$

$$\left(\frac{\ell_e}{d}\right)_x = \left(\frac{K_e\ell}{d}\right)_x = \frac{1.0(10)12}{3.5} = 34.3$$

34.3 > 0 strong axis governs

Ck capacity

$K_{cE} = 0.3$

$c = 0.8$

NDS T2.3.1

$$E' = EC_MC_t = (1.4e3)1.0(1.0) = 1.4e3 \text{ ksi}$$

$$F_{cE} = \frac{K_{cE}E'}{\left(\ell_e/d\right)^2} = \frac{.3(1.4e3)}{(34.3)^2} = .36 \text{ ksi}$$

$$F_c^* = F_cC_DC_MC_tC_F = .825(1.6)1.0(1.15) = 1.5 \text{ ksi}$$

It would be consv. to use $C_F = 1.0$

NDS 3.7.1.5

$$C_P = \frac{1+\left(F_{cE}/F_c^*\right)}{2c} - \sqrt{\left(\frac{1+\left(F_{cE}/F_c^*\right)}{2c}\right)^2 - \frac{\left(F_{cE}/F_c^*\right)}{c}}$$

$$C_P = \frac{1+\left(.36/1.5\right)}{2(.8)} - \sqrt{\left(\frac{1+\left(.36/1.5\right)}{2(.8)}\right)^2 - \frac{\left(.36/1.5\right)}{.8}} = .23$$

NDS T2.3.1

$$F_c' = F_cC_DC_MC_tC_P = .825(1.6)1.0(1.0)1.15(.23)$$

$= .35$ ksi

$P = F_c' A_n = .35(5.25-1.5) = 1.3^k < 2.3^k$ **NG!**

Try 2-2x4

$2P = 2(1.3) = 2.6^k > 2.3^k$ √

Compression chord ok if 2-2x4 used

Ck bearing of bottom plate

NDS T2.3.1

$$F_{c\perp}' = F_{c\perp}C_MC_tC_b = .625(1.0)1.0(1.0)$$

$= .625$ ksi $> .35$ stability governs by inspection.

Use 2-2x4 DF-L stud grade studs for shearwall chords

Shearwall 2 and 3

Use the dynamic approach which utilizes the top half of the shearwall DL for the walls inertial seismic force. The chord stresses are higher in these walls than in wall 1. Because of this, we could have eliminated the chord analysis for shearwall 1 and just performed the shearwall analysis here.

$$v = \frac{9.2}{34} = .271 \text{ klf}$$

The unit shear for each shearwall is equal because of the assumed equal deflection of the flexible vertical diaphragms (connected by the drag strut). Filler panels are placed for surface thickness continuity, and are therefore not used in the calcs in this problem.

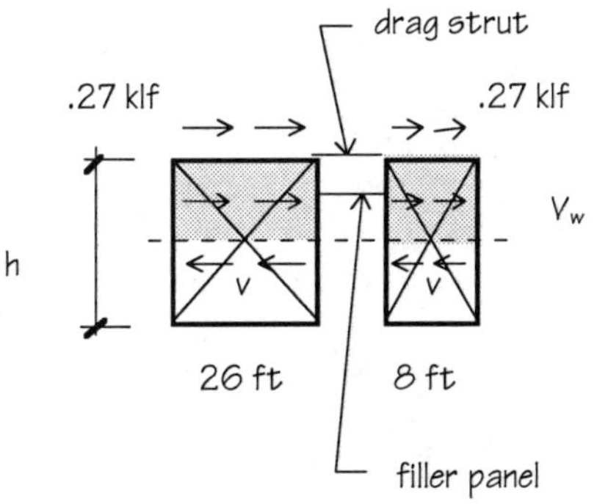

$$v_w = \frac{.12}{40} = .003 \text{ klf} \quad \text{from SW 1 (consv.)}$$

$$v_{base} = v + v_w = .27 \text{ klf} < .38 \text{ klf} \ \surd$$

Use 15/32 in C-D EXP 1 plywood with 8d at 4 in o/c, 12 in o/c in field with blocking required UBC T23-I-K-1

Calc T chord forces

Use the GOM to calc T and C forces. This is a conservative approach because it does not reduce the T force by the DL.

$$T = C = vh = .27(10) + .003(7.5) = 2.7^{k}$$

NDS T2.3.1

$$f_t = \frac{T}{A_n} = \frac{2.7}{5.25-(1(1.5))} = .72 \text{ ksi}$$

$$F_t' = F_t C_D C_M C_t C_F = .45(1.6)1.0(1.0)1.5$$

$$= 1.08 \text{ ksi} > .72 \text{ ksi} \ \surd$$

> 2x4 stud ok for tension chord

Calc C chord force

Since this is a very simplified example we will assume that the DL over the opening is supported by a separate post or trimmer. Assume that the wall has studs at 16 in o/c.

$$P_{DL} = 2.7 + 10(1.33/2).016 = 2.8^{k}$$

Note that some designers use the tributary length of the shearwall to calc the compression DL. This is a conservative approach that assumes that the wall studs do not carry any wall DL.

Ck 2x4 stud

Use conservative approach where P is calculated for the total height of the stud.

$F_c = .825$ ksi
$F_{c\perp} = .625$ ksi
$E = 1.4e3$ ksi
$A = 5.25$ in^2

Compare slenderness ratios

NDS 3.7.1.2

$$\left(\frac{\ell_e}{d}\right)_y = \left(\frac{K_e \ell}{d}\right)_y = \frac{1.0(0.0)12}{1.5} = 0.0$$

$$\left(\frac{\ell_e}{d}\right)_x = \left(\frac{K_e \ell}{d}\right)_x = \frac{1.0(10)12}{3.5} = 34.3$$

34.3 > 0 strong axis governs

Ck capacity

Same as shearwall 1

$$F_c' = .35 \text{ ksi}$$

$$P = 2.6^{k} < 2.8^{k} \text{ NG!}$$

Try 4x6 chord (see above)

$$F_c^* = F_c C_D C_M C_t C_F = .825(1.6)1.0(1.1) = 1.5 \text{ ksi}$$

$$C_P = \frac{1+\left(.36/_{1.5}\right)}{2(.8)} - \sqrt{\left(\frac{1+\left(.36/_{1.5}\right)}{2(.8)}\right)^2 - \frac{\left(.36/_{1.5}\right)}{.8}} = .23$$

$$F_c' = F_c C_D C_M C_t C_P = .825(1.6)1.0(1.0)1.1(.23) = .33 \text{ ksi}$$ NDS T2.3.1

$$P = F_c' A_n = .33(19.25 - 1.0(5.5))$$

$$= 4.5^{k} > 2.8^{k} \ \surd$$

> Chord ok if 4x4 used

Ck bearing of bottom plate

Similar to shearwall 1, stability governs by inspection.

> Use 4x6 DF-L stud grade post for shearwall chords at SW 2 and 3

The procedure outlined above is conservative as it did not use the resisting DL to reduce the chord T. If it were over stressed we could have added the resisting DL or analyzed the forces for 4x6 chord posts. Do not forget that the resisting DL is reduced by multiplying it by .67 for wind and .85 for seismic forces.

□
□
□

Losers visualize the penalties of failure. Winners visualize the rewards of success.

DR. ROB GILBERT

PROBLEM 5.5

Shearwall design with plywood on both sides with floor and header loads.

Determine the plywood shearwall thickness, and nailing, anchor bolts and spacing, HD's, chords and bearing for the force parallel to the wall for the building elevation shown below.

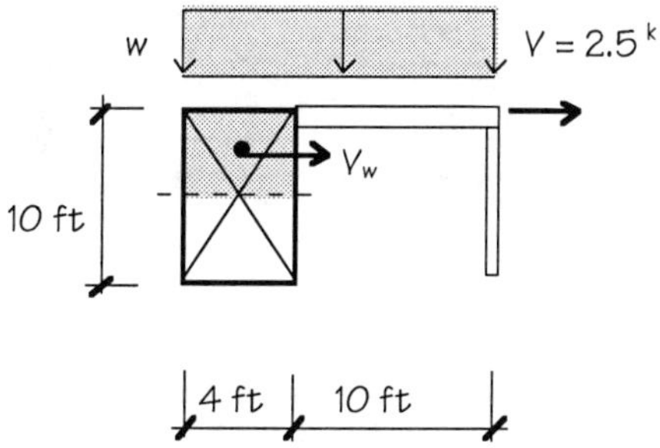

ASSUME

w_{RDL} = .16 klf.
w_{RLL} = . 2 klf.
Wall wt. = .016 ksf.
V_w= .183W.
Neglect wind.
MC < 19%.
2 ksi concrete footing.
2x4 DF-L stud grade at 16 in o/c.
1 in holes for holdowns if required.
1/2 in C-D EXP 1 plywood shearwall.
15/16 in AB shear capacity = 2.94 ^{k}.
Neglect seismic reversal.

SOLUTION

Ck aspect ratio

UBC T23-I-I

$$\frac{\ell}{b} = \frac{10}{4} = 2.5 < 3.5 \quad \surd$$

Shearwall

Recall that roof LL is omitted when checking overturning forces for the shearwalls.

Use the dynamic approach which utilizes the top half of the shearwall DL for the walls inertial seismic force.

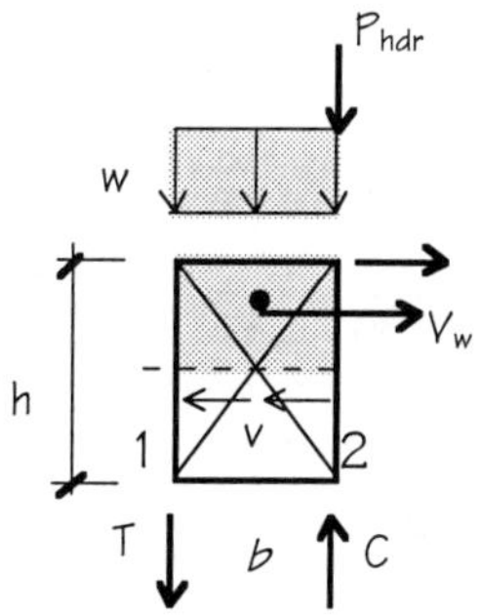

V_w= .183(10/2)4(.016) = .059 ^{k}

= $V_{w\perp}$ the seismic inertial force perpendicular to the wall.

$$v_w = \frac{.059}{4} = .015 \text{ klf}$$

$$V_{base} = V + V_w = 2.5 + .059 = 2.56^k$$

$$v_{base} = \frac{V_{base}}{b} = \frac{2.56}{4} = .64 \text{ klf} < 2(.38) = .76 \text{ klf} \quad \surd$$

UBC T23-I-K-1

> Use 15/32 in C-D EXP 1 plywood on both sides of shearwall with 8d at 4 in o/c, 12 in o/c in field with blocking required

Ck AB and spacing

The code stipulates that allowable shear tabular values that are used in the connection of wood members to concrete (or masonry) can be determined as 1/2 the double shear tabular value for a wood member twice the thickness of the attached member.

Try ⅝ in dia AB

capacity in concrete = 2.75 ^{k}

UBC T19-E, F

$$\text{capacity in wood } V_{AB\,||} = \frac{1.82}{2} = .91^k$$

$$\text{capacity in wood } V_{AB\,\perp} = \frac{.81}{2} = .41^k$$

Wood controls over concrete capacity in both directions

$$Ab_{reqd\,||} = \frac{V_{base}}{V_{AB}} = \frac{2.56}{.91} = 2.81 \quad \text{say 3 bolts}$$

$$Ab_{reqd\,\perp} = \frac{V_{base}}{V_{AB}} = \frac{.059}{.41} = .14 \quad \text{say 1 bolts}$$

> Use 3-5/8 in dia A307 AB equally spaced. 4 in. min. embedment

Calc T and C chord forces

$GOM = Vh = 2.5(10) + .059(7.5) = 25.4^{k\,ft}$

$$RM = \frac{w_{DL}b^2}{2} + \frac{w_{wall}\left(\ell/2\right)b^2}{2} = \frac{.16(4)^2}{2} + \frac{.016\left(10/2\right)(4)^2}{2}$$

$= 1.9^{k\,ft}$

$DOM = GOM - .85RM = 25.4 - .85(1.9) = 23.8^{k\,ft}$

Since the GOM is larger than the resisting moment we will need a holdown force calc.

$T_{design} = DOM/b = 23.4/4 = 5.9^{k}$

$$C_{design} = \frac{GOM}{b} + P_{trib} =$$

$$\frac{25.4}{4} + \frac{1.33(.16+.016(10))}{2} + .016\left(10/2\right)$$

$= 6.6^{k}$

Ck T chord

$F_t = .45$ ksi
$F_c = .825$ ksi
$F_{c\perp} = .625$ ksi

$E = 1.4e3$ ksi
$A = 5.25\ in^2$

Assume 1 in diameter hole for HD (consv.)

$$f_t = \frac{T}{A_n} = \frac{5.9}{5.25-(1(1.5))} = 1.6 \text{ ksi}$$

NDS T2.3.1 $F_t' = F_tC_DC_MC_tC_F = .45(1.6)1.0(1.0)1.5$

$= 1.08$ ksi > 1.6 ksi **NG!**

Try 4x4

$A = 12.25\ in^2$

$$f_t = \frac{5.9}{12.25-(1(3.5))} = .67 \text{ ksi} < 1.08 \text{ ksi} \quad \surd$$

$5.9^{k} < 6.8^{k}$ √

> 4x4 stud ok for tension chord with simpson HD6 with 3-3/4 in dia stud bolts and 1-1 in dia AB

Ck C chord

Note that some designers use the tributary length of the shearwall to calc the compression DL. This is a conservative approach that assumes that the wall studs do not carry any wall DL. Do not use the .85 multiplier for the compression force. To do so is not conservative. Use a conservative approach where C is calculated for the total height of the stud but the A is calculated at the base (the midpoint is where buckling will occur).

Compare slenderness ratios

Full lateral support implies

$$\left(\frac{\ell_e}{d}\right)_y = \left(\frac{K_e\ell}{d}\right)_y = \frac{1.0(0.0)12}{1.5} = 0.0$$ NDS 3.7.1.2

$$\left(\frac{\ell_e}{d}\right)_x = \left(\frac{K_e\ell}{d}\right)_x = \frac{1.0(10)12}{3.5} = 34.3$$

$34.3 > 0$ strong axis governs

Ck capacity

$K_{cE} = 0.3$

$c = 0.8$

$E' = EC_MC_tC_T = (1.4e3)1.0(1.0)1.0 = 1.4e3$ ksi

$$F_{cE} = \frac{K_{cE}E'}{\left(\ell_e/d\right)^2} = \frac{.3(1.4e3)}{(34.3)^2} = .36 \text{ ksi}$$ NDS T2.3.1

$F_c^* = F_cC_DC_MC_tC_F = .825(1.6)1.0(1.15) = 1.5$ ksi

It would be consv. to use $C_F = 1.0$

$$C_P = \frac{1+\left(F_{cE}/F_c^*\right)}{2c} - \sqrt{\left(\frac{1+\left(F_{cE}/F_c^*\right)}{2c}\right)^2 - \frac{\left(F_{cE}/F_c^*\right)}{c}}$$ NDS 3.7.1.5

NDS T2.3.1

$$C_P = \frac{1+\left(.36/_{1.5}\right)}{2(.8)} - \sqrt{\left(\frac{1+\left(.36/_{1.5}\right)}{2(.8)}\right)^2 - \frac{\left(.36/_{1.5}\right)}{.8}} = .23$$

$F_c' = F_cC_DC_MC_tC_P = .825(1.6)1.0(1.0)1.15(.23)$

$= .35$ ksi

$P = F_c' A_n = .35(12.25) = 4.3^k < 6.6^k$ **NG!**

Try 4x6 chord

$A = 19.25$ in^2

NDS 3.7.1.2

$$\left(\frac{\ell_e}{d}\right)_x = \left(\frac{K_e\ell}{d}\right)_x = \frac{1.0(10)12}{5.5} = 21.8$$

$$F_{cE} = \frac{K_{cE}E'}{\left(\ell_e/_d\right)^2} = \frac{.3(1.4e3)}{(21.8)^2} = .88 \text{ ksi}$$

$F_c^* = F_cC_DC_MC_tC_F = .825(1.6)1.0(1.1) = 1.5$ ksi

It would be consv. to use $C_F = 1.0$

NDS 3.7.1.5

$$C_P = \frac{1+\left(F_{cE}/_{F_c*}\right)}{2c} - \sqrt{\left(\frac{1+\left(F_{cE}/_{F_c*}\right)}{2c}\right)^2 - \frac{\left(F_{cE}/_{F_c*}\right)}{c}}$$

NDS T2.3.1

$$C_P = \frac{1+\left(.88/_{1.5}\right)}{2(.8)} - \sqrt{\left(\frac{1+\left(.88/_{1.5}\right)}{2(.8)}\right)^2 - \frac{\left(.4.883/_{1.5}\right)}{.8}} = .49$$

$F_c' = F_cC_DC_MC_tC_P = .825(1.6)1.0(1.0)1.1(.49) = .71$ ksi

$P = F_c' A_n = .71(19.25 - (5.5(1.0))) = 9.8^k > 6.6^k$ √

Compression ok for 4x6 chord

Ck bearing of bottom plate

NDS T2.3.1

$F_{c\perp}' = F_{c\perp}C_MC_tC_b = .625(1.0)1.0(1.0)$

$= .625$ ksi $< .71$ bearing governs

$P = 13.75(.625) = 8.6^k > 6.6^k$ √

Use 4x6 DF- L stud grade chord for shearwall

□
□
□

Until one is committed, there is hesitancy, the chance to draw back, always ineffectiveness. Concerning all acts of initiative (and creation) there is one elementary truth, the ignorance of which kills countless ideas and splendid plans: that the moment one definitely commits oneself, then Providence moves too. All sorts of things occur to help one that would never otherwise have occurred. A whole stream of events issues from the decision, raising in one's favor all manner of unforeseen incidents and meetings and material assistance, which no man could have dreamed would have come his way. I have learned a deep respect for one of Goethe's couplets:

Whatever you can do, or dream you can, begin it. Boldness has genius, power and magic in it.

W. H. MURRAY
THE SCOTTISH HIMALAYAN EXPEDITION

PROBLEM 5.6

Shearwall design for 2-story configuration.

Determine the shearwall forces for the wall shown below. Consider lateral force reversal. Neglect RDL + FDL + FLL + seismic load case.

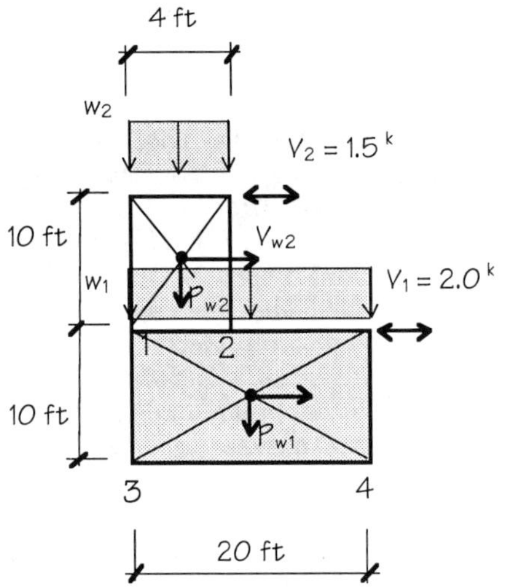

ASSUME

w_{RDL} = .12 klf.
w_{RLL} = . 2 klf.
w_{FDL} = .16 klf.
w_{FLL} = . 4 klf.
Wall wt. = .016 ksf (included in V below).
$V_{w1} = .59^k$.
$V_{w2} = .12^k$.
$P_{w1} = 3.2^k$.
$P_{w2} = .64^k$.
MC < 19%.

SOLUTION

Ck aspect ratios

UBC T23-I-I

$$\frac{\ell_1}{b_1} = \frac{10}{4} = 2.5 < 3.5 \ \checkmark$$

$$\frac{\ell_2}{b_2} = \frac{10}{20} = 0.5 < 3.5 \ \checkmark$$

Shearwall 2

All forces are symmetrical T = C for lateral force reversal.

Recall that roof LL is omitted when checking overturning forces for the shearwalls.

Use the conservative approach which utilizes the full height of the shearwall DL for the walls inertial seismic force.

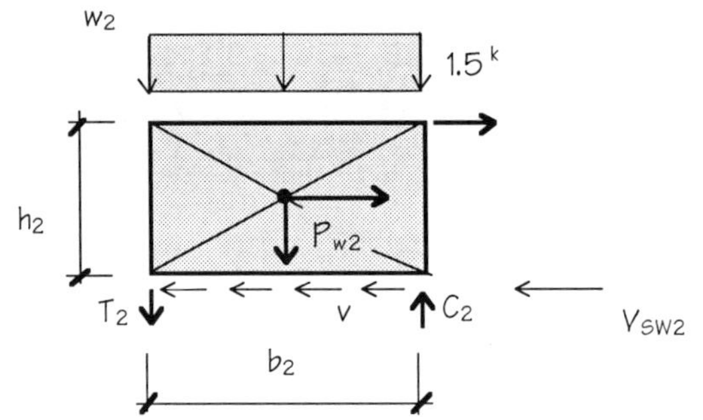

$$V_{SW2} = V_2 + V_{w2} = 1.5 + .12 = 1.6^k$$

$$v_{sw2} = \frac{V_{SW2}}{b} = \frac{1.6}{4} = .4 \text{ klf}$$

> $V_{SW2} = 1.6^k$, force added to V_{SW1} at first floor level.
> v_{SW2} = .4 klf , force used for shearwall design and shear transfer connection design

Calc T and C chord forces

$$GOM = V_2 h_2 + V_{w2}\left(\frac{h_2}{2}\right) = 1.5(10) + .12(5) = 15.6^{k\,ft}$$

$$RM = \frac{w_{RDL} b_2^2}{2} + P_{w2}\left(\frac{b_2}{2}\right) = \frac{.12(4)^2}{2} + .64\left(\frac{4}{2}\right)$$

$= 2.2^{k\,ft}$

$DOM = GOM - .85R = 15.6 - .85(2.2) = 13.7^{k\,ft}$

Since the GOM is larger than the resisting moment we will need a holdown force calc.

$T_2 = DOM/b_2 = 13.7/4 = 3.4^k$

> $T_2 = 3.4^k$ design force is used to check f_t stress of chord and to select the tension transfer connection hardware at the shearwall boundaries

$$C_2 = \frac{GOM}{b_2} + P_{trib} = \frac{15.6}{4} + \frac{1.33(.12 + .64/4)}{2} = 4.1^k$$

> $C_2 = 4.1^k$ design force is used to check f_c stress of chord compared to D + L case to see which governs. It is also used to select the tension transfer connection hardware at the shearwall boundaries, column stability and bearing

Shearwall 1 (⟶ Lateral load direction)

Recall that roof or floor LL is omitted when checking overturning forces for the shearwalls.

Use the conservative approach which utilizes the full height of the shearwall DL for the walls inertial seismic force.

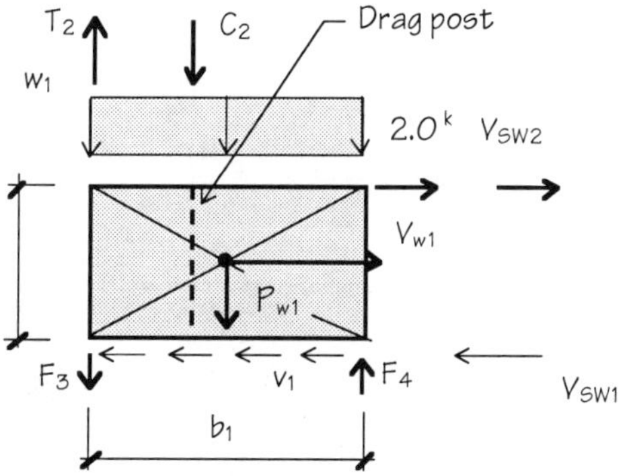

$V_{SW1} = V_{SW2} + V_{w1} + V_1$

$= 1.6 + .12 + 2.0 = 3.72^k$

$$v_{sw2} = \frac{V_{SW1}}{b_1} = \frac{3.72}{20} = .186 \text{ klf}$$

> $V_{SW1} = 3.72^k$, base shear.
> $v_{sw2} = .186$ klf , force used for shearwall design and shear transfer (AB) connection design

Calc T and C chord forces

Calculate about location 4.

$$GOM = (V_1 + V_{SW2})h_1 + V_{w1}\left(\frac{h_1}{2}\right) + T_2 b_1$$

$$= (2.0 + 3.72)10 + .59(5) + 3.4(20) = 128.2^{k\,ft}$$

$$RM = 16C_2 + \frac{w_{FDL} b_1^2}{2} + P_{w1}\left(b_1/2\right)$$

$$= 16(4.1) + \frac{.16(20)^2}{2} + 3.2\left(20/2\right) = 129.6^{k\,ft}$$

$DOM = GOM - .85RM = 123.2 - .85(129.6) = 13.0^{k\,ft}$

Since the GOM is larger than the resisting moment we will need a holdown force calc.

$F_3 = DOM/b_1 = 13.0/20 = .65^k$

> $F_3 = .65^k$ design force is used to check f_t stress of chord and to select the tension transfer connection hardware at the shearwall boundaries

Sum forces in vertical direction

$F_4 = 3.4 + .65 - 4.1 - .16(20) - 3.2 = -6.5^k$

> $F_4 = -6.5^k$ design force is used to check f_c stress of chord compared to D + L case to see which governs. It is also used to select the compression transfer connection hardware at the shearwall boundaries, column stability and bearing

Shearwall 1 (⟵ Lateral load direction)

Recall that roof or floor LL is omitted when checking overturning forces for the shearwalls. Use the conservative approach which utilizes the full height of the shearwall DL for the walls inertial seismic force.

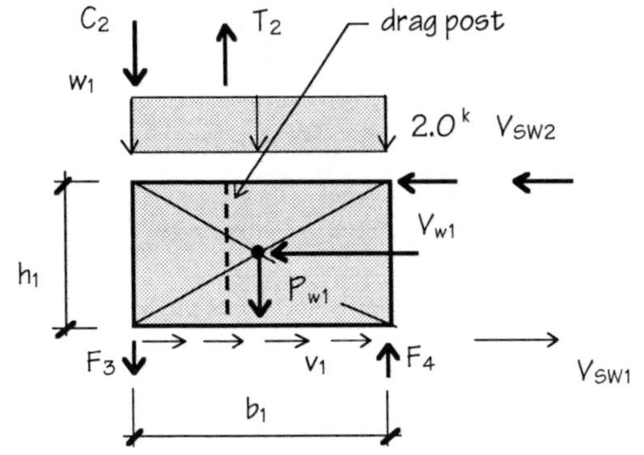

$V_{SW2} = 3.72^k$ (same as above)

$v_{sw2} = .186$ klf (same as above)

Calc T and C chord forces

Calculate about location 3.

$$GOM = (V_1 + V_{SW2})h_1 + V_{w1}\left(\frac{h_1}{2}\right) + 4T_2$$

$$= (2.0 + 3.72)10 + .59(5) + 3.4(4) = 73.8^{k\,ft}$$

$$RM = \frac{w_{FDL}b_1^2}{2} + P_{w1}\left(b_1/2\right) = \frac{.16(20)^2}{2} + 3.2\left(20/2\right)$$

$$= 64.0^{k\,ft}$$

$$DOM = GOM - .85RM = 73.8 - .85(64) = 19.4^{k\,ft}$$

Since the GOM is larger than the resisting moment we will need a holdown force calc.

$F_4 = DOM/b_1 = 19.4/20 = .97^k$

> $F_3 = .97^k$ design force is used to check f_t stress of chord and to select the tension transfer connection hardware at the shearwall boundaries

Sum forces in vertical direction

$F_4 = 3.4 + .72 - 4.1 - .16(20) - 3.2 = -6.4^k$

> $F_4 = -6.4^k$ design force is used to check f_c stress of chord compared to D + L case to see which governs. It is also used to select the compression transfer connection hardware at the shearwall boundaries, column stability and bearing

▯
▯
▯

The thing always happens that you believe in; and the belief in a thing makes it happen.

FRANK LLOYD WRIGHT

PROBLEM 5.7

Wood moment frame investigation.

Investigate the possiblity of using a wood shearwall moment frame for the loads given below.

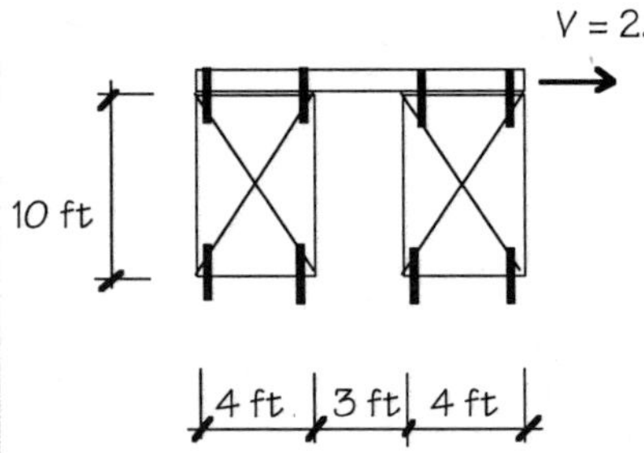

ASSUME

Neglect seismic reversal.
Neglect inertial load of wall.
Neglect vertical weight of wall or roof.

UBC T23-1-1

SOLUTION

Ck aspect ratio

$\frac{\ell}{b} = \frac{10}{4} = 2.5 < 3.5$ √

Shearwall

To achieve moment frame-like action, the shearwalls must act like vertical beams. The chords of the shearwalls act like the flanges of the beam while the plywood diaphragm acts like the web. Modeling similar to a steel moment frame gives:

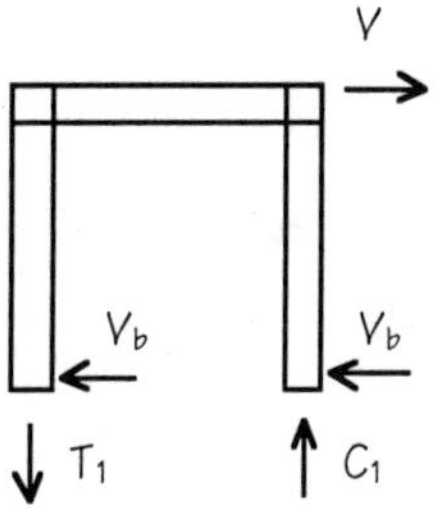

$T_1 = C_1 = 5(10)/7 = 7.14^k$

$V_b = 5/2 = 2.5^k$

Use the approximate approach of the portal method to arrive at the frame moments.

Portal analysis gives:

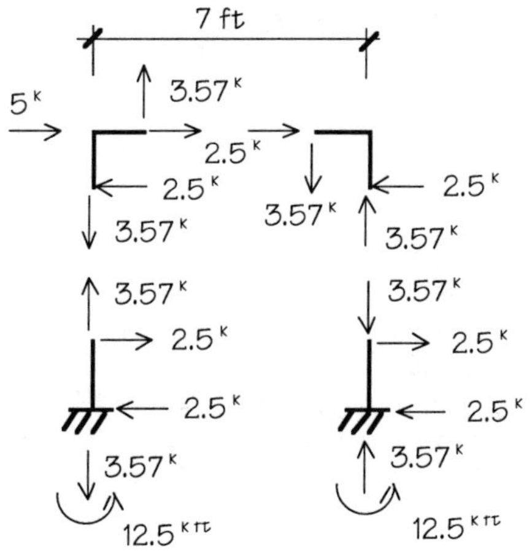

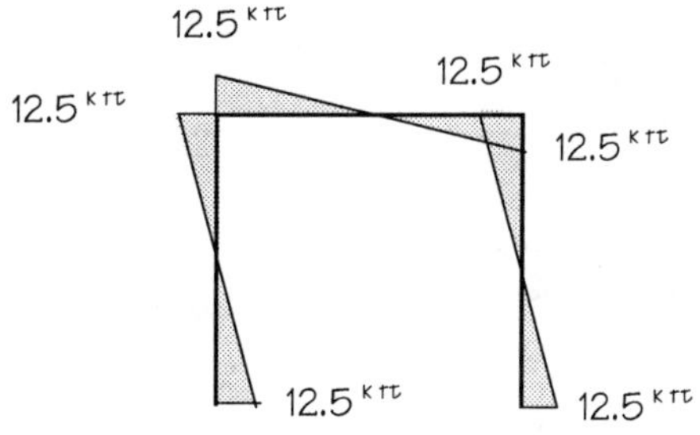

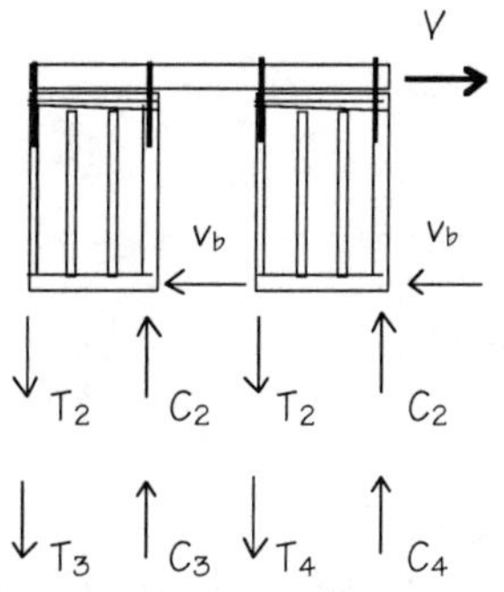

$T_2 = C_2 = M_b/4 = 12.5/4 = 3.13^k$

$T_3 = T_1/2 + T_2 = 7.14/2 + 3.13 = 6.7^k \Rightarrow (T)$

$C_3 = C_2 - T_1/2 = 3.13 - 7.14/2 = -.44^k \Rightarrow (T)$

$T_4 = T_2 - C_1/2 = 3.13 - 7.14/2 = -.44^k \Rightarrow (C)$

$C_4 = C_2 + C_1/2 = 7.14/2 + 3.13 = 6.7^k \Rightarrow (C)$

$v_b = V_b/4 = 2.5/4 = .63$ klf

> Strap force = T2 = 3.13^k
> Plywood shear = .63 klf
> HD force = $T_3 = 6.7^k$
> Beam M = $12.5^{k\,ft}$

The question arises as to how this compares to a drag strut beam with two shearwalls. A quick analysis gives:

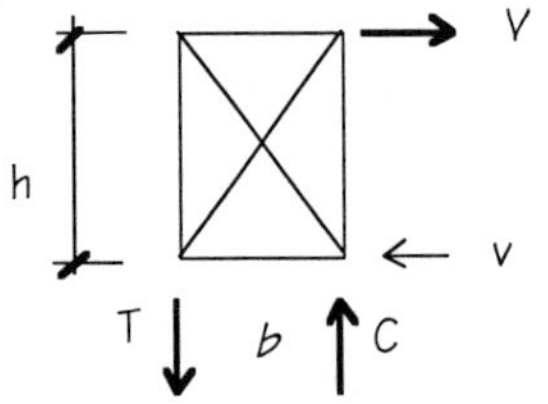

Since the two shear walls have the same length:

$v = \dfrac{5}{4(2)} = .63$ klf

$GOM = Vh = 2.5(10) = 25^{k\,ft}$

$T = C = GOM/b = 25/4 = 6.25^{k}$

Comparing to our moment frame model gives:

Plywood shear	=	.63 klf (same)
HD force	=	6.7^k and 6.25^k

From the above we can see that there is little actual difference between the two methods. If we continued with either of the methods we would have to consider inertial wall loads, vertical loads, and connective hardware (with their effect upon the connected element).

Will the moment frame even act like a moment frame before it acts like a drag strut with two shearwalls? In simple terms, frame action depends upon the stiffness of the members and, hence, their tendency to deflect. It seems likely that V will be transferred first by the beam acting like a drag (or column). Once the shearwalls begin to deflect and rotate you will get some frame action.

But, practically speaking, how much? And quite frankly, although an argument can be made that some frame action occurs, why bother with it when it is easier to use the drag strut methodology.

□
□
□

Yeah, but, your scientists were so preoccupied with whether or not they could, they didn't stop to think if they should.

DR. MALCOM
JURASSIC PARK

o PROBLEM 5.8

Shearwall with a hole designed as 2 cantilevers.

Design the transverse shearwall shown below with a hole as 2 cantilevers.

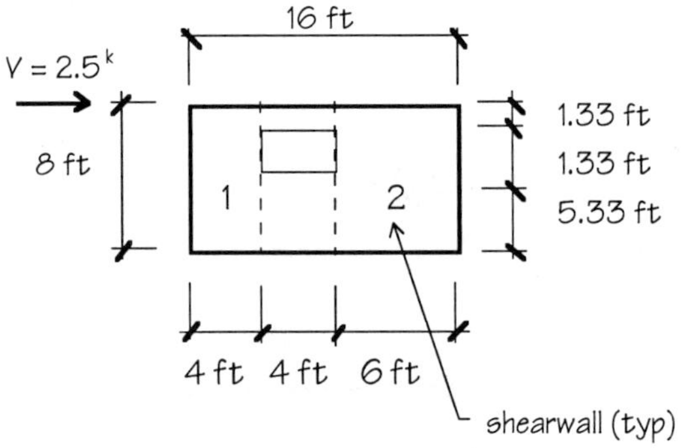

ASSUME

- V = wind.
- Wall wt. = .016 ksf.
- $V_w = .183W$.
- MC < 19%.
- 2x4 DF-L stud grade studs.
- 1 in holes for holdowns.

SOLUTION

Ck aspect ratios

UBC T23-I-I

$$\frac{h}{\ell_1} = \frac{8}{4} = 2.0 < 3.5 \quad \checkmark$$

$$\frac{h}{\ell_2} = \frac{8}{6} = 1.33 < 3.5 \quad \checkmark$$

Shearwall 1

Use the dynamic approach which utilizes the top half of the shearwall DL for the walls inertial seismic force.

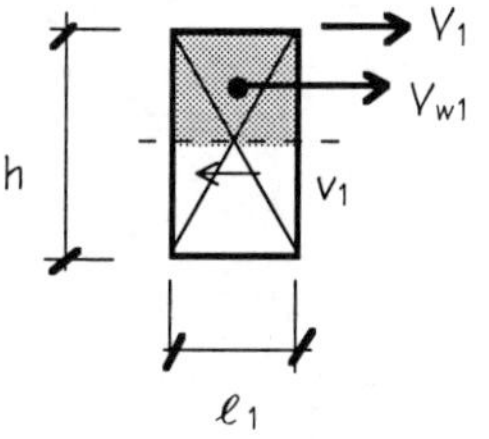

$V_1 = 2.5(4/10) = 1.0^k$

$$v_1 = \frac{1.0}{4} = .25 \text{ klf}$$

$V_{w1} = .183(8/2)4(.016) = .05^k$

$$v_w = \frac{.05}{4} = .013 \text{ klf}$$

$V_{base} = V_1 + V_w = 1.0 + .05 = 1.05^k$

$$v_{base} = \frac{V_{base}}{\ell} = \frac{1.05}{4} = .26 \text{ klf} < .27 \text{ klf} \quad \checkmark$$

UBC T23-I-K-1

> Use 15/32 in Str 1, EXP 1 plywood with 8d at 6 in. o/c, 12 in. o/c in field

Calc T chord forces

Use the GOM to calc T and C forces. This is a conservative approach because it does not reduce the T force by the DL. Since there is no DL other than the wall wt. itself, use the full T force for holdown requirement.

$T = vh = .25(8) + .013(4) = 2.05^k$

$$f_t = \frac{T}{A_n} = \frac{2.1}{5.25-(1(1.5))} = .56 \text{ ksi}$$

$F_t' = F_tC_DC_MC_tC_F = .45(1.6)1.0(1.0)1.5$ NDS T2.3.1

$= 1.08 \text{ ksi} > .56 \text{ ksi} \quad \checkmark$

> 2x4 stud ok for tension chord. Provide holdown = 2.05^k

Calc C chord force

Assume that the studs are at 16 in o/c.

$P_{DL} = 2.1 + 8(1.33/2).016 = 2.2^k$

Do not use the .85 multiplier for the compression force. To do so is not conservative.

Ck 2x4 stud

Use conservative approach where P is calculated for the total height of the stud but the A is calculated at the base.

$F_c = .825$ ksi
$F_{c\perp} = .625$ ksi
$E = 1.4e3$ ksi
$A = 5.25 \text{ in}^2$

Compare slenderness ratios

NDS 3.7.1.2

$$\left(\frac{\ell_e}{d}\right)_y = \left(\frac{K_e\ell}{d}\right)_y = \frac{1.0(0.0)12}{1.5} = 0.0$$

$$\left(\frac{\ell_e}{d}\right)_x = \left(\frac{K_e\ell}{d}\right)_x = \frac{1.0(8)12}{3.5} = 27.4$$

$27.4 > 0$ strong axis governs

Ck capacity

$K_{cE} = 0.3$

$c = 0.8$

$E' = EC_MC_t = (1.4e3)1.0(1.0) = 1.4e3$ ksi NDS T2.3.1

$$F_{cE} = \frac{K_{cE}E'}{\left(\ell_e/d\right)^2} = \frac{.3(1.4e3)}{(27.4)^2} = .56 \text{ ksi}$$

$F_c^* = F_cC_DC_MC_tC_F = .825(1.6)1.0(1.15) = 1.5$ ksi

It would be consv. to use $C_F = 1.0$

NDS 3.7.1.5

$$C_P = \frac{1+\left(F_{cE}/F_c{}^*\right)}{2c} - \sqrt{\left(\frac{1+\left(F_{cE}/F_c{}^*\right)}{2c}\right)^2 - \frac{\left(F_{cE}/F_c{}^*\right)}{c}}$$

$$C_P = \frac{1+\left(.56/1.5\right)}{2(.8)} - \sqrt{\left(\frac{1+\left(.56/1.5\right)}{2(.8)}\right)^2 - \frac{\left(.56/1.5\right)}{.8}} = .34$$

NDS T2.3.1

$F_c' = F_cC_DC_MC_tC_P = .825(1.6)1.0(1.0)1.15(.34)$

$= .52$ ksi

$P = F_c{}' A_n = .52(5.25\text{-}1.5) = 1.95^k < 2.3^k$ NG!

Try 2-2x4

$2P = 2(1.95) = 3.9^k > 2.2^k$ √

> Compression chord ok if 2-2x4 used. Note that nailing should be provided to transfer P to each 2x4

Ck bearing of bottom plate

NDS T2.3.1

$F_{c\perp}' = F_{c\perp}C_MC_tC_b = .625(1.0)1.0(1.0)$

$= .625$ ksi $> .35$ stability governs by inspection.

> Use 2-2x4 DF-L stud grade studs for shearwall chords

Shearwall 2

It was shown in previous examples that the shorter wall will provide the more critical case. In practice it is customary to use the shorter shearwall specifications for both walls. This practice results in less confusion in the field.

> Use shearwall 1 specifications for both shearwall 1 and 2 (see above)

□
□
□

It is easier to fight for one's principles than to live up to them.

ALFRED ADLER

○ PROBLEM 5.9

Shearwall with a hole designed as one panel.

Design the transverse shearwall shown below with a hole as one shearwall panel.

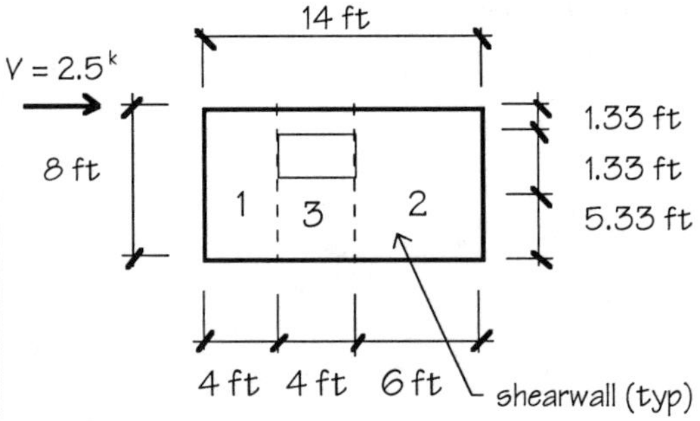

ASSUME

V = seismic.
Wall wt. = .016 ksf.
$V_w = .183W$.
MC < 19%.
2x4 DF-L stud grade studs.
1 in holes for holdowns.
Diaphragm drag ok.

SOLUTION

Ck aspect ratio

UBC T23-I-I

$\frac{h}{\ell} = \frac{8}{14} = .57 < 3.5$ √

Shearwall

The custom of assuming a 2-cantilever system with filler panels in between is widely used in professional practice (see previous problem). The performance of this methodology has been good. It does, however, have its problems. Consider a wall with many openings like the one shown below. The cantilever method would have us believe that all the panels have the same stiffness. This assumption is obviously wrong when we add the consideration of the panel below the windows. The free standing panel will be over-designed while the panel between the windows will be under-designed, because it is indeed stiffer and will "draw" more lateral load. We can improve performance of the system by taking into consideration the panels (below the window) as shown in this example:

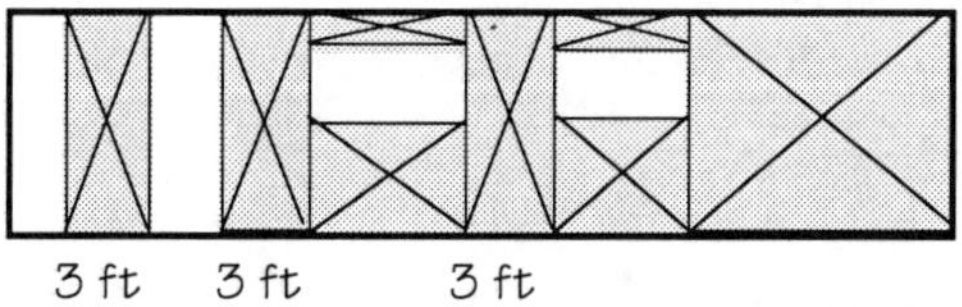

Use the conservative approach which utilizes the total height of the shearwall DL for the walls inertial seismic force.

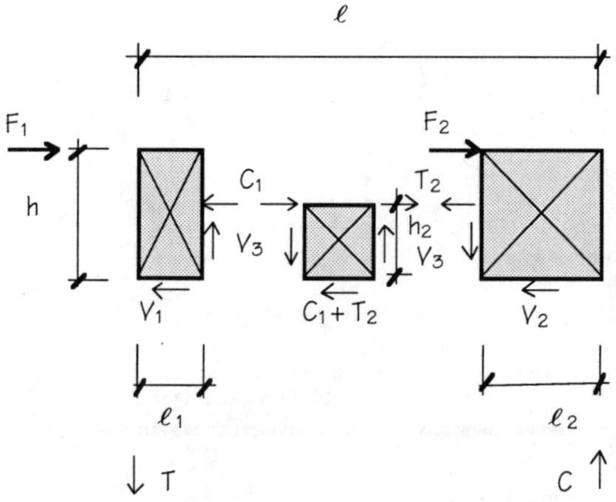

Assume wall DL inertial load without a hole. It is convenient for calculations to translate the walls inertial load to the F force h level thus:

$V_w = .183(14)(8)(4/8).016 = .16^k$

$F = V + V_w = 2.5 + .16 = 2.66^k$

$F_1 = 2.66(4/10) = 1.06^k$

$F_2 = 2.66(6/10) = 1.6^k$

Neglect wall DL as in previous problem (conservative). The following diagram sums the statics.

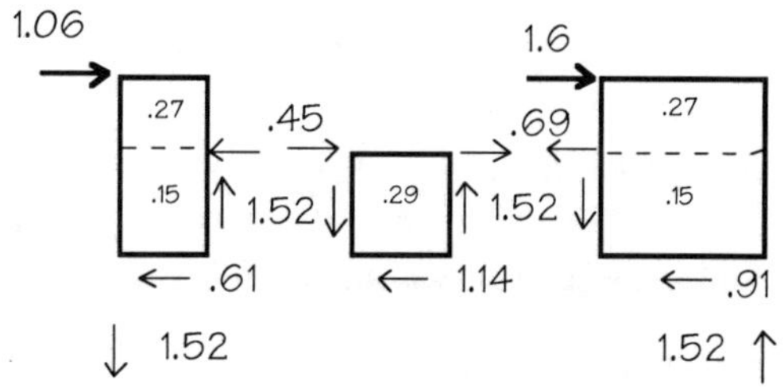

Assume forces to the right and clockwise moments are positive and solve by statics.

$T = C = (F_1 + F_2)h/L = (2.66)8/14 = 1.52^k$

$C_1 = (F_1h - TL_1)/h_2 = (1.06(8) - 1.52(4))/5.33 = .45^k$

$T_2 = (F_2h - CL_2)/h_2 = (1.6(8) - 1.52(6))/5.33 = .69^k$

$V_4 = C_1 + T_2 = .45 + .69 = 1.14^k$

$V_3 = (F_1h - C_1h_2)/L_2 = (1.06(8) - .45(5.33))/4 = 1.52^k$

$V_1 = (TL_1 - F_1(h - h_2))/h_2 = (1.52(4) - 1.06(2.66))/5.33 = .61^k$

$V_2 = (CL_2 - F_2(h - h_2))/h_2 = (1.52(6) - 1.6(2.66))/5.33 = .91^k$

Statics Check

$1.06 + 1.6 = 2.66^k = .61 + 1.14 + .91 = 2.66^k$ √

Using the proximate V and dividing by the shearwall length gives the unit shear as summarized above. Calculating the forces for seismic reversal gives:

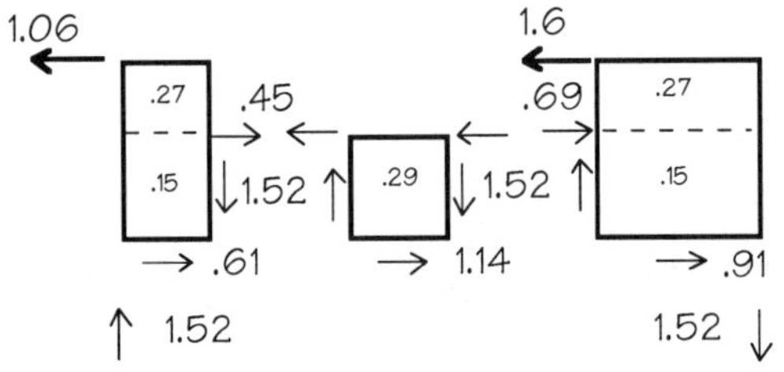

The largest unit shear = .29 klf < 430 klf

UBC T23-I-K-1

> Use 15/32 in Str 1, EXP 1 plywood with 8d at 4 in o/c, 12 in o/c in field

Calc T chord forces

Use the GOM to calc T and C forces. This is a conservative approach because it does not reduce the T force by the DL. Since there is no DL other than the wall wt. itself, use the full T force for holdown requirement.

$T = 1.52^k$

$$f_t = \frac{T}{A_n} = \frac{1.52}{5.25-(1(1.5))} = .41 \text{ ksi}$$

NDS T2.3.1

$F_t' = F_tC_DC_MC_tC_F = .45(1.6)1.0(1.0)1.5$

$= 1.08 \text{ ksi} > .41 \text{ ksi}$ √

> 2x4 stud ok for tension chord. Provide holdown = 1.52^k

Calc C chord force

Assume that the studs are at 16 in o/c.

$P_{DL} = 1.52 + 8(1.33/2).016 = 1.61^k$

Do not use the .85 multiplier for the compression force. To do so is not conservative.

Ck 2x4 stud

Use conservative approach where P is calculated for the total height of the stud but the A is calculated at the base.

$F_c = .825$ ksi
$F_{c\perp} = .625$ ksi
$E = 1.4e3$ ksi
$A = 5.25 \text{ in}^2$

Compare slenderness ratios

$$\left(\frac{\ell_e}{d}\right)_y = \left(\frac{K_e\ell}{d}\right)_y = \frac{1.0(0.0)12}{1.5} = 0.0$$ NDS 3.7.1.2

$$\left(\frac{\ell_e}{d}\right)_x = \left(\frac{K_e\ell}{d}\right)_x = \frac{1.0(8)12}{3.5} = 27.4$$

27.4 > 0 strong axis governs

Ck capacity

$K_{cE} = 0.3$

$c = 0.8$ NDS T2.3.1

$E' = EC_MC_t = (1.4e3)1.0(1.0) = 1.4e3$ ksi

$$F_{cE} = \frac{K_{cE}E'}{\left(\ell_e/d\right)^2} = \frac{.3(1.4e3)}{(27.4)^2} = .56 \text{ ksi}$$

$F_c^* = F_cC_DC_MC_tC_F = .825(1.6)1.0(1.15) = 1.5$ ksi

It would be consv. to use $C_F = 1.0$

$$C_P = \frac{1+\left(F_{cE}/F_c^*\right)}{2c} - \sqrt{\left(\frac{1+\left(F_{cE}/F_c^*\right)}{2c}\right)^2 - \frac{\left(F_{cE}/F_c^*\right)}{c}}$$ NDS 3.7.1.5

$$C_P = \frac{1+(.56/1.5)}{2(.8)} - \sqrt{\left(\frac{1+(.56/1.5)}{2(.8)}\right)^2 - \frac{(.56/1.5)}{.8}} = .34$$

$F_c' = F_cC_DC_MC_tC_P = .825(1.6)1.0(1.0)1.15(.34)$ NDS T2.3.1

$= .52$ ksi

$P = F_c'A_n = .52(5.25-1.5) = 1.95^k < 1.61^k$ √

> Compression chord ok with 2x4.

Ck bearing of bottom plate

$F_{c\perp}' = F_{c\perp}C_MC_tC_b = .625(1.0)1.0(1.0)$ NDS T2.3.1

$= .625 \text{ ksi} > .52$ stability governs by inspection.

> Use 2x4 DF-L stud grade studs for shearwall chords

Window drags

It was shown above that the maximum T or C is $.69^k$. For the compressive force we need to block (tightly fit) the shearwall to transmit the drag force into the diaphragm. The tensile force can be transmitted into the shearwall via a metal tension strap and blocking. Block for a length of:

$.69/.34 = 2.02$ ft

> Use manufactured steel strap with cap. $= .7^k$ with blocking at window drag height for a minimum of 2.0 ft each side

Compare with cantilever method

The present problem utilizes a larger inertial load. This effectively raises the unit shear and force level and is considered conservative.

	Present	Cantilever
T or C (k)	1.52	2.05
v (klf)	.29	.27
Chord size	2x4	2-2x4

We can see by the above that the present method will give smaller values for the chord forces and sizes.

□
□
□

You grow up the day you have the first laugh - at yourself.

ETHEL BARRYMORE

PROBLEM 5.10

Shearwall deflection.

Determine the deflection of the shearwall for the building shown below.

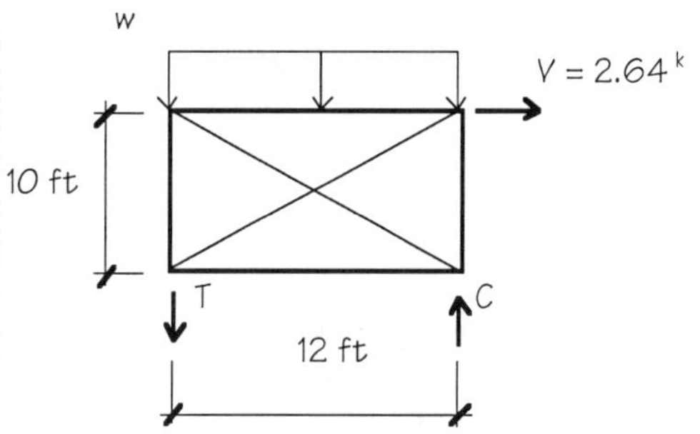

ASSUME

- Neglect wind.
- MC < 19%.
- 2x6 DF-L stud grade at 16 in o/c.
- 4x6 DF-L No 1 chords.
- 1 in "net" holes for holdowns.
- 1/2 in Str 1 ply with 8d @ 4 in o/c (blk'd).

SOLUTION

Ck aspect ratio

(used for comparison in this prob.)

The aspect ratio is the basic rule of thumb for determining acceptability of shearwall deflection. It is also the most widely used method because of its ease of employment. This approach relies on the notion that deflection will be reasonable as long as the relative proportions of the diaphragm are limited by traditional ratios. These ratios have historically performed well when used in wood-type structures. UBC T23-I-I

$$\frac{\ell}{b} = \frac{12}{10} = 1.2 < 3.5 \quad \checkmark$$

Shearwall

The formula for the estimated deflection of shearwalls can be found in Section 25.923 of the 1991 UBC Standard 25-9. The formula is as follows:

$\Delta = \Delta_{bending} + \Delta_{shear} + \Delta_{nail\ slip} + \Delta_{chord\ bolt\ slip}$

$$\Delta = \frac{8vh^3}{EAb} + \frac{vh}{Gt} + 0.75he_n + d_a$$

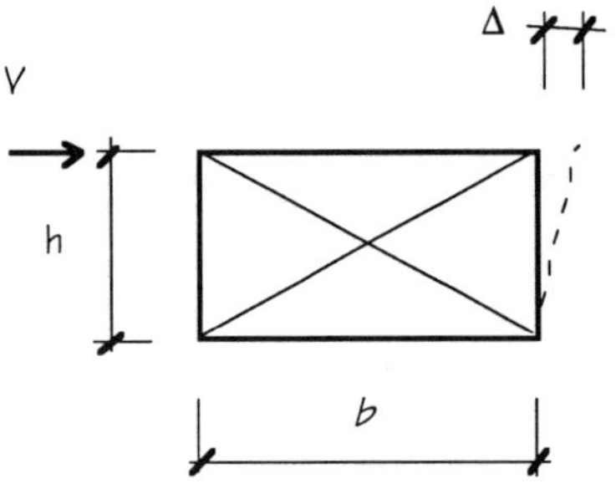

$V = 2.64^k$

In this example, we will use the imposed seismic load V (at the top of the wall). We could opt to use the dynamic approach. In this method, we would add the inertial weight from the top half of the wall to the seismic load above. (It is conservative to assume that the seismic load of the wall acts at the top of the wall). Note that in order to use this formula the shearwall must be uniformly nailed and blocked.

$v = \frac{2.64}{12} = .22$ klf (max. unit shear)

$A = 19.25\ in^2$ (chord boundary element)

h = 10 ft (wall height)

b = 12 ft (wall width)

Estimate the rotation and slip for the tie-down anchorage. Assume 1/16 in. = .0625 in net holes:

$d_a = .0625$ in. (rotation and slip of tie-down anchorage)

E = 1.6e3 ksi (chord boundary element)

Plywood modulus of rigidity.

G = 90.0 ksi (Table No. 25-9-J)

Plywood effective thickness.

t = .535 in., (Table No. 25-9-H, I)

nail deformation (Table B-4, APA research report # 138).

$$\frac{load}{nail} = \frac{v}{\#\ 8d/ft} = \frac{.22}{3} = .073^k$$

$$\left(\frac{v_n}{616}\right)^{3.018} = \left(\frac{73}{616}\right)^{3.018} = .002 \text{ in.}$$

$e_n = .002$ in.

$$\Delta = \frac{8(.22)10^3}{1.6e3(19.25)12} + \frac{.22(10)}{90(.535)} + 0.75(10).002 + .0625$$

= .128 in.

Shearwall deflection = .98 in.

Note that the aspect ratio is a code requirement and must be satisfied. The calculated deflection of .98 in is difficult to evaluate due to a lack of limiting criteria. The Designer must use her own judgment and experience as to whether the deflection will have deleterious effects on the shearwall or the structure as a whole.

We cherish our friends not for their ability to amuse, but for ours to amuse them.

EVELYN WAUGH

PROBLEM 5.11

Shearwall supported by a beam design.

Do a preliminary design analysis of the shearwall and beam shown below (one direction). Obtain beam load criteria only.

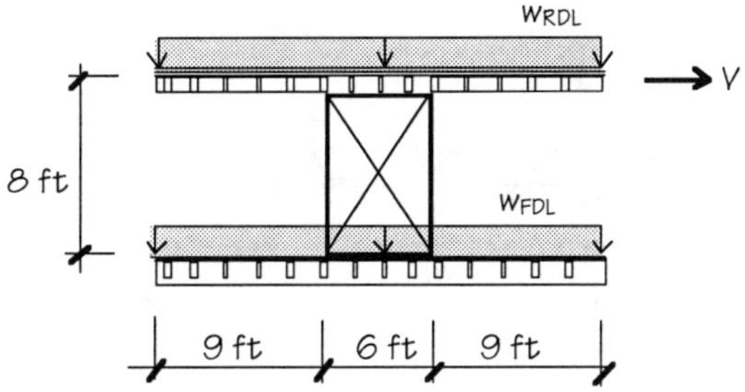

ASSUME

$V = 1.5^k$.
$w_{RDL} = .12$ klf.
$w_{FDL} = .12$ klf.
Wall wt. = .016 ksf.
$V_w = .183W$.
Seismic only.
MC < 19%.
2x4 DF- L stud grade at 16 in o/c.
1 in holes for holdowns if required.
1/2 in C-D EXP 1 plywood shearwall.
Neglect seismic reversal.

SOLUTION

Ck aspect ratio

UBC T23-I-I

$$\frac{\ell}{b} = \frac{8}{6} = 1.33 < 3.5 \quad \surd$$

Shearwall

Recall that roof LL is omitted when checking overturning forces for the shearwalls.

Use the conservative approach which utilizes the full height of the shearwall DL for the walls inertial seismic force.

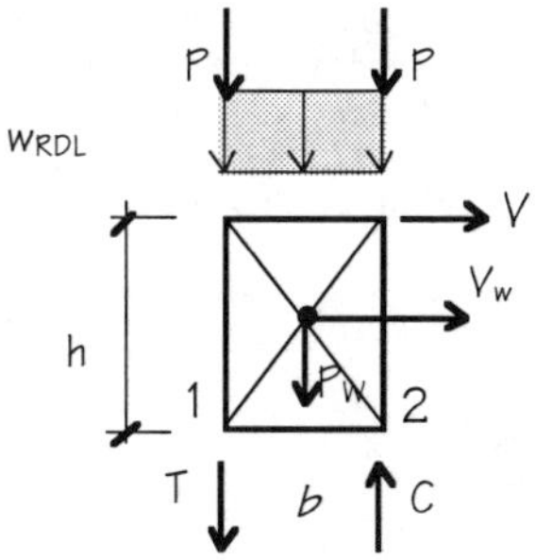

Spec. plywood:

$V_w = .183(8)6(.016) = .141^k$

$V_{base} = V + V_w = 1.5 + .141 = 1.64^k$

$$v_{base} = \frac{V_{base}}{b} = \frac{1.64}{6} = .27 \text{ klf} < .31 \quad \surd$$

UBC T23-I-K-1

> Use 15/32 in C-D EXP 1 plywood shearwall with 10d at 6, 12 in o/c

Spec. sill nailing and spacing:

The code stipulates 16d @ 16 in. o/c. Try 16d.

Z (per NDS table 12.3B) = $.141^k$

UBC T19-E, F

$$C_d = \frac{1.5}{12(.162)} = .77$$

$Z' = .141(1.33).77 = .141^k$

$$\text{spacing required} = \frac{.141}{.27} = .52 \text{ ft}$$

> Use 16d @ 6 in o/c for sill

Calc T and C chord forces

$GOM = Vh = 1.5(8) + .14(4) = 12.56^{k\,ft}$

Use conservative approach. Do not include RM.

$T = C = GOM/b = 12.7/6 = 2.12^k < 2(1.27) = 2.54^k$ $\surd$

> Use Simpson 2- CS18 coiled strap with 18-10d and L = 9 in min for tiedown for each side

Ck T chord

$F_t = .45$ ksi
$F_c = .825$ ksi
$F_{c\perp} = .625$ ksi
E = 1.4e3 ksi
A = 5.25 in^2

$$f_t = \frac{T}{A_n} = \frac{2.54}{5.25} = .48 \text{ ksi}$$

NDS T2.3.1

$F_t' = F_t C_D C_M C_t C_F = .45(1.33)1.0(1.0)1.5$

$= .9 \text{ ksi} > .48 \text{ ksi}$ $\surd$

2x4 stud ok for tension chord

Ck C chord

Use conservative approach.

$P = 9(.12)/2 = .54^k$

$$C_{design} = \frac{GOM}{b} + P_{trib} = \frac{12.7}{6} + \frac{6(.12+.016(8))}{2} + .54$$

$= 3.4^k$

Note: Do not use the .85 multiplier for the compression force. To do so is not conservative. Use conservative approach where C is calculated for the total height of the stud but the A is calculated at the base. Since this is a preliminary design (what we call in the field "quick and dirty"), use the Preliminary Column Design Chart found in the appendix.

2x4 cap. for 8 ft = **NG!**

Try 4x4 cap. = $6.6^k > 3.4^k$ √

Compression ok for 4x4 chord

Ck bearing of bottom plate

NDS T2.3.1

$F'_{c\perp} = F_{c\perp} C_M C_t C_b = .625(1.0)1.0(1.0)$

$= .625$ ksi $< 3.4/12.25 = .28$ √

Use 4x4 DF- L stud grade chords for shearwall

Analyze free body above for beam sizing:

$P_w = 6(8).016 = .77^k$

$\sum M_{R1} = 0$ implies:

$6(1.2) + .12(6)^2/2 + 3(.77) + .14(4) + 1.5(8) - 6R_2 = 0$

$$R_2 = \frac{24.2}{6} = 4.04^k$$

$R_1 = 2(1.2) + .12(6) + .77 - 4.04 = -.15^k$

Beam sizing criteria:

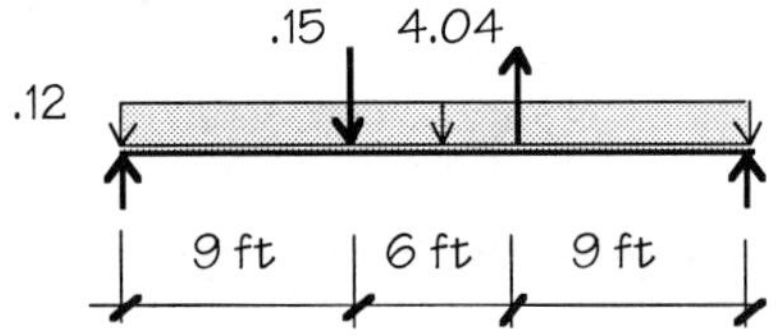

Use superposition:

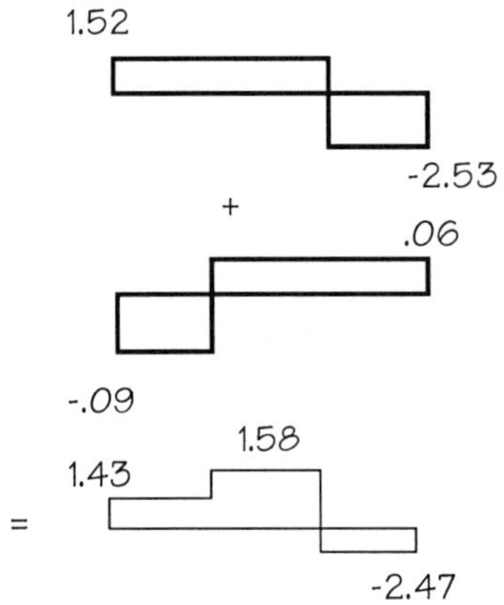

Adding the effects of the uniform load gives:

$V = 2.47 + .12(24)/2 = 3.91^k$

$M = 1.43(9) + 1.58(6) + .12(24)^2/8 = 31^{k\,ft}$

Rotation/deflection of the beam is a concern because of the shearwall defection (story drift) criteria from UBC Sec. 2334(h). This is best done via a computer model where you can look at the rotation of the middle of the beam and compare it to the rotation of the UBC generated story drift.

□
□
□

A noble person attracts noble people, and knows how to hold on to them.

GOETHE

PROBLEM 5.12

Shearwall with opening on one side.

Determine the plywood shearwall thickness, and nailing, anchor bolts and spacing, HD's, chords and bearing for the force parallel to the wall for the building elevation shown below. For this problem neglect all vertical and wall inertial loads.

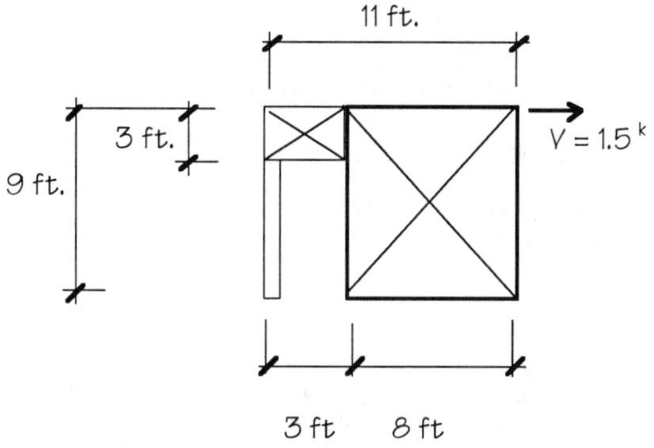

ASSUME

- MC < 19%.
- 2 ksi concrete footing.
- 2x4 DF- L stud grade at 16 in o/c.
- 1 in holes for holdowns if required.
- 1/2 in C-D EXP 1 plywood shearwall.
- Consider seismic reversal.

SOLUTION

Ck aspect ratio

$$\frac{\ell}{b} = \frac{9}{8} = 1.13 < 3.5 \quad \checkmark$$

UBC T23-I-I

Shearwall

Perform analysis with free bodies:

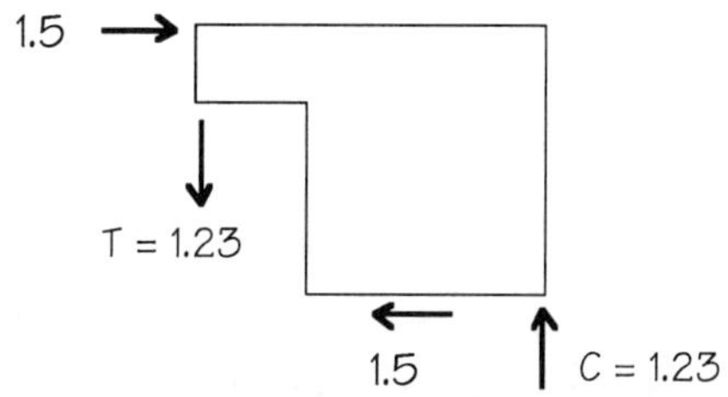

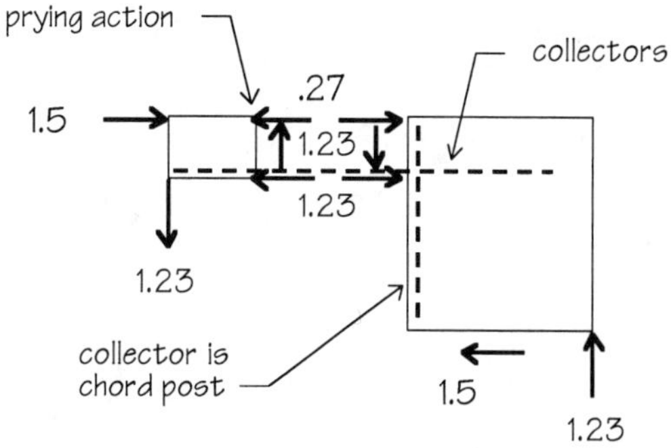

$$v_w = \frac{1.23}{3} = .41 \text{ klf} < .46 \text{ klf} \quad \checkmark \text{ controls}$$

$$v_{base} = \frac{1.5}{8} = .19 \text{ klf} < .46 \text{ klf} \quad \checkmark$$

> Use 15/32 in C-D EXP 1 plywood with 10d at 4,12 in. o/c (blocked), 3x at adjoining edges

UBC T19-E, F

Ck AB and spacing

stipulates that allowable shear tabular values that are used in the connection of wood members to concrete (or masonry) can be determined as 1/2 the double shear tabular value for a wood member twice the thickness of the attached member.

Try ½ in dia. AB

capacity in concrete = 2.0^k

capacity in wood $V_{AB\,||} = \frac{1.26}{2} = .63^k$

(UBC Table-25F)

Wood controls over concrete.

$$Ab_{reqd\,||} = \frac{V_{base}}{V_{AB}} = \frac{1.5}{.63} = 2.38 \quad \text{say 3 bolts}$$

> Use min 3-1/2 in dia A307 AB equally spaced. 4 in min. embedment

Ck T chord

Since this must be at least a 3x try 4x4 post (Normally this would be ok by inspection).

$T = 1.23^k < 1.56^k$ √

$F_t = .45$ ksi
$F_c = .825$ ksi
$F_{c\perp} = .625$ ksi
$E = 1.4e3$ ksi
$A = 12.25$ in^2

Assume 1 in diameter hole for HD (consv.)

$$f_t = \frac{T}{A_n} = \frac{1.23}{12.25-(1(3.5))} = .141 \text{ ksi}$$

NDS T2.3.1

$F_t' = F_tC_DC_MC_tC_F = .45(1.33)1.0(1.0)1.5$

$= .89$ ksi > .14 ksi √

> 4x4 stud ok for tension chord with simpson HD2A with 2-5/8 in dia. stud bolts and 1-5/8 in dia. AB

Ck C chord

$$\left(\frac{\ell_e}{d}\right) = \left(\frac{K_e\ell}{d}\right) = \frac{1.0(9)12}{3.5} = 30.9$$

Ck capacity

$K_{cE} = 0.3$

$c = 0.8$

$E' = EC_MC_tC_T = (1.4e3)1.0(1.0)1.0 = 1.4e3$ ksi NDS T2.3.1

$$F_{cE} = \frac{K_{cE}E'}{\left(\ell_e/d\right)^2} = \frac{.3(1.4e3)}{(30.9)^2} = .44 \text{ ksi}$$

$F_c^* = F_cC_DC_MC_tC_F = .825(1.33)1.0(1.15) = 1.26$ ksi

NDS 3.7.1.5

$$C_P = \frac{1+\left(F_{cE}/F_c^*\right)}{2c} - \sqrt{\left(\frac{1+\left(F_{cE}/F_c^*\right)}{2c}\right)^2 - \frac{\left(F_{cE}/F_c^*\right)}{c}}$$

$$C_P = \frac{1+\left(.44/1.26\right)}{2(.8)} - \sqrt{\left(\frac{1+\left(.44/1.26\right)}{2(.8)}\right)^2 - \frac{\left(.44/1.26\right)}{.8}} = .32$$

NDS T2.3.1

$F_c' = F_cC_DC_MC_tC_P = .825(1.33)1.0(1.0)1.15(.32) = .4$ ksi

$P = F_c'A_n = .4(12.25) = 4.9^k > 1.23^k$ √

> Compression ok for 4x4 chord

Ck bearing of bottom plate

NDS T2.3.1

$F_{c\perp}' = F_{c\perp}C_MC_tC_b = .625(1.0)1.0(1.0)$

$= .625$ ksi

$P = 12.25(.625) = 7.66^k > 1.23^k$ √

> Use 4x4 DF- L stud grade chords for shearwall

Collector straps

Tight blocking is required to transfer the compressive force into the large diaphragm. It will be seen that with seismic reversal a tie is also required here.

Collector drag force = $1.23^k < 1.65^k$ (CS16)

Length required = $\frac{1.23}{.46} = 2.67$ ft. min.

> Use simpson CS16 coiled strap with blocking as required

Ck for seismic reversal

Perform analysis with free bodies:

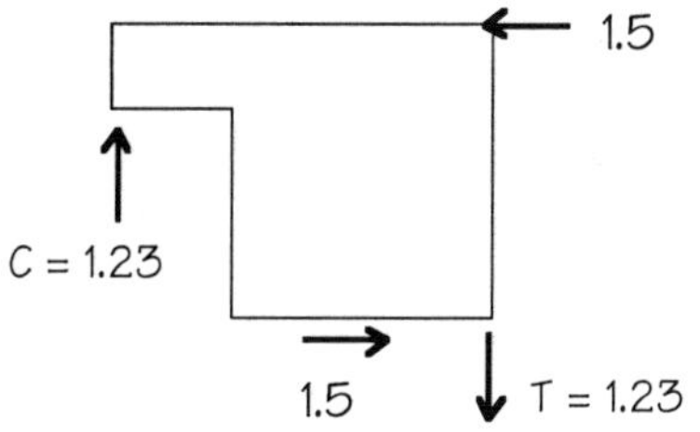

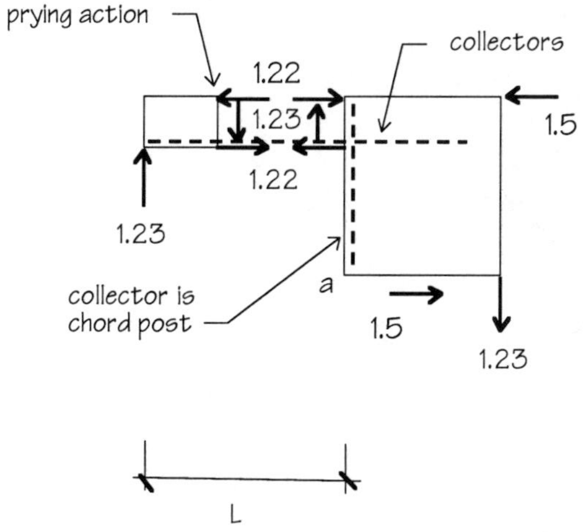

In this case, we can see that seismic reversal effects little except the tie strap as noted above. Therefore, the preceding analysis and specification is ok.

The wall would look something like this.

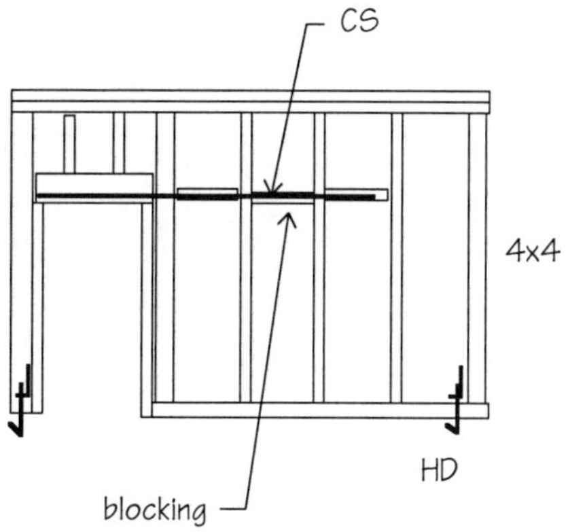

Note, however, that as L gets longer the greater the tendency is for point "a" to draw load for a seismic force in this direction (it is, after all, in contact with the foundation). The question arises as to whether this shearwall configuration will act as a kind of "L-shaped" shearwall or whether point "a" will draw enough load to practically make the large shearwall act "alone". It seems reasonable to me, that since we know there will be some nail slip at the CS connection, point "a" will indeed draw load. But how much? It is obvious that this "L" configuration only works if the post, studs and diaphragm buckle enough to allow engagement of the "L" arm. So, the stiffer the post the more the configuration acts like a simple 9x8 shearwall with a filler panel. Let's compare the 9x8 shearwall with the "L" configuration.

$$T = C = \frac{1.5(9)}{8} = 1.7^{k}$$

The percent increase is $= \frac{1.7}{1.23} = 1.38$ or 38%

$$v_{base} = \frac{1.5}{8} = .19 \text{ klf} \quad \text{(same as before)}$$

The net effect is that we would use a larger HD, but with no requirement for CS or blocking, and less stringent criteria for the diaphragm nailing. The tradeoffs are obvious, use the simple method unless you want an exercise in statics.

This page intentionally left blank.

To become the spectator of one's own life is to escape the suffering of life.

OSCAR WILDE

6. Timber Connections with Nails

Chapter Problems	Page	Prob.
Nailed spacing for shear type connection	6-21	6.13
Scaffold rigging using nailed conn. of different species and nail penetration reduction	6-26	6.15
Shearwall drag post continuity connection	6-12	6.7
Shearwall toenail transfer conn. for wind load perpendicular to wall and ceiling joists	6-15	6.8
Shed wall with nailed end grain connection	6-18	6.10
Shear toenail transfer connection for floor joist blocking and top plates	6-17	6.9
Single shear conn. with diff. species and nail penetration reduction using Yield Limit Eq	6-7	6.5
Single shear connection using Yield Limit Equations	6-2	6.1
Single shear connection with different species using Yield Limit Equations	6-4	6.3
Single shear connection with metal side plate using Yield Limit Equations	6-3	6.2
Single shear knee brace conn. for a free standing patio using Yield Limit Equations	6-5	6.4
Toenail withdrawal capacity of a nailed connection	6-21	6.12
Top plate design utilizing nailed connection for both chord and drag forces	6-9	6.6
UBC Table 23-I-Q nailing schedule capacity for typical wood connections	6-22	6.14
Withdrawal load capacity of nailed connection	6-20	6.11

PROBLEM 6.1

Single shear connection using Yield Limit Equations.

Determine the nominal value for the nail portion of the connection shown below by using the Yield Limit Equations.

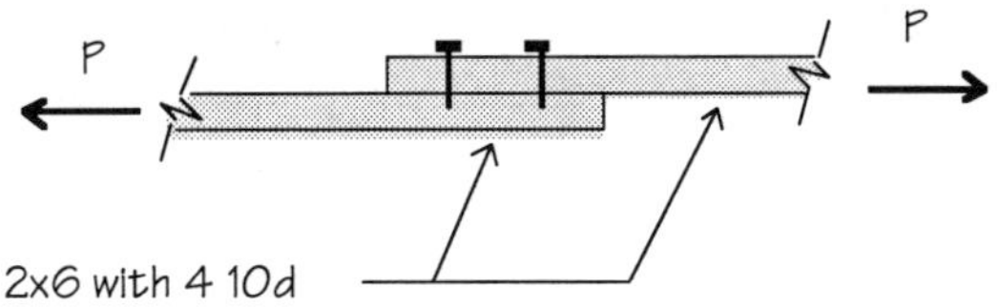

ASSUME

Common nails (10d).
DF-L lumber.
MC < 19%.
F_{yb} = 90 ksi.

SOLUTION

Obtain required values for Yield Equations

t_s = 1.5 in
t_m = 1.5 in
ℓ = 3.0 in
F_{es} = 4650 psi
F_{em} = 4650 psi
D = .148
K_D = 2.2 since D < .17 in

Calc preliminary coefficients values

$p = \ell - t_s \le t_m$

= 3 - 1.5 = 1.5 in √

NDS T12.3B, 12A

12D = 12(.148) = 1.8 in > 1.5 in

min. penetration NG use $C_d = p/12D$ when $6D \le p < 12D$

C_d = .84 in (not used in this example)

$$R_e = \frac{F_{em}}{F_{es}} = \frac{4650}{4650} = 1.0$$

NDS 12.3.1

$$k_1 = -1 + \sqrt{2(1+R_e) + \frac{2F_{yb}(1+2R_e)D^2}{3F_{em}p^2}}$$

$$= -1 + \sqrt{2(1+1) + \frac{2(90000)(1+2(1))(.148)^2}{3(4650)(1.5)^2}} = 1.0921$$

$$k_2 = -1 + \sqrt{\frac{2(1+R_e)}{R_e} + \frac{2F_{yb}(2+R_e)D^2}{3F_{em}t_s^2}}$$

$$= -1 + \sqrt{\frac{2(1+1)}{1} + \frac{2(90000)(2+1)(.148)^2}{3(4650)(1.5)^2}} = 1.0921$$

Calc Failure Equation Mode Values

Mode I_s

$$Z = \frac{Dt_sF_{es}}{K_D} = \frac{.148(1.5)4650}{2.2} = 469 \text{ lb}$$

Mode I_s Z = 469 lb

Mode III_m

$$Z = \frac{k_1DpF_{em}}{K_D(1+2R_e)} = \frac{1.0921(.148)1.5(4650)}{2.2(1+2(1))} = 171 \text{ lb}$$

Mode III_m Z = 171 lb

Mode III_s

$$Z = \frac{k_2Dt_sF_{em}}{K_D(2+R_e)} = \frac{1.0921(.148)1.5(4650)}{2.2(2+1)} = 171 \text{ lb}$$

Mode III_s Z = 171 lb

Mode IV

$$Z = \frac{D^2}{K_D}\sqrt{\frac{2F_{em}F_{yb}}{3(1+R_e)}}$$

$$= \frac{(.148)^2}{2.2}\sqrt{\frac{2(4650)90000}{3(1+1)}} = 118 \text{ lb}$$

Mode IV Z = 118 lb

The smallest value of the four is found in Mode IV.

Z = 118 lbs

If you want a quality, act as if you already had it. Try the "as if" technique.

WILLIAM JAMES

PROBLEM 6.2

Single shear connection with metal side plate using Yield Limit Equations

Determine the nominal value for the nail portion of the connection shown below by using both the Yield Limit Equations and NDS Table 12.3F.

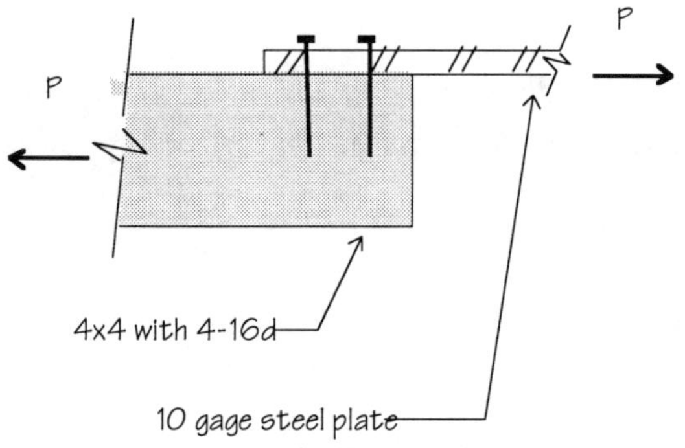

ASSUME

Common nails.
DF-L lumber.
MC < 19%.
F_{yb} = 90 ksi.

SOLUTION

Obtain required values for Yield Equations NDS T12.3B,12A

t_s = .134 in
t_m = 3.5 in
ℓ = 3.5 in
F_{es} = 45000 psi
F_{em} = 4650 psi
D = .162
K_D = 2.2 since D <.17 in

Calc preliminary coefficients values NDS 12.3.2

$p = \ell - t_s \le t_m$

$= 3.5 - .134 = 3.37 \text{ in} < 3.5 \text{ in } \surd$

$12D = 12(.162) = 1.9 \text{ in} < 3.4 \text{ in } \surd$

min. penetration ok.

$R_e = \frac{F_{em}}{F_{es}} = \frac{4650}{45000} = .1033$ NDS 12.3.4

$$k_1 = -1 + \sqrt{2(1+R_e) + \frac{2F_{yb}(1+2R_e)D^2}{3F_{em}p^2}}$$

$$= -1 + \sqrt{2(1+.1033) + \frac{2(90000)(1+2(.1033))(.162)^2}{3(4650)(3.37)^2}}$$ NDS 12.3.1

$= .4976$

$$k_2 = -1 + \sqrt{\frac{2(1+R_e)}{R_e} + \frac{2F_{yb}(2+R_e)D^2}{3F_{em}t_s^2}}$$

$$= -1 + \sqrt{\frac{2(1+.1033)}{.1033} + \frac{2(90000)(2+.1033)(.162)^2}{3(4650)(.134)^2}}$$

$= 6.812$

Calc Failure Equation Mode Values

<u>Mode</u> I_s

$$Z = \frac{Dt_sF_{es}}{K_D} = \frac{.162(.134)4500}{2.2} = 444 \text{ lb}$$

Mode I_s Z = 444 lb

Mode III_m

$$Z = \frac{k_1 D p F_{em}}{K_D(1+2R_e)} = \frac{.4976(.162)3.37(4650)}{2.2(1+2(.1033))} = 475 \text{ lb}$$

Mode III_m Z = 475 lb

Mode III_s

$$Z = \frac{k_2 D t_s F_{em}}{K_D(2+R_e)} = \frac{6.812(.162)1.34(4650)}{2.2(2+.1033)} = 149 \text{ lb}$$

Mode III_s Z = 149 lb

Mode IV

$$Z = \frac{D^2}{K_D}\sqrt{\frac{2F_{em}F_{yb}}{3(1+R_e)}} = \frac{(.162)^2}{2.2}\sqrt{\frac{2(4650)90000}{3(1+.1033)}}$$

= 190 lb

Mode IV Z = 190 lb

The smallest value of the four is found in Mode III_S.

Z = 149 lbs

Determine by the NDS Table 12.3F

Z = 149 lb

□
□
□

Creativity can solve almost any problem. The creative act, the defeat of habit by originality, overcomes everything.

GEORGE LOIS

PROBLEM 6.3

Single shear connection with different species using Yield Limit Equations.

Determine the nominal value for the nail portion of the connection shown below by using both the Yield Limit Equations.

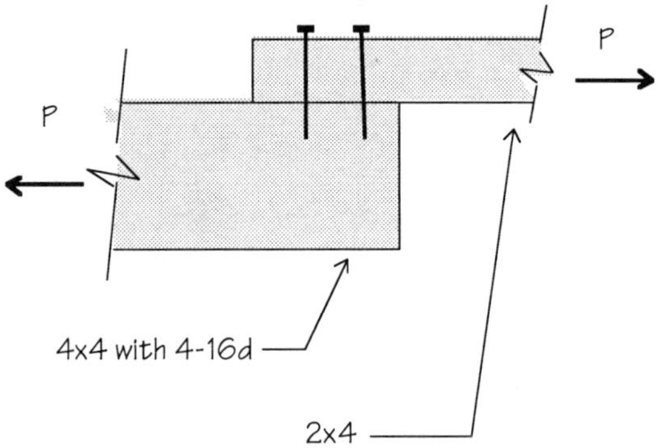

ASSUME

Box nails.
DF-L 4x4.
Hem-fir 2x4.
MC < 19%.
F_{yb} = 100 ksi.

SOLUTION

Obtain required values for Yield Equations NDS T12.3B, 12A

t_s = 1.5 in
t_m = 3.5 in
ℓ = 3.5 in
F_{es} = 3500 psi
F_{em} = 4650 psi
D = .135 in
K_D = 2.2 since D <.17 in

Calc preliminary coefficients values NDS 12.3.4

$p = \ell - t_s \le t_m$

= 3.5 - 1.5 = 2 in < 3.5 in √

12D = 12(.135) = 1.62 in < 2.0 in √

min pennetration ok.

NDS 12.3.1

$$R_e = \frac{F_{em}}{F_{es}} = \frac{4650}{3500} = 1.3286$$

$$k_1 = -1+\sqrt{2(1+R_e)+\frac{2F_{yb}(1+2R_e)D^2}{3F_{em}p^2}}$$

$$= -1+\sqrt{2(1+1.3286)+\frac{2(100000)(1+2(1.3286))(.135)^2}{3(4650)(2)^2}}$$

$=1.213$

$$k_2 = -1+\sqrt{\frac{2(1+R_e)}{R_e}+\frac{2F_{yb}(2+R_e)D^2}{3F_{em}t_s^2}}$$

$$= -1+\sqrt{\frac{2(1+.1.3286)}{1.3286}+\frac{2(100000)(2+1.3286)(.135)^2}{3(4650)(1.5)^2}}$$

$=.9728$

Calc Failure Equation Mode Values

Mode I_s

$$Z = \frac{Dt_sF_{es}}{K_D} = \frac{.135(1.5)3500}{2.2} = 322 \text{ lb}$$

Mode I_s Z = 322 lb

Mode III_m

$$Z = \frac{k_1DpF_{em}}{K_D(1+2R_e)} = \frac{1.213(.135)2(4650)}{2.2(1+2(1.329))} = 189 \text{ lb}$$

Mode III_m Z = 189 lb

Mode III_s

$$Z = \frac{k_2Dt_sF_{em}}{K_D(2+R_e)} = \frac{.9728(.135)1.5(4650)}{2.2(2+1.329)} = 125 \text{ lb}$$

Mode III_s Z = 125 lb

Mode IV

$$Z = \frac{D^2}{K_D}\sqrt{\frac{2F_{em}F_{yb}}{3(1+R_e)}} = \frac{(.135)^2}{2.2}\sqrt{\frac{2(4650)100000}{3(1+1.329)}}$$

$= 96$ lb

Mode IV Z = 96 lb

The smallest value of the four is found in Mode IV.

Z = 96 lbs

□
□
□

Any activity becomes creative when the doer cares about doing it right, or better.

JOHN UPDIKE

PROBLEM 6.4

Single shear knee brace connection for a free-standing patio using Yield Limit Equations.

Determine the design value for the nail portion of the connection shown below by using the Yield Limit Equations.

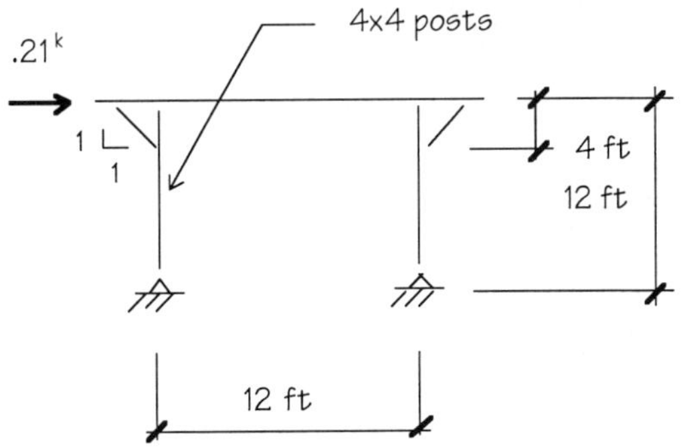

ASSUME

- Common nails (16d).
- DF-L 4x4.
- DF-L 2x4 knee braces.
- MC < 19%, but outdoor conditions.
- Seismic load.

SOLUTION

Since the posts are of equal length, assume that the lateral load is equally shared between the two posts.

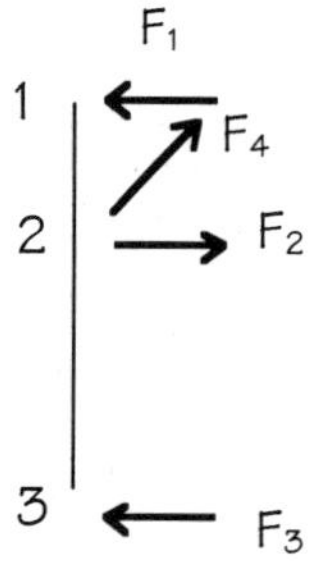

$F_3 = .21/2 = .105$ From above

$$\sum M_2 = 0 \Rightarrow F_1 = \frac{.105(8)}{4} = .21^k$$

$$\sum M_1 = 0 \Rightarrow F_2 = \frac{.105(12)}{4} = .315^k$$

Force in knee brace:

$$F_4 = F_2\sqrt{2} = .315\sqrt{2} = .445^k$$

Obtain required values for Yield Equations

NDS 12.3B,12A

$t_s = 1.5$ in
$t_m = 3.5$ in
$\ell = 3.5$ in
$F_{es} = 4650$ psi
$F_{em} = 4650$ psi
$D = .162$ in

$F_{yb} = 90$ ksi
$K_D = 2.2$ since $D < .17$ in

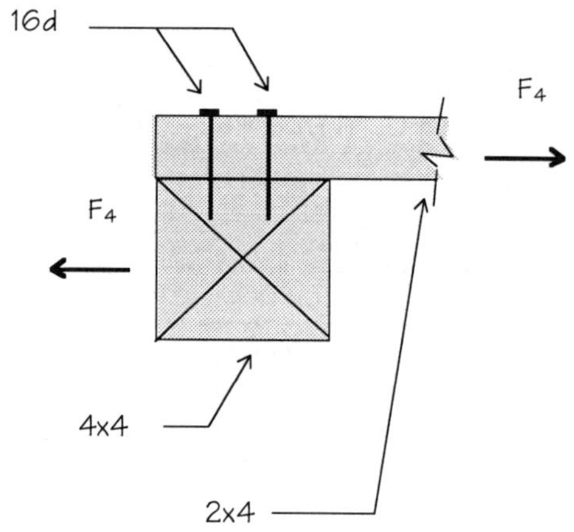

Calc preliminary coefficients values

$p = \ell - t_s \le t_m$ NDS 12.3.4

$= 3.5 - 1.5 = 2.0 \text{ in} < 3.5 \text{ in} \checkmark$

$12D = 12(.162) = 1.94 \text{ in} < 2.0 \text{ in} \checkmark$

min. penetration ok.

$$R_e = \frac{F_{em}}{F_{es}} = \frac{4650}{4650} = 1.0$$

$$k_1 = -1 + \sqrt{2(1+R_e) + \frac{2F_{yb}(1+2R_e)D^2}{3F_{em}p^2}}$$

$$= -1 + \sqrt{2(1+1.0) + \frac{2(90000)(1+2(1.0))(.162)^2}{3(4650)(2)^2}} = 1.063$$ NDS 12.3.1

$$k_2 = -1 + \sqrt{\frac{2(1+R_e)}{R_e} + \frac{2F_{yb}(2+R_e)D^2}{3F_{em}t_s^2}}$$

$$= -1 + \sqrt{\frac{2(1+1.0)}{1.0} + \frac{2(90000)(2+1.0)(.162)^2}{3(4650)(1.5)^2}} = 1.109$$

Calc Failure Equation Mode Values

Mode I_s

$$Z = \frac{Dt_s F_{es}}{K_D} = \frac{.162(1.5)4650}{2.2} = 514 \text{ lb}$$

Mode I_s Z = 514 lb

Mode III_m

$$Z = \frac{k_1 D p F_{em}}{K_D(1+2R_e)} = \frac{1.063(.162)2(4650)}{2.2(1+2(1.0))} = 243 \text{ lb}$$

Mode III_m Z = 243 lb

Mode III_s

$$Z = \frac{k_2 D t_s F_{em}}{K_D(2+R_e)} = \frac{1.109(.162)1.5(4650)}{2.2(2+1.0)} = 190 \text{ lb}$$

Mode III_s Z = 190 lb

Mode IV

$$Z = \frac{D^2}{K_D}\sqrt{\frac{2F_{em}F_{yb}}{3(1+R_e)}} = \frac{(.162)^2}{2.2}\sqrt{\frac{2(4650)900000}{3(1+1.0)}}$$

= 141 lb

Mode IV Z = 141 lb

The smallest value of the four is found in Mode IV.

Z = 141 lbs / nail

Calc Z´ (exterior conditions, $C_M = .75$)

NDS T7.3.1

$Z' = ZC_DC_MC_tC_dC_{eg}C_{di}C_{tn}$

=.141(1.6).75(1.0)1.0(1.0)1.0(1.0)

= .169 ^{k}

$$16d_R = N = \frac{F_4}{Z'} = \frac{.445}{.169} = 2.6 \text{ nails} \qquad \text{say 3 nails}$$

Use 3-16d common nails at each end of the knee brace

Follow your desire as long as you live; do not lessen the time of following desire, for the wasting of time is an abomination to the spirit.

PTAHHOTPE
2350 B.C.

PROBLEM 6.5

Single shear connection with different species and nail penetration reduction using Yield Limit Equations.

Determine the nominal value for the nail portion of the connection shown below by using both the Yield Limit Equations.

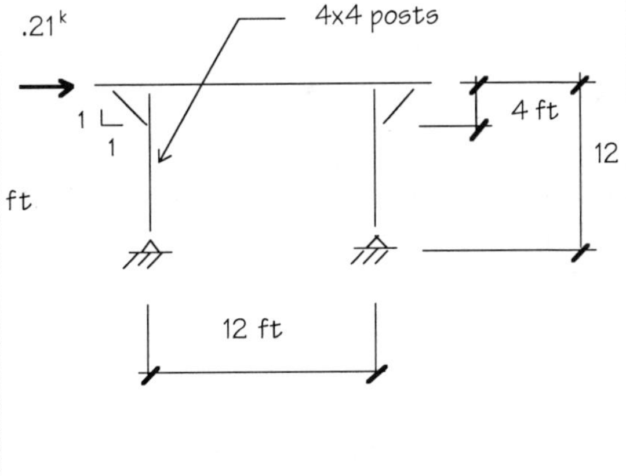

ASSUME

Common (10d).
DF-L 4x4.
DF-L (n) 2x4 knee braces.
MC < 19%, but outdoor conditions.

SOLUTION

Since the posts are of equal length assume that the lateral load is equally shared between the two posts.

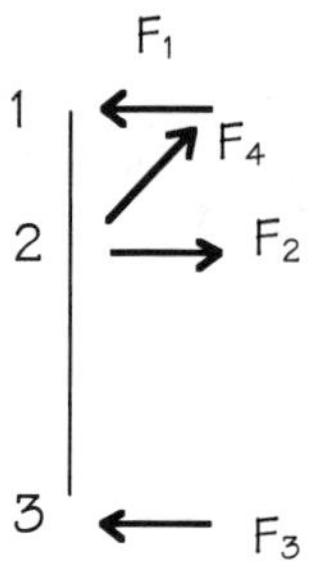

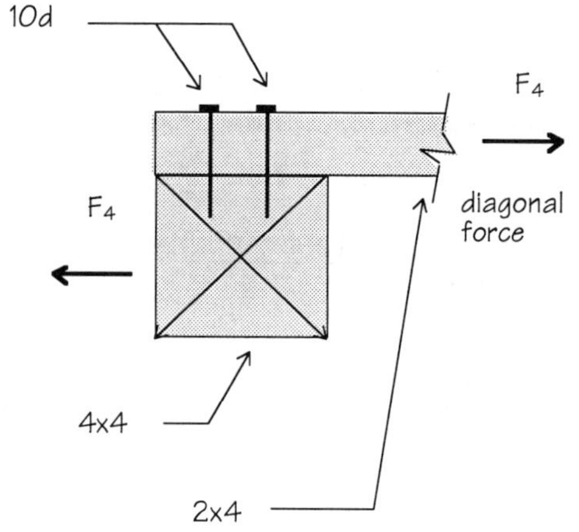

$F_3 = .21/2 = .105$ From above:

$$\sum M_2 = 0 \Rightarrow F_1 = \frac{.105(8)}{4} = .21^k$$

$$\sum M_1 = 0 \Rightarrow F_2 = \frac{.105(12)}{4} = .315^k$$

Force in knee brace:

$F_4 = F_2\sqrt{2} = .315\sqrt{2} = .445^k$

Obtain required values for Yield Equations

NDS T12.3B, 12A

$t_s = 1.5$ in
$t_m = 3.5$ in
$\ell = 3.0$ in
$F_{es} = 4650$ psi
$F_{em} = 4650$ psi

$D = .148$ in
$F_{yb} = 90$ ksi
$K_D = 2.2$ since D <.17 in

Calc preliminary coefficients values

$p = \ell - t_s \leq t_m$ NDS 12.3.4

$= 3.0 - 1.5 = 1.5$ in < 3.0 in √

$12D = 12(.148) = 1.78$ in > 1.5 in

min. penetration NG use $C_d = p/12$ when $6D \leq p < 12D$

$C_d = 1.5/1.78 = .84$

$$R_e = \frac{F_{em}}{F_{es}} = \frac{4650}{4650} = 1.0$$

NDS 12.3.1

$$k_1 = -1 + \sqrt{2(1+R_e) + \frac{2F_{yb}(1+2R_e)D^2}{3F_{em}p^2}}$$

$$= -1 + \sqrt{2(1+1.0) + \frac{2(90000)(1+2(1.0))(.148)^2}{3(4650)(1.5)^2}} = 1.092$$

$$k_2 = -1 + \sqrt{\frac{2(1+R_e)}{R_e} + \frac{2F_{yb}(2+R_e)D^2}{3F_{em}t_s^2}}$$

$$= -1 + \sqrt{\frac{2(1+1.0)}{1.0} + \frac{2(90000)(2+1.0)(.148)^2}{3(4650)(1.5)^2}} = 1.092$$

Calc Failure Equation Mode Values

Mode I_s

$$Z = \frac{Dt_sF_{es}}{K_D} = \frac{.148(1.5)4650}{2.2} = 469 \text{ lb}$$

Mode I_s Z = 469 lb

Mode III_m

$$Z = \frac{k_1DpF_{em}}{K_D(1+2R_e)} = \frac{1.092(.148)2(4650)}{2.2(1+2(1.0))} = 171 \text{ lb}$$

Mode III_m Z = 171 lb

Mode III_s

$$Z = \frac{k_2Dt_sF_{em}}{K_D(2+R_e)} = \frac{1.092(.148)1.5(4650)}{2.2(2+1.045)} = 171 \text{ lb}$$

Mode III_s Z = 171 lb

Mode IV

$$Z = \frac{D^2}{K_D}\sqrt{\frac{2F_{em}F_{yb}}{3(1+R_e)}} = \frac{(.148)^2}{2.2}\sqrt{\frac{2(4650)900000}{3(1+1.0)}}$$

= 118 lb

Mode IV Z = 118 lb

The smallest value of the four is found in Mode IV.

Z = 118 lbs / nail

NDS T7.3.1

Calc Z´ (exterior conditions)

$Z' = ZC_DC_MC_tC_dC_{eg}C_{di}C_{tn}$

$=.118(1.6).75(1.0).84(1.0)1.0(1.0)$

$= .119^k$

$$16d_R = N = \frac{F_4}{Z'} = \frac{.445}{.119} = 3.7 \text{ nails}$$ say 4 nails

Use 4-10d common nails at each end of the knee brace

It is common sense to take a method and try it. If it fails, admit it frankly and try another. But above all, try something.

FRANKLIN D. ROOSEVELT

PROBLEM 6.6

Top plate design utilizing nailed connection for both chord and drag forces.

Design the top plate splice shown in the structure below. Neglect compressive forces.

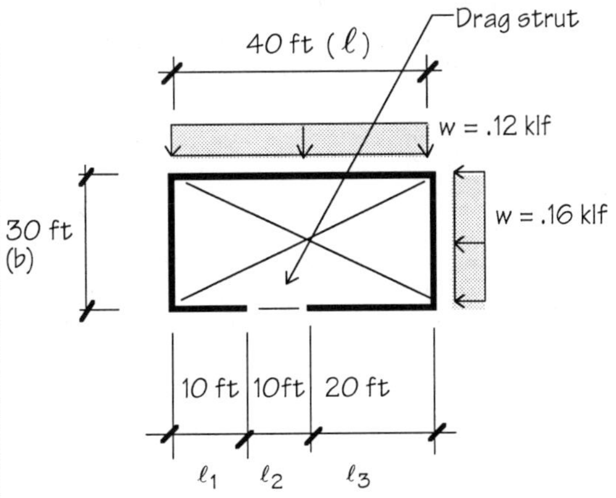

ASSUME

2x4 DF-L double top plates.

Roof sloped for drainage.
16d common nails.
EMC <19%.
Roof trusses at 24 in o/c.

SOLUTION

The top plate acts as the chord of the diaphragm. Since this problem is to show connection design, abbreviate the analysis to the essentials.

N/S direction (transverse)

$$M = \frac{w\ell^2}{8} = \frac{.12(40)^2}{8} = 24^{k\,ft}$$

$$T/c \text{ chord force} = \frac{M}{b} = \frac{24}{30} = .8^{k}$$

E/W direction (longitudinal)

$$R = \frac{w\ell}{2} = \frac{.16(30)}{2} = 2.4^{k\,ft}$$

$$v_{roof} = \frac{R}{\ell} = \frac{2.4}{40} = .06 \text{ klf}$$

$$v_{wall} = \frac{R}{\ell_{wall}} = \frac{2.4}{30} = .08 \text{ klf}$$

Max T/C force = .8^{k}

Calc drag force

The wall top plate (or hdr) acts as a drag strut over the opening and is a critical drag strut force carrying member.

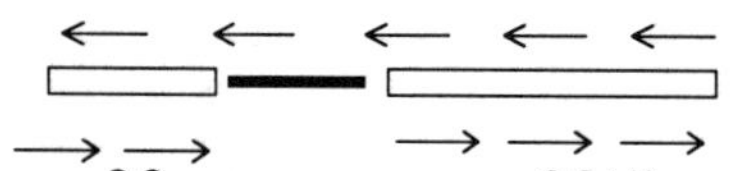

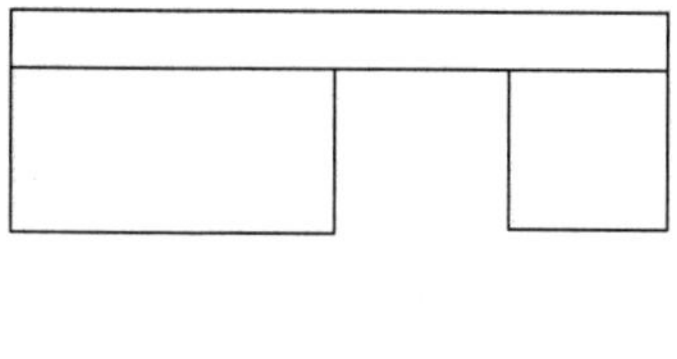

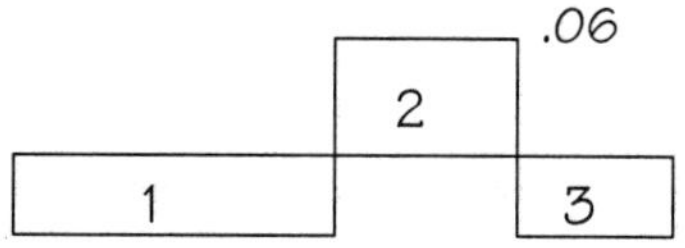

$A_1 = -.02(10) = -.2^{k}$

$A_2 = .06(10) = .6^{k}$

$A_3 = -.02(20) = -.4^{k}$

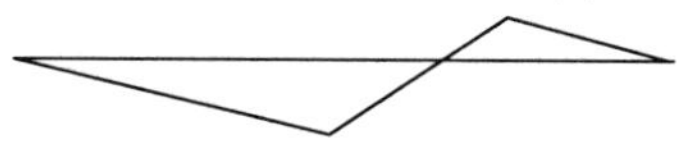

Max drag strut force = .4^{k} which is less than .8^{k} so the chord force controls connection

Obtain required values for Yield Equations

NDS T12.3B, 12A

$t_s = 1.5$ in
$t_m = 1.5$ in
$\ell = 3.5$ in
$F_{es} = 4650$ psi
$F_{em} = 4650$ psi
$D = .162$ in
$F_{yb} = 90$ ksi
$K_D = 2.2$ since $D < .17$ in

Note that in this configuration only one top plate is engaged to transmit the tensile force. A metal strap is required for simultaneous engagement of both plates. The concept of transfer force flow is illustrated in the diagram below. The tension or compression is transferred from top plate to top plate via the nails in the 4 ft minimum lap zone of the connection. If only one top plate is engaged as in this example, the full force must be transmitted within this zone.

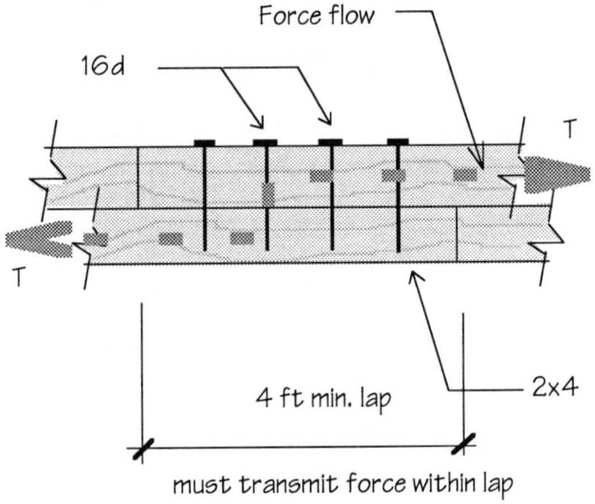

NDS 12.3.4

Calc preliminary coefficients values

$p = \ell - t_s \le t_m$

$= 3.5 - 1.5 = 2.0$ in > 1.5 use $p = 1.5$

$12D = 12(.162) = 1.94$ in $> t_m$

min. Penetration NG, use $C_d = p/12D$ when $6D \le p < 12D$

$C_d = 1.5/1.94 = .77$ in

$$R_e = \frac{F_{em}}{F_{es}} = \frac{4650}{4650} = 1.0$$

Note which equations are dependent upon "p" and which are dependent upon "t_m".

NDS 12.3.1

$$k_1 = -1 + \sqrt{2(1+R_e) + \frac{2F_{yb}(1+2R_e)D^2}{3F_{em}p^2}}$$

$$= -1 + \sqrt{2(1+1.0) + \frac{2(90000)(1+2(1.0))(.162)^2}{3(4650)(1.5)^2}} = 1.1099$$

$$k_2 = -1 + \sqrt{\frac{2(1+R_e)}{R_e} + \frac{2F_{yb}(2+R_e)D^2}{3F_{em}t_s^2}}$$

$$= -1 + \sqrt{\frac{2(1+1.0)}{1.0} + \frac{2(90000)(2+1.0)(.162)^2}{3(4650)(1.5)^2}} = 1.1099$$

Calc Failure Equation Mode Values

__Mode__ I_s

$$Z = \frac{Dt_sF_{es}}{K_D} = \frac{.162(1.5)4650}{2.2} = 514 \text{ lb}$$

Mode I_s Z = 514 lb

__Mode__ III_m

$$Z = \frac{k_1DpF_{em}}{K_D(1+2R_e)} = \frac{1.109(.162)1.5(4650)}{2.2(1+2(1.0))} = 190 \text{ lb}$$

Mode III_m Z = 190 lb

__Mode__ III_s

$$Z = \frac{k_2Dt_sF_{em}}{K_D(2+R_e)} = \frac{1.109(.162)1.5(4650)}{2.2(2+1.0)} = 190 \text{ lb}$$

Mode III_s Z = 190 lb

__Mode__ IV

$$Z = \frac{D^2}{K_D}\sqrt{\frac{2F_{em}F_{yb}}{3(1+R_e)}} = \frac{(.162)^2}{2.2}\sqrt{\frac{2(4650)900000}{3(1+1.0)}}$$

= 141 lb

Mode IV Z = 141 lb

The smallest value of the four is found in Mode IV.

Z = 141 lbs / nail

Calc Z´

$Z' = ZC_DC_MC_tC_dC_{eg}C_{di}C_{tn}$

$= .141(1.6)1.0(1.0).77(1.0)1.0(1.0)$

$= .174^k$

Be sure to verify the 1.6 factor with you local building officials.

NDS T7.3.1

$16d_R = N = \frac{T}{Z'} = \frac{.8}{.174} = 4.6$ nails   say 5 nails

> Use 5-16d common nails at each side of splice of walls 1 and 2

Note that III_m and III_s are the same because the length of the nail in the members is the same in both, $p = t_s$.

The essential conditions of everything you do must be choice, love, passion.

NADIA BOULANGER

PROBLEM 6.7

Shearwall drag post continuity connection.

Design the continuity tie nailing between shearwall 1 and shearwall 2 of the building shown below.

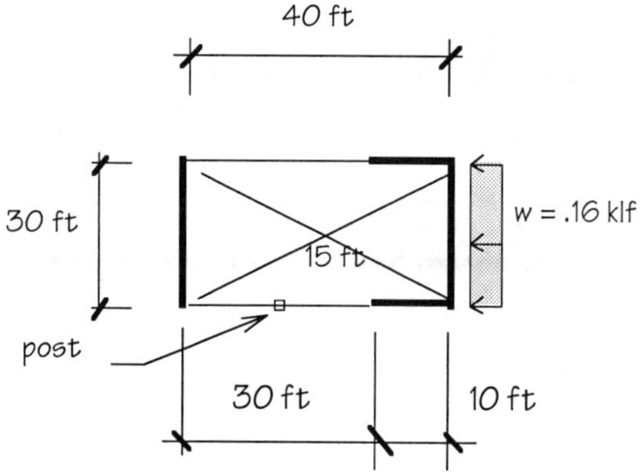

Second Floor Plan

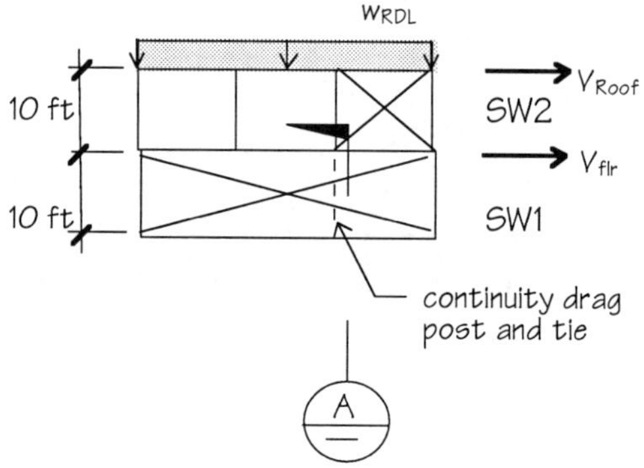

Elevation

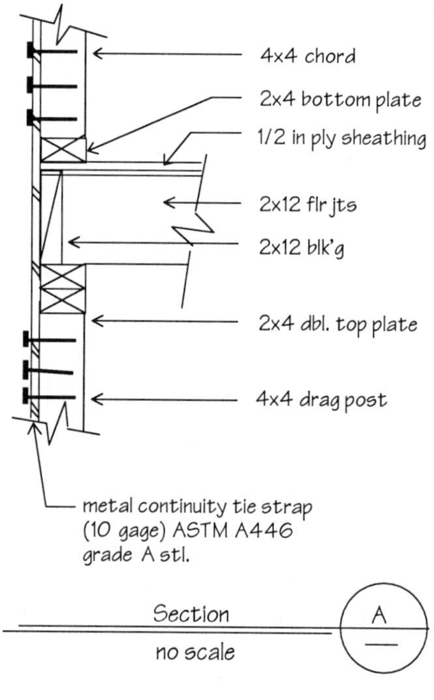

Section

no scale

UBC T23-1-1

ASSUME

$V_{ROOF} = 2.4^k$.
2^k continuity strap capacity.
10d common nails.
DF-L lumber.
EMC <19%.
Roof trusses at 24 in o/c.
$w_{RDL} = .12$ klf.
$V_w = .183W$.
Wall wt. = .016 ksf.
Seismic loading.

SOLUTION

This tie is required because in platform type construction the wall studs are not continuous from the 1st floor to the 2nd floor.

Ck aspect ratio

$$\frac{\ell_2}{b_2} = \frac{10}{10} = 1.0 < 3.5$$

Shearwall 2 (→ direction)

Since this problem is concerned with the showing of connection design, the analysis is abbreviated to the essentials. All the resisting forces are not symmetrical so we must check for lateral force reversal. Recall that roof LL is omitted when checking overturning forces for the shearwalls.

Use the conservative approach which utilizes the full height of the shearwall DL for the walls inertial seismic force.

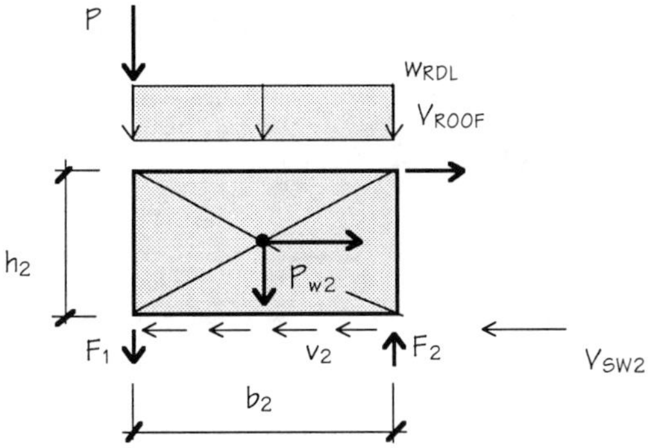

$$P = .12\left(\frac{15}{2}\right) = .9^k$$

$$V_w = .016(.183)10(10) = .293^k$$

$$P_w = .016(10)10 = 1.6 \text{ klf}$$

Calc T and C chord forces

We could use either GOM (conservative) without the effects of RM or DOM to calculate these forces.

$$GOM = V_2h_2 + V_{w2}\left(\frac{h_2}{2}\right) = 2.4(10) + .293(5)$$

$$= 25.5^{k\,ft}$$

$$RM = Pb_2 + \frac{w_{RDL}b_2^2}{2} + P_{w2}\left(b_2/2\right)$$

$$= .9(10) + \frac{.12(10)^2}{2} + 1.6(10/2) = 23.0^{k\,ft}$$

$$DOM = GOM - .85RM$$

$$= 25.5 - .85(23) = 5.95^{k\,ft}$$

Since the GOM is larger than the resisting moment we will need a holdown force calc.

$$F_1 = T = DOM/b_2 = 5.95/10 = .6^k$$

> $T = .6^k$ and will be compared to the chord force in the other direction and the largest will be used to select the tension transfer connection hardware at the shearwall boundaries

Shearwall 2 (← direction)

$GOM = 25.5^{k\,ft}$

We could assume that some portion of the attached (right) wall will contribute a resisting force to the overall RM. This varies from designer to designer. It is not unusual to assume a DL tributary length of between 2 to 6 feet depending upon the circumstances. Check with your engineer of record in your office for your firm's policy. In this example, we will omit the RM from this possibility. If you use it, the DL (contributing to the RM) would be treated as a point load, as in the other end of the wall.

$$RM = \frac{.12(10)^2}{2} + 1.6(10/2) = 14.0^{k\,ft}$$

$$DOM = GOM - .85RM = 25.5 - .85(14) = 13.6^{k\,ft}$$

Since the GOM is larger than the resisting moment we will need a holdown force calc.

$F_2 = T = DOM/b_2 = 13.6/10 = 1.4^k > .6^k$

It is often desirable to match the chord sizes and their respective connective hardware. This is done to ease field complications and to cut down on the possibility of errors.

Use T = 1.4ᵏ for chord design of both chord force transfer connections

NDS T12.3B, 12A

Obtain required values for Yield Equations

$t_s = .134$ in
$t_m = 3.5$ in
$\ell = 3.0$ in
$F_{es} = 45000$ psi
$F_{em} = 4650$ psi
$D = .148$ in
$F_{yb} = 90$ ksi
$K_D = 2.2$ since $D < .17$ in

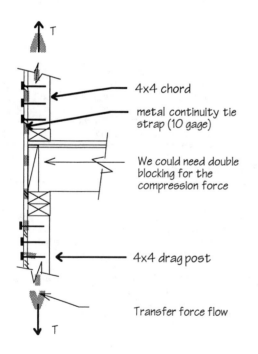

NDS 12.3.2

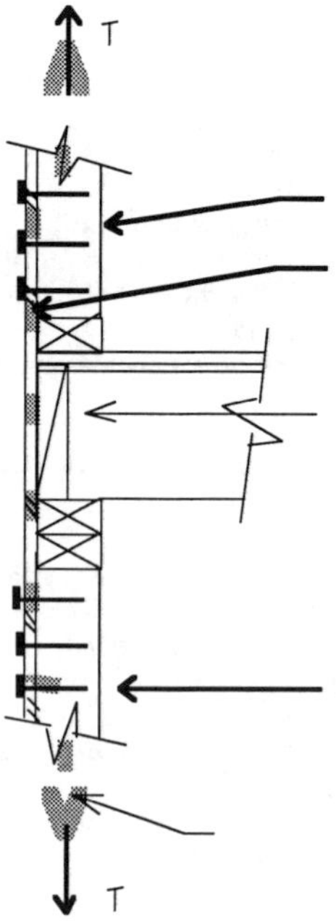

Calc preliminary coefficients values

$p = \ell - t_s \le t_m$

$= 3.0 - .134 = 2.87 \text{ in} < 3.5 \text{ in}$ √ NDS 12.3.4

$12D = 12(.148) = 1.78 \text{ in} < 2.87 \text{ in}$ √

min. penetration ok

$$R_e = \frac{F_{em}}{F_{es}} = \frac{4650}{45000} = .1033$$

$$k_1 = -1+\sqrt{2(1+R_e)+\frac{2F_{yb}(1+2R_e)D^2}{3F_{em}p^2}}$$

NDS 12.3.1

$$= -1+\sqrt{2(1+.1033)+\frac{2(90000)(1+2(.1033))(.148)^2}{3(4650)(2.87)^2}}$$

$= .4994$

$$k_2 = -1+\sqrt{\frac{2(1+R_e)}{R_e}+\frac{2F_{yb}(2+R_e)D^2}{3F_{em}t_s^2}}$$

$$= -1+\sqrt{\frac{2(1+.1033)}{.1033}+\frac{2(90000)(2+.1033)(.148)^2}{3(4650)(.134)^2}}$$

$= 6.3798$

Calc Failure Equation Mode Values

Mode I_s

$$Z = \frac{Dt_sF_{es}}{K_D} = \frac{.148(.134)45000}{2.2} = 406 \text{ lb}$$

Mode I_s Z = 406 lb

Mode III_m

$$Z = \frac{k_1DpF_{em}}{K_D(1+2R_e)} = \frac{.4994(.148)2.87(4650)}{2.2(1+2(.1033))} = 371 \text{ lb}$$

Mode III_m Z = 371 lb

Mode III_s

$$Z = \frac{k_2Dt_sF_{em}}{K_D(2+R_e)} = \frac{6.379(.148).134(4650)}{2.2(2+.1033)} = 127 \text{ lb}$$

Mode III$_s$ Z = 127 lb

<u>Mode</u> IV

$$Z = \frac{D^2}{K_D}\sqrt{\frac{2F_{em}F_{yb}}{3(1+R_e)}} = \frac{(.148)^2}{2.2}\sqrt{\frac{2(4650)900000}{3(1+.1033)}}$$

= 158 lb

Mode IV Z = 158 lb

The smallest value of the four is found in Mode III$_s$.

Z = 127 lbs / nail

<u>Calc Z´</u>

NDS 7.3.1

$Z' = ZC_DC_MC_tC_dC_{eg}C_{di}C_{tn}$

=.127(1.6)1.0(1.0)1.0(1.0)1.0(1.0)

= .203 k

$16d_R = N = \frac{T}{Z'} = \frac{1.4}{.203} = 6.9$ nails   say 7 nails

Use 7-10d common nails at each side of continuity transfer connection

▯
▯
▯

The strangest and most fantastic fact about negative emotions is that people actually worship them.

P. D. OUSPENSKY

PROBLEM 6.8

Shearwall toenail transfer connection for wind load perpendicular to wall and ceiling joists.

Determine the wind load capacity of the toenail portion of the abbreivated connection shown below by using the Yield Limit Equations.

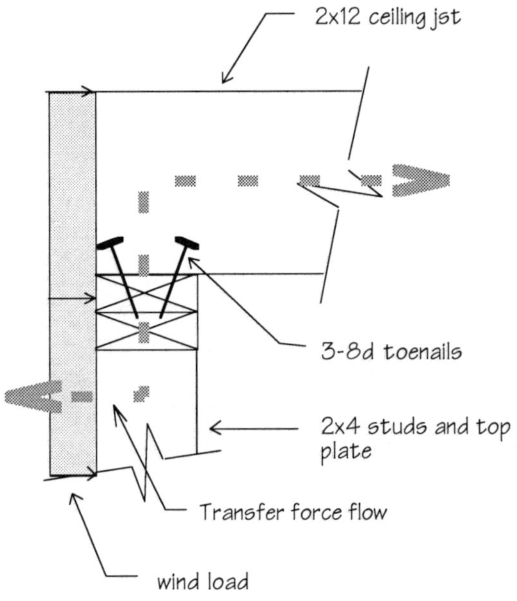

ASSUME

Common nails.
DF-L lumber.
MC < 19%.

SOLUTION

In this connection the toenail runs though the side grain of the ceiling joists. It is referred to as a slant nail and some designers believe it should not require a toenail reduction. However, the 91 NDS does not as yet recognize this distinction and the reduction is required.

Obtain required values for Yield Equations

$\ell = 2.5$ in

$t_s = \frac{\ell}{3} = .83$ in

$t_m = 1.5$ in

NDS T12.3B, 12A

F_{es} = 4650 psi
F_{em} = 4650 psi
D = .131 in
F_{yb} = 100 ksi
K_D = 2.2 since D <.17 in

$p_L = \ell \cos 30 - t_s = 1.34$ in $\le t_m = 1.5$ in √

12D = 12(.131) = 1.57 in > 1.33 in NG!

NDS 12.3.4

min. penetration ok, use C_d =

$p/_{12D}$ when $6D \le p < 12D$ min.

C_d = 1.33/1.57 = .85

Calc preliminary coefficients values

$$R_e = \frac{F_{em}}{F_{es}} = \frac{4650}{4650} = 1.0$$

NDS 12.3.1

$$k_1 = -1+\sqrt{2(1+R_e)+\frac{2F_{yb}(1+2R_e)D^2}{3F_{em}p^2}}$$

$$= -1+\sqrt{2(1+1.0)+\frac{2(100000)(1+2(1.0))(.131)^2}{3(4650)(1.33)^2}} = 1.102$$

$$k_2 = -1+\sqrt{\frac{2(1+R_e)}{R_e}+\frac{2F_{yb}(2+R_e)D^2}{3F_{em}t_s^2}}$$

$$= -1+\sqrt{\frac{2(1+1.0)}{1.0}+\frac{2(100000)(2+1.0)(.131)^2}{3(4650)(.83)^2}} = 1.25$$

Calc Failure Equation Mode Values

Mode I_s

$$Z = \frac{Dt_sF_{es}}{K_D} = \frac{.131(.83)4650}{2.2} = 231 \text{ lb}$$

Mode I_s Z = 231 lb

Mode III_m

$$Z = \frac{k_1DpF_{em}}{K_D(1+2R_e)} = \frac{1.102(.131)1.33(4650)}{2.2(1+2(1.0))} = 135 \text{ lb}$$

Mode III_m Z = 135 lb

Mode III_s

$$Z = \frac{k_2Dt_sF_{em}}{K_D(2+R_e)} = \frac{1.25(.131).83(4650)}{2.2(2+1.0)} = 96 \text{ lb}$$

Mode III_s Z = 96 lb

Mode IV

$$Z = \frac{D^2}{K_D}\sqrt{\frac{2F_{em}F_{yb}}{3(1+R_e)}} = \frac{(.131)^2}{2.2}\sqrt{\frac{2(4650)1000000}{3(1+1.0)}}$$

= 97 lb

Mode IV Z = 97 lb

The smallest value of the four is found in Mode III_s.

Z = 96 lbs / nail

Calc Z′

Verify C_D = 1.6 for wind or seismic with local building department. C_{tn} = .83 NDS 12.3.7

$Z' = ZC_DC_MC_tC_dC_{eg}C_{di}C_{tn}$

=.96(1.6)(1.0)1.0(.85)1.0(1.0)(.83)

= .108 ^{k}

3-8d = R = N Z′ = 3(.108) = .33 ^{k} NDS 17.3.1

Capacity of toenail connection at each ceiling joist = .33^k

□
□
□

How many cares one loses when one decides not to be something but to be someone.

COCO GABRIELLE CHANEL

PROBLEM 6.9

Shear toenail transfer connection for floor joist blocking and top plates.

Determine the wind or seismic load capacity of the toenail portion of the abbreviated connection shown below by using the Yield Limit Equations.

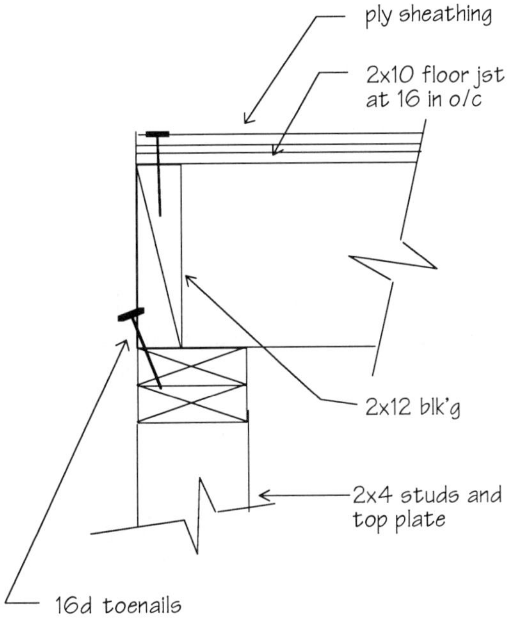

ASSUME

$v = .263$ klf.
Common nails.
DF-L lumber.
MC < 19%.

SOLUTION

In this connection the toenail runs though the side grain of the blocking. It is referred to as a slant nail and many designers believe that it should not require a toenail reduction. However, the 91 NDS does not as yet recognize this distinction and the reduction is required.

Obtain required values for Yield Equations

$\ell = 3.5$ in

$t_s = \frac{\ell}{3} = 1.17$ in

NDS T12.3B, 12A

$t_m = 1.5$ in
$F_{es} = 4650$ psi
$F_{em} = 4650$ psi
$D = .162$ in
$F_{yb} = 90$ ksi
$K_D = 2.2$ since $D < .17$ in

$p_L = \ell \cos 30 - t_s = 1.86$ in > 1.5 in, use $p_L = 1.5$ in

$12D = 12(.162) = 1.94$ in > 1.5 in **NG!**

min. penetration ok use $C_d =$

$p/12D$ when $6D \le p < 12D$ min.

$C_d = 1.5/1.94 = .77$

NDS 12.3.4

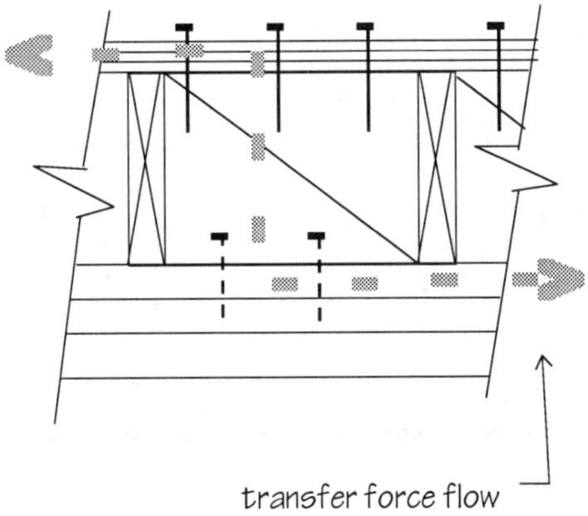

Calc preliminary coefficients values

$$R_e = \frac{F_{em}}{F_{es}} = \frac{4650}{4650} = 1.0$$

$$k_1 = -1 + \sqrt{2(1+R_e) + \frac{2F_{yb}(1+2R_e)D^2}{3F_{em}p^2}}$$

NDS 12.3.1

$$= -1 + \sqrt{2(1+1.0) + \frac{2(90000)(1+2(1.0))(.162)^2}{3(4650)(1.86)^2}} = 1.11$$

$$k_2 = -1 + \sqrt{\frac{2(1+R_e)}{R_e} + \frac{2F_{yb}(2+R_e)D^2}{3F_{em}t_s^{\,2}}}$$

$$= -1 + \sqrt{\frac{2(1+1.0)}{1.0} + \frac{2(90000)(2+1.0)(.162)^2}{3(4650)(1.17)^2}} = 1.179$$

Calc Failure Equation Mode Values

<u>Mode</u> I_s

$$Z = \frac{Dt_sF_{es}}{K_D} = \frac{.162(1.17)4650}{2.2} = 399 \text{ lb}$$

> Mode I_s Z = 399 lb

<u>Mode</u> III_m

$$Z = \frac{k_1DpF_{em}}{K_D(1+2R_e)} = \frac{1.11(.162)1.86(4650)}{2.2(1+2(1.0))} = 190 \text{ lb}$$

> Mode III_m Z = 190 lb

<u>Mode</u> III_s

$$Z = \frac{k_2Dt_sF_{em}}{K_D(2+R_e)} = \frac{1.179(.162)1.17(4650)}{2.2(2+1.0)} = 157 \text{ lb}$$

> Mode III_s Z = 157 lb

<u>Mode</u> IV

$$Z = \frac{D^2}{K_D}\sqrt{\frac{2F_{em}F_{yb}}{3(1+R_e)}} = \frac{(.162)^2}{2.2}\sqrt{\frac{2(4650)900000}{3(1+1.0)}}$$

= 141 lb

> Mode IV Z = 141 lb

The smallest value of the four is found in Mode IV.

> Z = 141 lbs / nail

<u>Calc Z'</u>

Verify C_D = 1.6 for wind or seismic with local building department. C_{tn} = .83 NDS 12.3.7

$$Z' = ZC_DC_MC_tC_dC_{eg}C_{di}C_{tn}$$

$$=.141(1.6)1.0(1.0).77(1.0)1.0(.83)$$

$$=.144^k$$

$$16d_R = N = \frac{v}{Z'} = \frac{1.33(.263)}{.144} = 2.4 \text{ nails}$$ Say 3-16d NDS T7.3.1

> 3-16d required at each 2x blk
> to transfer diaphragm shear
> to shearwall top plate

▯
▯
▯

I like long walks, especially when they are taken by people who annoy me.

FRED ALLEN

PROBLEM 6.10

Shed wall with nailed end grain connection.

Determine the wind load capacity of the nailed portion of the abbrevated connection shown below by using the Yield Limit Equations.

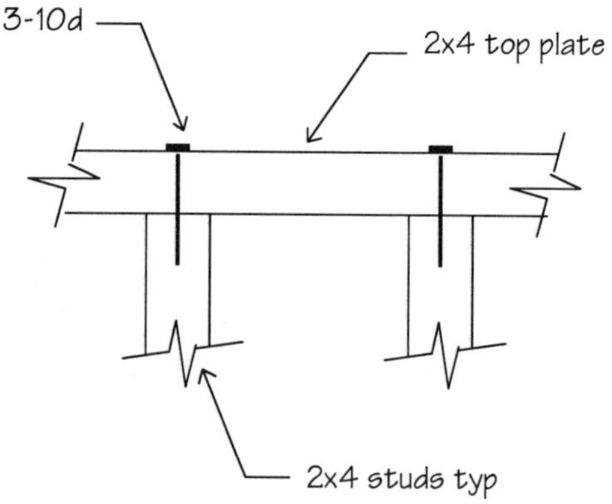

ASSUME

Common nails.
DF-L lumber.
MC < 19%.

SOLUTION

In this connection the nail runs though the end grain of the main member. An end grain reduction is required.

Obtain required values for Yield Equations

$\ell = 3.0$ in
$t_s = 1.5$ in
$t_m = 3.5$ in (or greater)

This t_m is simply made larger than that of the length of the nail for convenience of calculation. By inspection it is seen that it will not play a role in the final outcome of the calc if it is longer.

NDS T12.3B, 12A

$F_{es} = 4650$ psi
$F_{em} = 4650$ psi
$D = .148$ in
$F_{yb} = 90$ ksi
$K_D = 2.2$ since $D < .17$ in

$p = \ell - t_s \leq t_m$

$= 3.0 - 1.5 = 1.5 \text{ in} < t_m$

$12D = 12(.148) = 1.78 \text{ in} > 1.5 \text{ in}$ NG!

NDS 12.3.4

min. penetration ok, use C_d =

$p/_{12D}$ when $6D \leq p < 12D$ min.

$C_d = 1.5/1.78 = .84$

Calc preliminary coefficients values

$$R_e = \frac{F_{em}}{F_{es}} = \frac{4650}{4650} = 1.0$$

NDS 12.3.1

$$k_1 = -1 + \sqrt{2(1+R_e) + \frac{2F_{yb}(1+2R_e)D^2}{3F_{em}p^2}}$$

$$= -1 + \sqrt{2(1+1.0) + \frac{2(90000)(1+2(1.0))(.148)^2}{3(4650)(1.5)^2}} = 1.092$$

$$k_2 = -1 + \sqrt{\frac{2(1+R_e)}{R_e} + \frac{2F_{yb}(2+R_e)D^2}{3F_{em}t_s^2}}$$

$$= -1 + \sqrt{\frac{2(1+1.0)}{1.0} + \frac{2(90000)(2+1.0)(.148)^2}{3(4650)(1.5)^2}} = 1.092$$

Calc Failure Equation Mode Values

Mode I_s

$$Z = \frac{Dt_sF_{es}}{K_D} = \frac{.148(1.5)4650}{2.2} = 469 \text{ lb}$$

Mode I_s Z = 469 lb

Mode III_m

$$Z = \frac{k_1DpF_{em}}{K_D(1+2R_e)} = \frac{1.092(.148)1.5(4650)}{2.2(1+2(1.0))} = 171 \text{ lb}$$

Mode III_m Z = 171 lb

Mode III_s

$$Z = \frac{k_2Dt_sF_{em}}{K_D(2+R_e)} = \frac{1.092(.148)1.5(4650)}{2.2(2+1.0)} = 171 \text{ lb}$$

Mode III_s Z = 171 lb

Mode IV

$$Z = \frac{D^2}{K_D}\sqrt{\frac{2F_{em}F_{yb}}{3(1+R_e)}} = \frac{(.148)^2}{2.2}\sqrt{\frac{2(4650)900000}{3(1+1.0)}}$$

= 118 lb

Mode IV Z = 118 lb

The smallest value of the four is found in Mode IV.

Z = 118 lbs / nail

Calc Z´

Verify $C_D = 1.6$ for wind or seismic with local building department. $C_{eg} = .67$ NDS 12.3.5

$Z' = ZC_DC_MC_tC_dC_{eg}C_{di}C_{tn}$

$= .118(1.6)(1.0)(1.0).84(.67)1.0(1.0)$

$= .106^k$

$3\text{-}10d = R = N Z' = 3(.106) = .319^k$ NDS T7.3.1

Capacity of nail end grain connection at each stud = .32^k

If at first you don't succeed, you're running about average.

M. H. ALDERSON

PROBLEM 6.11

Withdrawal load capacity of a nailed connection.

Determine the withdrawal load capacity of the connection shown.

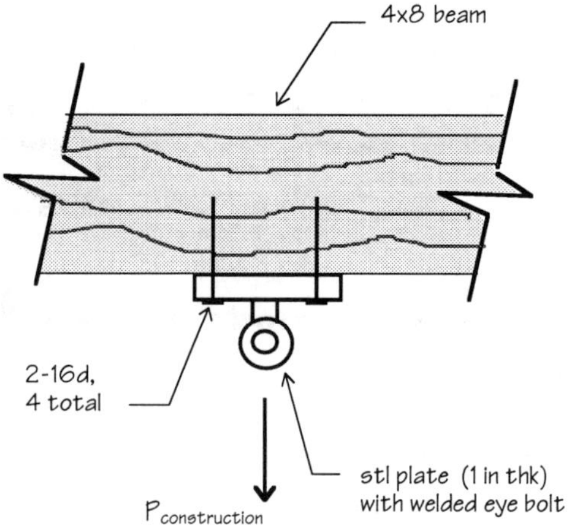

ASSUME

Common nails.
DF-L lumber.
MC < 19%.
Stl plate and eye have > cap than nails.

SOLUTION

Yield Limit Equations only apply to shear type connections. Withdrawal type connections are based on empirical data from extensive testing. Use NDS Table 12.2A for the nominal design value. NDS 12.2.1

$\ell = 3.5$ in

$t_s = 1.0$ in

$t_m = 7.25$ in NDS 12.3.4

$D = .162$ in

$p = \ell - t_s \le t_m$

$= 3.5 - 1.0 = 2.5 \text{ in} < t_m$ √

$12D = 12(.162) = 1.94 < t_m$ √ NDS T12.2A

$w = 40$ lb/in

$W = pw = 2.5(40) = 100$ lb/nail

W = 100 lbs / nail

Calc W′

$C_D = 1.25$

$W' = WC_DC_MC_tC_{tn} = .100(1.25)(1.0)\,1.0(1.0) = .125^k$ NDS T7.3.1

$4\text{-}16d = P = N\,W' = 4(.125) = .5^k$

Capacity of withdrawal connection = .5^k

Passion is in all great searches and is necessary to all creative endeavors.

W. EUGENE SMITH

PROBLEM 6.12

Toenail withdrawal capacity of a nailed connection.

Determine the toenail withdrawal load capacity of the connection shown.

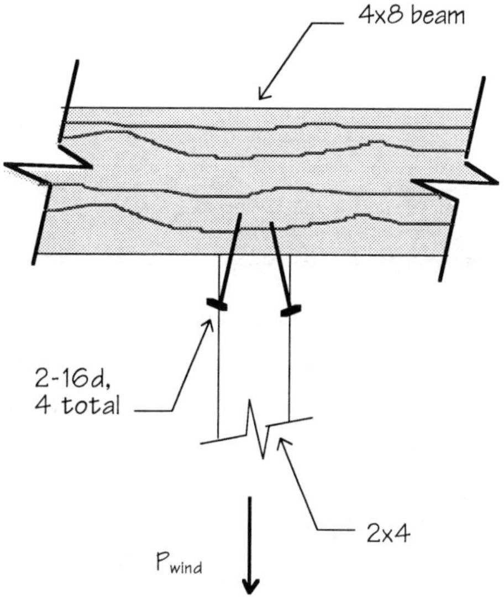

ASSUME

Common nails.
DF-L lumber.
MC < 19%.

SOLUTION

NDS 12.2.2

Yield Limit Equations only apply to shear type connections. Withdrawal type connections are based on empirical data from extensive testing. Use NDS Table 12.2A for the nominal design value.

$\ell = 3.5$ in
$t_m = 7.25$ in
$D = .162$ in

NDS T12.2A

$$p_w = \ell - \frac{\ell/3}{\cos 30} \le \frac{t_m}{\cos 30} = 3.5 - \frac{3.5/3}{\cos 30} \le \frac{7.25}{\cos 30}$$

$= 2.15$ in $< t_m = 8.37$ in

$w = 40$ lb/in

$W = p_w w = 2.15(40) = 86$ lb/nail

W = 86 lbs / nail

Calc W′

$C_D = 1.6$ NDS 12.2.3

$W' = WC_DC_MC_tC_{tn} = .086(1.6)(1.0)\,1.0(.67) = .092^k$

$4\text{-}16d = P = N\,W' = 4(.092) = .37^k$

Capacity of withdrawal connection = $.37^k$ NDS T7.3.1

Many persons have a wrong idea of what constitutes true happiness. It is not attained through self-gratification but through fidelity to a worthy purpose.

HELEN KELLER

PROBLEM 6.13

Nail spacing for shear type connection.

Determine if the spacing requirements for the UBC are fulfilled for the connection shown.

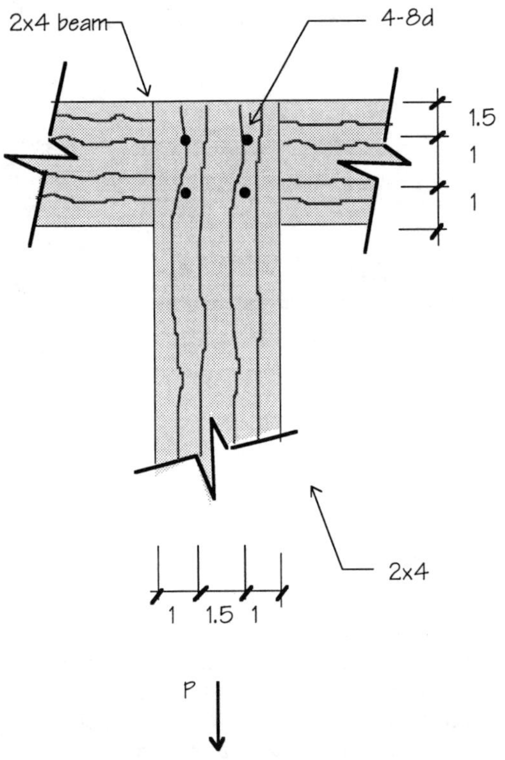

ASSUME

Common nails.
DF-L lumber.
2x members.
MC < 19%.

NDS 12.2.4

SOLUTION

t_m = 1.5 in

D = .131 in

p = 12D = 12(.131)= 1.57 in say 1.5 in = t_m

UBC 2311.3.3

Parallel to load spacing

Min. end distance = p/2 = 1.5/2 = .75 in

Min. edge distance = p/2 = 1.5/2 = .75 in

Min. spacing = p = 1.5 in

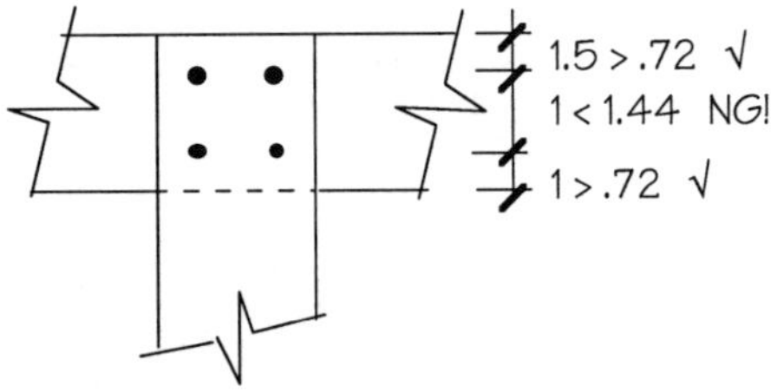

> Center to center spacing NG for parallel to load

Perpendicular to load spacing

The UBC is silent on this except that the splitting of the wood is to be avoided. However, spacing perpendicular to load meets the more stringent parallel to load requirements. Say ok.

> Nail spacing perpendicular to load ok

I know of no more encouraging fact than the unquestionable ability of man to elevate his life by conscious endeavor.

THOREAU

PROBLEM 6.14

UBC Table 23-I-Q nailing schedule capacity for typical *wood connections.*

Determine the lateral (wind) load capacity of common nails for each connection of the UBC Table 23-I-Q

Nailing Schedule numbers 1,2,6thru 21 (omit 11,12,19,20 and face nail only for6,11).

ASSUME

Common nails.
2x DF-L lumber.
MC < 19%.

SOLUTION

Due of the extent of the problem, the calculations will be abbreviated and will use the NDS Table where possible. For references see similar problems.

1. Jst to sill or girder (3-8d toenail)

$\ell = 2.5$ in
$t_s = .83$ in
$t_m = 1.5$ in
$F_{es} = 4650$ psi
$F_{em} = 4650$ psi
$D = .131$ in
$F_{yb} = 100$ ksi
$K_D = 2.2$ since $D < .17$ in
$p_L = 1.33$ in $< t_m = 1.5$ in
$12D = 1.57$ in > 1.33 in **NG!**
$C_d = .85$
$R_e = 1.0$
$k_1 = 1.1015$
$k_2 = 1.25$

Mode I_s $Z = 231$ lb
Mode III_m $Z = 135$ lb
Mode III_s $Z = 96$ lb
Mode IV $Z = 97$ lb

The smallest value of the four is found in Mode III_s.

$Z = 97$ lbs / nail

Verify $C_D = 1.6$ for wind or seismic with local building department. $C_{tn} = .83$

$Z' = .108^k$

$R = .325^k$

Connection capacity $= .325^k$

2. Bridging to joist (2-8d toenail each end)

$\ell = 2.5$ in
$t_s = .83$ in
$t_m = 1.5$ in
$F_{es} = 4650$ psi
$F_{em} = 4650$ psi
$D = .131$ in
$F_{yb} = 100$ ksi
$K_D = 2.2$ since $D < .17$ in
$p_L = 1.33$ in $< t_m = 1.5$ in
$12D = 1.57$ in > 1.33 in **NG!**
$C_d = .85$
$R_e = 1.0$
$k_1 = 1.1015$
$k_2 = 1.25$

Mode I_s $Z = 231$ lb
Mode III_m $Z = 135$ lb
Mode III_s $Z = 96$ lb
Mode IV $Z = 97$ lb

The smallest value of the four is found in Mode III_s.

$Z = 96$ lbs / nail

Verify $C_D = 1.6$ for wind or seismic with local building department. $C_{tn} = .83$

$Z' = .108^k$
$R = .216^k$

Connection capacity $= .216^k$ at each end

6. Sole plate to joist or blk'g (16d at 16 in o/c face nail)

$\ell = 3.5$ in
$t_s = 1.5$ in
$t_m = 9.25$ in (assume 2x10)
$D = .162$ in
$p = 2.0$ in $< t_m$
$12D = 1.94$ in < 2.0 in

Determine by the NDS Table 12.3F

$Z = 141$ lb

$Z' = .23^k$
$R = .17$ k/ft

Connection capacity =.17 k/ft

7. Top plate to stud (2-16d, end nail)

$\ell = 3.5$ in
$t_s = 1.5$ in
$t_m = 3.5$ in (assume at least ℓ)
$D = .162$ in
$p = 2$ in $< t_m$ √
$12D = 1.94$ in < 2 in √

Determine by the NDS Table 12.3F

Z = 141 lb

$Z' = .151^k$
$R = .3^k$

Connection capacity $.3^k$

8. Stud to sole plate (4-8d toenail or 2-16 end nail)

Toenail

$\ell = 2.5$ in
$t_s = .83$ in
$t_m = 1.5$ in
$F_{es} = 4650$ psi
$F_{em} = 4650$ psi
$D = .131$ in
$F_{yb} = 100$ ksi
$K_D = 2.2$ since $D < .17$ in
$p_L = 1.33$ in $< t_m = 1.5$ in √
$12D = 1.57$ in > 1.33 in NG!
$C_d = .85$
$R_e = 1.0$
$k_1 = 1.1015$
$k_2 = 1.25$

Mode I_s Z = 231 lb
Mode III_m Z = 135 lb
Mode III_s Z = 96 lb
Mode IV Z = 97 lb

The smallest value of the four is found in Mode III_s.

Z = 96 lbs / nail

Verify $C_D = 1.6$ for wind or seismic with local building department. $C_{tn} = .83$

$Z' = .108^k$
$R = .433^k$

End nail

From 7 above:

$R = .3^k < .433^k$ end nail governs

Connection capacity = $.3^k$

9. Double studs. (16d at 24 in o/c face nail)

$\ell = 3.5$ in
$t_s = 1.5$ in
$t_m = 1.5$ in
$D = .162$ in
$p = 1.5$ in $= t_m$ √
$12D = 1.94$ in > 1.5 in NG!
$C_d = .77$

Determine by the NDS Table 12.3F

Z = 141 lb

$Z' = .174^k$
$R = .087$ k/ft

Connection capacity =.087 k/ft

10. Doubled top plates (16d at 16 in o/c face nail)

From 9 above:

$Z' = .174^k$
$R = .13$ k/ft

Connection capacity = .13 k/ft.

13. Top plates, laps and intersections (2-16d face nail)

From 9 above:

$Z' = .174^k$
$R = .348^k$

Connection capacity = $.348^k$

14. Continuous header, two pieces
(16d at 16 in o/c face nail along each edge)

From 10 above:

$Z' = .174^k$
$2R = 2(.13) = .26$ k/ft

Connection capacity = .26 k/ft

15. Ceiling joists to plate (3-8d, toenail)

From 1 above:

$Z' = .108^k$
$R = .325^k$

Connection capacity = $.325^k$

16. Continuous header to stud (4-8d toenail)

$\ell = 2.5$ in
$t_s = .83$ in
$t_m = 1.5$ in
$F_{es} = 4650$ psi
$F_{em} = 4650$ psi
$D = .131$ in
$F_{yb} = 100$ ksi
$K_D = 2.2$ since $D < .17$ in
$p_L = 1.33$ in $< t_m = 1.5$ in
$12D = 1.57$ in > 1.33 in NGI
$C_d = .85$
$R_e = 1.0$
$k_1 = 1.1015$
$k_2 = 1.25$

Mode I_s Z = 231 lb
Mode III_m Z = 135 lb
Mode III_s Z = 96 lb
Mode IV Z = 97 lb

The smallest value of the four is found in Mode III_s.

Z = 96 lbs / nail

Verify $C_D = 1.6$ for wind or seismic with local building department. $C_{tn} = .83$

$Z' = .108^k$
$R = .433^k$

Connection capacity = $.433^k$

17. Ceiling joists, laps over partitions
(3-16d, face nail)

From 13 above:

$Z' = .174^k$
$R = .52^k$

Connection capacity = $.52^k$

18. Ceiling joists to parallel rafters
(3-16d, face nail)

From 17 above:

$Z' = .174^k$
$R = .52^k$

Connection capacity = $.52^k$

19. Rafter to plate (308d, toenail)

From 1 above:

$Z' = .108^k$
$R = .325^k$

Connection capacity = $.325^k$

20. 1 in brace to each stud and plate
(2-8d, face nail)

$\ell = 2.5$ in
$t_s = 1.5$ in
$t_m = 3.5$ in
$D = .131$ in
$p = 1.0$ in $< t_m$
$12D = 1.57$ in > 1.0 in NGI

$C_d = .64$

Determine by the NDS Table 12.3F

Z = 97 lb

$Z' = .099^k$
$R = .198$ k/ member

Connection capacity = .12 k/mem

23. Built-up corner studs (12d at 24 in o/c)

From 9 above:

$Z' = .174^k$
$R = .087$ k/ft

Connection capacity = .087 k/ft

The control man has secured over nature has far outrun his control over himself.

ERNEST JONES

PROBLEM 6.15

Scaffold rigging using nailed connections of different species and nail penetration reduction

Determine the 10d nailing requirements for the connections of the temporary scaffold rig load shown below by using the Yield Limit Equations.

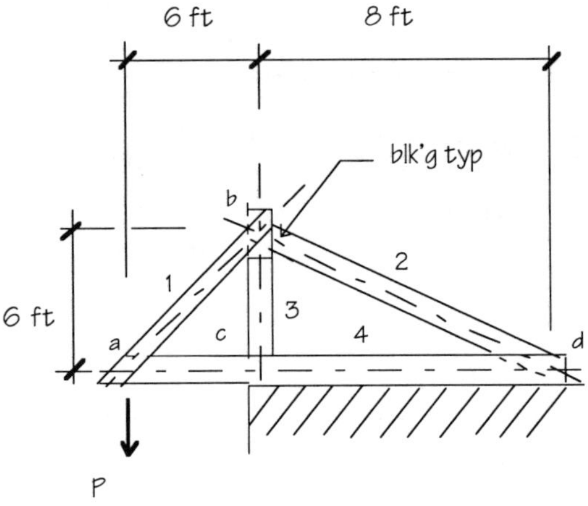

ASSUME

Common (10d).
DF-L No 1.
All lumber is 2x6.
Lateral stability ok.
Neglect member weight.
$P = 2.0^k$.
$C_D = 1.0$.
MC < 19%.

SOLUTION

Resolve forces

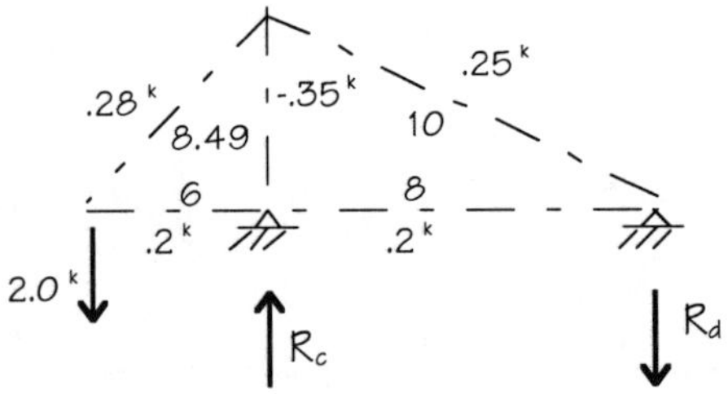

$\sum M_d = 0 \Rightarrow R_c = \frac{.2(14)}{8} = .35^k$

$\sum M_c = 0 \Rightarrow R_d = \frac{.2(6)}{8} = .15^k$

Connection a (member 1 to 4)

Obtain required values for Yield Equations

NDS T12.3B, 12A

$t_s = 1.5$ in
$t_m = 1.5$ in
$\ell = 3.0$ in
$F_{es} = 4650$ psi
$F_{em} = 4650$ psi
$D = .148$ in
$F_{yb} = 90$ ksi
$K_D = 2.2$ since $D < .17$ in

Calc preliminary coefficients values

NDS 12.3.4

$p = \ell - t_s \le t_m$

$= 3.0 - 1.5 = 1.5 \text{ in} = 1.5 \text{ in}$

$12D = 12(.148) = 1.78 \text{ in} > 1.5 \text{ in}$

min. penetration NG, use $C_d = p/12D$ when $6D \le p < 12D$

$C_d = 1.5 / 1.78 = .84$

$R_e = \frac{F_{em}}{F_{es}} = \frac{4650}{4650} = 1.0$

NDS 12.3.1

$$k_1 = -1 + \sqrt{2(1+R_e) + \frac{2F_{yb}(1+2R_e)D^2}{3F_{em}p^2}}$$

$$= -1 + \sqrt{2(1+1.0) + \frac{2(90000)(1+2(1.0))(.148)^2}{3(4650)(1.5)^2}} = 1.092$$

$$k_2 = -1 + \sqrt{\frac{2(1+R_e)}{R_e} + \frac{2F_{yb}(2+R_e)D^2}{3F_{em}t_s^2}}$$

$$= -1 + \sqrt{\frac{2(1+1.0)}{1.0} + \frac{2(90000)(2+1.0)(.148)^2}{3(4650)(1.5)^2}} = 1.092$$

Calc Failure Equation Mode Values

Mode I_s

$$Z = \frac{Dt_sF_{es}}{K_D} = \frac{.148(1.5)4650}{2.2} = 469 \text{ lb}$$

Mode I_s Z = 469 lb

Mode III_m

$$Z = \frac{k_1DpF_{em}}{K_D(1+2R_e)} = \frac{1.092(.148)2(4650)}{2.2(1+2(1.0))} = 171 \text{ lb}$$

Mode III_m Z = 171 lb

Mode III_s

$$Z = \frac{k_2Dt_sF_{em}}{K_D(2+R_e)} = \frac{1.092(.148)1.5(4650)}{2.2(2+1.0)} = 171 \text{ lb}$$

Mode III_s Z = 171 lb

Mode IV

$$Z = \frac{D^2}{K_D}\sqrt{\frac{2F_{em}F_{yb}}{3(1+R_e)}} = \frac{(.148)^2}{2.2}\sqrt{\frac{2(4650)90000}{3(1+1.0)}}$$

= 118 lb

Mode IV Z = 118 lb

The smallest value of the four is found in Mode IV.

Z = 118 lbs / nail

Calc Z′ (exterior conditions)

NDS T7.3.1

$Z' = ZC_DC_MC_tC_dC_{eg}C_{di}C_{tn}$

$= .118(.75)1.0(1.0).84(1.0)1.0(1.0)$

$= .074^k$

$16d_R = N = \frac{F_1}{Z'} = \frac{.28}{.074} = 3.8$ nails say 4 nails

Use 4-10d common nails at joint a

Connection b

member 1 to blk'g controls and blk'g to 3.

From “a” above:

> Use 4-10d common nails at joint b, member 1 to blk'g and blk'g to 3

member 2 to 3

$Z' = .074^{k}$

$16d_R = N = \frac{F_{2-3}}{Z'} = \frac{.25}{.074} = 3.4$ nails say 4 nails

> Use 4-10d common nails at joint b, member 2-3

<u>Connection c</u>

member 2 to 4.

From “a” above:

$Z' = .074^{k}$

$16d_R = N = \frac{F_{3-4}}{Z'} = \frac{.35}{.074} = 4.5$ nails say 5 nails

> Use 5-10d common nails at joint c, member 3-4

<u>Connection d</u>

member 2 to blk'g and blk'g to 4

From “b” above:

> Use4-10d common nails at joint d, member to blk'g and blk'g to 4

No one would remember the Good Samaritan if he only had good intentions. He had money as well.

MARGARET THATCHER

7. Timber Connections with Bolts and Lag Screws

Chapter Problems	Page	Prob.
Bolted 2- row connection capacity with spacing requirements and steel side plates	7-23	7.12
Bolted connection capacity considering spacing requirements with steel side plates	7-21	7.11
Bolted connection capacity with wood side plates and steel main member	7-25	7.13
Bolted double shear connection	7-5	7.3
Bolted double shear connection capacity considering spacing requirements	7-19	7.10
Bolted double shear connection using hankinson formula	7-16	7.9
Bolted double shear connection with steel side plates using hankinson formula	7-14	7.8
Bolted double top plate connection design considering spacing requirements	7-10	7.6
Bolted double top plate connection design with drag strut forces and four bolts	7-8	7.5
Bolted single shear connection using hankinson formula	7-3	7.2
Bolted top plate connection design with drag strut forces	7-6	7.4
Bolted trellis with steel side plates	7-12	7.7
Handrail base plate connection using lag bolts in withdrawal	7-30	7.16
Lag bolt subject to both lateral and withdrawal forces for temp. canopy tie down	7-32	7.17
Lag bolt tension connection considering spacing requirements	7-28	7.14
Lag bolts in withdrawal	7-29	7.15
Shear plate continuity brag force connection	7-34	7.18
Lag bolt connection of ledger to stud wall	7-35	7.19
bolted leaf truss connectin	7-36	7.20
Moment splice for beam	7-40	7.21
Single shear bolted connection	7-2	7.1

PROBLEM 7.1

Single shear bolted connection.

Determine the nominal design value using both Yield Limit Equations and NDS Tables.

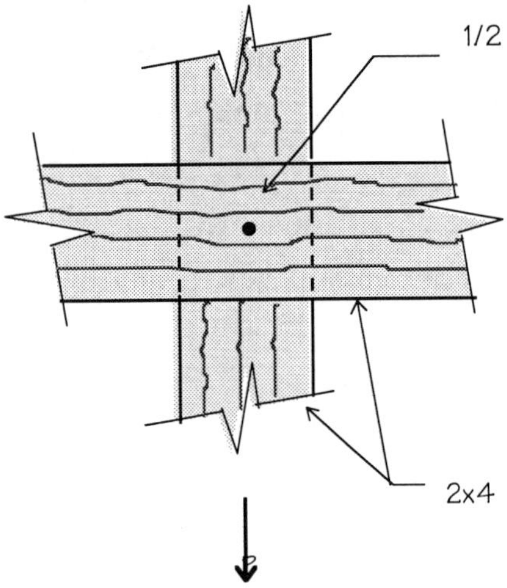

ASSUME

Horizontal member = main member.
DF-L stud grade.
1/2 in dia. A307 MB.
EMC <19%.

SOLUTION

Ck nominal bolt capacity using NDS Tables

From given above Z = 300 lb.

Obtain required values for Yield Equations

NDS T8A, 8.2A

$t_s = 1.5$ in
$t_m = 1.5$ in
$F_{es} = 5600$ psi
$F_{em} = 3150$ psi
$D = .5$ in
$F_{yb} = 45$ ksi
$\theta_m = 90$
$\theta_s = 0$

Calc preliminary coefficients values

$$R_e = \frac{F_{em}}{F_{es}} = \frac{3150}{5600} = .5625$$

$$R_t = \frac{t_m}{t_s} = \frac{1.5}{1.5} = 1.0$$

NDS 8.2.1

$$k_1 = \frac{\sqrt{R_e + 2R_e^2(1+R_t+R_t^2) + R_t^2 R_e^3} - R_e(1+R_t)}{(1+R_e)}$$

$$= \frac{\sqrt{.563+2(.563)^2(1+1+(1)^2)+(1)^2(.563)^3} - .563(1+1)}{(1+.563)}$$

$$= .3197$$

$$k_2 = -1 + \sqrt{2(1+R_e) + \frac{2F_{yb}(1+2R_e)D^2}{3F_{em}t_m^2}}$$

$$= -1 + \sqrt{2(1+.563) + \frac{2(45000)(1+2(.563))(.5)^2}{3(3150)(1.5)^2}} = 1.318$$

$$k_3 = -1 + \sqrt{\frac{2(1+R_e)}{R_e} + \frac{2F_{yb}(2+R_e)D^2}{3F_{em}t_s^2}}$$

$$= -1 + \sqrt{\frac{2(1+.563)}{.563} + \frac{2(45000)(2+.563)(.5)^2}{3(3150)(1.5)^2}} = 1.875$$

Calc Failure Equation Mode Values

Mode I_m

$$Z = \frac{Dt_mF_{em}}{4K_\theta} = \frac{.5(1.5)3150}{4(1.25)} = 473 \text{ lb}$$

Mode I_m Z = 473 lb

Mode I_s

$$Z = \frac{Dt_sF_{es}}{4K_\theta} = \frac{.5(1.5)5600}{4(1.25)} = 840 \text{ lb}$$

Mode I_s Z = 840 lb

Mode II

$$Z = \frac{k_1Dt_sF_{es}}{3.6K_\theta} = \frac{.3197(.5)1.5(3150)}{3.6(1.25)} = 298 \text{ lb}$$

Mode II Z = 298 lb

Mode III_m

$$Z = \frac{k_2 D t_m F_{em}}{3.2(1+2R_e)K_\theta} = \frac{1.318(.5)1.5(3150)}{3.2(1+2(.563))1.25} = 366 \text{ lb}$$

Mode III_m Z = 366 lb

Mode III_s

$$Z = \frac{k_3 D t_s F_{em}}{3.2(2+R_e)K_\theta} = \frac{1.875(.5)1.5(3150)}{3.2(2+.563)1.25} = 432$$

Mode III_s Z = 432 lb

Mode IV

$$Z = \frac{D^2}{3.2K_\theta}\sqrt{\frac{2F_{em}F_{yb}}{3(1+R_e)}} = \frac{(.5)^2}{3.2(1.25)}\sqrt{\frac{2(3150)450000}{3(1+.563)}}$$

=486 lb

Mode IV Z = 486 lb

The smallest value of the four is found in Mode II.

Z = 298 lbs / bolt

Compare both values

Z =298 approx. = 300 lb √

Be bold - and mighty forces will come to your aid.

BASIL KING

PROBLEM 7.2

Bolted single shear connection using hankinson formula.

Determine the nominal design value using Yield Limit Equations.

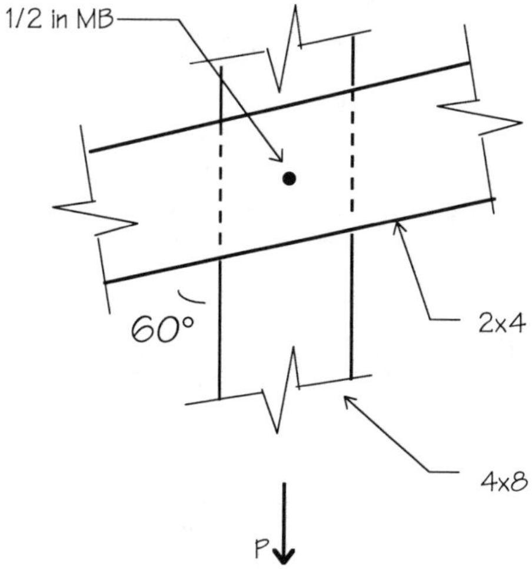

ASSUME

Vertical. member = main member.
DF-L stud grade.
1/2 in dia. A307 MB.
EMC <19%.

SOLUTION

Obtain required values for Yield Equations

NDS T8A, 8.2A

$D = .5$ in
$F_{yb} = 45$ ksi
$t_s = 1.5$ in
$\theta_s = 60$
$t_m = 3.5$ in
$\theta_m = 0.0$
$F_{em} = 5600$ psi, $F_{es} = 3150$ psi

Calc preliminary coefficients values

NDS 8.2.1

$$F_{e\theta} = \frac{F_{e\parallel} F_{e\perp}}{F_{e\parallel}\sin^2\theta + F_{e\perp}\cos^2\theta}$$

$$= \frac{5600(3150)}{5600\sin^2(60) + 3150\cos^2(60)} = 3537 \text{ psi}$$

$$R_e = \frac{F_{em}}{F_{es}} = \frac{5600}{3537} = 1.583$$

$$R_t = \frac{t_m}{t_s} = \frac{3.5}{1.5} = 2.333$$

$$k_1 = \frac{\sqrt{R_e + 2R_e^2\left(1 + R_t + R_t^2\right) + R_t^2 R_e^3} - R_e(1 + R_t)}{(1 + R_e)}$$

$$= \frac{\sqrt{1.58 + 2(1.58)^2\left(1 + 2.33 + (2.33)^2\right) + (2.33)^2(1.58)^3} - 1.58(1 + 2.33)}{(1 + 1.58)}$$

$$= 1.13$$

$$k_2 = -1 + \sqrt{2(1 + R_e) + \frac{2F_{yb}(1 + 2R_e)D^2}{3F_{em}t_m^2}}$$

$$= -1 + \sqrt{2(1 + 1.583) + \frac{2(45000)(1 + 2(1.583))(.5)^2}{3(5600)(3.5)^2}} = 1.371$$

$$k_3 = -1 + \sqrt{\frac{2(1 + R_e)}{R_e} + \frac{2F_{yb}(2 + R_e)D^2}{3F_{em}t_s^2}}$$

$$= -1 + \sqrt{\frac{2(1 + 1.583)}{1.583} + \frac{2(45000)(2 + 1.583)(.5)^2}{3(5600)(1.5)^2}} = 1.323$$

Calc Failure Equation Mode Values

Mode I_m

$$Z = \frac{Dt_mF_{em}}{4K_\theta} = \frac{.5(3.5)5600}{4(1.17)} = 2100 \text{ lb}$$

Mode I_m Z = 2100 lb

Mode I_s

$$Z = \frac{Dt_sF_{es}}{4K_\theta} = \frac{.5(1.5)3537}{4(1.17)} = 568 \text{ lb}$$

Mode I_s Z = 568 lb

Mode II

$$Z = \frac{k_1Dt_sF_{es}}{3.6K_\theta} = \frac{1.13(.5)1.5(3537)}{3.6(1.17)} = 714 \text{ lb}$$

Mode II Z = 714 lb

Mode III_m

$$Z = \frac{k_2Dt_mF_{em}}{3.2(1 + 2R_e)K_\theta} = \frac{1.371(.5)3.5(5600)}{3.2(1 + 2(1.583))1.17} = 864 \text{ lb}$$

Mode III_m Z = 864 lb

Mode III_s

$$Z = \frac{k_3Dt_sF_{em}}{3.2(2 + R_e)K_\theta} = \frac{1.583(.5)1.5(5600)}{3.2(2 + 1.583)1.17} = 415 \text{ lb}$$

Mode III_s Z = 415 lb

Mode IV

$$Z = \frac{D^2}{3.2K_\theta}\sqrt{\frac{2F_{em}F_{yb}}{3(1 + R_e)}} = \frac{(.5)^2}{3.2(1.17)}\sqrt{\frac{2(5600)45000}{3(1 + 1.583)}}$$

$$= 540 \text{lb}$$

Mode IV Z = 540 lb

The smallest value of the four is found in Mode III_s.

Z = 415 lbs / bolt

□
□
□

If you have built castles in the air, your work need not be lost; that is where they should be. Now put the foundations under them.

HENRY DAVID THOREAU

PROBLEM 7.3

Bolted double shear connection.

Determine the nominal design value using both Yield Limit Equations and NDS Tables.

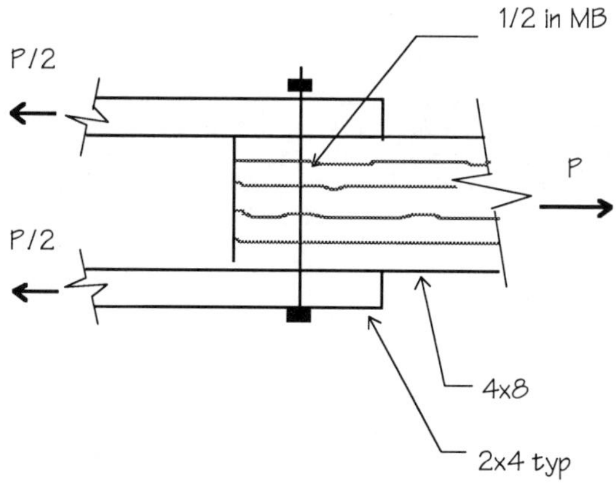

ASSUME

DF-L stud grade.
1/2 in dia. A307 MB.
EMC <19%.

SOLUTION

Ck nominal bolt capacity using NDS Tables

From given above Z_{II} = 1210 lb.

Obtain required values for Yield Equations

t_s = 1.5 in
t_m = 3.5 in
F_{es} = 5600 psi
F_{em} = 5600 psi
D = .5 in
F_{yb} = 45 ksi
$\theta_m = 0$
$\theta_s = 0$ NDS T8A, 8.2A

Calc preliminary coefficients values

$$R_e = \frac{F_{em}}{F_{es}} = \frac{5600}{5600} = 1.0$$

$$K_\theta = 1 + \frac{\theta}{360} = 1 + \frac{0}{360} = 1.0$$

$$k_3 = -1 + \sqrt{\frac{2(1+R_e)}{R_e} + \frac{2F_{yb}(2+R_e)D^2}{3F_{em}t_s^{\,2}}}$$ NDS 8.3.1

$$= -1 + \sqrt{\frac{2(1+1.0)}{1.0} + \frac{2(45000)(2+1.0)(.5)^2}{3(5600)(1.5)^2}} = 1.405$$

Calc Failure Equation Mode Values

Mode I_m

$$Z = \frac{Dt_mF_{em}}{4K_\theta} = \frac{.5(3.5)5600}{4(1.0)} = 2450 \text{ lb}$$

Mode I_m Z = 2450 lb

Mode I_s

$$Z = \frac{Dt_sF_{es}}{2K_\theta} = \frac{.5(1.5)5600}{2(1.0)} = 2100 \text{ lb}$$

Mode I_s Z = 2100 lb

Mode III_s

$$Z = \frac{k_3Dt_sF_{em}}{1.6(2+R_e)K_\theta} = \frac{1.405(.5)1.5(5600)}{1.6(2+1.0)1.0} = 1230 \text{ lb}$$

Mode III_s Z = 1230 lb

Mode IV

$$Z = \frac{D^2}{1.6K_\theta}\sqrt{\frac{2F_{em}F_{yb}}{3(1+R_e)}} = \frac{(.5)^2}{1.6(1.0)}\sqrt{\frac{2(5600)45000}{3(1+1.0)}}$$

= 1432 lb

Mode IV Z = 1432 lb

The smallest value of the four is found in Mode III_s.

Z = 1230 lbs / bolt

Compare both values

Z =1230 approx. = 1210 lb √

Laziness is nothing more than the habit of resting before you get tired.

JULES RENARD

PROBLEM 7.4

Bolted top plate connection design with drag strut forces.

Determine the maximum wind tension drag force capacity of the double top plate splice single shear connection shown below. Neglect spacing requirements. Do not use adjustment factors. Use Yield Limit Equations.

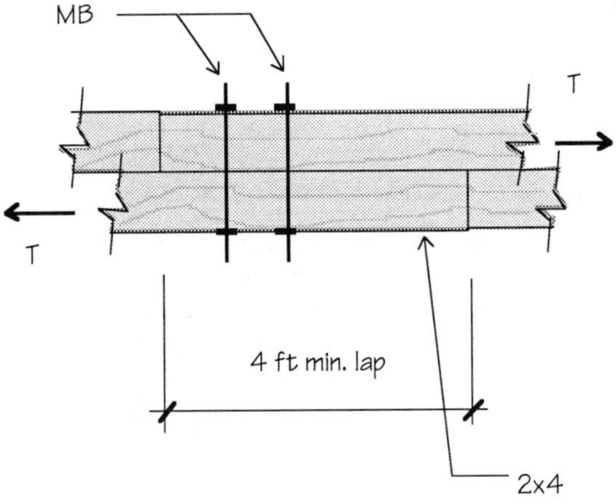

ASSUME

Spacing = s = 2 in.
2x4 double top plates.
DF- L stud grade.
1/2 in dia. A307 MB.
EMC <19%.
C_Δ = 1.0 (base dimensions).

SOLUTION

One member must transmit total drag force through the splice. In order for both top plate members to transmit one half the drag or chord force, the diaphragm shear (from moment tension or compression) must first be transmitted by nails into the bottom plate as well as the top plate.

Tension

$C_F = 1.5$

$F_t' = F_T C_D C_M C_t C_F = .45(1.6)1.0(1.0)1.5 = 1.08$ ksi

$A_n = 5.25 - \left(\frac{1}{2}+\frac{1}{8}\right)1.5 = 4.31\ in^2$

$T_{max} = F_t' A_n = 1.08(4.31) = 4.65^k$

Max tension force in wood = 4.65^k

NDS T2.3.1

NDS T8A, 8.2A

Ck bolt capacity

Obtain required values for Yield Equations

$t_s = 1.5$ in
$t_m = 1.5$ in
$F_{es} = 5600$ psi
$F_{em} = 5600$ psi
$D = .5$ in
$F_{yb} = 45$ ksi
$\theta_m = 0$
$\theta_s = 0$

Calc preliminary coefficients values

$$R_e = \frac{F_{em}}{F_{es}} = \frac{5600}{5600} = 1.0$$

$$R_t = \frac{t_m}{t_s} = \frac{1.5}{1.5} = 1.0$$

NDS 8.2.1

$$k_1 = \frac{\sqrt{R_e + 2R_e^2\left(1+R_t+R_t^2\right)+R_t^2R_e^3} - R_e(1+R_t)}{(1+R_e)}$$

$$= \frac{\sqrt{1.0+2(1.0)^2\left(1+1.0+(1.0)^2\right)+(1.0)^2(1.0)^3} - 1.0(1+1.0)}{(1+1.0)}$$

$$= .4142$$

$$k_2 = -1+\sqrt{2(1+R_e)+\frac{2F_{yb}(1+2R_e)D^2}{3F_{em}t_m^2}}$$

$$= -1+\sqrt{2(1+1)+\frac{2(45000)(1+2(1))(.5)^2}{3(5600)(1.5)^2}} = 1.405$$

$$k_3 = -1+\sqrt{\frac{2(1+R_e)}{R_e}+\frac{2F_{yb}(2+R_e)D^2}{3F_{em}t_s^2}}$$

$$= -1+\sqrt{\frac{2(1+1.0)}{1.0}+\frac{2(45000)(2+1.0)(.5)^2}{3(5600)(1.5)^2}} = 1.405$$

Calc Failure Equation Mode Values

Mode I_m

$$Z = \frac{Dt_mF_{em}}{4K_\theta} = \frac{.5(1.5)5600}{4(1.0)} = 1050 \text{ lb}$$

Mode I_m $Z = 1050$ lb

Mode I_s

$$Z = \frac{Dt_sF_{es}}{4K_\theta} = \frac{.5(1.5)5600}{4(1.0)} = 1050 \text{ lb}$$

Mode I_s $Z = 1050$ lb

Mode II

$$Z = \frac{k_1Dt_sF_{es}}{3.6K_\theta} = \frac{.4142(.5)1.5(5600)}{3.6(1.0)} = 483 \text{ lb}$$

Mode II $Z = 483$ lb

Mode III_m

$$Z = \frac{k_2Dt_mF_{em}}{3.2(1+2R_e)K_\theta} = \frac{1.405(.5)1.5(5600)}{3.2(1+2(1.0))1.0} = 615$$

Mode III_m $Z = 615$ lb

Mode III_s

$$Z = \frac{k_3Dt_sF_{em}}{3.2(2+R_e)K_\theta} = \frac{1.405(.5)1.5(5600)}{3.2(2+1.0)1.0} = 615 \text{ lb}$$

Mode III_s $Z = 615$ lb

Mode IV

$$Z = \frac{D^2}{3.2K_\theta}\sqrt{\frac{2F_{em}F_{yb}}{3(1+R_e)}} = \frac{(.5)^2}{3.2(1.0)}\sqrt{\frac{2(5600)450000}{3(1+1.0)}}$$

$= 716$ lb

Mode IV $Z = 716$ lb

The smallest value of the four is found in Mode II.

$Z = 483$ lbs / bolt

Calc Z′

$$\gamma = 180000D^{1.5} = 180000(.5)^{1.5} = 63640$$

$E_s = E_m = 1400000$ psi

$A_s = A_m = 5.25$ in^2

$$R_{ea} = \min\left[\frac{E_sA_s}{E_mA_m} \text{ or } \frac{E_mA_m}{E_sA_s}\right]$$

same size members ⇒ $R_{ea} = 1.0$

$$u = 1+\gamma\left(\frac{s}{2}\right)\left(\frac{1}{E_mA_m}+\frac{1}{E_sA_s}\right)$$

$$= 1+63640\left(\frac{2}{2}\right)\left(\frac{1}{1400000(5.25)}+\frac{1}{1400000(5.25)}\right)$$

$= 1.0177$

NDS 7.3.6

$$m = u-\sqrt{u^2-1} = 1.0177-\sqrt{(1.0177)^2-1} = .884$$

$$C_g = \left[\frac{m(1-m^{2n})}{n\left[(1+R_{EA}m^n)(1+m)-1+m^{2n}\right]}\right]\left[\frac{1+R_{EA}}{1-m}\right]$$

NDS T7.3.1

$$= \left[\frac{.884(1-.884^{2(2)})}{2\left[(1+1.0(.884)^2)(1+.884)-1+(.884)^{2(2)}\right]}\right]\left[\frac{1+1.0}{1-.884}\right]$$

$= 1.0$

$Z' = ZC_DC_MC_tC_gC_\Delta = .483(1.6)1.0(1.0)1.0(1.0) = .773^k$

$P = NZ' = 2(.773) = 1.546^k < 4.65^k$

Bolts govern.

Capacity of splice = 1.55 ^{k}

□
□
□

Have no fear of perfection - you'll never reach it.

SALVADOR DALI

PROBLEM 7.5

Bolted double top plate connection design with drag strut forces and four bolts.

Determine the maximum wind tension drag force capacity of the double top plate splice single shear connection shown below. Neglect spacing requirements. Use Yield Limit Equations.

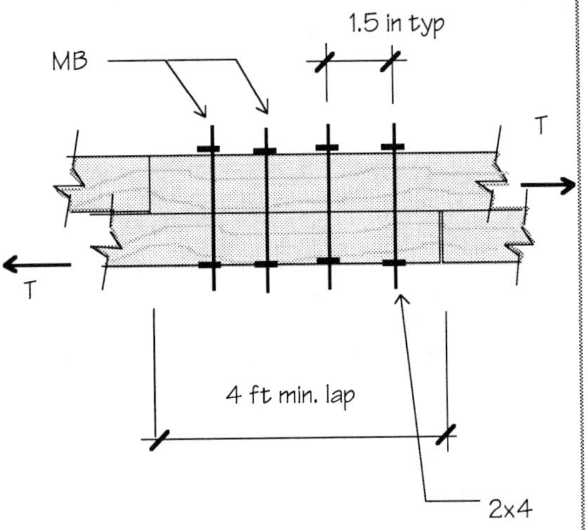

ASSUME

Spacing = s = 1.5 in.
2x4 double top plates.
DF-L stud grade.
5/8 in dia A307 MB.
EMC <19%.
C_Δ = 1.0 (base dimensions).

SOLUTION

One member must transmit total drag force through the splice. In order for both top plate members to transmit one half the drag or chord force, the diaphragm shear (from moment tension or compression) must first be transmitted by nails into the bottom plate as well as the top plate.

Tension

$C_F = 1.5$ NDS T2.3.1

$F_T' = F_T C_D C_M C_t C_F = .45(1.6)1.0(1.0)1.5 = 1.08$ ksi

$$A_n = 5.25 - \left(\frac{5}{8}+\frac{1}{8}\right)1.5 = 4.125 \text{ in}^2$$

$$T_{max} = F_T' A_n = 1.08(4.125) = 4.46^k$$

Max tension force in wood = 4.46^k

Ck bolt capacity

Obtain required values for Yield Equations

NDS T8A, 8.2A

$t_s = 1.5$ in
$t_m = 1.5$ in
$F_{es} = 5600$ psi
$F_{em} = 5600$ psi
$D = .625$ in
$F_{yb} = 45$ ksi
$\theta_m = 0$

$\theta_s = 0$

Calc preliminary coefficients values

NDS T2.3.1

$$R_e = \frac{F_{em}}{F_{es}} = \frac{5600}{5600} = 1.0$$

$$R_t = \frac{t_m}{t_s} = \frac{1.5}{1.5} = 1.0$$

$$k_1 = \frac{\sqrt{R_e + 2R_e^2(1+R_t+R_t^2)+R_t^2R_e^3} - R_e(1+R_t)}{(1+R_e)}$$

$$= \frac{\sqrt{1+2(1)^2(1+1+(1)^2)+(1)^2(1)^3} - 1(1+1)}{(1+1)} = .4142$$

$$k_2 = -1+\sqrt{2(1+R_e)+\frac{2F_{yb}(1+2R_e)D^2}{3F_{em}t_m^2}}$$

$$= -1+\sqrt{2(1+1)+\frac{2(45000)(1+2(1))(.625)^2}{3(5600)(1.5)^2}} = 1.606$$

$$k_3 = -1+\sqrt{\frac{2(1+R_e)}{R_e}+\frac{2F_{yb}(2+R_e)D^2}{3F_{em}t_s^2}}$$

$$= -1+\sqrt{\frac{2(1+1.0)}{1.0}+\frac{2(45000)(2+1.0)(.625)^2}{3(5600)(1.5)^2}} = 1.606$$

Calc Failure Equation Mode Values

Mode I_m

$$Z = \frac{Dt_mF_{em}}{4K_\theta} = \frac{.625(1.5)5600}{4(1.0)} = 1313 \text{ lb}$$

Mode I_m Z = 1313 lb

Mode I_s

$$Z = \frac{Dt_sF_{es}}{4K_\theta} = \frac{.625(1.5)5600}{4(1.0)} = 1313 \text{ lb}$$

Mode I_s Z = 1313 lb

Mode II

$$Z = \frac{k_1Dt_sF_{es}}{3.6K_\theta} = \frac{.4142(.625)1.5(5600)}{3.6(1.0)} = 604 \text{ lb}$$

Mode II Z = 604 lb

Mode III_m

$$Z = \frac{k_2Dt_mF_{em}}{3.2(1+2R_e)K_\theta} = \frac{1.606(.625)1.5(5600)}{3.2(1+2(1.0))1.0} = 878 \text{ lb}$$

Mode III_m Z = 878 lb

Mode III_s

$$Z = \frac{k_3Dt_sF_{em}}{3.2(2+R_e)K_\theta} = \frac{1.606(.625)1.5(5600)}{3.2(2+1.0)1.0} = 878 \text{ lb}$$

Mode III_s Z = 878 lb

Mode IV

$$Z = \frac{D^2}{3.2K_\theta}\sqrt{\frac{2F_{em}F_{yb}}{3(1+R_e)}} = \frac{(.625)^2}{3.2(1.0)}\sqrt{\frac{2(5600)45000}{3(1+1.0)}}$$

$= 1119$

Mode IV Z = 1119 lb

The smallest value of the six is found in Mode II.

Z = 604 lbs / bolt

Calc Z′

$\gamma = 180000D^{1.5}$

$= 180000(.625)^{1.5} = 88939$

$E_s = E_m = 1400000$ psi

$A_s = A_m = 5.25$ in^2

$R_{ea} = \min\left[\frac{E_s A_s}{E_m A_m} \text{ or } \frac{E_m A_m}{E_s A_s}\right]$

same size members $\Rightarrow R_{ea} = 1.0$

$u = 1+\gamma\left(\frac{s}{2}\right)\left(\frac{1}{E_m A_m}+\frac{1}{E_s A_s}\right)$

$= 1+88939\left(\frac{1.5}{2}\right)\left(\frac{1}{1400000(5.25)}+\frac{1}{1400000(5.25)}\right)$

$= 1.0182$

NDS 7.3.6

$m = u-\sqrt{u^2-1} = 1.0182-\sqrt{(1.0182)^2-1} = .827$

$C_g = \left[\frac{m(1-m^{2n})}{n\left[(1+R_{EA}m^n)(1+m)-1+m^{2n}\right]}\right]\left[\frac{1+R_{EA}}{1-m}\right]$

$= \left[\frac{.827(1-.827^{2(4)})}{4\left[(1+1.0(.827)^4)(1+.827)-1+(.827)^{2(4)}\right]}\right]\left[\frac{1+1.0}{1-.827}\right]$

$= .98$

NDS 7.3.1

$Z' = ZC_DC_MC_tC_gC_\Delta = .604(1.6)1.0(1.0).98(1.0) = .95^k$

$P = NZ' = 4(.95) = 3.8^k < 4.46^k$

Bolts govern.

Capacity of splice = 3.8 k

□
□
□

When in doubt, make a fool of yourself. There is a microscopically thin line between being brilliantly creative and acting like the most gigantic idiot on earth. So what the hell, leap.

CYNTHIA HEIMEL

PROBLEM 7.6

Bolted double top plate connection design considering spacing requirements.

Determine the maximum wind tension drag force capacity of the double top plate splice single shear connection shown below. Use NDS tables.

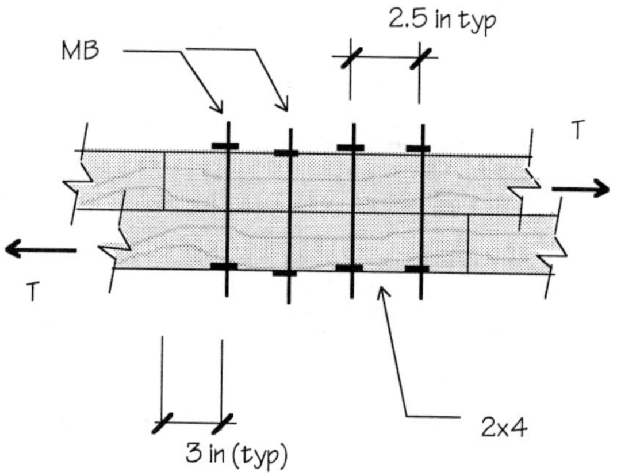

ASSUME

2x4 double top plates.
DF-L No 1.
3/4 in dia. A307 MB.
EMC <19%.
$C_\Delta = 1.0$ (base dimensions).

SOLUTION

Tension

NDS T2.3.1

$C_F = 1.5$

$F_T' = F_T C_D C_M C_t C_F = .675(1.6)1.0(1.0)1.5 = 1.62$ ksi

$A_n = 5.25 - \left(\frac{3}{4}+\frac{1}{8}\right)1.5 = 3.94\text{ in}^2$

$T_{max} = F_T' A_n = 1.62(3.94) = 6.38^k$

> Max tension force capacity in wood = 6.38^k

Ck bolt capacity

Obtain Nominal Capacity

NDS T8A, 8.2A

$t_s = 1.5$ in
$t_m = 1.5$ in
$D = .75$ in
$F_{yb} = 45$ ksi
$\theta_m = 0$
$\theta_s = 0$

> $Z_{II} = .72^k$ / bolt

Calc Z′

$\gamma = 180000D^{1.5} = 180000(.75)^{1.5} = 116913$

$E_s = E_m = 1700000$ psi

$A_s = A_m = 5.25\text{ in}^2$

$R_{ea} = \min\left[\frac{E_sA_s}{E_mA_m} \text{ or } \frac{E_mA_m}{E_sA_s}\right]$

same size members $\Rightarrow R_{ea} = 1.0$

$u = 1+\gamma\left(\frac{s}{2}\right)\left(\frac{1}{E_mA_m}+\frac{1}{E_sA_s}\right)$

$= 1+116913\left(\frac{2.5}{2}\right)\left(\frac{1}{1700000(5.25)}+\frac{1}{1700000(5.25)}\right)$

$= 1.0327$

$m = u-\sqrt{u^2-1} = 1.0327-\sqrt{(1.0327)^2-1} = .775$

$C_g = \left[\frac{m(1-m^{2n})}{n\left[\left(1+R_{EA}m^n\right)(1+m)-1+m^{2n}\right]}\right]\left[\frac{1+R_{EA}}{1-m}\right]$ NDS 7.3.6

$= \left[\frac{.775(1-.775^{2(4)})}{4\left[\left(1+1.0(.775)^4\right)(1+.775)-1+(.775)^{2(4)}\right]}\right]\left[\frac{1+1.0}{1-.775}\right]$

$= .97$

We have one row of 4 bolts in tension in softwood. The end distance is 3.5D minimum allowable and 7D for maximum value. Our value is in-between, so we can interpolate. NDS 8.5.4

End $C_\Delta = \frac{3}{7D} = \frac{3}{7(.75)} = .57$

Edge distance is = 3.5/2 = 1.75 in. NDS 8.5.3

$\frac{\ell}{D} = \frac{1.5}{.75} = 2 < 6$

$\Rightarrow 1.5D = 1.5(.75) = 1.125\text{ in} < 1.75\text{ in}$ √

Edge distance ok.

The spacing requirements for bolts in a row is 3D for minimum allowable and 4D for Maximum. NDS 8.5.5

Spc'g $C_\Delta = \frac{2.5}{4D} = \frac{2.5}{4(.75)} = .83 > .57$

End distance governs.

$Z' = ZC_DC_MC_tC_gC_\Delta = .72(1.6)1.0(1.0).97(.57) = .64^k$ NDS 7.3.1

$P = NZ' = 4(.64) = 2.56^k < 6.38^k$

Bolts govern.

> Capacity of splice = 2.56^k

□
□
□

The superior man thinks always of virtue; the common man thinks of comfort.

CONFUCIUS

○ PROBLEM 7.7

Bolted trellis with steel side plates.

Determine the size of the designated bolts required for the lateral force on the trellis bottom member shown below. Neglect spacing requirements and combined stress. Use Yield Limit Equations.

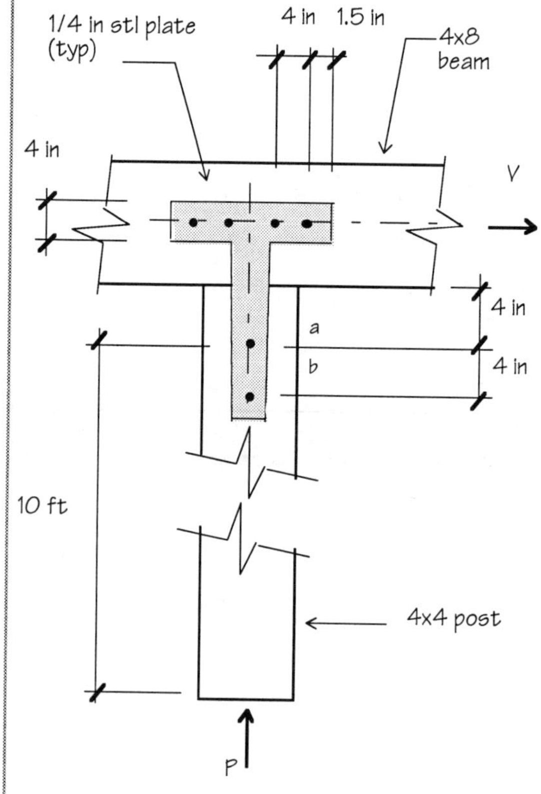

ASSUME

$V = .05^{k}$
$P = 1^{k}$
DF-L No 1
A307 MB
EMC > 19%
C_{Δ} = 1.0 (base dimensions)

SOLUTION

Calc Forces to bolts

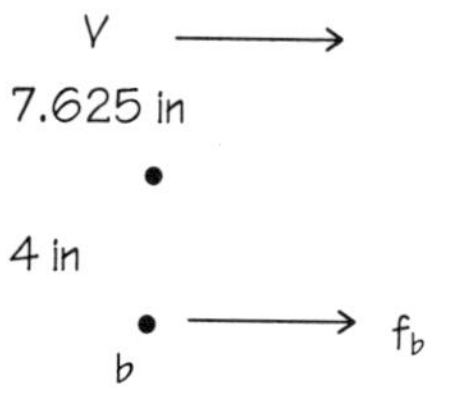

Consider the steel plate as a constraint making the bolts act as a force couple, counteracting the .05 k force at the end of the post.

10(12) - 2 = 118 in

Sum of the moments about "a" with respect to the post gives:

$f_b = .05(118)/2(2) = 1.48^{k}$

Force to bolt = 1.48^{k}

Try 3/4 in dia. bolt

Obtain required values for Yield Equations NDS T8A, 8.2A

t_s = .25 in
t_m = 3.5 in
F_{es} = 58000 psi
F_{em} = 2600 psi
D = .75 in
F_{yb} = 45 ksi
θ_m = 90 NDS 8.3.2

Calc preliminary coefficients values

$$R_e = \frac{F_{em}}{F_{es}} = \frac{2600}{58000} = .045$$

NDS 7.3.1

$$k_3 = -1 + \sqrt{\frac{2(1+R_e)}{R_e} + \frac{2F_{yb}(2+R_e)D^2}{3F_{em}t_s^2}}$$

$$= -1 + \sqrt{\frac{2(1+.045)}{.045} + \frac{2(45000)(2+.045)(.75)^2}{3(2600)(.25)^2}} =$$

15.092

$$K_\theta = 1 + \frac{\theta}{360} = 1 + \frac{90}{360} = 1.25$$

Calc Failure Equation Mode Values

Mode I_m

$$Z = \frac{Dt_mF_{em}}{4K_\theta} = \frac{.75(3.5)2600}{4(1.25)} = 1365$$

Mode I_m Z = 1365 lb

Mode III_s

$$Z = \frac{k_3Dt_sF_{em}}{1.6(2+R_e)K_\theta} = \frac{15.092(.75)1.5(2600)}{1.6(2+.045)1.25} = 1799 \text{ lb}$$

Mode III_s Z = 1799 lb

Mode IV

$$Z = \frac{D^2}{1.6K_\theta}\sqrt{\frac{2F_{em}F_{yb}}{3(1+R_e)}} = \frac{(.75)^2}{1.6(1.25)}\sqrt{\frac{2(2600)45000}{3(1+.045)}}$$

=2430lb

Mode IV Z = 2430 lb

The smallest value of the six is found in Mode I_m.

Z = 1365 lbs / bolt

Calc Z′

$$\gamma = 270000D^{1.5} = 270000(.75)^{1.5} = 175370$$

E_s = 29000000 psi

E_m = 1700000 psi

$A_s = 2(.25)4 = 2 \text{ in}^2$

$A_m = 12.25 \text{ in}^2$

$$R_{ea} = \min\left[\frac{E_sA_s}{E_mA_m} \text{ or } \frac{E_mA_m}{E_sA_s}\right]$$

$$= \min\left[\frac{29e6(2)}{1.7e6(12.25)} \text{ or } \frac{1.7e6(12.25)}{29e6(2)}\right] = .359$$

$$u = 1 + \gamma\left(\frac{s}{2}\right)\left(\frac{1}{E_mA_m} + \frac{1}{E_sA_s}\right)$$

$$= 1 + 175370\left(\frac{4}{2}\right)\left(\frac{1}{1700000(12.25)} + \frac{1}{29000000(4)}\right)$$

= 1.023

$$m = u - \sqrt{u^2-1} = 1.01 - \sqrt{(1.01)^2-1} = .808$$

NDS 7.3.6

$$C_g = \left[\frac{m(1-m^{2n})}{n\left[(1+R_{EA}m^n)(1+m)-1+m^{2n}\right]}\right]\left[\frac{1+R_{EA}}{1-m}\right]$$

$$= \left[\frac{.808(1-.808^{2(1)})}{1\left[(1+.401(.808)^1)(1+.808)-1+(.808)^{2(1)}\right]}\right]\left[\frac{1+.401}{1-.808}\right]15$$

= .99

NDS 7.3.1

$$Z' = ZC_DC_MC_tC_gC_\Delta = 1.365(1.6).75(1.0).99(1.0)$$

$=1.62^k$

$P = NZ' = 1(1.62) = 1.62^k > 1.48^k$ √

Use 3/4 in dia. A307 MB bolts

Success is not the result of spontaneous combustion. You must set yourself on fire.

REGGIE LEACH

PROBLEM 7.8

Bolted double shear connection with steel side plates using hankinson formula.

Determine the maximum tensile load T for the connection shown below using Yield Limit Equations.

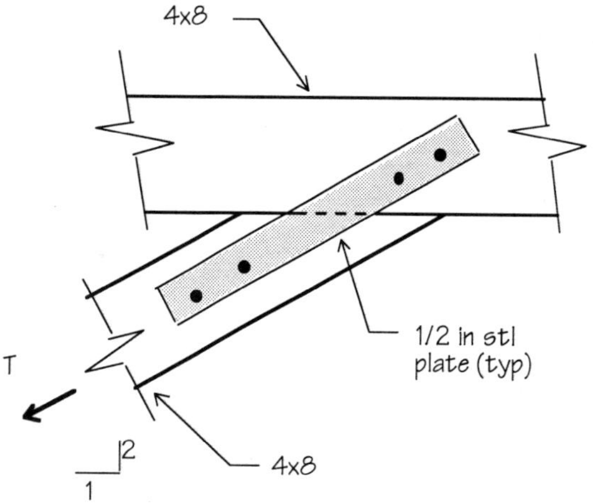

ASSUME

1/2 in dia. A307 MB at 4 in o/c.
DF-L No 1.
4x.5 in A36 stl plates.
EMC < 19%.
C_Δ = 1.0 (base dimensions).

SOLUTION

$\theta = \tan^{-1}(1/2) = 26.57$

Ck capacity of bolts

We must ck both the diagonal strut and the horizontal beam separately, then compare to see which governs for the bolts.

Ck bolts in strut

Obtain required values for Yield Equations NDS T8A,8.2A

t_s = .5 in
t_m = 3.5 in
F_{es} = 58000 psi
F_{em} = 5600 psi
D = .5 in
F_{yb} = 45 ksi
$\theta_m = 0$

Calc preliminary coefficients values NDS 8.3.2

$$R_e = \frac{F_{em}}{F_{es}} = \frac{5600}{58000} = .097$$

NDS 7.3.1

$$k_3 = -1+\sqrt{\frac{2(1+R_e)}{R_e}+\frac{2F_{yb}(2+R_e)D^2}{3F_{em}t_s^2}}$$

$$= -1+\sqrt{\frac{2(1+.097)}{.097}+\frac{2(45000)(2+.097)(.5)^2}{3(5600)(.5)^2}}$$

$=4.826$

$$K_\theta = 1+\frac{\theta}{360} = 1+\frac{0}{360} = 1.0$$

Calc Failure Equation Mode Values

Mode I_m

$$Z = \frac{Dt_mF_{em}}{4K_\theta} = \frac{.5(3.5)5600}{4(1.0)} = 2450 \text{ lb}$$

Mode I_m Z = 2450 lb

Mode III_s

$$Z = \frac{k_3Dt_sF_{em}}{1.6(2+R_e)K_\theta} = \frac{4.826(.5).5(5600)}{1.6(2+.096)1.0} = 2014 \text{ lb}$$

Mode III_s Z = 2014 lb

Mode IV

$$Z = \frac{D^2}{1.6K_\theta}\sqrt{\frac{2F_{em}F_{yb}}{3(1+R_e)}} = \frac{(.5)^2}{1.6(1.0)}\sqrt{\frac{2(5600)45000}{3(1+.097)}}$$

= 1934 lb

Mode IV Z = 1934 lb

The smallest value of the six is found in Mode IV.

Z = 1934 lbs / bolt

Calc Z′

$\gamma = 270000D^{1.5} = 270000(.5)^{1.5} = 95459$

$E_s = 29000000$ psi

$E_m = 1700000$ psi

$A_s = 2(.5)4 = 5 \text{ in}^2$

$A_m = 25.38 \text{ in}^2$

$$R_{ea} = \min\left[\frac{E_sA_s}{E_mA_m} \text{ or } \frac{E_mA_m}{E_sA_s}\right]$$

$$= \min\left[\frac{29e6(4)}{1.7e6(25.38)} \text{ or } \frac{1.7e6(25.38)}{29e6(4)}\right] = .298$$

$$u = 1+\gamma\left(\frac{s}{2}\right)\left(\frac{1}{E_mA_m}+\frac{1}{E_sA_s}\right)$$

$$= 1+95459\left(\frac{4}{2}\right)\left(\frac{1}{1700000(25.38)}+\frac{1}{29000000(4)}\right)$$

$=1.006$

$$m = u-\sqrt{u^2-1} = 1.006-\sqrt{(1.006)^2-1} = .898$$

NDS 7.3.6

$$C_g = \left[\frac{m\left(1-m^{2n}\right)}{n\left[\left(1+R_{EA}m^n\right)(1+m)-1+m^{2n}\right]}\right]\left[\frac{1+R_{EA}}{1-m}\right]$$

$$= \left[\frac{.898\left(1-.898^{2(2)}\right)}{2\left[\left(1+.416(.898)^2\right)(1+.898)-1+(.898)^{2(2)}\right]}\right]\left[\frac{1+.416}{1-.898}\right]$$

$= 1.0$

$Z' = ZC_DC_MC_tC_g C_\Delta = 1.934(1.6)1.0(1.0)1.0(1.0)$

NDS 7.3.1

$= 3.09^k$

$P = NZ' = 2(3.09) = 6.18^k$

Strut bolt capacity = 6.18^k

Ck bolts in horizontal beam

Obtain required values for Yield Equations

NDS 8.3.2

$t_s = .5$ in
$t_m = 3.5$ in
$F_{es} = 58000$ psi
$F_{em\parallel} = 5600$ psi
$F_{em\perp} = 3150$ psi
$D = .5$ in
$F_{yb} = 45$ ksi

$\theta_m = 26.57$

Calc preliminary coefficients values

$$F_{e\theta} = \frac{F_{e\parallel}F_{e\perp}}{F_{e\parallel}\sin^2\theta+F_{e\perp}\cos^2\theta}$$

$$= \frac{5600(3150)}{5600\sin^2(25.57)+3150\cos^2(25.67)} = 4846 \text{ psi}$$

$= F_{em}$

$$R_e = \frac{F_{em}}{F_{es}} = \frac{4846}{58000} = .084$$

NDS 8.3.1

$$k_3 = -1+\sqrt{\frac{2(1+R_e)}{R_e}+\frac{2F_{yb}(2+R_e)D^2}{3F_{em}t_s^2}}$$

$$= -1+\sqrt{\frac{2(1+.084)}{.084}+\frac{2(45000)(2+.084)(.5)^2}{3(4846)(.5)^2}} = 5.232$$

$$K_\theta = 1+\frac{\theta}{360} = 1+\frac{25.57}{360} = 1.07$$

Calc Failure Equation Mode Values

Mode I_m

$$Z = \frac{Dt_mF_{em}}{4K_\theta} = \frac{.5(3.5)4846}{4(1.07)} = 1974 \text{ lb}$$

Mode I_m Z = 1974 lb

Mode III_s

$$Z = \frac{k_3Dt_sF_{em}}{1.6(2+R_e)K_\theta} = \frac{5.232(.5).5(4846)}{1.6(2+.084)1.07} = 1771 \text{ lb}$$

Mode III_s Z = 1771 lb

Mode IV

$$Z = \frac{D^2}{1.6K_\theta}\sqrt{\frac{2F_{em}F_{yb}}{3(1+R_e)}} = \frac{(.5)^2}{1.6(1.07)}\sqrt{\frac{2(4846)45000}{3(1+.084)}}$$

$=1685$ lb

Mode IV Z = 1685 lb

The smallest value of the three is found in Mode IV.

Z = 1685 lbs / bolt

Calc Z′

$\gamma = 270000D^{1.5} = 270000(.5)^{1.5} = 95459$

$E_s = 29000000$ psi

$E_m = 1700000$ psi

$A_s = 2(.5)4 = 5 \text{ in}^2$

$A_m = 25.38 \text{ in}^2$

$$R_{ea} = \min\left[\frac{E_s A_s}{E_m A_m} \text{ or } \frac{E_m A_m}{E_s A_s}\right]$$

$$= \min\left[\frac{29e6(4)}{1.7e6(25.38)} \text{ or } \frac{1.7e6(25.38)}{29e6(4)}\right] = .298$$

$$u = 1 + \gamma\left(\frac{s}{2}\right)\left(\frac{1}{E_m A_m} + \frac{1}{E_s A_s}\right)$$

$$= 1 + 95459\left(\frac{4}{2}\right)\left(\frac{1}{1700000(25.38)} + \frac{1}{29000000(4)}\right)$$

$= 1.006$

$m = u - \sqrt{u^2 - 1} = 1.006 - \sqrt{(1.006)^2 - 1} = .898$

NDS 7.3.6

$$C_g = \left[\frac{m(1 - m^{2n})}{n\left[(1 + R_{EA} m^n)(1 + m) - 1 + m^{2n}\right]}\right]\left[\frac{1 + R_{EA}}{1 - m}\right]$$

$$= \left[\frac{.898(1 - .898^{2(2)})}{2\left[(1 + .416(.898)^2)(1 + .898) - 1 + (.898)^{2(2)}\right]}\right]\left[\frac{1 + .416}{1 - .898}\right]$$

$= 1.0$

NDS 7.3.1

$Z' = Z C_D C_M C_t C_g C_\Delta = 1.685(1.6)1.0(1.0)1.0(1.0) = 2.7^k$

$P = NZ' = 2(2.7) = 5.4^k < 6.18^k$

Bolts in horizontal beam govern.

Connection capacity for bolts = 5.4^k

Minds, like bodies, will often fall into a pimpled, ill-conditioned state from mere excess of comfort.

CHARLES DICKENS

PROBLEM 7.9

Bolted double shear connection using hankinson formula.

Determine if the proposed bolted connection is adequate for the catwalk for the D+ L load shown below using Yield Limit Equations.

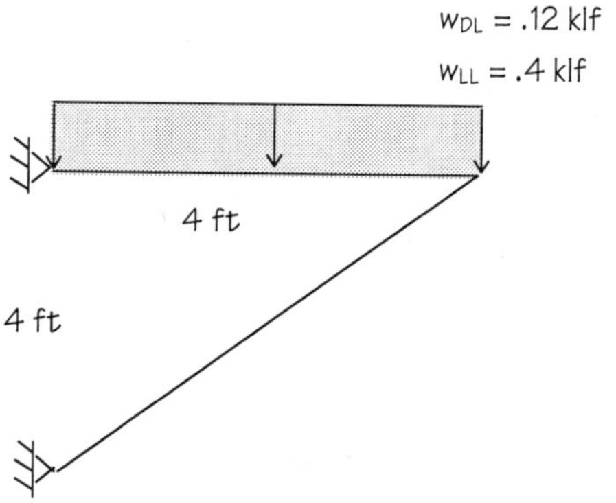

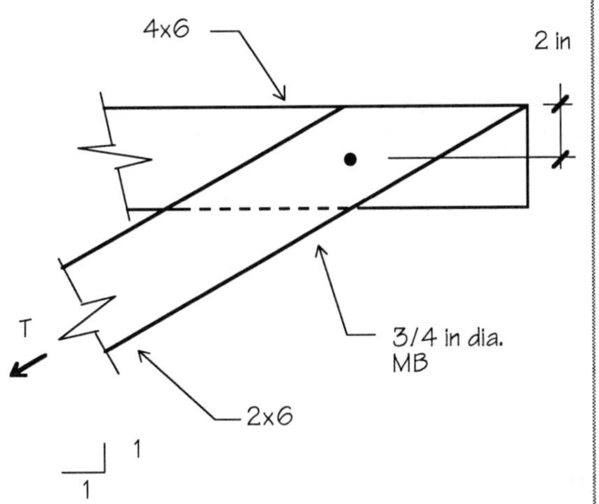

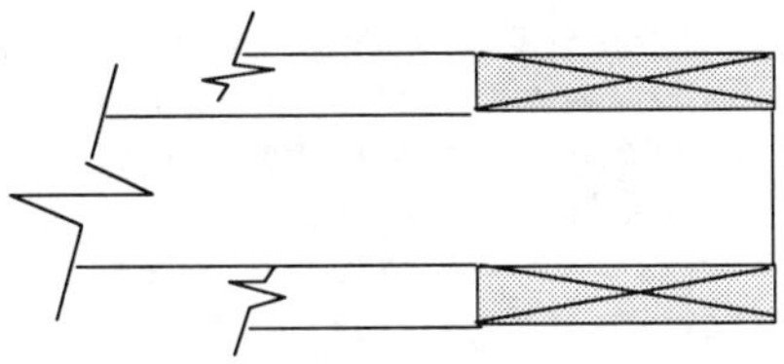

ASSUME

3/4 in dia. A307 MB.
DF-L No 1.
Beam and diagonal strut ok.
EMC < 19%.
C_Δ = 1.0 (base dimensions).

SOLUTION

$\theta = \tan^{-1}(1/1) = 45$

$w_{D+L} = .12 + .4 = .52$ klf

$R = \frac{w\ell}{2} = \frac{.52(4)}{2} = 1.04^k$

strut force = $R\sqrt{2} = 1.04\sqrt{2} = 1.47^k$

Ck capacity of bolts

Obtain required values for Yield Equations NDS T8A, 8.2A

$t_s = 1.5$ in
$t_m = 3.5$ in
$F_{es} = 5600$ psi
$F_{em\parallel} = 5600$ psi
$F_{em\perp} = 2600$ psi
$D = .75$ in
$F_{yb} = 45$ ksi
$\theta_m = 45$
$\theta_s = 0$

Calc preliminary coefficients values

$$F_{e\theta} = \frac{F_{e\parallel}F_{e\perp}}{F_{e\parallel}\sin^2\theta + F_{e\perp}\cos^2\theta} =$$

$$\frac{5600(2600)}{.5600\sin^2(45)+2600\cos^2(45)} = 3551 \text{ psi} = F_{em}$$

$$R_e = \frac{F_{em}}{F_{es}} = \frac{3155}{5600} = .634$$

NDS 8.3.1

$$k_3 = -1+\sqrt{\frac{2(1+R_e)}{R_e}+\frac{2F_{yb}(2+R_e)D^2}{3F_{em}t_s^2}}$$

$$= -1+\sqrt{\frac{2(1+.634)}{.634}+\frac{2(45000)(2+.634)(.75)^2}{3(3551)(1.5)^2}} = 2.274$$

$$K_\theta = 1+\frac{\theta}{360} = 1+\frac{45}{360} = 1.13$$

Calc Failure Equation Mode Values

Mode I_m

$$Z = \frac{Dt_mF_{em}}{4K_\theta} = \frac{.75(3.5)3551}{4(1.13)} = 2072 \text{ lb}$$

Mode I_m Z = 2072 lb

Mode I_s

$$Z = \frac{Dt_sF_{es}}{2K_\theta} = \frac{.75(1.5)5600}{2(1.13)} = 2800 \text{ lb}$$

Mode I_s Z = 2800 lb

Mode III_s

$$Z = \frac{k_3 D t_s F_{em}}{1.6(2+R_e)K_\theta} = \frac{2.274(.75)1.5(3551)}{1.6(2+.634)1.13} = 1916 \text{ lb}$$

Mode III_s Z =1916 lb

Mode IV

$$Z = \frac{D^2}{1.6K_\theta}\sqrt{\frac{2F_{em}F_{yb}}{3(1+R_e)}} = \frac{(.75)^2}{1.6(1.13)}\sqrt{\frac{2(5600)45000}{3(1+.634)}}$$

=2523lb

Mode IV Z = 2523 lb

The smallest value of the four is found in Mode III_s.

Z = 1916 lbs / bolt

Calc Z′

NDS 7.3.1 Since C_Δ = 1.0 from the given statement of the problem, assume that the dimensions for the connections are ok, or will be chosen to be so.

$Z' = ZC_DC_MC_tC_gC_\Delta$=1.916(1.0)1.0(1.0)1.0(1.0)=1.916^k

P = NZ′ = 1(1.916)= 1.916^k > 1.47^k √

Connection ok for D + L load

Ck. shear stress in 4x6

Here we can eyeball the dimensions by inspection.

NDS 3.4.5.1 d_e = 2 in

5d = 5(5.5) = 27.5 in > actual end distance by insp.

$$f_v = \left(\frac{3V}{2bd_e}\right)\left(\frac{d}{d_e}\right) = \left(\frac{3(1.04)}{2(3.5)2}\right)\left(\frac{5.5}{2}\right) = .613 \text{ ksi}$$

NDS T2.3.1 $F_v' = F_vC_DC_MC_tC_H$ = .095(1.0)1.0(1.0)1.0

=.095 ksi < .613 ksi **NG!**

Try increasing beam size to 4x8

min. edge distance perpendicular to grain is:

1.5D = 1.5(.75) = 1.125 in (unloaded edge)

try d_e = 7.25 - 1.25 = 6.0 in

$$f_v = \left(\frac{3V}{2bd_e}\right)\left(\frac{d}{d_e}\right) = \left(\frac{3(1.04)}{2(3.5)6.0}\right)\left(\frac{7.25}{6.0}\right)$$ NDS 3.4.5.1

= .089 ksi < .095 ksi √

Since the above shear stress is ok, the shear stress on the gross section is ok by inspection.

Use 4x8 beam with d_e = 6 in for above connection

One of the best ways to properly evaluate and adapt to the many environmental stresses of life is to simply view them as normal. The adversity and failures in our lives, if adapted to and viewed as normal corrective feedback to use to get back on target, serve to develop in us an immunity against anxiety, depression, and the adverse responses to stress. Instead of tackling the most important priorities that would make us successful and effective in life, we prefer the path of least resistance and do things simply that will relieve our tension, such as shuffling papers and majoring in minors.

DENIS WAITLEY

PROBLEM 7.10

Bolted double shear connection capacity considering spacing requirements.

Determine the maximum wind tension force capacity of the connection shown below.

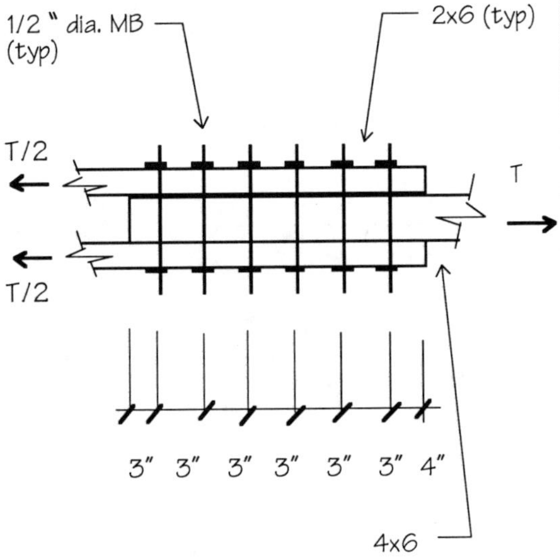

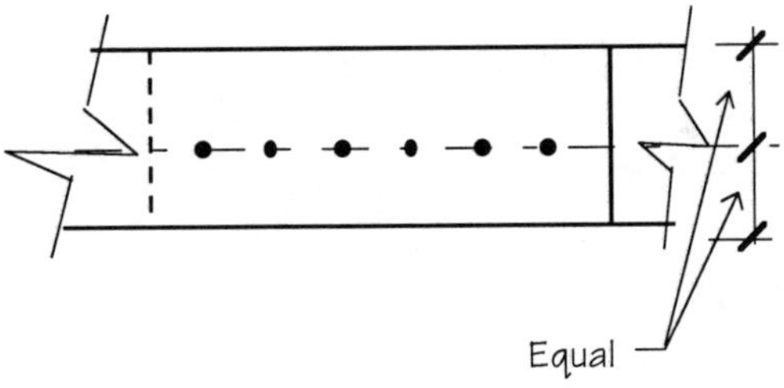

ASSUME

- Hem-fir No 1 2x6.
- DF-L No 1 4x6.
- Exposed to weather.
- A307 MB.
- EMC >19%.
- D + wind load.

SOLUTION

Ck 2x6 tension capacity

NDS T2.3.1

$F_T' = F_T C_D C_M C_t C_F = .6(1.6)1.0(1.0)1.3 = 1.25$ ksi

$A_n = 8.25 - \left(\frac{1}{2}+\frac{1}{8}\right)1.5 = 7.31\ in^2$

$T_{max} = 2\,F_T'\,A_n = 2(1.25)7.31 = 18.28^k$

> Max tension force capacity in 2-2x6 = 18.28^k

Ck 4x6 tension capacity

NDS T2.3.1

$F_T' = F_T C_D C_M C_t C_F = .675(1.6)1.0(1.0)1.3 = 1.4$ ksi

$A_n = 19.25 - \left(\frac{1}{2}+\frac{1}{8}\right)3.5 = 17.1\ in^2$

$T_{max} = F_T'\,A_n = 1.4(17.1)$

$= 23.9^k > 18.28^k$ 2-2x6 governs

> Max tension force capacity in 4x6 = 23.9^k

Ck capacity of bolts

Obtain required values for Yield Equations

NDS T8A, 8.2A

$t_s = 1.5$ in
$t_m = 3.5$ in
$F_{es} = 4800$ psi
$F_{em} = 5600$ psi
$D = .5$ in
$F_{yb} = 45$ ksi
$\theta_m = 0$
$\theta_s = 0$

Calc preliminary coefficients values

$$R_e = \frac{F_{em}}{F_{es}} = \frac{5600}{4800} = 1.167$$

NDS 8.3.1

$$k_3 = -1+\sqrt{\frac{2(1+R_e)}{R_e}+\frac{2F_{yb}(2+R_e)D^2}{3F_{em}t_s^2}}$$

$$= -1+\sqrt{\frac{2(1+1.167)}{1.167}+\frac{2(45000)(2+1.167)(.5)^2}{3(5600)(1.5)^2}} = 1.366$$

$$K_\theta = 1+\frac{\theta}{360} = 1+\frac{0}{360} = 1.0$$

Calc Failure Equation Mode Values

Mode I_m

$$Z = \frac{Dt_mF_{em}}{4K_\theta} = \frac{.5(3.5)5600}{4(1.0)} = 2450 \text{ lb}$$

Mode I_m Z = 2450 lb

Mode I_s

$$Z = \frac{Dt_sF_{es}}{2K_\theta} = \frac{.5(1.5)4800}{2(1.0)} = 1800 \text{ lb}$$

Mode I_s Z = 1800 lb

Mode III_s

$$Z = \frac{k_3Dt_sF_{em}}{1.6(2+R_e)K_\theta} = \frac{1.266(.5)1.5(5600)}{1.6(2+1.167)1.0} = 1133 \text{ lb}$$

Mode III_s Z =1133 lb

Mode IV

$$Z = \frac{D^2}{1.6K_\theta}\sqrt{\frac{2F_{em}F_{yb}}{3(1+R_e)}} = \frac{(.5)^2}{1.6(1.0)}\sqrt{\frac{2(5600)45000}{3(1+1.167)}}$$

= 1376 lb

Mode IV Z = 1376 lb

The smallest value of the four is found in Mode III_s.

Z = 1133 lbs / bolt

Calc Z′

Calc C_g

$$\gamma = 180000D^{1.5} = 180000(.5)^{1.5} = 63640$$

E_s = 1500000 psi

E_m = 1700000 psi

A_s = 8.25 in^2

A_m = 19.25 in^2

$$R_{ea} = \min\left[\frac{E_sA_s}{E_mA_m} \text{ or } \frac{E_mA_m}{E_sA_s}\right]$$

$$\min\left[\frac{1500000(8.25)}{1700000(19.25)} \text{ or } \frac{1700000(19.25)}{1500000(8.25)}\right] = .378$$

$$u = 1+\gamma\left(\frac{s}{2}\right)\left(\frac{1}{E_mA_m}+\frac{1}{E_sA_s}\right)$$

$$= 1+63640\left(\frac{3}{2}\right)\left(\frac{1}{1700000(19.25)}+\frac{1}{1500000(8.25)}\right)$$

$$= 1.011$$

$$m = u-\sqrt{u^2-1} = 1.011-\sqrt{(1.011)^2-1} = .864$$ NDS 7.3.6

$$C_g = \left[\frac{m(1-m^{2n})}{n\left[\left(1+R_{EA}m^n\right)(1+m)-1+m^{2n}\right]}\right]\left[\frac{1+R_{EA}}{1-m}\right]$$

$$= \left[\frac{.864\left(1-.864^{2(6)}\right)}{6\left[\left(1+1.0(.864)^6\right)(1+.864)-1+(.864)^{2(6)}\right]}\right]\left[\frac{1+.378}{1-.864}\right]$$

$$= .91$$

Calc C_Δ

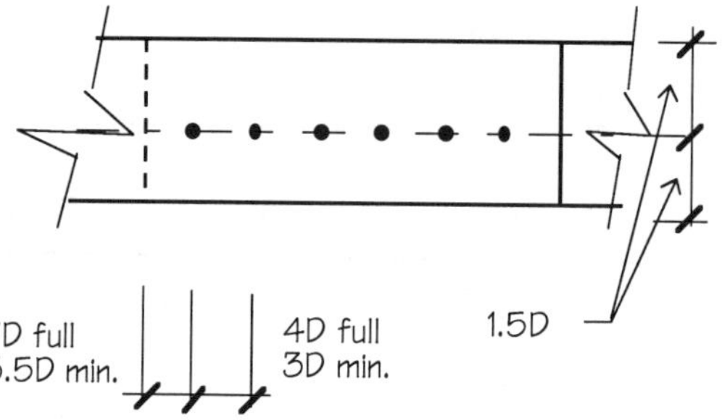

We have one row of 6 bolts in tension in softwood.

1.5D = 1.5(.5) = .75 in < 5.25/2 = 2.75 in √

7D = 7(.5) = 3.5 in > 3 in

3D = 3(.5) = 1.5 in < 3 in ⇒ reduce

spacing $C_\Delta = \frac{3}{7D} = \frac{3}{3.5} = .86$

edge for 2x6

NDS 8.5.5

$4D = 4(.5) = 2.0 \text{ in} < 4 \text{ in}$ √

edge for 4x6

$4D = 4(.5) = 2.0 \text{ in} < 3 \text{ in}$ √

$Z' = ZC_DC_MC_tC_g\,C_\Delta = 1.133(1.6).75(1.0).91(.86)$

NDS T7.3.1

$= 1.06^k$

$P = NZ' = 6(1.06) = 6.36^k < 18.28^k$

Bolts govern.

Capacity of connection governed by bolts = 6.36^k

Guilt is never a rational thing; it distorts all the faculties of the human mind, it perverts them, it leaves a man no longer in the free use of his reason, it puts him into confusion.

EDMUND BURKE

PROBLEM 7.11

Bolted connection capacity considering spacing requirements with steel side plates.

Determine the maximum wind tension force capacity of the connection shown below.

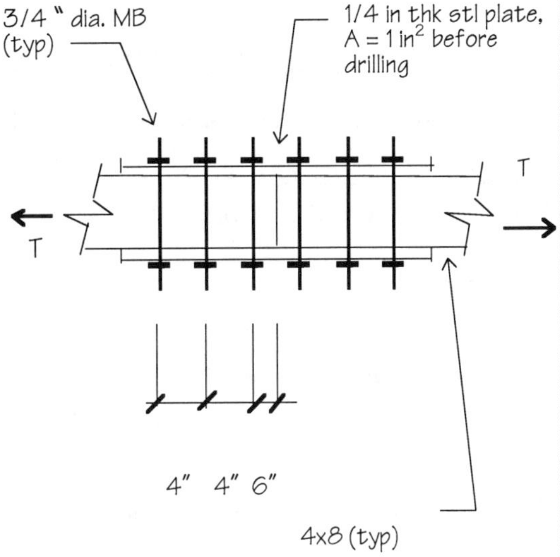

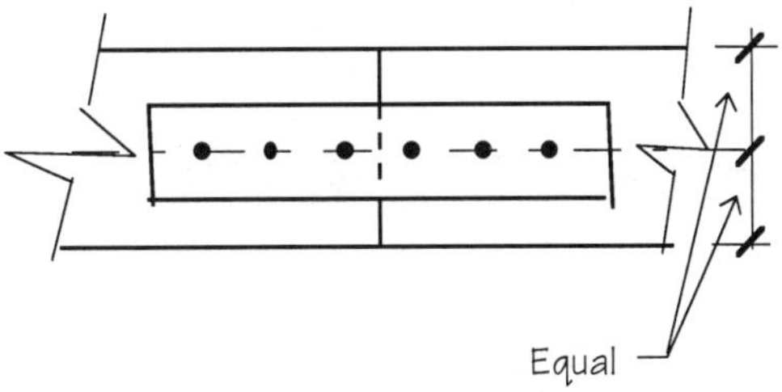

ASSUME

DF-L No 2.
A307 MB.
A36 stl.
EMC < 19%.
D + wind load.

SOLUTION

Ck 4x8 tension capacity

NDS T2.3.1

$F_t' = F_TC_DC_MC_tC_F = .575(1.6)1.0(1.0)1.3 = 1.2 \text{ ksi}$

$A_n = 25.38 - \left(\frac{3}{4}+\frac{1}{8}\right)3.5 = 22.32\ in^2$

$T_{max} = F_T' A_n = 1.2(22.32) = 26.8^k$

> Max tension force capacity in 4x8 = 26.8^k

Ck capacity of bolts

Obtain required values for Yield Equations

NDS T8A, 8.2A

$t_s = .25$ in
$t_m = 3.5$ in
$F_{es} = 58000$ psi
$F_{em} = 5600$ psi
$D = .75$ in
$F_{yb} = 45$ ksi
$\theta_m = 0$
$\theta_s = 0$

NDS 8.3.2

Calc preliminary coefficients values

$R_e = \frac{F_{em}}{F_{es}} = \frac{5600}{58000} = .0966$

NDS 8.3.1

$k_3 = -1+\sqrt{\frac{2(1+R_e)}{R_e}+\frac{2F_{yb}(2+R_e)D^2}{3F_{em}t_s^2}}$

$= -1+\sqrt{\frac{2(1+.097)}{.097}+\frac{2(45000)(2+.097)(.75)^2}{3(5600)(.25)^2}}$

$=10.13$

$K_\theta = 1+\frac{\theta}{360} = 1+\frac{0}{360} = 1.0$

Calc Failure Equation Mode Values

Mode I_m

$Z = \frac{Dt_mF_{em}}{4K_\theta} = \frac{.75(3.5)5600}{4(1.0)} = 3675$ lb

> Mode I_m Z = 3675 lb

Mode III_s

$Z = \frac{k_3Dt_sF_{em}}{1.6(2+R_e)K_\theta} = \frac{10.13(.75).25(5600)}{1.6(2+.097)1.0} = 3170$ lb

> Mode III_s Z = 3170 lb

Mode IV

$Z = \frac{D^2}{1.6K_\theta}\sqrt{\frac{2F_{em}F_{yb}}{3(1+R_e)}} = \frac{(.75)^2}{1.6(1.0)}\sqrt{\frac{2(5600)45000}{3(1+.097)}}$

$=4352$ lb

> Mode IV Z = 4352 lb

The smallest value of the three is found in Mode III_s.

> Z = 3170 lbs / bolt

Calc Z'

Calc C_g

$\gamma = 270000D^{1.5} = 270000(.75)^{1.5} = 175370$

$E_s = 29000000$ psi
$E_m = 1600000$ psi
$A_s = 2.0\ in^2$
$A_m = 25.38\ in^2$

$R_{ea} = \min\left[\frac{E_sA_s}{E_mA_m}\ or\ \frac{E_mA_m}{E_sA_s}\right]$

$\min\left[\frac{29000000(2)}{1600000(25.38)}\ or\ \frac{1600000(25.38)}{29000000(2)}\right] = .7$

$u = 1+\gamma\left(\frac{s}{2}\right)\left(\frac{1}{E_mA_m}+\frac{1}{E_sA_s}\right)$

$= 1+175370\left(\frac{4}{2}\right)\left(\frac{1}{1600000(25.38)}+\frac{1}{29000000(2)}\right)$

$=1.015$

$m = u-\sqrt{u^2-1} = 1.015-\sqrt{(1.015)^2-1} = .843$

$C_g = \left[\frac{m(1-m^{2n})}{n\left[(1+R_{EA}m^n)(1+m)-1+m^{2n}\right]}\right]\left[\frac{1+R_{EA}}{1-m}\right]$ NDS 7.3.6

$$= \left[\frac{.843\left(1-.864^{2(3)}\right)}{3\left[\left(1+1.0(.843)^3\right)(1+.843)-1+(.843)^{2(3)}\right]} \right] \left[\frac{1+.7}{1-.843} \right]$$

$= .99$

Calc C_Δ

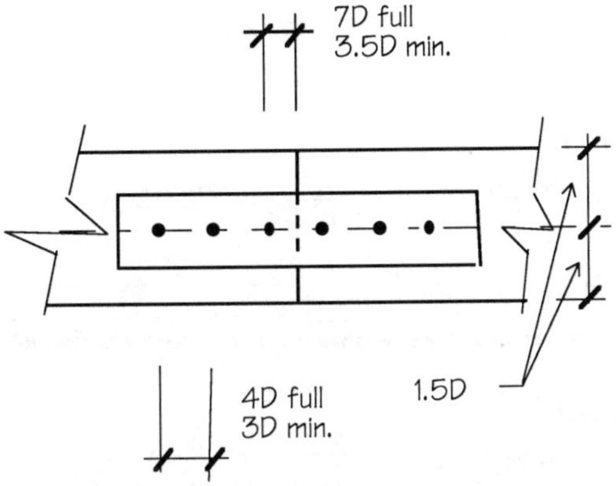

We have one row of 3 bolts in tension in softwood.

NDS 8.5.5

$1.5D = 1.5(.75) = 1.125 \text{ in} < 7.25/2 = 3.6 \text{ in}$ √

$7D = 7(.75) = 5.25 \text{ in} < 6 \text{ in}$ √

$4D = 4(.75) = 3.0 \text{ in} < 4 \text{ in}$ √

NDS T7.3.1

$Z' = ZC_DC_MC_tC_g C_\Delta = 3.17(1.6)1.0(1.0).99(1.0) = 5.02^k$

$P = NZ' = 3(5.02) = 15.06^k < 26.8^k$

Bolts govern.

> Capacity of connection governed by bolts = 15.06^k

□
□
□

If you're going to do something wrong, at least enjoy it.

LEO ROSTEN

PROBLEM 7.12

Bolted 2- row connection capacity with spacing requirements and steel side plates.

Determine the maximum seismic tension force capacity of the proposed connection shown below. Check spacing.

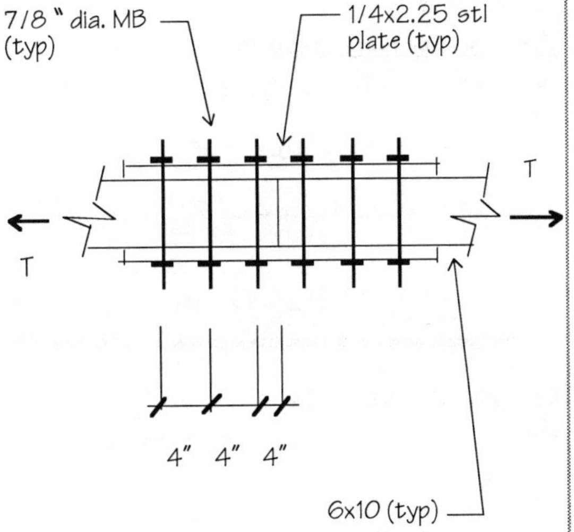

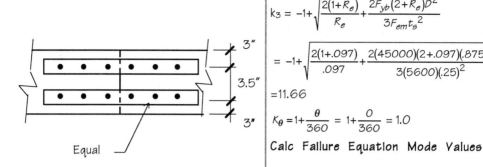

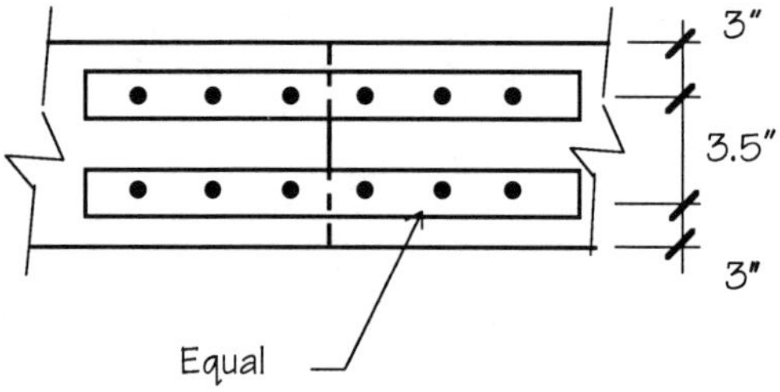

ASSUME

DF-L select str.
A307 MB.
A36 stl.
Initial dry/wet exposure.

SOLUTION

Ck 6x10 tension capacity

NDS T2.3.1

$F_T' = F_T C_D C_M C_t C_F = .95(1.6)1.0(1.0)1.0 = 1.52$ ksi

$A_n = 52.25 - 2\left(\frac{7}{8}+\frac{1}{8}\right)5.5 = 41.25\ in^2$

$T_{max} = F_T' A_n = 1.52(41.25) = 62.7^k$

> Max tension force capacity in 6x10 = 62.7^k

Ck capacity of bolts

NDS T8A, 8.2A

Obtain required values for Yield Equations

$t_s = .25$ in
$t_m = 5.5$ in
$F_{es} = 58000$ psi
$F_{em} = 5600$ psi
$D = .875$ in
$F_{yb} = 45$ ksi
$\theta_m = 0$
$\theta_s = 0$

Calc preliminary coefficients values

$R_e = \frac{F_{em}}{F_{es}} = \frac{5600}{58000} = .0966$

$$k_3 = -1+\sqrt{\frac{2(1+R_e)}{R_e}+\frac{2F_{yb}(2+R_e)D^2}{3F_{em}t_s^2}}$$ NDS 8.3.1

$$= -1+\sqrt{\frac{2(1+.097)}{.097}+\frac{2(45000)(2+.097)(.875)^2}{3(5600)(.25)^2}}$$

$=11.66$

$K_\theta = 1+\frac{\theta}{360} = 1+\frac{0}{360} = 1.0$

Calc Failure Equation Mode Values

Mode I_m

$Z = \frac{Dt_mF_{em}}{4K_\theta} = \frac{.875(5.5)5600}{4(1.0)} = 6738$ lb

> Mode I_m Z = 6738 lb

Mode III_s

$Z = \frac{k_3Dt_sF_{em}}{1.6(2+R_e)K_\theta} = \frac{11.66(.875).25(5600)}{1.6(2+.097)1.0} = 4258$ lb

> Mode III_s Z = 4258 lb

Mode IV

$Z = \frac{D^2}{1.6K_\theta}\sqrt{\frac{2F_{em}F_{yb}}{3(1+R_e)}} = \frac{(.875)^2}{1.6(1.0)}\sqrt{\frac{2(5600)45000}{3(1+.097)}}$

$=5923$lb

> Mode IV Z = 5923 lb

The smallest value of the three is found in Mode III_s.

> Z = 4258 lbs / bolt

Calc Z'

Calc C_g

$\gamma = 270000D^{1.5} = 270000(.875)^{1.5} = 220992$

$E_s = 29000000$ psi

$E_m = 1600000$ psi

$A_s = 2.25\ in^2$

$A_m = 52.25\ in^2$

$$R_{ea} = \min\left[\frac{E_sA_s}{E_mA_m} \text{ or } \frac{E_mA_m}{E_sA_s}\right]$$

$$\min\left[\frac{29000000(2.25)}{1600000(52.25)} \text{ or } \frac{1600000(52.25)}{29000000(2.25)}\right] = .781$$

$$u = 1+\gamma\left(\frac{s}{2}\right)\left(\frac{1}{E_mA_m}+\frac{1}{E_sA_s}\right)$$

$=$

$$1+220992\left(\frac{4}{2}\right)\left(\frac{1}{1600000(52.25)}+\frac{1}{29000000(2.25)}\right)$$

$= 1.012$

$$m = u-\sqrt{u^2-1} = 1.012-\sqrt{(1.012)^2-1} = .856$$

NDS 7.3.6

$$C_g = \left[\frac{m\left(1-m^{2n}\right)}{n\left[\left(1+R_{EA}m^n\right)(1+m)-1+m^{2n}\right]}\right]\left[\frac{1+R_{EA}}{1-m}\right]$$

$$= \left[\frac{.856\left(1-.856^{2(3)}\right)}{3\left[\left(1+1.0(.856)^3\right)(1+.856)-1+(.856)^{2(3)}\right]}\right]\left[\frac{1+.781}{1-.856}\right]$$

$= .99$

Calc C_Δ

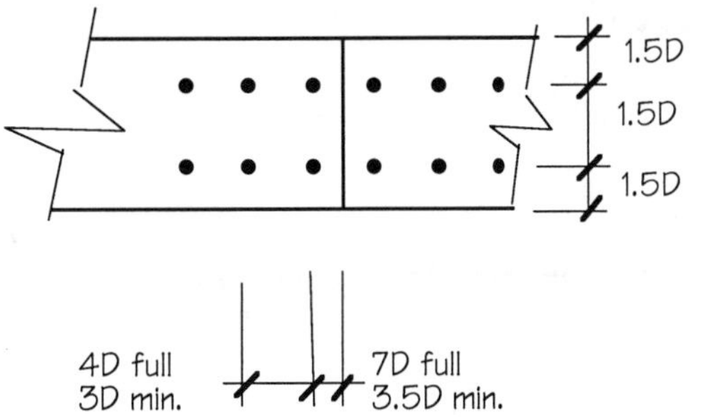

We have 2 rows of 3 bolts in tension in softwood.

Edge/row distance NDS 8.5.3

$$\min\left[\frac{\ell_m}{D} \text{ or } \frac{\ell_s}{D}\right] = \frac{3.5}{.875} = 4 < 6$$

$1.5D = 1.5(.875) = 1.313$ in < 3.0 in √ NDS 8.5.4

end distance (softwood)

$7D = 7(.875) = 6.13$ in > 4 in

$3.5D = 3.5(.875) = 3.06$ in < 4 in

end distance $C_\Delta = \frac{4}{6.13} = .65$ NDS 8.5.5

spacing

$4D = 4(.875) = 3.5$ in < 4 in

$Z' = ZC_DC_MC_tC_g\,C_\Delta = 4.258(1.6).67(1.0).99(.65) =$ NDS 7.3.1

2.94^k

$P = NZ' = 6(2.94) = 17.6^k < 62.7^k$

Bolts govern.

Capacity of connection governed by bolts = 17.6^k

If you are distressed by anything external, the pain is not due to the thing itself, but to your estimate of it; and this you have the power to revoke at any moment.

MARCUS AUREOLES

PROBLEM 7.13

Bolted connection capacity with wood side plates and steel main member.

Determine the capacity of the proposed connection shown below. Check spacing required and horizontal shear in side members.

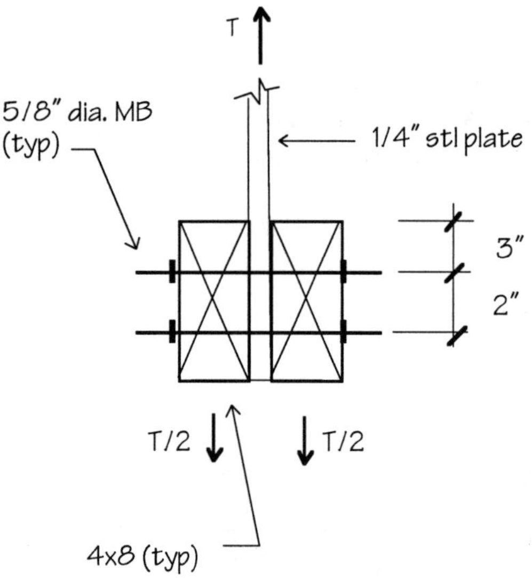

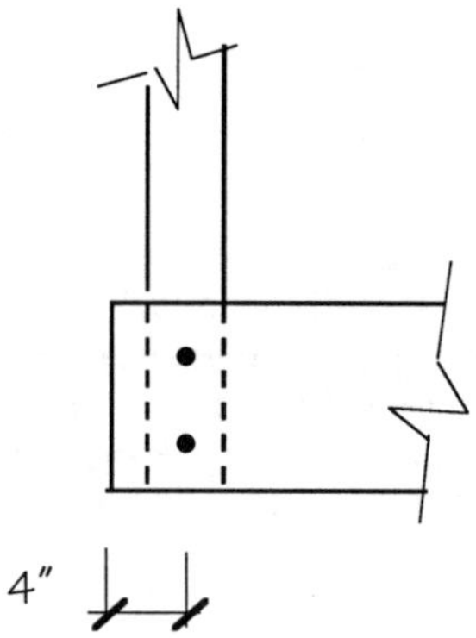

ASSUME

DF-L No 3 ok.
A307 MB.
A36 stl ok.
Dry/exposed to weather.
DL only.

SOLUTION

Ck capacity of bolts

Obtain required values for Yield Equations NDS T8A, 8.2A

$t_s = 3.5$ in
$t_m = .25$ in
$F_{es} = 2800$ psi
$F_{em} = 58000$ psi
$D = .625$ in
$F_{yb} = 45$ ksi
$\theta_m = 0$
$\theta_s = 90$

Calc preliminary coefficients values NDS 8.3.2.2

$$R_e = \frac{F_{em}}{F_{es}} = \frac{58000}{2800} = 20.71$$

$$k_3 = -1 + \sqrt{\frac{2(1+R_e)}{R_e} + \frac{2F_{yb}(2+R_e)D^2}{3F_{em}t_s^2}}$$ NDS 8.3.1

$$= -1 + \sqrt{\frac{2(1+20.71)}{20.71} + \frac{2(45000)(2+20.71)(.625)^2}{3(58000)(3.5)^2}} = .572$$

$$K_\theta = 1 + \frac{\theta}{360} = 1 + \frac{90}{360} = 1.25$$

Calc Failure Equation Mode Values

Mode I_m

$$Z = \frac{Dt_sF_{es}}{2K_\theta} = \frac{.625(3.5)2800}{2(1.25)} = 2450 \text{ lb}$$

Mode I_m Z = 2450 lb

Mode III_s

$$Z = \frac{k_3 D t_s F_{em}}{1.6(2+R_e)K_\theta} = \frac{.572(.625)3.5(58000)}{1.6(2+20.714)1.25} = 1598 \text{ lb}$$

Mode III_s Z = 1598 lb

Mode IV

$$Z = \frac{D^2}{1.6K_\theta}\sqrt{\frac{2F_{em}F_{yb}}{3(1+R_e)}}$$

$$= \frac{(.625)^2}{1.6(1.25)}\sqrt{\frac{2(58000)45000}{3(1+20.714)}} = 1748 \text{ lb}$$

Mode IV Z = 1748 lb

The smallest value of the three is found in Mode III_s.

Z = 1598 lbs / bolt

Calc Z´

Calc C_g

$$\gamma = 270000D^{1.5} = 270000(.625)^{1.5} = 133409$$

$E_s = 1400000$ psi

$E_m = 29000000$ psi

$A_s = 50.75\ in^2$

$A_m = .25\ in^2$

$$R_{ea} = \min\left[\frac{E_sA_s}{E_mA_m}\ or\ \frac{E_mA_m}{E_sA_s}\right]$$

$$\min\left[\frac{1400000(50.75)}{29000000(.25)}\ or\ \frac{29000000(.25)}{1400000(50.75)}\right]$$

$= .102$

$$u = 1+\gamma\left(\frac{s}{2}\right)\left(\frac{1}{E_mA_m}+\frac{1}{E_sA_s}\right)$$

$$= 1+133409\left(\frac{2}{2}\right)\left(\frac{1}{29000000(.25)}+\frac{1}{1400000(50.75)}\right)$$

$= 1.02$

$$m = u-\sqrt{u^2-1} = 1.02-\sqrt{(1.02)^2-1} = .818$$

NDS 7.3.6

$$C_g = \left[\frac{m\left(1-m^{2n}\right)}{n\left[\left(1+R_{EA}m^n\right)(1+m)-1+m^{2n}\right]}\right]\left[\frac{1+R_{EA}}{1-m}\right]$$

$$= \left[\frac{.818\left(1-.818^{2(2)}\right)}{2\left[\left(1+1.0(.818)^2\right)(1+.818)-1+(.818)^{2(2)}\right]}\right]\left[\frac{1+.102}{1-.818}\right]$$

$= .98$

Calc C_Δ

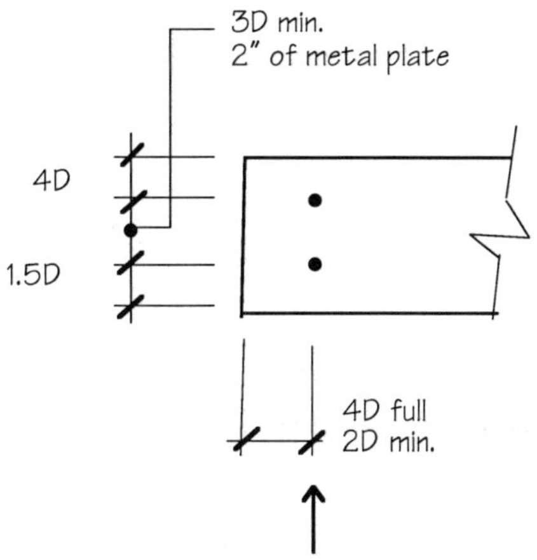

We have one row of 2 bolts in tension in softwood. NDS 8.5.3
unloaded edge distance

1.5D = 1.5(.625) = .938 in < 7.25-5 = 2.25 in √

loaded edge distance

4D = 4(.625) = 2.5 in < 4 in √ NDS 8.5.4

end distance

2D = 2(.625) = 1.25 in < 4 in √

4D = 2.5 in < 4 in √

spacing NDS 8.5.5

3D = 3(.625) = 1.875 in < 2 in √

spacing of plate = 2 in ok

$Z' = ZC_DC_MC_tC_g\,C_\Delta = 1598(.9).75(1.0).98(1.0)$ NDS 7.3.1

$= 1061^k$

$P = NZ' = 2(1.061) = 2.122^k$

Capacity of bolts = 2.122 ^{k}

Ck shear stress in 4x8

Here we can eyeball the dimensions by inspection. NDS 2.3.1

$d_e = 5$ in

$5d = 5(7.25) = 36.25$ in > actual end distance by insp.

$F_v' = F_v C_D C_M C_t C_H = .095(.9).97(1.0)1.0 = .083$ ksi

NDS 3.4.5.1

$$f_v = \left(\frac{3V}{2bd_e}\right)\left(\frac{d}{d_e}\right)$$

solve for V of 2 4x8 (V/2)

$$V = \frac{Fv'4bd_e^2}{3d} = \frac{.083(4)3.5(5)^2}{3(7.25)} = 1.34^k < 2.18^k$$

Horizontal shear governs connection.

Connection capacity = 1.34 ^{k}

My philosophy is that not only are you responsible for your life, but doing the best at this moment puts you in the best place for the next moment.

OPRAH WINFREY

PROBLEM 7.14

Lag bolt tension connection considering spacing requirements.

Determine the number of 4" long 1/2" dia. lag bolts that are required in the continuity connection shown below.

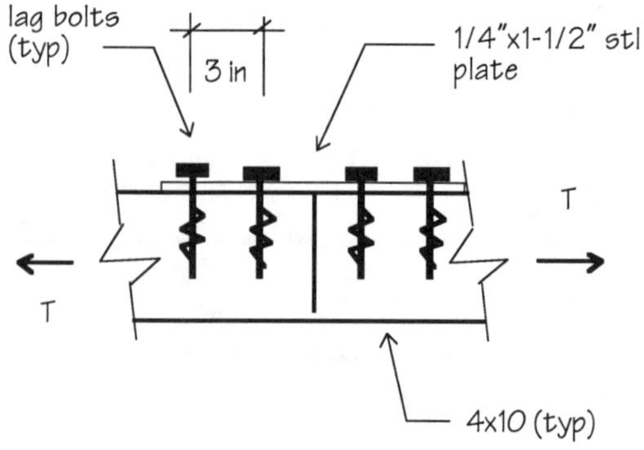

ASSUME

T = 3.0 ^{k} (seismic).
Neglect eccentricity.
DF-L No 1.
EMC < 19%.
Spacing ok.
$C_\Delta = 1.0$ (base dimensions).

SOLUTION

Ck bolt capacity

Obtain required values for Yield Equations NDS T9A, 9.3A

$t_s = .25$ in
$t_m = 9.25$ in
$F_{es} = 58000$ psi
$F_{em} = 5600$ psi
$D = .5$ in
$F_{yb} = 45$ ksi NDS 9.3.2
$\theta_m = 0$

Calc preliminary coefficients values

$$R_e = \frac{F_{em}}{F_{es}} = \frac{5600}{58000} = .0966$$

$$k = -1 + \sqrt{\frac{2(1+R_e)}{R_e} + \frac{F_{yb}(2+R_e)D^2}{2F_{em}t_s^2}}$$ NDS 9.3.1

$$= -1 + \sqrt{\frac{2(1+.0966)}{.0966} + \frac{(45000)(2+.0966)(.5)^2}{2(5600)(.25)^2}} = 6.511$$

$$K_\theta = 1 + \frac{\theta}{360} = 1 + \frac{0}{360} = 1.0$$

Calc Failure Equation Mode Values

Mode III_s

$$Z = \frac{kDt_sF_{em}}{2.8(2+R_e)K_\theta} = \frac{6.511(.5).25(5600)}{2.8(2+.0966)1.0} = 776 \text{ lb}$$

Mode III_s Z = 776 lb

Mode IV

$$Z = \frac{D^2}{3K_\theta}\sqrt{\frac{1.75F_{em}F_{yb}}{3(1+R_e)}} = \frac{(.5)^2}{3(1.0)}\sqrt{\frac{1.75(5600)45000}{3(1+.0966)}}$$

$= 965$ lb

Mode IV Z = 965 lb

The smallest value of the two is found in Mode III_s.

Z = 776 lbs / bolt

<u>Calc Z´</u> (without group factor for trial size)

Penetration

NDS 9.3.3

$p = L - t_s - t_{washer} - E = 4 - .25 - 0 - .3125 = 3.438''$

$8D = 8(.5) = 4'' > 3.438''$ NG!

$4D = 4(.5) = 2'' < 3.438''$ √ reduction ok

NDS T7.3.1

$$C_d = \frac{p}{8D} = \frac{3.438}{4} = .86$$

$Z' = ZC_DC_MC_tC_g\,C_\Delta C_dC_{eg}$

$= .776(1.6)1.0(1.0)1.0(1.0).86(1.0) = 1.07^k$

$N = P/Z' = 3/1.07 = 2.8$ say 3 lag bolts

Group action factor

$\gamma = 270000D^{1.5} = 270000(.5)^{1.5} = 95459$

$E_s = 29000000$ psi

$E_m = 1600000$ psi

$A_s = .25\ in^2$

$A_m = 32.38\ in^2$

$$R_{ea} = \min\left[\frac{E_sA_s}{E_mA_m}\ or\ \frac{E_mA_m}{E_sA_s}\right]$$

$$= \min\left[\frac{29000(.25)}{1600000(32.38)}\ or\ \frac{1600000(32.38)}{29000(.25)}\right] = .14$$

$$u = 1+\gamma\left(\frac{s}{2}\right)\left(\frac{1}{E_mA_m}+\frac{1}{E_sA_s}\right)$$

$$= 1+95459\left(\frac{3}{2}\right)\left(\frac{1}{1600000(32.38)}+\frac{1}{29000000(.25)}\right)$$

$= 1.023$

NDS 7.3.6

$m = u-\sqrt{u^2-1} = 1.023-\sqrt{(1.023)^2-1} = .809$

$$C_g = \left[\frac{m\left(1-m^{2n}\right)}{n\left[\left(1+R_{EA}m^n\right)(1+m)-1+m^{2n}\right]}\right]\left[\frac{1+R_{EA}}{1-m}\right]$$

$$= \left[\frac{.809\left(1-.809^{2(2)}\right)}{2\left[\left(1+.14(.809)^2\right)(1+.809)-1+(.809)^{2(2)}\right]}\right]\left[\frac{1+.14}{1-.809}\right]$$

$= .95$

$Z' = ZC_DC_MC_tC_g\,C_\Delta C_dC_{eg}$ NDS T7.3.1

$= .776(1.6)1.0(1.0).95(1.0).86(1.0) = 1.014^k$

$P = NZ' = 3(1.014) = 304^k > 3^k$ √

Use 3-1/2" dia. x4" long lag bolts
Capacity = 3.04^k

The greatest discovery of my generation is that a human being can alter his life by altering his attitudes of mind.

WILLIAM JAMES

<u>PROBLEM</u> 7.15

Lag bolts in withdrawal.

Determine the size of the lag bolts required.

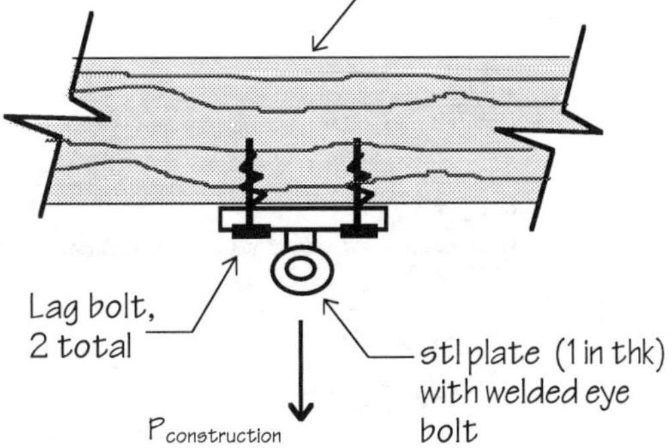

ASSUME

DF-L No 1.
Initially dry, exposed to weather.
Neglect stl plate weight.
$P = .4^k$.

SOLUTION

Ck lag bolt effective thread length

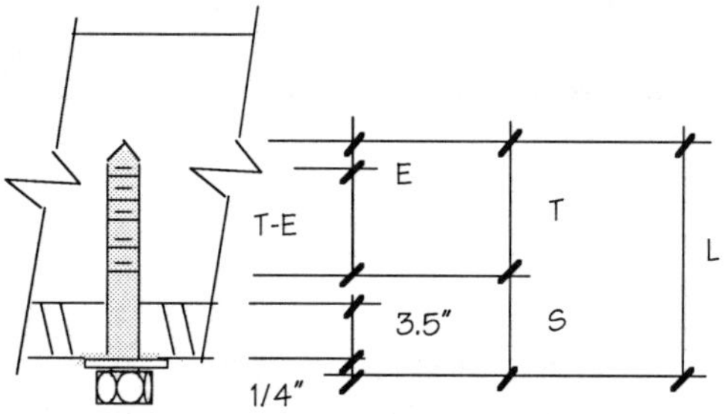

penetration = $L - t_s - t_{washer} - t_{plate}$
$= L - 1.0 - .25 = L - 1.25$

NDS 9.3.3

Try 3/8" dia. 3" long lag bolt

$p_w = T - E = 1.78'' < L - 1.25 = 3 - 1.25 = 1.75''$ √

All threads within main member

Calc W

NDS T9.2A

For DF-L, SG = .5

w = .305

$W = wp_w = .305(1.78) = .543^k$

W= .543 lbs / bolt

Calc W′

NDS T7.3.1

$W' = WC_DC_MC_tC_{eg} = .543(1.25).75(1.0)1.0 = .509^k$

$P = NZ' = 2(.509) = 1.018^k > .4^k$ √

Use 2-3/8" dia. x3" long lag bolts with 1/4" thk washer. Capacity = 1.02^k

Next week there can't be any crisis. My schedule is already full.

HENRY A. KISSINGER

○ PROBLEM 7.16

Handrail base plate connection using lag bolts in withdrawal.

Determine the required size of the lag bolts for the handrail shown below.

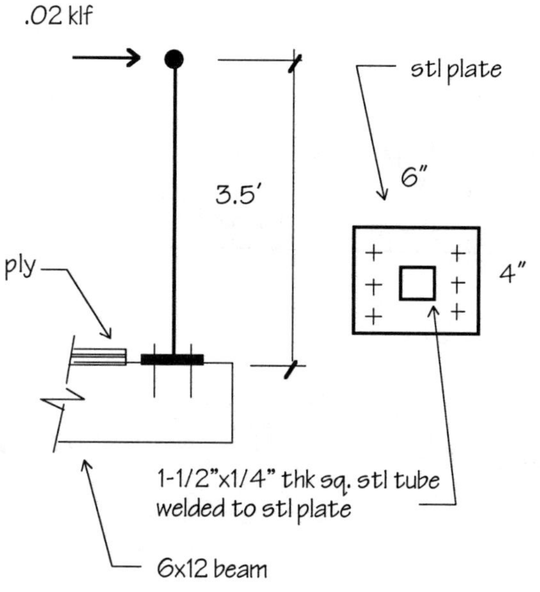

ASSUME

Stl tube ok.
Hr post at 8' o/c.
Hr wt. = .015 klf.
Neglect ply defl.
DF-L No 1.
Initially dry, exposed to weather.
Neglect stl plate weight.
$C_D = 1.0$.
Lag bolts as required (six max.).
Neglect lag shear.

SOLUTION

Find forces

$P = .015(8) = .12^k$

$P_V = .02(8) = .16^k$

$M = 3.5(.16)12 = 6.72^{k\,in}$

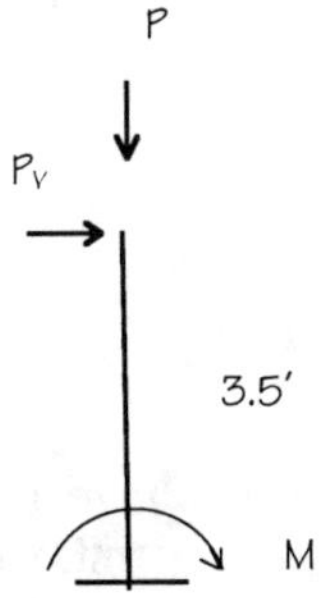

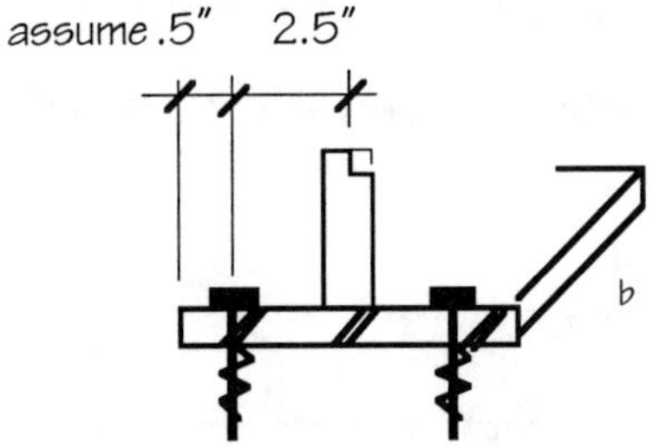

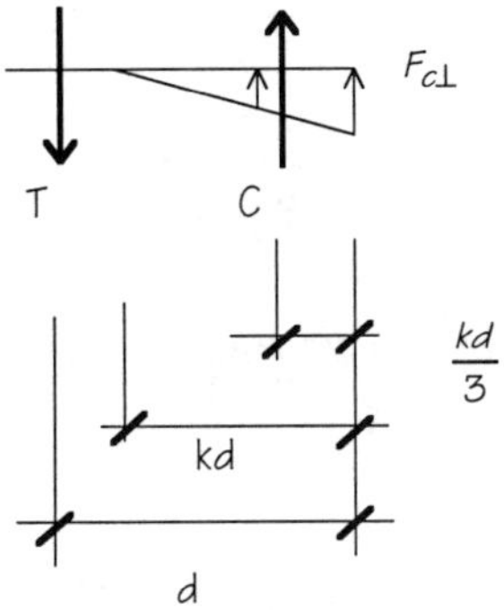

Neglect P (consv)

$F_{c\perp} = .625$ ksi

$$\sum M = 2.5T - M + C\left(3 - \frac{kd}{3}\right)$$

$$C = \left(\frac{kd}{2}\right)F_{c\perp}b = \left(\frac{kd}{2}\right).625(4) = 1.25kd$$

$$\sum F_y = 0 = T - C \;\Rightarrow\; T = C$$

$$0 = 2.5(1.25)kd - 6.72 + 1.25kd\left(3 - \frac{kd}{3}\right)$$

$= 3.125kd - 6.72 + 3.75kd - .417(kd)^2$

$= 6.875kd - 6.72 - .417(kd)^2$ divide by $-.417$

$= (kd)^2 - 16.49kd + 16.12$

Using quadratic

$$\frac{-b \pm \sqrt{b^2 - 4ac}}{2a} = \frac{16.49 \pm \sqrt{(-16.49)^2 - 4(1)16.12}}{2(1)}$$

$= 15.45,\ 1.04$ by insp. implies 1.04

$C = 1.25(1.04) = 1.3^k = T$

Group T required = 1.3^k

Select stl base plate

Although the design of a base plate is beyond the scope of this book, it is included with the intent to provide continuity of the design process.

$M = 2.75T = 2.75(1.3) = 3.58^{k\,in}$

$$t = \left(\frac{6M}{bF_b}\right)^{.5} = \left(\frac{6(3.58)}{4(27)}\right)^{.5} = .45''$$

Or from center line of tube wall:

$$M = \left(2.75 - \left(\frac{1.5}{2} - \frac{.25}{2}\right)\right)1.3 = 2.76^{k\,in}$$

$$t = \left(\frac{6M}{bF_b}\right)^{.5} = \left(\frac{6(2.76)}{4(27)}\right)^{.5} = .39''$$

Because of incremental sizing:

> Use 1/2" thk A-36 stl base plate

Select trial lag

Assume 3 lags each side of base plate with at least 2 in effective thread length. Remember that C_m will be .75 because of the environmental conditions.

Cap/in req'd = $1.3/(3(2).75) = .289^{k}$/in

NDS T9.2A

Use NDS Tables to get a preliminary size by looking at the withdrawal values.

Try 3/8" dia. x 4" long lag bolts with 1/8" thk washer.

NDS 9.3.3

$p_w = T - E = 2.28'' < L - t_s - t_{washer}$
$4 - .5 - .125 = 3.38''$ √

All threads within main member.

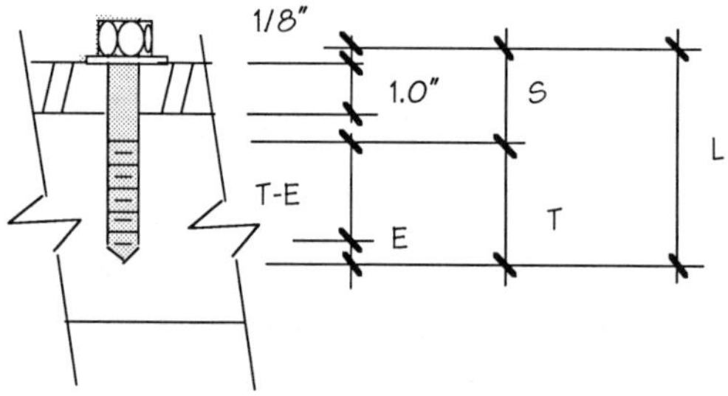

Calc W

For DF-L, SG = .5

w = .305 k/in

$W = wp_w = .305(2.28) = .696^{k}$

> W= .696 k / bolt

Calc W′

NDS T7.3.1

$W' = WC_DC_MC_tC_{eg} = .696(1.0).75(1.0)1.0 = .522^{k}$

$P = NZ' = 3(.522) = 1.57^{k} > 1.3^{k}$ √

> Use 6-3/8" dia. x4" long lag bolts with 1/8" thk washer.
> Capacity = 1.57^{k}

Note that the above did not include the weight of the Handrail. This is a conservative approach that simplifies the process somewhat.

▯
▯
▯

Life means to have something definite to do - a mission to fulfill - and in the measure in which we avoid setting our life to something, we make it empty. Human life, by its very nature, has to be dedicated to something.

JOSE ORTEGA Y GASSET

PROBLEM 7.17

Lag bolt subject to both lateral and withdrawal forces for temporary canopy tie down.

Determine the required size of the lag bolt for the temporary tent canopy tie down shown below.

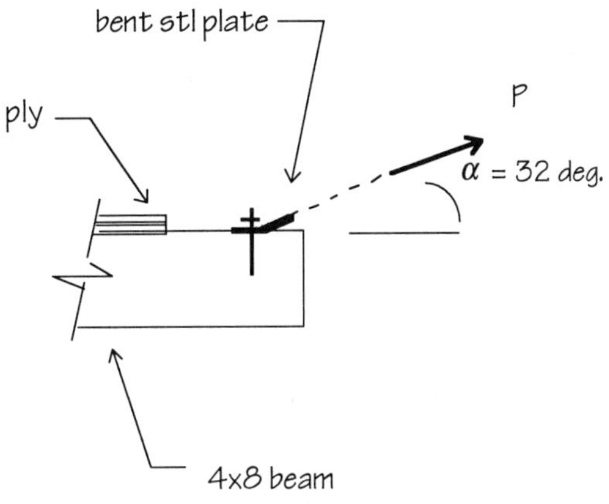

ASSUME

Bent stl plate ok.
Hem fir No 1.
Initially dry, exposed to weather.
$C_D = 1.6$ (wind).
Lag bolt size as required.
$P = 1.2^k$.

SOLUTION

This problem involves the simultaneous utilization of both Yield Limit Equations and the NDS Withdrawal Table values in hankinson's interaction formula. To get an idea for a trial size, resolve the force P into its components and check the values in the NDS tables.

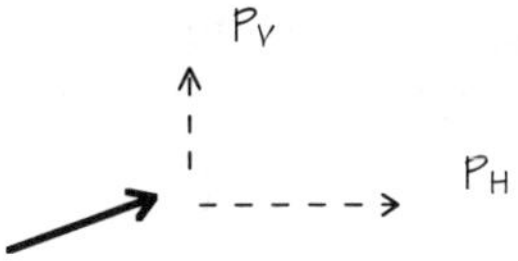

$P_V = P \sin\alpha = 1.2 \sin 32 = .64^k$

$P_H = P \cos\alpha = 1.2 \cos 32 = 1.02^k$

Hem fir SG = .43

From the tables select 5/8" dia. x 4" long lag

W = .357 kli of effective thread penetration

$Z = 1.07^k$ (table with 1/4" stl side plate)

Ck lag bolt capacity

Obtain required values for Yield Equations

$t_s = .25$ in
$t_m = 9.25$ in
$F_{es} = 58000$ psi
$F_{em} = 4800$ psi
$D = .625$ in
$F_{yb} = 45$ ksi
$\theta_m = 0$

NDS T9A, 9.2A

Calc preliminary coefficients values

NDS 9.3.1

$$R_e = \frac{F_{em}}{F_{es}} = \frac{4800}{58000} = .0828$$

$$k = -1+\sqrt{\frac{2(1+R_e)}{R_e}+\frac{F_{yb}(2+R_e)D^2}{2F_{em}t_s^2}}$$

$$= -1+\sqrt{\frac{2(1+.0828)}{.0828}+\frac{(45000)(2+.0828)(.625)^2}{2(4800)(.25)^2}} = 8.337$$

$$K_\theta = 1+\frac{\theta}{360} = 1+\frac{0}{360} = 1.0$$

Calc Failure Equation Mode Values

Mode III_s

$$Z = \frac{kDt_sF_{em}}{2.8(2+R_e)K_\theta} = \frac{8.337(.625).25(4800)}{2.8(2+.0828)1.0} = 1072 \text{ lb}$$

Mode III_s Z = 1072 lb

Mode IV

$$Z = \frac{D^2}{3K_\theta}\sqrt{\frac{1.75F_{em}F_{yb}}{3(1+R_e)}} = \frac{(.625)^2}{3(1.0)}\sqrt{\frac{1.75(4800)45000}{3(1+.0828)}}$$

= 1405 lb

Mode IV Z = 1405 lb

The smallest value of the two is found in Mode III_s.

$Z = 1072$ lbs / bolt

Calc Z'

NDS 9.3.3

Penetration (assume 1/8" washer)

$p = L - t_s - t_{washer} - E = 4 - .25 - .125 - .40625$

$= 3.219$ "

$8D = 8(.625) = 5" > 3.219"$ **NG!**

$4D = 4(.625) = 2.5" < 3.219"$ √ reduction ok

$$C_d = \frac{p}{8D} = \frac{3.219}{5} = .64$$

NDS T7.3.1

$Z' = ZC_DC_MC_tC_gC_\Delta C_dC_{eg}$

$= 1.072(1.6).75(1.0)1.0(1.0).64(1.0)$

$= 828^k < 1.06^k$ **NG!**

try 6" long lag

$p = 5.219" > 8D = 5"$ √

$C_d = 1.0$

NDS T7.3.1

$Z' = ZC_DC_MC_tC_gC_\Delta C_dC_{eg}$

$= 1.072(1.6).75(1.0)1.0(1.0)1.0(1.0) = 1.287^k$

$P = NZ' = 1(1.287) = 1.287^k > 1.06^k$ √

$Z' = 1.287^k$

Calc W

$p_w = T - E = 3.094" < L - t_s - t_{washer}$

$6 - .25 - .125 = 5.625"$ √

All threads within main member.

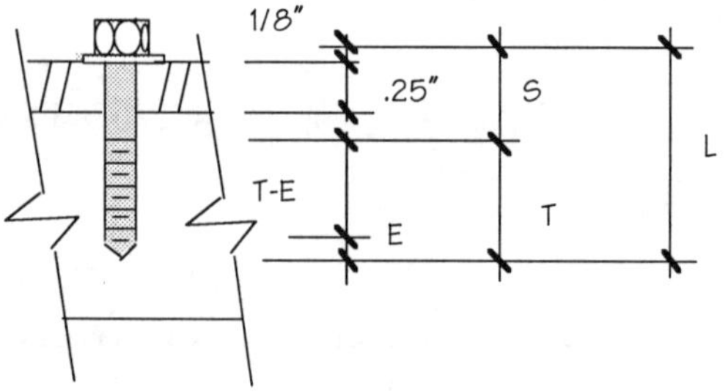

For DF-L, SG = .43

$w = .357$

$W = wp_w = .357(3.094) = 1.105^k$

$W = 1.105$ lbs / bolt

Calc W'

NDS T7.3.1

$W' = WC_DC_MC_tC_{eg} = 1.105(1.6).75(1.0)1.0 = 1.326^k$

$P = NZ' = 1(1.326) = 1.326^k > .64^k$ √

$W' = 1.326^k$

Use hankinson formula to calc Z'_α

NDS 9.3.5

Let $W' = W_p'$

$$Z'_\alpha = \frac{Z'W'}{Z'\sin^2\alpha + W'\cos^2\alpha}$$

$$= \frac{1.29(1.33)}{1.29\sin^2(32) + 1.33\cos^2(32)} = 1.3^k > 1.2^k \ \surd$$

Use 5/8 " dia. x 6 " long lag

The highest possible stage in moral culture is when we recognize that we ought to control our thoughts.

CHARLES DARWIN

PROBLEM 7.18

Shear plate continuity drag force connection.

Determine the maximum capacity of the continuity drag force connection shown below.

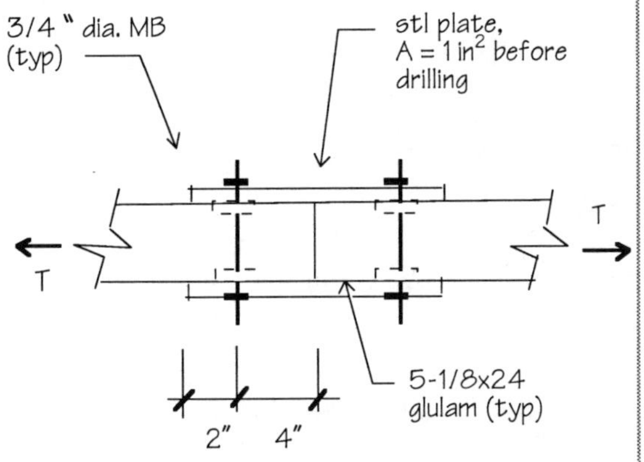

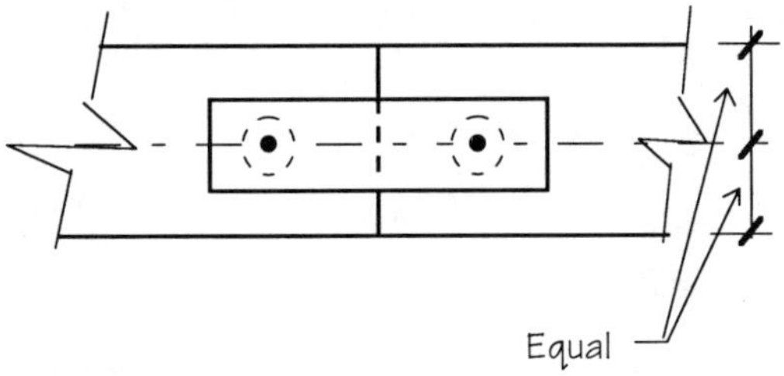

ASSUME

- Side plates, and glulam ok.
- 24F- V8 glulam.
- 2 5/8 in. shear plate with 3/4 in. dia. MB.
- EMC < 19%.
- Wind load.
- Building Dept. requires $C_D = 1.33$.

SOLUTION

Ck 4x8 tension capacity

24F - V8 has DF - DF laminations which implies Group B from NDS Table 10A.

$P_{tab} = 2.67^k$

$C_g = 1.0$ (one shear plate)

$C_\Delta = 1.0$ (NDS Table 10.3)

$C_{st} = 1.11$ (side plate factor NDS Table 10.2.4)

$P' = P C_D C_M C_t C_g C_\Delta C_{st} = 2.67(1.33)1.0(1.0)1.0(1.0)1.11$

$= 3.94^k$

$P = NP' = 2(3.94) = 7.88^k$

Capacity of connection = 7.88^k

> **Some people have greatness thrust upon them. Very few have excellence thrust upon them.**
>
> JOHN GARDNER

PROBLEM 7.19

Lag bolt connection of ledger to stud wall.

Determine the number of 5" long 3/8" dia. lag bolts that are required for the loft shown below.

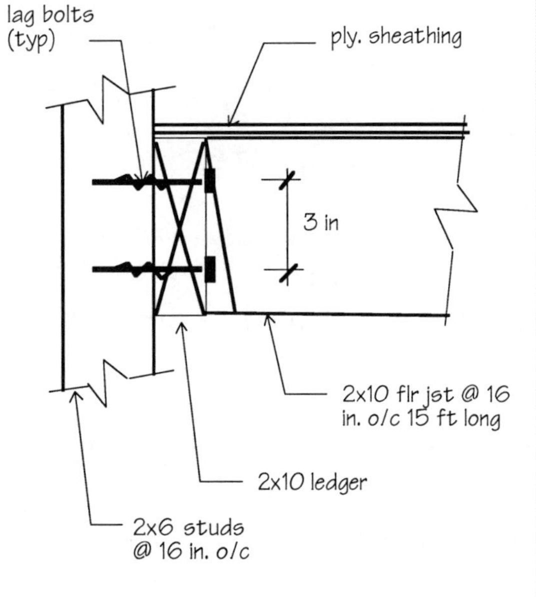

ASSUME

w_{TL} = .052 ksf.
All beams, studs, lag spacing and hardware ok.
DF-L No 2.
EMC < 16%.
D + L only.

SOLUTION

Calc load to ledger

$$w = \frac{.052(15)}{2} = .39 \text{ klf}$$

$$\text{load to stud} = .39\left(\frac{16}{12}\right) = .52^k$$

NDS T9A, 9.3A

Ck bolt capacity (assume 2 - lags per stud)

Obtain required values from NDS Table 9.3A

t_s = 1.5 in
t_m = 5.5 in
D = . 375 in
$\theta_m = 0$
$\theta_s = 90$

NDS 9.3.2

Z = 270 lbs / bolt

NDS 9.3.3

Calc Z′ (without group factor for trial number)

Penetration

$$p = L - t_s - t_{washer} - E = 5 - 1.5 - 0 - .219 = 3.28''$$

$$8D = 8(.375) = 3'' < 3.28'' \ \surd$$

NDS T7.3.1

$C_d = 1.0$

$$Z' = ZC_DC_MC_tC_gC_\Delta C_dC_{eg}$$

$$= .27(1.0)1.0(1.0)1.0(1.0)1.0(1.0) = .27^k$$

$N = P/Z' = .52/.27 = 1.9$ say 2 lag bolts

Group action factor

$$\gamma = 180000D^{1.5} = 180000(.375)^{1.5} = 41335$$

E_s = 1600000 psi

E_m = 1600000 psi

A_s = 13.88 in^2

A_m = 8.25 in^2

NDS 7.3.6

$$R_{ea} = \min\left[\frac{E_sA_s}{E_mA_m} \text{ or } \frac{E_mA_m}{E_sA_s}\right]$$

$$= \min\left[\frac{1600000(13.88)}{1600000(8.25)} \text{ or } \frac{1600000(8.25)}{1600000(13.88)}\right] = .594$$

$$u = 1+\gamma\left(\frac{s}{2}\right)\left(\frac{1}{E_mA_m}+\frac{1}{E_sA_s}\right)$$

$$= 1+41335\left(\frac{3}{2}\right)\left(\frac{1}{1600000(8.25)}+\frac{1}{1600000(13.88)}\right)$$

$$= 1.01$$

$$m = u-\sqrt{u^2-1} = 1.01-\sqrt{(1.01)^2-1} = .885$$

$$C_g = \left[\frac{m\left(1-m^{2n}\right)}{n\left[\left(1+R_{EA}m^n\right)(1+m)-1+m^{2n}\right]}\right]\left[\frac{1+R_{EA}}{1-m}\right]$$

$$= \left[\frac{.885\left(1-.885^{2(2)}\right)}{2\left[\left(1+.594(.885)^2\right)(1+.885)-1+(.885)^{2(2)}\right]}\right]\left[\frac{1+.594}{1-.885}\right]$$

$$= 1.0$$

NDS T7.3.1

$$Z' = ZC_DC_MC_tC_gC_\Delta C_dC_{eg}$$

$$= .27(1.0)1.0(1.0)1.0(1.0)1.0(1.0) = .27^k$$

$$P = NZ' = 2(.27) = .54^k > .52^k \ \surd$$

Use 2-3/8″ dia. x 5″ long lag bolts

□
□
□

The best thing about the future is that it comes only one day at a time.

ABRAHAM LINCOLN

PROBLEM 7.20

Bolted leaf truss connection.

Determine the bolt size for the forces in the leaf truss connection shown below using Yield Limit Equations.

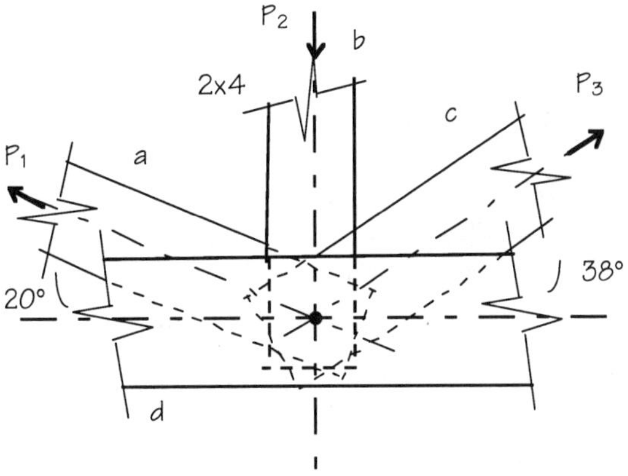

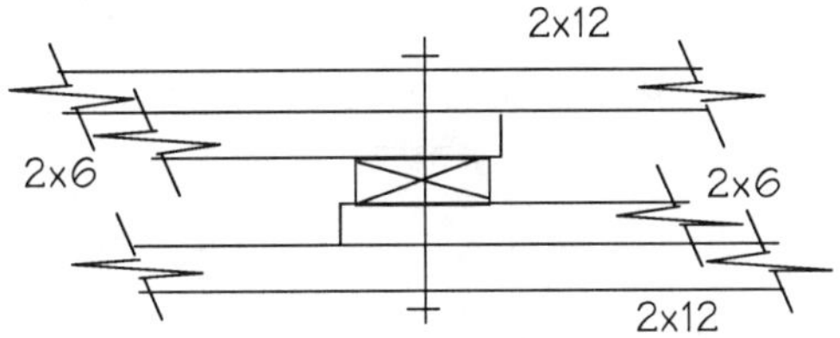

ASSUME

Roof loads.
$P_1 = .89^K$.
$P_2 = .98^K$.
$P_3 = 1.7^K$.
End and edge distance ok.
EMC < 16%..
DF-L No 1 grade.
A307 MB.
Buckling ok in post.
All adjustment factors equal 1.0.

SOLUTION

We have a 5 member connection with equal thickness and 4 shear planes. NDS Sec 8.4 states that the design value shall be based upon the lowest nominal design value of any single shear plane times the number of shear planes. In this problem we must examine 4 cases, then select the lowest value and multiply it by 4

Shear plane ad

Since we must assume a trial bolt at each shear plane (to obtain the nominal value), try 1/2 in o/c. This assumes a iterative process.

Obtain required values for Yield Equations

NDS T8A, 8.2A

$D = .5$ in
$F_{yb} = 45$ ksi
$t_s = 1.5$ in
$t_m = 1.5$ in
$\theta_s = 0$
$\theta_m = 20$
$F_{em} = 5133$ psi
$F_{es} = 5600$ psi

Calc preliminary coefficients values

$$F_{e\theta} = \frac{F_{e//} F_{e\perp}}{F_{e//} \sin^2\theta + F_{e\perp}\cos^2\theta} = 5132.99 \text{ psi} = F_{em}$$

NDS 8.2.1

$$R_e = \frac{F_{em}}{F_{es}} = .9166$$

$$R_t = \frac{t_m}{t_s} = 1.0$$

$$k_1 = \frac{\sqrt{R_e + 2R_e^2\left(1+R_t+R_t^2\right)+R_t^2R_e^3} - R_e(1+R_t)}{(1+R_e)}$$

$= .3968$

$$k_2 = -1 + \sqrt{2(1+R_e) + \frac{2F_{yb}(1+2R_e)D^2}{3F_{em}t_m^2}} = 1.3818$$

$$k_3 = -1 + \sqrt{\frac{2(1+R_e)}{R_e} + \frac{2F_{yb}(2+R_e)D^2}{3F_{em}t_s^2}} = 1.465$$

Calc Failure Equation Mode Values

Mode I_m Z = 912 lb
Mode I_s Z = 995 lb
Mode II Z = 439 lb
Mode III_m Z = 556 lb
Mode III_s Z = 572 lb
Mode IV Z = 663 lb

The smallest value of the four is found in Mode II.

Z = 439 lbs / bolt

NDS T8A, 8.2A

Shear plane cd

Obtain required values for Yield Equations

$D = .5$ in
$F_{yb} = 45$ ksi
$t_s = 1.5$ in
$t_m = 1.5$ in
$\theta_s = 0$
$\theta_m = 38$
$F_{em} = 4325$ psi
$F_{es} = 5600$psi

NDS 8.2.1

Calc preliminary coefficients values

$$F_{e\theta} = \frac{F_{e//}F_{e\perp}}{F_{e//}\sin^2\theta + F_{e\perp}\cos^2\theta} = 4324.97 \text{ psi}$$

$$R_e = \frac{F_{em}}{F_{es}} = .7723$$

$$R_t = \frac{t_m}{t_s} = 1.0$$

$$k_1 = \frac{\sqrt{R_e + 2R_e^2(1+R_t+R_t^2) + R_t^2R_e^3} - R_e(1+R_t)}{(1+R_e)}$$

$= .3662$

$$k_2 = -1 + \sqrt{2(1+R_e) + \frac{2F_{yb}(1+2R_e)D^2}{3F_{em}t_m^2}} = 1.3464$$

$$k_3 = -1 + \sqrt{\frac{2(1+R_e)}{R_e} + \frac{2F_{yb}(2+R_e)D^2}{3F_{em}t_s^2}} = 1.5935$$

Calc Failure Equation Mode Values

Mode I_m Z = 734 lb
Mode I_s Z = 950 lb
Mode II Z = 386 lb
Mode III_m Z = 485 lb
Mode III_s Z = 527 lb
Mode IV Z = 605 lb

The smallest value of the four is found in Mode II.

Z = 386 lbs / bolt

NDS T8A, 8.2A

Shear plane ab

Obtain required values for Yield Equations

$D = .5$ in
$F_{yb} = 45$ ksi
$t_s = 1.5$ in
$t_m = 1.5$ in
$\theta_s = 0$
$\theta_m = 70$
$F_{em} = 3320$ psi
$F_{es} = 5600$ psi

NDS 8.2.1

Calc preliminary coefficients values

$$F_{e\theta} = \frac{F_{e//}F_{e\perp}}{F_{e//}\sin^2\theta + F_{e\perp}\cos^2\theta} = 3319.91 \text{ psi}$$

$$R_e = \frac{F_{em}}{F_{es}} = .5928$$

$$R_t = \frac{t_m}{t_s} = 1.0$$

$$k_1 = \frac{\sqrt{R_e + 2R_e^2(1+R_t+R_t^2) + R_t^2R_e^3} - R_e(1+R_t)}{(1+R_e)}$$

$= .3266$

$$k_2 = -1 + \sqrt{2(1+R_e) + \frac{2F_{yb}(1+2R_e)D^2}{3F_{em}t_m^2}} = 1.3195$$

$$k_3 = -1 + \sqrt{\frac{2(1+R_e)}{R_e} + \frac{2F_{yb}(2+R_e)D^2}{3F_{em}t_s^2}} = 1.8243$$

Calc Failure Equation Mode Values

Mode I_m Z = 521 lb
Mode I_s Z = 879 lb
Mode II Z = 319 lb
Mode III_m Z = 393lb
Mode III_s Z = 458 lb
Mode IV Z = 517 lb

The smallest value of the four is found in Mode II.

Z = 319 lbs / bolt

<u>Shear plane cb</u>

Obtain required values for Yield Equations

NDS T8A, 8.2A

D = .5 in
F_{yb} = 45 ksi
t_s = 1.5 in
t_m = 1.5 in
$\theta_s = 0$
$\theta_m = 52$
F_{em} = 3776 psi
F_{es} = 5600 psi

Calc preliminary coefficients values

NDS 8.2.1

$$F_{e\theta} = \frac{F_{e//}F_{e\perp}}{F_{e//}\sin^2\theta + F_{e\perp}\cos^2\theta} = 3776.21 \text{ psi}$$

$$R_e = \frac{F_{em}}{F_{es}} = .6743$$

$$R_t = \frac{t_m}{t_s} = 1.0$$

$$k_1 = \frac{\sqrt{R_e + 2R_e^2\left(1+R_t+R_t^2\right)+R_t^2R_e^3} - R_e(1+R_t)}{(1+R_e)}$$

$= .3448$

$$k_2 = -1 + \sqrt{2(1+R_e) + \frac{2F_{yb}(1+2R_e)D^2}{3F_{em}t_m^2}} = 1.3285$$

$$k_3 = -1 + \sqrt{\frac{2(1+R_e)}{R_e} + \frac{2F_{yb}(2+R_e)D^2}{3F_{em}t_s^2}} = 1.7068$$

Calc Failure Equation Mode Values

Mode I_m Z = 619 lb
Mode I_s Z = 917 lb
Mode II Z = 351 lb
Mode III_m Z = 437 lb
Mode III_s Z = 494 lb
Mode IV Z = 562 lb

The smallest value of the four is found in Mode II.

Z = 351 lbs / bolt

Calc nominal bolt value (members a,b,c)

The least value of the 4 is = .319^k

nominal bolt value = 4(.319) = 1.28^k > 1.07^k √

1/2 in. MB ok for members a,b,c

Calc nominal bolt value (members d)

Resolve forces at joint

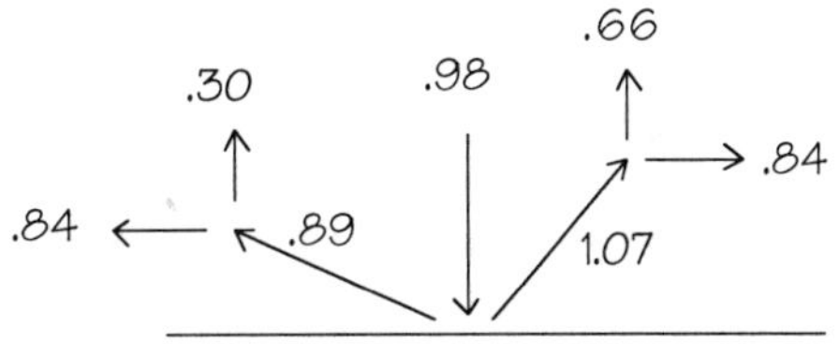

Note that the load comes into the joint in an unbalanced manner. This causes eccentric loading and hence creates couples member d.

Horizontal couple:

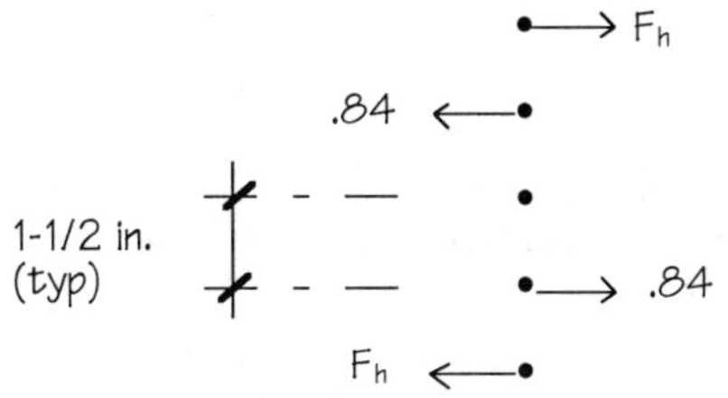

$$Fh = \frac{3(.84)}{6} = .42^k$$

Vertical couple:

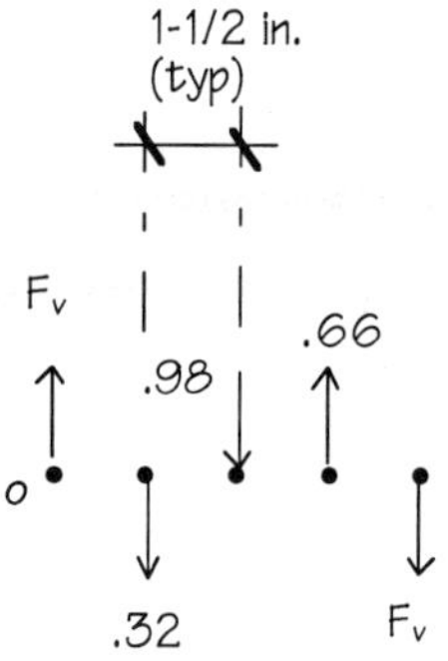

$$\sum M_o = 1.5(.32) + 3(.98) - 4.5(.66) - 6F_v$$

$$F_v = \frac{.45}{6} = .075^k$$

1/2 in. MB ok for members d

Although this problem does not require checking the wood member capacity, it is required to design the joint.

No man chooses evil because it is evil, he only mistakes it for happiness, the good he seeks.

MARY WOLLSTONECRAFT

PROBLEM 7.21

Moment splice for beam.

Design the moment connection shown below.

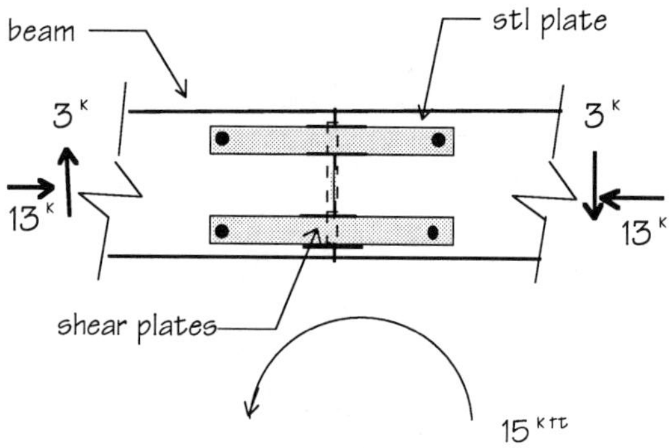

ASSUME

- DF-L No 1.
- A307 MB.
- A36 stl.
- EMC < 19%.
- Roof D + L load only.
- Neglect deflection.
- Full lateral support.
- Beam column ok.

SOLUTION

Moment connections are rarely used because of the manufacturing capabilities of glulam beams. If this type of connection is required it must be capable of resisting the potential forces of moments, shears, uplift, axial and stress reversals. The moment connection must also be capable of holding the alignment of the joint. Tight tolerances for installation are required to reduce inelastic deformation (slip). If the forces and members are small, plywood splice plates with glue, nails or bolts may be used for moment connections.

Member properties

10x16 (9.5x15.5)

$A = 147.3 \text{ in}^2$

$S = 380.4 \text{ in}^3$

$I = 2948 \text{ in}^4$

$F_b = 1.35$ ksi

$F_t = .675$ ksi

$F_v = .085$ ksi

$F_{c\perp} = .625$ ksi

$F_c = .925$ ksi

E = 1.6e3 ksi

Assume continuous member

$$f_c = \frac{P}{A} = \frac{13}{147.3} = .088 \text{ ksi}$$

$$C_F = \left(\frac{12}{d}\right)^{1/9} = \left(\frac{12}{15.5}\right)^{1/9} = .97$$

NDS T2.3.1

$$F_c' = F_c C_D C_M C_t C_F C_p$$

$$= .925(1.25).97 = 1.12 \text{ ksi} > .088 \text{ ksi } \checkmark$$

$$f_c = \frac{M}{S} = \frac{15(12)}{380.4} = .473 \text{ ksi}$$

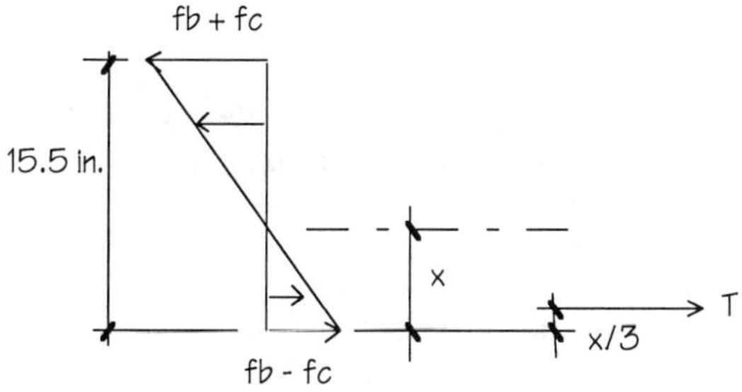

$$fb + fc = .473 + .088 = .561 \text{ ksi}$$

$$fb - fc = .473 - .088 = .385 \text{ ksi}$$

$$x = \frac{15.5(.385)}{.561+.385} = 6.31 \text{ in.}$$

x/3 = 2.1 in.

$$T = \frac{.385(6.31)}{2} = 1.21^k$$

Try 3/4 in dia. bolts using NDS Table 8.3 and 1/4 in. stl. side plates.

$3.17(1.25) = 3.96^k < 1.21^k$

$1.21^k < 4.65^k$ for simpson HST3 (with 3-3/4 bolts)

Because of potential stress reversals and handling stresses use same hardware at top of beam.

> Use Simpson HST3 with one 3/4 in. dia. bolt each side, top and bott. of beam.

Shear plates

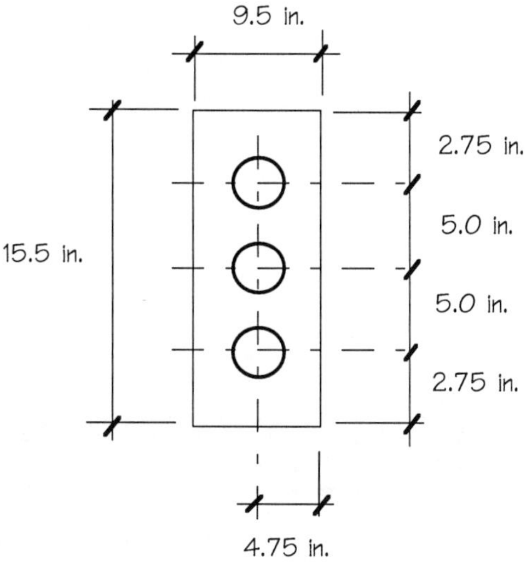

Preliminary values

NDS T8A, 8.2A

With square end cut surface (NDS eq. 10.2-2)

$Q_{90}' = .6\,Q'$

$Q = 1.99^k$ (NDS Table 10.2B)

$Q' = QC_D.6 = 1.99(1.25).6 = 1.49^k$

shear plates required = 3/1.49 = 2.01 try 3

The spacing requirements (NDS Table 10.3) for full values of C_Δ are:

unloaded edge = 1.75 in. < 2.75 in. √

loaded edge = 2.75 in. = 2.75 in. √

spacing = 4.25 in. < 5.0 in. √

Calc $C_\Delta = 1.0$

Use NDS Table 7.3.6B for $C_g = .87$

$Q' = QC_DC_MC_tC_g C_\Delta C_d$

$= 1.99(1.25).87(.6) = 1.3^k$

3 plates = $3(1.3) = 3.9^k > 3^k$ √

Dowel length

Use standard penetration (NDS Table 10.2.3) for 3/4 in. dia. lags plus 1 in.

penn. =(5(.75) +1)2 = 9.5 in.

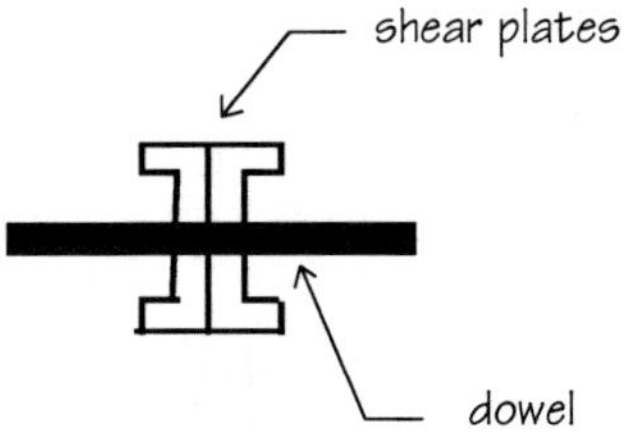

Use 3- 2-5/8 in. dia. shear plates with 3/4 in dia. 9.5 in. long dowels.

Inelastic deformation (slip) can be eased by using a bolted tension connection as shown below. By tightening the bolts we can help to eliminate the initial slip in the connection. The amount of tightening is based upon actual movement during the tighten process.

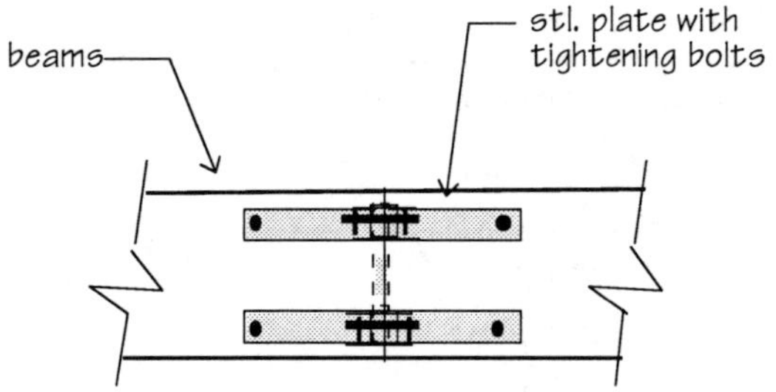

People are always blaming their circumstances for what the are. I don't believe in circumstances. The people who get on in this world are the people who get up and look for the circumstances they want, and, if they can't find them, make them.

GEORGE BERNARD SHAW

8. Horizontal Diaphragm to Shearwall Connections, Subdiaphragms and Continuity

○ PROBLEM 8.1

Tilt-up concrete wall ledger to timber roof diaphragm connection configuration.

Determine if the connection is adequate for the forces shown below.

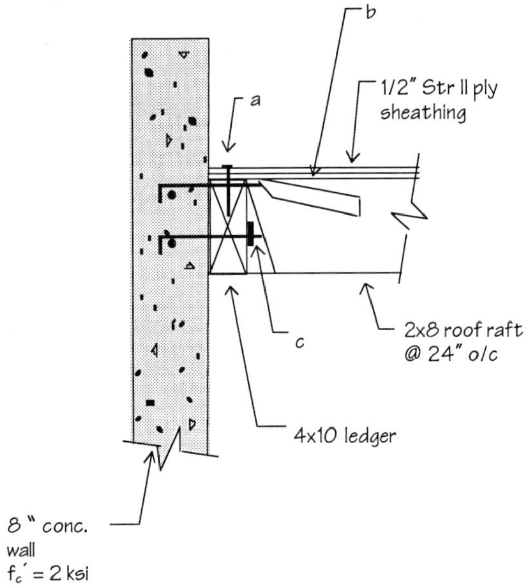

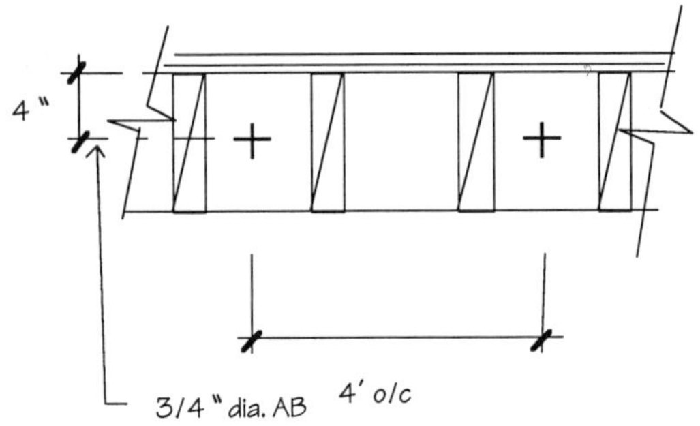

ASSUME

DF-L lumber.
EMC <19%.
Common nails.
Blocked diaphragms.
$C_D = 1.33$.
$v_{diaph} = .35$ klf.
$v_{\perp wall} = .2$ klf (code min.).
$w_{DL} = .048$ klf (along ledger).
$w_{LL} = .08$ klf (along ledger).
Ledger ok.
Rafter ok.
Neglect chord forces.

SOLUTION

We need to look at two separate load cases, DL + LL and DL + Lateral. It is believed that by looking element by element rather than case by case, the readers understanding will be broadened and the case will be easier to follow.

a. Diaphragm nailing (UBC case 3)

$v_{diaph} = .35$ klf < .36 klf √

> Use 1/2" Str II EXP 1 plywood with 8D @ 4" o/c, boundary and continuous edges 6" o/c, other edges, 12" o/c, field

b. Wall anchor

Assume the section is not in center half of a flexible diaphragm wall.

$v_{\perp wall} = .2$ klf

Assume anchors at 4' o/c.

$P = .2(4) = .8^k$ < prefab

> Use manufacturers anchor at 4' o/c (every other rafter)

c. Ledger bolts

Ck DL + LL case (bolt in conc.)

Assume 3/4" dia. AB with 5" min. embedment.

$w_{DL+LL} = .048 + .08 = .128$ klf

$P_{DL+LL} = 4(.128) = .512^k$

UBC T19-E

NDS T8A, 8.2A

$P_{all} = 2.94^k > .512^k$ √

Ck DL + LL case (bolt in ledger)

Per NDS 8.2.3, $t_m = 2t_s$, and $F_{em} = F_{es}$

Values for Yield Equations

$t_s = 3.5$ in
$t_m = 7.0$ in
$F_{es} = 2600$ psi
$F_{em} = 2600$ psi
$D = .75$ in
$F_{yb} = 45$ ksi
$\theta_s = 90$

Calc preliminary coefficients values

$$R_e = \frac{F_{em}}{F_{es}} = \frac{2600}{2600} = 1.0$$

$$R_t = \frac{t_m}{t_s} = \frac{7.0}{3.5} = 2.0$$

NDS 8.2.1

$$k_1 = \frac{\sqrt{R_e + 2R_e^2\left(1 + R_t + R_t^2\right) + R_t^2 R_e^3} - R_e(1 + R_t)}{(1 + R_e)}$$

$$= \frac{\sqrt{1.0 + 2(1.0)^2\left(1 + 2.0 + (2.0)^2\right) + (2.0)^2(1.0)^3} - 1.0(1 + 2.0)}{(1 + 1.0)}$$

$= .6794$

$$k_2 = -1 + \sqrt{2(1 + R_e) + \frac{2F_{yb}(1 + 2R_e)D^2}{3F_{em}t_m^2}}$$

$$= -1 + \sqrt{2(1 + 1.0) + \frac{2(45000)(1 + 2(1.0))(.75)^2}{3(2600)(7.0)^2}} = 1.097$$

$$k_3 = -1 + \sqrt{\frac{2(1 + R_e)}{R_e} + \frac{2F_{yb}(2 + R_e)D^2}{3F_{em}t_s^2}}$$

$$= -1 + \sqrt{\frac{2(1 + 1.0)}{1.0} + \frac{2(45000)(2 + 1.0)(7.5)^2}{3(2600)(3.5)^2}} = 1.364$$

Calc Failure Equation Mode Values

Mode I_m

$$Z = \frac{Dt_mF_{em}}{4K_\theta} = \frac{.75(3.5)2600}{4(1.25)} = 2730 \text{ lb}$$

Mode I_m Z = 2730 lb

Mode I_s

$$Z = \frac{Dt_sF_{es}}{4K_\theta} = \frac{.75(3.5)2600}{4(1.25)} = 1365 \text{ lb}$$

Mode I_s Z = 1365 lb

Mode II

$$Z = \frac{k_1Dt_sF_{es}}{3.6K_\theta} = \frac{.6794(.75)3.5(2600)}{3.6(1.25)} = 1030 \text{ lb}$$

Mode II_m Z = 1030 lb

Mode III_m

$$Z = \frac{k_2Dt_mF_{em}}{3.2(1 + 2R_e)K_\theta} = \frac{1.097(.75)7.0(26000)}{3.2(1 + 2(1.0))1.25} = 1248 \text{ lb}$$

Mode III_m Z = 1248 lb

Mode III_s

$$Z = \frac{k_3Dt_sF_{em}}{3.2(2 + R_e)K_\theta} = \frac{1.264(.75)3.5(2600)}{3.2(2 + 1.0)1.25} = 776 \text{ lb}$$

Mode III_s Z = 776 lb

Mode IV

$$Z = \frac{D^2}{3.2K_\theta}\sqrt{\frac{2F_{em}F_{yb}}{3(1 + R_e)}} = \frac{(.75)^2}{3.2(1.25)}\sqrt{\frac{2(2600)450000}{3(1 + 1.0)}}$$

$= 878$ lb

Mode IV Z = 878 lb

The smallest value of the six is found in Mode III_s.

Z = 776 lbs / bolt

Calc Z′

NDS T7.3.1

$Z' = ZC_DC_MC_tC_gC_\Delta = .776(1.25)1.0(1.0)1.0(1.0)$

$= .970^k > .512^k$ √

3/4" dia. AB ok for DL + LL case.

Ck DL + Lateral case (bolt in conc.)

$P_{DL} = .048(4) = .192$ k/bolt

$v_{ll} = .35(4) = 1.4$ k/bolt

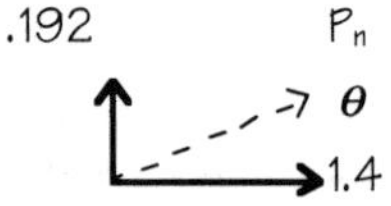

$\theta = \tan^{-1}(.192/1.4) = 7.81$

$P_n = \sqrt{(.192)^2+(1.4)^2} = 1.41^k < P_{all\,conc} = 2.94^k$

Ck DL + Lateral case (bolt in ledger)

Per NDS 8.2.3, $t_m = 2t_s$, and $F_{em} = F_{es}$

Values for Yield Equations

NDS 8.2.1

Same as above except the angle.

$\theta_s = 7.81$

Calc preliminary coefficients values

$$F_{e\theta} = \frac{F_{e\parallel}F_{e\perp}}{F_{e\parallel}\sin^2\theta + F_{e\perp}\cos^2\theta}$$

$$= \frac{5600(2600)}{5600\sin^2(7.81)+2600\cos^2(7.81)} = 5483 \text{ psi} = F_{em}$$

$$R_e = \frac{F_{em}}{F_{es}} = \frac{5483}{5483} = 1.0$$

$$K_\theta = 1+\frac{\theta}{360} = 1+\frac{7.81}{360} = 1.02$$

$$R_t = \frac{t_m}{t_s} = \frac{7.0}{3.5} = 2.0$$

$$k_1 = \frac{\sqrt{R_e+2R_e^2\left(1+R_t+R_t^2\right)+R_t^2R_e^3} - R_e(1+R_t)}{(1+R_e)}$$

$$= \frac{\sqrt{1.0+2(1.0)^2\left(1+2.0+(2.0)^2\right)+(2.0)^2(1.0)^3} - 1.0(1+2.0)}{(1+1.0)}$$

$= .6794$

$$k_2 = -1+\sqrt{2(1+R_e)+\frac{2F_{yb}(1+2R_e)D^2}{3F_{em}t_m^2}}$$

$$= -1+\sqrt{2(1+1.0)+\frac{2(45000)(1+2(1.0))(.75)^2}{3(5483)(7.0)^2}} = 1.047$$

$$k_3 = -1+\sqrt{\frac{2(1+R_e)}{R_e}+\frac{2F_{yb}(2+R_e)D^2}{3F_{em}t_s^2}}$$

$$= -1+\sqrt{\frac{2(1+1.0)}{1.0}+\frac{2(45000)(2+1.0)(.75)^2}{3(5483)(3.5)^2}} = 1.18$$

Calc Failure Equation Mode Values

Mode I_m

$$Z = \frac{Dt_mF_{em}}{4K_\theta} = \frac{.75(7.0)5483}{4(1.02)} = 7044 \text{ lb}$$

Mode I_m Z = 7044 lb

Mode I_s

$$Z = \frac{Dt_sF_{es}}{4K_\theta} = \frac{.75(3.5)5483}{4(1.02)} = 3522 \text{ lb}$$

Mode I_s Z = 3522 lb

Mode II

$$Z = \frac{k_1Dt_sF_{es}}{3.6K_\theta} = \frac{.6794(.75)3.5(5483)}{3.6(1.02)} = 2659 \text{ lb}$$

Mode II Z = 2659 lb

Mode III_m

$$Z = \frac{k_2Dt_mF_{em}}{3.2(1+2R_e)K_\theta} = \frac{1.047(.75)7.0(5483)}{3.2(1+2(1.0))1.02} = 3072 \text{ lb}$$

Mode III_m Z = 3072 lb

Mode III_s

$$Z = \frac{k_3 D t_s F_{em}}{3.2(2+R_e)K_\theta} = \frac{1.18(.75)3.5(5483)}{3.2(2+1.0)1.02} = 1732 \text{ lb}$$

Mode III_s Z = 1732 lb

Mode IV

$$Z = \frac{D^2}{3.2K_\theta}\sqrt{\frac{2F_{em}F_{yb}}{3(1+R_e)}} = \frac{(.75)^2}{3.2(1.02)}\sqrt{\frac{2(5483)45000}{3(1+1.0)}}$$

= 1560 lb

Mode IV Z = 1560 lb

The smallest value of the six is found in Mode IV.

Z = 1560 lbs / bolt

Calc Z´

NDS 8.2.1

$$Z' = ZC_DC_MC_tC_gC_\Delta = 1.560(1.6)1.0(1.0)1.0(1.0)$$

$$= 2.497^k > 1.41^k \quad \surd$$

Use 3/4 " dia. AB at 48 " o/c

All men should try to learn before they die what they are running from, want, and why.

JAMES THURBER

O PROBLEM 8.2

Shear transfer from 2-nd story shearwall thru floor diaphragm to 1st floor shearwall.

Determine the connective anchorage for the detail and forces shown below.

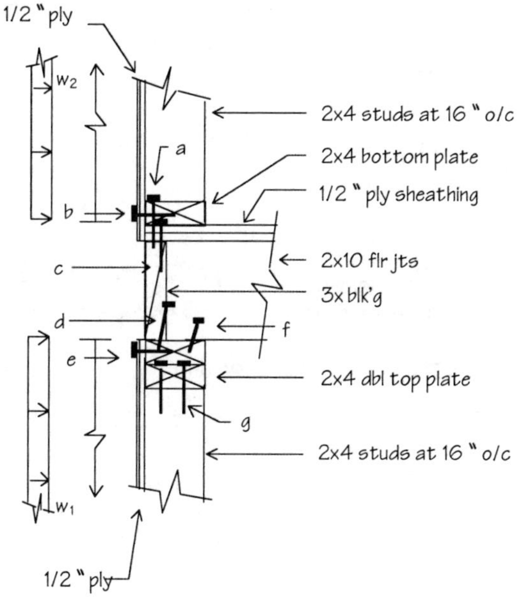

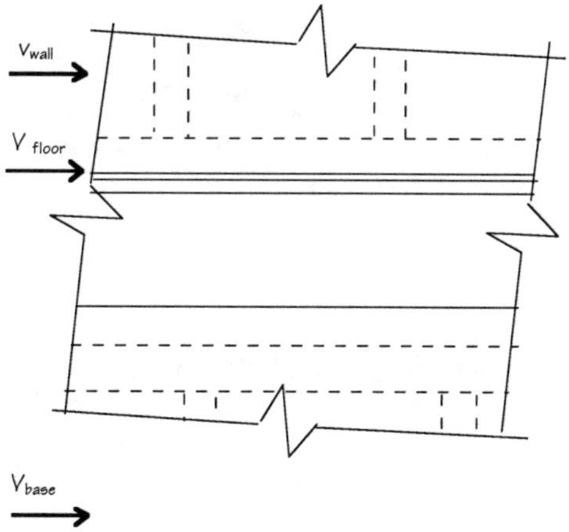

ASSUME

v_{wall} = .18 klf.
v_{flr}= .24 klf.
v_{base}= .47 klf.
w = .183W (seismic).
Wind = 20 psf.
Wt. of walls = .016 psf.
DF-L lumber.
EMC <19%.
Common nails.
Field nailing ok for all loads.

SOLUTION

Shear Transfer parallel to wall

b. 2nd flr shearwall nailing

UBC T23-I-K-1

v_{wall} = .18 klf < .26 klf √

Use 15/32 C-D EXP 1 plywood
8D @ 6" o/c and 12" o/c field

a. v_{wall} transfer into blocking

v_{wall} = .18 klf

t_s = 1.5 + .5 = 2.0" try 16d

Required values for Yield Equations

NDS T12A, 12.3B

ℓ = 3.5 in
t_s =2.0 in
t_m = 9.25 in
F_{es} = 4650 psi
F_{em} = 4650 psi
D = .162 in
F_{yb} = 90 ksi
K_D = 2.2 since D <.17 in

$p = \ell - t_s \le t_m = 3.5 - 2 \le t_m = 1.5 \text{ in} < t_m$ √

12D = 12(.162) = 1.94 in > 1.5 in NG!

min. penetration NG use C_d =

$p/12D$ when $6D \le p < 12D$ min.

$C_d = 1.5/12(.162) = .77$

Calc preliminary coefficients values

$$R_e = \frac{F_{em}}{F_{es}} = \frac{4650}{4650} = 1.0$$

NDS 12.3.1

$$k_1 = -1+\sqrt{2(1+R_e)+\frac{2F_{yb}(1+2R_e)D^2}{3F_{em}p^2}}$$

$$= -1+\sqrt{2(1+1.0)+\frac{2(90000)(1+2(1.0))(.162)^2}{3(4650)(1.5)^2}} = 1.1099$$

$$k_2 = -1+\sqrt{\frac{2(1+R_e)}{R_e}+\frac{2F_{yb}(2+R_e)D^2}{3F_{em}t_s^2}}$$

$$= -1+\sqrt{\frac{2(1+1.0)}{1.0}+\frac{2(90000)(2+1.0)(.162)^2}{3(4650)(1.5)^2}} = 1.063$$

Calc Failure Equation Mode Values

Mode I_s

$$Z = \frac{Dt_sF_{es}}{K_D} = \frac{.162(1.5)4650}{2.2} = 685 \text{ lb}$$

Mode I_s Z = 685 lb

Mode III_m

$$Z = \frac{k_1DpF_{em}}{K_D(1+2R_e)} = \frac{1.109(.162)1.5(4650)}{2.2(1+2(1.0))} = 190 \text{ lb}$$

Mode III_m Z =190 lb

Mode III_s

$$Z = \frac{k_2Dt_sF_{em}}{K_D(2+R_e)} = \frac{1.063(.162)1.5(4650)}{2.2(2+1.0)} = 243 \text{ lb}$$

Mode III_s Z = 243 lb

Mode IV

$$Z = \frac{D^2}{K_D}\sqrt{\frac{2F_{em}F_{yb}}{3(1+R_e)}} = \frac{(.162)^2}{2.2}\sqrt{\frac{2(4650)900000}{3(1+1.0)}}$$
= 141 lb

Mode IV Z = 141 lb

The smallest value of the four is found in Mode IV.

Z = 141 lbs / nail

Verify C_D = 1.6 for wind or seismic with local building department.

Calc Z´

NDS 12.3.5, T7.3.1

$C_{eg} = .67$

$Z' =$

$ZC_DC_MC_tC_dC_{eg}C_{di}C_{tn} = .141(1.6)(1.0)1.0(.77)1.0(1.0)1.0$

$= .174^k$

$$16d_{spc'g} = Z'/v_{wall} = \frac{.174}{\left(.18/12\right)} = 11.6 \text{ in}/16d$$

say 8 " o/c consv.

Use 16d at 8 " o/c to transfer unit shear into blocking

c. Diaphragm shear transfer into blocking

UBC T23-I-J-1

v_{flr}= .24 klf < .27 klf √

Use 15/32 C-D EXP 1 plywood 8D @ 6,6,12

d. Shear transfer form block to top plate

$v = v_{wall} + v_{flr}$ = .18 + .24 = .42 klf

NDS 12.2.3

Try 16d toe nailed.

Required values for Yield Equations

ℓ = 3.5 in

$$t_s = \frac{\ell}{3} = 1.17 \text{ in}$$

NDS T12A, 12.3.3

t_m = 1.5 in

F_{es} = 4650 psi

F_{em} = 4650 psi

D = .162 in

F_{yb} = 90 ksi

K_D = 2.2 since D <.17 in

NDS 12.3.4

$p_L = \ell \cos 30 - t_s$ = 1.86 in > t_m = 1.5 in

use p_L = 1.5 in

12D = 12(.162) = 1.94 in > 1.5 in **NG!**

min. penetration ok use

$C_d = p/12D$ when $6D \le p < 12D$ min

$$C_d = \frac{1.5}{1.94} = .77$$

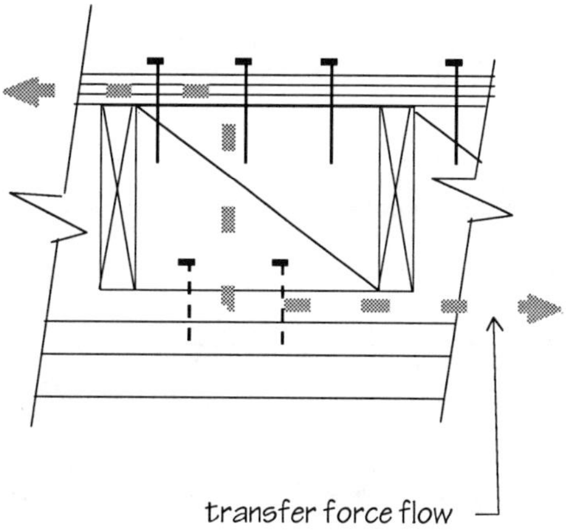

Calc preliminary coefficients values

NDS 12.3.1

$$R_e = \frac{F_{em}}{F_{es}} = \frac{4650}{4650} = 1.0$$

$$k_1 = -1 + \sqrt{2(1+R_e) + \frac{2F_{yb}(1+2R_e)D^2}{3F_{em}p^2}}$$

$$= -1 + \sqrt{2(1+1.0) + \frac{2(90000)(1+2(1.0))(.162)^2}{3(4650)(1.5)^2}} = 1.109$$

$$k_2 = -1 + \sqrt{\frac{2(1+R_e)}{R_e} + \frac{2F_{yb}(2+R_e)D^2}{3F_{em}t_s^2}}$$

$$= -1 + \sqrt{\frac{2(1+1.0)}{1.0} + \frac{2(90000)(2+1.0)(.162)^2}{3(4650)(1.17)^2}}$$

$= 1.179$

Calc Failure Equation Mode Values

Mode I_s

$$Z = \frac{Dt_sF_{es}}{K_D} = \frac{.162(1.17)4650}{2.2} = 399\text{ lb}$$

Mode I_s Z = 399 lb

Mode III_m

$$Z = \frac{k_1DpF_{em}}{K_D(1+2R_e)} = \frac{1.109(.162)1.5(4650)}{2.2(1+2(1.0))} = 190\text{ lb}$$

Mode III_m Z = 190 lb

Mode III_s

$$Z = \frac{k_2Dt_sF_{em}}{K_D(2+R_e)} = \frac{1.179(.162)1.17(4650)}{2.2(2+1.0)} = 157\text{ lb}$$

Mode III_s Z = 157 lb

Mode IV

$$Z = \frac{D^2}{K_D}\sqrt{\frac{2F_{em}F_{yb}}{3(1+R_e)}} = \frac{(.162)^2}{2.2}\sqrt{\frac{2(4650)900000}{3(1+1.0)}}$$

= .141 lb

Mode IV Z = .141 lb

The smallest value of the four is found in Mode IV

Z = 141 lbs / nail

Calc Z′

Verify C_D = 1.6 for wind or seismic with local building department. C_{tn} = .83

NDS T7.3.1

$Z' = ZC_DC_MC_tC_dC_{eg}C_{di}C_{tn}$

=.141(1.6)(1.0)1.0(.77)1.0(.83)

= $.144^k$

$$16d_{spc'g} = Z'/v = \frac{.144}{(.42/12)} = 4.1\text{ in/16d}$$

$$\#/blk = \frac{1.33(.42)}{.144} = 3.9 \text{ say 4/ blk}$$

Use 4-16d (toe nailed) at each block to transfer unit shear into top plate

e. Shear transfer and v_{base} for shearwall

v_{base}= .47 klf <.43 klf

UBC T23-I-K-1

Use 15/32 Str 1 plywood with 10d @ 4,6,12

Shear Transfer perpendicular to wall

Calc force

$$v_{wind} = \frac{wl}{2} = \frac{.02(10)}{2} = .1\text{ klf}$$

$$v_{seismic} = \frac{wl}{2} = \frac{.183(.016)10}{2} = .015\text{ klf} < .1\text{ klf}$$

Wind governs at .1 klf

a. perpendicular shear transfer

Perpendicular load transfer into diaphragm via stud to sole plate to plywood diaphragm. UBC minimum nailing Table 23-I-Q stipulates 4-8d toenailed or 2-16d end nailed from stud to sole plate. See Chapter 6, UBC Table 23-I-Q nailing schedule problem.

$Z = .141^k > 1.33(.1) = .133^k$ √ (without adjustments)

And the UBC minimum nailing Table 23-I-Q stipulates 16d at 16" o/c for sole plate to joist or blocking. This minimum may appear to work thus:

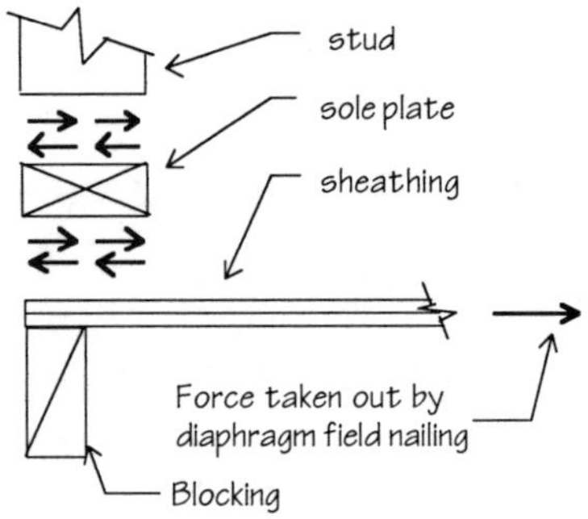

A conservative approach is to assume that the blocking acts like the main (locking) member and the plywood and the soleplate acts as the side member. The penetration is thus:

$p = 3.5 - (1.5 + .5) = 1.5$ in

$Z' = .141(1.6).77 = .174^k > 1.33(.1) = .133^k$ √

> Use 16d at 16 in o/c

g. Perpendicular load transfer

top plate to stud, UBC min. 2-16d,

end nail Z (without adjustment)= $.141^k > .133^k$ √

Dbl top plate, UBC min. 16d @ 16 " o/c,

face nail Z (without adjustment)
= .13 k /ft < .1 k/ft √

> Use UBC min. nailing requirements 2-16d end nailed at top plate to stud and 16d @ 16 " o/c at dbl. top plate connections.

f. load transfer top plate to joist

$V_r = .1(16/12) = .133^k$

UBC min. nailing is 3-8d

Z (without adjustment) = $.141^k > .133^k$ √

> Use 3-8d toenailed at each joist

Don't play for safety - It's the most dangerous thing in the world.

HUGH WALPOLE

PROBLEM 8.3

Shear transfer through roof diaphragm overhang 1st-floor shearwall configuration.

Determine the lateral capacity of the connective anchorage for the detail shown below. Force may move both in and out of plane.

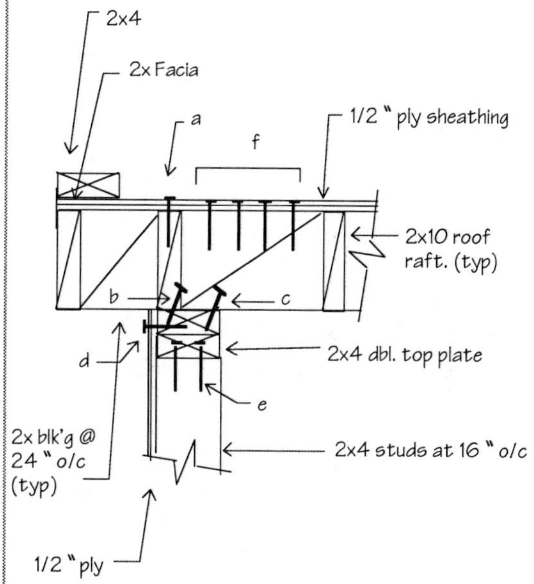

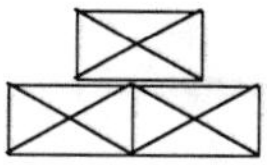
blocked diaphragm

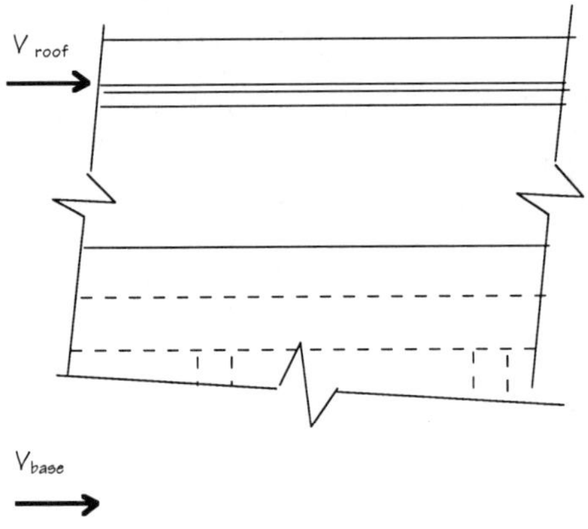

ASSUME

DF-L lumber.
EMC <19%.
Common nails.
Blocked diaphragms.
C_D = 1.33.
a. 10d @ 6,6,12.
b. 10d @ 12 " o/c toe nailed.
c. 3-8d toe nailed.
d. 10d @ 6,12.
e. 2-16d face/4-8d toe nailed.
f. 3-10d

SOLUTION

UBC T23-I-J-1

Shear Transfer parallel to wall capacities

a. 10d @ 6,6,12_{cap} = .32 klf

Capacity at a = .32 klf

b. 10d @ 12 " o/c toe nailed

Required values for Yield Equations

NDS T12A, 12.3B

$\ell = 3.0$ in

$t_s = \frac{\ell}{3} = 1.0$ in

$t_m = 1.5$ in
F_{es} = 4650 psi
F_{em} = 4650 psi
D = .148 in

F_{yb} = 90 ksi
K_D = 2.2 since D <.17 in

$p_L = \ell \cos 30 - t_s = 1.5$ in $= t_m = 1.5$ in

12D = 12(.148) = 1.78 in > 1.5 in **NG!**

min. penetration ok, use C_d =

$p/_{12D}$ when $6D \le p < 12D$ min. NDS 12.3.4

$$C_d = \frac{1.5}{1.78} = .84$$

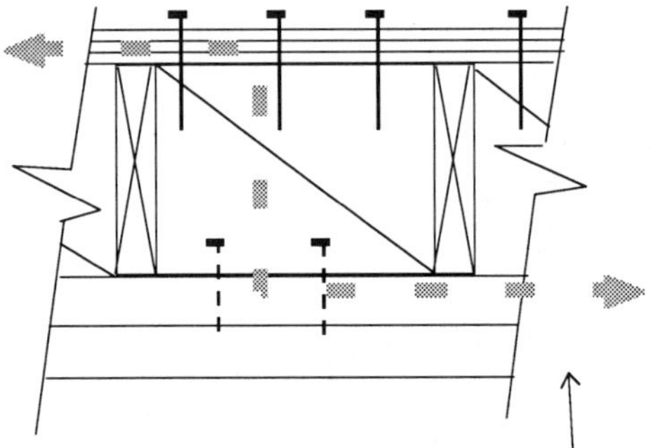

Calc preliminary coefficients values

NDS 12.3.1

$$R_e = \frac{F_{em}}{F_{es}} = \frac{4650}{4650} = 1.0$$

$$k_1 = -1 + \sqrt{2(1+R_e) + \frac{2F_{yb}(1+2R_e)D^2}{3F_{em}p^2}}$$

$$= -1 + \sqrt{2(1+1.0) + \frac{2(90000)(1+2(1.0))(.148)^2}{3(4650)(1.5)^2}} = 1.092$$

$$k_2 = -1 + \sqrt{\frac{2(1+R_e)}{R_e} + \frac{2F_{yb}(2+R_e)D^2}{3F_{em}t_s^2}}$$

$$= -1 + \sqrt{\frac{2(1+1.0)}{1.0} + \frac{2(90000)(2+1.0)(.148)^2}{3(4650)(1.0)^2}} = 1.202$$

Calc Failure Equation Mode Values

Mode I_s

$$Z = \frac{Dt_sF_{es}}{K_D} = \frac{.148(1.0)4650}{2.2} = 313 \text{ lb}$$

> Mode I_s Z = 313 lb

Mode III_m

$$Z = \frac{k_1DpF_{em}}{K_D(1+2R_e)} = \frac{1.092(.148)1.5(4650)}{2.2(1+2(1.0))} = 171 \text{ lb}$$

> Mode III_m Z = 171 lb

Mode III_s

$$Z = \frac{k_2Dt_sF_{em}}{K_D(2+R_e)} = \frac{1.202(.148)1.0(4650)}{2.2(2+1.0)} = 125 \text{ lb}$$

> Mode III_s Z = 125 lb

Mode IV

$$Z = \frac{D^2}{K_D}\sqrt{\frac{2F_{em}F_{yb}}{3(1+R_e)}} = \frac{(.148)^2}{2.2}\sqrt{\frac{2(4650)900000}{3(1+1.0)}}$$

= 118 lb

> Mode IV Z = 118 lb

The smallest value of the four is found in Mode IV.

> Z = 118 lbs / nail

Calc Z′

$C_D = 1.33$
$C_{tn} = .83$

$Z' = ZC_DC_MC_tC_dC_{eg}C_{di}C_{tn}$

$=.118(1.33)(1.0)1.0(.84)1.0(.83) = .109^k$

10d @ 12 " o/c toe nailed$_{cap}$ = .109 klf < .32klf

> Capacity at b = = .109 klf

d. 8d @ 6,12$_{cap}$ = .28 klf > .109 klf

Nailed blocking governs

> Max inplane (parallel) unit shear = .109 klf

UBC T23-I-K-1

Shear Transfer perpendicular to wall capacity

c. 3-8d toe nailed

Required values for Yield Equations

$\ell = 2.5$ in

$t_s = \frac{\ell}{3} = .83$ in

$t_m = 1.5$ in
$F_{es} = 4650$ psi
$F_{em} = 4650$ psi
$D = .131$ in
$F_{yb} = 90$ ksi
$K_D = 2.2$ since $D < .17$ in

NDS T12A, 12.3B

$p_L = \ell \cos 30 - t_s = 1.33 \text{ in} < t_m$ √

12D = 12(.131) = 1.57 in > 1.33 in NG!

min penetration ok use C_d =

$p/12D$ when $6D \le p < 12D$ min.

NDS 12.3.4

$$C_d = \frac{1.33}{1.57} = .85$$

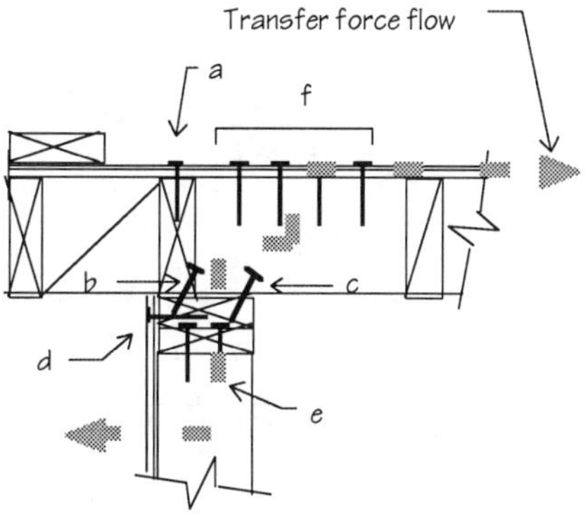

NDS 12.3.1

Calc preliminary coefficients values

$$R_e = \frac{F_{em}}{F_{es}} = \frac{4650}{4650} = 1.0$$

$$k_1 = -1+\sqrt{2(1+R_e)+\frac{2F_{yb}(1+2R_e)D^2}{3F_{em}p^2}}$$

$$= -1+\sqrt{2(1+1.0)+\frac{2(90000)(1+2(1.0))(.131)^2}{3(4650)(1.33)^2}} = 1.102$$

$$k_2 = -1+\sqrt{\frac{2(1+R_e)}{R_e}+\frac{2F_{yb}(2+R_e)D^2}{3F_{em}t_s^2}}$$

$$= -1+\sqrt{\frac{2(1+1.0)}{1.0}+\frac{2(90000)(2+1.0)(.131)^2}{3(4650).83^2}} = 1.25$$

NDS T7.3.1

Calc Failure Equation Mode Values

Mode I_s

$$Z = \frac{Dt_sF_{es}}{K_D} = \frac{.131(1.0)4650}{2.2} = 231 \text{ lb}$$

> Mode I_s Z = 231 lb

Mode III_m

$$Z = \frac{k_1DpF_{em}}{K_D(1+2R_e)} = \frac{1.102(.131)1.33(4650)}{2.2(1+2(1.0))} = 135 \text{ lb}$$

> Mode III_m Z = 135 lb

Mode III_s

$$Z = \frac{k_2Dt_sF_{em}}{K_D(2+R_e)} = \frac{1.25(.131).83(4650)}{2.2(2+1.0)} = 96 \text{ lb}$$

> Mode III_s Z = 96 lb

Mode IV

$$Z = \frac{D^2}{K_D}\sqrt{\frac{2F_{em}F_{yb}}{3(1+R_e)}} = \frac{(.131)^2}{2.2}\sqrt{\frac{2(4650)900000}{3(1+1.0)}}$$

= 97 lb

> Mode IV Z = 97 lb

The smallest value of the four is found in Mode III_s

> Z = 96 lbs / nail

NDS 12.3.7

Calc Z´

$C_D = 1.33$
$C_{tn} = .83$

NDS T7.3.1

$Z' = ZC_DC_MC_tC_dC_{eg}C_{di}C_{tn}$

$= .096(1.33)(1.0)1.0(.85)1.0(.83) = .09^k$

since blocking at 24 " o/c

$w = 3(.09)/(2) = .135$ klf

NDS T7.3.1

> Capacity at c = .135 klf

e. 2-16d end nailed

From NDS tables

NDS 12.3B

$Z = .141^k$

$p = \ell - t_s \le t_m$

$= 3.5 - 1.5 \le t_m$

$= 2.0 \text{ in} < t_m = 1.5 \text{ in}$ √

NDS 12.3.4

$12D = 12(.162) = 1.94 \text{ in} < 2.0 \text{ in}$ √

$Z' = ZC_DC_MC_tC_dC_{eg}C_{di}C_{tn}$

$= .141(1.33)(1.0)1.0(.67)1.0(1.0) = .126^k < .141^k$

NDS T7.3.1

Since studs are at 16 " o/c:

$w = .126(12/16)2 = .189$ klf

> Capacity at e = .189

NDS T12.3B

f. 3-10d

From NDS tables

$Z = .09^k$

Penetration ok by insp.

NDS T7.3.1

$Z' = ZC_DC_MC_tC_dC_{eg}C_{di}C_{tn}$

$= .09(1.33)(1.0)1.0(1.0)1.1(1.0) = .132^k$

The APA recommends a 10% reduction when diaphragm nailing is in 2x main member.

Since blocks are at 24 " o/c:

w = .132(4).9/2= .238 klf > .189 klf

Nailed blocking governs.

Max out of plane (perpendicular) unit shear = .189 klf

□
□
□

The greatest obstacle to discovery is not ignorance - it is the illusion of knowledge.

DANIEL J. BOORSTIN

● PROBLEM 8.4

Shear transfer of wood diaphragm to sole plate of concrete wall.

Determine if the connection is adequate for the forces shown below.

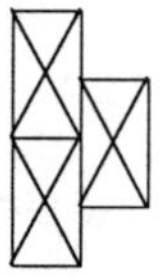

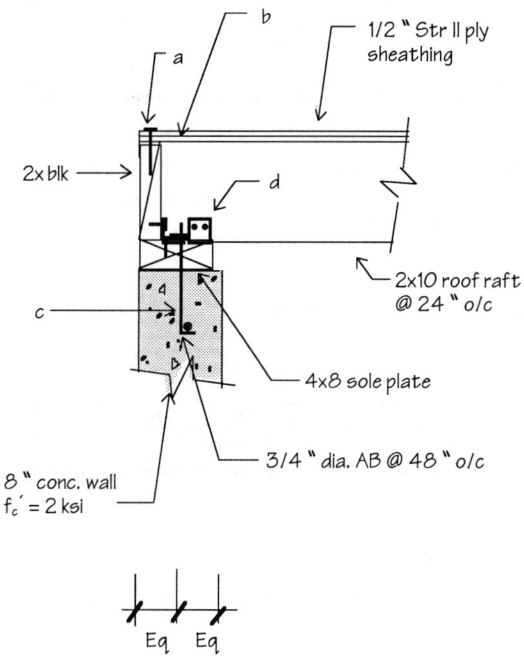

ASSUME

Horizontal shear ok.
DF-L lumber.
EMC <19%.
Common nails.
Blocked diaphragms.
C_D = 1.6.
v_{diaph} = .25 klf.
$v_{\perp wall}$ = .2 klf (code min. UBC Sec. 2310).
Rafter ok.
Neglect chord forces.

SOLUTION

Shear transfer parallel to wall

a. Diaphragm nailing (case 3)

v_{diaph}= .25 klf < .27 klf √

UBC T23-I-K-1

> Use 1/2 " Str II EXP 1 plywood
> with 8D @
> 6 " o/c, boundary and continuous edges
> 6 " o/c, other edges
> 12 " o/c, field

b. Framing anchor

Toe nailing is not permitted for anchorage of concrete or masonry walls.

v = .25 klf

A34 manf. clip cap = .365 ^{k}

$A34_R$ = .24(2)/.365 = 1.32 say 2/ blk

> Use manufacturers A34 anchor with .365^k cap. 2 required per blk.

c. Anchor bolts

Bolt in conc.

Assume 3/4 " dia. AB with 5 " min. embedment.

UBC T19-E

$P_R = 4(.25) = 1.0^k$

$P_{all\ conc} = 2.94^k > 1.0^k$ √

Bolt in wood

Per NDS 8.2.3, $t_m = 2t_s$, and $F_{em} = F_{es}$

Values for Yield Equations

NDS T8A, 8.2A

$t_s = 3.5$ in
$t_m = 7.0$ in
$F_{es} = 2600$ psi
$F_{em} = 2600$ psi
$D = .75$ in
$F_{yb} = 45$ ksi
$\theta_s = 0$

Calc preliminary coefficient values

$$R_e = \frac{F_{em}}{F_{es}} = \frac{5600}{5600} = 1.0$$

$$R_t = \frac{t_m}{t_s} = \frac{7.0}{3.5} = 2.0$$

$$k_1 = \frac{\sqrt{R_e + 2R_e^2\left(1+R_t+R_t^2\right)+R_t^2R_e^3} - R_e(1+R_t)}{(1+R_e)}$$

NDS 8.2.1

$$= \frac{\sqrt{1.0+2(1.0)^2\left(1+2.0+(2.0)^2\right)+(2.0)^2(1.0)^3} - 1.0(1+2.0)}{(1+1.0)}$$

$= .6794$

$$k_2 = -1 + \sqrt{2(1+R_e) + \frac{2F_{yb}(1+2R_e)D^2}{3F_{em}t_m^2}}$$

$$= -1 + \sqrt{2(1+1.0) + \frac{2(45000)(1+2(1.0))(.75)^2}{3(5600)(7.0)^2}} = 1.046$$

$$k_3 = -1 + \sqrt{\frac{2(1+R_e)}{R_e} + \frac{2F_{yb}(2+R_e)D^2}{3F_{em}t_s^2}}$$

$$= -1 + \sqrt{\frac{2(1+1.0)}{1.0} + \frac{2(45000)(2+1.0)(.75)^2}{3(5600)(3.5)^2}} = 1.177$$

Calc Failure Equation Mode Values

Mode I_m

$$Z = \frac{Dt_mF_{em}}{4K_\theta} = \frac{.75(7.0)5600}{4(1.0)} = 7350 \text{ lb}$$

> Mode I_m Z = 7350 lb

Mode I_s

$$Z = \frac{Dt_sF_{es}}{4K_\theta} = \frac{.75(3.5)5600}{4(1.0)} = 3675 \text{ lb}$$

> Mode I_s Z = 3675 lb

Mode II

$$Z = \frac{k_1Dt_sF_{es}}{3.6K_\theta} = \frac{.6794(.75)3.5(5600)}{3.6(1.0)} = 2774 \text{ lb}$$

> Mode II Z = 2774 lb

Mode III_m

$$Z = \frac{k_2Dt_mF_{em}}{3.2(1+2R_e)K_\theta} = \frac{1.046(.75)7.0(5600)}{3.2(1+2(1.0))1.0} = 3202 \text{ lb}$$

Mode III_m Z = 3202 lb

<u>Mode</u> III_s

$$Z = \frac{k_3 D t_s F_{em}}{3.2(2+R_e)K_\theta} = \frac{1.177(.75)3.5(5600)}{3.2(2+1.0)1.0} = 1802 \text{ lb}$$

Mode III_s Z = 1802 lb

<u>Mode</u> IV

NDS 17.3.1

$$Z = \frac{D^2}{3.2K_\theta}\sqrt{\frac{2F_{em}F_{yb}}{3(1+R_e)}} = \frac{(.75)^2}{3.2(1.0)}\sqrt{\frac{2(5600)45000}{3(1+1.0)}}$$

= 1611 lb

Mode IV Z = 1611 lb

The smallest value of the six is found in Mode IV.

Z = 1611 lbs / bolt

Calc Z´

NDS 17.3.1

$$Z' = ZC_DC_MC_tC_gC_\Delta$$

$$=1.611(1.6)1.0(1.0)1.0(1.0)= 2.578^k > 1.0^k \ \surd$$

3/4 " dia. AB ok for parallel to wall forces

Shear transfer perpendicular to wall

<u>c. Anchor bolts</u>

Bolt in conc.

UBC 1919-E

$P_R = 4(.2) = .8^k$

$P_{all\ conc} = 2.94^k > .8^k \ \surd$

Bolt in wood

Per NDS 8.2.3, $t_m = 2t_s$, and $F_{em} = F_{es}$

Values for Yield Equations

Same as above but angle changes

$\theta_s = 90$

Calc preliminary coefficients values

$$R_e = \frac{F_{em}}{F_{es}} = \frac{2600}{2600} = 1.0$$

$$K_\theta = 1+\frac{\theta}{360} = 1+\frac{90}{360} = 1.25$$

$$R_t = \frac{t_m}{t_s} = \frac{7.0}{3.5} = 2.0$$

NDS 8.2.1

$$k_1 = \frac{\sqrt{R_e+2R_e^2(1+R_t+R_t^2)+R_t^2R_e^3} - R_e(1+R_t)}{(1+R_e)}$$

$$= \frac{\sqrt{1.0+2(1.0)^2(1+2.0+(2.0)^2)+(2.0)^2(1.0)^3} - 1.0(1+2.0)}{(1+1.0)}$$

$= .6794$

$$k_2 = -1+\sqrt{2(1+R_e)+\frac{2F_{yb}(1+2R_e)D^2}{3F_{em}t_m^2}}$$

$$= -1+\sqrt{2(1+1.0)+\frac{2(45000)(1+2(1.0))(.75)^2}{3(2600)(7.0)^2}} = 1.097$$

$$k_3 = -1+\sqrt{\frac{2(1+R_e)}{R_e}+\frac{2F_{yb}(2+R_e)D^2}{3F_{em}t_s^2}}$$

$$= -1+\sqrt{\frac{2(1+1.0)}{1.0}+\frac{2(45000)(2+1.0)(.75)^2}{3(2600)(3.5)^2}} = 1.364$$

Calc Failure Equation Mode Values

<u>Mode</u> I_m

$$Z = \frac{Dt_mF_{em}}{4K_\theta} = \frac{.75(7.0)2600}{4(1.25)} = 2730 \text{ lb}$$

Mode I_m Z = 2730 lb

<u>Mode</u> I_s

$$Z = \frac{Dt_sF_{es}}{4K_\theta} = \frac{.75(3.5)2600}{4(1.25)} = 1365 \text{ lb}$$

Mode I_s Z = 1365 lb

<u>Mode</u> II

$$Z = \frac{k_1Dt_sF_{es}}{3.6K_\theta} = \frac{.6794(.75)3.5(2600)}{3.6(1.25)} = 1030 \text{ lb}$$

Mode II Z = 1030 lb

Mode III$_m$

$$Z = \frac{k_2 D t_m F_{em}}{3.2(1+2R_e)K_\theta} = \frac{1.097(.75)7.0(2600)}{3.2(1+2(1.0))1.25} = 1248 \text{ lb}$$

Mode III$_m$ Z = 1248 lb

Mode III$_s$

$$Z = \frac{k_3 D t_s F_{em}}{3.2(2+R_e)K_\theta} = \frac{1.364(.75)3.5(2600)}{3.2(2+1.0)1.25} = 776 \text{ lb}$$

Mode III$_s$ Z = 776 lb

Mode IV

$$Z = \frac{D^2}{3.2K_\theta}\sqrt{\frac{2F_{em}F_{yb}}{3(1+R_e)}} = \frac{(.75)^2}{3.2(1.25)}\sqrt{\frac{2(2600)45000}{3(1+1.0)}}$$

= 878lb

Mode IV Z = 878 lb

The smallest value of the six is found in Mode III$_s$.

Z = 776 lbs / bolt

Calc Z´

NDS T7.3.1

$Z' = Z C_D C_M C_t C_g C_\Delta$

$=.776(1.6)1.0(1.0)1.0(1.0)= 1.241^k > .8^k$ √

3/4 " dia. AB at 48 " o/c ok for perpendicular to wall forces

d. Framing anchor

Toe nailing is not permitted for anchorage of concrete or masonry walls. We must avoid connections that exhibit the possibility of cross grain tension. If we assume that the clips are at 2 ft o/c then:

$P_R = 2(.2) = .4$ klf

A34 manf. clip cap = $.365^k$

$A34_R = .4/.365 = 1.1$ say 2/ blk

But look at what happens during seismic reversal of the force direction perpendicular to the wall.

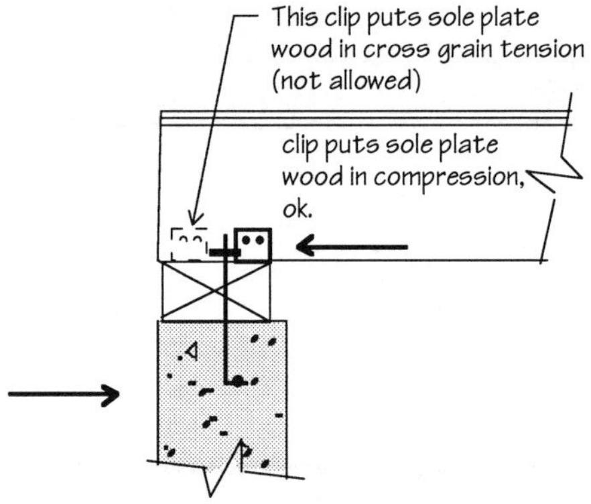

This clip puts sole plate wood in cross grain tension (not allowed)
clip puts sole plate wood in compression, ok.

Only one of the two required framing anchor clips is working in compression. We, therefore, should have 4 clips at each rafter so that at least two clips will be working for the above force ($.4^k$) during seismic force reversal.

Use manf. A34 anchor with $.365^k$ cap. 4 required per rafter.

It is the commonest of mistakes to consider that the limit of our power of perception is also the limit of all there is to perceive.

C.W. LEADBEATER

● PROBLEM 8.5

Subdiaphragm analysis of a building.

Perform a subdiaphragm analysis for the structure shown below.

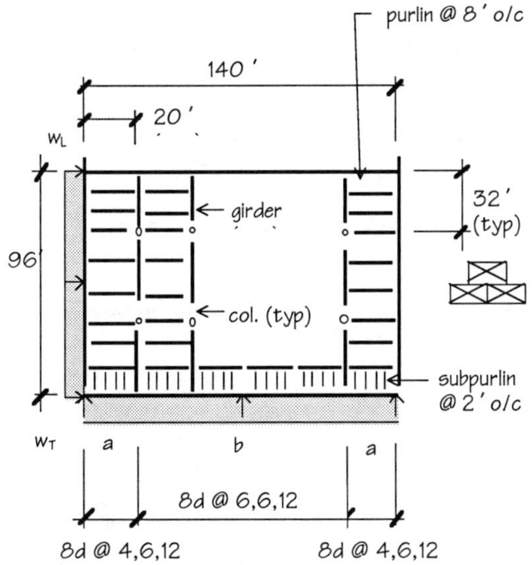

zone nailing

ASSUME

- RDL = .012 ksf.
- Wall DL = .09 ksf, ht = 16 ′.
- w = .183W, zone 4.
- wT = .474 klf.
- wL = .571 klf.
- 1/2 ′ Str II ply with zone nailing.
- 8d @ 4,6,12 cap = .36 klf.
- 8d @ 6,6,12 cap = .27 klf.
- Neglect wind.
- Roof sloped for drainage.

SOLUTION

Longitudinal direction

Try 96 ′ x 20 ′ subdiaphragm

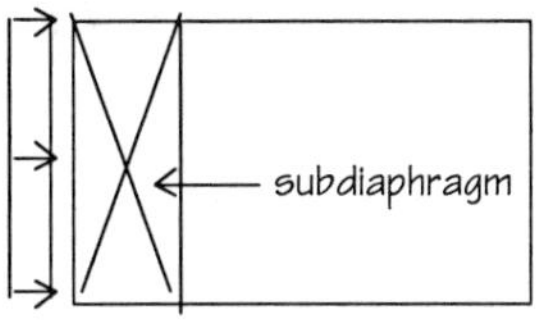

Seismic force of wall to diaphragm anchorage:

$F_p = ZIC_pW_p = .4(1.0).75W_p = .3W_p$

Force normal to wall:

w = .3(.09)16/2 = .216 klf > .2 klf code min. √

UBC Table 16-O footnote 3 specifies the C_P for anchorage is to be increased 50% in the center half of the flexible diaphragm. This will cause the anchorage design forces to increase proportionally.
1.5w = 1.5(.216) = .324 klf

This implies a 24 ′ zone on both sides of the middle half of the diaphragm. Technically we could have used a lower value here. But it would only be for one purlin on each side of the middle half, because the next one is an extrapolation of the two values. Therefore, use a larger value over the entire longitudinal length.

Ck aspect ratio

aspect ratio = 96/20 = 4.8 > 4 **NG!**

try 96 ′ x 40 ′ subdiaphragm

aspect ratio = 96/40 = 2.4 < 4 √ UBC T23-1-I

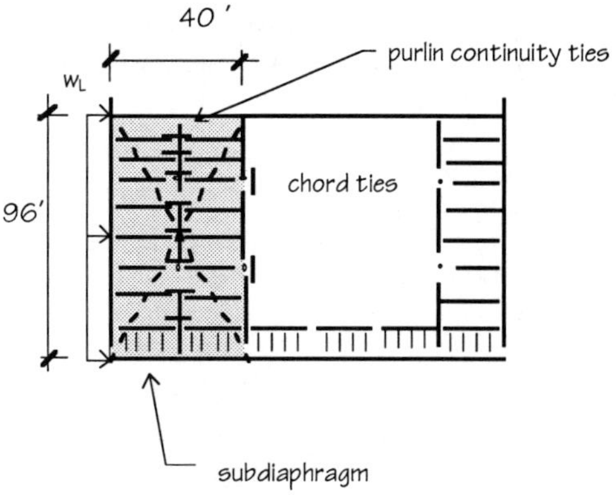

Calc subdiaphragm v force

$$v = \frac{w\ell}{2b} = \frac{.324(96)}{2(40)} = .389 \text{ klf} > .36 \text{ klf} \quad \textbf{NG!}$$

Upgrade plywood diaphragm.

.39 klf < .425 klf √

> Upgrade plywood diaphragm to 1/2 " STR 1 EXP1 grade 10d @4,6,12 for zone a

Calc girder chord tie forces

$$T = \frac{M}{b} = \frac{w\ell^2}{8b} = \frac{.324(96)^2}{8(40)} = 9.33^k$$

> Chord tie cap required = 9.33^k

Calc purlin continuity tie force

$T = 8(.324) = 2.6^k$

> Purlin continuity tie cap required = 2.6^k

Calc purlin anchorage to wall force.

Since purlins are at 8 ' o/c > 4 ' o/c, the wall must be designed as 8 ' long beams along the entire longitudinal length of both sides of the building.

$T = 2.6^k$

> Use manf. ties with cap $= 2.6^k$

Transverse direction

Try 29 ' x 8 ' subdiaphragm.

ck aspect ratio

aspect ratio = 20/8 = 2.5 < 4 √

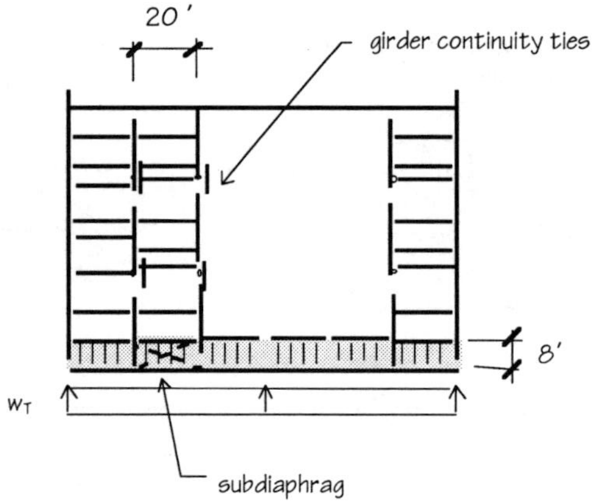

Since we upgraded the diaphragm, the anchorage force for zone b is now = .32 klf.

Ck subdiaphragm v

$$v = \frac{w\ell}{2b} = \frac{.324(20)}{2(8)} = .405 \text{ klf} > .32 \text{ klf} \quad \textbf{NG!}$$

We can either change the depth of the subdiaphragm (b) or change the zone nailing requirements. If we change b then we must provide continuity ties for the subpurlins. In these circumstances it is usually economical to change the zone nailing. Use 10d @ 4,6,12 at zone a, capacity = .425 klf.

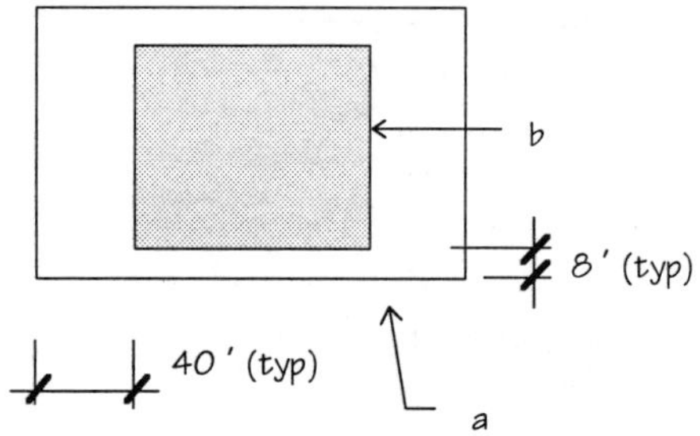

Change zone nailing to above

Ck girder continuity tie force

$T = 20(.324) = 6.84^k$

Girder continuity tie cap required = 6.84^k

Purlin chord force

$$T = \frac{w\ell^2}{8b} = \frac{.324(20)^2}{8(8)} = 2.03^k$$

Since purlin is continuous, no continuity ties are required

Calc subpurlin anchorage to wall force

Assume purlins are at 4′ o/c so that wall does not have to be designed as a beam along the entire length of both sides of the building.

$T = 4(.324) = 1.3^k$

Use manf. ties with cap = 1.3^k

Note that it is possible that an anchor will be installed at a subpurlin that is not at the boundary of a plywood panel. Therefore, we should provide special field nailing requirements for the nailing along these walls so that the anchorage force will transfer into the diaphragm.

NDS 12.3.6

$Z' = ZC_DC_MC_tC_dC_{eg}C_{di}C_{tn}$

$= .090(1.6)1.0(1.0)1.0(1.0)1.1(1.0) = .158$ k/nail

The APA recommends a 10 percent reduction in nail value for diaphragm nailing.

NDS T7.3.1

Z' modified = .9(.158) = .143 k/nail

N = 1.3/.143 = 9.1 say 10 nails

spacing = 8(12)/10 = 9.6 in o/c

Here we could revise the zone nailing by either adding another zone with 10d @ 4,6,9 and have three zones, or make all of the zones have the new field nailing. In practice it is common to simplify connections to save labor in the field and to lessen the possibility of error.

Use 10d @ 4,6,9 at zone "a"

The higher up you go, the more mistakes you're allowed. Right at the top, if you make enough of them, it's considered to be your style.

FRED ASTAIRE

PROBLEM 8.6

Continuity connection for drag strut.

Determine if the hanger and continuity connection is adequate for the forces shown below.

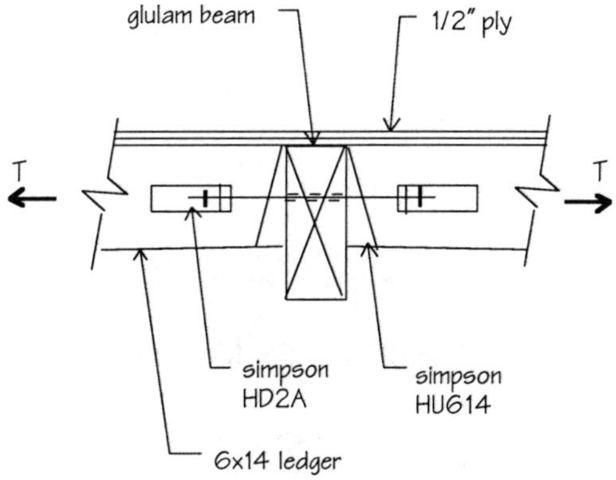

ASSUME

DF-L lumber.
EMC <19%.
$C_D = 1.33$.
$T = 2^k$.
$P = 2^k$.
Rafters, glulam and diaphragm are ok.

SOLUTION

Check hanger

HU614 capacity = $3.0^k > 2^k$ √

Hanger HU614 with 8-16d ok

Check continuity connection

HD2A capacity = $2.8^k > 2^k$ √

Simpson HD2A with 2-3/4 in dia.
A307 MB continuity connection ok

Note: If it seems that this problem is too easy, good. It is important to realize that most of the difficulty in structural engineering comes from the analysis and detailing phases. The actual specification is relatively easy. It is merely a matter of looking up the required force in some manufacturers catalog. However, do not lose sight that you must understand the limitations of the connective hardware you are specifying. This means you must be familiar with the material in the catalog. If you have any doubt about a products application, don't assume, call the manufacturer and find out the answer you require.

The price of greatness is responsibility.

WINSTON CHURCHILL

PROBLEM 8.7

Wall anchorage connection.

Determine if the connection is adequate for the forces shown below.

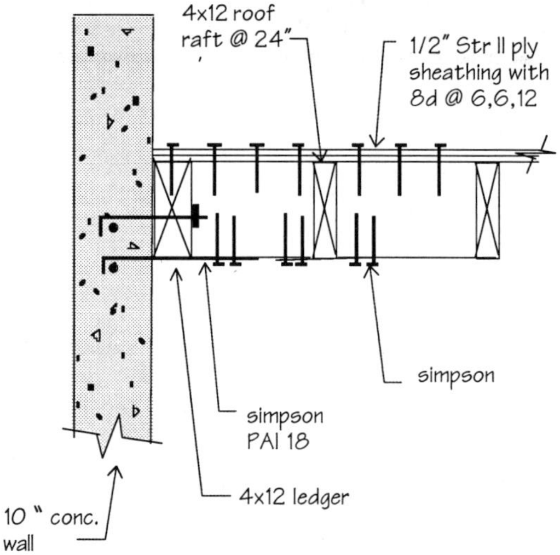

ASSUME

DF-L lumber.
EMC <19%.
Common nails.
Blocked diaphragms.
$C_D = 1.33$.
$v_{\perp wall} = .3$ klf.
Ledger, rafter and diaphragm are ok.
Neglect chord forces.
$Z' = .108^k$ for 8d.

SOLUTION

Wall anchor

Assume section is not in the middle 1/2 of a flexible diaphragm.

$v_{\perp wall} = .2$ klf

Assume anchors at 4' o/c.

$P = .3(4) = 1.2^k <$ prefab $= 1.5^k$ √

> Use manufacturers anchor at 4′ o/c
> Simpson PAI 18 = 1.5^k capacity
> with 12-10d

Check diaphragm

The diaphragm must be capable of taking the transferred load from the wall. In this problem we are looking at the connection that will allow that transfer to be completed. Since it is possible that the field might place the wall anchorage where diaphragm field nailing will occur, we must either calculate the transfer using nails spaced at 12 in. o/c, or require the field to have boundary nailing equal to the amount specified. It is usually more efficient to use the full amount of diaphragm shear available than to block extra bays for the reduced load transfer capacity of field nailing. The diaphragm capacity = .27 klf.

Calc number of bays required to block and nail.

$$\# = \frac{force}{v} = \frac{1.2}{.27(2)} = 2.2 \text{ bays} > 2 \quad \textbf{NG!}$$

> Use 8d @ 6 in. o/c for 3 bays at
> all wall anchorage locations

Check LST

LSTA9 cap = $.6^k < 1.2 - .27(2) = .66^k$ **NG!**

Try LSTA12 = $.76^k > .66^k$ √

> Use 2 - Simpson LSTA12 strap ties
> for 3 transfer bays

Check blocking

The detail given did not show what kind of nailing was required for the blocking to prevent rotation from occuring. Assume code minimum nailing and check. Assume block ok by inspection.

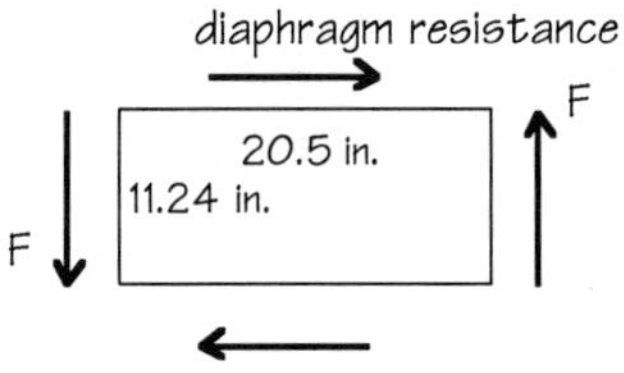

wall transfer force

$$F = 1.2\left(\frac{11.25}{20.5}\right) = .66^k$$

Assume UBC Table 25-Q, 2. Bridging to joist, 2-8d each end.

$2Z' = 2(.108) = .22^k < .66^k$ **NG!**

$$8d \text{ required} = \frac{.66}{.108} = 6.1$$

Try Simpson hanger U410

uplift capacity = $.89^k > .66^k$ √

roof capacity = $1.94^k > .66^k$ √

> Use 2- Simpson U410 hangers with
> 6-10d at each block

Note: When the seismic force reverses the blocks will be in compression. Rotation will not be a problem. However, a note should be placed on the plans that states that the blocking shall be tight fit. If this is not done, the diaphragm might take some of the compressive load - not a good idea.

You'll get no laurel crown for outrunning a burro.

MARTIAL
40 - 104 A.D.

PROBLEM 8.8

Continuity connection for drag strut.

Quickly determine if the drag at "a" is adequate for the forces shown below.

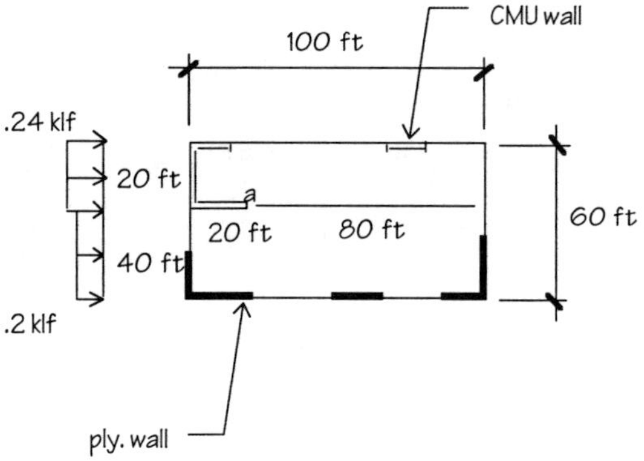

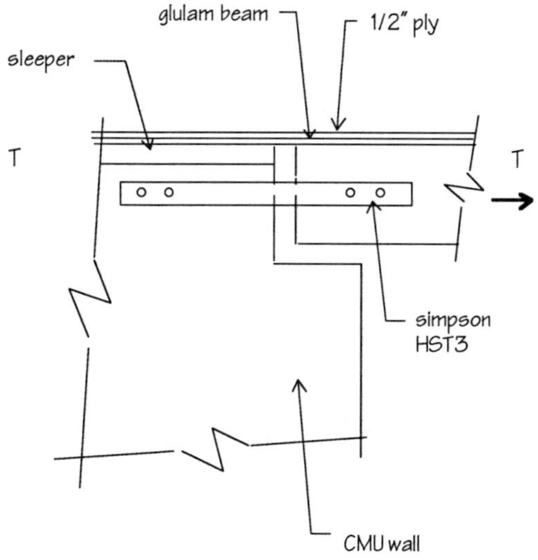

ASSUME

DF-L lumber.
EMC <16%.
C_D = 1.33.
Rafters, glulam and diaphragm are ok.

SOLUTION

Calculate the force required (T)

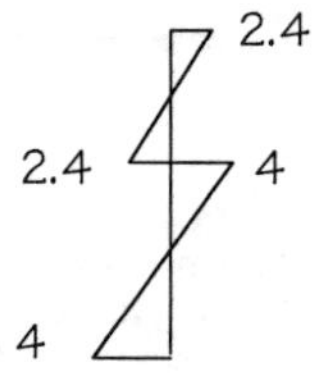

$R = 2.4 + 4 = 6.4^k$

$T = 80\left(\frac{6.4}{100}\right) = 5.12^k$

Check continuity connection

The simpson HST3 capacity = $6.2^k > 5.12^k$ √

> The simpson HST3 with 6-3/4in dia. A307 MB ok for glulam tension forces shown.

Design notes:

Simpson assumes a minimum lumber of DF- L No. 2 (based upon $F_{c\perp}$ 625 psi) under continuously dry conditions. The glulam in this problem has not been specified. The bolts are most likely to be located near the neutral axis of the glulam beam. In many cases, this is the zone of lesser quality material. It is possible that the 625 psi minimum will not be met and the allowable for the HST must be adjusted accordingly. For example, say we have a value of 500 psi. The adjustment factor is 500/625 = .8 or 80% of the value given in the simpson catalog.

Also recall that the length of the HST must allow for the force transfer in the CMU wall (development length).

If the load gets too large consideration should be given to the eccentricity of the one-sided connection.

Seismic reversal requires that the plate must transfer compressive forces. Therefore, the HST must be capable of transferring the force or blocking must be provided.

9. Advanced Topics

● PROBLEM 9.1

Nailed wood "I" beam maximum capacity using shear flow.

Determine the maximum uniform load for the built-up "I" beam configuration shown below.

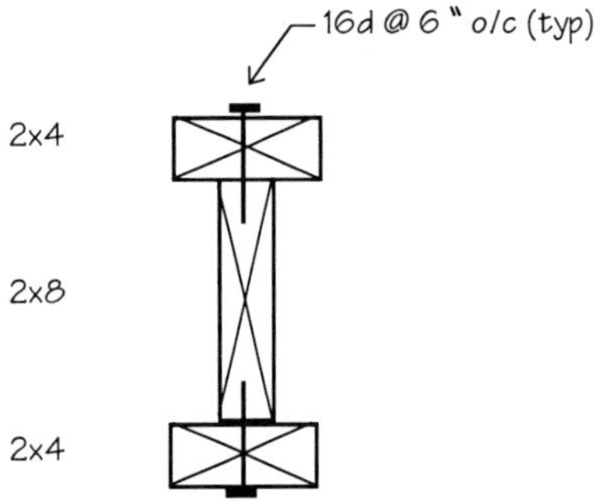

Assume

- DF- L No 1.
- EMC < 19%.
- Span = 15 ′.
- $C_D = 1.0$.
- Neglect deflection.
- Full lateral support.
- $Z' = .096^k$.
- $F_v' = .095$ ksi.
- $F_b' = 1.5$ ksi.

SOLUTION

$A_{2x4} = 5.25\ in^2$ $\quad A_{2x8} = 10.875\ in^2$

$I_{2x4} = 2.039\ in^4$ (flat) $\quad I_{2x8} = 47.635\ in^4$

$S_{2x4} = 2.719\ in^3$ (flat) $\quad S_{2x8} = 13.14\ in^3$

Calc I of composite

Determine the spatial relationships of the three components of the composite member so that you may use the parallel axis theorem.

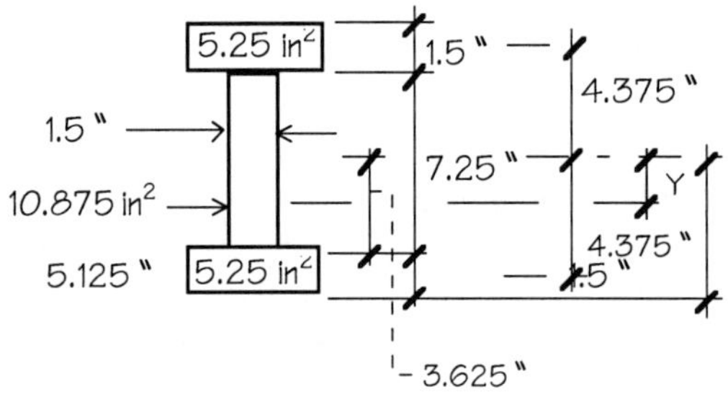

Using parallel axis theorem

$$I = \sum A\left(\frac{h^2}{12} + d^2\right)$$

$$= 2(5.25)\left(\frac{1.5^2}{12} + 4.375^2\right) + 10.875\left(\frac{7.25^2}{12} + 0\right)$$

$$= 250.58\ in^4$$

Or alternately

$$I = I_{solid} - I_{space}$$

$$= \frac{3.5(7.25+3)^3}{12} - \frac{2(7.25)^3}{12} = 250.58\ in^4$$

From shear flow

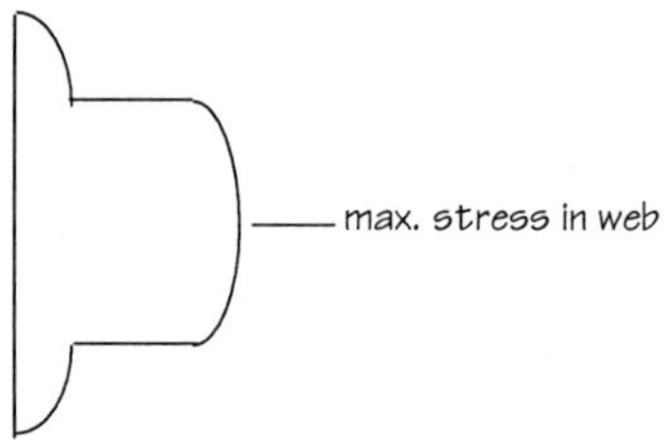

We must examine both the web and the flange for shear.

Flange

$$Q = A'\bar{Y} = 3.5(1.5)4.375 = 22.97\ in^3$$

$$q = \frac{VQ}{I} = \frac{P}{spacing}$$

$$V = \frac{PI}{Qspacing} = \frac{.096(250.58)}{22.97(6)} = .175^k$$

flange shear = $.175^k$

Web

area = 1.5(3.625 - Y)

lever arm = Y + (3.625 - Y)/2 = (3.625 +Y)/2

$$Qweb = 1.5(3.625 - Y)\frac{3.625+Y}{2} = .75(13.14 - Y^2)$$

$$Q_{web}\big|_{Y=0} = .75(13.14 - 0) = 9.86 \text{ in}^3$$

$$f_v = \frac{VQ}{It} \Rightarrow V = \frac{f_v It}{Q} = \frac{.095(250.58)1.5}{9.86} = 3.62^k > V_{flg}$$

V_{flg} controls.

Calc w_{max}

$$V = \frac{w\ell}{2} \Rightarrow w = \frac{2V}{\ell} = \frac{2(.175)}{15} = .023 \text{ klf}$$

Calc Flexure stress

$$f_b = \frac{Mc}{I} \Rightarrow M = \frac{f_b I}{c} = \frac{w\ell^2}{8}$$

$$w = \frac{8 f_b I}{c\ell^2} = \frac{8(1.5)250.58}{5.125(15(12))^2} = .018 \text{ kli}$$

= .217 klf > .023 klf

V_{flg} controls.

Max uniform load based upon nails = 23 plf

They always say that time changes things, but you actually have to change them yourself.

ANDY WARHOL

PROBLEM 9.2

Composite beam (wood side plates and steel main members) stresses.

Determine the bending stress of each material for the composite beam shown below.

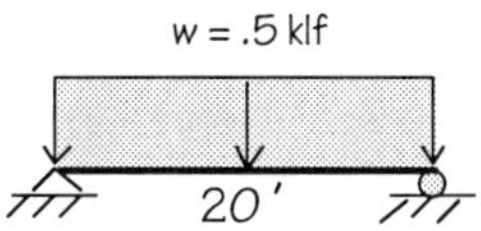

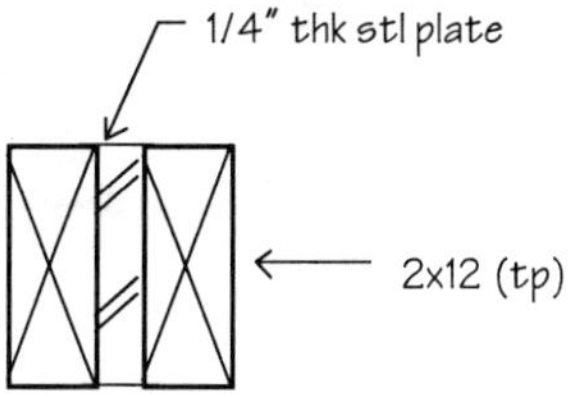

ASSUME

DF-L No 1 and btr.
A-36 stl.
EMC < 19%.
Connection between stl and wood ok.

SOLUTION

A_{2x12} = 16.875 in^2
I_{2x12} = 177.979 in^4
S_{2x12} = 31.641 in^3

Transfer Section

$$\eta = \frac{E_s}{E_w} = \frac{29E6}{1.8E6} = 16.1$$

Transform steel

b_{stl} = 16.1(.25) = 4.03"

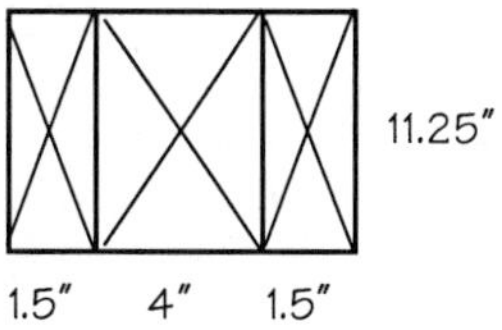

$$I_{trans} = \frac{7(11.25)^3}{12} = 830.57 \text{ in}^4$$

Stress in wood

$$M = \frac{w\ell^2}{8} = \frac{.5(20)^2}{8} = 25^{\text{ k ft}}$$

$$f_{b\,wood} = \frac{12Mc}{I} = \frac{12(25)\frac{11.25}{2}}{830.57} = 2.03 \text{ ksi}$$

Wood stress = 2.03 ksi

Stress in stl

$$f_b \text{ stl} = \eta f_{b\ wood} = 16(2.03) = 32.5 \text{ ksi}$$

Stl stress = 32.5 ksi

It is a good idea to obey all the rules when you're young just so you'll have the strength to break them when you're old.

MARK TWAIN

○ PROBLEM 9.3

Bolted built-up "T" beam.

Determine the bolt spacing for the built-up beam shown below. Check beam.

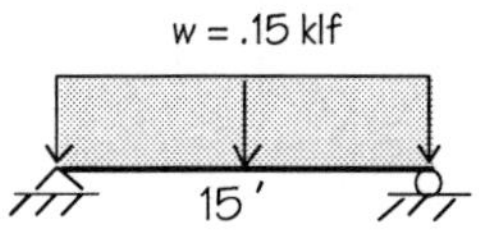

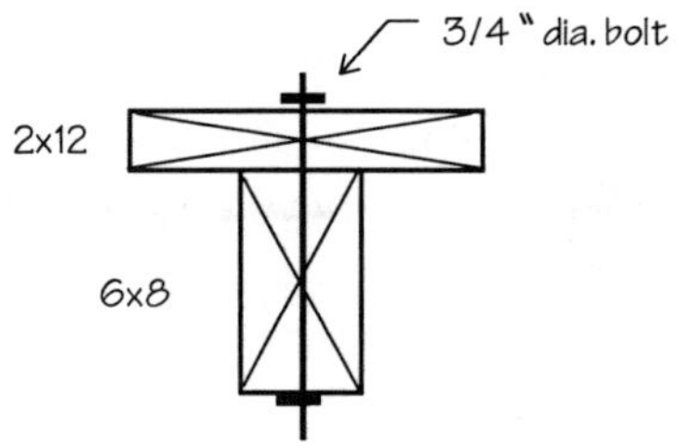

ASSUME

DF-L - No 1.
EMC < 19%.
$C_D = 1.0$.
L/240 criteria.
Full lateral support.

SOLUTION

$A_{2x12} = 16.88 \text{ in}^2$ (flat)
$I_{2x12} = 178.0 \text{ in}^4$ (flat)
$S_{2x12} = 31.64 \text{ in}^3$ (flat)

$A_{6x8} = 41.25 \text{ in}^2$
$I_{6x8} = 193.4 \text{ in}^4$
$S_{6x8} = 51.56 \text{ in}^3$

Calc I of composite (find NA)

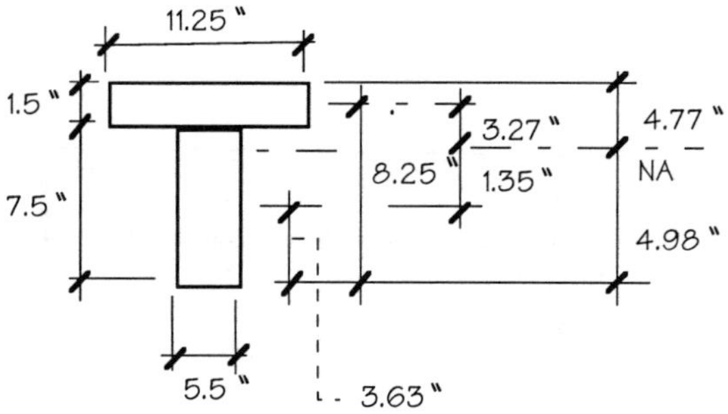

$$\bar{Y} = \frac{\sum Ax}{\sum A}$$

$$\bar{Y} = \frac{7.5(5.5)3.63 + 1.5(11.25)8.25}{16.8 + 41.25} = 4.98''$$

Find I

using parallel axis theorem

$$I = \sum A\left(\frac{h^2}{12} + d^2\right)$$

$$= 41.25\left(\frac{7.5^2}{12} + 1.35^2\right) + 16.88\left(\frac{1.5^2}{12} + 3.27^2\right)$$

$$= 452.2 \text{ in}^4$$

From shear flow

$$Q = A'\bar{Y} = 16.88(3.27) = 55.2 \text{ in}^3$$

$$V = \frac{w\ell}{2} = \frac{.15(15)}{2} = 1.23^k$$

$$q = \frac{VQ}{I} = \frac{1.23(55.2)}{452.2} = .15 \text{ kli}$$

> shear flow = .15 kli

Bolts (single shear)

Obtain required values for Yield Equations

NDS T8A, 8.2A

$t_s = 1.5$ in
$t_m = 7.5$ in
$D = .75$ in
$\theta_m = 0$
$\theta_s = 0$

> Z = 1200 lbs / bolt

Calc Z′

NDS T7.3.1

$$Z' = ZC_DC_MC_tC_g C_\Delta = 1.2(1.0)1.0(1.0)1.0(1.0) = 1.2^k$$

$$\text{spacing required} = \frac{1.2}{.15} = 8.0'' \text{ o/c say } 6'' \text{ o/c}$$

> Use 3/4 " dia. bolts at 6 " o/c in net holes

Since v is the maximum shear at the NA of the composite beam, and the bolt must be able to take that force on a per length basis. We use $C_{eg} = 1$.

Calc Bending stress

$$M = \frac{w\ell^2}{8} = \frac{.15(15^2)}{8} = 4.22^{k\,ft}$$

$$S_{top} = \frac{I}{c} = \frac{452.2}{4.77} = 94.8 \text{ in}^3$$

$$S_{bott} = \frac{I}{c} = \frac{452.2}{4.98} = 90.8 \text{ in}^3$$

NDS T2.3.1

$$F_b' = C_DC_MC_tC_LC_FC_VCf_uC_rC_cC_f$$

$$= 1.35(1.0)1.0(1.0)1.0(1.0)1.0(1.0)1.0(1.0) = 1.35 \text{ ksi}$$

$$S_R = \frac{12M}{F_b'} = \frac{12(4.22)}{1.35} = 37.51 \text{ in}^3 < S_{bott} < S_{top} \quad \checkmark$$

> Bending ok

Ck deflection

$$\Delta = \frac{5w\ell^4}{384EI} = \frac{5(.15)15^4 1728}{384(1.7E3)452.2} = .22 \text{ in}$$

$$l/240 = 12(15)/240 = .75 \text{ in} > .22 \text{ in} \quad \checkmark$$

> Built-up beam ok with spacing of bolts indicated

Life is like playing a violin in public and learning the instrument as one goes on.

SAMUEL BUTLER

○ PROBLEM 9.4

Built-up beam fiber stress with slippage prevented.

Determine the adequacy of the proposed beam shown. Re-design as required using 1 " dia. bolts. Is this a good design?

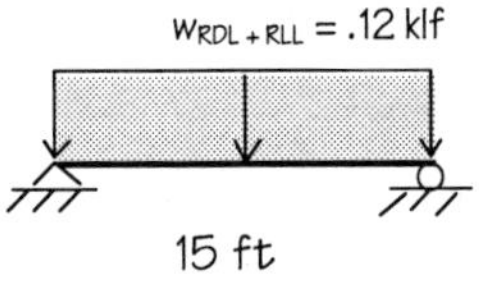

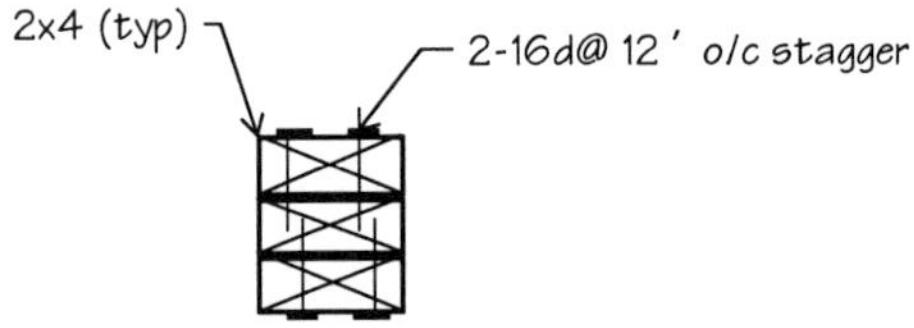

ASSUME

Common nails.
EMC < 19%.
Full lateral support.
single member use.
$\Delta < L/180$.

SOLUTION

$A_{2x4} = 5.25$ in^2
$I_{2x4} = 5.359$ in^4
$S_{2x4} = 3.063$ in^3

Check Bending

NDS T2.3.1

$$M = \frac{wL^2}{8} = \frac{.12(15)^2}{8} = 3.38^{k'}$$

$$F_b' = F_b C_D C_M C_t C_F C_{fu} = 1.0(1.25)1.0(1.0)1.0(1.1)$$

$= 1.38$ ksi

$$S_R = \frac{12M}{F_b'} = \frac{12(3.38)}{1.38} = 29.39 \text{ in}^3$$

If we consider the built-up beam as a non-composite;
$S_{3\text{-}2x4} = 3(2.06) = 6.18$ in^3 $< S_R$ NG!

We must consider it as a composite member.

$$S = \frac{bd^2}{6} = \frac{5.5(3(1.5))^2}{6} = 18.56 \text{ in}^3 < S_R \text{ NG!}$$

Try adding another 2x6

$$S = \frac{5.5(4(1.5))^2}{6} = 33.0 \text{ in}^3 > 29.4 \text{ in}^3 \ \checkmark$$

> Bending ok with the addition of another 2x6 and composite action

Ck Deflection (assume composite action)

$$I = \frac{bd^3}{12} = \frac{5.5(4(1.5))^3}{12} = 99 \text{ in}^4$$

$$\Delta = \frac{5w\ell^4}{384EI} = \frac{5(.12)(15)^4 1728}{384(1.7E3)99} = .81 \text{ in}$$

$$\ell/180 = \frac{15(12)}{180} = 1.0'' > .81'' \ \checkmark$$

> Deflection ok with additional member and composite action

Check Shear

$$V = \frac{w\ell}{2} = \frac{.12(15)}{2} = .9^k$$

Shear flow

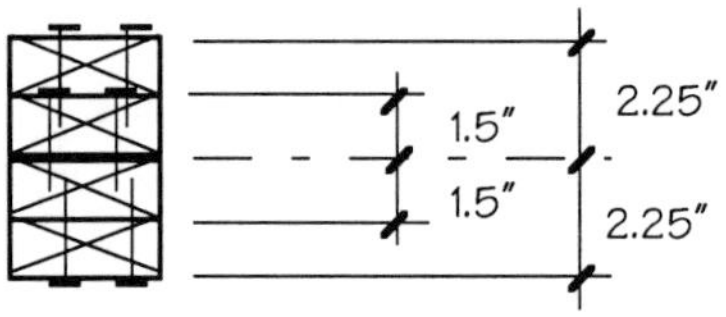

$$Q = A'\bar{Y} = 8.25(2.25) = 18.56 \text{ in}^3$$

$$v = q = \frac{VQ}{I} = \frac{.9(18.56)}{99} = .17 \text{ kli}$$

> Required shear flow = .17 kli

Calc Nail Capacity

Obtain required values for Z′ for nails NDS T12A, 12.3B

$t_s = 1.5$ in
$t_m = 1.5$ in

Z = 141 lbs / nail

Calc Z´

NDS 12.3.4 $p = \ell - t_s \le t_m$

$= 3.5 - 1.5 = 2.0$ in $> t_s = 1.5$ in use $p = 1.5$ in

$p < 12D = 12(.162) = 1.94$ in

min. penetration NG use $C_d = P/12D$ *when* $6D \le p < 12D$

$$C_d = \frac{1.5}{1.94} = .77$$

NDS T7.3.1 $Z' = ZC_DC_MC_tC_dC_{eg}C_{di}C_{tn}$

$= .141(1.25)1.0(1.0).77(1.0)1.0(1.0) = .136^k$

$$\text{spc'g } 16d_R = \frac{2(.136)}{.17} = 1.6'' \quad \text{to close, NG!}$$

Increasing nail size will not give us better spacing because the maximum penetration is 1.5". What we will have is an ever increasing penalty (C_d) for the larger nail penny size. Try 1" dia. bolt in net holes.

Ck bolt capacity

Obtain required values for Yield Equations

$t_s = 1.5$ in
$t_m = 1.5$ in
NDS T8A, 8.2A $D = 1.0$ in
$\theta_m = 0$
$\theta_s = 0$

Z = 950 lbs / bolt

Calc Z´

NDS T7.3.1 $Z' = ZC_DC_MC_tC_gC_\Delta$

$= .95(1.25)1.0(1.0)1.0(1.0) = 1.188^k$

$$\text{spac'g required} = \frac{1.188}{.17} = 6.99'' \text{ o/c} \quad \text{say } 6'' \text{ o/c}$$

Use 4-2x6 DF-L No 1 (flat) with 1" dia. bolts at 6" o/c in net holes

Note that the above is a "multiple shear connection" with 4 members and 3 shear planes. The NDS stipulates that we may take the lowest nominal design value of any of the shear planes and multiply it times the number of shear planes to arrive at our nominal design value for the connection. However, since v is the maximum shear at the N.A. of the composite beam, and the bolt must be able to take that force, we can't use the multiplier. It makes more sense if you think about it in a typical multiple shear connection. In that type of connection each member takes a share of the total load, like in tension on the bottom of a truss. Our case is different because there is no total "load" to share. We have horizontal shear at different locations within the depth of the beam. So the bolt must be able to take the maximum "load" at the N.A., since it is not distributed among the other members.

You can't build a reputation on what you're GOING to do.

HENRY FORD

PROBLEM 9.5

Bolted built-up beam fiber stress.

Determine the maximum fiber bending stress of the built-up beam shown below.

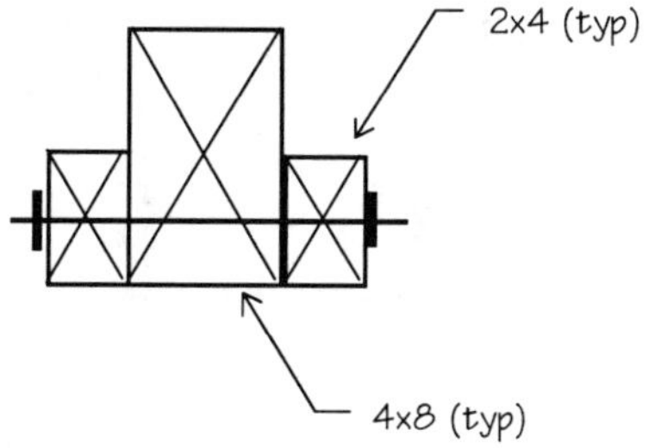

ASSUME

Equal deflection.
Horizontal slippage allowed.
Uniform load of .4 klf.
15 ′ span.
Bolts and connection ok.
E is equal for both members.

SOLUTION

$A_{2x4} = 5.25\ in^2$ $A_{4x8} = 25.375\ in^2$
$I_{2x4} = 5.359\ in^4$ $I_{4x8} = 111.148\ in^4$
$S_{2x4} = 3.063\ in^3$ $S_{4x8} = 30.661\ in^3$

Loads will be distributed in proportion to the stiffness of the individual members. In general:

$\bar{k} = EI$ = Relative Stiffness

E is constant so

$\bar{k}_{2x4} = 2(5.4) = 10.8\ in^3$

$\bar{k}_{4x8} = 111.1\ in^3$

$\sum \bar{k} = 111.1 + 10.8 = 121.9\ in^3$

Distribution of Loads

$$w_{2\text{-}2x4} = \left(\frac{\bar{k}_{2-2x4}}{\sum \bar{k}}\right) w = \left(\frac{10.8}{121.9}\right).4 = .035\text{ klf}$$

$$w_{4x8} = \left(\frac{111.1}{121.9}\right).4 = .365\text{ klf}$$

Calc stress

$$f_{b2x4} = \frac{12M}{S} = \frac{12\left(\frac{w}{2}\right)\ell^2}{8S} = \frac{12\left(\frac{.035}{2}\right)(15)^2}{8(3.06)} = 1.93\text{ ksi}$$

$$f_{b4x8} = \frac{12(.365)(15)^2}{8(30.66)} = 4.02\text{ ksi}$$

$f_{b2x4} = 1.93$ ksi
$f_{b4x8} = 4.02$ ksi

Alternate method

$$M = \frac{wL^2}{8} = \frac{.4(15)^2}{8} = 11.25^{k'} = 135^{k''}$$

Since w is distributed based upon rigidity and continuity of deformation, this implies M is as well.

$M = 2M_{2x4} + M_{4x8} = 2(f_{b2x4}S_{2x4}) + f_{b4x8}S_{4x8}$

$= 2(fb2x4(3.06)) + f_{b4x8}(30.66)$

$= 6.12fb2x4 + 30.66f_{b4x8}$

Combining the above equations implies:

$135 = 6.12fb2x4 + 30.66f_{b4x8}$ (EQ 1)

Equal deflection of the members implies:

$\Delta_{2x4} = \Delta_{4x8}$

$$\Delta = \frac{5w_{2x4}\ell^4}{384EI}$$

$$\frac{5w_{2x4}\ell^4}{384EI_{2x4}} = \frac{5w_{4x8}\ell^4}{384EI_{4x8}}$$

Substitute in their respective M gives:

$$5\left(\frac{w_{2x4}\ell^2}{8}\right)\frac{\ell^2}{48EI_{2x4}} = 5\left(\frac{w_{4x8}\ell^2}{8}\right)\frac{\ell^2}{48EI_{4x8}}$$

Since $M = \frac{f_b I}{c}$ gives:

$$5\left(\frac{f_{b2x4}I_{2x4}}{c_{2x4}}\right)\frac{\ell^2}{48EI_{2x4}} = 5\left(\frac{f_{b4x8}I_{4x8}}{c_{4x8}}\right)\frac{\ell^2}{48EI_{4x8}}$$

Cancelling:

$$\frac{f_{b2x4}}{c_{2x4}} = \frac{f_{b4x8}}{c_{4x8}}$$

$$f_{b2x4} = f_{b2x4}\left(\frac{c_{2x4}}{c_{4x8}}\right) = f_{b4x8}\left(\frac{3.5}{7.25}\right)$$

$= .483f_{b4x8}$ (EQ 2)

Substitute EQ 2 into EQ 1 and solve.

$135 = 6.12(.483f_{b4x8}) + 30.66f_{b4x8}$

$f_{b4x8} = 135/33.62 = 4.02$ ksi √

$$f_{b2x4} = \frac{135 - 30.66(4.02)}{6.12} = 1.92\text{ ksi}$$

These results compare well with the above.

$f_{b2x4} = 1.92$ ksi
$f_{b4x8} = 4.02$ ksi

Drawing on my fine command of the English language, I said nothing.

ROBERT BENCHLEY

PROBLEM 9.6

Built-up (composite) beams fiber stress with slippage prevented.

Determine the maximum fiber bending stress of the built-up beam shown below. Slippage is prevented.

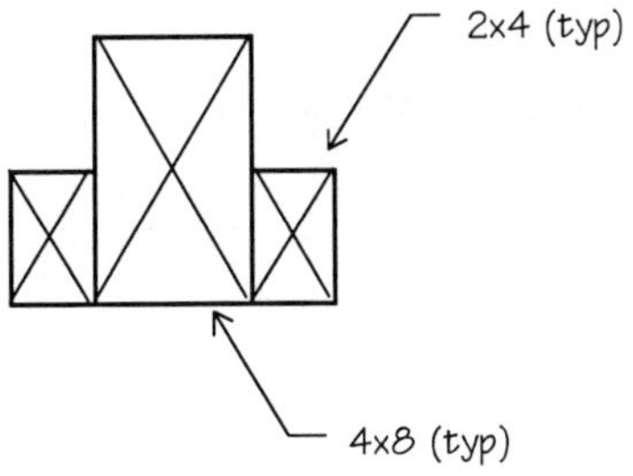

ASSUME

- Equal deflection.
- Horizontal slippage prevented.
- Uniform load of .4 klf.
- 15 ′ span.
- Glue at connection provides homogeneity.
- E is equal for both members.

SOLUTION

$A_{2x4} = 5.25\ in^2$ $A_{4x8} = 25.375\ in^2$
$I_{2x4} = 5.359\ in^4$ $I_{4x8} = 111.148\ in^4$
$S_{2x4} = 3.063\ in^3$ $S_{4x8} = 30.661\ in^3$

Loads are not distributed in proportion to the stiffness of the individual members, as in the previous example, because of composite action.

Find the C.G. and N.A.

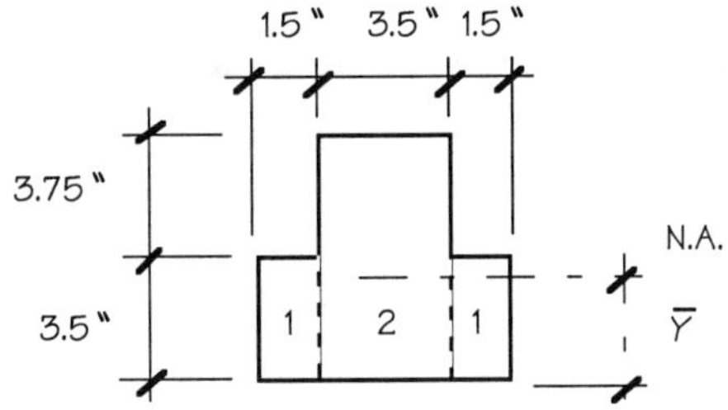

$$\bar{Y} = \sum_i \frac{A_i \bar{Y}_i}{A_i} = \frac{2(1.5)3.5(3.5/2) + 3.5(7.25)7.25/2}{2(1.5)3.5 + 3.5(7.25)}$$

$$= \frac{110.36}{35.88} = 3.08\ "$$

Calc M

$$M = \frac{wL^2}{8} = \frac{.4(15)^2}{8} = 11.25\ ^{k\prime} = 135\ ^{k\,"}$$

Calc I of composite

Use parallel-axis theorem

$$I_x \sum \bar{I} + Ad^2 = \sum \frac{bh^3}{12} + Ad^2 = \sum A\left(\frac{h^2}{12} + d^2\right)$$

$$= 2(5.25)\left(\frac{3.5^2}{12} + 1.33^2\right) + 25.375\left(\frac{7.25^2}{12} + .55^2\right)$$

$$= 148.12\ in^4$$

Calc stress ($f_{b\ top}$ and $f_{b\ bott}$)

$$f_{b\ 2x4\ bott} = MS = \frac{Mc_{2x4}}{I} = \frac{Mc_{4x8}}{I} = f_{b\ 4x8\ bott}$$

$$= \frac{135(3.08)}{148.12} = 2.81\ ksi$$

$$f_{b\ 2x4\ bott} = f_{b\ 4x8\ bott} = 2.81\ ksi$$

$$f_{b\ 4x8\ top} = \frac{135(7.25 - 3.08)}{148.12} = 3.8\ ksi$$

The stress varies from previous examples because the N.A. shifted up for the 2x4's and down with respect to the 4x8.

$f_{b\ 4x8\ top} = 3.8$ ksi

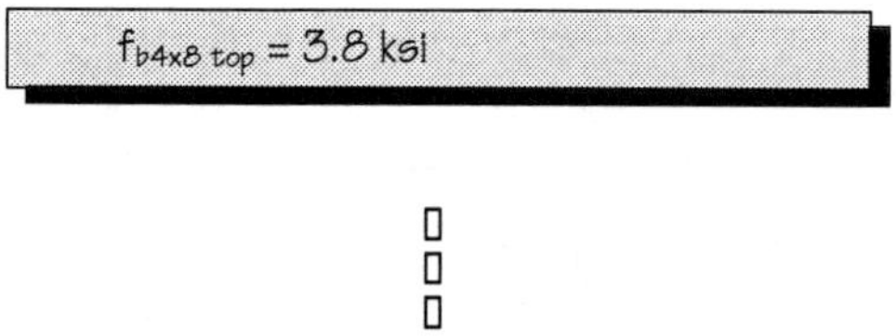

> *Opportunity is missed by most people because it is dressed in overalls and looks like work.*
>
> THOMAS EDISON

O PROBLEM 9.7

Bolted sandwich beam.

An architect requires that you check a wooden built-up beam with a steel plate sandwiched in between.

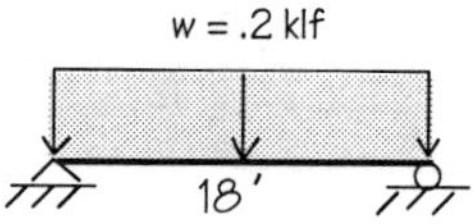

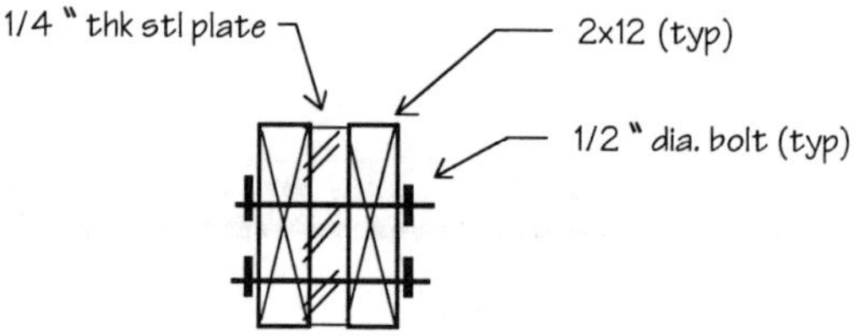

ASSUME

DF-L – No 1.
LL = 67% of TL.
EMC < 19%.
$C_D = 1.25$.
L/360 criteria.
A-36 stl.
4" stud wall supports beam.
$F_{b\ stl} = 22$ ksi.
Neglect bolts, spacing and holes.
Full lateral support.

SOLUTION

$A_{2x12} = 16.88$ in^2
$I_{2x12} = 178.0$ in^4
$S_{2x12} = 31.64$ in^3

Loads will be distributed in proportion to the stiffness of the individual members. In general:

$\bar{k} = EI$ = Relative Stiffness

Substituting values

$\bar{k}_{2-2x12} = E_w I_w = 1.7e3(178)2 = 605.2e3$ in^3

$\bar{k}_{stl} = E_s I_s = E_s \left(\dfrac{bd^3}{12}\right) = 29e3 \left(\dfrac{.25(11.25)^3}{12}\right)$

$= 860.2e3$ in^3

$\sum \bar{k} = 605.2e3 + 860.2e3 = 1465.4e3$ in^3

Distribution of Loads

$w_{2-2x12} = \left(\dfrac{\bar{k}_{2-2x12}}{\sum \bar{k}}\right) w = \left(\dfrac{605}{1465}\right) 2 = .083$ klf

$w_{stl} = \left(\dfrac{860}{1465}\right) 2 = .117$ klf

checking $.083 + .117 = .2 = w$ ✓

Ck 2-2x12 bending stress

$f_{b\ 2-2x4} = \dfrac{12M}{S} = \dfrac{12\left(\dfrac{w_w}{2}\right)\ell^2}{8S} = \dfrac{12(.083/2)(18)^2}{8(31.6)}$

$= .638$ ksi

$F_b' = C_D C_M C_t C_L C_F C_V C_{fu} C_r C_c C_f$

$= .875(1.25)1.0(1.0)1.0(1.0)1.0(1.0)1.0(1.0)$

$= 1.09$ ksi $> .638$ ksi ✓

Bending ok for 2-2x12

Ck stl bending stress

$$S = \frac{bd^2}{6} = \frac{.25(11.25)^2}{6} = 5.27 \text{ in}^3$$

$$f_{bstl} = \frac{12M}{S} = \frac{12(.117)(18)^2}{8(5.27)} = 10.8 \text{ ksi} < 22 \text{ ksi} = F_{b\,stl}$$

Bending ok for stl plate

Ck shear stress in wood

$$V = \frac{w\ell}{2} = \frac{(.083/2)(18)}{2} = .37^k$$

$$f_v = \frac{1.5V}{A} = \frac{1.5(.37)}{16.88} = .033 \text{ ksi}$$

NDS T2.3.1

$$F_v' = F_vC_DC_MC_tC_H$$

$$= .095(1.25)1.0(1.0)1.0$$

$$= .119 \text{ ksi} > .033 \text{ ksi}$$

Shear ok for 2-2x12

Ck shear stress in stl

$$V = \frac{w\ell}{2} = \frac{.117(18)}{2} = 1.05^k$$

$$f_v = \frac{V}{A} = \frac{1.05}{.25(11.25)} = .37 \text{ ksi}$$

$$F_{V\,stl} = 14.5 \text{ ksi} > .37 \text{ ksi}$$

Ck deflection

$$\Delta_w = \frac{5w\ell^4}{384EI} = \frac{5(.083)18^4 1728}{384(1.7E3)178(2)} = .32 \text{ in}$$

$$\Delta_s = \frac{5w\ell^4}{384EI} = \frac{5(.117)18^4 1728}{384(29E3)29.66} = .32 \text{ in}$$

$$l/360 = 12(18)/360 = .6 \text{ in} > .32 \text{ in}$$

Deflection ok for built-up beam

Ck bearing

The stl plate is carrying most of the shear and with a smaller bearing area with respect to the wall below.

$$F_{c\perp}' = F_{c\perp}C_MC_tC_b \quad \text{(no adjustment)}$$ NDS T2.3.1

$$= .625(1.0)1.0(1.0) = .625 \text{ ksi}$$

$$f_{c\perp\,stl} = \frac{R}{A} = \frac{1.05}{3.5(.25)} = 1.2 \text{ ksi} > .625 \text{ ksi} \quad \textbf{NG!}$$

Use bearing plate under built-up beam.

$$f_{c\perp} = \frac{R}{A} = \frac{1.05+2(.37)}{3.5(1.5+1.5+.25)} = .157 \text{ ksi} < .625 \text{ ksi}$$

Built-up beam ok with the use of a 3.5x3.25 stl bearing plate

If your parents didn't have any children, there is a good chance that you won't have any.

CLARENCE DAY

○ PROBLEM 9.8

Compatibility of deformation of a cantilever beam configuration.

Determine the maximum stresses (f_b,f_v) at the point of contact for the cantilever beam configuration shown below.

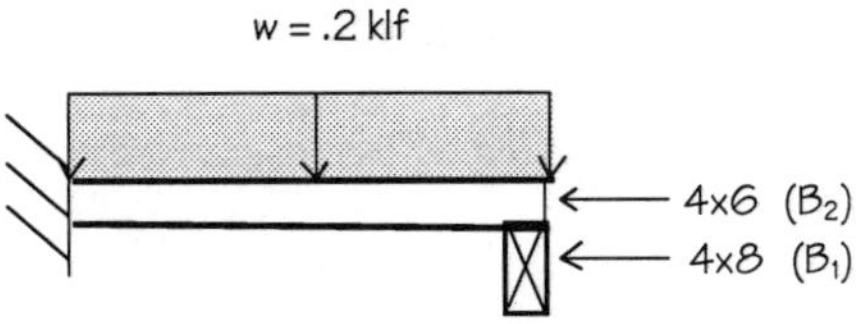

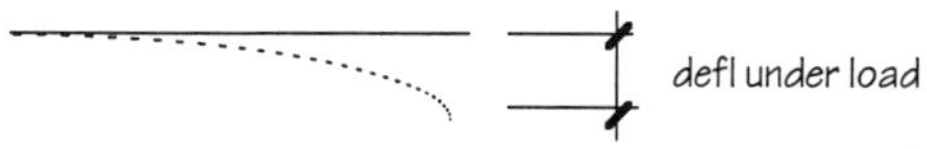

ASSUME

- Df - No 2.
- EMC < 19%.
- Defl under load = .75".
- BM_2 has unkown load and length.
- BM_1 and BM_2 connected.

SOLUTION

$A_{4x6} = 19.25\ in^2$ $\quad$ $A_{4x8} = 25.38\ in^2$

$I_{4x6} = 48.5\ in^4$ $\quad$ $I_{4x8} = 111.1\ in^4$

$S_{4x6} = 17.6\ in^3$ $\quad$ $S_{4x8} = 30.7\ in^3$

Check Bending

Since we know the deflection under load, use compatibility of deformation for analysis.

B_2 (4x6) ↓

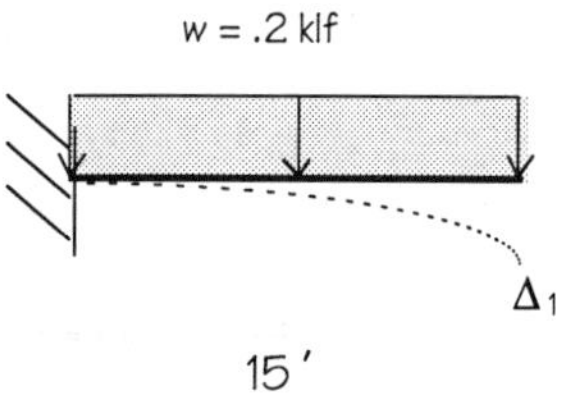

Solve deflection in terms of E:

$$\Delta_1 = \frac{w\ell^4}{84EI} = \frac{.2(15)^4 1728}{8(1.7e3)48.5} = 26.5 \text{ in}$$

This is how the beam would deflect if acting alone with the load.

B_1 (4x8) ↑

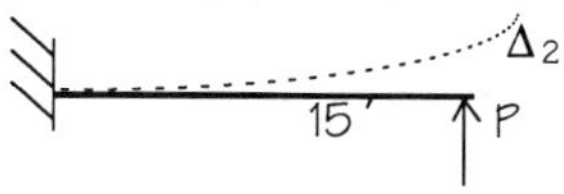

Solve deflection in terms of P,E

$$\Delta_2 = \frac{P\ell^3}{3EI} = \frac{P(15(12))^3}{3(1.7e3)48.5} = 23.58P$$

This is the "resistive" deflection offered by the 4x8.

B_1 (4x8) ↕

$\Delta_3 = 442P/E$

$\Delta_{actual} = \Delta_1 - \Delta_2 = \Delta_3$

$26.5 - 23.58P = .75$

$$P = \frac{(26.5+.75)}{23.58} = 1.16^k$$

Calc Flexure stress

B_2 (4x6)

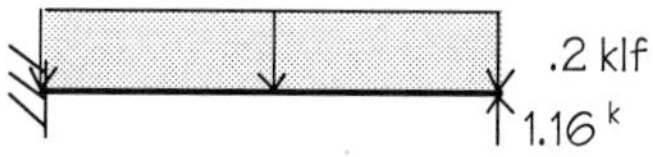

$$M = \frac{w\ell^2}{2} - P\ell = \frac{.2(15)^2 12}{2} - 1.16(15)12 = 61.2^{k'}$$

$$f_b = \frac{M}{S} = \frac{61.2}{17.6} = 3.48 \text{ ksi}$$

Beam B_2 yields f_b =3.48 ksi

Calc Shear stress

B_2 (4x6)

$V = w\ell - P = .2(15) - 1.16 = 1.84^k$

$$f_v = \frac{1.5V}{A} = \frac{1.5(1.84)}{19.25} = .143 \text{ ksi}$$

Beam B_1 yields $f_v = .143$ ksi

I am in earnest; I will not equivocate; I will not excuse; I will not retreat a single inch; and I will be heard.

WILLIAM LLOYD GARRISON

PROBLEM 9.9

King post with point load utilizing complementary strain energy analysis.

Determine the stress in each of the members of the king post truss shown below.

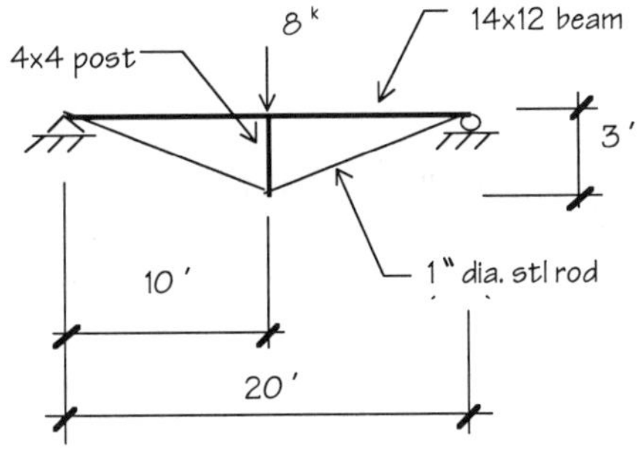

ASSUME

DF-L - No 1.
Connections ok.
EMC < 19%.
$C_D = 1.25$.
Connection at beam at NA.
A-36 stl.
w = .2 klf.
Full lateral support.

SOLUTION

$A_{4x12} = 39.38$ in^2
$I_{4x12} = 415.3$ in^4
$E_{4x12} = 1.7e3$ ksi

$E_R = 29e3$ ksi
$A_R = .196$ in^2

$E_P = 1.7e3$ ksi
$A_P = 12.25$ in^2

Ck Determinacy

M = 2j - 3

$4 \neq 2(4) - 3 = 5 \Rightarrow$ *one degree*

Use complementary strain to solve for P

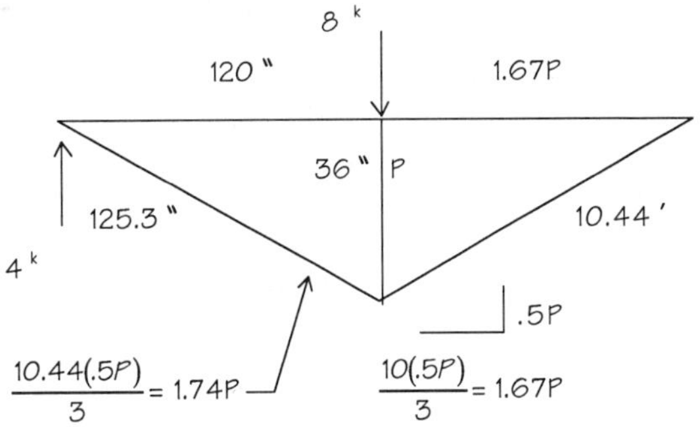

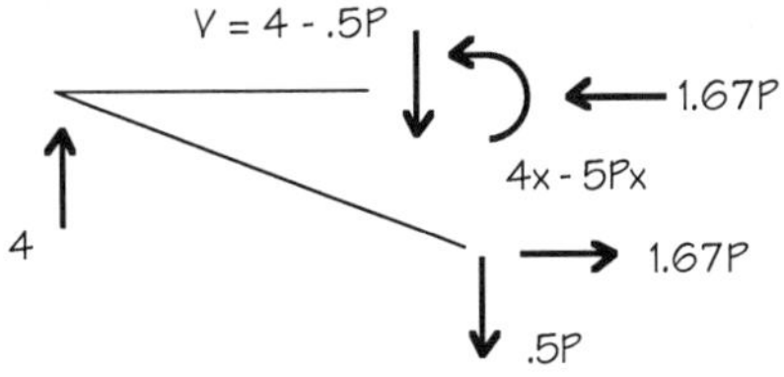

$$U_d = \sum\left[\int_0^{\ell} \frac{M^2 dx}{2EI} + \int_0^{\ell} \frac{P^2 dx}{2EA}\right]$$

$$= \frac{2}{2E_BA_B}\int_0^{120}(4x-.5P)^2dx + \qquad (M^2\ bm)$$

$$\frac{1}{2E_BA_B}\int_0^{240}(1.67)^2dx + \qquad (P^2\ bm)$$

$$\frac{1}{2E_pA_p}\int_0^{36}(P)^2dx + \qquad (P^2\ post)$$

$$\frac{2}{2E_RA_R}\int_0^{125.3}(1.74P)^2dx \qquad (P^2\ rod)$$

$$= \frac{1}{E_BA_B}\left[\frac{16(120)^3}{3} - \frac{4P(120)^3}{3} + \frac{.25P^2(120)^3}{3}\right] +$$

$$\frac{1}{2E_BA_B}\left[2.79P^2(240)\right] + \frac{1}{2E_pA_p}\left[P^2(36)\right] +$$

$$\frac{1}{E_RA_R}\left[3.03P^2(125.3)\right]$$

$$d\left(\frac{Ud}{dp}\right) \Rightarrow \text{yields } P$$

$$= \frac{1}{E_BA_B}\left[0 - \frac{4(120)^3}{3} + \frac{2(.25)P(120)^3}{3}\right] +$$

$$\frac{1}{2E_BA_B}\left[2(2.79)P(240)\right] + \frac{1}{2E_pA_p}\left[2P(36)\right] +$$

$$\frac{1}{E_RA_R}\left[2(3.03)P(125.3)\right] = .53P - 3.083 = 0$$

$P = 3.082/.53 = 5.816^k$

Solve for Δ

$$\Delta_{actual} = \Delta_{with\ 8^k\ down} - \Delta_{with\ P\ up}$$

$$= \frac{P_8\ell^3}{48EI} - \frac{P_p\ell^3}{48EI} = \frac{(P_8 - P_p)\ell^3}{48EI} = \frac{(8-5.82)(240)^3}{48(1.7e3)415.3}$$

$= .89$ in

<u>Calc bending stress</u>

$$f_b = \frac{12M}{S} = \frac{12P\ell}{4S} = \frac{12(8-5.82)20}{4(73.83)} = 1.77 \text{ ksi}$$

Bending stress = 1.77 ksi

<u>Calc axial stress</u>

Beam

$P_B = 1.67P = 1.67(5.82) = 9.72^k$

$$f_{c\perp} = \frac{P_B}{A} = \frac{9.72}{39.4} = .248 \text{ ksi}$$

Axial stress for beam = .248 ksi

Post

$P = 5.82^k$

$$f_{c\perp} = \frac{P}{A} = \frac{5.82}{12.25} = .475 \text{ ksi}$$

Axial stress for post = .475 ksi

Rods

$P_R = 1.74P = 1.74(5.82) = 10.13^k$

$$f_{c\perp} = \frac{P_R}{A} = \frac{10.13}{.196} = 51.67 \text{ ksi}$$

Axial stress for rod = 51.67 ksi

Many of life's failures are people who did not realize how close they were to success when they gave up.

THOMAS EDISON

● PROBLEM 9.10

Compatibility of deformation of a 2-beam configuration that has a point load.

Determine the maximum stresses (f_b, f_v) at the point of contact for the 2 beam configuration shown below.

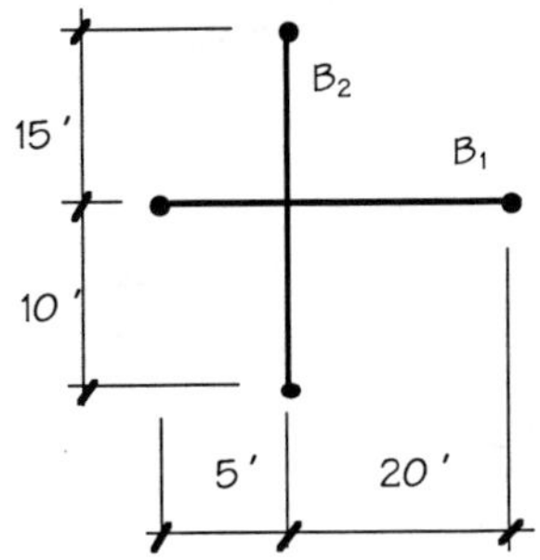

of B2

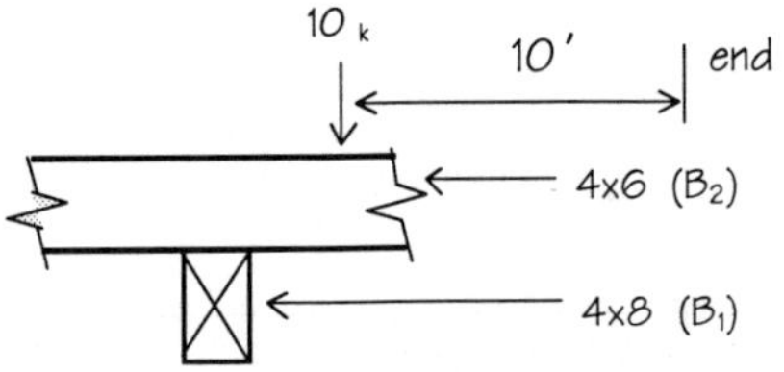

ASSUME

DF-L - No 2.
Slippage allowed at "a".
EMC < 19%.
Full lateral support at B_2 only.
Neglect beam weight.
$\Delta < L/180$ ok.

SOLUTION

$A_{4x6} = 19.25$ in^2
$I_{4x6} = 48.5$ in^4
$S_{4x6} = 17.6$ in^3

$A_{4x8} = 25.38$ in^2
$I_{4x8} = 111.1$ in^4
$S_{4x8} = 30.7$ in^3

Check Bending

From compatibility of deformation we have:

B_1 (4x6) ↓

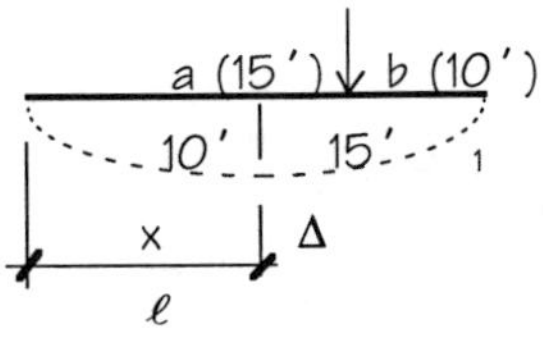

Solve deflection in terms of E:

Δ_1

$$= \frac{Pbx\left(\ell^2 - b^2 - x^2\right)}{6EI\ell} = \frac{10(10)10\left((25)^2 - (10)^2 - (10)^2\right)1728}{6E(48.5)25}$$

$= 100948.45/E$

This is how the beam would deflect if acting alone with the load.

B_1 (4x8)

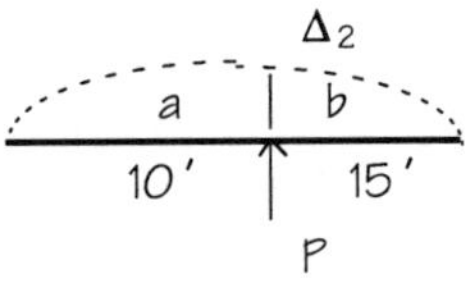

Solve deflection in terms of P,E:

$$\Delta_2 = \frac{Pa^2b^2}{3EI\ell} = \frac{P(10)^2(15)^2 1728}{3E(48.5)25} = 10688.66P/E$$

Which is the "resistive" deflection offered by the 4x8 below.

B_1 (4x8) ↕

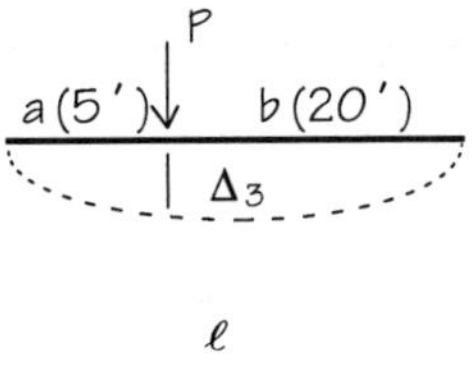

Solve deflection at point of load in terms of P,E:

$$\Delta_3 = \frac{Pa^2b^2}{3EI\ell} = \frac{P(5)^2(20)^2 1728}{3E111.1(25)} = 2073.81P/E$$

$\Delta_{actual} = \Delta_1 - \Delta_2 = \Delta_3$

$$\frac{100948.45}{E}-\frac{10688.66P}{E}=\frac{2073.81P}{E}$$

$$P=\frac{100948.45}{(10688.66+2073.81)}=7.91^k$$

Calc Flexure stress

B_1 (4x6)

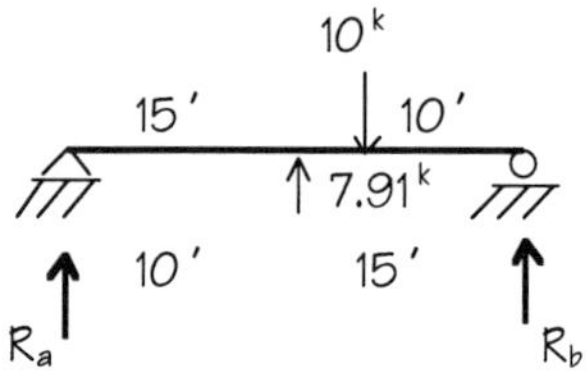

$$\sum M_a = 0 = -10(7.91)+15(10)-25R_b$$

$R_b = 70.9/25 = 2.84^k$

$$\sum M_b = 0 = 25R_a+15(7.91)-10(10)$$

$R_a = -18.65/25 = -.75^k$ up

Use simigraphical method

$-w$	0	0	0	dv/dx
$-\int wdx$	0	0	0	ΔV

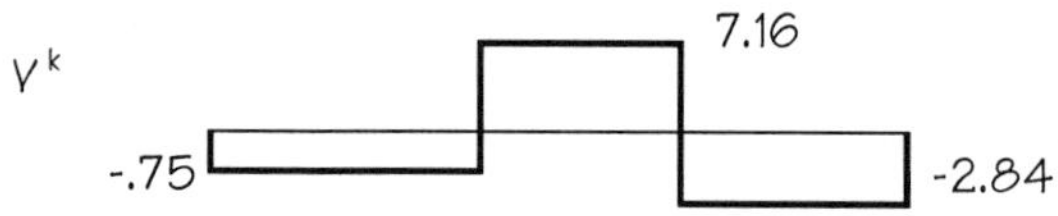

V	-.75	7.16	-2.84	dm/dx
$\int Vdx$	-7.5	35.8	-28.4	ΔM

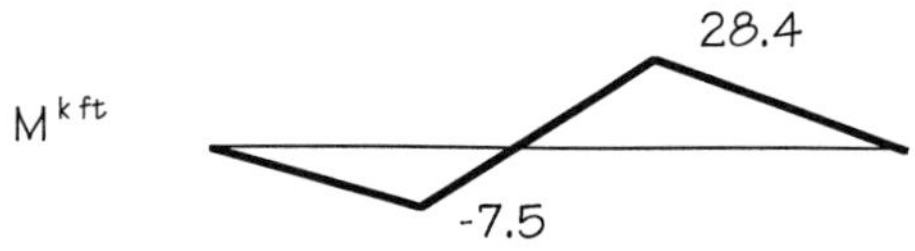

$$f_b=\frac{M}{S}=\frac{28.4(12)}{17.6}=19.36\text{ ksi}$$

Beam B_2 yields f_b = 19.36 ksi

B_1 (4x8)

$$f_b=\frac{M}{S}=\frac{12}{S}\left(\frac{Pab}{\ell}\right)=\frac{12}{30.7}\left(\frac{7.91(5)20}{25}\right)=12.37\text{ ksi}$$

Beam B_1 yields f_b = 12.37 ksi

Calc Shear stress

B_2 (4x6)

$$f_v=\frac{1.5V}{A}=\frac{1.5(7.16)}{19.25}=.056\text{ ksi}$$

Beam B_1 yields f_v = 056 ksi

B_2 (4x8)

$$f_v=\frac{1.5Pb}{\ell A}=\frac{1.5(7.91)20}{25.38(25)}=.37\text{ ksi}$$

Beam B_2 yields f_v = .37 ksi

My grandmother started walking five miles a day when she was sixty. She's ninety-five now, and we don't know where the hell she is.

ELLEN DEGENERES

○ PROBLEM 9.11

Compatibility of deformation of a 2-beam configuration.

Determine the maximum stresses (f_b,f_v) at the point of contact for the 2-beam configuration shown below.

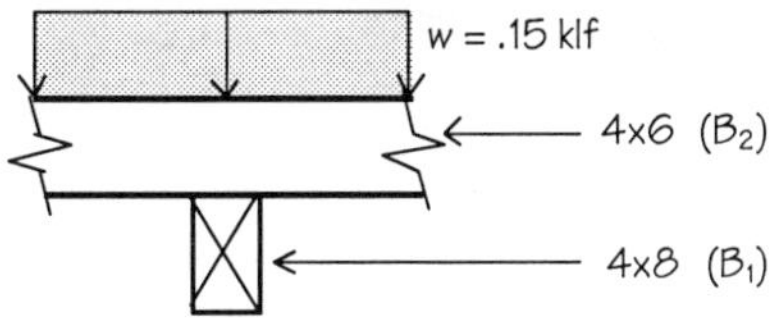

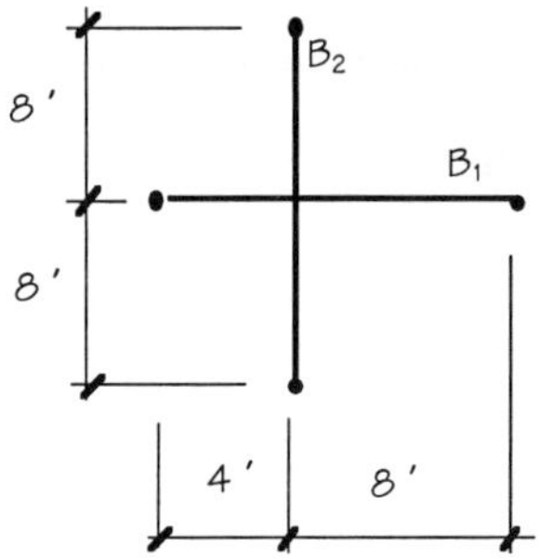

ASSUME

DF-L - No 2.
Slippage allowed at "a".
EMC < 19%.
Full lateral support at B_2 only.
Neglect beam weight.
$\Delta < L/180$.

SOLUTION

$A_{4x6} = 19.25\ in^2$
$I_{4x6} = 48.5\ in^4$
$S_{4x6} = 17.6\ in^3$

$A_{4x8} = 25.38\ in^2$
$I_{4x8} = 111.1\ in^4$
$S_{4x8} = 30.7\ in^3$

Check Bending

From compatibility of deformation we have:

B_2 (4x6) ↓

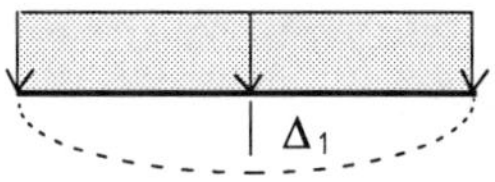

Solve deflection in terms of E.

$$\Delta_1 = \frac{5w\ell^4}{384EI} = \frac{5(.15)(16)^4 1728}{384(E)48.5} = 4560/E$$

This is how the beam would deflect if acting alone with the load.

B_1 (4x8) ↑

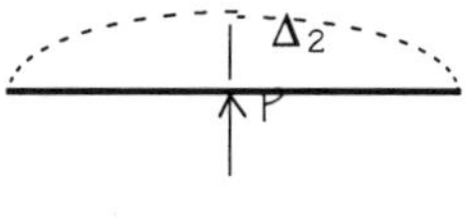

Solve deflection in terms of P,E:

$$\Delta_2 = \frac{P\ell^3}{48EI} = \frac{P(16(12))^3}{48(E)48.5} = 3040P/E$$

This is the "resistive" deflection offered by the 4x8.

B_1 (4x8) ↕

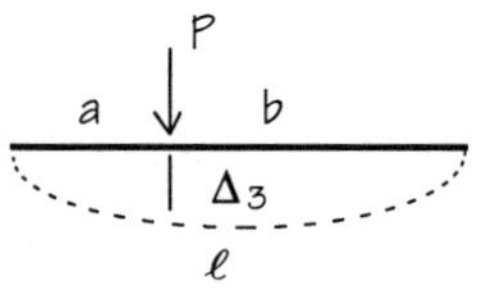

Solve deflection at point of load in terms of P,E:

$$\Delta_3 = \frac{Pa^2b^2}{3EI\ell} = \frac{P(4(12))^2(8(12))^2}{3(E)111.1(12)12} = 442P/E$$

$$\Delta_{actual} = \Delta_1 - \Delta_2 = \Delta_3$$

$$\frac{4560}{E} - \frac{3040P}{E} = \frac{442P}{E}$$

$$P = \frac{4560}{(3040+442)} = 1.31^k$$

Calc Flexure stress

B_1 (4x6)

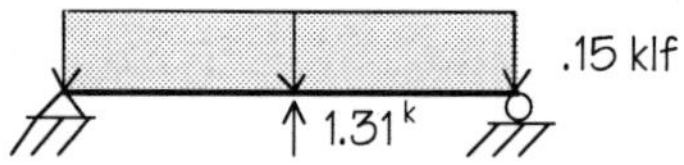

Note that this is not the maximum stress along beam B1 because we can think of B2 as a resistive spring with some spring constant that resists w. The moment diagram looks something like this.

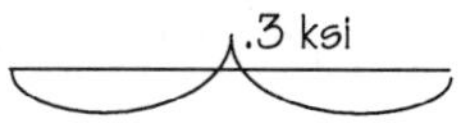

An exact solution would require the use of calculus. We can see this graphically thus:

Conservatively we have:

$$f_b = \frac{M}{S} = \frac{1}{S}\left(\frac{wL^2}{8} - \frac{P\ell}{4}\right) = \frac{12}{17.6}\left(\frac{.15(16)^2}{8} - \frac{1.31(16)}{4}\right)$$
$$= -.3 \text{ ksi}$$

Beam B_2 yields $f_b = .3$ ksi

B_1 (4x8)

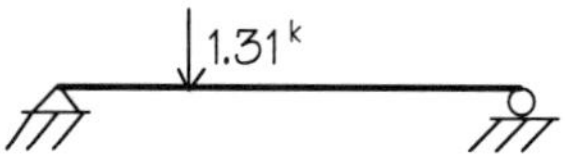

$$f_b = \frac{M}{S} = \frac{1}{S}\left(\frac{Pab}{\ell}\right) = \frac{1}{30.7}\left(\frac{1.31(4)8(12)}{12}\right) = 1.37 \text{ ksi}$$

Beam B_1 yields $f_b = 1.37$ ksi

Calc Shear stress

B_2 (4x6)

$$V = \frac{w\ell}{2} - \frac{P}{2} = \frac{.15(16)}{2} - \frac{1.31}{2} = .55^k$$

$$f_v = \frac{1.5V}{A} = \frac{1.5(.55)}{19.25} = .043 \text{ ksi}$$

Beam B_1 yields $f_v = 043$ ksi

B_2 (4x8)

$$f_v = \frac{1.5Pb}{\ell A} = \frac{1.5(1.31)8}{25.38(12)} = .052 \text{ ksi}$$

Beam B_2 yields $f_v = .052$ ksi

The hand is the cutting edge of the mind.

JACOB BRONOWSKI

PROBLEM 9.12

Torsional stress in a column.

A local contractor wants to erect a sign post from some extra material she has stockpiled in her laydown area of her construction yard. Determine if the proposed sign post can withstand the torsional stress due to the wind load on the surface of the commercial signage.

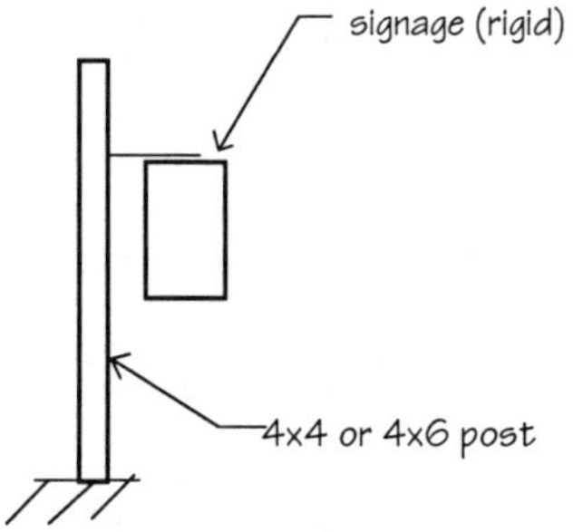

ASSUME

- Neglect combined load effects.
- DF - L No 1 post.
- EMC > 16%, wet exposure.
- Torsion (T) = 300 in lb.
- $F_{rt} = 15$ psi

SOLUTION

Torsional moments cause a member to twist and induce torsional stress. This occurs when design loads are offset from (eccentric to) the centroid of the member.

It is unusual for torsion to be a factor in the design of timber structures. In fact, as engineers, we try to avoid torsional stress in our designs. When large torsional stresses are expected in a design we try to modify the design to eliminate them. Torsion may be of concern in cantilevered signage, beams that support the lateral loads of handrailing and certain tower structures.

The information available on torsion in wood members is rather limited. The TCM recommends that the design value for torsional stress F_s be limited to the design value for radial stress.

Ck 4x4 for torsion

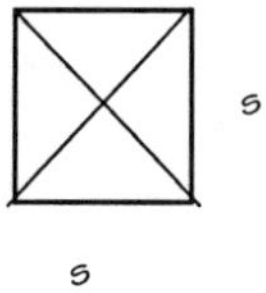

The formula for torsional stress for a square section is:

$$f_s = \frac{4.8T}{s^3} = \frac{4.8(300)}{(3.5)^3} = 33.6 \text{ psi}$$ TCM 5.5

It is conservative to use C_M for a glulam thus:

$F_s' = F_s C_D C_M = 15(1.6).875 = 21 \text{ psi} < 33.6 \text{ psi}$ **NG!**

4x4 post NG

Try 4x6 post for torsional stress

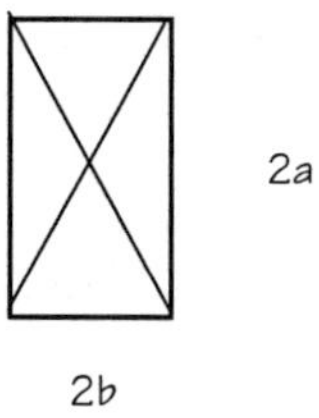

TCM 5.5

Torsional stress is given by the formula:

$$f_s = \frac{T(3a+1.8b)}{8a^2b^2} = \frac{300\left(3\left(5.5/2\right)+1.8\left(3.5/2\right)\right)}{8\left(5.5/2\right)^2\left(3.5/2\right)^2}$$

= 18.5 psi < 21 psi √

4x6 post ok for torsional stress

□
□
□

Once you accept your own death, all of a sudden you're free to live. You no longer care about your reputation. You no longer care except so far as your life can be used tactically - to promote a cause you believe in.

SAUL ALINSKY

○ PROBLEM 9.13

Fire damaged beam repair.

Your assignment is to determine if a fire damaged solid beam has to be replaced or can be retained with minor repair work.

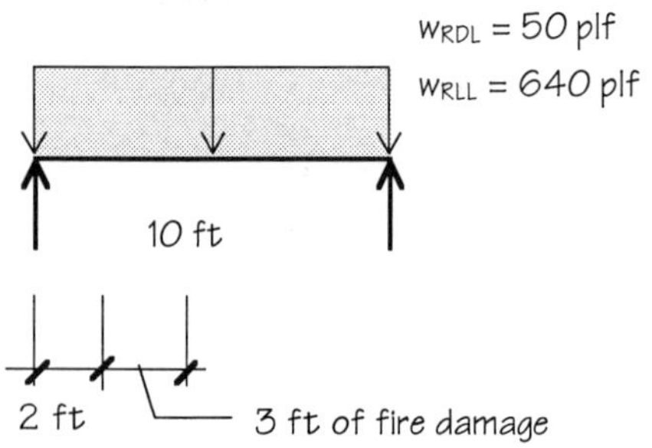

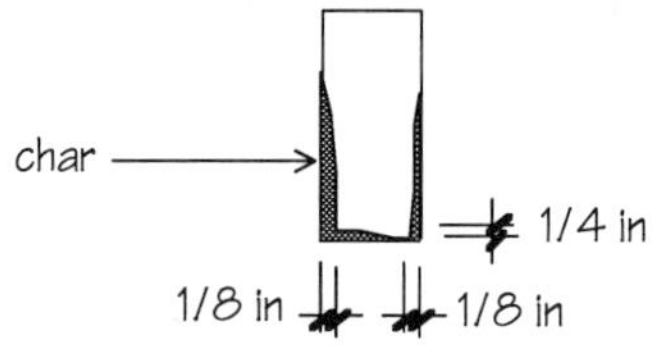

ASSUME

Original beam ok.
No ponding, no plaster.
6x12, DF - L No. 1.
Full Lat. support from plywood.
Neglect beam wt.
EMC <19%.
Normal temp. conditions.
Commercial building.

SOLUTION

The mechanical properties of wood are detrimentally altered by the elevated temperatures of fire. The amount of thermal degradation (wood mass loss) to the members' properties is dependent upon the location of the heat damage and the temperature history at that point.

Heavy timbers, like glulams, perform well in fires and are capable of simple restoration (due in part to the insulation properties of char). Unless the wood is well charred, the glue-line will maintain its integrity and has a thermal response similar to wood.

Residual strength and section properties

Per recommendation by *"Evaluation, Maintenance and Upgrading of Wood Structures"* assume the removal of 1/4 of an inch of wood below the char line by sandblasting. We may use 90 percent of the original of allowable tensile design stress and 100 percent of the compressive strength, or modulus of elasticity, to calculate the residual strength of the damaged member.

Fb = 1.35 ksi
Fv = .085 ksi
E = 1.6e3 ksi

Reduced b = 5.5 - 2(.125) - 2(.25) = 4.75 in

Reduced d = 11.5 - .25 - .25 = 11 in

$$S = \frac{bd^2}{6} = \frac{4.75(11)^2}{6} = 95.8 \text{ in}^3$$

$$I = \frac{bd^3}{12} = \frac{4.75(11)^3}{12} = 526.9 \text{ in}^4$$

$$A = bd = 4.75(11) = 52.3 \text{ in}^2$$

DL + RLL controls by inspection. Assume the rafter is relatively short and has a large loading so that V will control.

Ck shear without shear modification

NDS 2.3.1

$$F_v' = F_v(C_D)C_M(C_t)C_H = .085(1.25)1.0(1.0)1.0 = .11 \text{ ksi}$$

$$V = \frac{w\ell}{2} = \frac{(.050+.64)10}{2} = 3.45^k$$

NDS 3.4.2

$$A_R = \frac{1.5(V)}{F_v'} = \frac{1.5(3.5)}{.11} = 47.7 \text{ in}^2 < 52.3 \text{ in}^3$$

Shear ok

Bending

NDS 2.3.1

Assume the selected section has a C_F of 1.0 (4x12) and that the revised section properties exist the entire length of the beam.

NDS 3.3.2

$$F_b' = F_bC_DC_MC_tC_LC_FC_r = 1.35(1.25)1.0(1.0)1.0(1.0)$$

$$= 1.69 \text{ ksi}$$

$$M = \frac{w\ell^2}{8} = \frac{(.05+.64)10^2}{8} = 8.6^{\text{k-ft}}$$

$$S_R = \frac{12M}{F_b'} = \frac{12(8.6)}{1.69} = 61.1 \text{ in}^3 < 95.8 \text{ in}^3$$

Bending ok

Ck defl. (based on TCM)

NDS 2.3.1

$$E' = E(C_M)C_t = 1.6e3(1.0)1.0 = 1.6e3 \text{ ksi}$$

$$\Delta_{LL} = \frac{5w\ell^4}{384EI} = \frac{5(.64)10^4(1728)}{384(1.6e3)526}$$

$$= .17 \text{ in} < \ell/240 = 10(12)/240 = .5 \text{ in}$$

$$\Delta_{TL} = \Delta_{LL}\left(\frac{w_{TL}}{w_{LL}}\right) = .17\left(\frac{.69}{.64}\right) = .18 \text{ in}$$

$$\ell/180 = 10(12)/180 = .67 \text{ in} > .18 \text{ in}$$

Deflection ok. Sandblast the fire damaged area 1/4 in. beyond interior of char.

Perhaps the most valuable result of all education is the ability to make yourself do the thing you have to do, when it ought to be done, whether you like it or not.

THOMAS HENRY HUXLEY

○ PROBLEM 9.14

Fire damaged glulam beam repair.

A small fire has damaged an old glulam beam as indicated below. You are to see if the beam can be saved from being replaced and thus retained with minor repair work.

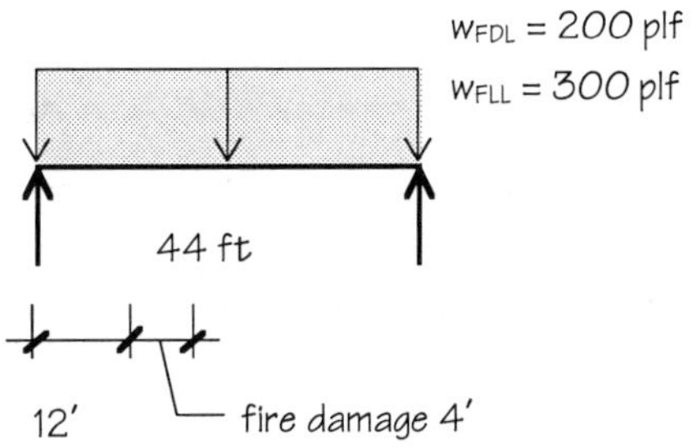

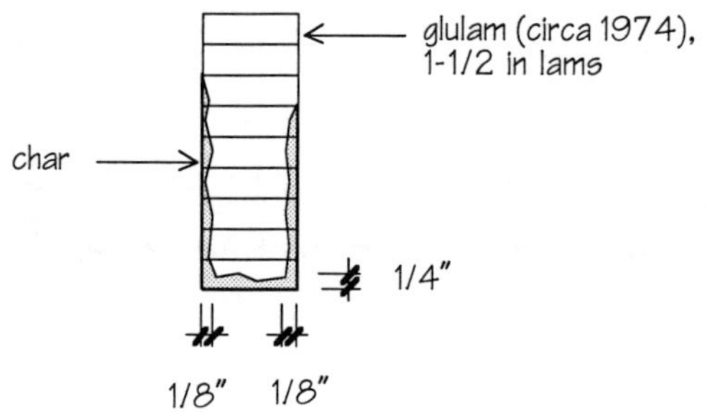

ASSUME

Building Dept. allows use of 1974 specification.
Original beam ok.
No ponding, plaster ceiling.
Full Lat. support from plywood.
w includes self wt.
EMC < 19%.
Normal temp. conditions.
Commercial building.
5-1/8 x 34-1/2, 24F-3 glulam, southern pine.

SOLUTION

As stated in the previous problem on fire damaged solid beams, the mechanical properties of wood are detrimentally altered by the elevated temperatures of fire. The amount of thermal degradation (wood mass loss) to the members' properties is dependent upon the location of the heat damage and the temperature history at that point. Glulams, perform well in fires and are capable of simple restoration (due in part to the insulation properties of char). Unless the wood is well charred, the glue-line will maintain its integrity and has a thermal response similar to wood.

Residual strength and section properties

Per recommendation by *"Evaluation, Maintenance and Upgrading of Wood Structures"* assume the removal of 1/4 of an inch of wood below the char line by sandblasting. We may use 90 percent of the original of allowable tensile design stress and 100 percent of the compressive strength, or modulus of elasticity, to calculate the residual strength of the damaged member. However, the determination of the residual strength of the glulam is more complicated than that of a solid beam. Since glulams are manufactured with the premium quality laminations placed in the maximum bending stress zones, damage to the outermost zones by fire severely reduces the tabular and, hence, the allowable stress of the subject member. From TCM 117-71 Table 3, Part B of Structural Glued Laminated Southern Pine we get:

$F_b = 2.4$ ksi
$F_v = .2$ ksi
$E = 1.8e3$ ksi

Calculating the reduced section properties gives:

Reduced $b = 5.125 - 2(.125) - 2(.25) = 4.38$ in

Reduced $d = 34.5 - .25 - .25 = 34.0$ in

$$S = \frac{bd^2}{6} = \frac{4.38(34)^2}{6} = 843.9 \text{ in}^3$$

$$I = \frac{bd^3}{12} = \frac{4.38(34)^3}{12} = 14346 \text{ in}^4$$

$A = bd = 4.38(34) = 148.9$ in^2

The lay-up requirements for TCM 117-71:

outer zone = 10% No.1 D = 34.5(.1) =3.5 in or 3 lams
intermed. zone = 5% No. 2 MG = 34.5(.05) =1.73 in or 2 lams
inner zone = No 3

Checking the lay-up after char removal gives:

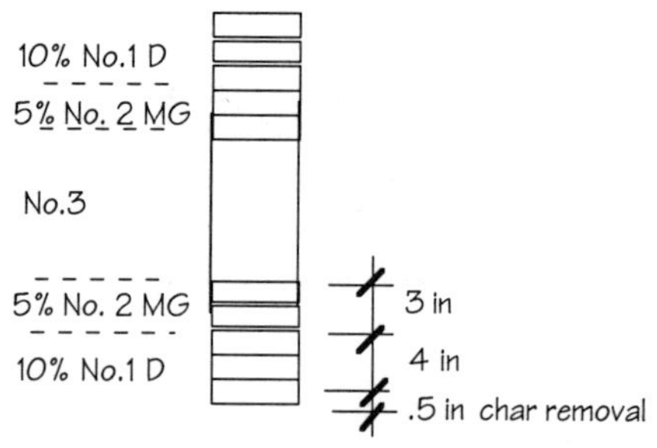

outer zone =10% < (4/34)100 = 11.8% √
intermed. zone =5% < (3/34)100 = 8.8% √
inner zone = No 3 √ by inspection

No stress reduction required for loss of outer lams

Note:

It is possible that a stress reduction is required due to the loss of the premium quality lams. If this occurs, it is customary to reduce the allowable stress to the next level that is verifiable by the appropriate agencies. Further guidelines may be found in ASTM Standards. If the Building Dept. does not permit the use of prior stress grading, you will need to use current TCM and ASTM Standards or have a grading inspector visually re-grade the glulam. If you are evaluating arch type members it is recommended that you consult the TCM for guidance of this very complex subject.

Bending

NDS T2.3.1

DL + LL controls by inspection. The beam is long so either M or Δ will control. Lateral stability implies:

$F_b' = F_b C_D C_M C_t C_L$

The plywood roof diaphragm fully supports the top compression side of the beam. The unbraced length is zero. Hence lateral buckling is prevented and C_L = 1.0. Therefore, we need only consider the volume factor (C_v).

Volume effect:

$F_b' = F_b C_D C_M C_t C_V$

NDS 3.3.4

Assume the selected glulam will have a C_V of .82. If the actual C_V is not .82, adjust it and re-ck the calc. This trial procedure is an iterative process.

$F_b = 2.4(1.0)1.0(1.0).82 = 1.97$ ksi

$$M = \frac{wx(\ell - x)}{2} = \frac{(.2+.3)16(44-16)}{2} = 112.0^{\text{k-ft}}$$

$$S_R = \frac{12M}{F_b'} = \frac{12(112)}{1.97}$$

= 682 in^3 < .9(843.9) = 759.5 in^3

Determine the actual C_V (K_L = 1.0)

$$C_V = K_L\left(\frac{21}{L}\right)^{1/10}\left(\frac{12}{d}\right)^{1/10}\left(\frac{5.125}{b}\right)^{1/10}$$

$$C_V = 1.0\left(\frac{21}{44}\right)^{1/10}\left(\frac{12}{34}\right)^{1/10}\left(\frac{5.125}{4.38}\right)^{1/10} = .85 > .82$$

Which implies that our assumption was conservative, and that our reduced size is ok.

Bending ok

Ck shear

NDS T2.3.1

$F_V' = F_V(C_D)C_M(C_t) = .2(1.0)1.0(1.0) = .2$ ksi

$$V = \frac{w\ell}{2} = \frac{(.5)44}{2} = 11.0^{k}$$

NDS 3.3.2

$$A_R = \frac{1.5(V)}{F_V'} = \frac{1.5(11)}{.2} = 82.5 \text{ in}^2 < 148.9 \text{ in}^2$$

Shear ok

Ck defl. (based on TCM)

Since our beam is only going to be sandblasted within the area of fire damage, it would be conservative to assume a reduced "I" throughout its length.

NDS T2.3.1

$E' = E(C_M)C_t = 1.8e3(1.0)1.0 = 1.8e3$ ksi

$$\Delta_{LL} = \frac{5w\ell^4}{384EI} = \frac{5(.3)44^4(1728)}{384(1.8e3)14346}$$

$$= .98 \text{ in} < \ell/360 = 44(12)/360 = 1.47 \text{ in}$$

If we did not consider the original camber in the beam our deflection would be:

NDS T4.3

$$\Delta_{TL} = \Delta w_{LL}\left(\frac{w_{TL}}{w_{LL}}\right) = .98\left(\frac{.5}{.3}\right)$$

$$= 1.6 \text{ in} < \ell/240 = 44(12)/240 = 2.2 \text{ in}$$

But since the original camber is:

$1.5\,\Delta_{DL} = 1.5(.98)14356(.2)/.3(17537)$

= .8 in

The beam is well within deflection limits.

Deflection ok

If we open a quarrel between the past and the present, we shall find that we have lost the future.

WINSTON CHURCHILL

● PROBLEM 9.15

Glued plywood box beam.

Perform a preliminary design of a glued plywood box beam for the following loading as shown.

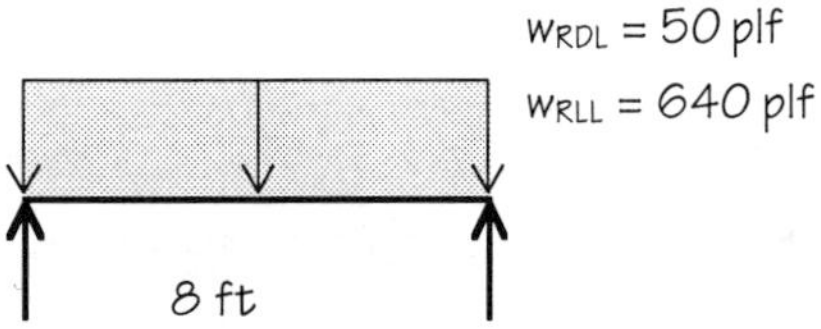

ASSUME

- No ponding, no plaster.
- DF - L No. 1 & btr.
- Full Lat. support from plywood or blocking.
- Neglect beam wt.
- EMC <19%.
- Normal temp. conditions.
- Commercial building.

SOLUTION

The solution presented here is based upon the methodology found in APA *Design and Fabrication of Glued Plywood-Lumber Beams* and *Plywood Design Specification (PDS).*

Trial section

The depth of plywood box beams range from 1/12 to 1/18 the span. A general rule for the gluing of the flange to the web, is to have the flange depth be a minimum of 4 times the abutting web thickness.

$$d = \frac{20(12)}{18} = 13.33 \text{ in. and}$$

$$d = \frac{20(12)}{12} = 20.0 \text{ in.}$$

Try 20 in. depth with 2 - DF-L No. 1 & btr, 2x4 flanges with unspliced webs of 23/32 in thick rated sheathing. Check Appendix B in the APA *Plywood Design Specification.*

$$M = \frac{w\ell^2}{8} = \frac{(.35)20^2}{8} = 17.5^{\text{ k-ft}}$$

From Appendix B (let p = footnote #4 factor):

$$M_{max} = 15.65 + 1.53 = 17.18$$

$$= C_D\left(M_{flg}\left(\frac{F_{t\ (actual)}}{F_{t\ (select\ str)}}\right) + M_{web}(p)\right)$$

$$= 1.25\left(15.65\left(\frac{.775}{1.0}\right) + 1.53(1.42)\right) = 17.9^{\text{ k ft}} > 17.5^{\text{ k ft}} \ \surd$$

$$V = \frac{w\ell}{2} = \frac{(.35)20}{2} = 3.35^{\text{ k}}$$

From Appendix B (let p = footnote #5 factor)

$$V_{max} = 2.14(p)C_D$$

$$= 2.14(1.49)1.25 = 3.98^{\text{ k}} > 3.35^{\text{ k}} \ \surd$$

The trial section is as follows:

To allow for good adhesion, the surfaces which will be glued must be sanded according to the recommendations found in 4.1.2 (see above ref.). Beams are also resurfaced to allow for their appearance or to provide for a uniformity of depth. The glue used should conform to ASTM D2559 for exterior applications and ASTM D3024 or D4689 for interior applications.

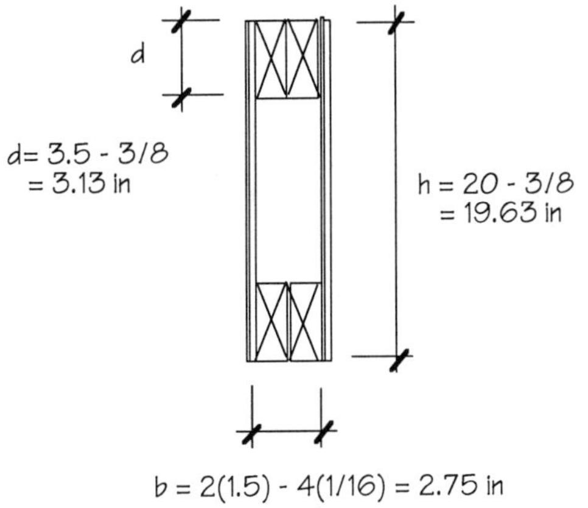

Note that "b" is reduced for 4 surfaces that will be sanded for gluing.

Calc. Properties

Net Moment of Inertia, I_n

$$I_{flg} = \frac{b}{12}\left(h^3 - (h-2d)^3\right)$$

$$= \frac{2.75}{12}\left(19.63^3 - (19.63 - 2(3.13))^3\right) = 1186 \text{ in}^4$$

For unsanded plywood parallel to grain, A = 4.219,

and $t_{//} = \frac{4.219}{12} = .352$ in.

$$I_{x\ each\ web} = \frac{t_{//}h^3}{12} = \frac{.352(19.63)^3}{12} = 221.9 \text{ in}^4$$

$I_t = I_{x\ flg} + I_{x\ webs}$

$= 1186 + 2(222) = 1630 \text{ in}^4$

$$Q_{flg} = bd\left(\frac{h}{2} - \frac{d}{2}\right) = 2.75(3.13)\left(\frac{19.63}{2} - \frac{3.13}{2}\right) = 71.0 \text{ in}^3$$

$$Q_{webs} = t_{//}\left(\frac{h}{2}\right)\frac{h}{4}(\#\ of\ webs)$$

$$= .352\left(\frac{19.63}{2}\right)\frac{19.63}{4}(2) = 33.91 \text{ in}^3$$

$Q = Q_{flg} + Q_{web} = 71.0 + 33.91 = 104.9 \text{ in}^3$

Ck bending NDS 2.3.1

The allowable stress for bending in box beams is based upon the direct compression and tension stresses in the flanges (see section 4.2 of the above reference). The selected section will have a C_F of 1.5 .

$F_t' = F_t C_D C_F = .775(1.25)1.5 = 1.45$ ksi

$$M_{allowable} = \frac{F_t'(I_t)}{.5h(12)} = \frac{1.45(1630)}{.5(19.63)(12)}$$

$= 20.07^{\text{k-ft}} > 17.5 \text{ in}^3$

Bending ok

Ck shear NDS 2.3.1

Assume that the shear is equally distributed in both webs. Shear stress is given from PDS Table 3. Note 19% increase for continuous glued edge framing parallel to face grain (PDS section 3.8.1).

$F_v' = F_v(C_D)1.19 = .19(1.19)1.25 = .283$ ksi

Rolling shear (50% reduction per PDS section 3.8.2)

$F_s' = F_s(.5)C_D = .075(.5)1.25 = .047$ ksi

Horizontal shear

$$V_h' = \frac{F_v' I_t \sum t_s}{Q} = \frac{.283(1630)\sum 2(.739)}{104.9}$$

$= 6.5^k > 3.35^k$

Flange web shear

$$V_s' = \frac{2F_s' d I_t}{Q_{flg}} = \frac{2(.047)3.13(1630)}{71.0}$$

$= 6.75^k > 3.35^k$

Shear ok

Ck defl. (approximate method)

The deflection of plywood box beams is taken from the sum of the deflections from both bending and shear. The approximate method is used to obtain a checking deflection. It supplies a deflection that controls or nearly controls the design of the beam. A further check must be made using the refined method found in the reference. The refined method is a bit complicated and the reader should refer to the reference for additional information.

$$\text{span/depth} = \frac{20(12)}{20} = 12$$

Interpolating:

10	1.5	
12	x	x = 1.38
15	1.2	

NDS 2.3.1

$E' = E(C_M)C_t = 1.8e3(1.0)1.0 = 1.8e3$ ksi

$$\Delta_A = \frac{5w\ell^4(1.38)}{384EI} = \frac{5(.2)20^4(1728)1.38}{384(1.8e3)1630}$$

$$= .34 \text{ in} < \ell/180 = {}^{20(12)}/_{180} = 1.33 \text{ in} \ \surd$$

Camber (1.5 Δ) can be incorporated into the design of box beams to produce the desired drainage for roofs or nearly level floors.

Deflection ok

Ck bearing stiffeners

Vertical stiffeners are used between flanges to distribute concentrated loads (like reactions) and to resist the buckling of the web or webs of the box beam. The APA has found that intermediate stiffeners placed at 48 in. o/c develop just about all the available shear strength of the normal beam.

$P = 2.0^k$

NDS T2.3.1

$F'_{c\perp} = .625$ ksi

let x = stiffener thickness required

$$x = \frac{P}{bF'_{c\perp}} = \frac{2.0}{2.75(.625)} = 1.16 \text{ in} < 1.5 \text{ in}$$

So one 2x4 is ok.

For rolling shear at bearing ends:

$$x = \frac{P}{2hF'_s} = \frac{2.0}{2(19.63).047} = 1.08 \text{ in} < 1.5 \text{ in}$$

Use 4-2x4 DF-L No. 1 & btr stiffeners at each end

□
□
□

Alas, I know if I ever became truly humble, I would be proud of it.

BENJAMIN FRANKLIN

PROBLEM 9.16

Sistered rafter repair.

An existing roof rafter is cracked. You determine that it should be repaired with the use of the sistering of additional rafters to its side. Design the sistering for the rafter shown below.

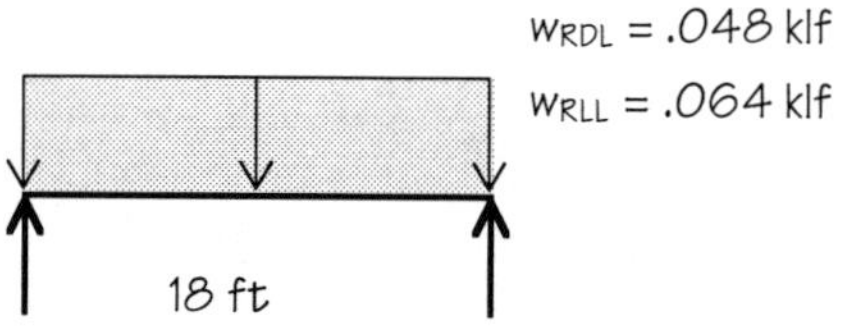

ASSUME

- No ponding, no plaster.
- 2x8 @ 48″ o/c.
- DF - L No. 2.
- Full Lat. support from plywood.
- Neglect rafter wt.
- EMC <19%.
- Normal temp. conditions.
- Commercial building.
- No fit up problems.

SOLUTION

$F_b = .875$ ksi
$F_v = .095$ ksi
$E = 1.6e3$ ksi

DL + RLL controls by inspection. Investigate existing loading to obtain potential failure mechanisms.

Bending

$F_b' = F_b C_D C_M C_t C_L C_F C_r$

$F_b = .875(1.25)1.0(1.0)1.0(1.2)1.0 = 1.31$ ksi

NDS 3.3.2

$M = \frac{w\ell^2}{8} = \frac{(.064+.048)18^2}{8} = 4.54^{k\text{-}ft}$

$S_R = \frac{12M}{F_b'} = \frac{12(4.53)}{1.31} = 41.5 \text{ in}^3$

$S_{2\times8} = 13.14 \text{ in}^3 < 41.5 \text{ in}^3$ **NG!**

$I = 47.63 \text{ in}^4$

$A = 10.88 \text{ in}^2$

Try 2 - 2x10

$F_b = .875(1.25)1.0(1.0)1.0(1.1)1.0 = 1.2$ ksi

NDS 3.3.2

$S_R = 41.5(1.31/1.2) = 45.3 \text{ in}^3$

$2S = 2(21.39) = 42.78 \text{ in}^3 > 45.3 \text{ in}^3$ **NG!**

Try No.1

$F_b = 1.0(1.25)1.0(1.0)1.0(1.1)1.0 = 1.38$ ksi

$S_R = 41.5(1.31/1.38) = 39.4 \text{ in}^3 < 45.3 \text{ in}^3$

Bending ok with 2 - No. 1 2x10

Ck shear

$F_v' = F_v(C_D)C_M(C_t)C_H = .095(1.25)1.0(1.0)1.0 = .119$ ksi

NDS 3.4.2

$V = \frac{w\ell}{2} = \frac{(.064+.048)18}{2} = 1.01^k$

$A_R = \frac{1.5(V)}{F_v'} = \frac{1.5(1.01)}{.119}$

$= 12.73 \text{ in}^2 < 2(13.88) = 27.76 \text{ in}^2$

But since we must notch the 2x10 to bear on the support,
Recheck with notched beam formula.

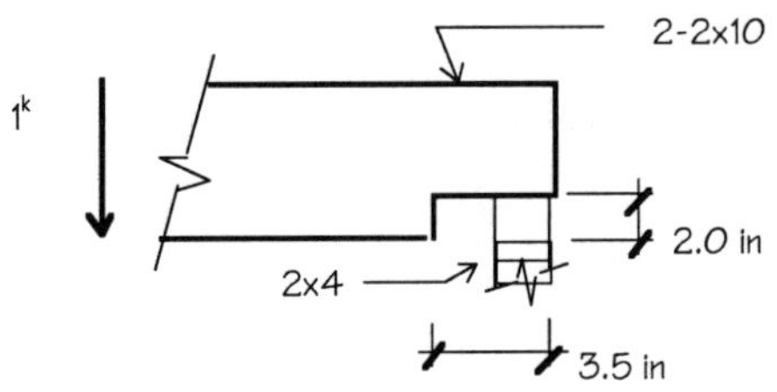

The NDS suggests that the notching of beams is to be avoided whenever possible. It's not that you cannot do it, it's that you shouldn't, especially on the tension side of the element. However, we do some notching when we retrofit or repair existing structures. Be careful and be conservative.

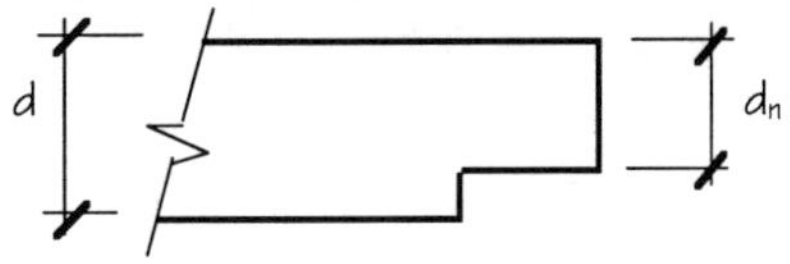

$f_v = \left(\frac{3V}{2bd_n}\right)\left(\frac{d}{d_n}\right)$ NDS 3.4.4

$= \left(\frac{3(1.01)}{2(1.5)(9.25-2)}\right)\left(\frac{9.25}{(9.25-2)}\right) = .178$ ksi

Since we have 2 loaded members (actually 3)

$f_v = .178/2 = .089$ ksi

$F_v' = F_v C_D C_M C_t C_H = .095(1.25)1.0(1.0)1.0$

$= .119 \text{ ksi} > .089$ ksi

Shear ok

Ck notch

$\frac{9.25}{4} = 2.31 \text{ in} < 2 \text{ in}$ NDS T2.3.1

Notch ok for the recommended ratio

NDS T4.3

Ck defl. (based on TCM)

$E' = E(C_M)C_t = 1.7e3(1.0)1.0 = 1.7\ e3$ ksi

$$\Delta_{LL} = \frac{5w\ell^4}{384EI} = \frac{5(.064)18^4(1728)}{384(1.7e3)98.93(2)}$$

$$= .45 \text{ in} < \ell/240 = 18(12)/240 = .9 \text{ in} \quad \checkmark$$

$$\Delta_{TL} = \Delta_{LL}\left(\frac{w_{TL}}{w_{LL}}\right) = .45\left(\frac{.112}{.064}\right) = .79 \text{ in}$$

$$\ell/180 = 18(12)/180 = 1.2 \text{ in} > .79 \text{ in} \quad \checkmark$$

Deflection ok with 2 - No. 1 2x10.

Ck bearing

Since the existing support conditions require that the 2x10's take the load, determine the minimum bearing length.

NDS T2.3.1

$$F'_{c\perp} = F_{c\perp}(C_M)C_t(C_b) = .625(1.0)1.0(1.0) = .625 \text{ ksi}$$

$$\ell_{b\ min} = \frac{R}{2bF'_{c\perp}} = \frac{1.01}{(2)1.5(.625)} = .54 \text{ in ok by inspection}$$

Bearing ok

Nailing

Since we are not trying to transfer the load from the cracked beam, use recommendation by UBC Table 23-I-Q no. 22. Built-up girder and beams.

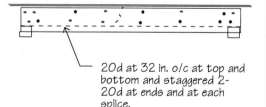

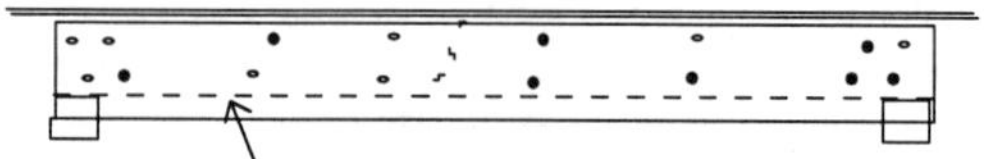

20d at 32 in. o/c at top and bottom and staggered 2-20d at ends and at each splice.

General notes

Consideration should be given to the following:

1. This seems to be a general overload which is systemic to the framing design. Require that all similar rafters be sistered as well. Furthermore, it would be recommended that a new analysis be performed on the building. This is recommended because the failure mechanism is to be found in the engineering design rather than as a result of a problem with the construction or material.
2. Insertion and fit-up must be investigated to insure that the sisters can be placed.
3. Jack rafters (at two points) to slightly above horizontal. Place sisters. install with nails. This will help to load the sisters simultaneously with the existing rafters.

Let us train our minds to desire what the situation demands.

SENECA
4 B.C. - 65 A.D.

References

1. Publications of the International Conference of Building Officials (ICBO), 5360 South Workman Mill Road, Whittier, CA 90601:
    1.1 **Uniform building Code**, 1991 and 1994 ed.
2. **National Design Specification for Wood Construction and Supplement**, 1991 ed., National Forest Products Association, 1250 Connecticut Avenue NW, Suite 200, Washington, DC 20036.
3. Publications of the American Institute of Timber Construction, 11818 S.E. Mill Plain Blvd., Suite 407, Vancouver, WA 98684:
    3.1 **Timber Construction Manual**, 4th ed., Wiley, New York, 1985
4. Publications of the Forest Products Laboratory (FPL), Forest Service, US Department of Agriculture, One Gifford Pinchot Drive, Madison, WI53705-2398:
    4.1 **Wood Handbook: Wood as an Engineering Material**, Agriculture Handbook 72, 1987.
5. Publications of MaGraw-Hill, Inc.,
    5.1 Breyer, Donald E., **Design of Wood Structures**, 3rd ed.
6. Publications of the American Institute of Steel Construction, Inc., 400 North Michigan Avenue, Chicago, IL 60611:
    6.1 **Manual of Steel Construction**, 9th ed., 1989
7. Amrhein, James E.: **Reinforced Masonry Engineering Handbook**, 3rd ed., 1978, Masonry Institute of America, 2550 Beverly Boulevard, Los Angeles, CA 90057.
8. Publications of the Applied Technology Council, Berkeley, California :
    8.1 **Guidelines For The Design Of Horizontal Wood Daiaphragms (ATC-7)**, 1981
9. Publications of the American Plywood Association, 7011 South 19th St., PO Box 11700, Tacoma, Wash. 98411-0700:
    9.1 **Diaphragms (Design/Construction Guide)**, 1995
    9.2 **138 Plywood Diaphragms (Research Report)**, 1993
    9.3 **Plywood Design Specification**, 1986
    9.4 **Design and Fabrication of Glued Plywood-Lumber Beams**, 1992
10. Publications of the California Board of Registration for Professional Engineers and Land Surveyors, PO Box 349002., Sacramento, CA 95834-9002:
    10.1 **Structural Engineer Examination**, 1993
    10.2 **Structural Engineer Examination**, 1994
    10.3 **Structural Engineer Examination**, 1995
11. Publications of the Simpson Strong-Tie Corporation, 4637 Chabot Drive Ste 200, Pleasanton, CA 94588:
    11.1 **Wood Construction Connectors**, 1996
12. Buckner, Dale C.: **246 Solved Structural Engineering Problems**, 1991, Professional Publications Inc., 1250 Fifth Ave, Belmont, CA 94002.
13. Li, Charles: **Professional Engineers (civil) License Reviewer**, 1990, Burdick & Landreth Co.
14. Chelapati, C. V.: **P.E. (Civil) License Review Manual** (volume IV), 3rd ed., 1990, Professional Engineering Development Publications, P.O. Box 15406, Long Beach, CA 90815-0406.

Seismic Coefficient Charts (Modified and Abridged from 1994 UBC Tables)

Importance Factor I = 1.0 (assume C = 2.75)	Zone				
A. Bearing Wall System	1	2A	2B	3	4
1. Light-framed walls with shear panels	(.075)	(.15)	(.2)	(.3)	(.4)
a. Plywood walls for structures three stories or less (8)	.026	.052	.069	.103	.138
b. All other light-framed walls (6)	.034	.069	.092	.138	.183
2. Shear walls					
a. Concrete (6)	.034	.069	.092	.138	.183
b. Masonry (6)	.034	.069	.092	.138	.183
B. Building Frame System					
2. Light-framed walls with shear panels					
a. Plywood walls for structures three stories or less (9)	.023	.046	.061	.092	.122
b. All other light-framed walls (7)	.029	.059	.079	.118	.157
3. Shear walls					
a. Concrete (8)	.026	.052	.069	.103	.138
b. Masonry (8)	.026	.052	.069	.103	.138

Importance Factor I = 1.25 (assume C = 2.75)	Zone				
A. Bearing Wall System	1	2A	2B	3	4
1. Light-framed walls with shear panels	(.075)	(.15)	(.2)	(.3)	(.4)
a. Plywood walls for structures three stories or less (8)	.032	.064	.086	.129	.172
b. All other light-framed walls (6)	.043	.086	.115	.172	.229
2. Shear walls					
a. Concrete (6)	.043	.086	.115	.172	.229
b. Masonry (6)	.043	.086	.115	.172	.229
B. Building Frame System					
2. Light-framed walls with shear panels					
a. Plywood walls for structures three stories or less (9)	.029	.057	.076	.115	.153
b. All other light-framed walls (7)	.037	.074	.098	.147	.196
3. Shear walls					
a. Concrete (8)	.032	.064	.086	.129	.172
b. Masonry (8)	.032	.064	.086	.129	.172

Reproduced from the Uniform Building Code, copyright 1994, with the permission of the publisher, the International Conference of Building Officials

Adjustment Factor Applicability (Modified and Abridged from 1991 NDS Table 2.3.1)

	BENDING		TENSION PARALLEL TO GRAIN		COMPRESSION PARALLEL TO GRAIN		COMPRESSION PERPENDICULAR TO GRAIN		SHEAR PARALLEL TO GRAIN		END GRAIN IN BEARING		MODULUS OF ELASTICITY		RADIAL TENSION	
	SAWN	GLULAM	SAWN	GLULAM	SAWN	GLULAM	SAWN	GLULAM	SAWN	GLULAM	SAWN	GLULAM	SAWN	GLULAM	SAWN	GLULAM
	F'_b	F'_b	F'_t	F'_t	F'_c	F'_c	$F'_{c\perp}$	$F'_{c\perp}$	F'_v	F'_v	F'_g	F'_g	E'	E'	F'_{rt}	F'_{rt}
TABULAR VALUE	F_b	F_b	F_t	F_t	F_c	F_c	$F_{c\perp}$	$F_{c\perp}$	F_v	F_v	F_g	F_g	E	E	•	F_{rt}
LOAD DURATION FACTOR	C_D	C_D	C_D	C_D	C_D	C_D	•	•	C_D	C_D	C_D	C_D	•	•	•	C_D
WET SERVICE FACTOR	C_M	C_M	C_M	C_M	C_M	C_M	C_M	C_M	C_M	C_M	•	•	C_M	C_M	•	C_M
TEMPERATURE FACTOR	C_t	C_t	C_t	C_t	C_t	C_t	C_t	C_t	C_t	C_t	C_t	C_t	C_t	C_t	•	C_t
BEAM STABILITY FACTOR (1)	C_L	C_L	•	•	•	•	•	•	•	•	•	•	•	•	•	•
SIZE FACTOR (2)	C_F	•	C_F	•	C_F	•	•	•	•	•	•	•	•	•	•	•
VOLUME FACTOR (1,3)	•	C_V	•	•	•	•	•	•	•	•	•	•	•	•	•	•
FLAT USE FACTOR (4)	C_{fu}	C_{fu}	•	•	•	•	•	•	•	•	•	•	•	•	•	•
REPETITIVE MEMBER FACTOR (5)	C_r	•	•	•	•	•	•	•	•	•	•	•	•	•	•	•
CURVATURE FACTOR(6)	•	C_c	•	•	•	•	•	•	•	•	•	•	•	•	•	•
FORM FACTOR	C_f	C_f	•	•	•	•	•	•	•	•	•	•	•	•	•	•
COLUMN STABILITY FACTOR	•	•	•	•	C_p	C_p	•	•	•	•	•	•	•	•	•	•
SHEAR STRESS FACTOR (7)	•	•	•	•	•	•	•	•	C_H	•	•	•	•	•	•	•
BUCKLING STIFFNESS FACTOR (8)	•	•	•	•	•	•	•	•	•	•	•	•	C_T	•	•	•
BEARING AREA FACTOR	•	•	•	•	•	•	C_b	C_b	•	•	•	•	•	•	•	•

<u>Note</u>

1. The beam stability factor, C_L, shall not apply simultaneously with the volume factor, C_V, for glued laminated timber bending members. Therefore the lesser of these adjustment factors shall apply.
2. The size factor, C_F, shall apply only to visually graded sawn lumber members and to round timber bending members.
3. The volume factor, C_V, shall apply only to glued laminated timber bending members.
4. The flat use factor, C_{fu}, shall apply only to dimension lumber bending members 2" to 4" thick and to glued laminated timber bending members.
5. The repetitive member factor, C_r, shall apply only dimension lumber bending members 2" to 4" thick.
6. The curvature factor, C_c, shall apply only to curved portions of glued laminated timber bending members.
7. Shear design values parallel to grain, F_V, for sawn lumber members shall be permitted to be multiplied by the shear stress factors, C_H.
8. The buckling stiffness factor, C_T, shall apply only to 2"x4" or smaller sawn lumber truss compression chords subjected to combined flexure and axial compression when 3/8" or thicker plywood sheathing is nailed to the narrow face.

Note: The TCM uses an additional adjustment factor for glulams in bending. It is referred to as the interaction stress factor C_I (see tapered end cut beam problem for example).

By permission of the National Forest Products Association, Washington, DC

Preliminary Shearwall Selection Chart

cap. (plf)	material	mem @ panel edges	nailing	sill bolts	sill	A-35 @"o/c	sill nailing @"o/c	91UBC Table
50	1/2" drywall	unblk'd, 2x	5d cooler @ 7,7	5/8"dia @ 72"o/c	2x	96	16d @ 16	47-I
50	3/8" lath and 1/2" gypsum plaster	unblk'd, 2x	13 gage 1-1/8" long, 19/64" head @ 5,5	5/8" dia @ 72" o/c	2x	96	16d @ 16	47-I
62	1/2" drywall	unblk'd, 2x	5d cooler @ 4,4	5/8"dia @ 72"o/c	2x	87	16d @ 16	47-I
75	1/2" drywall	blk'd, 2x	5d cooler @ 4,4	5/8"dia @ 72"o/c	2x	72	16d @ 16	47-I
87	5/8"drywall	blk'd, 2x	6d cooler @ 4,4	5/8"dia @ 72" o/c	2x	62	16d @ 16	47-I
180	7/8"stucco	unblk'd, 2x	11 gage 1-1/2" long, 7/16" head @ 6,6	5/8" dia @ 72"o/c	2x	30	16d @ 7	47-I
200	3/8" ply	2x	6d @ 6,12	5/8" dia @ 70" o/c	2x	27	16d @ 6	25-K-1
264	3/8" ply	2x	8d @ 6,12	5/8" dia @ 52"o/c	2x	20	16d @ 5	25-K-1
384	3/8" ply	2x	8d @ 4,12	5/8"dia @ 36"o/c	2x	14	2 - 16d @ 6	25-K-1
490	15/32" ply	3x	8d @ 3,12	3/4"dia @ 39" o/c	2x	11	2 - 16d @ 5	25-K-1
600	15/32" ply	3x	10d @ 3,12	3/4"dia @ 30"o/c	2x	9	2 - 16d @ 4	25-K-1
768	3/8" ply (2) sides	3x	8d @ 4,12	3/4"dia @ 24"o/c	2x	7	3 - 16d @ 5	25-K-1
980	15/32" ply (2) sides	3x	8d @ 3,12	3/4"dia @ 18" o/c	2x	2 @ 11	3 - 16d @ 4	25-K-1
1200	15/32" ply (2) sides	3x	8d @ 3,12	3/4"dia @ 15"o/c	2x	2 @ 9	3 - 16d @ 3	25-K-1

Note:

1. Charts is based on seismic zones 3 and 4 with DF-L timber.
2. Studs are at 16" o/c.
3. C_D = 1.33.
4. See UBC for requirements.
5. Charts should be used as a starting point for preliminary shearwall design. Check all applicable codes for final design.
6. See 91 - 94 UBC conversion chart for references.

Preliminary Column Sizing Chart

Area (in^2)	d (in)	size	Height (ft)											max bearing
			4.0	6.0	8.0	10.0	12.0	14.0	16.0	18.0	20.0	22.0	24.0	
5.25	1.5	2x4	2.2	1.0										7.8
8.25	1.5	2x6	3.4	1.6										12.2
10.88	1.5	2x8	4.5	10.8										16.1
13.88	1.5	2x10	5.8	2.8										20.5
16.88	1.5	2x12	7.0	3.4										25.0
8.75	2.5	3x4	7.2	4.3	2.6	1.7								13.0
13.75	2.5	3x6	11.3	6.8	4.2	2.7								20.4
18.13	2.5	3x8	14.9	9.0	5.5	3.6								26.8
23.13	2.5	3x10	19.0	11.5	7.0	4.6								34.2
28.13	2.5	3x12	23.1	14.0	8.5	5.6								41.6
12.25	3.5	4x4	12.0	9.5	6.6	4.5	3.3	2.4						18.1
19.25	3.5	4x6	18.8	14.9	10.3	7.1	5.1	3.8						28.5
25.38	3.5	4x8	24.8	19.6	13.6	9.4	6.8	5.1						37.6
32.38	3.5	4x10	31.7	25.0	17.4	12.0	8.6	6.5						47.9
39.38	3.5	4x12	38.5	30.4	21.1	14.6	10.5	7.9						58.3
30.25	5.5	6x6	32.0	30.0	26.6	22.0	17.4	13.7	10.9	8.8	7.2	6.0		62.9
41.25	5.5	6x8	43.6	40.9	36.2	30.0	23.7	18.6	14.8	12.0	9.9	8.2		85.8
52.25	5.5	6x10	55.2	51.8	45.9	37.9	30.0	23.6	18.8	15.2	12.5	10.4		108.7
63.25	5.5	6x12	66.9	62.7	55.6	45.9	36.3	28.6	22.7	18.4	15.1	12.6		131.6
56.25	7.5	8x8	60.6	58.9	56.1	51.8	46.2	39.7	33.4	27.9	23.5	19.9	17.0	117.0
71.25	7.5	8x10	76.8	74.6	71.0	65.7	58.5	50.2	42.3	35.4	29.8	25.2	21.6	148.2
86.25	7.5	8x12	93.0	90.3	86.0	79.5	70.8	60.8	51.2	42.9	36.0	30.5	26.1	179.4
90.25	9.5	10x10	98.1	96.4	93.9	90.3	85.2	78.6	70.8	62.5	54.6	47.4	41.3	187.7
109.3	9.5	10x12	118.8	116.8	113.8	109.3	103.2	95.2	85.8	75.7	66.1	57.4	50.0	227.3
132.3	11.5	12x12	144.3	142.8	140.4	137.1	132.6	126.7	119.3	110.5	100.7	90.6	81.0	275.2

Note:

1. Preliminary Column Chart is based upon the 1991 NDS Ylinen (C_P) formula and is to be used for preliminary sizing. Check all applicable codes for final design.
2. Charts assumes minimum of:
   $E = 1.6e3$ ksi
   $F_c = 1.1$ ksi
   $F_g = 1.48$ ksi (2x or 4x)
   $F_g = 2.02$ ksi (5x5 or larger)
3. $K_{cE} = .3$, $c = .8$, $K_e = 1.0$, $l_e/d \leq 50$, $C_D = 1.0$

Member Size Chart

	width b	depth d	A in	X-X Axis I in^4	X-X Axis S in^3	Y-Y Axis I in^4	Y-Y Axis S in^3	w plf	C_f	SC_f
2x4	1.5	3.5	5.25	5.359	3.063	0.984	1.313	1.458	1.500	4.595
2x6	1.5	5.5	8.25	20.8	7.563	1.547	2.063	2.292	1.300	9.832
2x8	1.5	7.5	10.88	47.64	13.14	2.039	2.719	3.021	1.200	15.77
2x10	1.5	9.25	13.88	98.93	21.39	2.602	3.469	3.854	1.100	23.53
2x12	1.5	11.25	16.88	178	31.64	3.164	4.219	4.688	1.000	31.64
2x14	1.5	13.25	19.88	290.8	43.89	3.727	4.969	5.521	0.900	39.5
3x4	2.5	3.5	8.75	8.932	5.104	4.557	3.646	2.431	1.500	7.656
3x6	2.5	5.5	13.75	34.66	12.6	7.161	5.729	3.819	1.300	16.39
3x8	2.5	7.5	18.13	79.39	21.9	9.44	7.552	5.035	1.200	26.28
3x10	2.5	9.25	23.13	164.9	35.65	12.04	9.635	6.424	1.100	39.22
3x12	2.5	11.25	28.13	296.6	52.73	14.65	11.72	7.813	1.000	52.73
3x14	2.5	13.25	33.13	484.6	73.15	17.25	13.8	9.201	0.900	65.84
3x16	2.5	15.25	38.13	738.9	96.9	19.86	15.89	10.59	0.900	87.21
4x4	3.5	3.5	12.25	12.51	7.146	12.51	7.146	3.403	1.500	10.72
4x6	3.5	5.5	19.25	48.53	17.65	19.65	11.23	5.347	1.300	22.94
4x8	3.5	7.5	25.38	111.1	30.66	25.9	14.8	7.049	1.300	39.86
4x10	3.5	9.25	32.38	230.8	49.91	33.05	18.89	8.933	1.200	59.89
4x12	3.5	11.25	39.38	415.3	73.83	40.2	22.97	10.94	1.100	81.21
4x14	3.5	13.25	46.38	678.5	102.4	47.34	27.05	12.88	1.000	102.4
4x16	3.5	15.25	53.38	1034	135.7	54.48	31.14	14.83	1.000	135.7
6x6	5.5	5.5	30.25	76.26	27.73	76.26	27.73	8.403	1.000	27.73
6x8	5.5	7.5	41.25	193.4	51.56	104	37.81	11.46	1.000	51.56
6x10	5.5	9.25	52.25	393	82.73	131.7	47.9	14.51	1.000	82.73
6x12	5.5	11.25	63.25	697.1	121.2	159.4	57.98	17.57	1.000	121.2
6x14	5.5	13.25	74.25	1128	167.1	187.2	68.06	20.63	0.989	165.2
6x16	5.5	15.25	85.25	1707	220.2	214.9	78.15	23.68	0.974	214.4
6x18	5.5	17.5	96.25	2456	280.7	242.6	88.23	26.74	0.959	269.2
6x20	5.5	19.5	107.3	3398	348.6	270.4	98.31	29.79	0.947	330.3
6x22	5.5	21.5	118.3	4555	423.7	298.1	108.4	32.85	0.937	397.1
6x24	5.5	23.5	129.3	5948	506.2	325.8	118.5	35903	0.928	469.8
8x8	7.5	7.5	56.25	263.7	70.31	263.7	70.31	15.63	1.000	70.31
8x10	7.5	9.25	71.25	535.9	112.8	334	89.06	19.79	1.000	112.8
8x12	7.5	11.25	86.25	950.5	165.3	404.3	107.8	23.96	1.000	165.3
8x14	7.5	13.25	101.3	1538	227.8	474.6	126.6	28.13	0.989	225.3
8x16	7.5	15.5	116.3	2327	300.3	544.9	143.3	32.29	0.972	291.9
8x18	7.5	17.5	131.3	3350	382.8	615.2	164.1	36.46	0.959	367.1
8x20	7.5	19.5	146.3	4634	475.3	684.5	182.8	40.63	0.947	450.4
8x22	7.5	21.5	161.3	6211	577.8	755.9	201.6	44.79	0.937	541.6
8x24	7.5	23.5	176.3	8111	690.3	826.2	220.3	48.96	0.928	640.6

91 - 94 UBC Cross Reference Chart

91 ref.	94 ref.
2303(d)	1603.5
2303(F)	1603.6
2304(C)4	2304.3.4.2
2304(d)	1604.4
2305(d)	1605.4
2306	1606
2310	1611
2316	1618
2317(a)	1619.1
2334(a)	1628.2
2334(b)	1628.2.1
2334(d)	1628.5
2334(G)2	1628.7.2
2334(j)	1628.10
2336(b)	1630.2
2337(a)	1631.1
2337(b)9	1631.2.9
2510(C)3	2311.3.3
2513(A)	2314.1
2513(c)	2314.3
T23-C	T16-C
T23-F,G,H,L	T16-F,G,H,K
T23-I,L,O	T16-I,L,O
T23-P	T16-O
T25-I	T23-I-I
T25-J-1	T23-I-J-1
T25-K-1	T23-I-K-1
T25-K-2	T23-I-K-2
T25-P	T23-I-P
T25-Q	T23-I-Q
T25-S-1	T23-I-S-1
T26-E,F	T19-E,F